COMPARATIVE POLITICS

Political Parties in Advanced Industrial Democracies

D0878607

COMPARATIVE POLITICS

Comparative Politics is a series for students and teachers of political science that
deals with contemporary issues in comparative government and politics. As
Comparative European Politics it has produced a series of high quality books since
its foundation in 1990, but now takes on a new form and new title for the new
millennium—Comparative Politics. As the process of globalisation proceeds, and as
Europe becomes ever more enmeshed in world trends and events, so it is necessary to
broaden the scope of the series.
The General Editors are Max Kaase, Vice President and Dean of Humanities and
Social Sciences, International University, Bremen, and Kenneth Newton,
Professor of Comparative Politics, University of Southampton. The series
is published in association with the European Consortium for Political Research.

OTHER TITLES IN THIS SERIES

Political Parties in Advanced Industrial Democracies

Edited by

PAUL WEBB,

DAVID M. FARRELL,

and

IAN HOLLIDAY

OXFORD

UNIVERSITY PRESS

OXFORD

UNIVERSITY PRESS

Great Clarendon Street, Oxford OX2 6DP

Oxford University Press is a department of the University of Oxford.
It furthers the University's objective of excellence in research, scholarship,
and education by publishing worldwide in

Oxford New York

Auckland Bangkok Buenos Aires Cape Town Chennai
Dar es Salaam Delhi Hong Kong Istanbul Karachi Kolkata
Kuala Lumpur Madrid Melbourne Mexico City Mumbai Nairobi
São Paulo Shanghai Taipei Tokyo Toronto

Oxford is a registered trade mark of Oxford University Press
in the UK and in certain other countries

Published in the United States
by Oxford University Press Inc., New York

A catalogue record for this title is available from the British Library

Library of Congress Cataloging in Publication Data

(Data available)

ISBN 0-19-924055-8 (hbk)
ISBN 0-19-924056-6 (pbk)

1 3 5 7 9 10 8 6 4 2

Typeset by Newgen Imaging Systems (P) Ltd, Chennai, India
Printed in Great Britain on acid-free paper by
T. J. International Ltd., Padstow, Cornwall

Acknowledgements

In the course of writing this book, a number of debts have been incurred which should be acknowledged. The book has benefited from the critical feedback which members of the group have been able to provide to each other, a process particularly facilitated by a meeting staged at Brunel University in March 1998. This was an invaluable experience, and one which was made possible by the financial generosity of the Ray C. Bliss Institute of Applied Politics at the University of Akron, the McDougall Trust, the journal *Party Politics*, and the Department of Government at Brunel University, where Paul Webb was a member of staff at the time the meeting was held. Though they are not contributors to this volume, we also gained from the valued participation at that meeting of Stephen White, David Stansfield, Lars Bille, Jim Tomlinson, Andrew Appleton, and Rei Shiratori. It should also be said that a debt of gratitude is owed to those scholars not directly involved in the making of this book, but whose intellectual efforts have proved a source of guidance and inspiration. There are, of course, many upon whose work, explicitly or implicitly, we have drawn, but two in particular—Dick Katz and Peter Mair—deserve thanks given the frequent reference made by our contributors to their ideas and to their party organizational data.

Feedback provided to Paul Webb at various conferences and seminar presentations over the years has also proved very helpful in respect of some of the themes and material included in the book: of particular note in this respect are the 'Party Politics in the Year 2000' conference staged in Manchester (January 1995), the British Politics Group panel at APSA Annual Meeting in Boston (September 1998) and research seminars held at the University of Copenhagen (May 1994), the University of Sheffield (March 1998), and the Sussex European Institute (January 2001). It would be invidious to single out individuals from any of these sessions for particular thanks, but each occasion helped evolve the understanding of political parties which is articulated in this book.

Significant intellectual debts are owed to the three anonymous referees who provided incisive and constructive feedback on the original proposal which was presented to Oxford University Press: without it, this would have been both a less ambitious and less well-conceived undertaking. Dominic Byatt has proved a very patient, encouraging and accommodating presence at OUP, while Amanda Watkins managed the transition from manuscript to published book with great efficiency.

Finally, a number of the book's contributors would like to offer individual acknowledgements in respect of their particular chapters. Ian Holliday is grateful to Ingrid van Biezen, David Farrell, Laura Morales, Luis Ramiro, and Paul Webb for very helpful comments on his chapter on Spanish parties. Andrew Knapp wishes to thank Nick Startin for his invaluable help in gathering data in Paris for the preparation of his chapter, and Colette Ysmal and Nonna Mayer, both of Centre d'Études sur la Vie Politique (CEVIPOF), for their insights into party membership in France. Ian McAllister wishes to acknowledge the Social Science Data Archive at the Australian National University for making available the following data sets: the 1987–98 Australian Election Studies, conducted by himself, David Gow, Clive Bean, and Roger Jones, and funded by the Australian Research Council; and the 1967 and 1979 Australian National Political Attitudes surveys, directed by Don Aitkin. In addition, he is grateful to Elim Papadakis and David Black for making available the 1995 Australian Values Survey. R. J. Murphy and David Farrell are grateful to Paul Webb, Michael Gallagher, Michael Marsh, Peter Mair, Fiachra Kennedy, the Public Offices Commission, the Central Statistics Office, Conor O'Reilly, and the main Irish political parties for advice and assistance in the writing of their chapter on Ireland. Jack Vowles is especially grateful to the following for providing data for his chapter on parties in New Zealand: Pat Day, Ian McLean, the New Zealand Electoral Commission (particularly Paul Harris), the NZ Broadcasting Standards Authority, and the NZ Parliamentary Service Commission. Paul Webb gratefully acknowledges the UK Data Archive at the University of Essex for supplying the 1987, 1992, and 1997 British Election Study data sets, and the current BES directors (David Sanders, Harold Clarke, Marianne Stewart, and Paul Whiteley) for providing the 2001 data set. He is also grateful to Justin Fisher for help and advice with party finance data in the UK, and to Ian Holliday for incisive comments on an earlier draft of his chapter. He is also much obliged to the British Academy for funding research on party employees (grant number APN8695), which proved helpful in writing parts of Chapter 2. Notwithstanding the intellectual and practical debts owed to the individuals, institutions and groups mentioned above, the usual disclaimer of responsibility applies, of course.

Paul Webb, David M. Farrell, and Ian Holliday

Contents

List of Figures

List of Tables

Notes on Contributors

Luciano Bardi is Professor of Political Science at the University of Pisa. His research interests include European Union politics and institutions, parties at the European Union level, and the Italian party system. He is the co-editor of an *International Political Science Review* special issue on enlargement of the European Union (2002), and of *Italian Politics: Mapping the Future* (Westview Press, 1998); co-author of *Il Parlamento Europeo* (Il Mulino, 1999), and of *Euroministri* (Il Saggiatore, 1994).

R. Kenneth Carty is Professor of Political Science in the University of British Columbia. He has published widely on questions of party and electoral organization and leadership in Europe, Australia, and Canada and is currently working on ecological models of local party organization and activity. His most recent book (co-authored) is *Rebuilding Canadian Party Politics* (UBC Press, 2000).

Kris Deschouwer is Professor of Politics at the Free University of Brussels and in the Department of Comparative Politics at the University of Bergen (Norway). He has published widely on political parties, consociationalism and regionalism, including (as co-editor) *Party Elites in Divided Societies* (Routledge, 1999).

David Farrell is Jean Monnet Professor of European Politics at the University of Manchester. A co-editor of *Party Politics*, his research focuses on campaigns, electoral systems, and representation in the European Parliament. His most recent books are *Electoral Systems: A Comparative Introduction* (Palgrave, 2001) and *Do Political Campaigns Matter?* (co-edited, Routledge, 2002).

John C. Green is Professor of Political Science and Director of the Ray C. Bliss Institute of Applied Politics at the University of Akron. His research interests include American political parties, campaign finance, and religion and politics. He is an editor of *Multiparty Politics in America* (Rowman & Littlefield, 2002), *The State of the Parties* (Rowman & Littlefield, 2002), *Financing the 1996 Election* (M. E. Sharpe, 1999), and co-author of *Religion and the Culture Wars* (Rowman & Littlefield, 1996).

Simon Hix is Reader in European Union Politics and Policy in the Government Department at the London School of Economics and Political Science. He is author of *The Political System of the European Union* (Palgrave, 1999) and co-author (with Christopher Lord) of *Political Parties in the European Union* (Palgrave, 1997). He is Associate Editor of the journal *European Union Politics*, has published articles on the EU in various leading political science journals, and is Director of the European Parliament Research Group.

Ian Holliday is Professor of Policy Studies and Head of the Department of Public and Social Administration at the City University of Hong Kong. He has written extensively on comparative politics, and is co-editor of the journal *Party Politics*.

Andrew Knapp is Senior Lecturer in French Studies at the University of Reading. He is author of *Le Gaullisme après de Gaulle* (Seuil, 1996), and co-author of *Government and Politics in Western Europe* (3rd edn, OUP, 1998) and of *The Government and Politics of France* (4th edn, Routledge, 2001), as well as of numerous articles on French party politics. He is currently preparing a general study of parties and the party system in France.

Ian McAllister is Professor of Politics and Director of the Research School of Social Sciences at the Australian National University in Canberra. His research interests lie in the areas of comparative political behaviour, political parties, and voters and electoral systems, with particular reference to Australia, the USA, Russia, Britain, and Northern Ireland. His recent publications include *How Russia Votes* (Macmillan, 1996) and *The Australian Political System* (Longman, 1998), both as co-author.

Ronan Murphy is Research Officer at the Local Government Services Board in Dublin and a doctoral researcher at Trinity College, Dublin. He previously worked on the Fine Gael membership survey, and his main area of interest is party membership and activism.

Susan E. Scarrow is Associate Professor of Political Science at the University of Houston. Among her main research interests are the development and impact of political parties in established democracies. She is the author of *Parties and their Members* (OUP, 1996) and *Perspectives on Political Parties* (Palgrave, 2002), and of many articles on political parties, German politics, electoral systems, and direct democracy.

Jan Sundberg is Professor of Political Science at the University of Helsinki. He has published widely in the field of comparative and Scandinavian party politics, and is editor of *Partier och interesseorganisationer in Nordern* (('Parties and Interest Organizations in Scandinavia') Nordisk Ministerråd, 2001). He is a member of the Executive of the European Consortium of Political Research and a former president of the Nordic Political Science Association.

Jack Vowles is Professor of Political Science at the University of Waikato. A native of New Zealand, he took his doctorate at the University of British Columbia in Canada. His research focuses on New Zealand politics, comparative public policy, political sociology, and electoral behaviour. He is Director of the New Zealand Election Study, and co-author of a number of books on recent elections in New Zealand, including *Proportional Representation on Trial: The 1999 Election in New Zealand and the Fate of MMP* (Auckland University Press, 2002).

Paul Webb is Professor of Politics at the University of Sussex. His research interests focus on representative democracy, particularly party and electoral politics. The author of *The Modern British Party System* (Sage Publications, 2000) and numerous articles and chapters on parties and electoral processes, he is Reviews and Associate Editor of *Party Politics* and co-editor of *Representation*.

1

Introduction

Political Parties in Advanced Industrial Democracies

Paul Webb

How relevant and vital are political parties in contemporary democracies? Do they fulfil the functions that any stable and effective democracy might expect of them? Do they represent citizens effectively? Do they help translate wants and needs into effective governmental outputs? Do they foster democratic involvement and support on the part of the citizen body? Or are they little more than moribund anachronisms, relics of a past age of political life, now superseded by other mechanisms of linkage between state and society? These are the central questions which this book aims to address through a rigorous comparative analysis of political parties operating in the world's advanced industrial democracies.

Parties have long since figured prominently in the canon of Western political science. Sartori (1976: 23) sees Max Weber as founder of the modern tradition of party scholarship, though reviews of the literature on parties generally tend to cite a well-known litany of studies which go back to the classic works of Ostrogorski (1902) and Michels (1915). It is equally evident that, while scholars have often expressed high hopes for the central roles played in democratic society by parties, they have just as frequently been perplexed by the realities of party politics. Indeed, this is apparent in the work of both Ostrogorski and Michels. More than half a century ago, the American Political Science Association felt parties were so vital to the US political system that a special committee was established to investigate and make recommendations on (the lack of) 'responsible' two-party politics in the country. Taking their cue from the well-known claims of previous authors like Bryce (1921: 119) and Schattschneider (1942: 1) that the operation of modern democracy was virtually inconceivable without parties, this committee emphasized the need for more clearly defined party programmes which would confront voters with clear choices (American Political Science Association 1950: 22–3).

Concern about the performance and popular standing of parties grew in the 1960s; for instance, a landmark review of individual-level attitudes towards parties at this time argued that 'anti-party norms and images are present as a living part of the political culture' in many Western political systems (Dennis 1966: 613). Towards the end of that decade, King (1969: 140), in reviewing party functions in Western democracies, concluded that 'we are entitled, at the very least, to a certain scepticism . . . concerning the great importance attached to parties in large segments of the political science literature'. He echoed the words of Kirchheimer (1966: 200), whose own seminal contribution to comparative scholarship suggested that 'the political party's role in Western industrial society today is more limited than it would appear from its position of formal preeminence'. Subsequently, propelled largely by evidence of partisan dealignment and electoral instability across Western democracies in the 1970s, concern developed into a fully-fledged debate about the alleged 'decline of party'. The epicentre of much of this debate lay in American political science, though it was by no means restricted exclusively to interpretation of the US case. A number of loosely connected arguments emerged, some normative, some empirical, categorized by Daalder (1992: 269–70) in the following terms:

1. A persistent body of thought which denied a legitimate role for party and saw parties as a threat to the good society (the normative *denial of party*).
2. The selective *rejection of certain parties* that were regarded as bad (on normative grounds), but not of party *per se*.
3. The selective rejection of certain party *systems* which were regarded as pathological.
4. A contention that parties were becoming increasingly irrelevant in democratic politics as other actors and institutions took over the major functions which they had once performed (an empirically based assertion of the *redundancy of party*).

While the academic literature on party decline has tended to be framed in terms of the last of these categories, political actors and critics have often expressed a normative rejection of parties or party systems. By the early 1990s, developments in a number of countries were stimulating a fresh round of speculation about the decline of party. For instance, in Germany, it became commonplace to refer to the phenomenon of *parteienverdrossenheit*, or a crisis of party legitimacy. Survey data in that country produced much evidence to suggest that citizens were disillusioned with the motivations, true concerns, and effectiveness of the parties (Poguntke 1996). This attitudinal trend reflected a mixture of the sentiments outlined above: while some citizens reacted against particular parties (typically the major established players in the system such as the SPD, CDU, or FPD), others took against the role and nature of parties in general. Even the President of the Federal Republic openly criticized the parties on some of these counts (Scarrow 1996). Some commentators conflated analytical statements of functional redundancy with a clear normative accusation against party.

This was implicit, for instance, in the position of the cultural critic Hans Magnus Enzensberger (cited in Giddens 1998: 51), who argued that the country's true political innovators now lay outside the orthodox domain of the governing parties, and claimed that Germany could 'afford an incompetent government, because ultimately the people who bore us in the daily news really do not matter'. At the same time, a similar, though far more intense, rejection of party was apparent in Italy. The roots of this ran deep, stemming from longstanding public scepticism about the immobilism that had characterized postwar governments in the country, but it was transformed into a fully-fledged systemic crisis by the collapse of the Berlin Wall and the widespread corruption among party elites which the *tangentopoli* (bribesville) scandals of the early 1990s brought to light (Ginsborg 1996).

However, criticism of party was by no means the exclusive preserve of countries experiencing overt crises. In most other advanced industrial democracies, parties were subject to allegations of weak performance, often from a left-wing or radical democratic perspective. Such observers of party life brought with them two major accusations in respect of party politics. First, parties were deemed to be failing when it came to fostering democratic political participation. Typically, the decline of participation in and through parties would be contrasted with burgeoning non-partisan forms of associative life through single-issue groups and new social movements (Lawson and Merkl 1988; Jacques 1993; Mulgan 1994*a,b*). Second, the prominence of neo-liberal political economy in the 1980s and a growing consciousness of the alleged effects of economic globalization in the 1990s served to convince some on the left that a political convergence was developing which undermined the ideological distinctiveness of party governments (Ahmin 1997). This effectively denied voters the clear policy choices for which the APSA Committee had so strongly indicated a need nearly half a century earlier.

Yet by no means all observers of party life have been so forcibly struck by signs of 'decline'. Although some focused on evidence of weakening party links with society (manifest in developments such as partisan dealignment, electoral instability, and membership decline (Dalton *et al.* 1984)), others asserted the resilience and adaptability of party organizations. This was initially apparent in studies of party organizational development in the USA (Cotter and Bibby 1980; Bibby 1998), and eventually an exhaustive comparative survey of three decades' worth of organizational material confirmed that in many other instances modern parties had succeeded in enhancing the supply of resources at their disposal in spite of weakening social linkages (Katz and Mair 1992, 1994, 1995). This suggests that we need to consider more than one dimension of the world of political parties in order to provide convincing answers to questions about their relevance and centrality for modern democratic politics. It also suggests that things are unlikely to be straightforward, which renders assertions of overall party decline in advanced western democracies simplistic.

THE AIMS OF THIS BOOK

Over thirty years ago, King (1969: 141) lamented the fact that scholars were inclined to be unsystematic about investigating the key questions relating to party performance: too often, he claimed, they relied on impressions and hunches when attempting to summarize the situation, and 'hunches are no substitute for disciplined inquiry'. To be sure, this judgement does not remain entirely valid today since a good deal of high-quality research has been conducted on voters' attitudes towards parties, party organizational development, parties' roles in governments, legislatures, political communications, and so on. However, as this knowledge has begun to accumulate there is a growing need for it to be reviewed and integrated. Hence, the central objective of this book is to meet the need for a rigorous, systematic, multi-dimensional comparison of the evidence concerning party performance, legitimacy, and organizational strength across the Western world.

It should be said that an important volume with a similar purpose to ours has been published recently; indeed, *Parties Without Partisans* (Dalton and Wattenberg 2000) is the result of a project whose timing and personnel have in part overlapped with our own. We welcome this and believe that to the extent that there is agreement between the conclusions of the two studies, it will be of obvious value to contemporary political science. When independent research projects arrive at similar conclusions, each corroborates the other and an accumulation of knowledge vital to the progression of the discipline is achieved. That said, it should also be stressed that a number of features distinguish this volume from *Parties Without Partisans*. First, while there are substantial areas of agreement between the two books, our conclusions differ in certain respects. For instance, we feel it is an exaggeration to imply that parties are 'no longer loyal to their policy commitments' (Dalton and Wattenberg 2000: 267), and neither do we feel that the parties' role has declined in respect of political recruitment (ibid: 276). We also doubt that parties have been as unresponsive to the challenges of dealigned politics as Dalton and Wattenberg claim (p. 284). Second, in the Conclusion of this book we seek to show how evaluations of party functioning today depend, in no small part, on the democratic vision of the beholder. In particular, we demonstrate that parties remain absolutely central in the view of those who feel that democracy is principally a means of facilitating popular control and choice over public affairs. For this reason, we are perhaps generally less critical of party performance than Dalton and Wattenberg. Finally, this book proceeds somewhat differently to *Parties Without Partisans* in a methodological sense. Whereas Dalton and Wattenberg's volume is organized thematically, ours provides a set of case studies which assess the standing and performance of parties in national contexts; general comparative inferences are only attempted in the final chapter. We hope that this will serve the needs of readers with special interests in particular systems, as well as those who wish to focus on the overall comparative picture.

THE SCOPE AND FRAMEWORK OF ANALYSIS

There is no intrinsic reason why the systematic comparative assessment of party status and performance should be restricted to long-established democracies in advanced industrial societies. The world has many less stable and recently transitional democracies which can be evaluated by the same criteria, even if the 'party decline' question makes little or no sense in the context of such regimes. So, although the perspective from which we ask the key questions would have to alter slightly in respect of parties in parts of Eastern Europe, Latin America, Africa and Asia, the overarching themes of the role, popular standing, organizational development, and functional relevance to democracy of political parties remain pertinent. Indeed, this book is to be understood as the first of two volumes of comparative scholarship addressing these themes and deploying a similar analytical framework: while we concentrate here on parties in established advanced industrial democracies,[1] a companion volume (Webb *et al.* forthcoming) will focus on recently transitional democracies in Eastern Europe and Latin America. The methodological purpose of such a division is to pursue a 'most similar systems design', thereby constraining extraneous sources of variance in the dependent variable (Peters 1998: 57). Ultimately, many readers may hone in on one volume while ignoring the other, according to their own interests, and indeed, each book can be read as a separate item in its own right. Equally, however, it should be understood that the books form twin components of an integrated package.

The analytical framework which our contributors have worked on challenges them to cover a considerable amount of ground. The chapters in this book are therefore necessarily long, at least by the usual standards of edited volumes of comparative scholarship. Given the inevitable space constraints within which we must operate, it has not been possible to devote a chapter to every case that might fall under the broad categorization of 'advanced industrial society'. However, the book presents a wide selection of relevant systems from Western Europe, North America, and Australasia. We believe that this array of cases offers a representative survey of the contemporary experience of political parties in the advanced industrial democratic world.

Two cases that are included in this collection—Spain and the European Union (EU)—require special explanation. In a sense, it might be argued that both could be more properly located in the companion volume on transitional democracies, since Spain only democratized after the death of General Franco in the

---

[1] 'Established' advanced industrial democracy is a term which we define operationally as any country which has enjoyed unbroken competitive democratic rule since 1945, or which has made a successful transition since then in so far as few would suggest any foreseeable prospect of authoritarian rule. In addition, each such country is a member of the OECD enjoying a high per capita income; such countries are often referred to as 'advanced industrial', 'post-industrial' (see, for instance, Dalton 1996), or even 'post-modern' in nature (Inglehart 1997).

mid-1970s, and the EU remains an inchoate transnational political actor, widely regarded to be suffering from the problem of 'democratic deficit'. On reflection, however, we feel that both are interesting cases worthy of inclusion in this book. Since the abortive coup attempt of 1981, Spain has consolidated its democratic status and has undoubtedly developed into an affluent industrial society; relevant to both these developments is the country's membership of the EU. Moreover, Spain's inclusion has some utility in terms of comparative logic. Further, while we are broadly adopting a most similar systems design, the inclusion of Spain also enables us to see if there are any resemblances between the status and role of parties there and in Latin America or Eastern Europe. If there are, this would strongly suggest a connection between party development and the stage of democratic development; if there are not, it would imply that the 'contagious' political impact of Spain's West European neighbours counts for more. This in itself is a significant point, though we will not be able to make the assessment until the companion volume on transitional democracies is complete. We would not justify the inclusion of the EU on precisely the same grounds; rather, we simply believe that it has become such a self-evidently important actor in European politics, and the role of parties is potentially and actually so significant for the democratic development of its institutions and processes, that it would be remiss to overlook it. In the European context it is no longer enough to focus on the politics of the nation state.

In order to achieve our stated objectives, an effective framework for comparative analysis is a paramount requirement. The one we have developed requires our contributors to produce an original synthesis of secondary material, new research, and critical comment. Two preliminary points are worth making about the way in which they have applied the framework. First, throughout, we are hoping to emphasize *change* over time. This raises the question of the date of reference against which to evaluate change; for long-established democracies, we focus on developments since 1960. As we have seen, it was in the 1960s that concerns about party performance (re)surfaced and the term 'party decline' emerged soon after. Moreover, much of the relevant source material dates from 1960 or thereabouts (for instance, on party organization, public opinion data, and so on).[2] Second, the precise indicators which authors discuss vary from case to case, mainly because of differences in what is available from each country. This is perhaps most obvious in the context of mass attitudes towards parties, since there is little or no consistency in the questions regarding parties which national election surveys pose of respondents. Nevertheless, we believe that our authors have managed to uncover evidence that taps the same underlying dimensions of analysis.

What are these dimensions? Implicit in the brief review of the literature outlined above is a distinction between three broad types of research inquiry into the

---

[2] For Spain, whose transition to democracy occurred more recently, we focus on the story since the initial year of democratization.

performance and standing of political parties:

1. Studies which focus on *party connections with the electorate* (by considering, for instance, partisan dealignment, electoral volatility, and membership change).
2. Studies which examine the *development of party organizations* over time.
3. Studies which investigate aspects of *party performance* on behalf of the wider political system.

To some extent, these different approaches give the impression of rather divergent perspectives on the decline of party controversy. Thus, while studies of 'parties-in-the-electorate' have often uncovered evidence of partisan dealignment or even anti-party sentiment, and taken this to signify party decline (Dalton *et al.* 1984), party organizational studies have tended to reveal ways in which parties have adapted and survived despite their weakening social linkages (Katz and Mair 1995). Then again, studies focusing on party performance have been somewhat mixed in their conclusions, some focusing on the perceived weaknesses (for instance, King 1969; Lawson 1980; Lawson and Merkl 1988), while others have offered notably more positive interpretations (Klingemann *et al.* 1994). It is curious to observe that most commentators, irrespective of their assessment, concur in the view that parties somehow remain important (Shonfeld 1983: 480). In any case, this threefold categorization of research on parties provides a cue for systematic comparative analysis.

Accordingly, each of the case studies which follows is divided into three sections, plus an introduction, and a conclusion. Our authors seek to use their **introductions** for two purposes. First, they draw a brief outline of the most notable features of the party system under consideration (emphasizing recent developments); this should provide readers who may lack country-expertise with a basic grasp of important contextual features such as the major actors in the party system and the prevailing pattern of party competition. For this reason, chapters routinely start with tables reporting national election results and the complexion of party governments. Where possible, authors will also use their introductions to summarize the main themes in the country-specific literature. Although there will not be space for an in-depth critique of such literature at this point, this introduction will serve both to outline key sources and references, and to raise themes to which authors may return in their chapter conclusions.

Following this, there are three major sections of empirical analysis, each dedicated to one of the dimensions implicit in the parties literature. The first is concerned with what we call the **popular legitimacy of parties**. This focuses on the vibrancy and health of linkages between parties and society at large. The central questions are: How stable and deep are links between party and society? And to what extent are parties generally held in esteem by citizens? These questions raise the issue of how one measures the popular legitimacy of political parties. We have taken our cue primarily from work on the theme of mass-level *anti-party sentiment* conducted by Poguntke and Scarrow (1996). In particular, we accept that Poguntke's behavioural indicators are as good as any available for gauging party–society linkages. These indicators comprise survey-based evidence of popular disaffection with parties in general, the erosion of partisan identification and affinity, declining electoral turnout, the growth of 'uncertainty' or 'hesitancy' within the electorate (in practice, a direct counterpart of the decline of partisan affinity), and declining party membership (Poguntke 1996: 325–38).[3] While these indicators do not necessarily constitute evidence of overt generalized mass-level antipathy towards parties, they are all consistent with a weakened sense of 'partyness' in society.

This is not to ignore the fact of a certain ambiguity in some of the measures. For instance, falling turnout, the erosion of partisanship, and the growth of voter 'hesitancy' could all be explained by temporary processes of ideological convergence between the major parties in a political system. Under such circumstances, deciding between the alternatives on offer becomes a more difficult but less consequential task for many citizens; equally, partisan loyalty and voting simply do not matter so much when the perceived differences between parties are not so great. Should the perception of ideological convergence prove a purely transient phenomenon, it is possible that partisanship and turnout would increase once more, while voter uncertainty could be expected to decline. Nevertheless, it is important to examine these indicators, for if we do find consistent developments across a number of them, and if we further discover that such developments persist over time, then it would surely be reasonable to conclude that party penetration of society had indeed eroded in a multifaceted and enduring fashion. In short, one could speak of the declining popular legitimacy of party.

Thus, each author has sought wherever possible to report and discuss the following indicators: survey evidence of antipathy, indifference, or cynicism towards political parties in general; survey evidence of levels of partisan identity; survey evidence of electoral uncertainty; individual party membership levels (both raw figures and membership/electorate ratios (Katz *et al.* 1992)); and national election turnout rates. In addition, these data will be set in the context of developments in national electoral behaviour and party competition in so far as we report rates of electoral volatility (Pedersen's (1979) well-known index of 'total net volatility' (TNV))[4] and party system fragmentation (Laakso and Taagepera's (1979) measure

---

[3] Poguntke includes one other indicator, support for 'anti-party parties'. We have decided to exclude this, however, on the grounds that it is questionable as to whether the existence of these organizations really represents any kind of retreat from party politics. In the final analysis, they remain parties themselves, and while they certainly stand against established parties, they could equally be interpreted as evidence of the adaptability and resilience of party politics.

[4] Note that some of our authors also refer to Bartolini and Mair's (1990) alternative measure of Bloc Volatility in discussing the evolution of party systems. However, we are primarily interested in the overall level of stability of electoral behaviour from one election to another, and thus focus on Pedersen's index of Total Net Volatility when summarizing the evidence in the Conclusion to this book.

of the 'effective number of parties'[5]). Though less unambiguous than some of the other measures, perhaps, indices of electoral volatility and party system fragmentation are aggregate-level indicators which could be expected to increase over the long term in line with the declining partyness of society. That is, the erosion of definite partisan orientations among voters should logically coincide with a greater likelihood of their switching party preferences from one election to another, while, though one would predict this with less confidence, it could also correlate with the emergence of new parties and/or the growth of support for small parties, both of which would generate a higher effective number of parties in a system. Although we suspect that it may be the least valid of our measures of overall party legitimacy, it is nevertheless interesting to examine how far there are consistent trends in the effective number of parties.

The second major dimension of analysis our authors investigate relates to **party organizational strength**. The central question here is: are parties persisting and developing as organizations? Are there signs of decay or might parties be adapting to changing social and political environments? As already mentioned, researchers focusing on this aspect of party life have often drawn rather different conclusions to those concentrating on the popular legitimacy dimension. The concept of organizational strength should be understood to imply both the quantity of resources at the disposal of a party, and the capacity to deploy those resources in a way that achieves the party's purposes. The latter criterion is important, for it is conceivable that the quantity of resources available to a party may decline without necessarily weakening its capacity to achieve its primary objectives (such as winning elections). Parties, like other organizations, change the way that they use resources over time; a *sine qua non* of party life thirty or forty years ago may now be regarded as virtually obsolete. The key thing, therefore, is whether or not a party has the resources it needs for its intended purposes; our country experts have

---

[5] This is probably the most widely used measure of party system fragmentation. Laakso and Taagepera's formula for counting the effective number of parties takes account of both the number of parties in the system and their relative strength. This is a very intuitive and useful technique of measurement since it tells us, for instance, that in any system comprised of just two equally strong parties, the effective number will indeed be 2.0, while a system consisting of three equally strong parties will generate an effective number of 3.0, and so on. This measure can be calculated either on the basis of party shares of the popular vote (the effective number of *electoral* parties (ENEP)), or on the basis of shares of seats won in parliament (the effective number of *parliamentary* parties (ENPP)). In this volume we are interested primarily in the former since it is the ENEP which is most likely to tap party penetration of society; by contrast, the ENPP can be quite heavily mediated by institutional factors like electoral systems. This is well illustrated by the case of the UK, where an increase in third-party support has produced a notable increase in the effective number of parties in the electorate since 1974. However, the Single-Member Plurality electoral system has prevented this surge in third-party support translating into a commensurate increase in parliamentary representation: consequently, the ENPP has not increased (Webb 2000: 6). So, while some of our authors find it useful to refer to the ENPP in introducing readers to the nature of a party system, we focus only on the effective number of electoral parties in the book's Conclusion.

therefore taken care to assess quantitative changes in resourcing in the light of this consideration.

Although the precise indications of party organizational development and strength may vary in significance from case to case, each chapter attempts to focus on a definite set of key measures of party organizational development. It should be said that the data in question are by no means universally and readily available, but our authors generally explain when this is the case. Specifically, each chapter seeks to uncover evidence of four aspects of organizational resourcing. The first is perhaps the most obvious: *party finance*. Specifically, overall changes in patterns of income and expenditure have been traced, and—wherever possible—the sources of funding (members, donors, or the state) identified. Second, *party staffing* has been examined where data are available in order to uncover changes in the number, type, and location of party employees. Third, *party membership* has been taken into consideration. Note, however, that here we are not so interested in simple trends in the sheer number of members, given that it may not be necessary for a party to recruit an especially high number in order for the organizational activities of the membership to be conducted. Rather, country experts discuss the implications of quantitative trends in party membership for organizational capacity; for instance, they may consider whether membership has fallen so far that local party organizations have become moribund and ineffectual, or whether parties have managed to adapt to membership losses by conducting activities in other ways. Finally, each chapter seeks to address the issue of party access to and/or control of the *media* (including publications and broadcast media).

The final dimension of analysis is in many ways the most challenging. It is concerned with **the systemic functionality of political parties**. What might the empirical indicators of party legitimacy and organizational strength imply about the broader utility of political parties for the political system? Where we find evidence of weakened legitimacy or organizational presence, does this reflect weak party functionality for the wider system? Conversely, where the indicators are more positive, could this reflect the resilience and continuing relevance of parties? In general, we would argue that it is hard to see how any serious attempt to consider the relevance of parties for modern democratic politics can avoid reflecting on how effectively they function. Although functional approaches to parties have sometimes been criticized (see, for instance, Shonfeld 1983), there is a very long tradition of paying attention to 'what parties do, what function, what role, or what purpose is served' by them (Scarrow 1957: 770). It is intuitive to ask these questions, and certainly very hard to overlook them when trying to assess the question of party decline. If parties really are in decline, then must it not reflect their failure to perform adequately some or all of the key tasks normally imputed to them? Perhaps, though it should be noted that sceptics have long doubted whether parties have really dominated the functions claimed for them (Sorauf 1964). This suggests that the sense of party decline which some observers experience might derive from the misperception that there was once a 'Golden Age' in which parties monopolized these systemic exigencies. Even if this is so, however, we still need to investigate party performance in order to assess whether it has really changed over time as much as some would have us believe.

But which functions should we examine? While Lowi (1963: 571) counsels against assuming an inventory of agreed functions of party 'as though these were as regularly a part of the political process as stages in the passage of a bill', it is clear from the considerable overlap between writers that something very like an 'agreed inventory' does in fact exist. True, they do not always use the same terminology, but frequently they are interested in the same phenomena. In view of the space constraints which must operate, the case studies in this volume do not address the most extensive list of party functions imaginable, but they do nevertheless engage with the following activities which we regard as central to modern democratic systems, all of which are explicit in the classic account of structural–functionalism articulated by Almond *et al.* (1993: Part 2).

Governance and political recruitment

While most of our authors choose to discuss these twin functions in separation from each other, it should be acknowledged that they are intimately connected. The central question around which the governing function revolves is: how far is government *party* government? Close consideration of this suggests that there are broadly two aspects to the governing function: personnel and policy. This is implicit, for instance, in Richard Katz's widely cited criteria for the 'partyness' of government: first, Katz suggests, all government decisions should be taken by individuals chosen in elections which are conducted along *party* lines; second, policy must clearly emanate from within parties (or definite coalitions of parties); and thirdly, 'positions in government must flow from support within the party rather than party positions flowing from electoral success' (Katz 1986: 43). While the first and third criteria prompt us to look at the personnel involved in the governing process, the second criterion points us towards the substance of policy. The recruitment function is intimately bound up with governance because, although it entails consideration of all kinds of elective and appointive political personnel, those who operate at the various levels of government lie at its heart. Hence, our contributors examine the extent to which recruitment to public—and especially governmental—office is channelled through political parties.

With respect to the policy aspect of governance, we have sought to address the question of how far public policy emanates from parties. There are a number of factors to bear in mind when discussing this question. One is the cohesion of legislative parties, for without this it can become impossible for 'governing' parties to leave their mark on public policy. A second issue is whether there are any significant alternatives to parties when it comes to shaping public policy. The most likely such alternatives would seem to be bureaucratic power, interest groups, and 'candidate-centred' forms of political agency. A further consideration is whether impersonal and structural constraints such as demographic developments, social trends, or economic forces can prevent parties from 'making a difference' to public policy (Rose 1980).

Interest articulation and aggregation

These functions require parties (among other political agents) to act as mechanisms of representative linkage between state and society.The articulation of interests refers to the role played by parties and other institutions (typically single-interest groups or social movements) in publicly expressing and pursuing the political demands of particular social groups. The aggregation of interests refers to a related but broader process by which parties bundle together the demands of a variety of social groups. This task is not quite so straightforward as the articulation of a narrower set of interests, since it requires the prioritization of demands and the maintenance of coalitions of support whose component elements may be in tension with each other.

A number of issues related to articulation and aggregation fall within the remit of our case studies. In particular, authors consider whether evidence of single-issue group and social movement activity suggests that parties are being challenged as articulators of social group interests, and in broad terms whether parties succeed in bundling together the demands of their various support constituencies in a coherent and stable fashion. One of the main questions to consider in relation to aggregation concerns the challenge posed by social change: where new cleavages emerge and society becomes more heterogeneous, does it become more difficult to aggregate incompatible demands from different components of a party's desired support base?

Political participation

As Almond *et al.* show (1993: ch. 4), this function overlaps with that of political recruitment, since holding elective public office is clearly a form of participation in politics. However, here we are more interested in the capacity of political parties to foster mass political participation through their members' activities and/or through mobilizing electoral turnout. Although it is true that we have already referred to party membership as an aspect of both party legitimacy and party organizational resourcing, now our primary focus switches to the activism levels of party members; this takes in the question of members' rights and powers within their parties. Some of our contributors also refer to the sociological profile of members here, where this bears upon party strategies to mobilize certain sectors of society.

Political communication and education

Political parties in democratic societies have traditionally played a significant role in helping to inform and educate citizens about public affairs. Prior to the era of widespread public access to television, this was accomplished largely through the activities of party members and through direct control of parts of the print media. Since then, parties have helped shape the agenda and substance of current affairs coverage by the broadcast media. Here our contributors consider how parties interpret their roles in political education, and the extent to which they have ceded agenda-setting and communication functions to non-partisan sources of political information.

It is apparent that there are points at which the three dimensions of our analytical framework overlap, most obviously perhaps, in the case of the party membership, which we have mentioned in the context of party legitimacy, organizational strength, and political participation. However, particular indicators have different meanings in different contexts and, where relevant, authors emphasize different aspects of indicators according to the dimension they are discussing. Thus, with respect to party membership, on the legitimacy dimension, the focus is primarily on trends in the *number* of party members; whereas on the organizational strength dimension, emphasis is placed on the *revenues and campaign work* flowing from party members (thus revealing something about how the party organization derives resource benefits from members); and in terms of the functionality dimension, authors focus on aspects such as the *number*, *sociology*, and *rights and activism* of party members, in order to say something about the degree to which parties succeed in fostering political participation.

CONCLUSION

Through the careful application of this framework, this book offers an insight into the changing nature and performance of modern political parties across the world's advanced industrial democracies. In the Conclusion to the book, we summarize the evidence and reflect on overall questions of party vitality and relevance. Moreover, we seek to draw attention to the links between perceptions of party legitimacy and performance and the observer's normative vision of democracy. There can be little real doubt that parties are here to stay for the foreseeable future, warts and all, yet it is equally evident that their nature and functioning has changed in a number of respects over the course of the past 40 years or so. Whether one looks at this and sees the glass half-empty (party decline) or half-full (party adaptation) ultimately depends on what one understands by, and expects of, the term 'democracy'.

REFERENCES

Ahmin, S. (1997) *Capitalism in the Age of Globalization* (London: Zed Press).

Almond, G. A., Powell, G. B., and Mundt, R. J. (1993) *Comparative Politics: A Theoretical Framework* (New York: Harper Collins).

American Political Science Association (1950) 'Toward a more responsible two-party system'. *American Political Science Review* 44 (Suppl.).

Bartolini, S. and Mair, P. (1990) *Identity, Competition, and Electoral Availability: The Stabilization of European Electorates 1885–1985* (Cambridge: Cambridge University Press).

Bibby, J. F. (1998) 'Party organizations, 1946–1996', in Bryon E. Shafer (ed.) *Partisan Approaches to Postwar American Politics* (New York: Chatham House), pp. 142–85.

Bryce, J. (1921) *Modern Democracies* (London: Macmillan).

Cotter, C. P. and Bibby, J. F. (1980) 'Institutional development of parties and the thesis of party decline'. *Political Science Quarterly* 95: 1–27.

Daalder, H. (1992) 'A crisis of party?' *Scandinavian Political Studies* 15(4).

Dalton, R. (1996) 'A divided electorate', in G. Smith et al. (eds) *Developments in German Politics* (Basingstoke: Macmillan).

Dalton, R. J. and Wattenberg, M. P. (2000) *Parties Without Partisans: Political Change in Advanced Industrial Societies* (Oxford: Oxford University Press).

Dennis, J. (1966) 'Support for the party system by the mass public'. *American Political Science Review* 60.

Giddens, G. (1998) *The Third Way: The Renewal of Social Democracy* (Cambridge: Polity Press).

Ginsborg, P. (1996) 'Explaining Italy's crisis', in S. Gundle and S. Parker (eds) *The New Italian Republic: From the Fall of the Berlin Wall to Berlusconi* (London: Routledge), pp. 19–39.

Inglehart, R. (1997) *Modernization and Post-Modernization: Cultural, Economic and Political Change in 43 Societies* (Princeton: Princeton University Press).

Jacques, M. (1993) *The Amazing Case of the Shrinking Politicians* BBC2 Television, Broadcast 25th October.

Katz, R. S. (1986) 'Party government: a rationalistic conception', in Francis G. Castles and Rudolf Wildenmann (eds) *The Future of Party Government: Visions and Realities of Party Government*, vol. 1 (Berlin: Walter de Gruyter), pp. 31–71.

—— and Mair, P. (1992) *Party Organizations: A Data Handbook on Party Organizations in Western Democracies, 1960–1990* (London: Sage Publications).

—— —— (1994) *How Parties Organize: Change and Adaptation in Party Organizations in Western Democracies* (London: Sage Publications).

—— —— (1995) 'Changing models of party organization and party democracy: the emergence of the cartel party'. *Party Politics* 1: 5–28.

King, A. (1969) 'Political parties in Western democracies: some sceptical reflections'. *Polity* 2: 111–41.

Kirchheimer, O. (1966) 'The transformation of West European party systems', in J. LaPalombara and M. Weiner (eds) *Political Parties and Political Development* (Princeton: Princeton University Press), pp. 177–200.

Klingemann, H. D., Hofferbert, R., and Budge, I. (1994) *Parties, Policy and Democracy* (Boulder, CO: Westview Press).

Laakso, M. and Taagepera, R. (1979) 'Effective number of parties: a measure with application to Western Europe'. *Comparative Political Studies* 12: 3–27.

Lawson, K. (1980) *Political Parties and Linkage: A Comparative Analysis* (New Haven: Yale University Press).

—— and Merkl, P. H. (1988) *When Parties Fail: Emerging Alternative Organizations* (New Jersey: Princeton University Press).

Lowi, T. J. (1963) 'Toward functionalism in political science: the case of innovation in party systems'. *American Political Science Review* 57.

Michels, R. (1915/1962) *Political Parties: A Sociological Study of the Oligarchical Tendencies of Modern Democracy* (New York: Free Press).

Mulgan, G. (1994*a*) 'Party-free politics?' *New Statesman & Society*, 15 April.

—— (1994*b*) *Politics in an Anti-Political Age* (Cambridge: Polity Press).

Ostrogorski, M. (1902) *Democracy and the Organisation of Political Parties*, vol. 1 (London: Macmillan).

Pedersen, M. (1979) 'The dynamics of European party systems: changing patterns of electoral volatility'. *European Journal of Political Research* 7: 1–26.

Peters, B. G. (1998) *Comparative Politics: Method and Theory* (Basingstoke: Macmillan).

Poguntke, T. (1996) 'Explorations into a minefield: anti-party sentiment. Conceptual thoughts and empirical evidence'. *European Journal of Political Research* 29: 319–44.

Poguntke, T. and Scaroow, S. (1996) 'Special issue on the theme of anti-party sentiment'. *European Journal of Political Research*, 29/2.

Rose, R. (1980) *Do Parties Make a Difference?* (London: Macmillan).

Sartori, G. (1976) *Parties and Party Systems: A Framework for Analysis* (Cambridge: Cambridge University Press).

Scarrow, H. (1957) 'The function of political parties: a critique of the literature and the approach'. *Journal of Politics* 29: 770–90.

Scarrow, S. (1996) *Parties and Their Members* (Oxford: Clarendon Press).

Schattschneider, E. E. (1942) *Party Government* (New York: Rhinehart).

Shonfeld, W. R. (1983) 'Political parties: the functional approach and the structural alternative'. *Comparative Politics* 15: 477–99.

Sorauf, F. J. (1964) *Political Parties in the American System* (Boston: Little Brown).

Webb, P. D. (2000) *The Modern British Party System* (London: Sage).

—— White, S., and Stansfield, D. (Forthcoming) *Political Parties in Transitional Democracies* (Oxford: Oxford University Press).

2

Political Parties in Britain

Secular Decline or Adaptive Resilience?

Paul Webb

INTRODUCTION

For thirty years following the end of the Second World War, it was orthodox to regard the UK as having one of the most stable and party-oriented political systems in the Western world. Parties penetrated state and society so significantly that it was virtually impossible to conceive of political life in the country without thinking first and foremost of *party* political life. Since the middle of the 1970s, however, old certainties have been challenged by a continuing and multi-dimensional debate about the transformation of British party politics. This challenge is predicated on a number of interconnected developments, including the apparent growth of electoral volatility; the spread of partisan and class dealignment; the emergence of nationalist cleavages in Scotland and Wales, which have threatened to fragment the national political culture; the erosion of two-party electoral domination; and the growing chorus of criticism levelled at the damaging iniquities of the electoral system and the adversarial 'winner-takes-all' political mentality that is closely associated with it. Despite this, the single-member plurality (SMP) (first-past-the-post) electoral system continues to ensure that single-party majority governments remain the norm (see Tables 2.1 and 2.2).

What do such changes imply for the general status of parties in the country? Those on the left have been especially prone to see evidence of party failure or decline in some of the changes noted. For instance, Jacques (1993) has contrasted the erosion of party–society links with the burgeoning non-partisan associative life of the country. In this context, he argues that the established model of representative politics which focuses on the parties in Westminster constitutes something of an impasse for democracy and it should be supplanted by the development of new forms of political participation. In a similar vein, Mulgan (1994*a*: 16)—ironically

Note that this chapter draws substantially on Chapter 9 of Webb (2000). I am grateful to Sage Publications for their kind cooperation in this matter

TABLE 2.1. *UK general election results since 1945*

Year	Conservative		Labour		Liberal Dem.		Others		ENEP	Turnout
	V	S	V	S	V	S	V	S		
1945	39.8	213	48.3	393	9.1	12	2.7	22	2.52	72.8
1950	43.5	299	46.1	315	9.1	9	1.3	2	2.40	83.9
1951	48.0	321	48.8	295	2.5	6	0.7	3	2.13	82.6
1955	49.7	345	46.4	277	2.7	6	1.1	2	2.16	76.8
1959	49.4	365	43.8	258	5.9	6	0.9	1	2.28	78.7
1964	43.4	304	44.1	317	11.2	9	1.3	0	2.53	77.1
1966	41.9	253	47.9	363	8.5	12	1.7	2	2.42	75.8
1970	46.4	330	43.0	287	7.5	6	3.1	7	2.46	72.0
1974F	37.8	297	37.1	301	19.3	14	5.8	23	3.13	78.8
1974O	35.8	277	39.2	319	18.3	13	6.7	26	3.16	72.8
1979	43.9	339	37.0	269	13.8	11	5.3	16	2.87	76.0
1983	42.4	397	27.6	209	25.4	23	4.6	21	3.45	72.7
1987	42.3	376	30.8	229	22.6	22	4.4	23	3.33	75.3
1992	41.9	336	34.4	271	17.8	20	5.8	24	3.03	77.7
1997	30.7	165	43.3	419	16.8	46	9.3	29	3.21	71.5
2001	31.7	166	40.7	413	18.3	52	9.3	28	3.25	59.5

Notes: V = % of the popular vote won; S = number of seats won in House of Commons; Liberal Democrat refers to the Liberal Party for the period 1974–79, and to the SDP–Liberal alliance in 1983 and 1987; ENEP = effective number of electoral parties.

Sources: Nuffield election studies; http://www.psr.keele.ac.uk/area/uk/uktable.htm; http://www.electionworld.org/unitedkingdom.htm.

in view of his subsequent role as advisor to Prime Minister Tony Blair—once asserted that 'it is hard to see the secular decline of the party reversing'. This, he claimed, reflected a gap between the ethos and practice of democracy; the blame for which could be placed squarely on the parties and parliament, who were 'centralised, pyramidal, national with strictly defined rules of authority and sovereignty' (see also Mulgan 1994*b*).

Evident in much of this line of criticism is a perspective on democracy which is essentially participationist; for the participationist critic, parties are a core compon-ent of a model which is based on the competitive elitism exemplified by the vision of Weber or Schumpeter (Held 1996: ch. 5). The participationist is exercised by the processes as much as by the outcomes of democracy, and any system which involves popular participation on the limited scale of the contemporary British model of party-dominated politics fails by at least two key criteria. The first of these is the criterion of personal development. That is, as participationists since Mill (at least) have argued, direct involvement by citizens in processes of political decision-making is critical to their sense of public responsibility and to their moral development. A further criterion by which the participationist evaluates any system is its legitimizing mechanisms, and here too, the elitist model is said to fall short, for 'people are more prone to accept decisions they help to make, even if they

TABLE 2.2. *Party composition of national government in the UK since 1945*

Dates	Party of government	Status	Prime minister
07/45–10/51	Labour	Majority	Attlee
10/51–04/55	Conservative	Majority	Churchill
04/55–01/57	Conservative	Majority	Eden
01/57–10/63	Conservative	Majority	Macmillan
10/63–10/64	Conservative	Majority	Douglas-Home
10/64–06/70	Labour	Majority	Wilson
06/70–02/74	Conservative	Majority	Heath
03/74–03/76	Labour	Minority/Majority[a]	Wilson
03/76–05/79	Labour	Majority/Minority[b]	Callaghan
05/79–11/90	Conservative	Majority	Thatcher
11/90–05/97	Conservative	Majority[c]	Major
05/97	Labour	Majority	Blair

[a] From March to October 1974 Harold Wilson led a minority government, but achieved a small overall majority in parliament at the general election held in the latter month.
[b] Labour lost its parliamentary majority in November 1976. Between March 1977 and August 1978, the Labour government's majority was effectively restored thanks to the negotiated support of Liberal MPs (the so-called 'Lib–Lab pact'). This was only an agreement on parliamentary support, however; the Liberals did not participate directly in government.
[c] John Major's government technically lost its parliamentary majority between November 1994 and April 1995 when 8 Eurosceptic Conservative backbenchers had the party whip removed, and a further backbencher voluntarily resigned the whip.

do not like the decisions reached' (Katz 1997: 67). From this perspective, the British model of democracy is frankly a disappointment, placing as it does far too much trust in the stultifying power of party elites. While these are themes to which we must necessarily return in the course of this chapter, they should be placed in perspective by the observation that debate about the positive and/or pathological features of political parties in general has not been the subject of widespread and notable debate in the way it has in some other countries included in this project (Germany, USA, and Italy, for instance). This is not to suggest, however, that evidence cannot be unearthed which hints at, or points directly to, public dissatisfaction with parties in Britain. It is to this evidence that we turn first.

THE POPULAR LEGITIMACY OF BRITISH POLITICAL PARTIES

If there is substance to the notion that British parties are in decline, then we should almost certainly expect to find evidence of their declining legitimacy within the citizen body at large. Taking our cue from the indicators of anti-party sentiment discussed in the book's Introduction, the first thing to address is *direct evidence*

TABLE 2.3. *Indications of popular dissatisfaction with parties in the UK*

Percentage of respondents feeling that	1987	1992	1997	2001
a Parties are only interested in votes	64.4	65.3	63.6	66.4
b Parties can be trusted to put national interest above party interest	36.8	33.2	—	—
c Governments can only sometimes, or never, be trusted	—	—	66.1	—
d Governments don't care what ordinary voters think	—	—	—	52.3
e MPs can only sometimes, or never, be trusted	—	—	91.5	—
f MPs lose touch with people once elected	—	—	—	67.7
g It does not matter which party governs	—	54.1	44.1	—
h No party can do much about unemployment	33.0	36.0	—	—
i No party can do much about inflation	27.0	38.0	—	—
j No party can do much about crime	34.0	41.0	—	—

Sources: British Social Attitudes Reports, British Election Surveys.

of popular disaffection with parties. Clearly, we need to call upon the findings of survey research in order to pursue this. Unfortunately, it is not easy to find long time-series of relevant variables, but we can at least use recent British Election Studies (BES) and British Social Attitudes Surveys in order to illuminate the state of British public opinion at the time of the recent general elections. Table 2.3 reveals a number of things about the popular standing of political parties and party elites since the 1980s.

This table suggests two kinds of problems which British voters have with political parties. First, a significant number of citizens distrust parties and party politicians in some respect or other. Thus, a very consistent two-thirds of the British electorate has been cynical about the motives of parties since the 1980s at least (item a in Table 2.1), while only one-third has claimed that parties place the national interest ahead of their own interest interest (item b). In general, one-third doubts that party governments can be trusted (item c), and less than half believes that governments even care what voters think (item d; see also Webb 2000, Figs 9.1 and 9.2). Staggeringly, fewer than 10 per cent are prepared to trust politicians, a level of disaffection which may in part reflect the numerous examples of adverse publicity which MPs have attracted concerning their sexual peccadilloes and financial misappropriations over the past few years (item e). Relatedly, perhaps, two-thirds feel that MPs lose touch with voters once elected (item f). The second problem which parties appear to have at the level of popular perception is that significant minorities doubt the distinctiveness and effectiveness of party government. Thus, while around half of respondents doubt that it really matters which party governs (item g), between one-quarter and two-fifths have expressed doubts about the ability of any party to resolve certain persistent policy problems (items h–j). Still, there is one comforting piece of news for parties; when all is said and done, the overwhelming majority of citizens find it hard to conceive of a political system which could operate without them (Webb 2000, Fig. 9.3).

It is possible that this sense of popular disaffection is also reflected in the second indicator of potential anti-party sentiment (or at least, of apartisanship), *the erosion of partisan affinity*. It is a frequently observed fact of British political science that partisan sentiment has eroded over the period since detailed attitudinal surveys of the electorate started in 1964. This partisan erosion occurs not so much in the sense that significantly fewer people are willing to identify themselves with a specific political party, but rather in that far fewer are inclined to express a very strong affinity with their preferred party, as Table 2.4 shows. Thus, whereas the proportion of British Election Survey respondents claiming to have a partisan identity only dropped from 93 to 86 per cent between 1964 and 2001, the number with a very strong identity fell from 44 to 13 per cent. This weakening of partisan sentiment is underlined if we add to the non-partisans the growing numbers (from 11 to 35 per cent) of those in the electorate who concede that their partisan identification is 'not very strong'. This gives us a sense of the proportional growth of the sector of the British electorate that lacks any clear affective partisan orientation; between 1964 and 2001 this sector increased in size from slightly less than one-fifth to half of the electoral sample. While a recent study of long-term trends in partisanship concedes that the circumstances surrounding the 1997 election offered Labour 'an exceptional opportunity to convert the demoralized refugees from the Conservative Party and capture a new generation of semi-detached but favourably inclined young voters' (Crewe and Thomson 1999: 84), it also stressed the short-term nature of Labour's window of opportunity in this respect; in essence, it is highly likely (particularly given that the proportion of very strong partisans did not grow either

TABLE 2.4. *Partisan sentiment in the UK*

	1964	1966	1970	1974	1979	1983	1987	1992	1997	2001
% with partisan identification	93	91	90	90	90	86	86	86	91	86
% identifying with Conservatives	38	35	40	35	38	38	37	35	30	25
% identifying with Labour	43	46	42	40	38	32	30	33	46	45
Total Cons + Labour identifiers	81	81	82	75	76	70	67	68	76	70
% very strong identifiers	44	44	42	26	22	26	19	17	16	13
% fairly strong identifiers	38	38	37	40	46	38	40	40	42	38
% not very strong identifiers	11	9	11	14	23	22	27	29	33	35

Note: The 1974 figure is for the February election only.

Sources: Crewe *et al.* (1995: 47); British Election Studies 1997, 2001.

in 1997 or 2001) that Labour's sudden surge in popularity since 1992 has been contingent rather than structural.

A rather different indication of the degree of party orientation within the British electorate (though not one for which we have a time-series, unfortunately) is provided by the information that 59 per cent of survey respondents suggested that they voted for a given party, regardless of the candidate choice in the 1987 general election (Jowell *et al.* 1987). Some 29 per cent indicated that candidate choice came into the reckoning to some extent or other (though only 5.5 per cent claimed to focus *primarily* on candidates). This is interesting in that it confirms the traditional view that the UK's political life is still predominantly party rather than candidate-centred. BES 2001, though using different question wording, conveys the same message even more emphatically: just 0.5 per cent of respondents spontaneously suggested that local candidate considerations entered into their decision-making processes. This lends an important sense of perspective to the discussion.

The third possible indicator of anti-party sentiment is *declining electoral turnout*. The significance of electoral turnout has long been debated by political scientists, of course, and it should be said that there is no clear consensus about overall transnational trends (Topf 1995; Poguntke 1996*a*; Wattenberg 2000). In the UK, turnout was actually higher in the 1992 general election than it was in that of 1945 (77.7 per cent compared to 73.3 per cent (refer again to Table 2.1)); the picture is essentially the same even if one focuses on a measure of turnout that is adjusted for the age of the electoral register (see Rose 1974: 494). In 1997, however, turnout dropped to its lowest level in any postwar general election up to that point in time (just 71.6 per cent); this, moreover, was the greatest decline in national turnout between any pair of elections since 1945 (Denver and Hands 1997*a*: 214). But this fall was easily outdone in 2001, as turnout plummeted to just 59.5 per cent, a collapse in mass participation which staggered most commentators. Even so, it may be too early to infer that Britain has experienced a secular trend of falling turnout in national elections. There may well have been reasons peculiar to the circumstances of the 1997 and 2001 elections which explain what happened then; as such, it is by no means assured that they will recur at future elections. For instance, one plausible explanation is that the vote has declined because a growing number of electors perceive a narrowing gap between the major parties in programmatic terms, and have thus concluded that, since it would make no great difference who was returned to office, there is simply little point in bothering to vote. The circumstantial evidence for this argument is unclear, however. On the one hand, there can be little doubt that voters have indeed, on the whole, seen ideological convergence between the major parties; thus, while 84 per cent of respondents perceived a 'good deal of difference' between Labour and the Conservatives in 1987, the figure was down to 57 per cent in 1992 and to just 33 per cent in 1997 (BES data). On the other hand, somewhat counter-intuitively, the proportion expressing indifference as to these governing alternatives actually dropped between 1992 and 1997, as we have already noted (see Table 2.3, item g). In fact, the most detailed analysis of the long-term pattern of general election turnout in the UK argues that 'the overall (lack of) closeness of the race, perhaps in conjunction with the ideological difference between the parties, seems the most convincing explanation for variations in turnout from one election to the next' (Taylor and Heath 1999: 180). In other words, there are no real 'trends' in turnout, but only fluctuations contingent on a variety of short-term factors relating to political context.

A fourth indication that the electoral roots of parties are eroding lies in evidence that *more voters are showing signs of uncertainty at election time*. Voters certain of their partisan orientation are, presumably, less likely to regard the electoral choice as a dilemma than those who lack a clear partisan allegiance. In this context, it is interesting to note that the first sophisticated panel study of British electoral behaviour across the course of a single general election campaign discovered that more than one-fifth of voters ended up by voting for a party other than the one they had initially inclined towards at the outset of that campaign (Miller *et al.* 1989: 111; 1990). Perhaps this should not surprise us in the light of the foregoing analysis showing the erosion of partisan affinity. Table 2.5 reports a variety of indications of voter hesitancy, using both aggregate-level and individual-level data. Aggregate-level data can be used to calculate the well-known measure of electoral volatility first devised by Mogens Pedersen in the 1970s—total net volatility (TNV). This does not appear to demonstrate anything other than trendless fluctuation over time; clearly, there are some high-volatility elections (February 1974, 1983, 1997), but once again, all of these can be readily explained by reference to short-term contextual factors. Survey data provide a number of possible individual-level indications of voter hesitancy, and while the pattern of these indicators is not entirely uniform, some interesting developments are apparent. Thus, the proportion of electors we

TABLE 2.5. *Indicators of electoral volatility and uncertainty in the UK*

Year	TNV	Partisans voting for another party	Considered voting for another party	Decided in election campaign	Switched vote from previous election
1964	6.0	8	25	12	18
1966	4.2	9	23	11	—
1970	5.9	10	21	12	16
1974 (F)	14.5	13	25	23	24
1974 (O)	3.0	11	21	22	—
1979	8.1	11	31	28	22
1983	11.6	13	25	22	23
1987	3.2	14	28	21	19
1992	5.2	17	25	24	19
1997	12.3	12	31	27	25
2001	2.6	12	—	25	22

Notes: TNV = total net volatility.

Sources: Heath *et al.* 1991: 15, 20; BES 1992, 1997, 2001.

might think of as 'disloyal partisans' (those who claim a certain partisan identifi-cation but vote for a different party) fluctuates, but it seems fair to conclude that it has increased moderately over the period as a whole since 1964 (see column 3); this conclusion is equally appropriate in respect of those who seriously considered voting for a party other than the one they finally chose (column 4). The percentage of voters only making their minds up during the final campaign itself shows a more definite upward trend, or rather a clear step-shift upwards after 1970 (column 5). On the other hand, there has been no clear pattern in the percentage claiming to have changed their vote from the previous election, although there was certainly an upwards lurch in 1997 (column 6); yet again, however, it is likely that this reflects the extraordinary nature of this particular election, given that an unusually high number of Conservative voters (one-third of the party's 1992 supporters) deserted John Major's party. Overall, there are few clear signs of a growth in electoral uncertainty. While it can be conceded that a significant minority of voters (between one-eighth and one-third) 'hesitate' at election time; there is no convincing reason for us to conclude that this signals a decline of party, though it may conceivably reflect the weakening partisan orientation of British electors since 1964.

However, perhaps the clearest evidence of popular alienation from parties lies in the indisputable fact of *declining party membership* since the 1960s. Even allow-ing for vagaries of accurate data (Webb 1992a: 847), party membership decline has been little short of precipitous. In 1964 over 9 per cent of all registered electors were members of the main three British parties with nationwide organizations; by the time of the 1992 general election, it was barely 2 per cent (an 80 per cent decline in proportional terms). Even allowing for the growth of certain minor parties not included in these calculations (notably the Scottish Nationalists) and the remark-able surge in Labour Party recruitment after Tony Blair was elected leader in the summer of 1994, it is quite evident that a significant trend is apparent. In any case, New Labour's burst of recruitment soon started to reverse itself after the election of May 1997, as Table 2.6 shows. This collapse of membership has a counterpart in declining levels of party activism, moreover. In the course of their research on major party membership in Britain, Patrick Seyd and Paul Whiteley uncovered a number of indications of declining activism among both Labour and Conservative Party members (Seyd and Whiteley 1992: 202; Whiteley *et al.* 1994: 223–4). The electorate, then, is notably less likely to engage in active partisan life in Britain.

What then is the overall picture in respect of party legitimacy in Britain? Trends in the key indicators of party membership and partisan identification undeniably suggest a real decline in partisan orientation among British electors; and although we lack relevant long-term time-series data, there are certainly some indications that voters are somewhat cynical about the motives, integrity, and governing effi-cacy of parties. There is also evidence to suggest that the minority of voters who make their choices late in the course of an election campaign has grown. On the other hand, the evidence of a variety of other indicators relating to electoral turnout, volatility, and 'uncertainty' is inconclusive. Indeed, the overwhelming majority of

TABLE 2.6. *Party membership in the UK since 1964*

Year	Labour	Conservative	Liberal/LD	M/E
1964	830,116	2,150,000	278,690	9.1
1966	775,693	2,150,000	234,345	8.8
1970	680,191	2,150,000	234,345	7.8
1974	691,889	1,500,000	190,000	5.9
1979	666,091	1,350,000	145,000	5.3
1983	295,344	1,200,000	145,258*	3.9
1987	288,829	1,000,000	137,500*	3.3
1992	279,530	500,000	100,000	2.0
1997	420,000	400,000	100,000	2.0
2001	361,000	350,000	90,000	1.9

*Includes SDP membership figures. M/E = membership/electorate ratio.

Sources: Labour Party NEC Annual Reports; Conservative National Union; Liberal Democrats' Information Office; Berrington and Hague 1997: 48; Walker 2001.

electors find the British system of government and politics inconceivable without parties, and continue to place party considerations well above candidate appeals when deciding how to vote. This, of course, places talk of 'party decline' in perspective. It is hardly the case, therefore, that empirical developments unanimously suggest a collapse of party legitimacy at the mass level in the country, though we cannot ignore the trends in party membership, partisan identity and, to some extent, electoral hesitancy. These trends may well be interrelated, and may be taken to reflect a certain detachment from political parties on the part of the electorate that did not exist a generation or so ago. Thus, although the overall case for declining party legitimacy is less than resounding, it cannot be wholly dismissed; at best, perhaps, a *prima facie* case for its development might be claimed.

THE ORGANIZATIONAL STRENGTH OF
BRITISH PARTIES

How far does this partial evidence of eroding party legitimacy find an echo at the level of party organization? Are British parties 'weakening' as organizations? Given the size and wealth of the country, British political parties have tended to be, in real terms, rather poorly resourced compared to other advanced industrial democracies (Webb 1995: 309–10). The UK has also been far more reluctant to regulate matters of party funding by law. However, this changed dramatically after the 1997 election, when the Labour government fulfilled an election pledge to reform what had become an increasingly controversial area of public life. Consequently, four months before the June 2001 election, a new Electoral Commission came into being, with powers to render more transparent the sources of party funding and to administer the provisions of the new *Political Parties, Elections and Referendums Act 2000* (Webb 2001). Among other things, this new regulatory framework imposed a ceiling on party expenditure in national general election campaigns. Initially set at a theoretical maximum of nearly £20 million per party, this represented a significant curb on the 'arms race' that culminated in the major parties spending approximately £55 million between them in 1997. Although official figures for party income and expenditure during the 2001 election campaign have not been published at the time of writing, media sources estimate that neither Labour nor the Conservatives could have spent more than £16 million (Hencke 2001). Thus, the new legal framework of party funding should reduce the financial pressure on the major parties. In any case, Tables 2.7 and 2.8 reveal that the parties were already better resourced in the 1990s than they had been thirty years previously, both in terms of money and staff.

Conservative Party real central income has fluctuated virtually trendlessly since the election of 1959, but the Labour Party has enjoyed a very definite growth in revenue; in fact, as the figures at the bottom of the final column of Table 2.7 make clear, Labour and the Liberal Democrats have gone a long way towards closing the traditional funding gap which has long existed between the Conservatives and themselves.[1] On average, therefore, it seems certain that the main British political parties are significantly better funded than hitherto and, not surprisingly, that they spend more in real terms. With respect to staff, it should be said that reliable time-series are very difficult to obtain, but there can be little doubt about the broad picture, for it is evident that while each of the parties has increased its establishment of personnel at the central level, the local story is generally one of substantial decline (see Table 2.8). Again, the Labour Party has experienced the most dramatic growth of central party resources (especially in the decade between the elections of 1987 and 1997). While the party did pursue a strategy of increasing the number of sub-national party organizers it employed after the 1997 election, press reports after the 2001 election suggest that this approach may not survive (Maguire 2001). Thus, even Labour has not been able to prevent the loss of full-time staff working at sub-national level over the period since the 1960s.

Does any of this point to the decline of party organization in Britain? Clearly, the local party figures suggest the possibility, at one level at least. Indeed, the impression of local organizational decline is confirmed when we turn to another indicator—or rather return to one we have already considered, albeit in a different context. For *party membership* is not only a measure of the popular legitimacy of parties, but it also bears directly upon the question of organizational development and presence. As we have already said, there is clear evidence of a very substantial

---

[1] This is probably not true of local party funding however. On average, local Conservative Associations appeared to be massively wealthier than either Constituency Labour Parties or local Liberal Democrat parties in the 1990s; at the time of the 1997 election, the average incomes for the three parties' local organizations were £33,305, £8,912, and £6,199 respectively (Neill 1998: 40).

TABLE 2.7. *UK party head office income and expenditure, 1959–97*

Year		Conservative		Labour		Liberals/LDs		Average	
		Money terms	Real terms	Money terms	Real terms	Money terms	Real terms	Money terms	Real terms
1959	Y	1,672,000	20,900,000	498,000	6,225,000	28,275	353,438	732,758	9,159,475
	X	1,180,000	14,750,000	485,000	6,062,500	27,057	338,213	564,019	7,050,238
1964	Y	2,092,000	22,740,040	573,000	6,228,510	82,965	901,830	915,988	9,956,790
	X	2,280,000	24,783,600	583,000	6,337,210	82,784	899,862	981,928	10,673,557
1966	Y	1,976,000	19,760,000	725,000	7,250,000	113,547	1,135,470	938,182	9,381,820
	X	2,450,000	24,500,000	420,000	4,200,000	115,582	1,155,820	995,194	9,951,940
1970	Y	1,860,000	15,493,800	1,034,000	8,613,220	213,630	1,779,538	1,035,877	8,628,855
	X	1,668,000	13,894,440	948,000	7,896,840	96,699	805,503	904,233	7,532,261
1974	Y	2,221,500	12,484,830	1,781,000	10,009,200	87,074	489,356	1,363,191	7,661,133
	X	2,519,500	14,159,590	1,865,000	10,481,300	119,241	670,134	1,501,247	8,437,008
1979	Y	5,292,000	14,394,240	3,113,000	8,467,360	299,101	813,555	2,903,131	7,896,516
	X	5,885,000	16,007,200	3,358,000	9,133,760	252,089	685,682	3,165,030	8,608,882
1983	Y	9,800,000	17,836,000	6,200,000	11,284,000	1,235,035	2,247,764	5,745,012	10,455,921
	X	8,600,000	15,652,000	6,100,000	11,102,000	4,704,000	8,561,280	6,468,000	11,771,760
1987	Y	15,013,000	23,270,150	9,843,000	15,256,650	1,896,640	2,939,792	8,917,547	13,822,197
	X	15,600,000	24,180,000	11,300,000	17,515,000	4,106,000	6,364,300	10,335,333	16,019,766
1992	Y	23,449,000	26,731,860	13,200,000	15,048,000	3,000,000	3,420,000	13,216,333	15,066,619
	X	19,600,000	22,344,000	19,000,000	21,660,000	2,500,000	2,850,000	13,700,000	15,618,000
1997	Y	42,500,000	42,500,000	24,100,000	24,100,000	3,800,000	3,800,000	23,466,666	23,466,666
	X	38,400,000	38,400,000	31,500,000	31,500,000	3,500,000	3,500,000	24,466,666	24,466,666
Change,	Y	+2442	+103	+4739	+287	+13339	+975	+3103	+156
1959–97 (%)	X	+3154	+160	+6395	+420	+12836	+935	+4238	+247

Notes: X = Expenditure, Y = Income.

All amounts are quoted in sterling; all years selected are general election years. Figures for 1974 are the average for financial years 1973/4 and 1974/5, thus taking in both the general elections of February and October 1974. Figures represent an attempt to total income to and expenditure from all central party funds, including both general and general election funds, where parties make such a distinction. Note that the figures for the old Liberal Party are almost certainly a significant underestimate of the party's true financial position (see Webb 1992a: 867). 'Liberal' figures for 1983 and 1987 are aggregated for both the Liberal Party and the SDP.

Sources: 1959–79 figures: Pinto-Duschinsky 1980; 1983–87 figures: Linton 1994; 1992–97 figures: Neill 1998. Ultimately, all these figures can be traced back to Conservative Party Annual Financial Statements, Labour Party NEC Annual Reports, Liberal Party Annual Reports, and Liberal Democrat Federal Party Annual Reports.

TABLE 2.8. *Party staffing in the UK*

Year	Conservatives		Labour		Liberals/LDs	
	Central	Sub-national	Central	Sub-national	Central	Sub-national
1964	97	580	50	248	19	74
1970	95	431	50	167	12	22
1979	—	350	—	128	17	—
1983	—	—	—	104	20	11
1987	100	291	71	95	25	8
1993	148	240	90	—	—	—
1998	167	221	179	150	35	5
Change 1964–98 (%)	+72	−62	+258	−40	+84	−77

Note: The figures cited for 1993 and 1998 are certainly lower for each of the parties than they would have been during the general election years of 1992 and 1997, respectively; for instance, the Conservatives managed to employ around 290–300 sub-national staff (i.e. full-time agents) during each of the election years of 1987, 1992, and 1997. Since I have been unable to gather central party staffing data for 1992 and 1997, I have cited the more complete 1993 and 1998 figures. The main implication of all this is that the general growth in the number of party employees has been almost certainly even greater than this table implies.

Sources: Conservative Central Office; Labour Party Personnel Department; Labour Party NEC Organization Committee minutes; Liberal Party Annual Reports; Liberal Democrats' Information and Personnel Offices; Finer 1980.

decline in major party membership in the UK since the 1960s, and a decline in the activist inclinations of many who do retain their party memberships. Taken together with the equally impressive decline in local party staffing, this paints a picture of political parties in decline at the local level, if not the central level.

There is no doubt that central party elites have noticed the decline of their local party organizations, and that this is of concern to them. Indeed, if they are to accept the assessment of Whiteley *et al.*, they should be profoundly worried:

We disagree with those who suggest that parties have less need today of their members . . . Without a participative grass-roots membership, political parties become dominated by legislative 'notables'. Such candidate-centred parties find it difficult to maintain their cohesion . . . notables are more likely to find personal reasons for why they are unable to remain loyal to collective decisions . . . (1994: 7)

Beyond this, the same authors have pointed to the importance of an active membership for constituency election campaigns (Whiteley and Seyd 1992; see also Denver and Hands 1992, 1997*b*; Johnston *et al.* 1995). Moreover, Susan Scarrow's close analysis of party strategists' thinking on these matters suggests that they have never accepted the notion of the insignificance of grass-roots members (Scarrow 1996*b*). Nevertheless, it is clear that the days of Duverger's mass party are long gone (if, indeed, they were ever here in the case of the UK (see

Webb 2000: ch. 7)) and it helps to view party change from the perspective of alternative and more contemporary models of party development; previously I have argued that Angelo Panebianco's archetype of the 'electoral-professional' party is instructive in interpreting the development of the major parties in the UK in what we might think of as a post-modern political environment (Webb 1992b; 2000: 208–9).

Notwithstanding the importance of the research cited above, it is still possible to argue that local party organization is most likely not as important to the national political party as was once the case. This is probably true at least in the crucial area of election campaigning, since contemporary campaigns are overwhelmingly televisually oriented. In such a context, communication with electors does not necessarily require large numbers of locally based officials and an army of volunteer member-activists. This is not to suggest that local campaigns are viewed as insignificant by the parties, but rather, that the careful targeting of resources and effort in certain localities is what counts. Indeed, this has become increasingly evident in recent election campaigns, with all parties concentrating their efforts on key seats (Berrington and Hague 1997: 52; Kavanagh 1997: 31). The crucial point about this is that such carefully targeted campaign efforts require central coordination, if not the centralization of resources. Seen in this light, the running down of local party organizations in the UK may not be as significant as it initially appears. This brings us back to the second criterion of party organizational strength alluded to earlier; that is, parties do not just require resources, but they need to deploy them in such a way as to achieve their primary purposes. Campaigning is a case in point, for if it is true that local staff and members are not so important as was once the case, then we should be careful about interpreting the reduction of these resources as part of an overall story of organizational 'decline'. And there is good evidence to suggest that parties might have more than made up for the loss of these local resources in other ways.

Since the 1960s British political parties have all drawn on the talent and advice of marketing and advertising professionals, a phenomenon which has increasingly attracted the attention of journalists and academics (Hughes and Wintour 1990; Webb 1992b; Seyd 1993; Shaw 1994; Scammell 1995; Lees-Marshment 2001). Initially, the Conservatives captured interest with their reliance upon the advertising skills of Saatchi and Saatchi during the 1979 and 1983 campaigns. However, more recently the focus has shifted towards Labour. Despite the habitual reservations of some on the left, Neil Kinnock decided in the mid-1980s that policy reform had to be complemented by a more professional approach to marketing if the message of the party was to get across. This professionalization has entailed the use of senior party employees with professional backgrounds in the mass media, advertising, or public relations; a commitment to far greater investment in and reliance upon the findings of (increasingly sophisticated) opinion research; and a more standardized approach to national campaigning, with overarching emphasis on the requirements of televisual communication (Shaw 1994: chs 3, 6;

Webb 2000: 157–8). The professionalization of political marketing has been a key element of Labour's organizational response to changing electoral markets, and it is central to the electoral-professional approach which the party has come to exemplify.

Historically, the Conservative Party was probably readier to adapted to the requirements of the modern electoral-professional than Labour, given its strong, relatively autonomous leadership and a highly developed willingness to invest heavily in marketing expertise. Indeed, this readiness to adapt to the needs of pro-fessional campaigning and political communication is hardly a new feature of the party. As Cockett (1994: 577) says

The record of the party's use of advertising and communications techniques for publicity is, therefore, one of extraordinary innovation—certainly compared to that of the other British political parties. Belying its name, the party had always been prepared to embrace the most modern publicity methods and techniques to gain political advantage . . .

The Conservatives have shown a willingness to employ professional agencies since the 1920s, but the era of partisan erosion and the arrival at the helm of Margaret Thatcher in the 1970s generated a new degree of investment in these methods. The role of the Saatchi and Saatchi advertising agency has attracted an enormous amount of attention over the years, and is widely regarded as having heralded a new age of professionalization in British political campaigning. While parties had used advertising professionals before, Saatchis were original in being the first to assume full-time control of all aspects of publicity and opin-ion research, and in being paid a retainer between elections. This enabled them to work with the leadership on long-term campaign strategies. Their sustained relationship with the party was later supplemented by the introduction of new public relations and marketing approaches to the staging of annual conferences, direct mailing of targeted supporters, telephone canvassing, and computer-aided communications.

Apart from staff formally on party payrolls, and professional consultants or limited-term fund-raising specialists hired by the parties, we should not over-look the possibility that modern British parties might benefit from professional research and policy assistance provided by independent policy research bodies. Formally, few of these 'think-tanks' (as they have generally come to be known) are linked to any of the parties or have representation within party structures. Informally, however, it is widely recognized that there are partisan and ideologi-cal sympathies as well as overlaps of personnel which to some extent connect parties to research bodies. Thus, these bodies should not be entirely dismissed when evaluating the overall picture of party resourcing in contemporary Britain. For instance, the Institute for Economic Affairs (IEA, founded in 1945), the Centre for Policy Studies (CPS, founded by former Conservative government minister Sir Keith Joseph in 1975), and the Adam Smith Institute (ASI, 1977) are essentially right-wing think-tanks, whose political outlooks were especially sympathetic to the governments of Margaret Thatcher. Less high-profile, but broadly right of centre, are the Social Market Foundation (1989) and Politeia (1995). Further left, there are long-established research foundations such as the Fabian Society (1884, and the one such body which is formally affiliated to Labour), the Policy Studies Institute (PSI since 1978, though its roots lie in Political & Economic Planning, which goes back to 1931), and the National Institute of Economic & Social Research (NIESR, 1938). Closer to New Labour in recent years, however, have been the Institute for Public Policy Research (IPPR, 1988) and Demos (1994). Just how valuable a resource to the parties have these bodies been? This is not easy to assess, but it seems most likely that they have been of less value than some commentators suppose. Scrutiny of policy development processes suggests that politicians are only willing to draw on the recommendations of think-tanks when these coincide closely with their own views. In other words, politicians gain intellectual support and credibility by pointing to the work of think-tanks, while the latter gain publicity, occasional research contracts, and publication sales in return (Denham and Garnett 1999). It should also be said that the parties sometimes recruit individuals to their own ranks from independent research bodies; David Willetts, for instance, moved from the PSI to Conservative Central Office's own Research Department before eventually being elected to parliament and becoming a minister in the Major government, while Neil Kinnock's former press secretary Patricia Hewitt travelled a not dissimilar path into the Blair government via the IPPR. More recently, Tony Blair has recruited both David Miliband (of IPPR) and Geoff Mulgan (of Demos) to his Downing Street policy unit. In these ways, think-tanks can act as occasionally useful resources for front-bench politicians, but only rarely provide direct staff or policy assistance.

To summarize overall patterns of development in party organizational strength in the UK, a number of features stand out. In real terms, central party organizations have become better off, especially in Labour's case as the party has tapped into new sources of support outside its traditional trade union sponsors. These new sources have largely been business corporations and wealthy individuals, but the state has also become more important in two ways: first, as a slightly more generous source of financial subvention in its own right (Webb 2001: 317); and second, as a regulatory force which reduces the financial pressure on parties by imposing legal constraints on their national campaign spending. Furthermore, resources have tended to shift away from local parties to the centre, and this has been complemented by a significant professionalization of central party organizations, at least in respect of the major parties. While British political parties face continuing struggles to resource their activities, it is nonetheless implausible to suggest that the evidence reviewed here constitutes 'party decline' in an organizational sense. Rather, it makes more sense to think in terms of the adaptation of party organization in Britain.

THE SYSTEMIC FUNCTIONALITY OF POLITICAL PARTIES
IN BRITAIN

What, if anything, do the empirical indicators of the party legitimacy and organizational strength tell us about the broader utility of parties for the political system in Britain? On the whole, evidence of party decline seems more persuasive with respect to popular legitimacy than to organizational strength, especially in respect of the erosion of party membership, the weakening of affective partisan sentiment and a consequent rise in voter hesitancy. But what do these phenomena say about the role played by parties in the modern political system?

Governance and political recruitment

We have seen (recall items g–j in Table 2.3) evidence that suggests a degree of voter cynicism about the impact of parties in government. In fact, two important aspects of the governing process need addressing, which draw us into the closely related functions of recruitment and governance: namely, the *personnel* and *policy* of government. Broadly speaking, parties cannot be regarded as central to the provision of governance unless they provide the key personnel and policies of government. Turning first to the question of government *personnel* (the recruitment function) it can be argued that party penetration of the British state in this sense is generally high and has become higher since 1960. In this context it is essential to recall that Cabinet ministers are, by longstanding convention, obliged to be parliamentarians—and the latter are almost entirely party politicians. In 1997, the election of the former BBC journalist Martin Bell as an Independent MP (on an anti-corruption ticket), constituted a rare counter-example to the domination of the House of Commons by party politicians.[2] Even the occasional selection of non-parliamentarians (and, indeed, of non-party members) for junior governmental posts is something entirely in the hands of the leading party politicians;[3] taken together with evidence that voters are overwhelmingly concerned with party rather than candidate considerations (see above), this seems to confirm unequivocally that national governmental recruitment is primarily a party-oriented rather than a candidate-centred process.

Furthermore, this has even become largely true of local government. While it was not uncommon for independent non-partisan councillors to play a significant

---

[2] Even then, his success depended on the decisions by the Labour and Liberal Democratic parties to withdraw their own candidates in the constituency and support him.

[3] Tony Blair demonstrated a certain proclivity for this practice on assuming office in 1997, in appointing one or two prominent businessmen with little or no background in party politics to junior ministerial posts: examples include Lord Simon, Lord Sainsbury, and Lord MacDonald. In order to maintain constitutional tradition, however, these men took their places on the Labour benches in the House of Lords.

role in local politics until the major reorganization of local government in 1973/4, this has now become comparatively rare, except at the lowest level of sub-national government (in the rural parishes, for instance). To this extent, therefore, there is actually a case for arguing that party penetration of the polity has increased since 1960. The constitutional reforms by which the new Labour government of 1997 introduced devolution and city-wide government in London are unlikely to alter the essential picture, since candidacies for these new offices will almost certainly be dominated by party nominees, though it should be said that the first London mayoral election did result in the remarkable victory of a non-party candidate (Startin 2001). Where cities opt to follow London's example of instituting directly elected mayors, some potential for candidate-centred politics may emerge at sub-national level; however, this seems unlikely to be the norm.

It should not be overlooked that there is a whole layer of non-elective public office which is part of the means by which Britain's public institutions are governed and resources allocated—that of the 'quangocracy'. Quango (an acronym for quasi-autonomous non-governmental organization) appointments may now number as many as 65,000 (though much depends on one's definition: Weir and Hall 1994; Viney and Osborne 1995) and cover an enormous range of activity and public provision, including school governorships, Training and Enterprise Councils (TECs), local health authorities and hospital trusts, and a variety of funding councils. Many of these positions are in the gift of the political parties, and it should be said that the increasingly naked exploitation of this vast reservoir of patronage by the Conservative governments between 1979 and 1997 became a subject of some controversy in the 1990s. Often the quangocracy's domain seemed to be enhanced at the expense of elective local authorities, and increasingly the Tories regarded it as vital to the exercise of power that sympathizers—especially from the world of business—outnumbered their rivals' appointees on all these bodies (Jenkins 1995: 264–5).

The second broad aspect of party government concerns *policy* rather than personnel: as Katz (1986: 43) puts it, under party government public policy should emanate from party sources which can clearly be identified and held to account by the citizenry. There are a number of potential challenges to this, however, the first of which is breakdown of party cohesion. That is, uncohesive, fluid, and unpredictable patterns of alignment in parliamentary parties can undermine the capacity of the executive to effect its legislative programme, and make it difficult for electors to hold accountable specific parties or coalitions of parties which might be regarded as the authors of policy. In the UK, though, this condition is still largely satisfied by the prevalence of single-party government. It is true that cross-party negotiations and collaboration are not entirely absent, and are likely to become more evident, especially in the government of Scotland, Wales, and Northern Ireland. But there is no evidence as yet that such coalitions will be especially uncohesive. Moreover, party discipline at Westminster is still strong enough for governments to enact most (and often all) of their preferred legislative programmes, notwithstanding evidence of a growth in backbench dissent since 1970 (Norton 1975, 1978, 1980, 1994; Norton and Cowley 1996). With the exception of certain authorities in local government, there is little difficulty in concluding that public policy can still generally be clearly identified as the policy of a given party or (occasionally) coalition of parties in Britain.

A further challenge to the idea that government policy is primarily party policy lies in the claim that the government is becoming increasingly 'prime ministerial'; the most notable example of this is Michael Foley's argument that a *de facto* 'presidentialization' of British politics has occurred as the prime minister has become far more than merely a 'first among equals' (Foley 1993). This presents us with the possibility that an essentially collegial form of party government is stealthily being usurped by a new form of candidate-centred executive leadership, a notion reinforced by evidence of the 'presidentialization' of campaigning and voter influences (Mughan 2000).

It should be said that there is solid evidence to support the view that 'prime ministerial government' has gradually come to inhere more structurally and less contingently in the British political system. This contention is not in itself novel; a well-known debate on this matter took place in the 1960s (Mackintosh 1962; Crossman 1964; Jones 1965). More recently, however, it has been persuasively demonstrated that a powerful prime ministerial department has come to exist in all but name. Burch and Holliday (1999: 43) contend that the development of the Prime Minister's Office and the Cabinet Office since 1970, and the growing connectedness between them, constitutes a transformation of the central state. The traditional fragmentation of the central state in Britain creates a pressing and persistent need for coordination, which is increasingly met by an 'integrated core which operates as the central point in the key policy networks'. This core lies clearly at the disposal of the prime minister and puts us in mind of Crossman's contention (1964: 189) that he or she is 'the hyphen which joins, the buckle which fastens' national policy-making. In recent years, Tony Blair has attracted particular attention (as did Margaret Thatcher before him) for his self-consciously 'presidential' style of government (Hennessy 1998; Kavanagh and Seldon 1999; Hencke 2000).

Even so, it must be said that while British prime ministers can often appear firmly in control of the ship of government, they still depend critically on the confidence of their Cabinet colleagues and backbench supporters in the Commons, as the reluctant departure from government of Margaret Thatcher in 1990 illustrated. Ultimately, and fatally, she lost the confidence of key Cabinet colleagues, while John Major's period at the helm of government was devastated by backbench dissent. Even Tony Blair is no monocrat, as his uneasy relationship with Chancellor of the Exchequer Gordon Brown attests (Rawnsley 2000). Therefore, we may conclude that while prime ministers can play an increasingly central role in developing and coordinating national policy, they are still constrained in various ways by the political impact of frontbench colleagues, backbenchers, and even extra-parliamentary 'sub-leaders'. To this extent, governmental policy remains party policy rather than prime ministerial policy.

A third challenge to party policy in government is posed by civil service power. In Britain, both central and local bureaucrats are career civil servants who are legally obliged to refrain from active engagement in party political activity. Clearly, there-fore, the official bureaucracy remains formally impervious to parties. However, though formally subservient to their political masters, it is certain that senior bureaucrats often play an influential role in influencing and implementing policy. Bureaucrats working closely with Cabinet ministers hold many advantages, in that they often have greater general knowledge of government and specific know-ledge of certain policy fields, control information flows to ministers, and influence their agendas. That said, there is equally little doubt that politicians retain the final word; moreover, experienced ministers and governments with a clear pro-grammatic purpose and electoral mandate can undoubtedly impose themselves on the civil servants, as the Thatcherite administrations of the 1980s demonstrated (Budge 1996: 44–5). In addition, ministers have increasingly sought to enhance their autonomy by appointing teams of political advisers answerable to them rather than the civil service. Thus, while it represents a significant constraint, the fact of civil service power should not be seen as fundamentally undermining the party government model in Britain.

So, national governmental policy in Britain is still predominantly *party* rather than prime ministerial or bureaucratic policy. However, we can delve deeper into the matter of party autonomy in government by addressing a question famously posed by Rose (1980): Do parties make a difference to public policy? This bears once again upon the issue of accountability, it should be noted, for if parties are fundamentally unable to shape public policy, who does (if anyone), and who should be held to account (if anyone)? In fact, it is well recognized that a variety of macro-social developments can seriously constrain the scope for autonomous action by party governments, including technological changes, demographic trends, social changes, and economic cycles. Indeed, the whole question of global economic constraints on national governmental autonomy has become one of the defining political themes of the contemporary era, and a highly vexed issue for politicians and intellectuals alike. The power of these implacable and impersonal forces can seem daunting, and they make it unsurprising that commentators should question the ability of parties to make any real difference. In fact, the broad question of whether or not they do breaks down into at least two more specific issues: first, do parties actually offer the electorate reasonably *distinct* policy alternatives, or are they so convergent as to render the idea of 'choice' meaningless? Second, irrespective of what they might promise to electors, do they actually generate real *differences in terms of policy outputs* once they get the opportunity to wield power?

The more straightforward issue to deal with is that of programmatic distinc-tiveness. Long-term manifesto analyses of shifting party ideologies demonstrate that ideological distance between the major UK parties tends to fluctuate. There have been times in the past two decades when the gap between Labour and the Conservatives has approximated a gulf, the early 1980s being the most obvious such occasion. However, more than one study shows that this gulf has diminished sharply since 1992, at least in terms of left–right ideology (Webb 2000: 113; Bara and Budge 2001: 28). Ideological convergence is particularly evident in matters of macro-economic management, and while it is certain that a degree of repolarization could occur at some point in the future, it is interesting to note that the long-term trend has been one of convergence in the UK (Caul and Gray 2000: 213–15). This should not lead us to the simplistic conclusion that there are no important differences between the major parties; it is not hard to demonstrate sharp contrasts over themes like constitutional reform, Europe, or welfare policy, but it does suggest that those electors who struggle to discern the differences have picked up on something tangible.

Does the growing indistinctness of ideological emphases, at least in certain areas, render insignificant party impacts on policy outcomes? Since Rose's initiatives in the early 1980s, a number of scholars have researched the impact of British party governments in the context of their various constraints, and the general conclusion is that parties can and do continue to make a difference. That said, this research is in need of updating. Hogwood (1992) discovered that while overall levels of public expenditure (relative to population size and GDP) tended to climb regardless of which party was incumbent between 1945 and 1990, certain policy fields (especially housing and defence) are clearly susceptible to party effects. This broad argument is confirmed in the far more theoretically ambitious and methodologically sophisticated approach of Klingemann *et al.* (1994: 70), who suggest that while party governments struggle to control spending in areas characterized by entitlement rights (for instance, the automatic right to benefit once a person is defined as unemployed or disabled), parties can and do implement meaningful policy changes in other areas. Overall, they claim that their evidence 'offers a clear picture of the operation of the party mandate in Britain'. Indeed, given the preponderance of single-party governments in the postwar era, Britain is precisely the sort of country in which one would expect to find a definite link between manifesto promises and government action. Interestingly, however, research demonstrates that party effects on policy are also apparent at the level of local government, where single-party control is far less pervasive (Sharpe and Newton 1984: ch. 9).

To the largely quantitative evidence supplied by researchers like Hogwood and Klingemann, two further points are worth adding. First, most observers would probably concur in the view that parties can effect quite distinctive qualitative shifts in public policy once in power. One need only think of the Conservative governments' legislative initiatives which constricted the powers of trade unions in the 1980s, or the various reforms affecting the agencies delivering social policy during the same period; similarly, New Labour's agenda of constitutional reform is less quantitative than qualitative in its implications for the British state, yet it is nonetheless profound for all that. Second, it should be borne in mind that the longer that parties are in power, the greater their policy impact is likely to be. As has often been pointed out, public policy tends to have a momentum of its own, and it can take considerable time and effort to change its direction. This fact may well explain an asymmetry in the party effects discovered by Klingemann, in that the Conservatives have tended to have a greater impact on policy outputs when in office than Labour. When one bears in mind that, between 1945 and 1997, the Conservatives enjoyed 35 years in office compared to Labour's 17, including unbroken spells of 18 and 13 years, compared to Labour's maximum incumbency of 6 years, it is readily apparent that the former have experienced significantly greater opportunities for wielding long-term influence over the development of national policy.

In essence, therefore, the overall conclusion must be that, while there have undoubtedly been significant areas of policy convergence between the parties, they remain central to the provision of meaningful and accountable governance in the UK. However, the (partly justified) perception of many voters that there are no great differences between the major parties probably contributes to the erosion of their popular standing.

Interest articulation and aggregation

It is fairly clear that British political parties do not fulfil the function of articulating and representing interests as effectively as might be desired, or might once have been the case. In part this could be taken to reflect the widespread perception that the party system fails to represent its citizens adequately. For instance, both the 1997 and 2001 general election results deviated from proportional outcomes in terms of party representation in the House of Commons by 21 per cent; by contrast, the deviation from proportionality at the last election before Liberal and nationalist party support rose significantly (June 1970) was only 8.6 per cent. Moreover, deviation from proportionality within certain regions of the country has often been far in excess of this national mean; at its most extreme, for instance, the Conservatives took 97 per cent of South East England's parliamentary seats in 1992, despite only winning 55 per cent of the votes there (Dunleavy *et al.* 1993: 186–7). Criticism of the adversarial and unrepresentative nature of the British party system is in itself part of a complex debate, but it is quite clear that such criticism has become more pervasive over the past thirty years, and for obvious reasons; the disproportional effects of the simple plurality system mattered relatively little when the major parties absorbed over 90 per cent of the national vote and alternated with some regularity in office, as was the case from 1945 to 1970. Since then, however, minor parties have come to account for a quarter of the vote on a regular basis, and, given their lack of particular regional strength, the centre parties (Liberals, Social Democrats, Liberal Democrats) have suffered particularly from the workings of the electoral system. Not surprisingly, therefore, the influential critiques of academics such as the late Samuel Finer (1975, 1980) and David Marquand

(1988) have been wholeheartedly expounded by the centre parties, and have found a certain resonance at the popular level. For instance, British Election Survey data in both 1992 and 1997 revealed that one-third or more of the electorate wanted the system reformed and two-fifths felt that the country would be better served by the introduction of coalition government to replace the single-party model that has been so characteristic of post-1945 Britain.[4] In effect, the question of electoral reform reveals doubts about whether the party system in the UK accords adequate weight to certain interests.

In December 1997 the Blair government established an Independent Commission on the Voting System (chaired by Lord Jenkins of Hillhead) to investigate and make recommendations on prospects of electoral reform for elections to Westminster; the Commission duly reported in October 1998. Although the government was initially expected to call a referendum on the question of replacing the present electoral system, this now seems far from certain, and it is even less likely that the government will endorse the alternative to SMP voting recommended by the Commission.[5] It should also be noted that Britain has in any case become an increasingly heterogeneous laboratory for those investigating the impact of different electoral systems; since 1999, a regional list-PR system has been employed for returning members to the European Parliament, while the new Scottish Parliament, Welsh Assembly, and Greater London Assembly use (slightly different versions of) the Additional Member System (AMS); London's directly elected mayor, on the other, is chosen by a variation of Alternative Vote (AV) known as the Supplementary Vote (SV). Thus, while it is certainly possible to make the case that the legitimacy of the political system has been undermined by the growing failure of the party system to provide a broadly accepted pattern of representation, it is not certain that the conditions producing this charge will remain indefinitely.

It should be added that perceptions of the representative 'decline' of British political parties stem not only from the vagaries of the electoral system, there is also the challenge which is said to be posed by alternative sources of interest articulation. As Mulgan and Jacques remind us (see chapter introduction), evidence of burgeoning single-issue group membership and activity suggest that, in the eyes of many citizens at least, other organizations better fulfil the representative function now. Circumstantially, this is persuasive since it would appear that the decline of party

---

[4] Note that these are relatively conservative estimates of the desire for electoral reform in the UK; Dunleavy and Margetts (1997: 240) claim that as many as 55 per cent of voters approve of reform.

[5] This is a peculiar hybrid referred to in the Jenkins Report as 'AV top-up' or 'limited AMS'. In essence, this proposes a system whereby the bulk of MPs (80–85 per cent) would be elected to single-member constituencies by the Alternative Vote, while the remainder would be allocated according to an open-list system based on existing local government areas. The express purpose of this system is to achieve 'broad proportionality without imposing a coalition habit on the country' (Jenkins 1998: ch. 9, para. 7). The Labour Party's National Policy Forum, however, has rejected this scheme. In so far as any kind of reform will be officially endorsed by the party, it seems likely to be straight AV.

membership coincides neatly with the growing number of interest group attachments and the emergence of new social movements (Byrne 1997: 3). Indeed, more
than this, it is often proposed that the two are part and parcel of a linked process;
when parties 'fail', Lawson and Merkl (1988) tell us, alternative organizations
of state–citizen linkage emerge to fulfil functions of interest articulation (1988).
Indeed, this perspective seems especially plausible in the context of centripetal
major party competition; that is, the more the major parties have sought to build
broad catch-all constituencies of social support, the more they have emphasized
the aggregation of interests while neglecting older traditions of articulating specific (class) constituency demands. Thus, it seems to make sense to suppose that
the effects of this are vitiated to some extent by the growth of single-issue group
activity. But how credible are such claims? Certainly, there is little denying the
evidence that, during the period in which party membership has palpably declined,
interest group membership has grown; Kees Aarts, for instance, has shown that
while 48 per cent of Britons surveyed in 1959 claimed membership of some kind
of civic or social organization, this had grown to 61 per cent by 1990 (Aarts 1995:
232).[6] Yet the same author provides further evidence which is profoundly damning for the 'when parties fail' perspective, for support for new social movements
and political parties seems to be anything but mutually exclusive; on the contrary,
across a range of west European countries, including Britain, supporters of new
social movements are significantly more likely to express a positive party preference than those not involved with new social movements. In 1989, for instance,
95 per cent of ecologists expressed such a partisan preference, compared to 89
per cent of non-ecologists; similarly, 93 per cent of CND supporters were partisans compared to 81 per cent of non-supporters (ibid: 251). Thus, commitment to
group activity is—as research on political participation has often pointed out—a
stimulant to partisanship.

   Processes of social and political change have almost certainly confronted the
parties with new challenges as articulators and aggregators of group interests. In
particular, the growing heterogeneity of British society has brought new social
group demands and issues on to the agenda of politics to which the parties have
sometimes struggled to respond adequately (Webb 2000: ch. 1). Nevertheless, it is
hard to see an alternative vehicle to the political party for the aggregation of political demands in a country like the UK. Though in principle demands can certainly
be aggregated into coherent legislative programmes by other actors (individual
politicians in candidate-centred presidential systems like the USA's, bureaucrats
in non-democratic systems), only parties can really do so legitimately in parliamentary democracies, and there is little doubt that the citizenry look overwhelmingly to
the parties to fulfil this function in Britain. Single-issue groups or social movements

---

   [6] Admittedly, these percentages include membership of political parties. However, since we know
that party membership has declined during the same period, the implication is of an even more
substantial increase in the proportion of the samples claiming membership of non-party organizations.

may be challenging parties as articulators of particular group demands, but by definition they are not in the business of bundling together a multiplicity of interests into ordered and coherent programmes of legislative action; interest aggregation, then, remains a core party function. To be sure, though, this task has become more complex given the growing number of cross-cutting cleavages; in effect, the major parties have been challenged to build increasingly broad coalitions of support at a time when such a task has become inherently more difficult. Moreover, not only have major parties struggled to aggregate interests as effectively as hitherto, but their attempts to do so may even have undermined their ability to articulate traditional group demands; for Labour at least, the adoption of a more broadly aggregative inter-class appeal (the catch-all strategy) has probably weakened its role as a working class tribune. In short, in attempting to develop its aggregative capacity, Labour may well have weakened its ability to articulate (some) demands.

Political communication

A role in which British parties have undoubtedly been challenged by other actors since 1960 is that of political communicator and educator. It is clear that reliance on non-partisan forms of media for political information and comment has increased dramatically in the country since 1960 (Dunleavy and Husbands 1985: 111). For instance, some 65.9 per cent of BES respondents indicated that they saw national TV news at least once a day during the 1997 election campaign, and all but 5 per cent claimed to see some TV news during the course of a week; over two-thirds claimed to pay at least 'some attention' to the political content of this news, moreover. By contrast, 43 per cent of respondents claimed to read a daily newspaper, and 58 per cent to see a paper at least once a week; the parties could only directly contact around a quarter of electors via canvassing.[7] All of this implies that the agenda-setting capacity of the political parties has most probably been reduced, and it certainly means that the most authoritative source of political information for most citizens is apt to criticize any and all of the political parties. Indeed, the standard manner in which the public broadcasting networks interpret their brief to provide 'balanced' (which is to say, non-partisan) coverage of politics is by adopting an acutely adversarial stance in dealing with party spokesmen and women. Ultimately, I suspect, this may serve to weaken the popular legitimacy of parties, though it is hard to think of a way in which this might be conclusively demonstrated. There is no doubt, though, that party politicians are often put squarely on the defensive in these encounters; this applies to politicians of all sides, but especially to those associated with governing parties. It may be, therefore, that indications of public cynicism about parties reflect in part the particular way in which parties are obliged to share the terrain of political communication with the mass media in Britain.

---

[7] Figures based on data from the British Election Study 1997.

That said, party politicians have no right to expect supine deference from the media in a competitive and pluralist democracy, and they are by no means entirely passive victims. Since the first 'television election campaign' of 1959, parties have taken enormous pains to transform themselves into highly sophisticated political communicators who exploit all the technological and professional resources available in their quest to inform and persuade voters (as we have already seen in the foregoing discussion of staff professionalization). It certainly seems reasonable to conclude that, in conjunction with the mass media, parties in contemporary Britain still manage to play a considerable role in defining the political agenda and providing an informational base for citizens' cognitive understanding of politics (see, for instance, Bowler *et al.* 1992).

Political participation

Do British political parties foster political participation to the extent that they once did? In some respects the answer would seem to be 'surely not'. The evidence we have already encountered regarding the decline of party membership and activism, and the more recent concerns about dwindling electoral participation, seem plainly damning. Of equal concern is the evidence of social imbalance in patterns of party political participation in advanced industrial societies like Britain's. As noted in the introduction to this chapter, it is precisely from the perspective of the participationist vision of democracy that political parties often tend to be regarded as 'failing'. Yet an overall assessment of the importance of political parties for political participation in the UK demands that a number of other factors should be borne in mind.

First, it should not be forgotten that the clear majority of voters still make the effort to vote for one party candidate or another, at least at national elections; notwithstanding the historically low turnout of 2001, it is not yet clear that this is part and parcel of a secular trend in mass political behaviour. Second, and perhaps more significantly, however, is the fact that a number of developments over the past two decades or more suggest that, at least for those who remain sympathetic to parties, the opportunities to participate are significantly greater. This is evident in a number of ways, some of which relate to sympathetic non-members as well as formally enrolled party activists; thus, the growth of the quangocracy offers a myriad of opportunities for participation in the governance of public sector institutions to thousands of individuals. Many of these positions, as we have already noted, remain in the gift of the parties. Even more notably, however, are the various reforms by which the main parties have sought to democratize their internal procedures over the years. These reforms have afforded ordinary members new rights of participation and influence in processes of candidate-selection, leadership-election, and policy making (Webb 2000: ch. 7). These new rights do not unambiguously empower the parties' grass roots at the expense of the elites; in particular, leaders have found ways to maintain or even enhance their autonomy in the policy-making processes which are crucial to strategic games of party competition. But neither have such reforms been entirely meaningless and cynical manipulations of followers by their leaders; ordinary party members have decidedly greater rights over the choice of party candidates and elites than was the case a generation ago.

It must be conceded that these arguments are hardly like to convince those who reject democratic elitism in favour of radical participatory visions of democracy. While it can be argued that parties should still be seen as central even to radically participatory models of direct democracy (Budge 1996), it is clear that many critics regard parties as fundamentally elitist devices which fail to engage enough citizens in processes of democratic participation. Even so, while parties may attract justified criticism in this respect, they remain vital to political participation in the UK. Party activity still offers one of the chief means by which ordinary British citizens can involve themselves in political life, and although fewer individuals may seek formally to exploit such channels than hitherto, the opportunities for activity and influence via parties are on the whole greater now for those who do wish to take advantage of them. In short, there can be little point in writing parties off, for they remain a vital ingredient in the institutional recipe of participation.

CONCLUSION

The evidence certainly leaves room to suggest a variety of challenges to the systemic functionality of British parties—for instance, in the emergence of non-partisan sources of political communication, or in the decline of partisan forms of political participation—yet, on reflection, it is just as evident that parties remain at the heart of the political system in a number of vital ways. While a degree of partisan dealignment and the decline of party membership cannot be denied, these developments need to be set in this broader functional context. That such a context makes it hard to sustain a simple declinist perspective should be apparent. We are able to reflect on several telling indicators of continuing party relevance. Thus, we have observed that the major parties have more than maintained their financial position since 1960; they have enhanced their professional sophistication in the areas of marketing and communication; the overwhelming majority of voters are still willing to declare a partisan identification (albeit a quite possibly weakened one); a similar proportion give a clear primacy to partisan rather than candidate considerations when they actually vote; and the major parties have reformed their procedures in a numbers of ways which extend the participatory rights of members. So why this apparent resilience?

In part, it could be said that, even where we have suggested a possible partial loss of functionality, parties must be given credit for adaptation. For instance, while it is true that parties share the political communication and education function to

Paul Webb

a greater extent than hitherto, it would be an exaggeration to represent them as being supplanted by an alternative set of communicators. The parties have worked hard to adapt to the reality of communicating principally through the medium of television, so that while TV may be formally independent of the parties, the latter are increasingly adept at its use. Similarly, the rise of single-issue groups not only challenges political parties as interest articulators, but it also offers parties new opportunities for political mobilization. For instance, Labour not only maintains its formal links with the trade unions, but it has forged less formal links with a host of groups concerned with the environment, nuclear energy and armaments, housing, social welfare, women's, and ethnic issues. This suggests that party penetration of society may be broader but shallower. Moreover, it is typical of parties to respond to electoral defeat or membership decline with a bout of intense organizational reform designed, among other things, to offer new participatory incentives to individual members. In short, even though political parties in the UK may have to contend with a variety of challenges, they are skilled at adapting and surviving; more than this, they remain of central importance to the structures and processes of democracy in the country. This record of survival and resilience, however, is almost certainly contingent upon the continuing willingness of party elites to recognize the remaining scope for reform, adaptation, and innovation.

REFERENCES

Aarts, K. (1995) 'Intermediate organizations and interest representation', in H. D. Klingemann and D. Fuchs (eds) *Citizens and the State* (Oxford: Oxford University Press).

Bara, J. and Budge, I. (2001) 'Party policy and ideology: still New Labour?' in Pippa Norris (ed.) *Britain Votes 2001* (Oxford: Oxford University Press), pp. 26–42.

Berrington, H. and Hague, R. (1997) 'The Liberal Democrat campaign', in P. Norris and N. T. Gavin (eds) *Britain Votes 1997* (Oxford: Oxford University Press), pp. 47–60.

Bowler, S., Broughton, D., Donovan, T., and Snipp, J. (1992) 'The informed electorate? Voter responsiveness to campaigns in Britain and Germany', in S. Bowler and D. Farrell (eds) *Electoral Strategies and Political Marketing* (Basingstoke: Macmillan), pp. 204–22.

Budge, I. (1996b) *The New Challenge of Direct Democracy* (Cambridge: Polity Press).

Byrne, P. (1997) *Social Movements in Britain* (London: Routledge).

Caul, M. L. and Gray, M. M. (2001) 'From platform declarations to policy outcomes: changing party profiles and partisan influence over policy', in R. S. Dalton and M. P. Wattenberg (eds) *Parties Without Partisans: Political Change in Advanced Industrial Democracies* (Oxford: Oxford University Press), pp. 208–37.

Cockett, R. (1994) 'The party, publicity and the media', in A. Seldon and S. Ball (eds) *The Conservative Century: The Conservative Party Since 1900* (Oxford: Oxford University Press), pp. 547–77.

Crewe, I., Fox, N., and Day, A. (1995) *The British Electorate: A Compendium of Data from the British Election Surveys 1963–1992* (Cambridge: Cambridge University Press).

Crewe, I. and Thomson, K. (1999) 'Party loyalties: dealignment or realignment?', in G. Evans and P. Norris (eds) *Critical Elections: British Parties and Voters in Long-term Perspective* (London: Sage).

Crossman, R. H. S. (1964) 'Introduction' to W. Bagehot *The English Constitution* (London: Watts). Reprinted in A. King (ed. 1985) *The British Prime Minister* (London: Macmillan), pp. 175–94.

Denham, A. and Garnett, M. (1999) 'Influence without responsibility? Think tanks in Britain'. *Parliamentary Affairs* 52, 46–57.

Denver, D. and Hands, G. (1992) 'Constituency campaigning'. *Parliamentary Affairs* 45: 528–44.

——, —— (1997a) 'Turnout', in P. Norris and N. T. Gavin (eds) *Britain Votes 1997* (Oxford: Oxford University Press), pp. 212–24.

——, —— (1997b) *Modern Constituency Campaigning* (London: Frank Cass).

Dunleavy, P. and Husbands, C. (1985) *British Democracy at the Crossroads* (London: Allen & Unwin).

——, Margetts, H., and Weir, S. (1993) 'The 1992 election and the legitimacy of British democracy', in D. Denver, P. Norris, D. Broughton and C. Rallings (eds) *British Elections and Parties Yearbook 1993* (Hemel Hempstead: Harvester Wheatsheaf), pp. 177–92.

——, —— (1997) 'The electoral system' in P. Norris and N. T. Gavin (eds) *Britain Votes 1997* (Oxford: Oxford University Press), pp. 225–41.

Finer, S. E. (1975) *Adversary Politics and Electoral Reform* (London: A. Wigram).

—— (1980) *The Changing British Party System* (Washington: American Enterprise Institute).

Foley, M. (1993) *The Rise of the British Presidency* (Manchester: Manchester University Press).

Heath, A., Jowell, R., Curtice, E. G., Field, J., and Witherspoon, S. (1991) *Understanding Political Change* (Oxford: Pergamon).

Held, D. (1996) *Models of Democracy*, 2nd edn (Cambridge: Polity Press).

Hencke, D. (2000) 'Special advisers tripled as No. 10 staff hits new high'. *The Guardian*, 2 March.

—— (2001) 'Super-rich lead party donor table'. *The Guardian*, 8 August.

Hennessy, P. (1998) 'The Blair style of government: an historical perspective and an interim audit'. *Government & Opposition* 33: 3–20.

Hogwood, B. (1992) *Trends in British Public Policy* (Buckingham: Open University Press).

Hughes, C. and Wintour, P. (1990) *Labour Rebuilt: The New Model Party* (London: Fourth Estate).

Jacques, M. (1993) *The Amazing Case of the Shrinking Politicians* BBC2 Television, Broadcast 25th October.

Jenkins, L. (1998) *Report of the Independent Commission on the Voting System* (London: HMSO).

Jenkins, S. (1995) *Accountable to None: The Tory Nationalization of Britain* (London: Penguin).

Johnston, R. and Pattie, C. (1995) 'The impact of spending on party constituency campaigns at recent British general elections'. *Party Politics* 1: 261–73.

Jones, G. W. (1965) 'The prime minister's power', *Parliamentary Affairs*, XVIII, pp. 167–85. Reprinted in A. King (ed., 1985) *The British Prime Minister* (London: Macmillan), pp. 195–220.

Jowell, R. *et al.* (1987) *British Social Attitudes Report* (Aldershot: Dartmouth Publishing).

Katz, R. S. (1986) 'Party government: a rationalistic conception', in Francis G. Castles and Rudolf Wildenmann (eds) *The Future of Party Government: Visions and Realities of Party Government*, vol. 1 (Berlin: Walter de Gruyter), pp. 31–71.

—— (1997) *Democracy and Elections* (New York: Oxford University Press).

Kavanagh, D. (1997) 'The Labour campaign', in P. Norris and N. T. Gavin (eds) *Britain Votes 1997* (Oxford: Oxford University Press).

Kavanagh, D. and Seldon, A. (1999) *The Powers Behind the Prime Minister: The Hidden Influence of Number 10* (London: Harper Collins).

Klingemann, H. D., Hofferbert, R., and Budge, I. (1994) *Parties, Policy and Democracy* (Boulder, CO: Westview Press).

Lawson, K. and Merkl, P. H. (1988) *When Parties Fail: Emerging Alternative Organizations* (New Jersey: Princeton University Press).

Lees-Marshment, J. (2001) *Political Marketing and British Political Parties: The Party's Just Begun* (Manchester: Manchester University Press).

Linton, M. (1994) *Money and Votes* (London: Institute for Public Policy Research).

Mackintosh, J. (1962) *The British Cabinet* (London: Stevens).

Maguire, K. (2001) 'Cash-strapped Labour steps up overdraft'. *The Guardian*, 1 August.

Marquand, D. (1988) *The Unprincipled Society: New Demands and Old Politics* (London: Fontana).

Miller, W., Broughton, D., Sonntag, N., and McLean, D. (1989) 'Political change in Britain during the 1987 campaign', in I. Crewe and M. Harrop (eds) *Political Communications: The General Election Campaign of 1987* (Cambridge: CUP).

Miller, W., Clarke, H., Harrop, M., Leduc, L., and Whiteley, P. (1990) *How Voters Change* (Oxford: Clarendon).

Mughan, A. (2000) *Media and the Presidentialization of Politics in Parliamentary Elections* (Basingstoke: Palgrave).

Mulgan, G. (1994*a*) 'Party-free politics?'. *New Statesman & Society*, 15 April.

—— (1994*b*) *Politics in an Anti-Political Age* (Cambridge: Polity Press).

Neill, L. (1998) *Report of the Committee on Standards in Public Life on the Funding of Political Parties in the UK, vol. 1, cm 4057-1* (London: The Stationery Office).

Norton, P. (1975) *Dissension in the House of Commons: Intra-Party Dissent in the House of Commons Division Lobbies 1945–74* (London: Macmillan).

—— (1978) *Conservative Dissidents: Dissent Within the Parliamentary Conservative Party 1970–74* (London: Temple-Smith).

—— (1980) *Dissension in the House of Commons 1974–79* (Oxford: Oxford University Press).

—— (1994) 'The parties in parliament', in L. Robins, H. Blackmore, and R. Pyper (eds) *Britain's Changing Party System* (London: Leicester University Press).

—— and Cowley, P. (1996) 'Are Conservative MPs revolting? Dissension by government MPs in the House of Commons, 1976–96'. *Centre for Legislative Studies Research Paper 2/96* (Hull: University of Hull).

Pinto-Duschinsky, M. (1980) *British Political Finance, 1932–1980* (Washington DC: American Enterprise Institute).

Rawnsley, A. (2000) 'How Gordon has trussed up Tony'. *The Observer*, 5 March.

Rose, R. (1974) *Electoral Behaviour: A Comparative Handbook* (NYC: Free Press).

—— (1980) *Do Parties Make a Difference?* (London: Macmillan).

Scammell, M. (1995) *Designer Politics: How Elections Are Won* (Basingstoke: Macmillan).

Seyd, P. (1993) 'Labour: the great transformation', in A. King *et al.* (eds) *Britain at the Polls 1992* (Chatham, NJ: Chatham House).

—— and Whiteley, P. (1992) *Labour's Grass Roots* (Oxford: Clarendon Press).

Sharpe, L. J. and Newton, K. (1984) *Does Politics Matter? The Determinants of Public Policy* (Oxford: Clarendon Press).

Shaw, E. (1994) *The Changing Labour Party Since 1979* (Oxford: Clarendon).

Startin, N. (2001) 'Candidate-centred and party-free elections: lessons from the Livingstone mayoral campaign'. *Representation* 38: 31–45.

Taylor, B. and Heath, A. (1999) 'Turnout and registration: new sources of abstention?' in G. Evans and P. Norris (eds) *Critical Elections: British Parties and Voters in Long-term Perspective* (London: Sage Publications), pp. 164–80.

Topf, R. (1995) 'Electoral participation', in H. D. Klingemann and D. Fuchs (eds) *Citizens and the State* (Oxford: OUP).

Viney, J. and Osborne, J. (1995) *Modernising Public Appointments* (London: Demos).

Walker, D. (2001) 'The party's over'. *The Guardian*, 16 January.

Webb, P. D. (1992*a*) 'The United Kingdom', in R. S. Katz and P. Mair (eds) *Party Organization: A Data Handbook* (London: Sage Publications), pp. 837–70.

—— (1992*b*) 'Election campaigning, organisational transformation and the professionalisation of the British Labour Party'. *European Journal of Political Research* 21: 267–88.

—— (1995) 'Are British political parties in decline?'. *Party Politics* 1: 299–322.

—— (2000) *The Modern British Party System* (London: Sage).

—— (2001) 'Parties and party systems: modernisation, regulation and diversity'. *Parliamentary Affairs* 54: 308–21.

Weir, S. and Hall, W. (1994) *Ego Trip* (London: Demos).

Whiteley, P. and Seyd, P. (1992) 'The Labour vote and local activism: the local constituency campaigns'. *Parliamentary Affairs*, October.

—— —— and Richardson, J. (1994) *True Blues: The Politics of Conservative Party Membership* (Oxford: Clarendon).

3

Italian Parties

Change and Functionality

Luciano Bardi

THE CHANGING STRUCTURE OF THE PARTY SYSTEM

For over forty years Italy was seen as a 'party government' system. The party system was extremely fragmented, consisting of up to ten national parties, at least seven of which could at any time be considered 'relevant': the five parties constituting most governmental coalitions from the early 1960s onwards (the dominant DC, the PSI, and three small secular centrist parties, the PSDI, PRI, and PLI), the largest opposition party, the communist PCI, and the neo-fascist MSI. As a consequence of various factors that found expression in the results of two crucial elections in 1992 and 1994, all of this has abruptly come to an end. Party organizations have literally fallen apart after at least thirty years of successful adaptation to societal and political system changes (Bardi and Morlino 1994). All parties and other electoral competitors have been deeply affected. A number of the traditional parties, including the three largest ones (DC, PCI, PSI) suffered divisions and transformations.[1] None of the thirteen major competitors in the 1994 Chamber of Deputies' race (for the list seats) had run with the same names and symbols in the 1987 election. Although only one of the thirteen lists, Forza Italia, led by Silvio Berlusconi, appeared to be, at least on the surface, completely new, the sheer number of these changes demonstrates the magnitude of the party system's transformation.

---

[1] The PCI finally underwent a long awaited transformation in 1991. The party abandoned all communist connotations and called itself Democratic Party of the Left (Ignazi 1992) and later on simply Democrats of the Left (DS). Its most orthodox wing did not accept the transformation and continued in the communist tradition as Communist Refoundation (RC). In 1993 the DC, in an attempt to re-found itself at least morally, changed its name to Italian People's Party (PPI), the party's original name in the pre-fascist period. This did not prevent the party's diaspora: in 1999, at least four different parties (PPI, CCD, CDU, and UDR) could be traced back to the pre-1993 DC. The PSI, also in a process of moral refoundation, after having been decapitated by political corruption investigations, completely changed its leadership and lost most of its apparatus.

The transformation was the result of three sets of direct causes. First, there had been shifts in political demand for specific parties or even parties in general, resulting from greater potential voter mobility. Second, there had been change in the political supply provided by the parties: (a) through the disappearance or transformation of individual parties resulting from scandals and judicial actions that exposed Italy's extended system of political corruption known as *tangentopoli* (kickback city); (b) as a consequence of the need for the parties to make new and different strategic choices in response to the new electoral law; and (c) as a response to the changing structure of political/electoral demand. Third, the new electoral law impacted directly on the parties' parliamentary delegations (Bardi 1996*b*). Some of these factors are arguably still effective, and the transformation of the Italian party system is far from complete.

The changes in political supply were nothing short of dramatic (Table 3.1). The most notable new party of the post-1992 party system has been Forza Italia. The creation of media tycoon Silvio Berlusconi, FI has consistently won over 20 per cent of the vote in recent elections, and contests closely with the ex-communist DS the position of Italy's largest party. The PCI's transformation initially resulted in the formation of two separate parties, the PDS and RC (and most recently a third formation, PdCI),[2] which between them in the last four general elections have attracted roughly the same electoral strength as their predecessor. The big difference is that parties of the left have now finally and definitively acquired sufficient legitimacy to be permanent and fundamental parts of governmental majorities, and even provide prime ministers. Similarly, the MSI's evolution has produced two offspring, the die-hard and small MSI-FT, and the much more mainstream and ostensibly respectable National Alliance (AN), which is now the fourth largest party in the system. The Lega Nord (Northern League) is a regionalist party that first made an electoral impact in the north during the 1987 national election; it had become, with approximately 10 per cent of the vote, one of the four big parties in the system by 1996, though it slipped back in 2001. The most important change, however, lies in the disappearance of the DC, whose political heritage was divided between the PPI and the CCD-CDU, which respectively joined the centre–left and centre–right coalitions. Both have comparatively modest electoral followings.[3] The only parties not to change very much between the two periods were regional parties, such as the Sardinian Action Party (PSdA), the Südtiroler Volkspartei (SVP), and the Greens. All of these parties, however, were forced to

---

[2] The PdCI was formed as a result of RC's split over the no-confidence vote to Romano Prodi's government in October 1998. About two-thirds of all RC MPs, led by Armando Cossutta, defied party secretary Fausto Bertinotti's instructions to vote against Prodi and seceded from the party going on to form the PdCI. The PdCI supported Prodi's successor, Massimo D'Alema, whereas RC moved in to the opposition. As PDS secretary, Massimo D'Alema had been responsible earlier in the year for dropping the word 'party' from the PDS' name and renaming it DS (Democrats of the Left).

[3] The CDU has since disappeared, having dissolved itself into the UDR, a centre party formed in 1997 by former President of the Republic and senator for life Francesco Cossiga.

TABLE 3.1. *National election results (Camera dei Deputati)*

Year		PSIUP PDUP DP RC[a]	VERDI	PCI PDS DS/ PdCI[b]	PSI SDI	PSDI	PRI	PR	DC PPI	CCD CDU	FI	PLI	MSI AN	PNM[c] PMP PDIUM	LN	Other
1963	%			25.3	13.8	6.1	1.4		38.3			7.0	5.1	1.7		1.3
	s			166	87	33	6		260			39	27	8		4
1968	%	4.4		26.9	14.5[d]		2.0		39.1			5.8	4.5	1.3		1.5
	s	23		177	91		9		266			31	24	6		3
1972	%	1.9		27.1	9.6	5.1	2.9		38.7			3.9	8.7			2.1
	s	0		179	61	29	15		266			20	56			4
1976	%	1.5		34.4	9.6	3.4	3.1	1.1	38.7			1.3	6.1			0.8
	s	6		227	57	15	14	4	263			5	35			4
1979	%	1.4		30.4	9.8	3.8	3.0	3.5	38.3			1.9	5.3			2.6
	s	6		201	62	20	16	18	262			9	30			6
1983	%	1.5		29.9	11.4	4.1	5.1	2.2	32.9			2.9	6.8		0.3	2.9
	s	7		198	73	23	29	11	225			16	42		1[e]	5
1987	%	1.7	2.5	26.6	14.3	2.9	3.7	2.6	34.3			2.1	5.9		1.3	1.9
	s	8	13	177	94	17	21	13	234			11	35		1[f]	6
1992	%	5.6	2.8	16.1	13.6	2.7	4.4	1.2	29.7			2.9	5.4		8.6	7.0
	s	35	16	107	92	16	27	7	206			17	34		55	18
1994	%	6.0	2.7	20.4	2.2			3.5	11.1[g]	—	21.0		13.5		8.4	6.6
	s	39	0	164[h]	14			6	33	27[i]	113		109		117	15
1996	%	8.6	2.5	21.1	0.4			1.9	6.8	5.8	20.6		15.7		10.1	6.5
	s	35	14	167					80	30	123		93		59	2
2001	%	5.0	2.2[j]	18.3	—			2.3	14.5[k]	3.2	29.4		12.0		3.9	9.2
	s[l]	11	8	146	9[m]			—	83	40	178		99		30	15

[a] PSIUP: 1968, 1972; PDUP: 1979; DP: 1976, 1983, 1987; RC: 1992, 1994, 1996, 2001; [b] PCI: 1963–87; PDS: 1992, 1994; DS: 1996; DS & PdCI: 2001; [c] PNM: 1948, 1953; PNM + PMP: 1958; PDIUM: 1963, 1968; [d] PSU (Partito Socialista Unificato); [e] Liga Veneta/Venetian League; [f] Lega Lombarda/Lombard League; [g] PPI + Patto Segni; [h] Includes seats assigned to La Rete, Verdi, and PSI candidates endorsed by the Progressisti, the PDS-led electoral alliance; [i] The CCD did not present its own candidate lists in the PR part of the election and consequently CCD vote percentages are not available for 1994. Twenty-seven CCD deputies were however elected in either the PR or the plurality parts of the election as FI candidates and went on to form a separate parliamentary group; [j] Il Girasole' alliance included Verdi and various socialist candidates; [k] La Margherita alliance (includes PPI, Democratici, RI, and UDEUR); [l] At the time of writing the allocation of eleven seats has yet to be decided by the courts; [m] SDI candidates only won seats in single-member plurality contests, so vote percentages are not available.

make explicit their support for the centre-left coalition. Finally, the Radical Party (PR) after the party's formal dissolution in 1989, became increasingly the expression of its charismatic leader, Marco Pannella, and lost importance and electoral support; the party enjoyed a modest recovery in 2001 thanks to the leading role taken by former EU Commissioner Emma Bonino.

All of this suggests the need for obtaining precise measures of party system change in Italy. Until recently, a high number of relevant parties, the presence of a strong centre party and of anti-system parties, considerable ideological distance and centrifugal competition, were all elements consistent with Sartori's (1976) classification of the Italian party system as polarized pluralism. But the ongoing transformation has revitalized the debate (Bartolini and D'Alimonte 1995; Melchionda 1995; Bardi 1996*a*,*b*; Morlino 1996; Pappalardo 1996; D'Alimonte and Bartolini 1997). According to at least two authors, the Italian party system has changed enough to warrant its re-classification. Pappalardo (1996: 140) argues that it is evolving towards moderate pluralism, as 'relevant actors, ideological distance, and number of poles' have changed. Morlino (1996: 25), on the other hand, supports the view that there is much continuity with the past but re-defines the present system as 'neo-polarized pluralism'. Clearly, not all authors are looking at the party system through the same lens. Pappalardo considers electoral coalitions as the relevant components of the party system whereas Morlino still privileges their individual party components. In reality, two different party systems seem to co-exist during the current phase: an electoral party system, consisting of the parties and the coalitions that participate in the electoral competition, and a parliamentary party system, consisting of the parties and groups that are formed in parliament after an election. This distinction is justified by the different competition rules they have to follow, respectively centripetal and centrifugal in the electoral and the parliamentary arenas.

Electoral competition now responds to what appear to be predominantly majoritarian pressures. Indeed, the new electoral law forced a multitude of parties to join electoral cartels. But post-election political dynamics (i.e. the formation of parliamentary parties) showed that some parties and groups interpreted electoral alliances as a means to obtain more seats in the election, and not as first steps towards the formation of more permanent common party structures, just as had been expected by critics of the new law (such as Sartori) even before the 1994 elections. But the new electoral law is not the only cause. The fact is that only electoral competition rules were changed, whereas parliamentary organization and procedure, government formation tactics and rules, coalition strategies and dynamics, all remained virtually unchanged. In other words, even if new electoral competition rules can foster tendencies towards a reduction in the number of relevant parties in the electoral party system, such pressures lose much of their importance after the election, and other sets of rules condition inter-party relations in the parliamentary party system. The two labels actually represent two facets of party systems that in the present Italian case appear to be particularly distinct: the 'electoral' one responds to the requirements of plurality competition and is structured accordingly around two major coalitions, the Casa delle Libertà (House of Freedoms, formerly il Polo per la Libertà) and the Ulivo (Olive Tree);[4] the 'parliamentary' one, on the other hand, is regulated by other features of the Italian political system and is still characterized by very high fragmentation. The two 'systems' coexist, with the electoral one surviving even between elections but, so far, with a limited impact on inter-election dynamics. In reality, both mathematical and qualitative criteria indicate that the number of relevant parties has not gone down (see Table 3.3 below), and ideological distance has declined only if one considers the differences between the poles—that is the coalitions— of the electoral party system (Bardi 1996*b*).

The parliamentary party system's transformation concerns its basic units more than its structure: the number of relevant parties and their ideological distance seem to be practically unchanged. Allowing for the trends referred to by Morlino (1996), it still appears to be very close to Sartori's classic mode of polarized pluralism. The electoral party system, on the other hand—viewed in terms of number of relevant parties and ideological distance—tends towards a form of moderate pluralism, as indicated by Pappalardo (1996). After the 1994 election it appeared that the electoral party system and its actors were playing a subordinate role. By 1996, however, it seemed that the electoral system was exerting some pressure on the parliamentary system. This was certainly visible in the efforts made by the various components of the two major electoral coalitions to present united fronts on most major questions. In the long run this could foster a reduction in the number of relevant parties in the parliamentary party system. It has certainly facilitated something which had not occurred in Italy prior to 1996, the alternation in power of centre-left and centre-right governing coalitions (see Table 3.2).

PARTY LEGITIMACY

As the data in Table 3.3 clearly show, since 1992 *electoral volatility* has been much higher than it was previously. Certainly, it can be surmised that in 1992 this was the exclusive consequence of changes in voters' party choices; in 1994, two more factors, the new electoral rules and the effects of the *Tangentopoli* investigations, were most likely at work. Both factors had dramatic effects on political supply. In fact, volatility levels have been greatly affected by changes in the field of parties contesting the election; that is, significant numbers of voters have been obliged to switch in the elections held since 1992 because of differences in party supply from one election to the next. Such change cannot necessarily be considered to have been caused by alterations in citizens' attitudes towards parties. While the

---

[4] In 2001, the victorious Casa delle Libertà coalition comprised Forza Italia, Alleanza Nazionale, Lega Nord, and CCD-CDU, while the Ulivo coaltion consisted of DS, PdCI, PPI, RI, Democratici, Unione Europea, SDI, and Verdi.

TABLE 3.2. *Party composition of Italian governments*

Dates	Party of Prime minister	Coalition parties	Status
25.III.60–19.VII.60	DC	—	Minority
26.VII.60–2.II.62	DC	—	Minority
21.II.62–16.V.63	DC	DC–PSDI–PRI	Majority
21.VI.63–5.XI.63	DC	—	Minority
4.XII.63–26.VI.64	DC	DC–PSI–PSDI–PRI	Majority
22.VII.64–21.I.66	DC	DC–PSI–PSDI–PRI	Majority
23.II.66–5.VI.68	DC	DC–PSI–PSDI–PRI	Majority
24.VI.68–19.XI.68	DC	—	Minority
12.XII.68–5.VII.69	DC	DC–PSI–PRI	Majority
5.VIII.69–7.II.70	DC	—	Minority
27.III.70–6.VII.70	DC	DC–PSI–PSDI–PRI	Majority
6.VIII.70–15.I.72	DC	DC–PSI–PSDI–PRI	Majority
17.II.72–26.II.72	DC	—	Minority
26.VI.72–12.VI.73	DC	DC–PSDI–PLI	Minority
7.VII.73–2.III.74	DC	DC–PSI–PSDI–PRI	Majority
14.III.74–3.X.74	DC	DC–PSI–PSDI	Majority
23.XI.74–7.I.76	DC	DC–PRI	Minority
12.II.76–30.IV.76	DC	—	Minority
29.VII.76–16.I.78	DC	—	Minority
11.III.78–31.I.79	DC	—	Minority
20.III.79–31.III.79	DC	DC–PRI–PSDI	Minority
5.VIII.79–19.III.80	DC	DC–PSDI–PLI	Minority
4.IV.80–27.IX.80	DC	DC–PRI–PSI	Majority
18.X.80–26.X.81	DC	DC–PRI–PSDI–PSI	Majority
28.VI.81–7.VIII.82	PRI	DC–PRI–PSDI–PSI–PLI	Majority
23.VIII.82–13.XI.82	PRI	DC–PRI–PSDI–PSI–PLI	Majority
1.XII.82–29.V.83	DC	DC–PSI–PSDI–PLI	Majority
4.VIII.83–26.VI.86	PSI	DC–PSI–PSDI–PLI–PRI	Majority
1.VIII.86–3.III.87	PSI	DC–PSI–PSDI–PLI–PRI	Majority
18.IV.87–28.IV.87	DC	—	Minority
28.VII.87–11.III.88	DC	DC–PSI–PSDI–PRI–PLI	Majority
2.IV.88–19.V.89	DC	DC–PSI–PSDI–PRI–PLI	Majority
22.VII.89–12.IV.91	DC	DC–PSI–PSDI–PRI–PLI	Majority
13.IV.91–3.VII.92	DC	DC–PSI–PSDI–PLI	Majority
4. VII.92–6.V.93	PSI	DC–PSI–PSDI–PLI–Ind.	Majority
7.V.93–9.V.94	Ind.	DC–PSI–PSDI–PLI–Ind.	Majority
10.V.94–16.I.95	FI	FI–LN–AN–CCD–Ind.–Oth.	Majority
17.I.95–30.V.96	Ind.	—	Minority
31.V.96–21.X.98	PPI	PPI–PDS–VER–Oth.–(RI)–(RC)[a]	Majority
22.X.98–13.VI.01	DS	DS–PDCI–PPI–VER–UDR–RI–Oth.	Majority
14.VI.01–	FI	FI–AN–LN–CCD–CDU	Majority

[a]RI and RC were not part of the governmental majority but gave the government led by Romano Prodi the necessary support for obtaining a vote of confidence.

Luciano Bardi

TABLE 3.3. *Measures of electoral change in Italy 1963–2001*

Year	Turnout %	Invalid votes %	Total net volatility	Effective number of electoral parties
1963	NA	NA	7.9	4.1
1968	92.8	1.6	3.4	4.0
1972	93.2	1.4	4.9	4.2
1976	93.4	1.1	8.2	3.5
1979	90.6	1.7	5.3	3.9
1983	89.0	3.1	8.5	4.5
1987	88.9	2.7	8.4	4.6
1992	87.3	2.8	14.2	6.4
1994	86.2	2.9	36.2	7.5/2.8
1996	82.9	4.1	18.2	7.2/3.0
2001	86.1	6.8	22.0	5.9/3.9

Notes: For 1994–2001, the first effective number of parties measure in the last column is based on vote distributions of all individual parties (as for 1963–92); the second measure is based on total votes obtained in the election by *coalitions* (e.g. Casa delle Liberta versus Ulivo in 2001) and individual parties not included in coalitions.

Sources: Turnout and invalid votes: 1968–87, Nuvoli and Spreafico (1990); 1992–2001, Electoral Service of the Italian Ministry for Internal Affairs; all other data calculated by the author.

effects of *Tangentopoli* may have been largely absorbed now, the supply of parties and candidates remains in a state of flux, as splits within the PPI and RC show. There remains relatively high potential for voter mobility. The *effective number of parties* in the system began to rise in 1983, and although the majoritarian logic of the reformed electoral system was designed to reverse this development, it cannot be said to have done so yet, unless one focuses on coalitions rather than individual parties (see second figure in final column of Table 3.3).

In effect, the dealignment of the 1980s was coupled with a major realignment. Its first manifestation was visible in 1992, with the resurgence, at least in the north/north-east, of the dormant centre–periphery cleavage. In that election the LN's ability to channel long-repressed popular dissatisfaction with the established parties was reflected in quasi-revolutionary results, at least by Italian standards. It would be a mistake, however, to attribute to the same factor the much greater changes that subsequently occurred. Whereas in 1992 shifting demand by the voters produced an instability in the party system, the greater magnitude of change in 1994 and 1996 was caused by exogenous factors (scandals and institutional reform) which operated on the supply side and totally transformed the range of choices offered to the electorate. It is highly unlikely that, without the scandals that affected most of their leaders, parties such as the DC or even the PSI would have collapsed as a result of one less-than-favourable election. Thus, the massive realignment that emerged from the 1994 election can be seen, at least in part, as the result of changes in the rules of the game, and of an almost complete restructuring of the supply side of the Italian electoral market. Electoral volatility remains very high, but given the changes Italian political parties have undergone, this is probably due more to difficulties in the development of new, permanent party loyalties, than to a decline of party attachment *per se*.

Time-series data on Italian *party identification* are practically non-existent, and trends can only be inferred on the basis of rather heterogeneous data. The general impression is that party identification declined significantly between 1985 and 1993 (Mannheimer and Sani 1987; Mannheimer 1989, 1994; Schmitt and Holmberg 1995). The slight reversal of the trend observed in 1994 (as shown in Table 3.4) cannot be monitored adequately as the relevant question has not always been included in subsequent surveys.

A similar situation exists with respect to other survey-based indicators designed to probe citizens' attitudes towards parties. Although many surveys include questions on political parties, these are hardly ever repeated over time. The only conclusion one can draw from these data is that the opinion of Italian citizens towards political parties has always been rather negative (Cartocci 1994). Again, *voter indecision* is very difficult to measure over time because of inconsistencies and ambiguities in data coding. Poguntke (1996*a*) tried to solve the problem by treating as voter indecision all answers not indicating a clear preference for one party. His Italian data show a very sharp increase in voter indecision, beginning in

TABLE 3.4. *Italian partisan attachment*

Year	Strong identifiers (%)	All identifiers (%)
1978	46	77
1979	45	78
1980	39	69
1981	44	73
1982	38	67
1983	41	71
1984	37	71
1985	37	67
1986	38	66
1987	36	64
1988	39	69
1989	35	62
1990	31	58
1991	29	51
1992	31	56
1993	26	51
1994	34	60
1996	30	56

Source: Eurobarometer.

the late 1980s and continuing through to 1994. Lack of data makes it impossible to update Poguntke's analysis. Overall, however, it would appear that, in recent years, attitudinal data do indicate a decline in party attachment.

Party membership trends appear less ambiguous. For most of the postwar period Italian membership–electorate ratios (M/E) were about average internationally (Katz *et al.* 1992). Between 1963–87 they declined slightly, from a high of almost 13 per cent to slightly less than 10 per cent (see Table 3.5). As absolute membership levels remained more or less unchanged, this was probably due to the expansion of the electorate. But by the early 1990s the legitimacy crisis of the traditional parties was clearly demonstrated by falling M/E ratios. These dropped to about 5 per cent in 1992 and 3.4 per cent in 1994—representing a decline of 40–60 per cent over 1987, more than double the total decline registered in the course of the previous 25 years. The ratio recorded in 1996, although marking a slight increase to 3.8 per cent, places Italy near the bottom of the scale for European democracies.

Voter turnout in Italy has always been considered an important manifestation of political participation and of party legitimization. Italy's traditionally high turnout (refer again to Table 3.3) was seen as representing the existence of some form of popular 'permissive consensus' towards the governmental coalition parties, and as revealing a commitment to the values of the Resistance-inspired Constitution by the leftist opposition. Voting was perceived more as a civic duty than a right by most Italian citizens, and average turnout in parliamentary elections between 1946–76 was second only to Austria's.[5] Thus the noticeable, though not dramatic, decline in turnout which manifested itself from 1979 onwards, along with an increase in the percentage of *invalid votes*, was viewed with concern by all major Italian parties. Conversely, the PR and other non-cartel parties and groups greeted the trend as an indicator of popular dissatisfaction with the established party-cartel (Katz and Mair 1995). Both positions justify an interpretation of these trends as a manifestation of dealignment, even if declining party loyalty is not the only cause (see Nuvoli and Spreafico 1990). From 1983–94, the percentage of invalid votes remained high at around 3 per cent of the total electorate, before doubling again over the two most recent elections.

Italy has long experience of citizen dissatisfaction with—even alienation from—party-based democracy (Morlino and Tarchi 1996), especially with regard to the traditional cartel parties (DC, PCI, PSI, PSDI, PLI, PRI). As a result, there has always been a number of anti-system, anti-party or, more simply, non-cartel parties (Bardi 1996*a*). *Support for anti-cartel parties* showed a gradual, if uneven, upward trend from the early 1970s, with a sharp surge between the end of the 1980s and the beginning of the 1990s. Where the early successes depended on support for the far left and far right, the Radicals and the Greens, the latter development was

---

[5] Voting is seen as a civic duty; non-voters are recorded in the elector's civil and criminal records but there are no other consequences.

TABLE 3.5. *Italian party membership, 1963–2001*

Year	PCI/PDS/DS	DP/RC	PSI/SI	SDI/LAB	DC/PPI	CCD/CDU	LN	PRI	PLI/FI	MSI/AN	M/E ratios
1963	1,615,112		501,176	150,717	1,621,620			52,499		240,063	12.67
1968	1,495,662				1,696,402			84,280	148,562	199,950	11.97
1972	1,573,956			284,772	1,827,925				139,725	239,075	12.77
1976	1,797,597				1,365,187					217,110	10.50
1979	1,761,297	2500	490,044	217,212	1,383,650			108,201	29,282	174,157	9.82
1983	1,635,264	4235	564,619	215,000	1,384,058			108,615	59,296	165,308	9.41
1987	1,508,140	9153	631,071	133,428	1,812,201				40,491	165,427	9.66
1992	769,944	119,094	51,224		NA		140,000	71,866		181,243	4.92
1994	698,287	113,495	43,052		233,377			20,916	5200	324,344	3.03
1996	675,114	126,600	38,472		172,701	140,000	100,000		116,000	486,911	3.81
1998	621,670	127,446	35,000		130,887	130,000	160,000		140,000	485,657	3.75

Sources: Bardi and Morlino (1992); D'Alimonte and Nelken (1997); *La Repubblica* (3-3-1998 and 18-12-1998); Mair and van Biezen (2001). M/E ratios: Katz *et al.* (1992) for 1963–87; author's calculations for 1992–98.

TABLE 3.6. *Support for non-cartel parties, Camera dei Deputati,*
1972–2001

	1972–79	1983	1987	1992	1994	1996	2001
LN	—	0.3	1.3	8.6	8.4	10.1	3.9
Pdup/DP	1.8	1.5	1.7	—	—	—	—
MSI/AN	6.7	8.8	5.9	5.4	13.5	15.7	12.0
MSI-FT	—	—	—	—	—	0.9	0.4
Greens	—	—	2.5	2.8	2.7	2.5	2.2
La Rete	—	—	—	1.9	1.9	—	—
PR	1.5	2.2	2.6	1.2	3.5	1.9	2.3
FI	—	—	—	—	21.0	20.6	29.4
AD	—	—	—	—	1.2	—	—
Patto Segni + RI	—	—	—	—	4.7	4.3	—
Italia dei Valori	—	—	—	—	—	—	3.9
Total	10.0	12.8	14.0	19.9	56.9	56.0	54.1

Note: Includes only those non-cartel parties which are positively identifiable as such.
With respect to 2001, much of the Margherita Alliance is also non-cartel; when added,
this pushes the total non-cartel vote to more than 60 per cent.

mostly due to the breakthrough of the LN. In the 1992 parliamentary elections
anti-cartel lists obtained about 20 per cent of the vote (see Table 3.6), the highest
level of such support in any western democracy (Poguntke 1994).

In 1994 and 1996 traditional and new non-cartel lists achieved sweeping successes, accounting in both elections for more than half of all valid votes. The figure
is even higher—reaching almost two-thirds of valid votes—if we include the results
for RC. This party is a splinter from the old PCI and as such not classifiable as
non-cartel, but its voters are among the most dissatisfied with democracy (Morlino
and Tarchi 1996: 53), and cannot be confused with supporters of the old regime.
In general, even those parties that express the highest degree of continuity with
the past (PDS, PPI, CCD/CDU) have gone out of their way to project a reformed
image as the champions of a regenerated, if unfinished, 'Second Republic'.

Referendum voting can also be regarded as an important electoral indicator of
anti-party sentiment; referendum proposals in Italy are 'abrogative' in that they can
only aim at repealing existing laws or parts of existing laws; that is, at undoing what
Parliament (dominated by the party cartel) has done. The referendum thus appears
to be very well suited to the expression of dissatisfaction with the dominant parties.
Moreover, all referenda, irrespective of their outcomes, have contributed to the
increasing inability of political parties to control their electorates: the dichotomous
nature of the voting choice makes it necessary for parties to take very clear positions
on issues, consequently permitting electors to appreciate differences that might
otherwise have gone unnoticed. Indeed, very often referenda have been invoked in
order to oblige Parliament to address issues that traditional parties have preferred
to ignore, thus exposing their unwillingness to respond to demands coming from
the electorate.

Referendum voting and outcomes dramatically revealed anti-party sentiment in 1991, when majority parties opposed a proposal to limit the number of preferences in Chamber of Deputies' elections. The referendum's positive outcome represented the first formal crack in Italy's party government system. In April 1993, on the crest of the anti-party tide caused by the *Tangentopoli* investigations, the majority parties were defeated in eight referenda, occasioning what many commentators saw as the end of a regime. In fact, two of the institutional cornerstones of the party regime, the Senate's proportional representation (PR) electoral law, which was modified to a mixed plurality/PR system, and the law regulating public funding of political parties, were substantially changed as a result of these referenda. The former inspired a similar reform of the Chamber of Deputies' electoral law, while the latter fully revealed the extent of popular anti-party sentiment. Indeed, of the eight referenda held in 1993, the one proposing abrogation of public funding recorded the highest percentage of 'yes' votes (over 90 per cent); a similar proposal had been defeated in 1978 (with 56.4 per cent voting 'no'). These referenda manifested perhaps the highest and most genuine expressions of mass anti-party sentiment yet seen in Italy. They certainly accelerated the collapse of traditional party organizations, and set the institutional and political conditions for the 1994 elections.

Overall, this brief review reveals more than enough evidence of eroding party legitimacy in Italy. On virtually every indicator examined we find signs of negative citizen orientations towards the parties: increased electoral volatility and voter indecision, reduced party identification and membership, lower electoral turnout and more invalid voting, greater support for anti-cartel parties and, through the institutional device of the referendum, for legislative changes designed to reform the old system of party democracy. That said, it is quite possible that anti-party sentiment in Italy may have been directed primarily at the old party-cartel rather than against party *per se*.

PARTY ORGANIZATIONAL STRENGTH

In reviewing party organizational strength in Italy, we start by turning again to *party membership*. In 1990, total membership was roughly at the same level as in 1960, at about 4,300,000 (refer again to Table 3.5). Even allowing for the considerable expansion of Italy's voting population (about 28 per cent), these data, if correct, could be taken to reflect a remarkable ability of Italian parties to maintain their position in society. But in the early 1990s the situation changed dramatically, with a noticeable collapse in the memberships of the three most important parties, the DC, the PDS, and the PSI. The PDS membership had dropped to about 700,000 in 1993, although the party had certainly consolidated its structure after the post-PCI transition. The DC reported a drop of almost 600,000 members in 1991, with

TABLE 3.7. *Income and expenditure of major Italian parties (in billions of lire)*

Year	PCI/PDS		DC/PPI		PSI		FI	
	Inc.	Exp.	Inc.	Exp.	Inc.	Exp.	Inc.	Exp.
1974	23.9	23.8	24.7	20.2	8.6	8.7	—	—
1984	104.7	109.3	68.9	61.8	22.1	33.9	—	—
1989	113.7	117.1	77.8	72.0	53.6	53.6	—	—
1994	58.1	55.0	17.0	31.3	—	—	38.6	35.8

Sources: Bardi and Morlino (1994); Caciagli and Kertzer (1996).

fourteen provincial committees not having yet reported their membership figures by the date (1 December 1992) that party secretary Mino Martinazzoli decided to have all membership records erased. The ensuing recruitment campaign yielded over 800,000 'new' members. After its transformation into the PPI, the party suffered multiple schisms: besides the CCD and the CDU, both of which became independent components of successive right-wing coalitions, another right-wing splinter headed by Publio Fiori joined AN, and Mario Segni formed the centrist group Patto per l'Italia. These developments were reflected in the 1994 election result (11.1 per cent for the PPI, a drop of 16.8 per cent on the DC's 1992 performance) and might even have had more serious consequences for membership levels. The situation was even more dramatic for the PSI—in many ways the party most damaged by the crisis of the political system. The PSI kept its name but lost even more electors, and certainly more members, than the PPI.

The membership collapse of the three traditional parties was only partially compensated by the growth of less traditional competitors. In 1998, the Lega claimed a total membership of approximately 160,000, but this has most likely declined since in line with the party's electoral support. In 1994, even considering the membership of Forza Italia clubs—which are sympathizers' associations and not party organizational units—the total number of party members in Italy was estimated as no higher than 2.5–3 million.[6] By the end of the decade the near-disappearance of the PSI and the continuing post-DC diaspora forced overall membership figures to drop below the two million mark, despite the sizeable expansion in AN's membership.

The reality of Italian party organization can be grasped only by exploring the complex, and often illegal, system of relationships between parties and interests—a system which can perhaps best be illustrated by a discussion of party finance (Bardi and Morlino 1994). Officially recorded incomes and expenditures (see Table 3.7)

[6] According to various, and contrasting, sources Forza Italia was supported by 8000/13000 sympathizers' clubs, whose membership size was deliberately kept rather low. In total, FI club members were probably no more than 500,000. More recently FI has introduced a more traditional form of membership, which attracted a much lower 140,000 subscribers in 1998. The party's stated objective then became the recruitment of 250,000 members.

only give a very superficial impression of actual party finances as they do not report illegal transactions which predominated in most parties prior to 1992, and which were estimated at some 3400 billion lire a year,[7] at least ten times the total official income of all Italian political parties. In recent years, the investigations of illegal party financing may have reduced these amounts to just a trickle, with the result that all of the traditional parties quickly approached bankruptcy. If we stick to the 'official story', then, the data suggest that the parties' financial resources have shrunk enormously, even if, at least in some cases (such as the PPI's), expenditures have not declined nearly so much. After the law on public financing of political parties was repealed by referendum, a new law was passed allowing party financing through citizens' voluntary contributions of up to 0.04 per cent of their income tax. In 1997 the projected total of such contributions was 160 billion lire, an amount that parties received as an advance. After the first calculations based on 1997 tax forms revealed that the initiative was much less popular with Italian taxpayers than anticipated, the advance for 1998 was reduced to 110 billion lire; in the event, the actual contributions amounted to no more than 50 billion lire. In theory the parties should return any excess advance payments to the state. In the interim, however, a new law providing for state financing of campaign expenditures on the basis of 4000 lire per voter should allow for the transfer to political parties of about 150 billion lire. Without even taking into account the impact of inflation, all of these figures are much lower than those afforded by the previous legislation.

A similar picture can be drawn regarding party *staff*. Although precise data on staffing levels are not available, in the early 1960s the PCI and the DC were estimated to employ several thousand staff between them, while the remaining parties jointly employed about one thousand (*La Repubblica*, 1998). Such figures, however, fail to give an adequate idea of the situation, in that there also existed a large number of civil servants who worked for parties with which they sympathized, and whose activities were substantially integrated within those of the formal party staff. Thus the DC, PCI, and PSI all profited from their positions in local and regional government, as well as from a mutual tolerance in the local branches of central administration (for instance, in the Postal Service, which was often staffed by large numbers of clientelistic appointees). Moreover, from the 1970s it became increasingly common for union representatives to be legally exempted from work duties; theoretically, this enabled them to undertake union responsibilities, but in reality time was also often spent on party activities. This regime was apparently (see below) terminated by the early 1990s investigations. In addition, as a result of their fiscal crisis, all parties were forced to downsize considerably their national and regional headquarters and to reduce the number of their local branches, thus reducing their staffing requirements. One estimate (*La Repubblica*, 1998) places current party staff needs at about one-tenth of pre-1992 levels.

---

[7] *La Repubblica*, 20 February 1993: 7.

Finally, we need to consider *party/media relations*. For a long time Italian parties had very precisely structured relations with the mass media. In fact they were among the most important news publishers. Besides publishing official newspapers, during the 1950s Italy's larger parties acquired control of some important 'independent' newspapers. The moderate, or even conservative, line of many these newspapers was guaranteed by the party-sponsored appointments of editors and journalists. Moreover, Italy's state-owned radio and television company, RAI, was controlled by the DC. A 1976 Constitutional Court ruling put an end to the state monopoly of radio and television broadcasts but did not substantially alter the relationship between parties and the media (Bardi and Morlino 1994). The ruling permitted an overnight explosion of private local TV stations which by the mid-1980s were concentrated into three national networks owned by media tycoon Silvio Berlusconi. Berlusconi's successful attempt to go beyond the limits posed by the Constitutional Court was made possible by the personal support of the PSI and Bettino Craxi. By this manoeuvre Craxi redressed TV's political balance which was at the time still heavily pro-DC. Eventually, a political balance was achieved whereby the DC controlled the presidency of RAI 1, the most viewed channel, while the PSI controlled RAI 2. This was done with the approval of the PCI, which obtained control of RAI 3, the most recently created and least popular RAI channel.

The situation changed enormously after the 1992–94 transformation. Although parties in government still have a privileged relationship with RAI, the political changes the country has experienced make their grip much weaker. Both coalitions proceeded to replace most of RAI's top executives soon after their respective electoral victories. The severe financial crisis experienced by all Italian parties after 1992 has somewhat paradoxically decreased their own involvement in media-related activities. Prior to 1992, the PCI/PDS for one, conducted its own pre-electoral and post-electoral surveys whose accuracy often rivalled that of the polling agencies. Now, party leaders limit themselves to commenting on surveys and projections commissioned by state-owned or private TV stations. The PPI has on the other hand helped the acquisition by PPI senator and movie producer Vittorio Cecchi Gori of two minor national networks, TMC1 and TMC2. The two networks' limited viewership and their financial problems have prevented them from being assets for the party.

Ironically, party-connected newspapers are still surviving and even increasing in number, even if they no longer seem to have much of an impact on contemporary Italian politics. Besides the traditional *l'Unità* (DS), *Il Popolo* (PPI), *l'Avanti* (PSI), *Il Secolo d'Italia* (AN), and *La Voce Repubblicana* (PRI), scores of minor newspapers and other periodicals are mushrooming right across Italy's party spectrum. This apparent paradox is due to the fact that the only form of direct public financing of non-electoral party activity still allowed by current legislation is the development of a party press. Party-connected publications received in 1995 a total of 52 billion lire in contributions, a very considerable amount given the current scarcity of financial resources. Any newspaper sponsored by a political group consisting of members of at least two of the Senate, the Chamber of Deputies, or the European Parliament's Italian delegation, is entitled to state subsidies. In practice, any two of Italy's elected members could together sponsor an official 'party organ' up to a theoretical limit of 539! Subsidies, calculated on the basis of a complex set of criteria, are to a large extent determined by official total circulation numbers (about 5000 lire a year per copy), an incentive for papers to exaggerate such figures.

Overall, the paradox which once characterized Italian parties—the existence of unpopular but strong and highly state-resourced party organizations—no longer holds. Party membership has declined precipitously along with party funding and staffing in the last decade. Media links have changed and in some cases eroded, although they remain important in others, most notably that of Forza Italia. In short, Italian party organizations survive but now find it harder to thrive on a network of state-derived patronage.

PARTY FUNCTIONALITY

Governance

As mentioned at the outset, Italy has always been seen as a quintessential example of party government. While, as yet there is not enough evidence to affirm whether significant alternatives to party government have developed in Italy in recent years, we may infer that the form of Italian party government has been modified. In particular, in order to govern, Italian parties now have to form extra-political coalitions—involving technocratic or societal actors—that depart sharply from those of the past. The relationship between interest groups and the policy-making apparatus always occurred through fairly permanent and institutionalized links with political parties that functioned as the gatekeepers of the system (Morlino 1991). And even the relative independence that Italy's chronic governmental instability afforded the highest echelons of public administration—especially the most 'technical' components such as the Treasury—was mitigated by the convergence of goals, interests, style, and ethos between bureaucrats and governing politicians. Parties were thus able to monitor closely, if not control, other actors' policy-making inputs. In the most extreme scenario, we can say that the parties manipulated politically their privileged societal and technocratic partners' demands and/or initiatives.

This entailed, for example, monetary policies favouring the country's export sector, whose international competitiveness was permitted through routine devaluations of the lira, while maintaining very generous pension and early retirement benefits for workers employed in the very same sector, and state salvaging of defaulting privately-owned industries for the benefit of owners (who passed on to the state their losses) and workers (who had their jobs preserved). Similarly, subsidies and, often unnecessary, investments benefiting the southern part of the country, were matched by the generous rewards accruing to (mostly northern) investors who subscribed to very high-yielding government bonds. Overall, this system implied generalized payoffs to all important economic and societal actors, while imposing an enormous burden on state finances. The price for what could be described as a fully-fledged social pact was a state debt which, by the early 1990s, exceeded the country's annual GDP.

The system was so articulated and complex as to make it impervious to attack. Not only were successive governments unwilling, let alone able, to reform it, but even those parties in the governmental coalition that prescribed more rigorous policies, such as the PRI and occasionally the PLI, were eventually forced to accept it. It is a widespread conviction that, in actuality, the 'system' survived with the full approval of the main opposition parties including the PCI. This was also reflected in the legislative behaviour of these parties, which was more often than not supportive of government-initiated bills (Cazzola 1972; Di Palma 1977). Although the *number* of parties officially making up Italy's government coalitions seems to have affected parliamentary output and governmental resort to decree-laws (Kreppel 1997), there is very little evidence that the *identity* of the parties in the coalition made much difference to sustained governance strategies.[8] The government headed by Giuliano Amato tried for the first time to change this course in 1992, not only through the usual tax and interest rate hikes, or the budget cuts generally resorted to in times of fiscal crisis, but also by attacking one of the cornerstones of Italy's social pact: the pension system. There was a widespread belief that Italy's fiscal crisis had virtually reached a point of no return. The country was essentially drifting out of the European Union because of the dismal performance of its economy. The only answer appeared to be a sharp departure from previous government trends through the adoption of *technically* adequate if unpopular decisions. Significantly, one of Amato's first initiatives was to ask the Italian parliament to give the Bank of Italy—the technical body *par excellence*—the power to declare economic emergencies, forcing the government to cut expenditure, raise taxation, and freeze civil servant salaries (Helman and Pasquino 1993).

Amato's new course was followed by all successive governments with the exception of the one headed by Silvio Berlusconi that reverted for 7 months in 1994 to the free-spending mode of the 1980s. The new course was also facilitated by the collapse of Italy's traditional parties that, as we know, began exactly in 1992. This eliminated any obstacles that the traditional parties would otherwise have created and virtually gave technicians unprecedented influence in governing the country. Independent bodies, defined with English terminology as 'Authorities', were established and given technical responsibilities in such crucial fields as energy

---

[8] Decree-laws are governmental acts having immediate legislative effect. To remain effective they must however be converted into law by parliament within sixty days.

and telecommunications. Economic rigour was certainly the initial distinguishing characteristic of Italy's new model of governance. Given the obvious emergency the country's economy was undergoing, it enjoyed a consensus to which most parties and societal actors (save the unions) were committed. But in more recent years demands for reform of the country's institutional and regulatory systems have created a division between supporters of change and supporters of the status quo. The former enjoy the powerful backing of Brussels for their commitment to liberalization and deregulation. Interestingly, reformist societal groups have often shunned institutionalized partnerships with specific political parties and have instead attracted *ad hoc* political backing from a range of actors with converging interests. These alliances have sometimes cut across governing coalitions, and have often favoured technically oriented governments (Mattina 1993).

This pattern continued even after the 1996 election produced a centre-left government, led by Romano Prodi, with a clear and lasting political mandate. Throughout the duration of the Prodi government (from mid-1996 to late 1998) technocrats relied on support for the most part from the DS vanguard around Massimo D'Alema. More generally, the government's commitment to meet the requirements for Italy's entry into European Monetary Union (EMU) was a sufficient incentive for a convergence between the overall positions of the technicians and politicians. Moreover, such convergence enjoyed a widespread consensus in society: EMU was in fact a goal equally important for both unions and industrialists, who were respectively attracted by its projected beneficial effects in terms of employment and business opportunities. Prodi's centre-left government thus uncharacteristically enjoyed the support of Italy's *poteri forti* (strong powers)—big industry, big finance, and banking—as well as that of the centre-left's traditional constituencies.

However, things changed considerably when D'Alema himself succeeded Prodi as prime minister, leading a coalition excluding RC and including the UDR, a newly formed centre-right mostly catholic grouping, headed by former President Francesco Cossiga. Italy's EMU success brought an end to the temporary political consensus, especially as the *Prodiani* were convinced that D'Alema had masterminded the downfall of the Prodi government, even though the DS was ostensibly its strongest supporter. As a consequence, Prodi went on to form yet another centre party (*i Democratici*) by joining forces with, among others, former *Mani Pulite* prosecutor and incumbent *Ulivo* senator Antonio Di Pietro, and Mayor of Rome Francesco Rutelli. Prodi himself left the Italian political scene to become President of the EU Commission, while another prominent 'technician' and ex-Prime Minister, Carlo Azeglio Ciampi, assumed a role 'above party' by being elected President of the Republic. This left Lamberto Dini as the only prominent technician in the D'Alema government. D'Alema seemed committed to a continuation of the fiscal rigour and broad consensus strategy pursued by his predecessors. But in the course of 1999 the main employers' confederation *Confindustria* appeared to be withdrawing its support, convinced that the government would not meet its demands for a more radical reform of Italy's rigid labour mobility, pension, and salary legislation.[9] Moreover, commentators thought that *Confindustria*'s new attitude towards the government was at least partly due to the (as it proved accurate) conviction that elections scheduled for 2001 would see a return to power of the centre-right. Thus, once the country's economy was back on the right track—something only the centre-left could achieve with the indispensable consent of the unions—the industrialists could start preparing an alliance which, it was believed, would represent Italy's future power-holders.

Given the accuracy of these predictions, it would appear that at least some of Italy's *poteri forti* have adapted remarkably to the less static nature of party dynamics in Italy's Second Republic. They, more than the parties formally alternating in power, seem to be making a difference to governance. Obviously, parties still have a role in governing the country, but more than hitherto it is necessary for alliances to be forged with forces outside parliament. The picture is complicated by the fact that parties can be in favour of change on some issues while defending the status quo on other issues.

In the public sector the division runs between more technical and more bureaucratic bodies, which are to be included respectively among the supporters of change and the supporters of the status quo. Foremost among the former is the Bank of Italy which, since Maastricht, is formally independent and which has maintained a tight monetary and fiscal policy, often at odds with governmental preferences. Its chief ally, the Treasury, headed in recent years by non-party ministers like Lamberto Dini and Carlo Azeglio Ciampi, has been asserting its own influence much more strongly than previously in areas that were traditionally left to party mediators. In doing do, it has shown itself to be a powerful supporter of a new style of public sector management, as outlined in the reforms proposed in 1998 by the Treasury committee on corporate governance, led by Mario Draghi. These far-reaching reforms are backed by Consob (the stock exchange regulator). Finally, another key ally of the Bank of Italy-Treasury-Consob axis is the Anti-trust Authority which (until recently headed by former Prime Minister Giuliano Amato) has addressed issues of civil service privileges and public sector inefficiency.

In other, more bureaucratic and conservative, parts of the public sector much needed and long awaited reforms, even if announced or approved, are rendered ineffective by lack of implementation (for instance, in the Ministry for Public Function and Regional Affairs) or the pre-emptive reactions by vested interests (Ministry of Education). Such resistance, of course, owes much of its effectiveness to the convergence of interests with political parties: most parties have some

---

[9] *Confindustria* was not impressed by D'Alema's successes, which included for the first time in many years projected income tax reductions for the year 2000. Besides more sweeping corporate tax and social security contribution cuts, it was demanding different minimum salaries in different parts of the country, and a further curbing of early retirement schemes. It was also opposing a governmental plan to use job-severance funds (considered in Italy as deferred salary) to increment ailing pension funds or even to increase current salaries.

issues on which they seek to resist change—even Forza Italia (on decentralization). A proposed reform of Italy's public administration which would introduce a sort of spoils system, allowing for the removal and substitution of top managers with every change of government, and job mobility for all public sector employees, would certainly reinforce prospects for party government and decrease bureaucratic discretion, especially if coalition alternation should continue.

The relationship between parties and private sector interest groups has also changed. The more progressive parts of the private sector have thrown their weight behind all governments since 1992, irrespective of their being technical or political in nature, or right- or left-wing in political orientation, in the hope that this might speed up the modernization of the country's fiscal and financial systems, thus reducing the paralysing effect of Italy's welfare state. But the private sector can be as closed and perhaps even more resistant to change than its state counterpart. In respect of reform of corporate governance, for instance, vested interests are particularly powerful: these include the might of the financial–industrial complex rooted in Italy's largest companies and largest investment bank, Mediobanca. Similarly, the largest and longer established trade union federations appear to be more willing to accept change in critical areas such as pensions or job protection than their sector-specific 'autonomous' affiliates, which prefer to defend entrenched interests. Here, relationships between parties and groups and their consequences for governance are more stable and are characterized by the continuing alliance between the major federations and the parties of the left.

Overall, it should be said that alternation in power between centre–left and centre–right coalitions—should it prove an enduring feature of Italian politics— carries with it the potential for more obvious party effects on policy outcomes. However, a more apparent development over the past decade has been the new set of relationships between parties and other potential governmental actors which has made Italian government more dynamic. In fact, the sectors in which non-party actors have become influential have tended to be precisely the ones in which policy change has been greatest, whereas sectors left to political actors are characterized by greater continuity and stagnation. This is especially visible in the field of institutional reform, in particular electoral reform, where the resistance of many smaller parties and their allies could frustrate the hopes of those seeking reform designed to reduce the number of parties. As was the case before the 1992/93 reforms, the referendum seems to be the only weapon against the defenders of the status quo. Thus, parties remain important to government in Italy, but the most dynamic sources of public policy today are often non-partisan.

Political recruitment

The conventional view is that prior to 1992 political recruitment in Italy was a function almost entirely performed by political parties. This included not only the formation of governments and the selection of political representatives, that is, political elites, but also, and just as importantly, the recruitment of personnel employed in all capacities (from janitorial to top executive) in public administration and in the ever-expanding state-owned sector of the economy. (Here we shall concern ourselves only with the recruitment of executives, broadly referred to as administrative elites.) Political elites were not only selected by political parties but usually recruited from within their own ranks. The selection of administrative elites, on the other hand, was part of a strategy aimed at securing both consensus (jobs) and resources (financial outlays from controlled companies and agencies) for cartel parties. This practice was so pervasive and important that Italy came to be known as the quintessential party-dominated polity or *partitocrazia* (Pasquino 1995).

As we have seen, independents or technocrats were very rarely allowed to access important governmental positions without serving as party card-holders first. For the first four or five postwar terms this also applied to parliamentary positions. But a departure from this rule took place from the mid-1970s when an increasing number of independents were presented as candidates in party lists and often elected as senators or deputies. Although all three major parties (DC, PCI, PSI) resorted to this practice in order to widen their contacts with civil society, the phenomenon had particular relevance for the PCI, whose independents went on to form separate parliamentary groups. During the 1980s the distinction between party members and independents became blurred as parties invited independents to join their extra-parliamentary organizations as well as their parliamentary groups. For example, the PSI reformed its internal organizational structure, changing the Central Committee into a much larger National Assembly in order to accommodate within its ranks 120 external members (out of about 500). This was part of party secretary Bettino Craxi's strategy for diluting internal opposition and opening up the party to civil society. In general, however, these exceptions were relatively unimportant and parties maintained a tight control over the recruitment of political personnel.[10]

Parties also had a quasi-monopoly over the selection of candidates for top jobs in public administration and state-owned or state-controlled companies. To be sure, the most important objectives of such control were tangible resources (jobs and money). But given the great political importance of the bureaucracy in a country with chronic governmental instability such as Italy, and the strategic importance of state-owned banks and agencies, the political significance of this practice cannot be underestimated. Begun during the fascist era (Pombeni 1984), it was continued by the DC after the Second World War. Italy's dominant party had almost exclusive control over civil servant selection and other state-level appointments until the early 1960s. With the extension of the governmental coalition to the PSI, a system

---

[10] On average only about one-fifth of all deputies elected between 1987 and 1992 had held no prior party office (Verzichelli 1997). It is reasonable to assume that at least some of them were party members.

of parcelling out public appointments (*lottizzazione*) was established. This allowed parties in the governing coalition (PSDI, PLI, and PRI besides DC and PSI) to fill administrative elite positions in proportion to their strength and strategic position (it is well known that the PSI was able to exploit this system better than its partners because of its key role in coalitions at all levels).[11] The situation was more complex at the municipal, provincial, and regional levels (in the last case only after 1970 when the first regional elections were held), at which other parties, most notably the PCI, had a governmental role. *Lottizzazione*, however, applied at these levels as well. This found an explicit political expression in the fact that in the early 1990s over 50 per cent of all regional ministers and at least one-third of all municipal councilmen were civil servants (Vannucci 1997).

The recruitment of political elites changed sharply after 1992. This is demonstrated intuitively by the fact that in 1994 parliamentary personnel turnover was about 70 per cent compared to 1992 and close to 90 per cent compared to 1987 (Verzichelli 1995). Even more telling is the fact that 44 per cent of the Chamber of Deputies elected in 1994 had never held any previous party office, as opposed to 17 per cent in 1976 (Verzichelli 1997). The slackening of party control over the recruitment of political personnel (both parliamentary and governmental) can be seen to result from at least three factors. By far the most important is the emergence of non-traditional parties. The effects of *tangentopoli* and the consequent demise of most traditional parties created a vacuum in Italy's political spectrum which was quickly filled by newly formed political groupings that, at least in the early stages of their existence, were extremely short of suitable candidates for political office. This facilitated and—given the bad press 'party' was getting at the time—even necessitated the resort to non-party candidates.[12] A second factor was Italy's fiscal crisis, which mostly affected the recruitment of governmental elites: technocrats, usually with financial or economic portfolios, were present in every government after 1992, with one, Lamberto Dini's, consisting entirely of technicians. As we have seen, it was felt that some of the economic policy objectives the country had to set itself, such as reforming the welfare and pension systems, as well as reducing deficits and debt, required technical competences political parties did not have; similar concerns were also felt at regional and municipal levels,

---

[11] In theory this should be made difficult by the fact that according to Italian law civil servants can only be hired if they win specially designated national competitions. In reality, the outcomes of such competitions are widely believed to have been controlled by parties and by members of the relevant administrations in order to favour the *raccomandati* (the well-connected ones). Moreover, as national competition procedures are extremely slow and inefficient, many positions are 'temporarily' filled through arbitrary appointments, which are often made permanent by successive laws. This latter procedure was applied to 60 per cent of all Italian civil servants hired between the late 1970s and the early 1990s (Vannucci 1997).

[12] To be sure, technically such individuals were still recruited by political parties. In reality the peculiar organizational nature of the 'new' parties has made for a substantial independence of many of the politicians recruited from civil society after 1992. The resort to independent personalities has been magnified by the decline of subcultures, and by the ensuing erosion of partisan identities.

as a consequence of citizens' demands for effective government after decades of ineffective administration. Third, there were the effects of electoral reform: the predominantly majoritarian system of election adopted in 1993 had an important impact on candidate selection; in some instances, popular personalities were selected as candidates as a means for the parties to attract non-politicized voters. It was felt that the new majoritarian competition would get more media attention and that well-known personalities who were already favourites with the media would hold an advantage. Actors, pop stars, sports and television personalities (Berlusconi himself a prominent manifestation of some of these) found their way into every major party's candidate list and parliamentary groups, except for the LN's; this factor may be relatively unimportant in terms of the number of such candidates who were actually recruited, but its effects were very visible.

Little research exists on post-1992 links between parties and public administration, although work has been done on the supposedly related phenomenon of corruption (Della Porta and Vannucci 1999). But in theory the ability of parties to control the recruitment of administrative elites should have declined for at least three reasons: first, the privatization of state-owned enterprises, which implies a reduction in the number of positions that parties can control; second, the collapse of traditional parties and the parallel emergence of new party-like actors, which may have undermined the stability of privileged links with parties which administrative elites had hitherto enjoyed; and third, a new electoral law that favours alternation in government. Coupled with the privatization of elite public administrators' contracts, this latter development has created something akin to a spoils system, whereby winning coalitions openly replace top managers after every election. Besides making such appointments short-lived, this situation makes the party-manager link a lot less political, as the main criterion for selection is now expertise rather than loyalty; moreover, it also makes *lottizzazione* much more difficult. Overall, it is clear that the old system by which cartel parties dominated political recruitment in Italy has been severely curtailed and altered since 1992.

Interest articulation and aggregation

The capacity of parties to articulate and aggregate interests was certainly declining in Italy for many years even before the great transformation of the early 1990s. This probably had a lot to do with a change in the very notion of interest. Traditionally, social interests in Italy could be broadly defined as political. Party-centred subcultures created 'collective identities within which interest systems were dependent upon solidarity systems and not vice versa' (Bellucci 1997: 264). In other words interests (and voting) were to a large extent determined by ideological and cultural identities. But by the 1980s, parties were progressively losing touch with society, as indicated by the decline of organizational presence. In fact the recent phenomenon of party membership decline was preceded by the progressive paralysis of grass-roots activity (Bardi and Morlino 1994). Up to that point, even economic interests had been articulated through organizations that maintained close, institutionalized, sometimes even subordinated, links with political parties. This was true of workers, industrialists, and even shopkeepers' unions.

The most interesting recent development, however, concerns the strengthening of interests stemming directly from civil society. These are articulated through various (cultural, environmental, welfare, religious, and recreational) citizens' associations; by the mid-1990s membership of such associations reached 21 per cent of the Italian population, an increase of 2 per cent on the previous decade (Meo 1996). This compounded with the growing relevance of less structured forms of citizen association. For a limited period, immediately before and after the 1994 election, when 'party' had become nothing short of a dirty word, single-issue groups and citizens' committees were considered to be in a position to become privileged conduits of interest aggregation and articulation. This was probably partly a consequence of the immediate political crisis, and partly of the erosion of subcultures. Potentially divergent interests could no longer be harnessed by common cultural identities, nor could they be pacified through generous public spending. On the contrary, the austerity policies embraced by Italian governments after 1992, which required tax increases and cuts in the welfare system, helped bring into the open societal conflicts which had been dormant for almost two decades. Parties have tried to establish links with new societal groups, or to tap directly the interests that express them. Already during the 1994 electoral campaign, a focus on economic issues and the presentation of different economic policy platforms became the instruments through which new parties like Forza Italia and the Lega Nord, but above all the newly created electoral coalitions, tried to attract those interests that had been liberated by collapse of the old parties (Bellucci 1997).

It would appear that electors and their interests now have an unprecedented range of party choices through which to find expression and articulation. This is not only due to the very high number of parties that have survived or emerged after the 1992/94 transformation, but above all to the presence of two electoral coalitions that are more than just collections of parties. The Polo/Casa and even more so the Ulivo, are both entities with lives of their own and seem to be able to attract voters and interests that would not be satisfied with any of the parties they include. This suggests a new kind of aggregative capacity that parties, or rather coalitions, in Italy are developing. Moreover, they are loose enough organizations to allow for the inclusion of very diverse components, not only in terms of policy or ideological orientations, but also in terms of their organizational nature. In fact, single-issue groups and new movements appear to be much more willing independently to join one of the two coalitions, rather than to establish tight links with individual political parties. The loose nature of the coalitions' organizational structures certainly allows such groups to preserve their identities much better than through association with specific parties. It should also be said that single-issue groups and new movements have lost much of the attractiveness they held for citizens in 1992–94 and would probably struggle to maintain a significant political impact were it not for the connections they have established with the coalitions. This is true even of the pro-referendum group, whose initiatives were so important to the beginning of the Italian transformation.

Political commmunication and education

Political parties had a quasi-monopoly over political communication and education for the first thirty years of the postwar Italian Republic. To be sure, for at least the first half of that period they had to share that privilege with the Catholic church and its flanking organizations, but at the time these coincided almost exactly with the organization of Italy's largest party, the DC. In other words, parties performed their functions as a consequence of their hegemonic positions in their respective subcultural areas. At a time when illiteracy still plagued vast regions of the country and poverty made newspapers a luxury, the cultural and recreational centres built around parishes and local party headquarters were the only sources of political information. There citizens would find party newspapers and magazines and other political literature, and would also be able to have access to small libraries with non-political books and 'cultural' events, such as conferences and film screenings. And when television broadcasts started in the mid-1950s, in most villages and working-class urban areas, party-connected cultural venues often owned the only television sets accessible to the general public. As politics in Italy was very ideological, parties, both in government and in opposition, did not need to justify and communicate to the public their positions on specific policies. As a consequence, political parties' agenda-setting powers were not only unchallenged but also not subject to public scrutiny. This has changed since the 1970s as a consequence of both the emergence of the referendum as a powerful agenda-setting instrument available to citizens' associations and interest groups, and of the growing importance of the media as a non-partisan source of political information. Although the impact of the latter appears to have more continuous effects, that of the former has definitely been more dramatic for the agenda-setting power of the parties. This is demonstrated by the fact that issues like electoral and/or institutional reform, which parties tried to ignore for almost four decades (since an ill-fated attempt at electoral reform in 1953), became prominent after they were successfully raised by a referendum in 1991.

Political participation

The clearest impact of party role in political education and communication was on electoral turnout. Parties obsessively reminded their potential sympathizers of the importance of voting, and may have even been responsible for spreading the mistaken belief that voting was compulsory. This obviously also had implications for party influence on political participation. As we have seen, turnout levels in Italy have remained very high until recently, even if direct party grip on the public started declining as of the mid-1970s. Turnout levels, though they have declined somewhat since 1980, remain relatively high (refer again to Table 3.3). These levels decline dramatically in two-stage elections, such as those sub-national ones which require a second vote 2 weeks after the first, and in referendum voting. Much has been said about voter fatigue and how detrimental so many electoral consultations can be for the sense of political engagement felt by citizens. While most observers seem to share this view, an argument can perhaps be made that frequent votes, especially if concerning well-known or local candidates (sub-national elections) or specific issues (referenda), can perhaps give those citizens who do participate a deeper sense of their importance for the system than voting once every 5 years for distant, party-imposed national candidates. It could be surmised that, when voting in national elections, citizens may feel that they are carrying out a civic duty, whereas when they are participating in other electoral events they are exercising a political privilege. Certainly parties do not seem to have the resources to mobilize citizens several times a year, as has become increasingly necessary.

We have seen too, of course, unmistakable evidence of party membership decline. Yet it is necessary to consider this in the context of membership duties and rates of activism. In Italy, party membership rarely entailed a very active commitment, but rather represented an expression of political identity, and this alone probably allowed the parties to maintain a constant membership bedrock through the years. Indeed, formal membership required no more than the annual payment of fees, an obligation which was often met by the heads of families or even by local leaders in need of undemanding support. Interviews with local cadres responsible for party organization confirm that by the 1970s membership had become a family affair, even for the PCI. Official conceptions of membership did not change much for most parties over the years; in practice, however, and even in the case of those parties such as the PDS or MSI which continued to prescribe an active role for their members, membership became an extremely weak notion. On the other hand, membership was perhaps more important for the new actors in the party system, albeit in a different sense. Thus, La Rete and PR viewed membership as their main source of income. The Verdi (Greens) are also somewhat unusual, maintaining a system of collective membership in which relationships with individuals are determined by the single lists making up the federation. The Lega maintains a more traditional, but rather undemanding, view of membership (at least on paper), characterized by low admission requirements and generic membership obligations. In practice, however, Lega members are actually divided into four hierarchical categories: supporters, who have no voting rights and no obligations (in effect, their role is simply to provide financial support); militants, who have voting rights at local level and also 'active militancy' obligations; full members, who are appointed by the National Assembly after having 'demonstrated excellent militant commitment' and who enjoy voting rights at national level; and founding members, who enjoy lifetime voting rights at national level. In general, contemporary notions of membership are very weak and do not entail many specific duties. Silvio Berlusconi's contention that the reliance of the PDS and the RC on member canvassing at election time gives those parties an unfair advantage, is very revealing in this context.

However, there may still be room for a qualitative revival of party membership. With the decline of public financing and the near disappearance of private contributions—legal or otherwise—parties are now again coming to view members as important sources of income. While precise data are not available, it can be confidently assumed that membership contributions now account for a much more sizeable portion of party income than in the past. For example, DS's 600,000 members contribute about two-thirds of the party's total official income. Even placing the average individual donation at a conservative 50,000 lire per year, that is on a level similar to the PCI in 1989 (Bardi and Morlino 1992). Members have also seen their roles as party campaigners restored as a consequence of the financial crisis which does not allow parties to invest in expensive press and television campaigns as much as in the past. Moreover, the desire of the parties to stimulate activism by members and sympathizers is becoming increasingly evident in consultations on various party internal and policy choice matters. That said, no significant changes have yet been made to party statutes to enhance members' participatory rights as a consequence of these developments.

CONCLUSION

Overall, the systemic functionality of political parties in Italy appears to have declined in a process that started more than two decades ago, but which has manifested its most dramatic effects in recent years. In addition, the means by which political parties express their residual functionality has also changed.

In this chapter, we have addressed the issue of how Italian parties perform five specific functions. In each of these areas, significant decline and change can be observed in the way Italian parties perform. A description and assessment of such change cannot be made without a prior consideration of the transformation experienced by the Italian party system in the last decade. The most visible consequence of the transformation has been the emergence of a whole new set of parties, often presenting neither ideological continuity with, nor organizational resemblance to, parties of the past. It could be argued that a decline in party functionality may have been one of the causes of the party system's transformation. But the novel characteristics of the parties that emerged from it may also be responsible for the changing way in which parties perform systemic functions.

Although quantitative indicators do not show an appreciable downward trend until the late 1980s, our qualitative assessment of party legitimacy reveals an earlier decline. Party performance of functions such as interest articulation and aggregation, political participation, and political communication deteriorated roughly at the same time, revealing, and also contributing to, the growing detachment of parties from their once privileged societal partners. This was coupled with an erosion of party-centred subcultures.

Once the transformation began, changes in party functionality have generally resulted from the different organizational characteristics of the new parties and from the new patterns of competition which emerged. Pre-transformation parties had stable relationships with other institutions in the political system and with societal groups. The government or opposition status of parties was more or less permanent, thus making for very stable patterns of governance. Similarly, whether they encapsulated specific social subcultures (according to the mass-party model) or had links with a plurality of interest groups (revealing a catch-all orientation), parties remained anchored to their societal referents; this stabilized patterns of interest aggregation and articulation. In the 1990s, the position of parties changed as a consequence of the new electoral law and because of changes in their organizational characteristics. The new, essentially majoritarian, electoral law opened up the competition for governmental status to more parties in the system. At the same time it forced the building of electoral coalitions, and not only of governmental ones. Alternation in government and the construction and maintenance of coalitions radically affected patterns of governance: not only were all parties potential players in government, but also non-party actors (technicians) were called upon to take a role.

The current situation is far from stabilized, resulting as it does from an unplanned and incomplete programme of institutional reform. As the Italian academic debate points out, it is unrealistic to expect a stabilization of the rules of the political game and of party behaviour at a time when one of the biggest preoccupations of the parties remains how to change those very rules through further institutional reform.

APPENDIX: GLOSSARY OF PARTY ACRONYMS

DP Democrazia Proletaria/Proletarian Democracy.
PSIUP Partito Socialista Italiano di Unità Proletaria/Italian Socialist Party of Proletarian Unity.
PDUP Partito di Unità Proletaria/Party of Proletarian Unity.
PCI Partito Comunista Italiano/Italian Communist Party.
RC Rifondazione Comunista/Communist Refoundation.
PDS Partito Democratico di Sinistra/Democratic Party of the Left.
PSI Partito Socialista Italiano/Italian Socialist Party.
PSDI Partito Socialista Democratico Italiano/Italian Social Democratic Party.
PSU Partito Socialista Unificato/Unified Socialist Party. Formed between 1966 and 1969 as a result of a short-lived merger between PSI and PSDI.
DC Democrazia Cristiana/Christian Democracy.

PPI   Partito Popolare Italiano/Italian People's Party.
CCD   Centro Cristiano Democratico/Christian Democratic Centre.
CDU   Cristiani Democratici Uniti/United Christian Democrats.
UDR   Unione dei Democratici Riformisti/Union of Reform Democrats.
PRI   Partito Repubblicano Italiano/Italian Republican Party.
RI   Rinnovamento Italiano—Lista Dini/Italian Renewal—Dini List.
FI   Forza Italia/'Way to go' Italy.
PLI   Partito Liberale Italiano/Italian Liberal Party.
AN   Alleanza Nazionale/National Alliance.
MSI   Movimento Sociale Italiano/Italian Social Movement.
PR   Partito Radicale/Radical Party.
VER   Verdi/Greens.
LN   Lega Nord/Northern League.
PPST   Südtiroler Volkspartei/Partito Popolare Sud Tirolese/South Tirolean People's Party.
PNM   Partito Nazionale Monarchico/Monarchist National Party.
PMP   Partito Monarchico Popolare/People's Monarchist Party.
PDIUM Partito Democratico Italiano di Unità Monarchica/Italian Democratic Party of Monarchic Unity.
UDEUR Unione Democratica Europea

REFERENCES

Bardi, L. (1996*a*) 'Anti-party sentiment and party system change in Italy'. *European Journal of Political Research* 29: 345–63.
——(1996*b*) 'Change in the Italian party system'. *Congrips Newsletter* 46: 9–23.
——and Mair, P. (forthcoming) 'What is a Party System?' *Unpublished manuscript.*
——and Morlino, L. (1992) 'Italy', in R. Katz and P. Mair (eds) *Party Organizations. A data handbook* (London: Sage Publications), 458–618.
——and Morlino, L. (1994) 'Italy: tracing the roots of the great transformation', in R. S. Katz and P. Mair (eds) *How Parties Organize: Adaptation and Change in Western Democracies* (London: Sage Publications), pp. 242–77.
Bartolini, S. and D'Alimonte, R. (1995) 'Il sistema partitico: una transizione difficile', in S. Bartolini and R. D'Alimonte (eds) *Maggioritario ma non troppo* (Il Bologna: Mulino).
Bellucci, P. (1997) 'Classi, identità politiche e interessi', in P. Corbetta and A. Parisi (eds) *A Domanda Risponde* (Bologna: Il Mulino).
Caciagli, M. and Kertzer, D. I. (1996) *Politica In Italia. I fatti dell'anno e le interpretazioni. Edizione 96* (Bologna: Il Mulino).
Cartocci, R. (1994) *Fra Lega e Chiesa* (Bologna: Il Mulino).
Cazzola, F. (1972) 'Consenso e opposizione nel Parlamento italiano. Il ruolo del PCI dalla I alla IV legislatura' *Rivista Italiana di Scienza Politica.* 2: 71–96.
D'Alimonte, R. and Bartolini, S. (1997) *Maggioritario per caso* (Bologna: Il Mulino).

D'Alimonte, R. and Nelken, D. (1997) *Politica In Italia. I fatti dell'anno e le interpretazioni. Edizione 97* (Bologna: Il Mulino).

Della Porta, D. and Vannucci, A. (1999) *Un paese anormale. Come la Classe Politica ha Perso l'Occasione di Mani Pulite* (Roma-Bari: Editori Laterza).

Di Palma, G. (1977) *Surviving without Governing: The Italian Parties in Parliament* (Berkeley: University of California Press).

Hellman, S. and Pasquino, G. (1993) *Politica In Italia. I fatti dell'anno e le interpretazioni. Edizione 93* (Bologna: Il Mulino).

Ignazi, P. (1992) *Dal PCI al PDS* (Bologna: Il Mulino).

Katz, R. S., Mair, P., *et al.* (1992) 'The membership of political parties in European democracies'. *European Journal of Political Research* 22: 329–45.

—— —— (1995) 'Changing models of party organization and party democracy: the emergence of the cartel party'. *Party Politics* 1: 5–28.

Kreppel, A. (1997) 'Impact of Parties on Legislative Output in Italy' *European Journal of Political Research* 31: 327–49.

Mair, P. and van Biezen, I. (2001) 'Party membership in twenty European democracies, 1980–2000'. *Party Politics* 7: 5–22.

Mannheimer, R. (1989) *Capire il Voto: Contributi per l'Analisi del Comportamento Elettorale in Italia* (Milano: Angeli).

—— (1994) 'Il mercato elettorale dei partiti tra il vecchio e il nuovo', in R. Mannheimer and G. Sani (eds) *La Rivoluzione Elettorale* (Milan: Anabasi).

—— and Sani, G. (1987) *Il Mercato Elettorale. Identikit dell'Elettore Italiano* (Bologna: Il Mulino).

Mattina, L . (1993) 'La Confindustria di Abete: dall'alleanza con la DC all'appello multipartitico' in S. Hellman and G. Pasquino (eds) *Politica In Italia. I fatti dell'anno e le interpretazioni. Edizione 93* (Bologna: Il Mulino), 265–283.

Melchionda, E. (1995) 'Il bipartitismo irrealizzato: Modelli di competizione nei collegi uninominali', in G. Pasquino (ed.) *L'Alternanza Inattesa: Le Elezioni del 27 Marzo 1994 e le loro Conseguenze* (Saveria Mannelli: Rubbettino).

Meo, A. (1996) 'Le associazioni volontarie e il volontariato', in P. Ginsborg (ed.) *Lo Stato dell'Italia* (Milano: Il Saggiatore).

Morlino, L. (1991) *Costruire la Democrazia. Gruppi e Partiti in Italia* (Bologna: Il Mulino).

—— (1996) 'Crisis of parties and change of party system in Italy'. *Party Politics* 2: 5–30.

—— and Tarchi, M. (1996) 'The dissatisfied society: the roots of political change in Italy'. *European Journal of Political Research* 30: 41–63.

Nuvoli, P. and Spreafico, A. (1990) 'Il partito del non voto' in M. Caciagli and A. Spreafico (eds) *Vent'anni di elezioni in Italia. 1968-1987* (Padova: Liviana Editrice), 223–257.

Pappalardo, A. (1996) 'Dal pluralismo polarizzato al pluralismo moderato. I modelli di Sartori e la tradizione italiana'. *Rivista Italiana di Scienza Politica* 26: 103–46.

Pasquino, G. (1995) 'La partitocrazia', in G. Pasquino (ed) *La Politica Italiana. Dizionario Critico 1945–95* (Bari: Laterza).

Poguntke, T. (1994) 'Parties in a legalistic culture: the case of Germany', in R. S. Katz and P. Mair (eds) *How Parties Organize: Change and Adaptation in Party Organizations in Western Democracies* (London: Sage), pp. 185–215.

—— (1996) 'Explorations into a Minefield: Anti-party Sentiment. Conceptual thoughts and empirical evidence' *European Journal of Political Research*, 29: 319–44.

Pombeni, P. (1984) *Demagogia e Tirannide: Uno Studio sulla Forma-Partito del Fascismo* (Bologna: Il Mulino).

Sartori, G. (1976) *Parties and Party Systems: A Framework for Analysis* (Cambridge: Cambridge University Press).

Schmitt, H. and Holmberg, S. (1995) 'Political parties in decline?', in H.-D. Klingemann and D. Fuchs (eds) *Citizens and the State* (Oxford: Oxford University Press).

Vannucci, A. (1997) *Il Mercato della Corruzione* (Milan: Società Aperta Edizioni).

Verzichelli, L. (1995) 'Gli eletti', in S. Bartolini and R. D'Alimonte (eds) *Maggioritario ma non Troppo* (Bologna: Il Mulino).

——(1997) 'La classe politica della transizione', in R. D'Alimonte and S. Bartolini (eds) *Maggioritario per Caso* (Bologna: Il Mulino).

4

Party Decline in the Parties State? The Changing Environment of German Politics

Susan E. Scarrow

The 1949 (West) German Basic Law established a system of party-based democracy which has now endured for more than half a century. Yet today's political system is not identical to that of earlier years. Since the beginning of the 1980s new party alternatives have made coalition politics harder to manage, the established parties have lost votes and members, and waning public support for all the parties has drawn unfavourable attention to the parties' entrenched positions. These changes grew more pronounced in the 1990s, exacerbated, though not caused, by German unification. Developments reached a new stage in 1998, when one of the new parties of the 1980s, the Greens, became a party of government—an event made possible at least as much by the transformation of the Green Party itself as by a revolution in German politics. Nevertheless, despite the recent challenges to traditional political patterns, Germany remains very much a parties state. Parties still serve as the central mechanisms for political linkage and political decision-making, and the same big parties—Christian Democrats, Christian Socialists, or Social Democrats—are the principal players in state and federal coalition politics.

GERMAN PARTIES AND POLITICAL INSTITUTIONS

Germany's parties and party system have been shaped by the country's legal and institutional frameworks. To begin with, the breadth of the German party system was intentionally limited by constitutional provisions which allowed the prohibition of anti-democratic parties, and by the 1953 and 1956 electoral laws, which raised the nation-wide electoral threshold.[1] These laws helped reduce the number of *Bundestag* parties from eleven after the 1949 election to four after the 1961 election, and the party system retained this configuration for the next two decades. The German parties' internal politics and structures have also been marked by

---

[1] Under Germany's mixed member electoral system, parties which win at least three direct seats receive a share of seats proportional to their list vote even if this is below 5 per cent.

the country's federal structures. The federal decentralization of political decision-making encourages politicians to build national careers by nurturing their own organizational and electoral bases at the state (*Land*) level. Finally, the 1949 constitution gave democratic parties the status of semi-constitutional organs, giving them some legal privileges as a result of their mandated role of 'helping to shape the public will'. The *Bundestag* parties did not get around to adopting legislation spelling out the details of this constitutional status until 1967, when the parties joined to secure public funds for their work. The resulting Parties Law provided a legal definition of political parties, one which affected the parties' organizational operations by specifying standards of intra-party democracy which were to be followed by all recognized parties. In return, the Parties Law established what was to become a very extensive system of public subsidies for legally-qualified parties.

Since the country's establishment in 1949, the Federal Republic's party competition has been dominated by struggles between left and right. Despite some initial concerns that Germany's proportional representation electoral system would promote the party system fragmentation that had characterized the Weimar Republic, from the 1950s through the 1970s only three parties played leading roles in this left/right dynamic: on the left the Social Democratic Party (SPD), and on the right the Christian Democratic Union (CDU) and its Bavarian partner, the Christian Social Union (CSU). The political centre was occupied by the much smaller Free Democratic Party (FDP), which alternately governed with both the left and the right in state as well as federal legislatures. Thus, until the 1980s the effective number of parties (in both electorate and parliament) fully justified the classification of the country as a two-and-a-half party system (see Table 4.1). As Table 4.2 shows, for the first two of these decades the West German republic was governed by CDU-led coalitions. In 1969, after a three-year interlude as part of a grand coalition, the SPD formed the country's first left-centre government when it allied with the FDP. This coalition broke apart in 1982, as the FDP switched its support back to the CDU/CSU. The ensuing right-centre alliance governed Germany for the next sixteen years.

This stable pattern of competition was disrupted by the emergence of the Greens at the beginning of the 1980s. Although this new party was clearly on the left, it was initially difficult to accommodate into the established left–right dynamic. It was only after a decade of both successful and unsuccessful coalition experiments at the state and local level that the Greens shed their original self-chosen image as an 'anti-party party'. Not until the mid-1990s did the Greens really establish their credentials as a pragmatic, office-seeking party with a will to govern; only then did they become a plausible federal coalition partner for the SPD. This change was cemented in 1998, when a new election gave the SPD and Greens the votes they needed to form their first federal-level coalition.

The advent of the Greens was not the end of the upheavals in the Federal Republic's party and political systems. The country's political dynamics were permanently altered by the opening of the Berlin Wall in November 1989, and by

TABLE 4.1. *Electoral results in the Federal Republic of Germany, 1961–98*

	1961	1965	1969	1972	1976	1980	1983	1987	1990[a,b]	1994[b]	1998[b]
CDU/CSU	45.3	47.6	46.1	44.9	48.6	44.5	48.8	44.3	43.8	41.4	35.2
	(242)	(245)	(242)	(225)	(243)	(226)	(244)	(223)	(319)	(302)	(245)
FDP	12.8	9.5	5.8	8.4	7.9	10.6	7.0	9.1	11.0	6.9	6.2
	(67)	(49)	(30)	(41)	(39)	(53)	(34)	(46)	(79)	(47)	(43)
Greens[c]	—	—	—	—	—	1.5	5.6	8.3	5.0	7.3	6.7
						(0)	(27)	(42)	(8)	(49)	(47)
PDS	—	—	—	—	—	—	—	—	2.4	4.4	5.1
									(17)	(30)	(36)
SPD	36.2	39.3	42.7	45.8	42.6	42.9	38.2	37.0	33.5	36.4	40.9
	(190)	(202)	(227)	(230)	(214)	(218)	(193)	(186)	(239)	(252)	(298)
Others	5.7	3.6	5.4	1.0	0.9	0.4	0.4	1.5	4.1	3.6	5.9
	(0)	(0)	(0)	(0)	(0)	(0)	(0)	(0)	(0)	(0)	(0)
TURNOUT	87.7	86.8	86.7	91.9	90.7	88.6	89.1	84.3	77.8	79.0	82.2
ENEP	2.86	2.56	2.50	2.38	2.38	2.56	2.56	2.94	3.13	3.13	3.33
ENPP	2.51	2.38	2.24	2.34	2.31	2.44	2.51	2.80	2.65	2.89	2.91

Notes: CDU/CSU—Christian Democratic Union/Christian Social Union; FDP—Free Democratic Party; SPD—Social Democratic Party of Germany. Top figure in each cell = % of the vote won, bottom figure = number of seats won in Bundestag. ENEP—Effective Number of Electoral Parties; ENPP—Effective Number of Parliamentary Parties.
[a] Major electoral system change this year.
[b] Results for unified Germany.
[c] Bündnis 90/Greens after 1990.

Sources: Schindler 1984, 1986, 1988, 1994; Statistisches Bundesamt Deutschland 1998.

TABLE 4.2. *Government composition in Germany since 1957*

Years in office	Governing coalition	Chancellor	Cabinet portfolios (%)
Oct. 1957–Sept. 1960	CDU, CSU, DP	1957–63 Konrad Adenauer (CDU)	CDU: 67 CSU: 22 DP: 11
Sept. 1960–Nov. 1961	CDU, CSU		CDU: 77 CSU: 23
Nov. 1961–Oct. 1965	CDU, CSU, FDP	1963–66 Ludwig Erhard (CDU)	CDU: 57 CSU: 19 FDP: 24
Oct. 1965–Dec. 1966			CDU: 59 CSU:23 FDP: 18
Dec. 1966–Oct. 1969	CDU, CSU, SPD	1966–69 Kurt Kiesinger (CDU)	CDU: 43 CSU:14 SPD: 43
Oct. 1969–Dec. 1972	SPD, FDP	1969–74 Willy Brandt (SPD)	SPD: 75 FDP: 19 Independent: 6
Dec. 1972–May 1974		1974–82 Helmut Schmidt (SPD)	SPD: 72 FDP: 28
May 1974–Oct. 1980			SPD: 75 FDP: 25
Oct. 1980–Oct. 1982			SPD: 77 FDP:23
Oct. 1982–Mar. 1993	CDU, CSU, FDP	1982–1998 Helmut Kohl (CDU)	CDU: 52 CSU: 24 FDP: 24
Mar. 1983–Nov. 1984			CDU: 52 CSU: 30 FDP: 18
Nov. 1984–June 1986			CDU: 56 CSU: 28 FDP: 16
June 1986–Feb. 1987			CDU: 58 CSU: 26 FDP: 16
Feb. 1987–Apr. 1989			CDU: 53 CSU: 26 FDP: 21
Apr. 1989–Oct. 1990			CDU: 50 CSU: 30 FDP: 20
Oct. 1990–Jan. 1991	CDU, CSU, FDP, DSU		CDU: 52 CSU: 24 FDP: 20 DSU: 4
Jan. 1991–Nov. 1994	CDU, CSU, FDP		CDU: 55 CSU: 20 FDP: 25
Nov. 1994–Oct. 1998			CDU: 61 CSU: 22 FDP: 17
Oct. 1998–present	SPD, Greens	1998–present Gerhard Schroeder (SPD)	SPD: 75 B'90/Greens: 19 Independent: 6

Note: DP—German Party.

Sources: Schindler 1994: 441; *European Journal of Political Research* Yearbooks.

the consequences of the unification that took place less than a year later. Such rapid unification was accomplished by transplanting eastward the basic constitutional and legal frameworks of western Germany. Yet although this transfer ensured institutional continuity between the old West Germany and the newly expanded Federal Republic, the political continuity was far from complete. Above all, the western German balance of powers and interests clearly was substantially altered by the addition of twelve million eligible voters and five new federal states, states whose shared problems and concerns were quite different than those of their western neighbours.

Given the enormous political changes associated with unification, the ensuing party system change was surprisingly small. In the months before unification the western German parties effectively colonized the new and newly democratized parties in the east, a process which culminated in formal mergers between eastern and western parties by the end of 1990. The only eastern party to survive on its own was the former ruling party of East Germany, the Socialist Unity Party (SED), now internally democratized and committed to constitutional politics, and renamed the Party of Democratic Socialism (PDS). The PDS defied initial predictions of its early obsolescence by stabilizing its regional support at levels high enough to win *Bundestag* seats in all the federal elections of the 1990s. It also established itself as the third largest party in the eastern states.

In contrast to the PDS, the position of the FDP grew ever more precarious as the 1990s progressed. Unable to break out from the shadow of its federal coalition partners, the FDP slipped below the 5 per cent hurdle in most state elections during the 1990s, and the party seemed increasingly vulnerable at the federal level as well. Relations between the FDP and its CDU/CSU partners grew increasingly tense in this decade as the FDP sought to re-establish its independent identity, primarily by emphasizing market liberal principles.

These changes in the party system coincided with other changes in the political system. Among the most important of these was the waning of the traditionally close links between German parties and distinct social sectors (trade unions with the SPD, the church-going public with the Christian Democratic parties, and the self-employed and small business owners with the FDP). The political importance of these social identities began to weaken as early as the 1960s, when the changing profile of Germany's parties helped to inspire Otto Kirchheimer's prediction of converging 'catch-all' parties (Kirchheimer 1966). In part, this shift among voters reflected the SPD's adoption of a more cross-class appeal, a move most notably symbolized by the party's 1959 Bad Godesberg programme. By the 1980s secular-ization and labour force changes had diminished but not erased the political reach of once-dominant religious and class cleavages. Unification further eroded the social delineations in German politics. The western parties initially attracted con-stituencies in the east which inverted traditional western loyalties, with unionized labour preferring the CDU to the SPD, and eastern church-goers preferring the SPD to the CDU (Dalton and Bürklin 1996; Gluchowski and Wilamowitz-Moellendorf 1998; Jung and Roth 1994; Schmitt 1998).

The weakening of traditional sectoral ties and the emergence of the Greens trig-gered ongoing debates about whether German politics was being transformed by a post-materialist realignment, or by the kind of generalized dealignment that had appeared earlier in other countries. Some pointed to increasing electoral volatility as confirmation of dealignment, but others disputed this interpretation, arguing that even if voters were more likely to abstain or to vote for different parties within the left/right party blocks, they continued to structure their choices in terms of left and right (Dalton and Rohrschneider 1990; Schmitt and Holmberg 1994; Schultze 1995; Veen 1994; Zelle 1994 (see Table 4.3)). As explained in the next section, still others viewed changing electoral behaviour as one of several indications that some-thing more than dealignment was occurring, arguing that public sentiment was turning against the institutions of party-dominated government. These questions of party legitimacy have had great resonance in Germany, where insufficient support for party democracy is still held responsible for undermining the Weimar Republic.

TABLE 4.3. *Electoral volatility and partisan attachment among German electors*

	1961	1965	1969	1972	1976	1980	1983	1987	1990	1994	1998
Party identifiers				75	81	75	74	72	71	67	64
Very strong and strong identifiers				55	47	46	39	41	40	36	—
Total net volatility	11.5	6.8	6.2	5.7	4.1	4.5	8.4	6.0	7.8	7.8	8.3
Block volatility[a]	4.3	3.2	2.7	2.7	3.0	0.1	4.8	1.5	0.9	2.4	5.2

Note: [a] 1960–83 scores from Bartolini and Mair 1990; PDS included as 'class left'.
Sources: Dalton 1996: 47; Forschungsgruppe Wahlen 1998.

PARTY LEGITIMACY

Given the centrality of parties in the German political system, and the democratic crises associated with the failed Weimar Republic's prevailing atmosphere of anti-party sentiment, Germans are particularly sensitive to the suggestion that parties might be losing the support of the citizens they are supposed to represent. Yet just such a diagnosis of popular disaffection with political parties gained great currency at the beginning of the 1990s, as Germans were adjusting to the new political and economic realities brought about by unification. Survey evidence from this period seemed to indicate that Germans were becoming increasingly disappointed with, and distrustful of, the parties that governed them (Haungs 1992; Rattinger 1993; Stöss 1990). Many suggested that this discontent reflected a new climate of political disenchantment, and commentators from the federal president downwards pointed to a variety of other behavioural and attitudinal indicators that seem consonant with claims of growing disapproval of parties.

One such indicator of apparent political disaffection is the decline in *party membership*. Throughout most of the past half century, Germany's most successful electoral parties have cultivated large membership organizations. The SPD helped invent mass-style organization in the late nineteenth century, and after 1945 it returned to its organizational roots when the party re-emerged from illegality. At first, the culture and hierarchy of the re-established party was dominated by earlier eras' visions of the SPD as the political arm of working-class comrades. By the 1960s, however, party life and membership began changing along with the party's increasingly cross-class political appeals. SPD membership grew rapidly in the 1960s and 1970s, including in rural and suburban areas where the Christian Democrats had previously faced only weakly organized competition.

The CDU membership grew even more quickly in this period. As early as the 1960s the CDU's central party managers began to put an increased emphasis on individual membership. In the 1970s, after the CDU went into opposition at the federal level, party organizers set their sights on constructing a membership-based organization to rival the SPD's grass roots networks. In a period of heightened

TABLE 4.4. *Party membership*

Year	CDU	CSU	SPD	FDP	Greens	PDS	Total members	Members/ Electorate
1961	248 (0.7)[a]	59 (0.2)	645 (1.7)				952	2.6
1965	288 (0.7)	81 (0.2)[b]	710 (1.8)	57 (0.1)[c]			1,136	2.8
1969	304 (0.8)	77 (0.2)	779 (2.0)	59 (0.2)			1,218	3.2
1972	423 (1.0)	107 (0.3)	954 (2.3)	58 (0.1)			1,542	3.7
1976	652 (1.6)	144 (0.3)	1022 (2.4)	79 (0.2)			1,897	4.5
1980	693 (1.7)	172 (0.4)	986 (2.3)	84 (0.2)	18 (0.1)		1,953	4.7
1983	735 (1.6)	185 (0.4)	926 (2.1)	72 (0.2)	25 (0.1)		1,943	4.4
1987	706 (1.3)	184 (0.4)	910 (2.0)	65 (0.1)	42 (0.1)		1,908	3.9
1990	790 (1.1)	186 (0.3)	950 (1.6)	179 (0.3)	41 (0.1)	285 (0.5)	2,431	3.9
1994	674 (1.1)	176 (0.3)	849 (1.4)	88 (0.1)	44 (0.05)	124 (0.2)	1,955	3.2
1998	638 (1.0)	180 (0.3)	775 (1.3)	68 (0.1)	52 (0.1)	94 (0.2)	1,745	3.0

Notes: Figures stated in thousands; figures in parenthesis = percentage of electorate enrolled as members.
[a] 1962.
[b] 1966.
[c] 1968.

political activism, the CDU's recruitment efforts paid off handsomely, and party membership doubled between the late 1960s and the mid-1970s. CSU membership also doubled in this period. Even the FDP, which has never aspired to enlist a mass membership, also saw its enrolments increase at this time (see Table 4.4). This period of general party growth came to an end in the early 1980s. At this point all the parties saw their memberships stagnate; by the end of the 1980s they had begun to plummet. The merger of eastern and western German parties provided a one-time boost in overall party enrolment. However, by the mid-1990s the downward trend was once again clearly evident, now reinforced by particularly sharp enrolment drops in the eastern states. In the 1990s only the CSU and the Greens were able to retain (and in the case of the Greens, boost) their membership strength. Recent drops look even starker when membership is described as a proportion of the eligible electorate: in the 1990s a smaller proportion of German voters chose to enrol in a political party than at any time since the 1960s.

The waning attractiveness of party enrolment also has been manifest in the ageing of the party memberships. Despite the big parties' increasingly urgent efforts to enrol young supporters, by the mid-1990s fewer than 5 per cent of CDU members and 9 per cent of SPD members were 30 years or younger (CDU 1997; SPD 1995). Though the Greens were somewhat more successful in enlisting younger supporters, the wider figures suggest a generational change that seems likely to perpetuate what appears to be a turn away from party-organized politics. This ageing and shrinking of party memberships has been a standard exhibit in arguments about the spread of political disaffection in Germany.

Changes in electoral behaviour over the same period also seem consistent with the portrait of growing dislike of partisan politics. To begin with, *turnout* in federal elections fell from over 90 per cent in the 1970s to under 80 per cent at the beginning

Susan E. Scarrow

of the 1990s (in both west and east (refer again to Table 4.1)). In the 1990s turnout routinely fell below 70 per cent in state elections, and sometimes even dropped below 60 per cent. Many connected this decline in electoral participation to popular discontent with the party alternatives (cf. Falter and Schumann 1993; Betz 1994). If so, the slight increase in turnout in the 1998 federal election, when the vote's outcome was considered too close to call, suggests that some voters overcome their disaffection when participation is most likely to make a difference.

A third behavioural pattern that is often cited as an indicator of weakening voter-party ties is voters' increasing *willingness to shift party support from election to election*. Reported vote-switching grew from 16 per cent in the 1980 federal election to 24 per cent in 1994, fuelled in part by the advent of new party alternatives (Conradt 1996). Particularly worrying to political observers have been the occasional flares of support for far-right parties in state, local, and European elections. Though the far-right parties found it difficult to consolidate such support, the fact that German voters express discontent through this sort of voting behaviour has been interpreted by some as a further sign of the declining legitimacy of the traditional parties (Rattinger 1993). These individual-level shifts in voting behaviour, plus the increasing abstention rates, helped boost aggregate measures of electoral volatility. Measures of total volatility in particular pointed to a change in the dynamics of the party system, although measures of block volatility suggested that the underlying shifts were much less dramatic (refer again to Table 4.3). Although some of the volatility might be explained away as loyalty to coalition partners more than to parties, the increasing unpredictability of electoral behaviour does contribute to the impression that traditional patterns of German partisan politics have changed significantly in recent years. Survey evidence about *party identification* has reinforced this picture of weakening partisan attachments. Although the proportion of citizens admitting ties to a particular party remained about the same from the 1970s through the 1990s, the strength of these reported ties weakened considerably, as Table 4.3 shows. Again, some have interpreted these shifts as signs of discontent, not merely as evidence of dealignment (Falter and Rattinger 1995).

Taken together these indicators clearly suggest a loosening of the bonds that join citizens with parties. What remains unclear, however, is whether these changes are merely the product of weakening cleavages and moderate catch-all politics, or whether they are, instead, warning signs of intense disaffection with party-organized politics (Poguntke 1994; Scarrow 1994). Under the latter interpretation, the one initially favoured by many journalists and politicians, the German parties and the party state were facing a crisis of legitimacy at the beginning of the 1990s, one that could be averted only by implementing democratizing changes to established political institutions (Starke 1993; von Arnim 1993; von Weizsäcker 1993). Under the former interpretation, the German Republic had become a 'normal' democracy in which citizens, though generally content with the system, nevertheless retained a healthy suspicion of their governors (Veen 1992). This normalization interpretation gained increasing support. By the end of the 1990s attention had shifted away from these supposed indicators of political discontent, even though most of them continued to develop in ways that do not contradict the thesis of growing disaffection with parties. Thus, party membership continued to fall, voters remained volatile, and Germans continued to register much higher support for the general political system than for the specifics of party politics (Pickel and Walz 1997; Wiesendahl 1998).

The apparent erosion of support for the traditional parties began appearing in West Germany several years before German unification burst onto the political agenda. After unification this western disaffection with parties seemed to spread to the east, where frustration with party politics was exacerbated by some specifically eastern problems. Of the parties that won eastern seats in the first post-unification federal election, only the eastern Social Democrats and the Federation '90 (later Federation '90/Greens) grew out of new movements that formed as the East German regime collapsed. Both parties initially tried to capitalize on their early opposition to the East German authorities, but they found that this issue was not enough to win them strong support. The Federation '90/Greens in particular discovered that their mixture of post-materialist and anti-materialist politics had little popular resonance in the east, where voters faced high economic uncertainty. The party won seats in four of the five eastern legislatures in 1990, but by 1998 its support no longer crossed the 5 per cent electoral threshold in any of the state elections in the east.

The remaining three parties grew out of organizations that had been part of the ruling coalition in the German Democratic Republic. The new eastern German CDU and FDP emerged out of pre-existing 'block parties', small parties which the dominant SED had permitted to exist in return for their complete and unquestioning loyalty. The PDS emerged as the democratized successor to the SED. All three parties began the unification era in an initially advantageous position, having inherited members, assets, and support from their East German predecessors. However, for the CDU and FDP these advantages proved to be short-lived, and many former members deserted these parties as the collapse of the old regime made obsolete the parties' previous identities as 'official' political alternatives. They, like the SPD and Federation '90, found it difficult to attract new members in the east. The eastern parties' recruitment problems were compounded by a lack of organizational tradition, and by the growing disenchantment with a system that brought such harsh economic realities as an eastern unemployment rate that stayed high, and well above the national average, throughout the 1990s. In this climate, parties faced a different kind of legitimacy problem, because easterners had good reason to view the 'established' parties as West German parties which showed little understanding of eastern states' problems.

The parties that benefited from this disaffection with the traditional western alternatives were those that were considered to be outside the mainstream, and above all the PDS. Although the PDS shed members at the beginning of the 1990s, by the end of the decade it was the only party which was increasing its organizational strength in the eastern region. Far-right parties also sporadically benefited from eastern dissatisfaction with the major parties, though much of this support took the form of occasional protest voting rather than consolidated support for a single far-right alternative. Even so, far-right parties retained the power to attract voters and to surprise the established parties by occasional successes in state elections; for instance, in the spring of 1998 the far-right German People's Union (DVU) gained a spectacular 12.9 per cent of the vote in state elections in Saxony-Anhalt.

It is somewhat hard to judge the import of easterners' distance from their new partisan institutions. Given the abrupt shift of regimes, it was perhaps not to be expected that citizens in eastern Germany would immediately develop strong ties to new parties and new political institutions. Seen in this light, German parties do not seem to be doing so badly in terms of their ability to establish and maintain links to citizens. By the time of the 1994 election more than half the eastern voters identified with some party, and the average intensity of this identification was only slightly below that of western voters (Falter and Rattinger 1994: 498). The 1998 election brought a sharp convergence—and mutual increase—of turnout levels in east and west. In short, it is plausible to argue that the parties have not done badly in the new states in consolidating their electoral support and in establishing their governing credentials, especially given that the integration of the eastern electorate began in a period when the legitimacy of the western parties was under attack, and given that the parties faced special difficulties in establishing their support in a period of economic crisis in the eastern states. Moreover, although in the western states the links between German parties and citizens are clearly not as strong as they once were, in neither west nor east can German citizens be said to have disowned party-dominated politics.

PARTY ORGANIZATIONAL STRENGTH

Notwithstanding recent slumps in party enrolments, in almost every other sense the German parties are organizationally stronger at the end of the 1990s than they were forty years earlier. All have more members, more employees, and much bigger budgets than at the beginning of the 1960s. However, the parties are finding it increasingly difficult to maintain their strength in these areas. In addition, all the parties are struggling to construct the most minimal of organizations in the five eastern German states.

Finance

German parties are the self-appointed beneficiaries of extraordinarily generous public subsidies. The first tentative experiments with public political funding started in the 1950s, but the Constitutional Court rejected a whole succession of plans as unfair and unauthorized. It was not until the end of the 1960s that the parliamentary parties finally united behind a plan which withstood Constitutional Court scrutiny. Though the precise subsidy formula has been altered frequently since then, one of its enduring features is to tie the size of each party's payment to its electoral success. This means that the large and well-established parties receive the largest share of public funds; even so, parties which win as little as one half of one per cent of the vote (0.5 per cent) also qualify for subsidies. These funds can be especially crucial for fledgling parties.

Rival legislative parties cooperated to steadily increase the level of political subsidies throughout the 1970s and 1980s. The cooperation was driven in part by the debts the parties incurred during increasingly expensive election campaigns. Between 1970 and 1990 campaign subsidies to the federal parties more than tripled. Such 'self-service' collusion was slowed in the early 1990s by the Constitutional Court, which set an inflation-adjustable cap on overall campaign subsidies (at the early 1990s level of DM 230 million). Yet even with this cap, public payments remain very generous in international terms (see Table 4.5). Moreover, these payments represent only one part of the subsidy picture. In addition to these funds for their federal organizations, German parties also receive public monies to support their state election campaigns, their parliamentary parties, and party-linked 'educational foundations' (described more fully below).

Thus, for the past three decades public subsidies have been a financial mainstay for all the German parties. In recent years public funds have provided on average 20–40 per cent of total party revenues during each election cycle. This level has been quite stable since the 1967 introduction of campaign subsidies

TABLE 4.5. *Party finance in Germany*

Year	CDU		CSU		FDP		Green		PDS		SPD	
	Inc.	Exp.	Inc.	Exp.	Inc.	Exp.	Inc.	Exp.	Inc.	Exp.	Inc.	Exp.
1969	45		13		9						65	
1972	114		23		23						113	
1976	145		29		28						123	
1980	159		38		35		7				156	
1983	252	221	68	53	41	39	19	26			233	198
1987	199	208	61	49	45	37	65	51			225	211
1990	174	170	44	40	33	26	48	49	192	954	354	352
1994	280	304	68	85	58	100	53	66	34	46	353	397
1998	252	302	66	81	49	59	57	67	39	49	304	355

Notes: All figures are national totals, in DM 100 millions. Election years only (excepting expenditure totals for 1983, which are in fact from 1984).

Source: Poguntke and Boll (1992); Deutscher Bundestag (2001) 'Parteienfinanzierung': http://www.bundestag.de/datbk.

(Landfried 1994: 370). Yet while these public payments eased the parties' financial worries, they did not free them from the need to find other funding sources.
Since the 1970s most of the German parties have been periodically indebted, and
have always wanted more funds than subsidies alone could provide. In addition,
Constitutional Court rulings have repeatedly stipulated that parties may not receive
more than half their revenues from the public purse: parties which cannot raise
sufficient matching funds from other sources must forfeit subsidies they otherwise
would be paid. For all these reasons, generous public subsidies have not freed the
German parties from funding worries.

To varying degrees all the parties have looked to large private and corporate
donations as a major source of revenue. However, in the 1980s and 1990s the parties
encountered new obstacles to fundraising. First, all the established parties (and
some of their reliable sponsors) were embarrassed as their extra-legal fundraising
efforts became targets of public investigations. In the 1980s there was the so-called
'Flick Affair', which entangled the FDP and CDU. In the same decade both the
SPD and CSU also confronted questions about their own funding irregularities
(Landfried 1994: ch. 5). Then towards the end of 1999 came the 'Kohl Affair',
a financial scandal involving unreported political donations in which the former
Chancellor refused to reveal the sources of these funds. These affairs have cast a
negative light on all political donations. Second, a series of Constitutional Court
rulings made political contributions less attractive by eliminating tax advantages
for corporate political donations, setting much lower limits on tax advantages for
private donations, and sharply restricting the amount donors could give anonym-
ously. The SPD and the centre–right parties have tried to counter the effects of
these changes by experimenting with such American-style fundraising techniques
as direct mailings, which aim to boost income from smaller donations; so far their
efforts have produced only limited financial returns (Römmele 1997a,b).

Given the problems with collecting donations, the parties continue to look to
membership dues and contributions from elected officials to provide a major portion of their revenues. As far as the latter are concerned, it is known that all the
parties expect their officeholders to contribute a portion of their salaries to party
coffers. These levies might be thought of as a kind of indirect public subsidy,
one that increases as representatives' salaries rise. However, the exact size of
such subsidies is not clear since financial reporting requirements no longer separate officeholders' contributions from membership dues. For the same reason it is
impossible to determine the precise extent to which membership dues contribute
to party revenues. It is nevertheless clear that party members continue to provide
a significant and steady source of revenue for at least the SPD, CDU, and CSU.
Throughout the 1980s and 1990s, the share of party revenues provided by dues
and contributions from officeholders ranged from about 50 per cent for the SPD
and 40 per cent for the CDU, to 25 per cent for the FDP.

Overall, we may say that, whatever the challenges German parties have faced
in raising financial resources, they are well off in comparative international terms

TABLE 4.6. *Party payroll staff in Germany*

Year	State-financed *Bundestag* fraktion staff				MdB's state-financed personal assistants				Central party staffs		
	CDU/CSU	SPD	FDP	Greens	CDU/CSU	SPD	FDP	Greens	CDU	SPD	Greens
1969	40	99	21		207	166	25		108		
1971/72	113	99	27		367	275	46		178	55	
1976/77	74[a]	141	50		405	422	62		233		
1980/81	175	159	59		651	567	105		218	67	
1983	192	190	51	75	606	587	130	75	199	63	12
1987	227	252	54	86	1145	776	241	146	205	76	19
1990					1641	1132	361	191			
1991	280	290	87		2026	1334	542	26			

[a]CDU only.

Sources: Schindler 1982, 1988, 1994; Poguntke 1993.

(Farrell and Webb 2000: 120), and certainly not getting any poorer. Thus, if we focus on the five main 'Western' parties, their combined income in 1980 was DM 395 million, while (constant at 1980 prices[2]) it was DM 462 million in 1998, a real terms increase of 17 per cent.

Staff

Until 1993, the party finance law stipulated that political subsidies were to be used exclusively to defray campaign costs, not for other organizational purposes. Even so, the 1967 introduction of these subsidies clearly fuelled the expansion of parties' permanent organizations. The CDU's central office staff expanded most rapidly, rising from around 100 at the end of the 1960s to over 200 by the mid-1970s (see Table 4.6). The central staffs of the other parties also grew in the same period, though precise employment figures are not available for all the parties. At the same time the parties expanded their state and local level organizations, growth that was supported in part by the introduction of state-level subsidies to the parties. All four parties maintained these relatively large party bureaucracies through the 1990s, although each party's staffing levels fluctuated along with its electoral (and hence financial) fortunes.

In addition to this subsidy-linked growth of the parties' extra-legislative offices, staffs in the state and federal legislatures also expanded markedly at the end of the 1960s. In the *Bundestag*, party staffs tripled in the 1960s, growing from about 70 in 1961 to over 220 in 1969 (Schindler 1984: 993). As Table 4.6 shows, high staffing levels have remained the norm ever since. In addition, since the mid-1960s every *Bundestag* member has received a budget that can be used to hire several

[2] Calculated using an inflator published at http://www.sunshinecable.com/~eisehan/V80-10en.htm.

assistants. These good support teams reduce the need for parliamentary parties or individual representatives to rely on the central party organizations for help in pursuing political or legislative agendas.

Because they have such large internal resources, the parties have been able to professionalize from within, and have not been forced to rely heavily on outside consultants to meet all the challenges of new communications technologies and new electoral environments. Even so, during the past two decades all the established parties have regularly sought the help of professional advertisers and market researchers. The parties commission extensive opinion polling to help them in planning campaign strategies, and they contract with independent advertising agencies to design campaign advertising. Despite this emphasis on the professionalism of their campaign presentations, party insiders have remained very much in control of the overall efforts, and have not ceded control over the presentation of party policies (Boll 1996).

Members

As discussed above, starting in the 1980s all the big German parties' membership organizations suffered first stagnation, and then decline. The traditional membership parties (the CDU, CSU, and SPD) responded to their enrolment losses by launching new recruitment drives, including ones targeted at young supporters. They also tinkered with the obligations and duties of party membership, hoping to make enrolment more attractive and less onerous (for instance, by creating special 'trial membership' programmes).

As such responses suggest, these parties have considered members to be a worthwhile organizational resource, though the reasons for which members are valued have somewhat altered since the beginning of the 1960s (Scarrow 1996b). For instance, in this period members' direct electioneering activities became much less central to federal campaign strategies, but campaign planners became more aware of how members' informal contacts might help mobilize party supporters. In recognition of this, recent campaigns have continued to attempt to engage the interest and enthusiasm of party members, sending them extra educational and publicity materials, holding rallies, and even producing election-oriented computer games in hopes of appealing to younger members. Similarly, over the past three decades party strategists have begun to place more emphasis on members' contributions to local politics, a reflection of growing partisanship in this arena. It is at this level in particular that the parties have been hurt by weaknesses in their membership organization. Such weakness has been especially evident in the eastern German states, where membership-poor parties have struggled to find sufficient candidates to fill local government offices (Clemens 1993; Poguntke 1996; Tiemann 1993).

Finally, all parties have shown some concern about changes in the size and demographic character of their memberships, in part because these widely reported figures have become indicators of party legitimacy and of party popularity with specific social sectors. Put differently, German party strategists clearly have regarded the legitimacy conveyed by membership as an organizational resource in its own right, one that should pay electoral dividends regardless of the activities of the party-sponsored activities in which the members engage.

Mass media

Until the 1980s, German parties had three primary vehicles for conveying their political messages: radio, television, and the many privately owned newspapers, most of which have regional readerships. Throughout the past forty years campaigning parties have been granted free broadcast time on the public channels, but until the 1980s they were unable to buy advertisements on either these or on the commercial stations. The biggest parties have received the bulk of this free media exposure, but even fledgling and tiny parties are allocated at least one free spot per election. Representatives of the legislative parties also have enjoyed extensive opportunities to present party positions during the many political talk shows which are a staple of German broadcasting both during and between campaigns. Moreover, although broadcasters are required to be politically neutral, German parties have become more savvy about tailoring sound-bites and staging events in order to influence the messages that get included in daily news bulletins. Since the end of the 1980s, parties have been able to supplement free media exposure by purchasing advertising spots on the increasingly important private television and radio stations. The largest (and richest) parties have experimented cautiously with this new option, attracted by the prospect of reaching wider audiences, but deterred by the high cost of these new advertising opportunities.

Party politics also receives extensive coverage in Germany's many regional newspapers and weekly news magazines. Although German newspapers are not overtly linked to particular parties, many of the leading papers undisguisedly favour the left or the right. Even so, parties cannot rely on friendly papers to act as mouthpieces for party messages. As a result, the parties must rely on advertising and stage-managed public events to ensure that readers are exposed to the party ideas and personalities (Semetko and Schoenbach 1993, 1995).

Parties in eastern Germany

As noted above, the eastern German parties entered into unification with very different organizational advantages and handicaps, but within a few years all except the PDS found their political efforts hampered by the intertwined weaknesses of their membership and professional organizations. The eastern CDU, FDP, and above all the PDS, started the 1990s with members, finances, and offices inherited from East German predecessors. The three parties retained the advantages provided by some of these physical assets, but all of them saw their memberships plunge.

Neither the CDU or SPD were able to sustain in the east even a shadow of the mass membership organizing style that remained the ideal in the western states. Their eastern state parties necessarily became 'electoral–professional' organizations, though in this case 'professionalization' was as much an indication of weakness as of strength.

Whatever their size, all the western-affiliated parties were slow in producing indigenous eastern leadership. In the newly founded SPD, as well as in the continuing CDU and FDP, many easterners were forced out of party and parliamentary leadership positions as their pasts were exposed to ever greater scrutiny. At the top levels, such losses were offset by the migration of political entrepreneurs from the western parties (most successfully, the long-serving CDU Minister President in the state of Saxony, Kurt Biedenkopf). However, the state and local parties were plagued by their small memberships and, particularly in the FDP and CDU, by tensions between those who joined before and after the collapse of the old regime. The scarcity of members made it hard for parties to recruit candidates for state and local offices, and lack of money and lack of volunteers made it all but impossible for local parties to campaign in ways that were likely to solidify electoral support. Their small size and mostly inexperienced leaders also made it more difficult for the eastern parties to fight against the domination of western priorities and personnel in the federal-level parties (Schmidt 1998: 48–51).

In a development that confounded many initial predictions, it was the PDS which best weathered the organizational attrition that affected the other parties in the region. The PDS was able to maintain a comparatively large, albeit ageing, membership and by the end of the 1990s it had established itself as the third strongest party in eastern state legislatures. The PDS organization was strong enough to develop a visible programme of outreach and constituency service, activities which were particularly evident in areas where the parties' electoral support was highest—especially in those districts where the party had a chance of winning or retaining the *Bundestag* seat.

As the above sections explain, generous public subsidies have sustained the parliamentary wings and central organizations of all the German parties. These resources have enabled the parties to take advantage of new communications opportunities and new advertising strategies without having to abandon more traditional approaches, many of which remain directed at, and supported by, the locally organized members. It was here, in their membership bases, that German parties have shown their greatest symptoms of weakness in recent years. Although all the parties have larger enrolments than at the beginning of the 1960s, the declining appeal of party membership is reflected in parties' diminished ability to attract younger recruits, and in the drop in membership as a proportion of the electorate. However, as the next section shows, despite such slippage in the parties' voluntary organizations, and despite the previously described attacks on party dominance, in terms of political agenda-setting, legislation, and governance, Germany remains very much a 'parties state'.

THE SYSTEMIC FUNCTIONALITY OF POLITICAL
PARTIES IN GERMANY

In the 1990s, as in the 1960s, German parties are the privileged channels to, and central players in, the political arena. In Germany, almost every important political dispute sooner or later becomes a party dispute, and almost every important political actor has known party allegiances or, at the very least, party allies.

Governance

Even in an environment of declining voter loyalties and new outlets for political activism, some of the biggest challenges to party governance actually arise within the party-based political system itself. They are the result of the difficulties of maintaining clear party identities under a constitution which has many institutional incentives for cross-party cooperation. Such cooperation is fostered above all by features of German federalism.

In the first place, federalism creates the possibility of disjunctions between coalitions at the state and federal level. Such disjunctions have been quite common in practice. This means that even when the FDP has governed with the CDU nationally, it has not ruled out cooperating with the SPD in state governments. Similarly, the CDU and SPD sometimes have been willing to form grand coalitions at the state level even while rejecting such alliances at the federal level. This tendency to blur lines of competition has been exacerbated in recent years by the expansion of the party system, which has increased the options for, and uncertainty about, government formation. Parties which campaign hard against one another may find after an election that they are the most likely candidates to form a joint coalition. This cross-party cooperation can reinforce voters' perception that there is little difference between the parties, and that none of the established parties offer real alternatives to 'politics as usual'. Put differently, although as a group the German parties are of central importance for shaping the way the country is governed, the pressures for rival parties to cooperate can make it difficult to disentangle the extent to which particular parties matter.

The states' institutional role in federal governance creates a second type of pressure for cross-party cooperation. State governments are directly represented in the upper house of the German parliament (the *Bundesrat*), which has either an absolute or a conditional veto over most legislation. Because of this, the federal government's ability to implement its agenda depends to a great extent on whether the upper house is sympathetic to government plans. This is usually the case when the *Bundesrat* and *Bundestag* are controlled by similar party blocks. However, when they are controlled by different blocks, the federal government must negotiate with opposition leaders to ensure passage of its proposals. This situation of divided government was experienced first in the 1960s, and then again for several years prior to the dissolution of the centre–left government in the 1980s. It prevailed again for most of the 1990s, sharply curtailing the CDU-led government's ability to react to the country's employment crisis by introducing rapid social or economic changes. During this period both the SPD and CDU were torn between the desire to avoid blame for creating policy gridlock, and the fear of losing politically valuable issues by compromising and cooperating to pass legislation.

Although parties are the major dividing line in German policy-making, no government has a guarantee that all its proposals will win the approval of the states even when the *Bundestag* and *Bundesrat* are controlled by similar coalitions. Cross-party alliances may form on issues, such as tax policy or regional subsidies, on which state and federal interests may conflict. In such cases conflicts between state and federal party leaders usually do not reach the legislature because intra-party compromises can generally be hammered out in advance of this stage (von Beyme 1997: 296–99).

Within the *Bundestag* itself, party discipline has been, and remains, the norm of parliamentary behaviour. It is hard to measure accurately the extent of party cohesion, because recorded votes are used for only a small fraction of the legislation considered by the *Bundestag*. Although the issues that do receive such treatment are generally the more controversial ones, even here deviation from the party line is quite rare. Whereas parties were seldom perfectly cohesive on such votes, the number of dissidents was never large: in the 1980s the average 'defection' level from party positions on recorded votes was under 5 per cent (see Table 4.7). This figure represented a slight increase for the CDU/CSU since the 1950s, and a slight decrease for the SPD. However, the main message of such figures is of the importance attached to party cohesion (Saalfeld 1995: 109; von Beyme 1997: 271–91).

Political parties not only dominate politics in the German legislative arena: they also have a privileged place in the country's judicial system. While the legal system itself is not run on partisan lines, parties are among the recognized 'governmental organs' which are constitutionally entitled to bring certain types of cases before the constitutional court. Parliamentary groups also play an important role in selecting the members of the constitutional court, with the Christian Democrats and Social Democrats acting as the primary bargainers in securing seats for their preferred nominees (Kommers 1997: 22). All this suggests that there have been no serious challenges to governance of and by the German parties. Legislating in Germany is above all a partisan affair. Occasionally intra-party discipline breaks down, particularly over regional economic differences. At other times, differences in the complexion of state and federal coalitions make it difficult for parties to take a single line. In most cases, however, even intra-party differences are negotiated within the framework of party politics.

Ballot initiatives and referendums offer a limited, but increasingly popular, route through which citizens can challenge party dominance of the legislative process.

TABLE 4.7. *Legislative party cohesion*

Legislative period	Number of named votes	Rice index of party cohesion[a]			% named votes without party dissent		
		CDU/CSU	SPD	FDP	CDU/CSU	SPD	FDP
1949–43	133	86.3	99.7	84.0	15.8	94.0	30.1
1953–57	169	90.0	99.3	80.5	26.6	95.3	40.5
1957–61	46	93.6	99.7	95.1	28.3	82.6	63.0
1961–65	37	89.6	98.5	84.9	32.4	81.1	45.9
1965–69	24	87.3	93.1	97.4	16.7	58.3	70.8
1969–72	38	98.8	99.9	97.9	78.9	92.1	71.1
1972–76	51	93.7	98.3	98.9	64.7	76.5	86.3
1976–80	59	97.4	98.4	94.9	86.4	78.0	89.8
1980–83	26	99.2	99.3	95.9	84.6	80.8	73.1
1983–87	343	99.7	96.0	97.7	89.6	58.5	77.8
1987–90	216	98.9	95.7	95.6	88.4	50.9	63.9
Total 1949–90	1142	94.3	97.8	91.4	58.1	74.7	59.7

[a]Per cent of party voting with majority minus per cent dissenting (excludes abstentions). A score of 100 indicates complete cohesion.

Source: Saalfeld 1995: 109–10.

Opportunities to hold state and local referendums began expanding in the 1980s, and by the mid-1990s it was possible for voters in every state to petition to call state or local ballots on public policy issues. In the 1990s citizens began making increasing use of such devices, often seeing them as a way to circumvent governing parties. This has been most evident in Bavaria, a state where the CSU has long held a majority in the state legislature. Here, what began as a non-partisan movement successfully petitioned to hold a referendum on amending the state constitution to provide for referendums on local issues and on non-constitutional statewide matters. Despite CSU opposition, the measure passed with a wide majority in 1995. Within three years, a non-party movement in the same state had petitioned to hold a referendum on abolishing the upper house of the Bavarian legislature; this change passed in 1998 despite the opposition of the governing CSU.

Bavaria's prominent instances of policy making outside party-controlled channels are not isolated occurrences. During the 1990s ballot initiatives emerged as a more recognized tool in German politics. However, such votes will never decide more than a very small number of political issues. They also are necessarily confined to the state and local levels, because the federal German constitution does not provide for this sort of direct democracy. Moreover, there are clear limits to the extent to which direct decision-making will erode party governance at sub-national levels, not only because most state laws limit the issues which may be addressed by referendums, but also because the parties themselves have become more alert to the advantages of employing the tools of direct democracy for partisan ends.

Interest articulation and aggregation

Under the system of cleavage-based politics that emerged in Germany in the 1950s, the big parties were central to the aggregation and articulation of the main interests around which politics revolved. In that period, the primary dividing lines were based on economic position and religious orientation. In the 1970s these traditional political divisions blurred and new concerns came to the fore. The established parties were slow to take up the 'new politics' issues. Their failure to react contributed to the proliferation of a new type of organization for interest articulation, the so-called 'citizens initiatives'. Initially, such groups were particularly active in support of environmental protection and in opposition to nuclear power and nuclear weapons.

In the 1970s and 1980s participation in citizens' initiatives burgeoned, and their activities on behalf of environmental protection and nuclear disarmament grabbed public attention. At this point, citizen initiatives seemed to threaten parties' dominance of the political agenda. For the first time, non-party groups were taking charge of functions more usually ascribed to political parties, such as political mobilization and interest articulation. In this light, the proliferation of citizen initiatives was construed by some as a sign of party 'failure' (Lawson 1988).

Several decades after the emergence of this non-party activism, it has become clear that these new actors are unlikely to push parties to the sidelines. They have, however, left several lasting marks on the German political system. It is perhaps ironic that one of the most striking legacies of non-party activism has been a shift in the party system itself, with the Green party emerging out of the milieu drawn into politics through the organized protests of the 1970s. In addition, non-party organizing through citizen initiatives remains an important and respected political technique in the 1990s, particularly in the realm of local politics. The post-1970s expansion of opportunities for direct democracy, discussed above, has provided new focal points for the efforts of such groups. According to one estimate there were about 50,000 citizens' initiatives with around 1.5 million members at the beginning of the 1990s—this was fewer members than the parties could claim, but the groups are nevertheless large and active enough to continue to stake a claim on public attention (von Beyme 1991: 160).

Party organizers responded to the popularity of these new movements by attempting to make party life more closely resemble work within a citizens' initiatives. They urged local branches to offer party members more opportunities to work on the kind of targeted projects that would give members the feeling of making a difference in their communities (Blessing 1993; CDU 1989). In keeping with this, the parties' conferences and membership publications highlighted such non-partisan local projects as cleaning up local streams and nature reserves, watering trees during the summer months, teaching traffic safety to children, and providing services for consumers. However much local parties actually have done to reorient intra-party life in this direction, it clearly has not been enough to boost party membership. On the other hand, by the 1990s the apparent threat posed by citizens' initiatives seemed also to have receded. While single-issue associations continue to be effective in bringing national, and particularly local, issues to public attention, as a whole the citizens' initiatives remain too loosely organized to supersede parties in their roles as interest aggregators or policy-makers.

Yet even the parties themselves are finding interest aggregation to be more challenging as old cleavage lines fade. As the divisions of class and religion have receded, and as opinion-polling techniques have improved, German parties have partially forfeited their role as champions of the interests of specific groups, and have instead pursued the more catch-all aim of tracking voters' preferences in order to assemble a winning coalition. Such efforts were particularly visible in the SPD's strategy debates of the 1980s, when the party commissioned research trying to calculate the net votes which would be gained or lost by shifting either towards the new left or towards the centre (Scarrow 1999). In this way the German parties are turning away from articulating the relatively fixed interests of pre-defined segments, and are instead attempting to aggregate the more fluid interests of short-term electoral coalitions.

Political participation

Although German parties still exercise unchallenged control over candidate selection and policy development, and although they remain important channels for political participation, rates of party membership are not particularly high in comparative terms. Since the 1960s overall party enrolment has ranged from about 3 to 5 per cent of the electorate. German party membership is not only relatively small; it is also rather unrepresentative of the general population. As mentioned earlier, most parties have found it increasingly difficult to attract younger members, though this is slightly less of a problem for the Greens than for the other parties. Women are under-represented in all the parties. Although membership in parties and legislatures always has been predominantly male, by the 1980s party strategists began to view this gender imbalance as a potential electoral problem. The catch-all parties in particular wanted to be able to proclaim that their enrolled supporters as well as their candidates resembled the voters they sought to attract.

As a result, in the 1980s and 1990s, both the CDU and SPD made special efforts to increase the participation of women and younger citizens in parties and in legislatures, participation deficits which party strategists viewed as inter-related problems. In 1988 the SPD introduced gender quotas for candidates, a step taken after the Greens more gender-balanced delegations drew attention to other parties' poor performance on this score. Eight years later, after party leaders' exhortation on this issue proved fruitless, the CDU reluctantly adopted its own gender quotas for candidates. In the 1990s, the SPD also tried to combat the greying of its membership by organizing special recruiting drives and party conferences for young supporters, and national leaders urged local parties to place more young members in local government. Although the party quotas did have the desired effect of increasing the number of female officeholders, their other efforts were, at best, only marginally successful. By the end of the 1990s even the Greens and the PDS estimated that fewer than 40 per cent of their members were female; for the SPD, CDU, and FDP the figure was under 30 per cent. These proportions were indeed somewhat higher than in the 1970s, but change in this regard came extremely slowly, especially in light of the rapid growth of party membership during the 1960s through early 1980s.

Those who do enrol in a German party are constitutionally entitled to have a say in some party decisions. The 1949 Basic Law stipulated that all parties must be democratically organized, and the 1967 Parties Law elaborated on this by requiring parties to use some form of intra-party democracy in selection procedures for party executives. Most parties have chosen to use representatives structures, with delegates to regional and national party conferences making personnel and policy decisions (Poguntke 1994). This pattern shifted slightly in the 1990s, as party strategists became concerned about their declining memberships and waning popularity. At this point many of the federal and state parties experimented with giving members a more direct say in party affairs. Among the most visible of these experiments were the SPD's 1993 advisory ballot of members to select the party chair, and the FDP's 1995 and 1997 member plebiscites on policy issues. In the same years many state parties introduced new procedures which gave members a more direct role in selecting party leaders and state and local government candidates. Some state parties also introduced the option of membership votes on policy issues (Beil and Lepsky 1995).

To the extent that these new options were used, they did seem to boost participation rates among enrolled members. However, the initial experiences of the 1990s provided little evidence that the new devices would expand overall party enrolment, or that they would boost the vote share of the parties which employed them (Scarrow 1999). Moreover, while rule changes may have boosted the possibilities for individual members to play important roles, such possibilities are little used: intra-party direct democracy remains an exceptional mode of decision-making in the federal or state parties, and party conference delegates still retain primary responsibility for debating and ratifying party programmes and electing party leaders.

Political recruitment and patronage

In Germany, political careers are party careers. No independent candidates are elected to federal or state legislatures, and even in local government the proportion of independents has declined sharply since the early 1970s. Moreover, when state and local parties select candidates and order their electoral lists, they almost invariably favour those who have demonstrated their political dedication through hard work within the party. National party organizers sometimes have pleaded with selection conventions to overcome their resistance to candidates who 'climb in sideways', without prior party service, arguing that such unwillingness to look outside their own ranks deprives parties of highly qualified, and more diverse, candidates (CDU 1989; Blessing 1993). During the 1998 federal election campaign SPD chancellor-candidate Gerhard Schroeder sought to emphasize his independence from party traditions when he announced that his nominee for economics minister was a business manager who not only was not a member of the SPD, but who had also declared that he had no intention of joining the party. In the event, this particular nominee chose not to take the ministerial appointment after he lost a brief struggle to define the power of the post. Though another non-party nominee accepted the job, this struggle highlighted the weakness of such outside appointees, who inevitably lack a power base within the party. In short, despite gestures in the direction of more openness, it remains true in all the parties that most elected officials and serious candidates continue to be drawn from the ranks of the existing party memberships. Once elected, politicians continue to depend on their standing within the party to secure a safe place on the party list at the next election (Wessels 1997).

In addition to controlling access to elected office, the German parties also have served as important conduits to jobs in the public and semi-public sector. At the federal, state, and local level governing parties control or influence top-level appointments in the civil service and in the oversight boards of publicly controlled utilities and media. Although the extent of these 'party-book' jobs is hard to ascertain, ties to governing parties clearly have played a role in many public appointments, and this politicization appears to have increased since the 1960s (Mayntz and Derlien 1989; Poguntke 1994: 198–99; Scheuch and Scheuch 1992; von Arnim 1993).

Political communication and education

In addition to establishing a system of subsidies for campaign expenses, the 1967 Parties Law authorized other subsidies to help parties fulfill their constitutionally mandated task of 'helping to form the public will'. Under the terms of this law, all parliamentary parties which receive at least 5 per cent of the popular vote may receive funds to support educational foundations. These subsidies grew almost as rapidly as the campaign funds, rising from the DM 74 million paid to four foundations in 1970, to the DM 544 million received by five foundations in 1990. Direct subsidies and other government grants constitute almost the entire revenue source for these foundations (von Arnim 1991: 102, 366).

The political foundations are legally independent of the parties, but are usually described as 'party linked'. They are not supposed to engage directly in day-to-day politics, but are rather to concentrate on the development of political ideas and opinions. This separation of educational from political tasks is fairly strictly adhered to, perhaps in part because the German parliamentary parties and party head offices are so generously funded in their own right. The foundations give university scholarships to German and foreign students, hold subsidized seminars open to all politically interested citizens (regardless of party membership), maintain party archives and libraries, produce research reports (often on issues of interests to their party sponsors), and issue journals and other publications with articles on political themes. They also sponsor active programmes of political education outside Germany. In addition to their other functions, these foundations provide valuable sources of employment for politically engaged academics and retired politicians.

Though these well-financed foundations provide a rather unusual dimension to political education in Germany, here, as elsewhere, the electronic media and newspapers are the primary sources of political information for most citizens. Both during and between elections, party politics and partisan conflicts receive extensive attention from the print and broadcast media, but the parties themselves are not in a position to dictate the content of this coverage. Although many newspapers are recognized as favouring one party or another, Germany no longer has any large-circulation newspapers which are operated by the parties. (The most important remaining party–press link is between the PDS and *Neues Deutschland*, once the organ of the East German Socialist Unity Party.) Political parties have representatives on the boards that oversee the national and regional public television stations, and known partisans fill many of the top positions in the public broadcasting networks. Such ties may help explain the amount of public affairs coverage, and put parties in a strong position to object to specific programmes or reports. However, they are not able to insist that the broadcast media convey particular messages, not least because the law requires stations to maintain political balance in their news coverage (Semetko and Schoenbach 1994: ch. 2).

The picture painted in this section is one of entrenched parties still dominating politics in the German 'parties state'. Despite hints of weakening public support for the partisan alternatives, and despite the increased prominence of new channels of interest articulation, Germany continues to have a high 'partyness' of government: political parties have retained their central role in political recruitment and governance (Katz 1986). As in many countries, German parties have a much less central role in political education and communication; the parties use, but cannot control, public and private media outlets. Even so, German parties have some advantages in this area not shared by their counterparts elsewhere; above all, they are helped by large public subsidies.

CONCLUSION

This chapter's overview of recent developments in the German 'parties state' shows a disjunction between popular regard for parties and parties' ability to dominate public resources and political agendas. While the former may be sinking, the latter seems to be solidly entrenched. What should be made of such contradictory developments?

In the first place, they are difficult to reconcile with the notion of 'party decline'. It is true that in the last three decades Germans' attachments to particular parties seem to have weakened, and in the last fifteen years participation in party-organized elections has indubitably declined. Yet although these are politically significant developments, they seem more indicative of dealignment than of the weakening of parties as such. After all, most definitions of parties do not even include voters, but rather describe parties as groups organized for the purpose of contesting elections—the parties are groups with a political product to sell, the voters are the potential customers. Declining 'customer loyalty' does indeed change the environment in which parties compete, but it by no means spells the obsolescence of the party-organized political marketplace.

Nor does the entrance of new parties into this marketplace signal the general decline of parties, though it may threaten the dominance of particular competitors. In Germany new parties have presented some of the strongest recent challenges to established patterns of politics. Yet while the expansion of the party system and the concomitant increase in electoral volatility has created more uncertainty for individual parties, it has not altered the country's character as a 'parties state'. Neither shifts in voters' loyalties nor the advent of new party actors have greatly diminished parties' roles in selecting political personnel, promoting policy alternatives, setting the contours of political debates, organizing electoral contests, or acting as decision-makers.

Finally, while the German parties have suffered from recent drops in membership, their organizations have adapted, and they remain seemingly as strong as ever in many other respects. Most importantly, the vast increase in public subsidies since the 1960s has allowed all the parties to build up professional bureaucracies that are somewhat, though by no means entirely, insulated from fluctuations in party enrolments and in party electoral fortunes. Within these organizations most responsibility for national campaigns has been centralized, and campaign tasks have been professionalized. Although German parties have not abandoned their pursuit of membership enrolment, they have indeed found good ways to make membership support less vital to their campaign strategies. Only in the area of candidate recruitment has the weakness of some local organizations (particularly in the eastern states) led to a real undermining of party-based political organizing.

If it is difficult to describe German parties or the German parties state as being in a condition of decline, it is nevertheless all too easy to be unsettled by the parties' ability to endure so well despite apparent losses of public support. As Elmar Wiesendahl has noted, this situation matches the condition of party privilege that Peter Mair considers culpable for the possibly eroding legitimacy of electoral democracies (Wiesendahl 1998: 27; Mair 1995). Yet the implications of the existence of strong parties and weak voter attachments are not necessarily so dire as these authors suggest. Although declining voter loyalties may indeed coincide with the emergence of a more politically sceptical public, this change may spur parties to be more, not less, responsive to public demands. After all, electoral competition does not vanish even when catch-all parties converge or when party cartels collude to strengthen the 'partyness' of the state, and to exclude new challengers (Katz and Mair 1995). Some cartel-like behaviour (such as proportionality in allocating patronage appointments) may indeed diminish the costs of electoral defeat, but even under these conditions parties still do better if they win more votes. When ties of voter loyalty weaken, parties and party politicians may have to work harder to gain these votes. They can no longer take for granted the support of particular segments of society; instead, they need to continually earn such support. In short, party entrenchment will not necessarily undermine support for representative institutions as long as parties retain incentives to compete with one another for popular support.

What seems to be occurring in Germany is a move towards parties that are organizationally more self-sufficient, but electorally more vulnerable. Whether such changes are considered desirable depends in part on one's views of the electorate. The most favourable way in which to view such changes is as developments which reinforce the 'responsible party' model of government. From this perspective, what we observe is parties that are becoming more sensitive to public opinion, and are also becoming stronger, and hence potentially more able to enact the promises they make. From other viewpoints, changes which lead parties to become more—or even 'overly'—attentive to public opinion may be more suspect, either because 'the people' are presumed to be more short-sighted than political elites, or because partisan adherence to political principles is considered to be a better basis for policy-making than 'opportunistic' trimming of the sails to match the political wind. Moreover, voters may find it harder to assess credit and blame when party profiles blur as they pursue centrist voters, and as they participate in variously shaded coalitions at the state and federal levels. Finally, such developments look undesirable to those who regret any strengthening of representative structures that weakens possibilities for more direct decision-making: from this view, popular government requires more direct democracy, not stronger parties—however 'responsible' these parties might be. Of course, at this point the debate is no longer about the extent of party decline, but has entered into the long-running and ultimately irreconcilable debate over appropriate models of democracy (Held 1996; Katz 1997).

Whatever the verdict on the import of ongoing changes in the status of German parties, it is clear that the possibilities for 'party decline' in Germany are narrowly constrained by the institutions and traditions which have given German parties their central roles. While the strength of particular parties fluctuates, parties as such are a well-integrated part of the German electoral and constitutional order.

REFERENCES

Arnim, H. H. von (1991) *Die Partei der Abgeordnete und das Geld* (Mainz: Hase und Koehler Verlag).

—— (1993) 'Ist die Kritik an den politischen Parteien berechtigt?' *Politik und Zeitgeschichte* 11: 14–23.

Bartolini, S. and Mair, P. (1990) *Identity, Competition, and Electoral Availability: The Stabilization of European Electorates 1885–1985* (Cambridge: Cambridge University Press).

Beil, S. and Lepsky, N. (1995) *Die Reformdiskussion in den Volksparteien* (Sankt Augustin: Konrad-Adenauer-Stiftung).

Betz, Hans-Georg (1994) 'Wahlenthaltung und Wählerprotest in Westeuropäischen Vergleich,' *Politik und Zeitgeschichte* 19: 31–41.

Beyme, K. von (1991) *Das politische System der Bundesrepublik Deutschland nach der Vereinigung* (Munich: Piper Verlag).

—— (1997) *Der Gesetzgeber: Der Bundestag als Entscheidungszentrum* (Opladen: Westdeutscher Verlag).

Blessing, K. (1993) *SPD 2000: Die Modernisierung der SPD.* (Marburg: Schüren Presseverlag).

Boll, B. (1996) 'Media communication and personality marketing: the 1994 German election campaign', in Geoffrey Roberts (ed.) *Superwahljahr: The German Elections in 1994* (London: Frank Cass), pp. 120–40.

CDU (1989) 'Moderne Parteiarbeit in den 90er Jahren', in *Parteitag Protokoll* (Bonn: CDU), pp. 454–69.

CDU (1997) *Bericht der Bundesgeschäftsstelle* (Bonn: CDU).

Clemens, C. (1993) 'Disquiet on the eastern front: the Christian Democratic Union in the Germany's new Länder'. *German Politics* 2: 200–23.

Conradt, D. (1996) *The German Polity* 5th edn (White Plains, NY: Longman).

Dalton, Russell (1996) 'A Divided Electorate,' in Gordon Smith *et al.*, (eds) *Developments in German Politics* (Basingstoke: Macmillan).

Dalton, R. and Bürklin, W. (1996) 'The two German electorates', in Russell Dalton (ed.) *Germans Divided* (Oxford: Berg), pp. 183–208.

Dalton, R. and Rohrschneider, R. (1990) 'Wählerwandel und die Abschwächung der Parteieigungen von 1972 bis 1987', in Max Kaase and Hans-Dieter Klingemann (eds) *Wahlen und Wähler: Analysen aus Anlaß der Bundestagswahl 1987* (Opladen: Westdeutscher Verlag).

Falter, J. and Rattinger, H. (1994) 'Die deutschen Partien im Urteil der öffentlichen Meinung 1977–1994', in Hans Rattinger, Oscar Gabriel, and Wolfgang Jagodzinski (eds) *Wahlen und politische Einstellungen in vereinigten Deutschland* (Bern: Peter Lang), pp. 495–513.

—— and Schumann, S. (1993) 'Nichtwähler und Protestwahl: Zwei Seiten einer Medaille'. *Politik und Zeitgeschichte* 11: 36–49.

Farrell, David and Webb, Paul (2000) 'Political Parties as Campaign Organizations,' in Russell Dalton and Martin Wattenberg (eds) *Parties without Partisans* (Oxford: Oxford University Press).

Forschungsgruppe Wahlen (1998) *Blitz-Umfrage zur Bundestagswahl 1998 West + Ost.*

Gluchowski, P. M. and Wilamowitz-Moellendorff, U. von (1998) 'The erosion of social cleavages in Western Germany, 1971–97', in Christopher J. Anderson and Carsten Zelle (eds) *Stability and Change in Germany Elections* (Westport, CT: Praeger), pp. 13–32.

Haungs, P. (1992) 'Aktuelle Probleme der Parteiendemokratie'. *Jahrbuch für Politik* 2: 37–63.

Held, D. (1996) *Models of Democracy*, 2nd edn (Cambridge: Polity Press).

Jung, M. and Roth, D. (1994) 'Kohls knappster Sieg'. *Politik und Zeitgeschichte* 51: 3–15.

Katz, R. S. (1986) 'Party government: a rationalistic conception', in Francis G. Castles and Rudolf Wildenmann (eds) *The Future of Party Government: Visions and Realities of Party Government*, vol. 1 (Berlin: Walter de Gruyter), pp. 31–71.

—— (1997) *Democracy and Elections* (New York: Oxford University Press).

—— and Mair, P. (1995) 'Changing models of party organization and party democracy: the emergence of the cartel party'. *Party Politics* 1: 5–28.

Kirchheimer, O. (1966) 'The transformation of West European party systems', in J. LaPalombara and M. Weiner (eds) *Political Parties and Political Development* (Princeton: Princeton University Press), pp. 177–200.

Kommers, D. (1997) *The Constitutional Jurisprudence of the Federal Republic of Germany*, 2nd edn (Durham: Duke University Press).

Landfried, Christine (1994) *Parteifinanzen und politische Macht*. 2nd edn. (Baden-Baden: Nomos Verlagsgesellschaft).

Lawson, K. (1988) 'When Linkage Fails', in K. Lawson and P. Merkel (eds) *When Parties Fail* (Princeton, N.J.: Princeton University Press), pp. 13–38.

Mair, P. (1995) 'Political parties, popular legitimacy and public privilege'. *West European Politics* 18: 40–57.

Mayntz, R. and Derlien, H.-U. (1989) 'Party patronage and politicization of the West German administrative elite 1970–1987—toward hybridization'. *Governance* 2: 384–404.

Pickel, G. and Walz, D. (1997) 'Politikverdrossenheit in Ost- und Westdeutschland: Dimensionen und Ausprägungen'. *Politische Vierteljahresschrift* 38: 27–49.

Poguntke, T. (1994) 'Parties in a legalistic culture: the case of Germany', in R. S. Katz and P. Mair (eds) *How Parties Organize: Change and Adaptation in Party Organizations in Western Democracies* (London: Sage), pp. 185–215.

—— (1996) 'Bündnis 90/Die Grünen', in Oskar Niedermayer (ed.) *Intermediäre Strukturen in Ostdeutschland* (Opladen: Leske und Büdrich), pp. 87–112.

—— and Boll, B. (1992) 'Germany', in R. S. Katz and P. Mair (eds) *Party Organizations: A Data Handbook on Party Organizations in Western Democracies, 1969–90* (London: Sage).

Rattinger, H. (1993) 'Abkehr von den Parteien? Dimensionen der Parteiverdrossenheit,' *Politik und Zeitgeschichte* 11: 24–35.

Römmele, A. (1997a) 'Communicating with their voters: the use of direct mailing by the SPD and CDU'. *German Politics* 6: 120–31.

—— (1997b) 'Campaign finance and linkage in U.S. and German parties'. Paper presented at the Annual Meetings of the American Political Science Association, Washington, DC.

Saalfeld, T. (1995) *Parteisoldaten und Rebellen* (Opladen: Leske und Budrich).

Scarrow, S. (1994) 'The paradox of enrollment: Assessing costs and benefits of party membership' *European Journal of Political Research* 25: 41–60.

Scarrow, S. (1996*a*) 'Politicians against parties: anti-party arguments as weapons of change in Germany'. *European Journal of Political Research* 29: 297–317.

—— (1996*b*) *Parties and Their Members.* (Oxford: Oxford University Press).

—— (1999) 'Der Rückgang von Parteibindungen aus der Sicht der deutschen Parteien: Chance oder Gefahr?', in Peter Mair, Wolfgang Mueller, and Fritz Plasser (eds) *Parteien auf komplexen Wählermärkten* (Vienna: Signum Verlag), pp. 71–102.

Scheuch, E. and Scheuch, U. (1992) *Cliquen, Klüngel und Karrieren* (Reinbek: Rowohlt Verlag).

Schindler, P. (1982) *Datenhandbuch zur Geschichte des Deutschen Bundestages 1949 bis 1980* (Baden-Baden: Nomos).

—— (1984) *Datenhandbuch zur Geschichte des Deutschen Bundestages 1949 bis 1984* (Baden-Baden: Nomos).

—— (1986) *Datenhandbuch zur Geschichte des Deutschen Bundestages 1980 bis 1984* (Baden-Baden: Nomos).

—— (1988) *Datenhandbuch zur Geschichte des Deutschen Bundestages 1980 bis 1987.* (Baden-Baden: Nomos).

—— (1994) *Datenhandbuch zur Geschichte des Deutschen Bundestages 1983 bis 1991* (Baden-Baden: Nomos).

Schmitt, H. and Holmberg, S. (1994) 'Political Parties in Decline?' in Hans-Dieter Klingemann and Dieter Fuchs (eds) *Citizens and the State* (Oxford: Oxford University Press).

Schmidt, U. (1998) 'Sieben Jahre nach der Einheit: Die ostdeutsche Parteienlandschaft im Vorfeld der Bundestagswahl 1998'. *Politik und Zeitgeschichte* 1–2: 37–53.

Schmitt, K. (1998) 'The social bases of voting behavior in unified Germany', in Christopher J. Anderson and Carsten Zelle (eds) *Stability and Change in Germany Elections* (Westport, CT: Praeger), pp. 33–54.

Schultze, R.-O. (1995) 'Widersprüchliches, Ungleichseitiges und kein Ende in Sicht: Die Bundestagswahl vom 16. Oktober 1994,' *Zeitschrift für Parlamentsfragen.* 26: 325–52.

Semetko, H. and Schoenbach, K. (1993) 'The campaign in the media', in Russell Dalton (ed.) *The New Germany Votes* (Providence: Berg), pp. 187–208.

—— and —— (1994) *Germany's Unity Election* (New Jersey: Hampton Press).

—— and —— (1995) 'The media and the campaign in the New Germany', in David Conradt *et al.* (eds) *Germany's New Politics* (Tempe, AZ: German Studies Review), pp. 51–68.

SPD (1995) *Anlage zum Ablschlußbericht der Arbeitsgruppe 'Mitgliederentwicklung'* (Bonn: SPD).

Starke, F. C. (1993) *Krise ohne Ende?* (Köln: Bund Verlag).

Statistisches Bundesamt Deutschland (1998) *Bundestagswahl 1998* (Bonn: SBD). See also http://www.statistik-bund.de/wahlen/btwahl3.htm.

Stöss, R. (1990) 'Parteikritik und Parteiverdrossenheit'. *Politik und Zeitgeschichte* 21. 14–36.

Tiemann, H. (1993) 'Die SPD in den neuen Bundesländern: Organisation und Mitglieder'. *Zeitschrift für Parlamentsfragen* 3: 415–22.

Veen, H.-J. (1992) 'Abschluß, Neubeginn und Übergang', in Erich Hübner and Heinrich Oberreuter (eds) *Parteien in Deutschland zwischen Kontinuität und Wandel* (Munich: Bayerische Landeszentrale für politische Bildungsarbeit), pp. 125–67.

Veen, H.-J. (1994) 'Zukunft und Gefährdung der Volksparteien', in Günther Rüther (ed.) *Politik und Gesellschaft in Deutschland* (Cologne: Verlag Wissenschaft und Politik), pp. 125–37.

Weizsäcker, R. von (1993) *Richard von Weizsäcker im Gespräch* (Frankfurt/M: Eichborn).

Wessels, B. (1997) 'Germany', in Pippa Norris (ed.) *Passages to Power* (Cambridge: Cambridge University Press), pp. 76–97.

Wiesendahl, E. (1998) 'Wie geht es weiter mit den Großparteien in Deutschland?'. *Politik und Zeitgeschichte* 1–2: 13–28.

Zelle, C. (1994) 'Steigt die Zahl der Wechselwähler? Trends des Wahlverhaltens und der Parteiidentifikation', in Hans Rattinger, Oscar Gabriel, and Wolfgang Jagodzinski (eds) *Wahlen und politische Einstellungen im vereinigten Deutschland* (Frankfurt/M: Peter Lang), pp. 47–91.

5

France

Never a Golden Age

Andrew Knapp

INTRODUCTION

'Political parties and groupings contribute to the expression of universal suffrage. Their formation and activities are freely undertaken. They are required to respect national sovereignty and democracy.' The Fifth Republic, founded in 1958, was the first French regime to include such an explicit reference to the role of political parties in its constitution. Yet its founder, General Charles de Gaulle, was a bitter opponent of the unchecked power of parties, for which he blamed the failures of earlier Republics—governmental instability, policy immobilism and, in 1940, national collapse in the face of the German invasion. His vision was of a France led by a president (himself, in the first instance) who would stand 'above parties' and maintain a direct dialogue, over the heads of politicians, with the voters, via referenda and, from the constitutional reform of 1962, through direct election. The prime minister and government, though requiring a supportive majority (or at least the absence of a hostile one) in parliament, would be chosen by the president in accordance with their competence and the national interest; none would be parliamentarians. Parties, as the expression of partial interests, would certainly have a role in the election of the legislature; but the legislature would henceforth be kept in its due place, balanced by a 'strong arbiter' who would ensure 'national continuity' in the midst of 'political contingencies' (de Gaulle 1946).

De Gaulle's vision of the future proved as naïve as his diagnosis of the past was tendentious. The problem of the Third and Fourth Republics (1870–1940 and 1946–58 respectively) was less the strength of parties than their weakness. Although the historical roots of the broad families of Left and Right in France are deep, indeed etched into the country's electoral geography (Bon and Cheylan 1988), France only developed political parties in the late nineteenth century. Even then they took a minimal form of cadre parties (Duverger 1951): agencies of electoral coordination for groups of local notables with broadly similar views but a deep aversion to such vulgar notions as membership dues or party discipline.

Until 1936, such parties filled four-fifths of all seats in the lower house of parliament; Communists and Socialists, mass parties at least in aspiration, were the exception rather than the rule. And although, in the early postwar years of the Fourth Republic, mass parties could appear (at least to Duverger) as the wave of the future, the cadre model showed great resilience; old-style conservative and Radical parties had revived by the early 1950s. The governing parties of the Fourth Republic, then, while strong in the sense of holding a monopoly on political recruitment, and internally united on general principles—secularism, defence of Catholicism, or opposition to *dirigisme*—were inclined to split on the major issues of the day, in particular foreign and colonial policy. It was their divisions, not their strength, that led to the crisis that brought de Gaulle back to power in 1958.

Under the Fifth Republic, the president 'above politics' of de Gaulle's dreams proved a chimera. Since 1965, when the General himself found he needed party support to campaign for re-election, the presidency itself has been a key stake of party competition. But the main surprise of the new regime was the emergence, from 1962, of the *fait majoritaire*—the secure parliamentary majorities that France had hitherto lacked. These two developments transformed the role of parties. From the unstable raw material of what Goldey and Williams (1983: 65) called the 'shifting and shifty alliances' of the Third and Fourth Republics, they became, instead, the sturdy bulwarks of 'presidential majorities' in parliament and in the country, as well as the indispensable organizational supports for any aspiring presidential candidate. The Gaullist party, re-founded in 1958 and developed thereafter with de Gaulle's tacit blessing, was the first exemplar of the new paradigm: committed to supporting a president (or, if in opposition, a presidential candidate), hegemonic on its own side (and, in the Gaullists' case, stronger and better organized than any previous right-wing party), appealing to a wide range of social categories, and capable of assuming power alone or (more frequently) with junior partners. It was imitated, very successfully by the Socialists, less so by the non-Gaullist moderate Right. Imitation by the Socialists led, in 1981, to alternation in power from Right to Left: another unprecedented development for the French, hitherto accustomed under the Fifth Republic to a permanent right-wing hegemony, and under the Third and Fourth to small government changes triggered by small coalition shifts. Alternation in power was followed by the disappointment with parties in general and by the partial dislocation of the party system that is part of the subject of this chapter. But the role played by the major parties, as stable supports of presidents (or presidential candidates) and of parliamentary majorities, has both distinguished the Fifth Republic from its predecessors and been fairly consistent throughout the present regime.

The party system of the Fifth Republic may be described as one of *bipolar multipartism*.[1] Its bipolar characteristics are most readily discerned in the relationship of parties to government. Alternation in power results from a clear electoral victory

---

[1] For a fuller discussion of bipolar multipartism, see Knapp and Wright 2001: ch. 9.

of a right-wing or a left-wing coalition, not from a pivot party changing partners in mid-legislature. There are no Grand Coalitions; if a left-wing president has to 'cohabit' with a right-wing prime minister and parliamentary majority, or vice versa, this is an accident caused by lack of synchronization between parliamentary elections, held every five years, and presidential ones, held every seven years (until the constitutional reform of 2000 reduced the presidential *septennat* to a *quinquennat* with effect from 2002). The multiparty characteristics are at least equally visible: the consistent presence of four (not two) major forces (Socialists, Communists, Gaullists, non-Gaullist conservatives) throughout the Republic's history; the periodic appearance of others, most recently the far right-wing Front National (FN) and the Greens; the ability of some parties (recently the FN) to survive outside the major coalitions of Left and Right; the growing multiplicity of candidacies (over eleven per seat in the 1997 parliamentary elections, double the level of 1981).

Bipolar multipartism also contains two distinct and opposed sets of dynamics. Bipolarity is encouraged in important ways by France's institutions. The second ballots of presidential elections have typically (though not always) been grand simplifying contests between one candidate of the Right and one of the Left, because only the top two candidates from the first round can take part in the run-off. A parallel to this is supplied at parliamentary elections, held on a single-member constituency, two-ballot system (Schlesinger and Schlesinger 2000), and even by the municipal electoral laws of 1964 and 1983. Parties have tailored their strategies to this framework, forming (at the least) second-ballot withdrawal agreements with allies (*désistements*) and (more frequently) more or less stable programmatic coalitions of Right or Left aimed at the conquest and the exercise of governmental power. It has also been suggested that two social developments in the early Fifth Republic, the acceleration of urbanization and the spread of television, helped to simplify and 'nationalize' French politics, moving voters away from local to national issues and reinforcing a bipolarity already well rooted in voter attitudes (most voters have little difficulty positioning themselves on a Left–Right scale).

Other forces in the party system, however, have pointed towards fragmentation and multipartism. The two-ballot electoral system itself offers a variety of temptations at first rounds: to voters, who may cast a protest vote in the expectation that the real decision will only be made at the run-off; to party leaders, who may wish to count the strength of their own forces against that of their allies; and to individual candidates, who may see parliamentary or even presidential elections as a way to measure their personal support, with a view to bargaining their endorsement of better-placed competitors at the run-off. Party strategies have therefore always involved fierce competition within coalitions as well as between them. The localism long characteristic of French politics, of which the most eloquent expression is the practice of multiple elective office-holding (the *cumul des mandats*) also encourages fragmentation by giving independent-minded politicians sufficient personal political resources to defy their parties. Institutional tendencies to fragmentation were reinforced after 1979. Proportional representation was introduced for direct elections to the European parliament (first held in 1979) and to France's regional councils (first held in 1986). Proportional representation diminishes the incentives for party alliances. And because voters see these elections as relatively inconsequential (regions have far fewer powers than, say, German *Länder*) they may use them as an opportunity for protest voting. Parodi (1997) has referred to the result of the juxtaposition of the two-ballot majority system and proportional representation as the 'accordion effect'. Voters spread their support widely (opening the accordion) at European and regional elections, but behave with more discipline at parliamentary and presidential ones (closing it). However, argues Parodi, the habits learned at 'open-accordion' elections tend, with time, to carry over into the others as well, causing fragmentation. Another institutional development has also furthered fragmentation: since 1993, public finance has been available to any party able to present fifty or more parliamentary candidates in mainland France—a rule that has contributed powerfully to the multiplication of candidacies. These institutional changes have been reinforced by changes within the electorate. France has faced 'new challenges' from postmaterialism and the extreme right (Ignazi 1997): the former rather less intensely than in some other West European countries, the latter, for a variety of reasons (including, for example, the unresolved legacies of the Algerian war) rather more so. European integration, moreover, has become a particularly divisive issue in an old state much attached to national sovereignty: France's voters accepted the single currency by a margin of 51 to 49 per cent at the September 1992 referendum on the Maastricht treaty, with every major party experiencing more or less deep divisions on the issue (Cole 1996; Shields 1996).

Pressures towards bipolarity and towards multipartism exist in every party system. The French case, however, is unusual because they are so evenly balanced. That means changes in the balance may affect the configuration of parties at any given time more readily than in more stable party systems. Indeed, we may distinguish a number of distinct systemic configurations during the relatively brief time of the Fifth Republic (see Tables 5.1–5.3). These include periods of dominance by single parties (the Gaullists from 1962 to 1974, the Socialists from 1981 to 1986) and more balanced periods of party interaction. The best known model of balanced competition was, in Duverger's term, the 'bipolar quadrille' of 1974–81, when two coalitions of roughly equal size confronted one another, one of the Right and one of the Left, each comprising two main parties, also of roughly equal size. On the Right, the Gaullists, diminished but relaunched by Jacques Chirac in 1976, competed with the parties of the non-Gaullist moderate Right, federated by President Valery Giscard d'Estaing into the Union pour la Démocratie Française (UDF) in 1978. On the Left, Francois Mitterrand's re-born Socialist Party achieved equivalent electoral support to the Communists, partners from 1972 in an alliance with a common programme.

TABLE 5.1. *Executives and parliamentary majorities in the Fifth French Republic*

Year	58 59 60 61 62 63 64 65 66 67 68	69 70 71 72 73	74 75 76 77 78 79 80	81 82 83 84 85 86	86 87 88	88 89 90 91 92 93	93 94 95	95 96 97	97 98 99 00 01
President	de Gaulle	Pompidou	Giscard d'Estaing	Mitterrand				Chirac	
Prime minister	Debré / Pompidou / Couve	Chaban-Delmas / Messmer	Chirac / Barre	Mauroy / Fabius	Chirac	Rocard / Cresson / Bérégovoy	Balladur	Juppé	Jospin
Parliamentary majority	Gaull. + Right + Soc. (till 1959) + Centre (till 1962) / Gaull. + Giscardians (Gaull. dominant)	Gaull. absolute + Giscardian support	Gaull. + Giscardian (closer to equal strengths especially after 1978)	PS absolute (PCF support till 1984)	Gaull. + Gisc.	PS govt with no absolute majority	Gaull. + Gisc.		Soc/PCF/Ecol.

TABLE 5.2. *Results of parliamentary elections in France, 1958–97*

	1958	1962	1967	1968	1973	1978	1981	1986	1988	1993	1997
Extreme Left											
Vote (%)	0.0	2.0	2.2	4.0	3.2	3.3	1.2	1.5	0.4	1.7	2.2
Seats (*n*)	0	0	0	0	0	0	0	0	0	0	0
Communist											
Vote (%)	18.9	21.9	22.5	20.1	21.4	20.6	16.1	9.7	11.3	9.1	9.9
Seats (*n*)	10	41	73	34	73	86	44	35	27	24	37
Moderate Left											
Vote (%)	26.3	19.9	18.9	16.5	21.2	26.3	38.3	32.8	37.5	19.9	28.7
Seats (*n*)	84	110	123	58	105	115	289	216	276	75	275
Green											
Vote (%)	—	—	—	—	—	2.0	1.1	1.2	0.3	10.9	6.4
Seats (*n*)	—	—	—	—	—	0	0	0	0	0	8
Moderate Right											
Vote (%)	51.7	55.4	55.8	58.9	53.7	46.7	42.9	44.6	40.4	44.0	35.8
Seats (*n*)	384	331	291	395	312	290	158	291	273	478	256
Extreme Right											
Vote (%)	2.6	0.8	0.6	0.1	0.5	0.8	0.3	10.1	9.8	12.8	15.4
Seats (*n*)	1	0	0	0	0	0	0	35	1	0	1
Others											
Vote (%)	0.5	—	—	0.5	—	0.2	—	0.1	0.2	1.5	1.6
Seats (*n*)	32	—	—	0	—	0	—	0	0	0	0
ENEP	2.7	2.5	2.5	2.4	2.6	3.0	2.8	3.1	3.1	3.7	4.0
TNV	—	8.8	1.2	5.3	6.4	7.7	12.0	12.0	6.5	19.8	12.7
Turnout	77.2	68.7	81.1	80.0	81.3	83.3	70.9	78.5	65.7	69.3	68.5
Spoilt ballots	2.0	2.1	1.9	1.4	1.8	1.6	1.0	3.4	1.4	3.7	3.4

Notes: Vote percentages are based on first ballot results. 'Others' seats for 1958 are chiefly overseas departments and territories. For later years, Deputies not registered with a parliamentary group have been distributed between Communists, Left and Right according to political sympathy and campaign backers. ENEP: Effective number of electoral parties; TNV: Total net volatility.

Sources: Lancelot 1988 for 1958–86; *Le Monde* for 1988–97.

Since 1981 the Socialists have remained, at most elections, France's largest single party, though their support has slumped after periods in office (1986 and 1993). While the mainstream Right has usually profited from the Socialists' difficulties, it has never recovered its pre-1981 levels of support. This is partly because of the electoral breakthrough of the far-right FN. The FN's emergence and the PCF's eclipse confirmed the end of the 'bipolar quadrille', and formed the basis of what Martin (2000: 217–327) has called a full-scale realignment of French politics.

Thus, in retrospect 1981 can be seen to have led, not to Socialist 'dominance', but to a period of instability without precedent under the Fifth Republic. Governing parties have consistently been subject to challenge, as alternation in power has become the norm: the voters changed president, parliamentary majority, or both, in 1981, 1986, 1988, 1993, 1995, and 1997. Only Mitterrand, who survived two seven-year presidential terms and left the Élysée as a moribund 77-year-old in 1995, resisted the trend, 'cohabiting' with right-wing premiers in 1986–88 and 1993–95. Chirac, who won the presidency in 1995 after defeating the Socialist candidate,

TABLE 5.3. *Results of French presidential elections (first ballots), 1965–95*

	Extreme Left	Communist	Socialist	Other moderate Left	Greens/Ecology	Non-Gaullist moderate Right	Gaullist	Other moderate Right	Extreme Right	Others	Total Right	Total Left	Turnout	Blank and spoilt ballots	TNV	BV
1965	0.0	0.0	32.2	0.0	0.0	15.9	43.7	1.7	5.3	1.2	66.6	32.2	85.0	0.9	—	—
1969	1.1	21.5	5.1	3.7	0.0	23.4	44.0	1.3	0.0	0.0	68.7	31.3	78.2	1.0	29.4	1.5
1974	2.7	0.0	43.4	0.0	1.3	32.9	14.6	3.9	0.8	0.4	52.2	47.4	84.9	0.8	36.8	16.3
1981	2.3	15.5	26.1	3.4	3.9	27.8	21.0	0.0	0.0	0.0	48.8	51.1	81.7	1.3	17.5	3.5
1988	4.5	6.9	33.9	0.0	3.8	16.5	19.8	0.0	14.6	0.0	50.9	49.1	82.0	1.6	19.1	2.1
1995	5.3	8.7	23.2	0.0	3.3	18.5	20.5	4.8	15.3	0.3	59.1	40.6	78.4	2.2	11.0	8.4

Lionel Jospin, at the run-off, himself suffered a major reverse in 1997 when he called parliamentary elections a year early, opening the way for the unexpected victory of Jospin's left-wing coalition and a third period of 'cohabitation' which lasted until the parliamentary and presidential elections of 2002.

Alternation was accompanied by a measure of policy convergence as formerly Marxist Socialists and formerly *dirigiste* Gaullists became fixated by the dreary goals of low budget deficits and inflation at home and monetary stability abroad. Both allowed unemployment to rise. Both incurred the voters' displeasure—at their record on joblessness above all, but also on issues relating to France's urban malaise, including crime and immigration. The periods 1983–85 and 1991–93 for the Socialists, and 1995–97 for the Right, saw record levels of public dissatisfaction with governments. Dissatisfaction had three obvious expressions: the frequency with which power changed hands, rising abstention, and a rise in votes cast for parties outside the 'bipolar quadrille'. Of these, the most successful was the FN, which from 1984 established its base level of support at 10 per cent, rising to 15 per cent in the late 1990s. Though it did limited deals with the mainstream Right, especially on regional councils, the FN remained above all a party outside, and against, the system. Also outside the system were the ecology groupings, which won a total of 10.7 per cent at the 1989 European elections; and the Hunters' Rights Party (Chasse, Pêche, Nature, Tradition (CPNT)), which has achieved at least 4 per cent at European and regional elections since 1989. These parties won growing support but no parliamentary seats. The gulf between votes and representation reached its extreme point in the 1993 parliamentary elections when, as Duhamel (1993) observed, the 'parties of government' were supported by fewer than 44 per cent of the voters.

The closing years of the twentieth century, on the other hand, provided some evidence of the continuing integrative power of the Fifth Republic's party system. This was most obvious on the Left, where the *gauche plurielle* coalition of Communists, Greens, and Socialists, constructed in the aftermath of Jospin's honourable defeat at the 1995 presidential elections, proved victorious in 1997. On the Right, the retreat of protest politics was signalled by the break-up of the FN in 1998–99. Yet neither the *gauche plurielle* nor the FN's split signalled a return to any *status quo ante*. No party is dominant: the Socialists, France's largest party, have an audience of some 25 per cent. Protest parties still count: at the 1999 European elections, the far Right, the Trotskyist far Left, and CPNT together won some 20 per cent of the vote. The 'bipolar quadrille' is rendered impossible by the proliferation of parties. Not only Communists, Socialists, and Greens, but also Left Radicals and the Mouvement des Citoyens jostle for position within the *gauche plurielle*, while on the Right, the UDF split in 1998 into its Christian Democrat component (which retains the UDF label) and a free-market conservative one, Démocratie Libérale, and a Eurosceptic party, the Rassemblement pour la France (RPF) was launched in 1999. The period since 1997 has therefore seen *both* more bipolarization *and* more fragmentation, illustrating the diversity of conflicting forces at work within bipolar multipartism.

Wilson's (1988: 528) contribution on France to Lawson and Merkl's volume *When Parties Fail* was entitled 'When Parties Refuse to Fail', and referred to 'a normal process of party decline and regeneration/replacement produced by problems and developments that are country-specific'. Other observers of parties (Offerlé 1991; Mayer and Perrineau 1992; Leyrit 1997) have been more ready to pose the question of a general crisis of parties. Work on political activism notes the diminishing capacity of parties to mobilize citizens, especially by comparison with 'the social movement' (a term used for the more or less spontaneous strikes and demonstrations of 1995 and their fall-out (Hewlett 1998)), or through a broader range of associations and pressure groups (Perrineau 1994). Of material on individual parties, a disproportionate amount is devoted to the new entrants—somewhat to the Greens (Bennahmias and Roche 1991; Faucher 1999; Sainteny 2000), above all to the FN (Camus 1996; Martin 1996, 2000; Perrineau 1997; Cambadélis and Osmond 1998; Mayer 1999, among many examples) or, occasionally to both (Appleton 1995). And yet few observers see the 'crisis' as terminal. Studies of voters' behaviour and attitudes, for example (Boy and Mayer 1997), while discerning rather new developments such as a 'tripartition' of the electorate on the basis of attitudes, still go back to the persistence of the old cleavages of class and religion. Others (Duhamel 1997) note not only the continued resilience of the Right–Left divide but even the persistent correspondence of party divisions to voter attitudes—surely a sign that parties, even in France, are fulfilling at least some sort of expressive function.

LEGITIMACY

Anti-party sentiment in France is nothing new. As has already been noted, the founder of the Fifth Republic was a master of invective against the 'regime of parties'. He was able to draw on a wide range of traditions, not all of them disreputable, as Charlot (1986) notes: revolutionary individualism, nationalist *apolitisme*, revolutionary syndicalism, and the rejection of the Fascist and Communist extremes that marked the mid-century. Nevertheless, there are signs that anti-party sentiment, or at least dissatisfaction with parties, has spread in France since 1981, and more specifically during the 1990s. The evidence is derived firstly from poll data. As Table 5.4 shows, well over two-thirds of the French in the 1990s felt that they were 'not well represented' by any political party or a political leader (or, for that matter, a trade union). Indeed, in one poll in 1995, as many as 40 per cent of respondents (compared to 53 taking the opposite view) declared that it 'would not be very serious' if political parties were abolished altogether (Le Gall 1996).

The French were, of course, far from unique in their views. But they appear to have held them rather more intensely than other West European nations. A Eurobarometer poll from 1997 (Bréchon 1999), for example, shows an average

TABLE 5.4. *Disappointment with the
quality of political representation in
France, 1989–2000*

Year	A party	A political leader	A trade union
1989	50	54	65
1990	70	74	78
1991	73	74	75
1992	70	71	80
1993	65	66	76
1994	70	69	77
1995	65	65	75
1997	64	64	NA
1999	68	70	74
2000	70	74	78

Note: Question: 'Do you feel that you are well
represented by …?' (per cent answering *No* in
each case).

Source: SOFRES, *L'état de l'opinion.*

75 per cent of EU respondents declaring they had no confidence in political
parties—but fully 83 per cent of French respondents adopted such a position.
This is borne out by figures on party identification. As Table 5.5 shows, party
identification, both in a close sense (respondents declaring a 'close attachment' to
a party) and in a loose one ('all attached plus sympathizers'), has declined more
or less steadily in France since 1978. Moreover, close identification in France has
always been substantially lower than the European average, and loose identification has almost always been somewhat lower—a finding consistent with earlier
work on party identification pioneered by Converse and Dupeux (Converse and
Dupeux 1962; Converse and Pierce 1986, p. 70). Table 5.6, moreover, suggests that
declining party identification carries over into a growing scepticism about the long-
standing cleavage between Left and Right. When Mitterrand became president in
1981, a plurality of the French believed that these notions were valid indicators
of political differences; by the time he left the Élysée fourteen years later, some
three-fifths of them considered that they were out of date.

A more fine-grained guide to opinions of parties between 1981 and 1995 is
provided by Table 5.7. It shows, first, that the popularity ratings of the more extreme
parties have been consistently negative (with the FN replacing the Communists as
France's most unpopular party almost as soon as it appeared in the polls). Second,
the parties of the mainstream Right, UDF, and Gaullists, succeeded only briefly,
after their electoral victory in 1993, in overcoming a balance of negative opinions.
The most striking findings, however, concern the Socialist Party, the president's
party throughout the period 1981–95 and the main party of government from May

TABLE 5.5. *Partisan attachment in France*

Year	France		EC(9) average		France minus EC	
	Closely attached	All attached plus sympathizers	Closely attached	All attached plus sympathizers	Closely Attached	All attached plus sympathizers
1978	28	69	37	68	−9	1
1979	29	69	34	69	−5	0
1980	19	59	32	66	−13	−7
1981	19	58	30	60	−11	−2
1982	20	59	30	62	−10	−3
1983	19	57	32	65	−13	−8
1984	18	57	30	64	−12	−7
1985	18	55	30	61	−12	−6
1986	18	58	28	59	−10	−1
1987	18	55	31	60	−13	−5
1988	24	64	31	63	−7	1
1989	19	57	28	58	−9	−1
1990	17	52	27	57	−10	−5
1991	18	45	27	51	−9	−6
1992	16	52	29	57	−13	−5
1993	23	60	24	57	−1	3
1994	18	56	28	60	−10	−4

Source: Schmitt and Holmberg 1995: 126–7; Eurobarometers 2346, 2490.

1981 to March 1986 and from May 1988 to March 1993. The Socialist Party is the only party to achieve a positive average balance of opinions (of 8.7 per cent) across the period. Its popularity also, however, varies more widely than that of other parties (as shown by the higher standard deviation values): high points, which follow the election victories of 1981 and 1988, contrast with troughs in 1984–85 (with the first negative rating in October 1983) and 1992–94 (with the first negative rating in November 1991). Both of the troughs coincide with economic downturns. In the first case, economic setbacks were compounded by clear policy failure (the monetary crisis of March 1983, and the failure of a major education bill in 1984). In the second case, they were greatly reinforced by the political disgrace of corruption, following the scandals that began to break around the Socialist Party in 1990. Other parties (chiefly the mainstream Right) benefited from the Socialists' misfortunes, but only to a modest degree. The variations in the Socialists' popularity, therefore, because they were especially wide, affected the *average* ratings of parties disproportionately. Overall, though, French voters are generally inclined to regard parties in a negative light; while the net balance of opinion fluctuates over time—often in line with overall governmental ratings—it was particularly negative in the mid-1980s and again in the early 1990s.

TABLE 5.6. *French views on the relevance of the Left/Right cleavage, 1981–96*

Year	Out of date	Still valid	Majority out of date	Don't know
1981	33	43	−10	24
1984	49	37	12	14
1986	45	42	3	13
1988	48	44	4	8
1989	56	36	20	8
1991 (April)	55	33	22	12
1991 (Sept.)	60	32	28	8
1992	60	31	29	9
1993	56	35	21	9
1994	57	34	23	9
1996	62	32	30	6

Note: Question: Do you feel that the notions of Right and Left are out of date, or that they are still valid? (%).

Source: SOFRES 1997: 83.

Drops in the Socialists' ratings in 1983–85 and 1991–94 also coincided with growing disenchantment with politics in general. But whereas the Socialists' popularity could recover (the figure for February 2000 in Table 5.7 demonstrates that it had done so again in the late 1990s), the overall image of politics and politicians remained tainted. Thus while a plurality (38 per cent) of the French claimed to think that politicians were 'generally corrupt' as early as 1977, by the end of the century this had risen to 61 per cent—well over twice the proportion perceiving them to be 'generally honest'. The French were also increasingly dismissive of politicians' capacities to share their concerns; though a small majority (53–42 per cent) still took a positive view on the question in 1977, this had turned to a clear negative majority (39–59 per cent) two decades later.[2] Moreover, as Bréchon (1999: 94) notes, hostility or indifference towards political parties was especially strong among younger age-groups—an element which, if explicable in terms of a cohort effect, would tend to amplify the phenomenon. By 1998, 84 per cent of the French agreed with the statement that politics was 'in crisis', a 10 per cent rise on the figure for 1989 (SOFRES 1999: 268); 57 per cent considered (at some risk of terminological inexactitude) the crisis to be a 'lasting' one. And more blamed the crisis on politicians—their incompetence to solve problems, rivalries, corruption—than on extraneous factors such as globalization or the growing power of Europe.

The declining legitimacy of parties can also be discerned in membership figures (Table 5.8). These should, it is true, be treated with caution, for two reasons. First, most parties have lied, regularly and sometimes outrageously, about their

---

[2] The source for these trends in public opinion is SOFRES, *L'état de l'opinion* (Paris: Éditions du Seuil, various dates).

TABLE 5.7. *France: Party popularities, 1981–95 (annual figures averaged from monthly polls)*

Year	Communists			Socialists			UDF			Gaullists			Front National			All including Front National (5 parties)			All excluding Front National (4 parties)		
	Good	Bad	Balance	Good	Bad	Balance	Good	Bad	Balance	Good	Bad	Balance	Good	Bad	Balance	Good	Bad	Balance	Good	Bad	Balance
1981*	28	60	−32	69	22	47	32	52	−20	34	52	−19	NA	NA	NA	NA	NA	NA	41	47	−6
1982	24	64	−40	60	30	30	34	47	−13	38	45	−7	NA	NA	NA	NA	NA	NA	39	47	−8
1983	21	66	−44	50	39	11	39	42	−4	41	42	−1	NA	NA	NA	NA	NA	NA	38	47	−10
1984	18	70	−53	44	45	0	40	43	−3	42	43	−1	13	65	−52	31	53	−22	36	50	−14
1985	14	74	−59	43	47	−4	40	43	−3	41	44	−3	13	72	−59	30	56	−26	34	52	−17
1986	15	73	−57	53	36	17	43	41	2	46	41	5	13	75	−61	34	53	−19	39	48	−8
1987	16	72	−56	55	33	22	42	42	0	44	44	0	12	76	−64	33	53	−20	39	48	−9
1988	20	66	−46	59	31	29	42	42	0	38	48	−10	11	79	−68	34	53	−19	40	47	−7
1989	18	68	−50	57	32	25	40	42	−2	38	47	−9	12	78	−66	33	53	−20	38	47	−9
1990	13	74	−61	53	36	17	38	43	−6	37	47	−10	13	77	−64	31	55	−25	35	50	−15
1991	13	74	−62	47	42	5	37	44	−6	38	48	−10	12	78	−66	29	57	−28	34	52	−18
1992	14	74	−60	37	53	−15	41	44	−2	39	43	−4	11	80	−69	29	59	−30	33	53	−20
1993	17	71	−54	34	57	−22	50	40	10	48	42	6	11	81	−70	32	58	−26	37	52	−15
1994	20	67	−47	39	52	−13	44	44	0	45	45	0	12	80	−68	32	58	−26	37	52	−15
1995†	26	62	−36	45	47	−3	45	44	1	48	45	3	14	79	−66	35	55	−20	41	50	−9
Average	17.7	69.5	−51.8	49.3	40.5	8.7	40.5	43.2	−2.7	40.8	44.9	−4.0	12.2	76.6	−64.4	31.8	55.4	−23.6	37.1	49.5	−12.4
SD	4.5	4.6	9.0	9.5	9.8	19.2	4.8	3.2	7.4	4.5	4.6	7.9	2.0	4.9	6.1	2.3	2.6	4.4	2.8	2.9	5.3
February 2000	21	55	−34	54	36	18	30	53	−23	35	53	−18	7	86	−79	29	57	−27	35	49	−14

Notes: Question: Do you have a good or bad opinion of the following parties?

*1981: June to December only.

†1995: January to April only.

Sources: Calculated from SOFRES, *L'état de l'opinion,* 1989 and 1996 (*Le Figaro Magazine* for February 2000).

membership. They have lied both in order to exaggerate their own influence and to give the (wholly false) impression of living from members' dues rather than from illegal business contributions or (in the case of the Communists) from subsidies from Moscow. The obligation, since 1988, to publish accounts, and the spread of direct leadership elections in parties, have diminished the scope of this mendacity, without eradicating it altogether. For that reason, membership figures rely to some degree on guesswork. Second, the French have rarely been inclined to join parties; indeed, observers of French society from Tocqueville to Michel Crozier have stressed their reluctance to join anything. In this light, the period of mass partisan mobilization just before and just after the Second World War should be seen as an exception. When Duverger wrote, in 1951, of the 'mass party' as the wave of the future, it was already, in France at least, past its peak. And as Table 5.8 suggests, the decade from the late 1940s to the foundation of the Fifth Republic saw overall party membership in France fall by more than three-quarters. It would never again reach as much as 3 per cent of the electorate.[3]

Nevertheless, the first two decades of the Fifth Republic saw a fairly steady revival, with membership probably doubling to reach a total of about 900,000 by the time of Mitterrand's presidential victory in 1981. Growth during the 1970s resulted from three factors. First, the Socialist revival under Mitterrand attracted significant numbers of recruits, including former activists of the May 1968 genera-tion now prepared to pursue their goals through conventional politics. Second, the Communist Party also attracted such activists, and also engaged in a vigorous membership drive to maintain their organizational superiority over the Socialists. Thirdly, after 1976 the Gaullists, under Chirac, sought to compensate for their lost positions in government by building a more viable party organization.

The decline in party membership under the Fifth Republic dates from the early 1980s, and accelerated as the century drew to a close. The *alternance* of 1981 clearly damaged recruitment on the Left: like his three predecessors in the Élysée, Mitterrand had no particular use for a large and therefore demanding presiden-tial party, while the Communists found that their attraction as a protest party was fatally undermined by their participation in government. Opposition to the 'Socialo-Communist' administration probably sustained Gaullist mobilization for a little longer; but Chirac had discovered that his control of the Paris Town Hall was a better logistical and financial substitute for state power than a large party, and a number of the most active members and cadres left the RPR for the FN in the mid-1980s. Neither of the new entrants compensated numerically for the decline in established parties' memberships; the FN has never claimed more than 60,000

---

[3] The years on which Table 5.8 is based are as follows: *Communist*: 1947, 1959, 1964, 1969, 1974, 1978, 1984, 1987, 1990, 1998; *Socialist*: 1946, 1958, 1963, 1968, 1974, 1978, 1983, 1988, 1992, 1999; *Green*: 1999; *Centrist*: 1946, 1958, 1962, 1968, 1974, 1979, 1983, 1986, 1992, 1997; *Non-Gaullist moderate Right*: 1947, 1958, 1961, 1970, 1979, 1983, 1986, 1992, 1999; *Gaullist*: 1947, 1958, 1963, 1969, 1973, 1978, 1985, 1989, 1994, 1999; *Eurosceptic Right*: 1999; *Front National*: 1979, 1985, 1992, 1999.

TABLE 5.8. *Party membership in France since 1945*

Year	Communist		Socialist		Green	Centrist		Non-Gaullist moderate Right		Gaullist		Eurosceptic Right (RPF)	Extreme Right (Front National)		Est. total*	M/E
	Claimed	Estimated	Claimed	Estimated	Estimated	Claimed	Estimated	Claimed	Estimated	Claimed	Estimated	Claimed	Claimed	Estimated		
Late 1940s	1,000,000	800,000		340,000			125,000		50,000		400,000				1,675,000	6.7
Late 1950s	425,150	300,000	85,000	60,000			40,000	10,000		280,000	20,000				430,000	1.7
Early 1960s	420,000	330,000	74,000	55,000		40,000	20,000	7500		150,000	86,000				498,500	1.8
Late 1960s		380,000	84,000	60,000		25,000	15,000	25,000		180,000	160,000				615,000	2.2
Early 1970s		450,000	146,000						3,000	238,000	100,000				724,000	2.4
Late 1970s	632,000	520,000	200,000	200,000		43,000	17,500	145,000	8,500	760,347	160,000			900	906,900	2.6
Early 1980s	600,000	380,000	200,000	180,000		49,000	12,500	60,000	10,000	850,000	200,000		65,000	10,000	792,500	2.8
Late 1980s	604,285	330,000	180,000						20,000	142,113				50,000	771,113	2.1
Early 1990s		220,000	150,000	125,000			12,500		25,000	148,000			48,000		578,500	1.5
Late 1990s	210,000	100,000	148,795		10,000	40,000		33,000	10,000	80,424		33,000	60,000	42,000	464,200	1.3

Notes: M/E: Membership/Electorate ratio.

* Annual totals are calculated on the basis of estimates where available, and of claimed figures where no estimates have been made.

Sources: Ysmal 1994: 48–9; Knapp 1996: 391; Mény and Knapp 1998: 55; Bréchon 1999: 107–8; *Le Monde*, 23 November 1999, 23–24 January 2000, 22 February 2000; documentation from parties; interviews with Colette Ysmal and Nonna Meyer, both of CEVIPOF (Centre d'Études sur la Vie Politique).

members (though initially at least they tended to be more active than those of other parties), the Greens never more than 10,000. By the late 1990s, the Greens were probably the only growing party in France—very slowly, and from a minute base. The membership of all other parties (including, after its split, the FN) was falling, bringing total party membership to levels comparable to those seen at the start of the Fifth Republic. This could not be explained in terms of a general French reluctance to join any sort of organization, for membership of associations of all kinds rose fast in the last quarter of the twentieth century (Archambault 1996). Part of the explanation clearly lies with the more general disenchantment with parties noted above—especially as it disproportionately affected the very age-groups most likely to supply new party recruits. Jean-Christophe Cambadélis, the Socialist Party's former deputy leader (and former Trotskyist student activist) has offered a more specific explanation: whereas earlier generations of young activists had crystallized around large political events—the Resistance, the Algerian war, or May 1968, nothing in the course of the Mitterrand presidency, not even the struggles of 'anti-fascist' organizations against the FN, appears to have offered a comparable experience (*Le Monde*, 5–6 March 2000).

The third type of evidence for the loss of legitimacy of parties is electoral (refer again to Tables 5.2 and 5.3). Figures for abstentions and spoilt ballots show a rising trend in both parliamentary and presidential elections. Abstention at parliamentary elections has regularly been high in those cases in which another electoral contest has preceded the vote by a few weeks, making the result appear a foregone conclusion: hence the low turnout in 1962 (after the successful referendum on the direct election of the president), and in 1981 and 1988 (when Mitterrand was elected or re-elected to the presidency, and proceeded to dissolve parliament). These 'abnormally' high levels of abstention, however, appear to have become increasingly common: abstentions and spoilt ballots in 1997, for example, an election which opinion polls suggested was wide open, exceeded those of 1962 or 1981. Similarly, at presidential elections, the 'exceptionally' high level of abstentions and spoilt ballots caused in 1969 by fragmentation and quarrelling on the Left was equalled in far more normal conditions in 1995.

The rise of abstentionism is paralleled, to some degree, by increased electoral volatility. Volatility is a delicate indicator in the French context, because the electoral system institutionalizes it: voters may actually be invited to switch parties between ballots, dropping their first choice for the better-placed candidate within their preferred political family. The frequency of joint candidacies between Gaullists and the non-Gaullist moderate Right makes volatility between these two groups impossible to measure, although they have at times been fierce competitors. With those caveats, the four highest levels for volatility at parliamentary elections between 1958 and 1997 were all recorded in the post-1978 period (refer again to Table 5.2). They correspond to developments outlined above: the Socialists' victory (and the Communist slump) in 1981; the FN's breakthrough in 1986; the strong Green showing (and the Socialist rout) in 1993; and the Socialist recovery in 1997.

A number of indices, then, appear to testify to the weakening capacity of French parties to function as a link between government and citizens. The French are massively, and increasingly, inclined to believe that politics is in crisis; increasingly critical of parties and politicians in a number of respects, including their basic honesty and their capacity to respond to the concerns of ordinary people; more mistrustful of the traditional landmarks of Left and Right; less and less inclined to join a political party; more inclined to switch their vote, notably towards a new entrant. Each of these indicators should nevertheless be treated with caution. In the first place, hostility to parties does not mean hostility to democracy, nor even, quite, to politics in general. Satisfaction with the workings of French democracy is certainly far from unanimous and is not especially high in international terms. Throughout the period between 1985 and 1999 an average of 50 per cent of respondents considered that French democracy worked quite or very well, while 46 per cent felt it did not work well. Even so, there are no signs of a downward trend in the country. It has slumped at times of unpopularity for governments of the Left (in 1991–93) or Right (especially in 1996), but it also showed a capacity to recover in the late 1990s: by 1999, 57 per cent felt democracy was working well, while 40 per cent took a contrary view. Furthermore, approval for the Fifth Republic as a regime actually *rose* from 56 per cent in 1976 to 71 per cent in 2000.[4] Second, the majority view of politicians as corrupt coexists, curiously, with a consistent majority view that politics is an honourable profession, as if the ideal remained, against the odds, untarnished by the practice: thus, in 1999 some 57 per cent of French respondents considered it an honourable activity compared to 35 per cent who regarded it in negative terms (figures close to average for the period since 1979). Third, the French are far more scornful of politicians or parties 'in general' than they are of politicians when given even a trace of personality. Thus 'Members of Parliament' receive higher approval ratings than 'politicians' or 'parties'; so do 'the President' and 'the Prime Minister', even in such a bad year for president and government as 1985. Mayors occupy an unrivalled place of trust among the French, as accessible figures close to the concerns of ordinary people (Mayer and Perrineau 1992)—despite the fact that the most prominent ones are also national politicians, and that much of the political corruption discovered in France has involved municipal building contracts. This inclination to personalize political loyalties does not facilitate the task of such a collective enterprise as a political party; but it results as much from the localism that has long been a feature of French politics as from a more recent 'crisis of representation'. Fourth, while the fall in membership is a cause for concern to all parties, it is neither wholly unprecedented, nor (despite the current unattractiveness of politics to the young) is it irreversible, as the example of the 1960s and 1970s indicates. Fifth and finally, the French appear very far from having lost their political landmarks.

---

[4] Unless otherwise stated, the figures cited in this paragraph are once again taken from various issues of *L'état de l'opinion*.

Though increasingly sceptical about the notions of Left and Right, they remain willing to place themselves on a Left–Right scale. The proportion of respondents to CEVIPOF polls who either placed themselves at the centre of the scale or refused to position themselves at all actually fell between 1978 and 1995 (Boy and Mayer 1997: 90). The resilience of the Left–Right divide may also be gauged from Jaffré and Chiche's finding (1997) that it was crossed by just 12 per cent of voters over three elections between 1993 and 1995 (the first rounds of the 1993 parliamentary elections and the 1995 presidential election, and the 1994 European election). The volatility of the 1980s and 1990s was chiefly due to new entrants, particularly the Greens and the FN; but as we have seen, the established parties, given time, proved quite successful at co-opting the former and contributing, at least, to the break-up of the latter. The relative resilience of established parties has also, to some degree, been demonstrated by their organizational survival—though at some cost to the taxpayer.

ORGANIZATIONAL STRENGTH

French parties in the late twentieth century, like many of their counterparts in Western Europe, became more prosperous and better staffed even as their roots in civil society were threatened.

Finance and staff

The greater prosperity of French political parties has been largely thanks to public finance, instituted, as in Germany and Italy, in an attempt to end political corruption by ending the financial penury of parties. In purely financial terms, parties were thus in a position to absorb a drop in membership, or a loosening of links with satellite organizations, with little difficulty. Political corruption, on the other hand, shows little sign of having abated.

The financial regime under which French parties laboured until 1988 might have been calculated to encourage illegal fund-raising. Public subsidies were practically non-existent, save for limited free television coverage and fairly token sums for election posters; business finance of parties was classified as 'abuse of company funds', and as such illegal both for donor and recipient; but parties were subject to no ceiling on spending and no obligation to publish accounts. In practice, all parties used business money. Most frequently, they extorted it in return for national or local building or utility contracts (even the Communists could do this, having controlled a number of local authorities since the 1920s), and used bogus 'consultancy' firms to conceal the transactions and funnel the funds to their recipients, sometimes through networks of offshore accounts. Other, less direct, funding methods have included the employment of party workers on local or (less frequently) national government payrolls, and the use of public assets such as vehicles or buildings for party purposes. All parties denied such practices and claimed to live off their members' dues, with steadily less plausibility as politics became more competitive and more expensive in the 1970s and 1980s. A striking example of one party's dependency on the perquisites of office came in 1974, when the Gaullists' daily paper, *La Nation*, turned weekly within two months of their losing the presidency. But the Socialists were the first to be caught, in 1989, through the national network of consultancies (Urba) they had set up two decades earlier. Urba's purpose was to prevent *personal* corruption by channelling set proportions of illegal funds to local and national party coffers. The coordination and book-keeping that this required made the system easy to unravel once a part of it was discovered. The systems of other parties (or indeed, in some areas, of factions within the Socialist Party) were less centralized and harder to unearth; but by 2000, all of the four established parties were under judicial investigation of one sort or another.

The first law on party finance was passed in 1988, shortly before the Urba affair broke publicly. Three more laws followed, in 1990, 1993, and 1995. They established a regime based around three principles. First, parties would receive public finance, both for running costs and for election campaigns. Campaign finance provision was quite generous—up to 100 million francs for a presidential candidate reaching the second round, for example. Running costs were calculated in 1988 on the basis of parliamentary representation, but the law of 1990 extended this: public finance is available on the basis of votes at parliamentary elections to all parties presenting fifty or more candidates at such elections in mainland France (with more liberal provisions applying to France's overseas departments and territories). Second, the financial affairs of parties and elected officials were subjected to increasing legal constraints, all monitored by a committee created in 1990 for the purpose. Parties must publish annual accounts; candidates must keep within spending ceilings, publish details of personal wealth, create separate campaign finance trusts, and publish campaign accounts. Third and most controversially, offences relating to political finance before 1988 were subject to an amnesty. Intended to facilitate a 'fresh start', the amnesty specifically excluded the parliamentarians who voted on it, as well as any cases of 'personal enrichment'. But these subtleties tended to escape the voters, especially when the Socialist Christian Nucci walked free after having helped to pillage a fund for overseas development for the benefit of the Socialist party (as a minister, and so not a parliamentarian, when the legislation was passed, Nucci came within the amnesty provisions). The coincidence of the amnesty with the emerging Urba scandal did much to discredit the Socialist party in the early 1990s.

A fourth provision, the legalization of business finance, was included in the 1990 law but reversed in 1995. The 1993 parliamentary elections were thus the only major election to have been openly financed, in part, by corporate donations. The accounts for this campaign show that of the total corporate finance involved (about 200 million francs), some three quarters came from firms in the public works and utilities sectors—in other words, firms involved in bidding for municipal contracts. The obvious implication is that the brief emergence into legality of corporate donations merely drew back a veil on earlier illegal practices. That the only major party to be excluded from corporate largesse was not the Communist Party, but the FN, suggested that donations were motivated not so much by ideological affinity as by well-calculated self-interest: unlike the FN, the Communists controlled town halls and thus contracts.

Table 5.9 shows the extent to which French parties depend on finance from public sources. The myth that they lived off membership dues was exploded as soon as they had to publish accounts; no party since 1993 has claimed to have received more than 20 per cent of its income from dues, and the average figure for all parties is roughly 10 per cent. The withdrawal of (legal) income from business after 1995 clearly hit all major parties, and especially the Gaullists (who ran up a deficit of 47 million francs in 1995); now restricted to personal donations only, the volume of 'gifts' has dropped by about three quarters. Commercial and investment income, though (apparently) much developed by the FN, has proved of relatively limited importance for other parties. All parties, especially those of the Left, also extract money from their elected officials. The extreme example is the Communist Party, which compels its parliamentarians and mayors to hand over their whole salaries in return for a skilled worker's wage, raising about a third of its funds in this way—a powerful incentive to retain town halls and parliamentary seats, and to keep up the alliance with the Socialists that is essential to do this. But public finance remains the single largest source of party income, accounting for over half of the total in 1997 and 1998. A total of 56 parties received public finance, amounting to over 900 million francs, in 1998. Thirty of them represented France's overseas departments and territories: the Polynesian Liberation Front, for example, received FF295,343. The bulk of the money, however, sustains the large parties. This dependence leads to sharp variations in income because public money is linked to electoral fortunes: the Socialists lost nearly half of their public finance after their rout of 1993, the Gaullists and UDF almost a third of theirs after losing in 1997.

It is far from clear, however, that public finance has achieved its aim of ending political corruption. Judicial investigations under way at the end of 1999 included the Communist Party's use of Gifco, a front organization comparable to Urba; the Socialists' dubious relationships with France's main student insurance firm, the MNEF, which had provoked the resignation of Finance Minister Dominique Strauss-Kahn in October; the Paris Town Hall, which had payrolled full-time RPR officials, and probably received kickbacks on council housing lift maintenance contracts (as well as falsifying electoral rolls) (Guédé and Liffran 1996; Madelin 1997); and the Paris Region, accused of receiving similar payments on contracts to renovate its high schools, and (as befits an assembly elected by proportional representation) distributing the profits to all parties represented on the regional council. All of these cases refer to post-amnesty years during which

TABLE 5.9. *Party finance in France, selected years*

	Communists			Socialists			Greens			UDF			Gaullists			Front National			Total		
	1993	1997	1998	1993	1997	1998	1993	1997	1998	1993	1997	1998	1993	1997	1998	1993	1997	1998	1993	1997	1998
Public finance	36.6	36.6	40.7	167.1	89.5	158.5	9.5	11.7	11.5	121.6	149.6	106.9	134.8	161.9	111.7	29.1	35.6	41.4	498.8	484.8	470.6
%	30.4	32.9	35.3	57.7	38.6	54.3	44.0	64.5	54.4	55.1	75.0	70.3	37.6	68.7	65.2	40.6	25.2	35.1	46.1	51.7	54.1
Membership dues	14.2	12.8	12.3	32.5	45.1	42.0	2.2	2.2	3.1	13.4	7.1	4.8	29.1	16.9	19.9	10.7	9.2	8.2	102.1	93.2	90.2
%	11.8	11.5	10.6	11.2	19.5	14.4	10.1	12.3	14.6	6.1	3.5	3.1	8.1	7.2	11.6	15.0	6.5	6.9	9.4	9.9	10.4
Elected officials	39.0	40.3	40.6	26.5	46.0	52.2	4.0	1.5	1.5	7.7	1.7	1.5	5.1	2.0	7.1	5.5	6.6	7.6	87.9	98.1	110.4
%	32.4	36.2	35.2	9.2	19.9	17.9	18.4	8.1	7.0	3.5	0.8	1.0	1.4	0.8	4.1	7.7	4.7	6.4	8.1	10.5	12.7
Gifts	21.6	10.3	13.1	37.3	2.5	1.9	0.0	0.8	0.9	44.9	2.6	2.7	124.5	38.6	14.0	13.6	6.5	6.7	241.9	61.3	39.2
%	17.9	9.3	11.3	12.9	1.1	0.7	0.0	4.5	4.2	20.3	1.3	1.8	34.7	16.4	8.2	19.0	4.6	5.7	22.3	6.5	4.5
Other, including commercial and investment income	9.1	11.2	8.8	26.1	48.7	37.4	6.2	1.9	4.2	33.0	38.6	36.2	64.9	16.3	18.8	12.7	83.0	54.1	152.0	199.8	159.4
%	7.5	10.0	7.6	9.0	21.0	12.8	28.7	10.6	19.8	15.0	19.3	23.8	18.1	6.9	11.0	17.7	58.9	45.9	14.0	21.3	18.3
Total income	120.5	111.2	115.4	289.6	231.9	292.0	21.7	18.1	21.1	220.6	199.5	152.1	358.4	235.7	171.4	71.7	140.9	118.0	1082.6	937.3	869.9
Spending	118.9	131.2	128.8	252.6	230.1	255.1	18.3	23.1	21.4	184.2	179.4	159.7	332.8	240.0	176.9	41.7	144.9	116.5	1052.6		

Note: Figures other than percentages are in millions of francs.

Source: Journal Officiel de la République Française, annexes, 19 November 1994, 18 November 1998, 6 November 1999.

parties have been in receipt of public money. Perhaps not surprisingly, individual parties have usually been restrained about exploiting scandals involving their opponents; for all of them would be damaged by a serious outbreak of mud-slinging. The suspicion remains, however, that French parties, like their German and Italian counterparts, have gratefully accepted the (rather unwilling) largesse of the French taxpayer while continuing to pocket large illegal donations as well.

That would help to account for the contrast between their *fin de siècle* prosperity and their mid-century penury. Nowhere is that contrast more striking than in the area of staffing. Under the Fourth Republic, according to Williams (1964: 66), apart from the Communists 'most French parties had no more than six or ten headquarters officials, with even fewer typists and doormen.' Forty years later, on the other hand, Socialists, Gaullists, and FN all claimed roughly a hundred full-time employees at party headquarters. To these should be added three other types of party workers, all paid out of public funds. First, the two houses of parliament (the National Assembly and the Senate) fund employees for parliamentary groups. Thus the Socialist group, the largest in the National Assembly, had 44 staff early in 2000, and the RPR group 25. Second, individual parliamentarians have, since the 1970s, received an allowance sufficient to employ a research assistant and a secretary. Third, parties and politicians may also find the (illegal) means to pay political assistants out of state, municipal, or other public funds, typically by appointing them to non-existent jobs. This practice is impossible to quantify because it is linked, above all, to local authorities, not national party headquarters. The probability is that while, in the case of the RPR, Chirac's control of France's capital city allowed local authority staff to be used directly by the Party's central office, elsewhere they have been controlled more by individual mayors and councillors.

By and large, their own employees, whether open or covert, suffice to meet the day to day needs of French parties. There are four exceptions, though, to this general rule. First, most parties other than the Communists have had links with, and drawn policies from, a variety of associations and think-tanks: the Club Jean-Moulin for the Socialists in the 1960s, the Club 89 for the Gaullists, and the Club de L'Horloge for the far Right in the 1980s. Second, parties use commercial organizations, usually created for the purpose, to undertake activities. Some of these, like Urba for the Socialists, have simply served to issue false invoices to cover illegal sources of finance. Others have managed less virtual areas of activity: for the RPR, for example, the Société de Diffusion de Presse handles individual donors, while Etape SA has dealt with the Party's publications. Their accounts are integrated into those of the Party. Third, French parties share the national addiction to opinion polls of all kinds, and regularly commission commercial polling firms: for example, the Communist Party has often used the IFOP and SOFRES polling organizations since the 1960s (Michelat and Simon 1996). Fourth, parties and especially candidates have had recourse to advertisers and image consultants, especially for campaigns. The sublime example of this remains Jacques Séguéla's 'La Force Tranquille' poster campaign for Mitterrand in 1981, but there have been many others. It is also of interest that as president, Mitterrand hired an image consultant, Jacques Pilhan, and that Pilhan's services were retained by Chirac (without great success) when he succeeded Mitterrand in 1995.

Activism and parties in civil society

The capital-intensive style of politics inherent in the reliance of French parties on large budgets extracted, legally or illegally, from the public purse, on paid employees and professional polling and advertising firms, has gone hand in hand with the shrinkage of more traditional party links with society that allowed a more labour-intensive (and volunteer-based) type of politics. The numerical fall in party membership since 1981 has already been noted. Just as important, though less easy to measure, has been the decline in activism (Bréchon 1999: 110). In particular, the anecdotal evidence suggests that party members have become steadily less available for the somewhat thankless duties traditionally assigned to the rank and file—bill posting, door to door canvassing, leafleting at Sunday morning markets (for the Gaullists, cf. Hecht and Mandonnet 1998). The first of these activities is increasingly assigned to professionals, and the others have been abandoned to a greater or lesser degree. One of the distinguishing features of the FN in its early years was the greater commitment it could draw on from its members (Tristan 1987)—an activism that led, in certain cases, to racist murders. But the militant force of the FN had already diminished by the time of the split in 1998.

For some parties, indeed, the question of why a mass membership should be recruited at all, and what it should be asked to do, has no very obvious answer. Those that place the most value on activism, the Communists, the far Left, and the FN, use them to project a sympathetic image of their party, typically at large and convivial fêtes (the Fête de l'Humanité for the Communists, the Fête de Lutte Ouvrière on the far Left, and the Fête des Bleus–Blancs–Rouges for the FN). Cadre parties, on the other hand, most notably on the non-Gaullist moderate Right, have managed happily for decades without a very active membership at all, relying on the 'notability' of their (often rural) candidates and on the (usually old) money they could raise at election times. This distaste for activism has carried over to some, though not all, Gaullists. Among Gaullist party leaders, one, Alain Peyrefitte, told journalists that '*les militants m'emmerdent*' (activists get on my wick), while another, Alain Juppé (1993), littered one of his books with complaints of their exasperating stupidity. Philippe Séguin, who succeeded Juppé as RPR president in 1997, observed (Séguin 1989) that 'joining a political party these days is like joining a supporters' club, for a sport that isn't even very interesting.' Perhaps the commonest contemporary use for party members is to supply a décor for party meetings, giving viewers of the main evening news an impression of dynamism that rubs off on the party or the candidate concerned. An alternative is to hire actors for this purpose. But when one junior minister, Olivier Stirn, did precisely that in

1990, his behaviour shocked even the French, and Stirn's ministerial career came to a premature close.

Parties have also relied on a variety of other organizations to maintain their influence in civil society. The Communists have been the most systematic about this. Aside from close links with the Confédération Générale du Travail (CGT), France's largest trade union confederation, whose leaders for half a century sat on the Communists' Political Bureau, they also possessed satellite organizations for every social group (notably women, the young, and students), and even had an agency to offer East European holidays to the faithful: the whole amounting, in the memorable phrase of Annie Kriegel (1968), to a veritable 'counter-society'. At the other end of the spectrum, the FN clearly tried to imitate this model (Fysh and Wolfreys 1992), as well as practising entryism in a whole range of unions, whether for policemen, workers, or council housing tenants (Darmon and Rosso 1998). Other parties, though less systematic, still had their networks. The Socialists, while lacking a really solid trade union link on the British or even German model, have always been close to the *laïc* (secular) movement, particularly among parents' associations and teachers in State schools. They also sought, in the 1980s, to use anti-fascist organizations such as SOS-Racisme or the Manifeste contre le Front National as seedbeds for their activists. Conversely, the Christian Democratic centre–right has benefited from its Catholic networks, both among parents of church schools and in organizations such as the various *Jeunesses Chrétiennes*. The Right, and especially the Gaullist Right, has also been more or less close to employers' organizations, with Pompidou being an important link in the early Fifth Republic.

These links have tended to weaken, in two main ways. First, 'subcultures', and the satellite organizations that went with them—whether Communist or Catholic—have withered. The CGT, for example, is a shadow of its former self with a total membership of some 700,000. Just as important has been the reluctance of such groups to be seen as the tools of political parties. Again, the CGT is a prime case; its leadership in the 1990s chose to sever direct links with the Communists. It is not alone, though. Parents of each camp have readily mobilized in defence of their preferred form of schooling, whether Catholic in 1984 or secular a decade later; they have not transferred their loyalties to parties. Committed anti-fascist activists have not joined the Socialist party. Even the FN's *démarches* had run into difficulties, both from the judiciary and from the target audience, before the break-up of 1998.

The second sign of subcultural erosion lies in the changing nature of the mass media. The postwar generation in France had a reasonably active partisan press, reinforced in 1944 by the takeover of former collaborationist papers by the left-wing *comités de Libération*. The prime example was the Communist *L'Humanité*, whose national sales ran into hundreds of thousands in the 1940s. Other news-papers, including regional dailies like Gaston Defferre's Socialist *Le Provençal*, were able to survive while still offering fairly partisan coverage. Indeed, when he returned to power in 1958, de Gaulle was sufficiently (and to a great extent rightly) convinced of the press's hostility towards him that he determined to make the emerging medium of television into a mouthpiece for the Government. Despite the demise of the Gaullist model (under which an Information Minister would dictate the day's lead stories to broadcasting chiefs) through successive reforms, few governments since then have resisted the temptation to take a hands-on approach to television, notably by placing their own partisans on private or privatized channels or in the supposedly arm's-length authorities designed to oversee them.

But partisanship in the media has become steadily more difficult to sustain. Readership of newspapers, and particularly of partisan newspapers, has slumped. *L'Humanité* now sells fewer than 60,000 copies, *Le Provençal* has merged into a non-party regional paper; *Le Matin*, an attempt at a national Socialist daily, stopped publication shortly after 1981; the far right-wing *Minute* and *Présent*, after a degree of revitalization in the 1980s, have settled to a low circulation. The televised media have become more or less non-partisan in three senses. First, the complexity of the system is now such that the sort of open manipulation across the board characteristic of the 1960s has become all but impossible. The role of party nominees in the management of television stations has helped to prevent the appearance of potentially embarrassing investigative journalism in the broadcast media; it is not enough to promote individual parties. Second, the political discussion that does occur tends to focus more readily on personalities than on parties: flagship interview programmes give hour-long coverage to individuals and to their suitability for the presidency or other high office (which viewers are frequently invited to pronounce on before and after the performance). Third, airtime cannot be purchased in France. Parties are, it is true, entitled to free election broadcasts: in 1997, twenty-one of them qualified by running candidates in more than seventy-five constituencies, so that the larger parties had to share the available airtime, proportionally, with the Humanist Party, the Natural Law Party, and the Union for the Four-Day Week. But party election broadcasts are treated with the same mixture of mockery and exasperation in France as elsewhere.

The Communist case is unique in France not only because the party's overall decline has been so precipitate; it is exceptional because no other party had anything like the Communists' comprehensive organizational base. Others—certainly the Socialists and the Gaullists—have aspired to a mass membership, or enjoyed the support of non-party organizations in civil society, or benefited from a more or less loyal press. But they have rarely if ever achieved all of these at the same time, and many crucial assets—the chance to employ staff, visibility with voters, links with associations—have been controlled to a greater or lesser extent by local elected officials, ensuring a sort of gravitational pull in France towards the notable-dominated cadre party. While the hold of parties on French society certainly loosened in the last quarter of the twentieth century, therefore, this was a relatively unspectacular event because it had not been terribly strong in the first place. At the same time, the growing financial demands placed on parties under the Fifth Republic contributed to the scandals of the late 1980s, and the scandals in turn to political funding reforms. The availability of public funding certainly placed parties, and especially their central offices, on a more secure financial footing than previously, allowing higher spending and more employees, though not—thanks to the linking of funding to election results—perfect immunity from need. This combination of a fairly limited decline in classical forms of organizational strength (limited because, if the Communists are excepted, the starting point was rather low) with the injection of new and legal public funding may help to explain why diminishing party allegiance has not necessarily meant diminishing party functionality.

FUNCTIONALITY

Parties, most analysts since Bagehot have broadly agreed, serve to recruit political personnel; to supply governments and play some role in defining their policies; to aggregate interests; to foster political participation; to help form the political ideas and choices of the voters. French parties have rarely done any of these things very exhaustively; but in some respects, and despite their weakened position within civil society, their ability to do them has improved rather than the reverse.

Political recruitment

Most elected officials in France are not party members at all. This is because most of them are among France's half-million or so municipal councillors. France has over 36,000 municipalities, of which the overwhelming majority are rural: over 32,000 have fewer than 2000 inhabitants, and over 25,000 have fewer than 700. The general political sympathies of candidates for the councils of these small rural communities are usually well known to the neighbours who vote for them; in Interior Ministry classifications they may be called *divers gauche* and *divers droite*; they rarely carry a party political label. *Notability*—prominence in a community gained through personal wealth, personal networks, or both—still counts for more, in politics at this level, than partisanship. It is projected into national politics because local councillors form 95 per cent of the electoral college that chooses the upper house of the French parliament. The Senate's composition reflects this. Rural areas are grossly over-represented among the Senators, who sit for nine-year terms, one-third of their number being renewed every three years. Over half of them are over sixty; 60 per cent are mayors; 97 per cent are men. Party labels differ slightly from those in the National Assembly. Although the Senate of 1998 contained sixteen Communists and seventy-eight Socialists on the Left, and ninety-nine Gaullists on the Right, it also included three groups without precise equivalents anywhere else: the Républicains Indépendants, the Union Centriste, and the Rassemblement Démocratique et Social Européen. In many ways, the 122 Senators of this central contingent give the Senate its dominant tone: men of the moderate centre and (mostly) centre–right, jealous of the prerogatives of their house and its role as a 'chamber of second thoughts', and not very amenable to party discipline. The Senate did, it is true, play a more politicized and confrontational role in the early years of the Mitterrand presidency, but even in the 1981–86 parliament, 46 per cent of Senate legislative amendments were retained by the left-wing National Assembly. The Senators, moreover, are not the only notables in national politics; multiple office-holding, the *cumul des mandats*, is common in the lower house too. Roughly half of all National Assembly members since 1958 have been mayors; over 80 per cent have held some sort of elective position, as councillor for a municipality, a department, region, or even several at once (though a law of 1985 set some limits on the *cumul*). Solid local bases form the basis of greater or lesser independence from parties. The case of Jean-Pierre Chevènement, a dissident socialist but well-implanted mayor of Belfort, whom Jospin appointed Interior Minister in 1997, is one illustration of this. Another is the number of National Assembly members, usually between 40 and 50, who choose a partly or wholly detached relationship with party groups (Table 5.10). A handful of these have no official links to any group; rather more maintain links that allow them considerable freedom. Some of these members represent constituencies in France's overseas departments and territories, where political pressures differ from those on the mainland; but few are in this category.

Parties, in short, have no monopoly in recruiting the political élite, and exert an imperfect discipline upon its activities. If the notable is one important reason for this, another is the technocrat, the non-political expert. The new constitutional incompatibility between ministerial and parliamentary office, included at de Gaulle's behest in 1958, broke the near-monopoly of the legislature on ministerial recruitment. Henceforth, not only did ministers appointed from the legislature have

TABLE 5.10. *Non-party members of the National Assembly, 1958–97*

	1958	1962	1967	1968	1973	1978	1981	1986	1988	1993	1997
*Non inscrits**	32**	13	9	9	13	15	12	9	15	25	5
Apparentés[†]	34	30	33	31	31	37	41	44	37	20	22
Total	66	43	42	40	44	52	53	43	52	45	27
Total Assembly	579	482	486	487	490	491	491	577	577	577	577
Total %	11.4	8.9	8.6	8.2	9.0	10.6	10.8	7.5	9.0	7.8	4.7

**Non inscrits*: National Assembly members belonging to no political group.
***Because the minimum size of a party group was thirty, the ten Communist members in 1958 had the status of *non inscrits*.
[†]*Apparentés*: Associate members of a political group, usually not subject to voting discipline but without a vote at group meetings.

TABLE 5.11. *Percentage of ministers without*
a parliamentary seat on their appointment,
1958–97

Year	PM	%
1958	Debré	37
1962	Pompidou	27
1968	Couve de Murville	3
1969	Chaban-Delmas	2
1972	Messmer	6
1974	Chirac	33
1976	Barre	29
1981	Mauroy	23
1984	Fabius	31
1986	Chirac	27
1988	Rocard	39
1991	Cresson	29
1992	Bérégovoy	28
1993	Balladur	3
1995	Juppé	14
1997	Jospin	17

to surrender their parliamentary seats; as Table 5.11 shows, they were regularly parachuted into government from outside the legislature altogether. This was true, for example, of de Gaulle's ministers for defence and foreign affairs, Pierre Messmer and Maurice Couve de Murville. Even more strikingly, when Georges Pompidou was appointed Prime Minister in 1962, he had managed de Gaulle's private office (and Rothschild's bank), but had never been elected to anything. A particularly well-trodden route to ministerial office under the Fifth Republic has been via the élite civil service school, the École Nationale d'Administration, and the private offices of ministers. This does not necessarily require the conquest of party positions at all. Chirac, for example, who entered politics through the Prime Minister's office under Pompidou in 1962, himself became Prime Minister twelve years later without ever having formally joined the Gaullist party (to the intense frustration of his many enemies in the party, who were thereby unable to expel him for his sabotage of the party's presidential candidate; he finally took his card in December 1974, the day after taking over the Party's leadership in a spectacular *coup*). Chirac was also able, in the early 1980s, to co-opt his adviser Édouard Balladur, the former secretary-general to the presidency under Pompidou, into the leadership of the Gaullist party, again without any formalities such as party cards. As Table 5.11 shows, governments led by Gaullists, Socialists, or the non-Gaullist moderate Right have all contained ministers from outside parliament; the downturn in their numbers since 1993, which had a precedent in 1968, has been too recent to represent a clear trend.

Parties do not, finally, control presidential candidacies. To run for the presidency, a candidate must attract the signatures of 500 mayors—a rule sufficiently liberal to leave eight or ten candidates in the field at most elections. De Gaulle's vision of a president 'above parties', involving a direct dialogue between candidates and voters, has never been fully realized, but it has left traces. Notable among these is the near-absence of established procedures of candidate-selection in parties. Lionel Jospin's adoption as the Socialist candidate in 1995 is revealing because it was the first time under the Fifth Republic that any party had held a clear contest between two candidates for a presidential nomination, especially on a one member, one vote basis. The absence of such accepted procedures has had particularly striking consequences for the Gaullists, the prototype 'presidentialized' party of the Fifth Republic. In 1974, while the Gaullist majority backed Chaban-Delmas, Chirac's minority supported Giscard. In 1981 three candidates, Chirac, Debré, and Garaud all claimed the Gaullist label. In 1995 Chirac, with the support of most but not all of the Gaullist party, fought a fierce first-round battle with Balladur, backed by a minority of Gaullists and most of the UDF. None of these cases provoked a full-scale party split; Balladur, for example, was returned to parliament for a safe Paris seat with his party's full backing in 1997. In presidential politics, a personal logic tends to prevail over a party logic, in three senses. First, parties (like Mitterrand's Socialists) may become, first and foremost, the instruments of an individual's presidential ambitions, rather than the individual being chosen to carry a more collective partisan project. Second, parties may decline into stables of warring *présidentiables* (Cole 1993), to the exasperation of voters. And third, French parties, unlike their British counterparts, have rarely been very good at removing their dead candidates from the field of battle: the brooding presence of Giscard after 1981, shattering the hopes of any *présidentiable* from the UDF, is a prime case in point.

Parties therefore control political recruitment rather imperfectly. They still, however, play an important role. In the first place, party activism remains one possible route to high political office. It was so, for example, for the Socialists' Pierre Mauroy, Mitterrand's first Prime Minister, and for the Gaullists' Charles Pasqua, Interior Minister from 1986–88 and 1993–95. Moreover, the invasion of politics by civil servants under the Fifth Republic has been part of a two-way process. For the higher reaches of the administration have been politicized as never before, and the party sympathies of top civil servants are increasingly 'marked' by the ministerial offices they have served in. Third, any non-political 'expert' minister seeking to prolong his political career must sooner or later seek election in a constituency (indeed, de Gaulle positively encouraged his unelected ministers, from Pompidou down, to run at parliamentary elections); and that will usually require a party's endorsement. Indeed, to reach the status of *présidentiables* they will need, like their competitors of more activist background, both a strong local base and leverage within their party. Fourth, while individuals like Chevènement have been able to use their local bases to build their own organizations and to survive outside the large established parties, attempts to 'break the mould' of such parties have failed. This was true, in particular, of the 'renovators' movement of 1989, which sought to break down what its protagonists saw as the artificial barriers between Gaullists and UDF and create a broader, more modern, conservative party, with a younger generation (themselves) in the saddle. The movement lasted barely three months before being torn apart by internal conflicts and the opposition of established parties. The attempt in Spring 2001 to launch 'Alternance 2002', a right-wing alliance designed to promote Chirac's re-election campaign regardless of party labels, also ran into opposition from established party officials, including those of Chirac's own Gaullist party. Finally, while presidential candidates operate with some independence from their own parties, they tend to need the backing of a major party to win. De Gaulle himself had to accept his party's help half-way through his re-election campaign in 1965. Thirty years later, Chirac's firmer party base was critical in giving him the first-ballot edge over Balladur that allowed him to go forward to a victorious run-off ballot.

The balance between party and other types of recruitment of politicians is therefore a complex one. It has been well conceptualized by Offerlé (1991), who describes parties as enterprises, with their own assets (such as the party label), to which individual politicians who join them may add personal assets of their own, such as expertise, networks, or notability. Within that framework, the balance between the individual and the party would appear to be more favourable to the former in the French case than in many others.

Governance

In one sense, the Fourth Republic could be seen as a prime example of party government. Parties made and unmade ministries; party leaders rather than premiers, on occasion, chose the ministers; and a prime minister who, like Pierre Mendès-France, sought to win greater freedom of action by establishing a direct relationship with the voters over and above party structures, was ousted at the earliest opportunity. In terms of policy outputs, on the other hand, the parties of the Fourth Republic were practically impotent. The constraints of coalition politics, the ideological rather than practical content of most programmes, and the indiscipline of parliamentarians (especially on the Centre and Right) rendered individual party manifestos impossible to apply, a situation that encouraged the 'outbidding' noted by Sartori (1976) as characteristic of polarized pluralism. Political accountability was minimal because the composition and policies of governments depended more on party negotiations than on direct voter choice.

The Fifth Republic, partly intentionally, reversed this situation. The emergence of the *fait majoritaire* and the greater constitutional authority of both president and prime minister have meant that the choice of governments depends, to a far greater extent than before 1958, on the heads of the executive rather than on party chiefs: that is, on the prime minister during cohabitation and on the president, in the last resort, at other times. It is true that prime ministers under cohabitation have had to be especially careful to give adequate representation in the government to each of the majority parties. But even in this case, they enjoy considerably greater freedom *vis-à-vis* the parties than their predecessors of the Fourth Republic—as Jospin showed in 1997 by keeping out of his government all but two or three of those Socialist heavyweights who had been closely associated with Mitterrand.[5] In other respects, though, party government has been greatly strengthened under the Fifth Republic. Discipline prevails in parliamentary groups to a greater extent than under the Fourth (this was long aided by absenteeism, since the constitutional rule that all parliamentary votes are cast in person was not applied until 1995, allowing group chairmen to vote for their absent colleagues, however numerous). And above all, a reasonably clear link was established between electoral choice and executive outcomes. The bipolarization characteristic of the Fifth Republic allowed voters to select between, and within, opposed coalitions; alternation in power between these coalitions, which had proved elusive under earlier regimes, became a possibility from 1962 and a reality in 1981.

Party government inevitably operates within constraints. These constraints include those imposed by the global economy and by European integration (in France as elsewhere); those imposed by street protest (in France rather more than elsewhere); and those resulting from a self-willed and powerful administration. Moreover, by the early 1990s a term—'la pensée unique'—had been coined to express the widespread view that right-wing and left-wing governments were producing the same results; in one poll shortly before the 1995 presidential election, the proposition that 'whether the Right or the Left is in government, the result is the same' won the agreement of 70 per cent of respondents (Le Gall 1996).

Despite these real convergences, the list of government policies of Right or Left that, having been included in party manifestoes, were enacted in the teeth of opposition and sometimes obstruction from their adversaries, testifies to the reality, however partial, of accountable party government. Such a list would include, for the Left, not only the nationalization programme but also decentralization, the abolition of the death penalty, and retirement at sixty in 1981, and the 35-hour week or the Civil Solidarity Pact (allowing a watered-down form of civil marriage between homosexual couples) in 1997; and for the Right, the launch of privatizations in 1986 or the tightening of immigration and nationality legislation in 1986 and 1993. Party proceedings were crucial in fixing these policies, even though they may have originated in think-tanks. Thus the Right's programmes of 1986 and 1993 were both negotiated between the Gaullists and the UDF, (being prepared well in advance, in the latter case, by meetings grandiosely referred to as 'Estates General'); that of the *gauche plurielle* had been extensively discussed between

---

[5] In Spring 2000, from a rather weakened political position, Jospin was forced to bring two major but hitherto excluded Mitterrand loyalists, Jacques Lang and Laurent Fabius, back into government.

Communists, Socialists, and Greens at conferences on 'social transformation' from 1993 on, before being negotiated between party leaders in early 1997.

In the 1960s, the Gaullists sought to encourage bipolarity at municipal level too, by passing a winner-takes-all majority list system for municipal elections in the 220 or so towns of over 30,000 inhabitants. With some adjustments, this system remains in place, and has led to clear alternation in power in most towns (as well as FN victories in three of them, in 1995). Such alternation has led to variable policy results, which may depend as much on the local context and on the mayor's personal visions for their localities as on party preferences. Nevertheless, parties have tried, if not to control, at least to provide a framework for, their local elected officials' activities; Communists, Socialists, and Gaullists all have local government associations for their mayors and local councillors. The Communists have traditionally been most systematic about the attempt, and did indeed produce a relatively homogeneous set of policy outputs during their municipal heyday of 1977–83 (Schain 1985).

While parties nationally (with the possible exception of the Communists) have allowed their local elected officials significant freedom over policy questions, they have sought to enforce alliance policies on the ground rather more strictly. Thus Socialist mayors were required by their party in the 1970s to abandon their old alliances with the centre-right, inherited from the Fourth Republic and join forces instead with the Communists. The few who refused left the Socialist party. More recently, the mainstream Right was faced with the problem of whether to join an alliance with the FN—an issue that was especially sensitive on regional councils, elected by proportional representation, where overall majorities for any force were rare. After initial hesitation, the Gaullists and UDF decided in 1988 to eschew any deals with the FN, a policy that was broadly respected with some small local lapses. But when, after the regional elections of 1998, four regional presidents of the non-Gaullist moderate Right accepted FN support to keep their presidencies, they were excluded from the UDF parliamentary group. That led, indirectly, to the 1998 split in the party, between the Christian Democratic group, which retains the UDF name and refuses any alliance with the FN, and Démocratie Libérale, which quietly welcomed the dissident regional presidents into its own ranks after an interval of a few months. The fact that the alliance question produced such a dramatic result is partly illustrative of the capacity of the ally in question to repel, but also indicates the limits to the otherwise fairly broad autonomy enjoyed by the local elected officials in France.

Interest articulation and aggregation

The Gaullist critique of the Fourth Republic included the claim that parties represented the selfish and partial interests of groups, not those of the nation as a whole. One of the problems of French parties, however, has been that organized interests have often not been very organized, and parties have had mixed success in aggregating them. Trade unionists were split, after the split of the CGT in 1947, into a pro-Communist majority and a vigorously anti-Communist minority; the picture was further complicated by a Catholic component, and above all, by a lively anarcho-syndicalist tradition in the French working class, suspicious of all party links. Catholics were divided between conservatives and Christian Democrats; the forces of secularism between Socialists and the declining Radicals; business between conservatives, Radicals, Gaullists, and, from 1953, the Poujadist movement, half-party, half-pressure group, which existed to defend the interests of small business threatened by competition and taxes.

The arrival of the Fifth Republic, and above all the rise of the Gaullist party, simplified the picture somewhat. Kirchheimer (1966) explicitly cites the revived Gaullist party as a leading example of a 'catch-all' party, strong, or at least able to win some support, in all sectors of the community: a view echoed by Charlot (1971), who refers to a 'voter-directed' party and underlines the novelty of such an entity in the French context. The Gaullists were able to appeal to modern and traditional conservatives— to small business, managers, Catholics, the retired, (most) peasants—as well as to the top end of the working class: a coalition held together by the reality of economic growth and the less tangible, but no less important appeals of national grandeur and anti-communism. It became a more obviously conservative coalition under Pompidou, attracting more farmers and fewer workers, but still able to win majorities in the new bipolarized context. Within a few years, the Gaullist-led coalition had provoked its opposite: a Left-wing assemblage of traditional leftist categories—blue-collar workers (still broadly loyal to the Communists before 1981), anti-clerical teachers, and peasants from 'red' areas—and newer ones, including the growing numbers of white-collar public service workers, working women, and baby-boomers whose formative political experience had been May 1968. To these groups, the Left's Common Programme of 1972 offered something close to the 'break with capitalism' to which Mitterrand had committed himself at the Socialists' Épinay congress the previous year.

The simplifying logic of the Fifth Republic did not long survive the *alternance* of 1981. The classic relationship between a social group and a single party during the postwar era, the Communists' hold on blue-collar workers, blew apart in the first half of the 1980s (Capdevielle 1998). Although this loyalty was briefly displaced onto the Socialists it soon began to dribble away from the Left as a whole, thanks to traumas both economic (the policy changes of 1983) and political (the Socialist government's backing for the Maastricht Treaty, which 58 per cent of blue-collar workers opposed at the 1992 referendum). By 1995, neither the Socialist nor the Communist candidates were doing much better among the working class than among the rest of the voters, and even the Left's second-ballot lead among workers had shrunk by half (Goldey and Knapp 1982; SOFRES 1989, 1996). Some disaffected blue-collar voters gravitated to the FN, which by 1995 had become the most working-class party in France in terms of its electoral composition (some of these voters, known as *gaucho-lepénistes*, chose to switch back to the Left at run-off ballots). Blue-collar abstention was also both higher and faster-growing than average: 24 per cent (2.5 per cent higher than the average) in the 1986 parliamentary elections, but 38 per cent (6.5 per cent above average) in 1997. As the Left lost working-class support it gained ground among other categories: by 1995, the Socialist candidate, Jospin, was doing better than average at both rounds among managers and professionals, in sharp contrast to Mitterrand's record. These voters, who were ready to accept the Socialists' claims of economic 'competence' and attracted to their greater cultural liberalism, were won from the mainstream Right. The mainstream Right's difficulties were compounded by losses to the FN, among the self-employed in particular and more generally among their most right-wing and most nationalist voters (here again, the Maastricht Treaty, opposed by the leaders of the moderate right-wing parties, played a role).

This new, relatively dealigned context rendered the aggregation of interests by parties or even coalitions of parties especially challenging. The mainstream Right can no longer count on the majority support of the better-off social groups, given the Left's (relative) reconciliation with the market, but protectionist farmers and right-wing nationalists among the ranks of its supporters act as a regular brake on the full-blown economic liberalism to which it has aspired, in varying degrees, since the early 1980s. The Gaullists' split of 1999, when Charles Pasqua left to launch a 'sovereignist' party, the Rassemblement pour la France, with the former UDF minister Philippe de Villiers, is illustrative of these tensions. The Left, on the other hand, can no longer take the working class for granted, but its efforts to regain their support are limited by the pro-European and even (relatively) free-market policies to which it is committed, and which remain necessary to maintain support among managerial groups whose backing was important in the Left's victory in 1997. Jospin's aspiration to forge a new coalition including the socially excluded, blue-collar workers, public service employees, and managers shows an awareness of the nature of the challenge facing him, but it does not point to an obvious solution. The lack of strong and influential interest groups does not simplify the task. Indeed, the lack of such a group to help win and retain Socialist support among workers makes it one of the most vulnerable of Europe's left-of-centre governing parties, with a normal electoral audience of barely 25 per cent.

The parties' indifferent performance in articulating and aggregating group demands raises the question of how far groups and social movements have by-passed parties and even usurped their functions. There is certainly evidence of the superior ability of social movements to channel citizen activism. One poll in 1989, for example, found that 51 per cent of respondents expressed greater trust in spontaneous, *ad hoc* movements to defend wage-earners than in formal union structures (Mayer and Perrineau 1992). Perrineau's study of 'political engagement' in France (1994) reveals a similar story: behind the appearance of a decline in political activism given, for example, by the erosion of party and traditional union membership, lies a displacement of such activism towards social movements and the burgeoning associative sector—whether a relatively classical NGO like Médecins sans Frontières (whose founder, Bernard Kouchner, became a Socialist minister) or the more openly political Droit au Logement (the movement for low-cost housing in Paris), Attac (the pressure group seeking French backing for the Tobin tax on international capital movements), or the wide range of anti-racist groups that have appeared since the rise of the FN. France is also littered with examples of more or less spontaneous social movements capturing and carrying forward a public mood in such a manner as to leave parties and established interest groups standing. The 'events' of May 1968 remain the classic example, but a more recent one is supplied by the movement that rose against the Prime Minister Juppé's Social Security reforms in late 1995, and retained the support of a majority of the French three weeks into a painful public-sector strike. In both cases the established unions and opposition parties were made to appear impossibly cautious and plodding. That pressure groups and social movements of various kinds have outflanked parties as mobilizers of citizens does not, however, mean that they have replaced parties to any very substantial extent either in political representation or in policy-making. France possesses three examples of pressure groups that have sought to become parties, at least in the sense of presenting candidates at elections. One was the Poujadist movement, which began to decline almost as soon as it had brought its rowdy brand of protest politics into parliament after the 1956 elections. CPNT, the tone if not the preoccupations of which resemble a latter-day Poujadism, has endured longer, but remains a single-issue group that presents candidates in defence of unrestricted wildfowl-shooting at elections held on proportional representation where it has a chance of winning seats (Traïni 2000). Its main effect has been to delay the implementation in France of European directives on conservation. Finally, there are the Greens, who, like their counterparts elsewhere in Europe, developed out of Friends of the Earth, and who have managed the transition from group to party more successfully, though they remain marked by their background of protest rather than electoralism. None of these cases is sufficient to suggest any substantial 'replacement' of parties by groups. Groups have not, it is true, been kept at the margins of policy-making as the Gaullist founders of the Fifth Republic would have liked. The co-management of agricultural policy by the FNSEA under Gaullist but also left-wing governments, in particular, is well documented (Keeler 1987). The *Mouvement des sans-papiers*, created in 1994 to defend immigrants threatened with expulsion under new legislation enacted by the conservative Balladur government, played an important role in setting the agenda for the immigration policy of the incoming Jospin government (though Jospin did not accept all of its demands). None of this, though, indicates anything more threatening to parties than the normal activity of groups. The one recent exception might be constituted by the employers' peak group, which changed its name in 1998 from CNPF to the Mouvement des Entreprises de France (MEDEF) and launched an aggressive proposal to redefine a wide range of social and employment legislation, including, for example, pensions and unemployment pay. This wide-ranging and highly political initiative may be explained in two ways. First, it arises from the employers' role, defined in postwar legislation in co-managing France's Social Security system with trade unions (which were thereby obliged to respond to the MEDEF plan in negotiations leading to a redefinition of the Social Security rules). Second, the mainstream right-wing parties were indeed too weak and too divided after their 1997 defeat to launch such a controversial programme. In that sense, the MEDEF initiative could be said to be an example of an interest group by-passing parties and exercising a policy-making function. But the example remains a somewhat specific and isolated one.

Political participation

The tendency of French parties to gravitate towards a cadre model, and the generally low membership levels mentioned above, indicate that French parties are not very effective in sustaining a high level of citizen participation in politics. A partial exception should be made for the Communist party, both because it was the only French party to sustain a membership of over 100,000 for any length of time and because it offered a wide range of opportunities to participate. True, the nature of participation could be menial—bill-sticking or leafleting; the Leninist organizational principles of democratic centralism ensured that no serious dissidence from the leadership's policies was tolerated; and the membership turnover was high (earning the epithet of a 'colander party'); but for a core of activists, the party offered a long-term commitment, purpose, and conviviality. Kriegel (1968) characterized the party and its satellites as a 'counter-society', cut off from the rest of France. In another sense, though, it fulfilled a function of social integration, offering a role and an identity to the least privileged, albeit in direct opposition to the rest of society: part of what Lavau (1981) called the Communists' 'tribunician' function. As late as 1979, moreover, the party could reasonably claim to have a membership that reflected the social base to which it aspired: of employed party members, 48 per cent were blue-collar workers, and a further 28 per cent white-collar employees (Ysmal 1989). Indeed, the PCF has always constituted a small but significant opportunity for upward social mobility for the best and brightest of its working-class members. The membership underwent gentrification, though, over the next two decades; by 1997, workers represented just 31 per cent of employed party members, and white-collar employees 33 per cent, with other growing categories including skilled public service employees, teachers, managers, and the self-employed (Platone and Ranger 1999). At least as worrying for the Communists, the membership aged: the proportion of under-30s shrank from 27 to 10.5 per cent, while the share of over-60s rose from 16 to 24.4 per cent.

   The Socialists of the 1970s were probably a more dynamic force than they had been at any time since the immediate postwar period. They were also, in 1973, a more middle-class one (Bell and Criddle 1988), with workers representing just

19 per cent of their members (against twice that in 1951), and teachers 17 per cent. By 1985 the proportion of workers among employed party members had dropped to just 10 per cent, with another 10 per cent for white-collar employees, and 26 per cent for teachers (Subileau *et al.* 1999). Socialist activism differed somewhat from that of Communists, being more open to a culture of debate but also, probably, less intense (Lagroye *et al.* 1976)—even if this was likely to vary considerably from one department to another, depending on the party's local leadership. By 1985, 50 per cent of respondents to a survey of the Socialist party claimed to spend five hours or less a month on party activism—the time for one or two meetings. These tendencies were prolonged into the 1990s. By 1998, the proportion of blue-collar workers had shrunk to 5 per cent, while 64 per cent of members gave five hours or less to the party (Subileau *et al.* 1999: 7, 57). Like the Communists, too, the Socialists were an ageing party by the century's end: just 7 per cent of the members were under 30, compared with 40 per cent who were over 60. In that respect, they resembled their predecessors of the 1960s—a decaying party, ripe for takeover.

The non-Gaullist moderate Right can be more or less discounted as a force allowing any large-scale political participation, having never aspired for long either to depart from the cadre model or to recruit a socially representative membership. The Gaullists, on the other hand, have aspired periodically to be a mass party, and did actively seek to recruit in the working class in the late 1970s, reaching a working-class membership of perhaps 20 per cent (Ysmal 1989). Successive studies of the Gaullist party, however, have underlined the limited opportunities it offers for rank and file activism and the domination of its activities by party office-holders and local and national elected officials (Lagroye *et al.* 1976; Ysmal 1984). The decline in membership since the mid-1980s will not have changed that. The FN, finally, briefly took over part of the Communists' 'tribunician' role in the late 1980s and early 1990s, but has had little to offer its diminished band of members since the split of 1998. Party cadres have, in general, been even less socially representative than members. Surveys of congress delegates from all major French parties in the early 1990s (Grunberg 1992) show high concentrations of professionals and managers, an almost negligible blue-collar representation, and even very few white-collar employees; the one exception, the Communist party, had roughly a quarter of each of these two categories among its delegates.

Yet as the membership of parties has become smaller and less socially representative and activism has tended to decline, party organizations have become somewhat more democratic. For most of the Fifth Republic, the Gaullists' leadership culture and the Communists' 'democratic centralism' effectively stifled internal debate on competing projects; only the Socialists possessed a well-rooted culture of debate, and even that often took the form of jousts between faction leaders, with rank and file members representing little more than numbers to be marshalled in support of one or another. All three changed somewhat in the 1990s, however. The Communists have progressively abandoned democratic centralism since 1994, when Robert Hue succeeded Georges Marchais as leader and committed the party to his policies of 'mutation'. Open dissent is now widely tolerated, with many of the dissenters being the Stalinists of yesteryear, and was particularly noticeable in the preparation of the 30th congress in March 2000. The Gaullists were provoked into democratization by electoral defeat, first in 1988 when separate 'currents' were allowed for the first time (an experiment that had effectively died out by late 1991), and then in 1997 when the process of leadership election was democratized. The first party president to be elected against a competitor on a one-member one-vote system was Michèle Alliot-Marie at the end of 1999. The Socialists, finally, also adopted one-member one-vote to choose Jospin as their presidential candidate in 1995, largely bypassing the more traditional manœuvrings of factions to produce a clear result which had the approval of activists. As Bréchon (1999: 121) sums it up, 'fewer members would appear to have more power.'

A final respect in which French parties have been very slow to promote political participation has been that of sexual equality. Michèle Alliot-Marie and the Greens' Dominique Voynet have been the only women leaders of a major party; parties typically have no more than a quarter of women among their members; the proportion of women in the National Assembly, at 10.9 per cent in 1997, was barely above that of Greece, and only 4 per cent higher than the level reached in France in November 1946. That is likely to change, with the law obliging the parties to do what they have failed to do spontaneously. A constitutional amendment passed in 1999 states that 'the law favours the equal access of men and women to elective offices' (article 3) and that political parties 'contribute to the implementation' of this principle (article 4). The law on 'parity' passed at the beginning of 2000 compels parties to run equal numbers of male and female candidates at all types of election, under pain of penalties in the calculation of State funding. Although the law has limitations—it does not, for example, oblige parties to offer women the same number of *winnable* seats in single-member constituency elections—it is still likely to change the face of France's elected assemblies within less than a decade.

Political education and communication

Many Third Republic politicians, operating in a period of rapidly spreading literacy and expanding newspaper circulation, took the task of political education seriously. The great Socialist tribune Jean Jaurès, assassinated in 1914, founded *L'Humanité*. His interwar successor Léon Blum was known for his ability to dictate his regular editorial for *Le Populaire* (the Socialist daily after the Communists had taken over *L'Humanité*) by telephone, without hesitation and without notes. The France of the 1920s had probably the most politically varied press in the world: as Orwell (1928: 36) noted: 'Paris alone has daily papers by the dozen, nationalist, Socialist and

Communist, clerical and anti-clerical, militarist and anti-militarist, pro-semitic and anti-semitic'. And the intense concern of the postwar *Comités de Libération* with controlling regional newspapers testifies to the central place occupied by the print media in the politics of the mid-century. As noted above, however, that place has been seriously eroded since the 1970s. When contemporary political leaders commit themselves to print, they do so far more frequently in the form of books, published at the approach of presidential elections to further a personal more than a partisan project.

Increasingly unable to command a loyal press reaching a mass audience, French parties have also lacked the infrastructure for political education represented by research foundations on the German model. The nearest approximations have been the Communists' research institute (long called the Institut de Recherches Maurice Thorez, after the leader Stalin picked for the party in the early 1930s), and the Socialists' Office Universitaire de Recherches Socialistes (OURS), but they are on a considerably smaller scale (OURS, for example, consists of a few rooms near the Socialist headquarters, and serves primarily as a historical documentation centre). Foundations have also been named after two dead presidents, de Gaulle and Mitterrand: the former has been very active in promoting conferences and publications on every aspect of de Gaulle's career. But both are publicly financed, broadly independent of party control (even though party figures may take a part in their management) and chiefly devoted to historical research on their subjects.

The direct educational efforts of parties are concentrated primarily on their own activists. For the Communists, the *école des cadres* was a vital tool in transforming able but untrained activists into seasoned party officials; in past years training periods here might be topped up, for the upper echelons, by a period in Moscow. Other parties, including the Gaullists, have imitated this type of training programme. Since the 1980s, however, the most widely adopted formula has been the 'summer university' which gives younger activists the chance to take part in party seminars of a relatively non-strenuous kind, usually in a holiday resort, and to meet party leaders in conditions of studied, and photogenic, informality.

That parties devote more effort to the education of their own dwindling faithful than to the sceptical majority may be reflected in the difference of political perceptions between activists and the rest of the population. Differences between parties are perceived very strongly by activists, but much less so even by party sympathizers, whose response to ideologically charged cue-words tends to be confused and contradictory (Bréchon 1999; Duhamel 1997). This problem is, arguably, most severe on the moderate Right, where the combination of joint candidacies at first rounds of parliamentary elections in most constituencies with fierce, but personal, competition at presidential elections deprives sympathizers of the benefits of right-wing unity without offering them the chance to choose regularly between competing policies.

CONCLUSION: NEVER A GOLDEN AGE

Many of the tendencies noted above have been noted elsewhere in Western Europe: widespread voter dissatisfaction with parties, expressed in poll data, in abstentions, in spoilt ballots, in electoral volatility; a declining, less active, less socially representative party membership, distinguished by an awareness of party difference that the general public appeared to have lost; the weakness and vulnerability of parties of government, taken individually, as witnessed by the Socialists' rather low electoral scores, and by the splits in both RPR and UDF. As elsewhere too, parties, like medieval kings, have manifestly failed to 'live off their own' and have made substantial calls on the taxpayer—without, in all probability, putting an end to the illegal practices of earlier years. There are also more specifically French features, however: the very long pedigree of anti-party sentiment, low party membership, and party organizations more virtual than real; the persistence of personal notability as a political resource capable, in some circumstances, of weighing in the balance against party discipline; and, since 1958, the curious balance in the party system between bipolarizing and centrifugal forces.

More than most other countries, France illustrates the danger of confusing the strength and mobilization of parties with the health of democracy. The peak period in France for the membership and mobilization of parties was just before, and again just after, the Second World War. Before 1939, the Third Republic had long since shown itself to be incapable of sustaining a government in power for more than a few months; the fiercest opponents of the left-wing government elected in 1936 openly invoked their preference for being governed by Hitler rather than the (Jewish) Socialist Prime Minister Léon Blum. After 1945, the uneasy postwar consensus was shattered by the onset of the Cold War; the Communists took advantage of very real deprivations suffered by the working class to urge insurrectionary strikes; the Interior Minister responded by sending tanks and troops to the coalfields of the Nord; André Malraux, acting as spokesman for de Gaulle's first party, the Rassemblement du Peuple Français, alarmed foreign diplomats by outlining the Gaullists' plans to evacuate Paris in the event of a Communist takeover, before starting a civil war from Brittany; the composite governments of the Fourth Republic were no better than their predecessors of the Third at achieving continuity in power or policy, the parties no more effective at articulating their ideological preferences with the practicalities of office. High party mobilization, in short, has coincided with extraordinarily dangerous times for the French Republic.

Since 1958, on the other hand, and despite low membership figures and mobilization, parties have become significantly more powerful, and not just because public finance has given them a (legal) income far beyond that of their predecessors. For under the Fifth Republic they have been able to supply the underpinning for more or less clear voter choices and thus for alternation in power. It may reasonably be asked, for example, whether the Communist Party was more powerful under the Fourth Republic, with a mass membership but confined to opposition, or under the Fifth, when it has had the chance to hold ministerial office and affect policy directly, albeit as a minority.

Alternation in power has, it is true, repeatedly disappointed—most notably when the Left discovered the constraints of a global economy and of European integration. It is perhaps here that the organizational weakness of French parties, their declining ability to root themselves in civil society, their proneness to prolonged personal feuding (especially but not exclusively on the Right), their incapacity to renew their leaderships, and their continuing corruption, may prove dysfunctional. In other systems with better integrated parties, voter disappointment with government may cause temporary damage to the party considered most responsible; in France, more readily than elsewhere, disappointment may affect the wider system, as it did, with damaging consequences, in the 1990s. The implosion of the FN (after it had reproduced, in caricatural form, the leadership struggles characteristic of its competitors) and falling unemployment offered more optimistic perspectives for the new century; but the claim made by Jospin's advisers that his premiership has 'rehabilitated politics' is perhaps premature.

REFERENCES

Appleton, A. (1995) 'Parties under pressure: challenges to "established" French parties'. *West European Politics* 18: 116–39.

Archambault, E. (1996) *Le Secteur sans but lucratif* (Paris: Economica).

Bell, D. S. and Criddle, B. (1988) *The French Socialist Party*, 2nd edn, (Oxford: Clarendon Press).

Bennahmias, J.-L. and Roche, A. (1991) *Des Verts de toutes les couleurs: Histoire et sociologie du mouvement écolo* (Paris, Albin Michel).

Bon, F. and Cheylan, J.-P. (1988) *La France qui vote* (Paris: Hachette).

Boy, D. and Mayer, N. (1997) 'Que reste-t-il des variables lourdes?', in D. Boy and N. Mayer (eds) *L'Électeur a ses raisons* (Paris: Presses de la FNSP), pp. 108–11.

Bréchon, P. (1999) *Les Partis Politiques* (Paris: Montchrestien).

Cambadélis, J.-C. and Osmond, E. (1998) *La France Blafarde* (Paris: Grasset).

Camus, J.-Y. (1996) *Le Front National: Histoire et Analyses* (Paris: Olivier Laurens).

Capdevielle, J. (1998) 'Les opinions et les comportement politiques des ouvriers: Une évolution inévitable? Irréversible?'. *Cahiers du CEVIPOF* 21. (Paris: Fondation Nationale des Sciences Politiques).

Charlot, J. (1971) *The Gaullist Phenomenon* (London: George Allen and Unwin).

—— (1986) 'La Transformation de l'image des partis politiques Français'. *Revue Française de Science Politique* 36(1): 5–13.

Cole, A. (1993) 'The presidential party and the fifth republic'. *West European Politics* 16(2) (April).

—— (1996) 'The French Socialists', in J. Gaffney (ed.) *Political Parties and the European Union* (London: Routledge), pp. 71–85.

Converse, P. and Dupeux, G. (1962) 'Politicization of the Electorate in France and the United States', *Public Opinion Quarterly*, 26, 1–23.

—— and Pierce, R. (1986) *Political Representation in France* (Cambridge, Mass: Belknap).

Darmon, M. and Rosso, R. (1998) *L'après Le Pen* (Paris: Éditions du Seuil).

de Gaulle, C. (1946) 'Discours prononcé à Bayeux, le 16 juin 1946', in C. de Gaulle, *Discours et Messages*, volume II (Paris: Plon 1970), 5–11 .

Duhamel, O. (1993) 'Les election legislatives', *Le Monde*, 7 April.

—— (1997) 'Derrière le brouillard, le bipartisme?'. *L'état de l'opinion 1997* (Paris: SOFRES), pp. 81–98.

Duverger, M. (1951) *Les Partis Politiques* (Paris: Armand Colin).

Faucher, F. (1999) *Les Habits Verts de la Politique* (Paris: Presses de Sciences Po).

Fysh, P. and Wolfreys, J. (1992) 'Le Pen, the National Front and the extreme right in France'. *Parliamentary Affairs* 45.

Goldey, D. and Knapp, A. (1982) 'Time for a change: the French elections of 1981. I: The Presidency'. *Electoral Studies* 1(1): 3–42.

—— and Williams, P. (1983) 'France', in V. Bogdanor and D. Butler (eds) *Democracy and Elections* (Cambridge: Cambridge University Press).

Grunberg, G. (1992) 'Les cadres des partis et la crise de la représentation'. *L'état de l'opinion 1992* (Paris: SOFRES), pp. 199–220.

Guédé, A. and Liffran, H. (1996) *Péril sur la Chiraquie: Enquête sur les Fausses Factures et les Affaires Immobilières du RPR* (Paris: Stock).

Hecht, E. and Mandonnet, E. (1998) *Au Cœur du RPR*. (Paris: Flammarion).

Hewlett, N. (1998) *French Politics since 1945: Conflict and Consensus* (Cambridge: Polity Press).

Ignazi, P. (1997) 'New challenges: postmaterialism and the extreme right', in M. Rhodes, P. Heywood, and V. Wright (eds) *Developments in West European Politics* (Basingstoke: Macmillan), pp. 300–19.

Jaffré, J. and Chiche, J. (1997) 'Mobilité, volatilité, perplexité', in D. Boy, and N. Mayer (eds) *L'électeur a ses raisons* (Paris: Presses de Sciences Po), pp. 285–325.

Juppé, A. (1993) *La Tentation de Venise* (Paris: Grasset).

Keeler, J. (1987) *The Politics of Neo-Corporatism in France* (Oxford: Oxford University Press).

Knapp, A. (1996) *Le Gaullisme après de Gaulle* (Paris: Éditions du Seuil).

—— and Wright, V. (2001) *The Government and Politics of France*, 4th edn. (London: Routledge).

Kirchheimer, O. (1966) 'The transformation of West European party systems', in LaPalombara, J., and Weiner, M. (eds) *Political Parties and Political Development*. (Princeton: Princeton University Press), pp. 177–200.

Kriegel, A. (1968) *Les Communistes Français* (Paris: Éditions du Seuil).

Lagroye, J., Lord, G., Mouneir-Chazel, L., and Palard, J. (1976) *Les Militants Politiques dans Trois Partis Français*. (Paris: Pedone).

Lancelot, A. (1988) *Les Élections sous la Cinquième République*, 2nd edn (Paris: Presses Universitaires de France).

Lavau, G. (1981) *A Quoi Sert le Parti Communiste Français ?* (Paris: Fayard).

Le Gall, G. (1996) 'La tentation du populisme'. *L'état de l'opinion 1996* (SOFRES) pp. 187–211.

Leyrit, C. (1997) *Les Partis Politiques: Indispensables et Contestés* (Paris: Marabout).

Madelin, P. (1997) *Le Clan des Chiraquiens* (Paris: Éditions du Seuil).

Martin, P. (1996) *La Montée du Front National* (Paris: Fondation Saint-Simon).

—— (2000) *Comprendre les évolutions électorales. La théorie des réalignements revisitée* (Paris: Presses de Sciences Po).

Mayer, N. (1999) *Ces Français qui Votent le Pen* (Paris: Flammarion).

—— and Perrineau, P. (1992) *Les Comportements Politiques* (Paris: Armand Colin).

Mény, Y. and Knapp, A. (1998) *Government and Politics in Western Europe*, 3rd edn (Oxford: Oxford University Press).

Michelat, G. and Simon, M. (1996) '1981–1995 : changements de société, changements d'opinion'. *L'état de l'opinion 1996* (SOFRES), pp. 167–86.

Offerlé, M. (1991) *Les Partis Politiques*, 2nd edn (Paris: Presses Universitaires de France).

Orwell, G. (1928) 'A farthing newspaper', in *The Collected Essays, Journalism and Letters of George Orwell*, Volume 1 (Harmondsworth: Penguin Books, 1970), 34–7.

Parodi, J.-L. (1997) 'Proportionnalisation périodique, cohabitation, atomisation partisane: un triple défi pour le régime semi présidentiel de la Cinquième République'. *Revue Française de Science Politique* 47: 292–312.

Perrineau, P. (1994) *L'Engagement Politique: Déclin ou Mutation?* (Paris: Presses de la Fondation Nationale des Sciences Politiques).

—— (1997) *Le Symptôme Le Pen: Radiographie des electeurs du Front National* (Paris, Fayard).

Platone, F. and Ranger, J. (1999) *Enquête auprès des adhérents du parti communiste français* (Paris: Fondation Nationale des Sciences Politiques).

Sainteny, G. (2000) *L'introuvable écologisme français?* (Paris: Presses Universitaires de France).

Schlesinger, J. and Schlesinger, M. (2000) 'The Stability of the French Party System: The Enduring Impact of the Two-Ballot Electoral Rules', in Lewis-Beck, M. (ed.) *How France Votes* (New York: Chatham House), pp. 130–52.

Sartori, G. (1976) *Parties and Party Systems: A Framework for Analysis* (Cambridge: Cambridge University Press).

Schain, M. (1985) *French Communism and Local Power.* (London: Frances Pinter).

Schmitt, H. and Holmberg, S. (1995) 'Political Parties in Decline?', in Klingemann, H.-D. and Fuchs, D. (eds) *Citizens and the State*. (Oxford: Oxford University Press).

Séguin, P. (1989) *La Force de Convaincre, Entretiens avec Pierre Servent* (Paris: Payot).

Shields, J. (1996) 'The French Gaullists', in J. Gaffney (ed.) *Political Parties and the European Union* (London: Routledge), pp. 86–109.

SOFRES (1989–2000) *L'état de l'opinion* (Paris: Éditions du Seuil).

Subileau, F., Ysmal, C., and Rey, H. (1999) 'Les Adhérents Socialistes en 1998'. *Cahiers du CEVIPOF* 23 (Paris: Fondation National des Sciences Politiques).

Traïni, C. (2000) 'Les braconniers de la politique: les ressorts de la conversion à Chasse, Pêche, Nature et Traditions', *Cahiers du CEVIPOF no. 28* (Paris: Fondation Nationale des Sciences Politiques).

Tristan, A. (1987) *Au Front* (Paris: Gallimard).

Williams, P. (1964) *Crisis and Compromise: Politics in the Fourth Republic* (London: Longmans).

Wilson, F. L. (1988) 'When parties refuse to fail: the case of France', in K. Lawson and P. Merkl (eds) *When Parties Fail: Emerging Alternative Organizations* (Princeton, N.J: Princeton University Press), pp. 503–32.

Ysmal, C. (1989) *Les Partis Politiques sous la V^eRépublique* (Paris: Montchrestien).

——(1994) 'Transformations du militantisme et déclin des partis', in P. Perrineau, (ed) *L'Engagement Politique: Déclin ou Mutation?* (Paris: Presses de la Fondation Nationale des Sciences Politiques), pp. 41–66.

6

The Colour Purple

The End of Predictable Politics in the Low Countries

Kris Deschouwer

INTRODUCTION: PARTIES AND PARTY SYSTEMS IN FLUX

Belgium and the Netherlands are often taken and presented together as the 'Low Countries', and there are good reasons for treating the two countries as part of a single category. Both are textbook examples of divided societies which display the subcultural vertical segmentation that has travelled conceptually as *verzuiling* (or pillarization (Rokkan 1977)) and share the well-known features of consociational democracy. Being neighbours, moreover, Belgium and the Netherlands share much common history. Yet the border separating the two countries is highly significant, and explains a number of important differences between them.

The border goes back to the religious wars of the sixteenth century, and was formalized by the Treaty of Münster in Westphalia in 1648, thus creating a Dutch state with a very definite Protestant identity, although the political borderline ran south of the religious borderline, leaving a Catholic minority within the Netherlands. The southern provinces remained under various foreign rulers, until the Congress of Vienna reunited north and south as the Kingdom of the Netherlands in 1815. Fifteen years later the Catholic and Francophone elites of the south broke away and created an independent Belgian state. This new state was Catholic and officially French speaking, though the majority of the population did not in fact speak French. History matters greatly in understanding the subsequent development of democratic politics in both countries, and many relevant aspects of this history derive from the separations of 1648 and 1830 (Andeweg and Irwin 1993: 7). In particular, it is impossible to describe the Low Countries without making reference to religion and language.

In both the Netherlands and Belgium, the major parties can be grouped into three party families: religious (Christian), liberal, and socialist. Religion is crucial for the Netherlands, where three religious minorities—Catholics, Protestants, and orthodox Protestants (Gereformeerden)—organized themselves and created political parties, respectively the KVP, the CHU, and the ARP, together with a number of smaller religious parties. Cutting across these religious divisions is the class cleavage, giving birth to the liberal VVD and the socialist PvdA.[1] These five parties were, until the 1960s, the major players of the political game, and as such can be labelled the 'pillar parties', because they organized the subcultural segments in Dutch society and played the consociational game of sharing power (Andeweg 1999; Luther 1999). They remain at the core of the contemporary Dutch party system and will be discussed in this chapter.

In Belgium, there has been no religious division within the Christian family, since the country is homogeneously Catholic. As in the Netherlands, the religious cleavage has been cut across by the class cleavage, resulting in the three main party families. However, there are more than three parties, for each of these political families has split internally along linguistic lines into Francophone and Dutch-speaking variants, each covering its own linguistic zone of the country. Hence, there are six major 'traditional' parties in Belgium: CVP/PSC (Christian Democrat), SP/PS (socialist), and PRL/VLD (liberal).[2] So, while religious fragmentation within the Christian party family was a crucial feature of Dutch party politics throughout much of the twentieth century, linguistic fragmentation became a notable characteristic of the Belgian party system. But whereas the key source of fragmentation has faded in Dutch politics, most tangibly illustrated by the fusion of the three major religious parties into the CDA during the 1970s, in Belgium the language issue has become increasingly salient, and still weighs very heavily in daily political life.

Since the 1960s both countries have experienced party system change, which is evident from a careful reading of the national election results reported in Tables 6.1 and 6.2. The nature and extent of change becomes clearer when reorganized by party family. First and foremost, change can be seen in terms of the decline of the pillar parties. Four decades ago (1959 for the Netherlands and 1961 for Belgium) these parties polled exactly 91 per cent of the votes; thereafter this aggregate score dropped rapidly and, after a slight recovery in the 1980s, fell below 70 per cent. In the Netherlands the pillar parties' electoral nadir came in 1994 when they returned just 66 per cent of the vote (recovering to 72 per cent in 1998), while the traditional parties in Belgium gained their lowest ever collective score (64 per cent) in June 1999.

The real losers in this process of electoral change have been the Christian and Socialist parties, whereas the Liberals in both countries have been gradually gaining in support. The Christian parties have experienced particularly steep decline: in the early 1960s they absorbed nearly half the popular vote in the Low Countries, but today win 20 per cent or (in the case of the CDA) less. Socialist party (SP)

---

[1] I am using here the current party names. For a more detailed account of their history and of their name changes, see Andeweg and Irwin 1993; Koole and van der Velde 1992. A full list of the parties is also in the appendix to this chapter.

[2] A more detailed history of the Belgian parties can be found in Deschouwer 1993, 1994.

TABLE 6.1. *Election results in the Netherlands, 1963–98 (Lower House)*

Year	CDA	ARP	CHU	KVP	PvdA	VVD	D66	Groen Links	SP	Other	ENEP	TNV	Turnout
1963	V	8.7	8.6	31.9	28.0	10.3				12.5	4.8	5.0	95.1
	S	13	13	50	43	16				8			
1967	V	9.9	8.1	26.5	23.6	10.7	4.5			16.7	4.8	10.8	94.9
	S	15	15	42	37	17	7			21			
1971	V	8.6	6.3	21.8	24.6	10.3	6.8			21.6	6.2	12.0	79.1
	S	13	10	35	39	16	11			14			
1972	V	8.8	4.8	17.7	27.3	14.4	4.2			22.8	7.1	12.2	83.5
	S	14	7	27	43	22	6			17			
1977	V 31.9				33.8	17.9	5.4			11.0	6.9	12.8	88.0
	S 49				53	28	8			8			
1981	V 30.8				28.3	17.3	11.1			12.5	4.0	8.8	87.0
	S 48				44	26	17			10			
1982	V 29.4				30.4	23.1	4.3			12.8	4.6	9.4	81.0
	S 45				47	36	6			10			
1986	V 34.6				33.3	17.4	6.1		0.4	8.2	4.2	9.9	85.8
	S 54				52	27	9		0	5			
1989	V 35.3				31.9	14.6	7.9	4.1	0.4	5.8	3.8	4.3	80.3
	S 54				49	22	12	6	0				
1994	V 22.2				24.0	20.0	15.5	3.5	1.3	13.5	3.9	21.4	78.7
	S 34				37	31	24	5	2	7			
1998	V 18.4				29.0	24.7	9.0	7.1	3.5	8.3	5.7	16.0	73.2
	S 29				45	38	24	11	5	8			

Notes: ENEP: Effective Number of Electoral Parties; TNV: Total Net Volatility. V: Per cent of the vote won; S: Number of seats won in the lower House.

losses have been less spectacular, with the Dutch PvdA results fluctuating over time, but the Belgian parties enduring clear decline in the 1960s and then again in the 1990s. By contrast, the Liberal parties have enjoyed a steady climb up to and then beyond the 20 per cent threshold.

It is important to note that a pattern of regional differentiation underlies the Belgian data. Christian Democratic decline is primarily a Flemish affair: in the late 1950s, the Christian Democrats polled the support of as many as 60 per cent of voters in Flanders, but in 1999 won only 22 per cent and were surpassed by the liberal VLD as the first party of the region. By contrast, the story of socialist decline is centred largely on Francophone Wallonia in the south of the country: whereas the socialists were supported by 50 per cent of Walloon voters in the late 1950s, they currently reap only 30 per cent. The significance of these regional variations cannot be underestimated, for they imply that Belgium in effect has two party systems in the electoral arena, which must then merge in the federal governmental arena. This has far-reaching consequences for party legitimacy, as we shall see in due course.

If the traditional parties (bar the liberals) have declined, then others have necessarily been successful. Although the timing of changes has been similar in both countries, the specific patterns have been quite different. In the Netherlands

TABLE 6.2. *Election results in Belgium 1961–99 (Lower House)*

		1961	1965	1968	1971	1974	1977	1978	1981	1985	1987	1991	1995	1999
CVP–PSC	V	41.5	34.8											
	S	96	77											
CVP	V			22.3	21.9	23.3	26.2	26.1	19.7	21.3	19.5	18.4	19.3	14.1
	S			50	46	50	56	57	43	49	43	39		22
PSC	V			9.4	9.0	9.1	9.8	10.1	7.1	8.0	8.0	8.5	8.0	5.9
	S			19	21	22	24	25	18	20	19	18	12	10
BSP–PSB	V	36.7	28.2	28.0	27.2	26.7	27.1							
	S	84	64	59	61	59	62							
SP	V							12.4	12.4	14.6	14.9	13.2	13.3	9.6
	S							26	26	32	32	28	20	14
PSB	V							13.0	12.7	13.8	15.7	13.5	12.7	10.1
	S							32	35	35	40	35	21	19
PVV–PLP	V	12.3	21.6	20.9	16.5									
	S	20	48	47	34									
PVV–VLD	V					9.6	8.5	10.3	13.1	10.7	11.5	12.3	13.2	14.3
	S					19	17	22	28	22	25	26	21	23
PRL	V					5.6	5.9	5.2	8.2	10.2	9.4	8.1	10.3	10.1
	S					11	14	14	23	24	23	20	18	18
VU	V	3.5	6.4	9.8	11.1	10.2	10.0	7.0	9.9	8.0	8.0	5.9	4.7	5.6
	S	5	12	20	21	22	20	14	20	16	16	10	5	8
AGALEV	V								2.3	3.7	4.5	4.9	4.4	7.0
	S								2	4	6	7	5	9
ECOLO	V								2.2	2.5	2.6	5.1	4.0	7.3
	S								2	5	3	10	6	11
VB	V							1.4	1.1	1.4	1.9	6.6	7.8	9.9
	S							1	1	1	2	12	11	15
FN	V											0.5	1.3	1.5
	S											1	2	1
Other	V	6.0	9.0	9.6	14.3	15.5	12.5	14.5	11.3	5.8	4.0	1.5	1.0	4.6
	S	5	9	15	27	27	17	19	12	2	3	3	0	0
ENEP		3.1	3.9	5.2	5.6	6.1	5.6	7.4	8.9	8.1	8.1	9.8	9.3	10.1
TNV		4.8	16.1	7.1	6.5	3.5	6.1	6.0	14.4	10.0	4.5	12.2	7.7	10.8
Turnout		92.3	91.6	90.0	91.5	90.3	95.1	94.9	94.6	93.6	93.4	92.7	91.1	90.6

Notes: ENEP: Effective Number of Electoral Parties; TNV: Total Net Volatility; V: Per cent of the vote won; S: Seats won in the lower House.

two new relevant parties have emerged: D66 and Green-Left. The former is a prototype of post-pillarization politics, expressly aiming to attract cross-cultural support. Its electoral support has proved volatile, but the party has established itself and is a regular partner in the government. Green-Left is a Dutch variety of Green party, being created relatively late (1989) as a fusion of the Communist Party and three smaller parties. Its level of electoral support is fairly typical of Green parties in Europe, but (unlike D66) Green-Left is not (yet) a governing party. More recently, a party defending pensioners' rights (AOV) enjoyed modest success, as did the left-wing SP in 1998. It remains to be seen how long these newcomers survive, though the SP is doing relatively well (see below) in attracting new members.

In Belgium the party-political changes of the 1960s revolved around the language issue: as new regionalist parties (VU, FDF, RW) broke through, they exerted enough pressure on the traditional parties to force all three into bifurcations along linguistic lines. In the early 1980s the Greens broke through, as two separate unilingual organizations (Ecolo in the south and Agalev in the north). Later in the 1980s a right-wing extremist party, Vlaams Blok, gained momentum in the north of the country, while the Front National emerged in the south, though it lacked the organizational coherence, adept leadership, and electoral success of the Vlaams Blok. Again, change occurred assymetrically across the country, proceeding much further in Flanders: in 1999 support for the traditional parties stood at just 59 per cent in Flanders, compared to 71 per cent in Wallonia.

Most symptomatic of the passing of the old politics has been the formation of the so-called 'purple' governments, which exclude Christian Democrats but draw together the 'red' Socialists and the 'blue' Liberals. Such a coalition was created in 1994 in the Netherlands, and renewed in 1998. In Belgium the Christian Democrats lost power in 1999. While the Dutch purple coalition consists of the PvdA, VVD, and D66, the Belgian variant is composed of the two Liberal parties, the two Socialist parties and the two Green parties, and was formed simultaneously at the federal and regional levels (though in Flanders, Volksunie was also included in order to produce a minimal winning coalition). The innovative nature of these coalitions becomes clear on inspection of Tables 6.3 and 6.4, which report the composition of national governments in the Low Countries since 1960.

Depillarization and the erosion of consociationalism

Though such changes are by no means unique, in the Low Countries they have occurred in polities that have long been classified as stable and predictable.

TABLE 6.3. *Composition of Dutch governments since 1959*

Period	Prime minister	Parties
1959–63	J. de Quay	KVP–ARP–CHU–VVD
1963–65	V. G. M. Marijnen	KVP–ARP–CHU–VVD
1965–66	J. M. L. Th. Cals	KVP–PvdA–ARP
1966–67	J. Zijlstra	ARP–KVP
1967–71	P. J. S. de Jong	KVP–ARP–CHU–VVD
1971–72	B. W. Biesheuvel	ARP–KVP–CHU–VVD–DS70
1972–73	B. W. Biesheuvel	ARP–KVP–CHU–VVD
1973–77	J. M. den Uyl	PvdA–D66–PPR (–ARP–KVP)
1977–81	A. A. van Agt	CDA–VVD
1981–82	A. A. van Agt	CDA–PvdA–D66
1982	A. A. van Agt	CDA–D66
1982–86	R. F. M. Lubbers	CDA–VVD
1986–89	R. F. M. Lubbers	CDA–VVD
1989–94	R. F. M. Lubbers	CDA–PvdA
1994–98	W. Kok	PvdA–D66–VVD
1998	W. Kok	PvdA–D66–VVD

Note: Party of Prime minister is mentioned first.

TABLE 6.4. *Composition of Belgian governments since 1958*

Period	Prime minister	Parties
1958–61	G. Eyskens	CVP/PSC–LP/PL
1961–65	T. Lefèvre	CVP/PSC–BSP/PSB
1965–66	P. Harmel	CVP/PSC–BSP/PSB
1966–68	P. Vanden Boeynants	CVP/PSC–PVV/PLP
1968–72	G. Eyskens	CVP–PSC–BSP/PSB
1972–73	G. Eyskens	CVP–PSC–BSP/PSB
1973–74	E. Leburton	BSP/PSB– CVP–PSC–PVV–PLP
1974	L. Tindemans	CVP–PSC–PVV–PLP
1974–77	L. Tindemans	CVP–PSC–PVV–PLP–RW
1977	L. Tindemans	CVP–PSC–PVV–PRLW
1977–78	L. Tindemans	CVP–PSC–BSP/PSB–VU–FDF
1978–79	P. Vanden Boeynants	PSC–CVP–BSP/PSB –VU–FDF
1979–80	W. Martens	CVP–PSC–SP–PS–FDF
1980	W. Martens	CVP–PSC–SP–PS
1980	W. Martens	CVP–PSC–SP–PS–PVV–PRL
1980–81	W. Martens	CVP–PSC–SP–PS
1981	M. Eyskens	CVP–PSC–SP–PS
1981–85	W. Martens	CVP–PSC–PVV–PRL
1985–88	W. Martens	CVP–PSC–PVV–PRL
1988–91	W. Martens	CVP–PSC–SP–PS–VU
1991–92	W. Martens	CVP–PSC–SP–PS
1992–95	J. L. Dehaene	CVP–PSC–SP–PS
1995–99	J. L. Dehaene	CVP–PSC–SP–PS
1999	G. Verhofstadt	VLD–PRL–SP–PS–Agalev–Ecolo

Note: Party of Prime minister is mentioned first.

In effect, they mark the erosion of consociational politics. The extent to which this erosion has occurred differs in the two countries, however, and in order to assess exactly what has happened, how it has happened and, in particular, how it has affected the role and position of the political parties, we need to decompose the concept of consociationalism into its societal and political dimensions (Luther and Deschouwer 1999). The societal dimension refers to subcultural segmentation and the manner in which it is institutionalized through networks of organizations providing (state) services to rank and file members of the various subcultures. The political dimension refers to the style and techniques of elite decision-making which typify consociational democracy, including power-sharing, mutual vetoes, proportional allocation of patronage and resources, and the granting of segmental autonomy. It is useful to bear in mind the analytical distinction between these two dimensions when seeking to understand some of the more striking differences between Belgium and the Netherlands.

Since the 1960s, both countries have experienced *desegmentation* or *depillar-ization* as the once sharp demarcations between the subcultures have eroded. As a result, it has become very difficult for the parties representing these segments of

TABLE 6.5. *Size and party-political loyalty of the five main subcultural segments in the Netherlands*

	1956		1968		1977		1989		1998	
	Size	Vote	Size	Vote	Size	Vote	Size	Vote	Size	Vote
Practising Catholics (KVP)	30	95	30	72	24	67	14	72	11	53
Practising Dutch-reformed (CHU)	12	63	16	55	9	51	8	53	6	44
Practising Re-reformed (ARP)	10	93	12	78	9	75	8	59	6	44
Secular working class (PvdA)	33	68	25	65	28	68	22	63	17	51
Secular middle class (VVD)	15	32	18	25	30	29	48	23	60	31
Total/average	100	70	100	59	100	58	100	54	100	45

Notes: Size = percentage of the electorate belonging to the subculture; Vote = percentage of the subculture voting for the relevant political party.

Source: Andeweg 1999.

society to mobilize voters by referring to traditional identities (Deschouwer 1990). Although there are no systematic data available for Belgium, Table 6.5 neatly illustrates this process for the Netherlands: since 1956 all the subcultural segments, except for the 'secular middle class', have shrunk, while loyalty to the pillar parties has fallen dramatically; thus, on average 70 per cent of each subculture voted for 'its' party in the 1950s, but only 45 per cent did in the 1990s.

This explains the dramatic decline of the religious parties, and the PvdA's increasingly volatile support. On the other hand, less 'pillarized' organizations like VVD, D66, and the other new parties have enjoyed fertile conditions for mobilizing new support. Despite the lack of systematic data on Belgium, analyses of the size and loyalty of the Catholic pillar suggest a very similar story (Billiet 1981; Dobbelaere 1988), while of course the electoral fate of the traditional pillar parties resembles precisely that of their counterparts in the Netherlands.

These changes, and the increasing 'availability' of the electorates (Bartolini and Mair 1990) in the Low Countries, are further illustrated by the measures of electoral volatility and party system fragmentation reported in Tables 6.1 and 6.2. These reveal how Belgium experienced high-volatility elections in 1965, 1981, 1991, and again in 1999; however, the Belgian parties have all become so small that even relatively heavy losses like those sustained in 1999 do not add up to high-volatility scores any more.[3] The Belgian party system is now highly fragmented,

---

[3] The discussion here focuses only on net volatility, since the concept of block volatility cannot meaningfully be applied to polities which do not divide neatly into Left and Right. In particular, the Christian Democrats, who were for so long the critical actors in the party systems of the Low Countries, have never belonged unambiguously to either block.

with an effective number of ten parties. Note that this has occurred not because of the linguistic bifurcation of the system only. This is illustrated by the fact that in 1999 even Belgium's largest party (the VLD), won a mere 22 per cent of the votes in Flanders; thus, even within linguistically defined zones, fragmentation is high. In fact, while the linguistic cleavage has had an obvious impact, party system fragmentation has been exacerbated both by the development of non-traditional parties motivated by linguistic issues (such as Volksunie, RW, FDF, and to some extent Vlaams Blok) and by the emergence of post-materialist politics (in the form of Agalev and Ecolo). The Netherlands experienced one very high-volatility election in the 1960s (1967), followed by a series of relatively high-volatility affairs in the 1970s and 1980s, and a new peak in the 1990s (1994). Clearly, neither is any longer a polity in which the party elites can rely on a visible and stable rank and file. Paraphrasing the commercial slogan of a well-known distribution company, in Belgium it is often the case that 'you have to earn your voters every day'.

Desegmentation has occurred at different rates and in different ways in the two countries, carrying a variety of implications for party politics. The process has gone further in the Netherlands, where organizational networks associated with the subcultures have lost their coherence, strength, and functions. The societal aspects of consociational democracy have thus almost completely disappeared. Yet the political practices have not. After a brief intermezzo of more adversarial politics in the 1970s, mainly inspired by the PvdA, the Dutch political system resumed its style of accommodation and continues to function as a 'depoliticized democracy' (Lijphart 1975). Some have disputed whether this style really does derive from the segmentation of society (see, for instance, Andeweg 1999), but it is clear that the Netherlands is still very much a country of minorities, a scenario which requires a great capacity for political compromise. The major difference is that the minorities are now almost purely party political rather than denominational. Thus, the power-sharing game is played solely by party elites, and the centrality of parties has therefore certainly not declined (a theme to which we shall return).

In Belgium the process of depillarization has been much slower. The party-related social networks still exist and continue to play an important role. In particular, they retain privileged links with the state on behalf of which they channel services to their members. For instance, the system of health insurance still depends on party-related mutual societies. Indeed, these members tend to be attracted by such services as much as by ideological or religious convictions, and patronage and clientelism were until very recently common practices (Huyse 1987; Deschouwer 1998, 1999a). Thus, although the subcultures have been eroded in Belgium, many of their organizational structures remain intact, and the parties retain their traditional relevance.

A number of factors help explain these different experiences of depillarization in Belgium and the Netherlands and bear upon the general issue of legitimacy. First, the presence of Protestantism helps explain why patronage and clientelism never really developed in the Netherlands, for such practices are difficult to defend in a strict rule-bound Protestant culture (Andeweg 1999; Luther and Deschouwer 1999). Furthermore, Protestantism accounts for the relatively early creation of the Dutch state, and thus for the greater legitimacy which the state bureaucracy enjoys there. Belgium is a Catholic country that was from the outset confronted with a deep cleavage between church and state which made it far harder for the state to be regarded as neutral and legitimate. In this sense, Belgian political culture is closer to the Austrian variant of consociationalism than to the Dutch model, and even bears a surprising resemblance to Italian political culture (Deschouwer *et al.* 1996).

A second factor which explains differences between the two countries is the electoral system. The Dutch system is highly centralized, with the entire country in effect treated as a single constituency. This places national politicians at some distance from their electorate. By contrast, in Belgium 150 seats are contested across 20 constituencies, and this creates a much closer link between elected members and their voters. Indeed, Belgian national politicians are (like their French counterparts) embedded in municipal politics, the offices they hold at this level (councillors or mayors) helping to generate the popularity they need to contest national elections. Thus, Belgian parties are much more deeply entrenched in local politics, which further enhances the prospects for patronage and clientelism.

The third, and probably most important, difference between the two countries is Belgium's regional divide. This has had at least two effects. First, it has delayed depillarization, and to some extent even reinforced existing pillarization. The two parts of the country not only speak different languages, but also have very different political landscapes, with Christian Democracy dominant in the north and socialism dominant in the south. Regionalization has reinforced this ideological split, providing the two major partisan forces each with one part of the territory. State reform was to a great extent an affair of compromises between these two political families and, as parties of government, neither felt inclined to undermine the pillar structures which they utilized to organize state services. In short, the regional divide has kept pillarization alive and has maintained the two major parties' control over their pillars (Deschouwer 1999*a*). It is possible that the 1999 elections signal something of a turning point, at least in Flanders where the Christian Democrats lost their traditional status as the largest party and were ousted from government. However, the socialists narrowly retained their leading position in Wallonia, and the formation of new federal and regional governments followed the traditional political logic.

The second effect of the regional divide has been to reinforce the political dimension of consociationalism. Belgium has become, through a series of ongoing constitutional reforms initiated in 1963, a federal state. This federal state is highly consociational. It depends on constant power-sharing between the two linguistic communities, grants them far-reaching segmental (which is to say, territorial) autonomy, allows them mutual vetoes and relies on proportional allocation of the spoils of office. The political parties, which are all unilingual and uniregional, are obliged simultaneously to mobilize support in their respective segments and to bridge the gap between them at the federal level (Deschouwer 1999*b*). That is no easy task. Not surprisingly, perhaps, the governing parties are often criticized for being 'traitors' or for acting duplicitously. Until 1999 this was particularly the fate of the Flemish Christian Democrats (CVP) and the Walloon socialists (PS): since the change of coalition which followed the election, however, the Flemish Liberals (VLD) and, to a lesser extent, their Walloon counterparts (PRL) have also attracted such criticism. In order to keep political and social tensions to a minimum, the parties have always taken care to construct congruent coalitions: that is, they have formed the same coalitions at regional and federal levels. This, however, creates at least two problems for their political legitimacy. The first is that such coalitions cannot fully respond to changes in electoral support, since this varies across the two regional party systems. The second problem is that very broad, innovative, and cleavage-bridging coalitions have to be formed, thus trivializing publicized differences between the parties over policy. For instance, after the 1999 election, socialists and liberals governed together for the first time since 1954, after a prolonged period of fierce political debate between the two which had not even been attenuated in the preceding election campaign. Similarly, bridging the gap—especially over questions of security and immigration—between liberals and Greens is fraught with difficulty. Yet it has to be done for the sake of keeping the whole together. In an immediate sense this seems to work, but to the detriment of the legitimacy of the political system in general and of the political parties in particular.

PARTY LEGITIMACY

In Belgium—especially in Flanders—and the Netherlands there has been considerable public debate about the basic legitimacy of the respective political systems during the 1990s. In both countries it has become commonplace to speak of a 'gap' (*de kloof*) opening up between citizens and the political elites. That said, the problem of legitimacy is greater and far more salient in Belgium. A basic indication of this is furnished by the Eurobarometer survey's measurement of overall satisfaction with the way democracy works in the Low Countries: although popular sentiment has varied over time in both countries in this respect, the percentage claiming to be very or fairly satisfied has been consistently higher in the Netherlands (where it averages 67 per cent since 1973) than in Belgium (where it averages 56 per cent). Thus, the overall legitimacy of the Dutch political system is far higher than that of its Belgian neighbour, something which must be borne in mind when comparing the popular standing of political parties in the two countries. This is manifest, for instance, in the Eurobarometer data on party attachment; while the relevant figures fluctuate trendlessly since 1975, they do so from a much higher baseline in the Dutch case: on average some 77 per cent of Dutch respondents claim some kind of partisan attachment (32 per cent a 'close' attachment) while only 51 per cent of Belgians (22 per cent 'close') do (Schmitt and Holmberg 1995: 126–7: Eurobarometers 2346, 2490).

Voter turnout

Low turnout is a Dutch problem, as reference to Table 6.1 reveals. The steep drop in 1971 reflects the abolition of compulsory voting in the country, after which turnout levels soon recovered. In the 1990s, however, turnout dropped twice in succession. Moreover, a parallel decline in turnout at local elections has added to the impression that parties face a structural problem in mobilizing the vote. At the local elections of 1994 turnout was 65.3 per cent, but in 1998 it slumped to 59.5 per cent. The provincial elections—which indirectly produce the upper house of Parliament—generated a turnout of 52.3 per cent in 1991, 50.2 per cent in 1995 and 45.6 per cent in 1999. Turnout for the European elections of 1994 was 35.6 per cent, and just 29.9 per cent in 1999; only the UK (at 23.3 per cent) produced a lower turnout on the last occasion. These developments are of concern to politicians since they are often regarded as indicators that political elites are out of touch with electors. Consequently, proposals for institutional reform have surfaced (a theme to which we shall return).

By contrast, low turnout is not a problem in Belgium where voting is compulsory. Formally, electors are obliged to show up at the polling booth but not necessarily to vote, since blank or invalid votes may be cast. Election results in Belgium count blank and invalid votes together (unfortunately for scientific research), and unsurprisingly these figures tend to be higher than in countries where voting is not compulsory; however, they do not reveal any significant trends, fluctuating at around 8 per cent of the vote. That said, it should be noted that the obligation to turn out is no longer enforced in practice, which means that abstention has gradually become a *de facto* option, and here it is possible to discern signs of a very modest trend. By summing together all those not voting and those casting blank or invalid votes, we obtain a figure that stood at approximately 12 per cent of the electorate until 1985, before rising to 12.8 per cent in 1987, 13.7 per cent in 1991, and 15.7 per cent in 1995: in 1999 it fell slightly to 15.4 per cent, suggesting the slight increase in abstention might have reached a plateau.[4]

---

[4] Note that one effect of extreme and anti-system parties gaining in strength has been a renewed debate about compulsory voting in Belgium. Those proposing its abolition argue that it would afford anti-system voters the opportunity of abstaining, whereas they are currently more likely to turn out but vote for extremist parties. Such a reform would, however, constitute a constitutional change requiring a two-thirds majority in parliament. While the majority of parties (especially the Liberals and Greens) favour an end to compulsory voting, Vlaams Blok and the Socialists object, fearing that their voters might be particularly inclined to stay home, an impression reinforced by survey research (Ackaert and de Winter 1993; Hooghe and Pelleriaux 1998). This makes a change in the electoral law unlikely in the foreseeable future.

TABLE 6.6. *Party membership in the Netherlands*

	1960	1970	1980	1990	1999
KVP	385.500	97.300			
ARP	97.980	80.695			
CHU	43.873	28.900			
CDA			143.000	123.530	86.000
PvdA	142.853	98.671	112.929	91.784	61.600
VVD	35.000	38.000	85.881	59.074	51.265
D66		6.400	14.638	9.829	13.391
Groen-Links				15.900	13.821
SGP	12.300	15.400	20.300	23.062	23.800
GPV	6.311	8.702	12.922	12.917	14.121
SP					25.052
M/E	9.41	4.24	4.29	3.19	2.51

Note: M/E = Membership/Electorate ratio.

Sources: Voerman 1995; De Boer *et al.* 1997, 1998; Katz *et al.* 1992; Mair and van Biezen 2001.

Party membership

Membership decline is also primarily a Dutch problem. The traditional pillar parties there have never organized high numbers of card-carrying members. While the KVP enrolled as many as 7 per cent of its voters in the early postwar years (Andeweg 1999: 111), it subsequently became the party which suffered most from membership decline: while it claimed almost 400,000 members in 1959,[5] immediately prior to merging into the CDA in 1977 it reported only 54,000. Today the CDA has just 86,000 members, compared to almost 150,000 at the time of its foundation. By 1998 less than 3 per cent of voters in the Netherlands were party members, the lowest membership/electorate ratio in Europe (Katz *et al.* 1992). While some of the smaller parties (notably the SGP and the GPV) have gained members over the years, this does not compensate for the losses of the pillar parties (Table 6.6).

The collapse of party memberships is perceived as a problem: when added to the evidence of declining turnout, it seems to point to a structural difficulty for parties in inspiring citizens' interest in politics, mobilizing them, and acting as an effective channel for political participation. Hence, it is often taken as further evidence of the 'gap', or the disconnection between citizens and politics. Moreover, the parties are especially concerned because membership dues are their most important source of income (Koole 1994). Consequently, membership decline has activated a debate about the state funding of parties (a subject to which we return below).

In Belgium membership decline has not been an issue until recently. Indeed, prior to the 1980s Belgium seemed to be an exception to the rule of membership

---

[5] Note, however, that there are doubts about the reliability of these figures (Koole 1992: 167).

decline in western Europe (Katz *et al.* 1992): approximately 10 per cent of Belgian electors were card-carrying party members. It is interesting to note, however, that of the new regionalist political parties that emerged in the 1960s and 1970s—Volksunie, Rassemblement Wallon (RW), FDF, and Vlaams Blok—only the first really became a membership movement. RW disappeared rapidly, while the Brussels regionalist party FDF and the Flemish Vlaams Blok each now claim to have about 10,000 members—hardly an impressive figure. Similarly, neither of the two Green parties could claim to have become large membership organizations. After a prolonged period of relative stability in party membership numbers (probably explained largely by clientelism), a decline set in during the early 1990s. Since then, the figures have diminished for all except the Liberal parties, which have also been able to increase their electoral appeal. Table 6.7 clearly illustrates these developments.

As in the Dutch case, the numbers are decreasing in both real and relative terms. In 1980 the Belgian parties organized 9 per cent of the electorate, in 1990 8.3 per cent and in 1999 6.4 per cent. Nevertheless, this remains much higher than in the Netherlands: moreover, the decline of party memberships has not yet become an issue for public debate in Belgium, largely, perhaps, because parties there are far less dependent financially on their members, given that they are heavily subsidized by the state.

TABLE 6.7. *Party membership in Belgium*

	1960	1970	1980	1990	1999
CVP/PSC	213,751	—	—	—	—
CVP	—	103,158	125,141	131,719	92,000
PSC	—	39,336	57,904	43,322	28,942
SPB/PSB	199,000	225,073	—	—	—
SP	—	—	113,922	99,112	78,000
PS	—	—	154,798	153,400	109,194
PRL/PVV	48,200	77,654	—	—	—
VLD	—	—	58,625	71,051	80,000
PRL	—	—	45,000	40,000	39,000
VU	2511*	36,326	49,563	40,779	15,500
VL.BLOK.	—	—	1231	6500	14,000
AGALEV	—	—	925	2376	3772
ECOLO	—	—	1248	2096	2240
M/E	7.77	8.01	8.97	9.15	6.55

Note: M/E = Membership/Electorate ratio.
*Figure for 1961.

Sources: Maes; *Res Publica* Yearbooks; Party headquarters (1999 is most recent figure available: 97, 98, or 99); Katz *et al.* 1992; Mair and van Biezen 2001.

Partisan identification

There are no reliable time-series data for the Low Countries which are directly comparable to those from places such as the USA or Britain (Deschouwer 1992; Koole and van der Velde 1992). The best approximation is provided by the Eurobarometer series on party attachment which runs from 1975. This reveals relatively little change in the case of the Netherlands; the average percentage of Dutch respondents claiming some kind of attachment (including the 'very' and 'fairly' close as well as mere 'sympathisers') in the 1970s was 75.6, whereas it was 77.4 in the 1980s and 76.2 in the 1990s. If we exclude sympathizers, however, there is evidence of a slight decline in the number of those with a close attachment: on average 36 per cent of Dutch respondents claimed this status in the 1970s, but this fell to 31.8 per cent in the 1980s and 28.4 per cent in the 1990s, the first marked fall (from 33 to 25 per cent) occurring in 1981. In the Belgian case, the erosion of partisan sentiment is somewhat more clear-cut, at least in so far as the closely attached categories are concerned. Whereas an average of 27.6 per cent of Belgian respondents could be classified thus in the 1980s, this fell to 19.8 per cent in the 1980s and 20.6 per cent in the 1990s. The overall numbers including sympathizers show less obvious decline, with the 1970s average of 53.6 per cent dropping to 48.4 per cent in the 1980s before recovering very slightly to 51.6 per cent in the 1990s (Schmitt and Holmberg 1995: 126–7).

Bridging the 'gap'

Indications of electoral volatility, support for the far right (in Belgium at least), membership and turnout decline, have been taken as evidence of a legitimacy problem by political elites and media commentators in both countries. Many agree that institutional changes have to be introduced in order to enhance participatory opportunities for citizens. In particular, debates about institutional renewal focus very much on the electoral system and the use of referenda.

In October 1995, the Dutch government (supported by D66, a party created to pursue the idea of institutional innovation) proposed reforms in both of these areas. With respect to the electoral system, a number of revisions were envisaged. In order to combat the supposed gulf between voters and office-holders, the government wanted to introduce a new 'two-vote' system, according to which half the seats would be distributed in the existing 'national' way, and the other half through five regional lists. Although this proposal was ultimately not enacted, the voters were handed a greater say in determining the list-order of party candidates: under the old system, a candidate required a number of preference votes equal to 50 per cent of the simple quota in order to be elected 'autonomously', but this threshold was now lowered to 25 per cent. In addition, polling stations were to remain open later and mobile polling stations were introduced in order to facilitate voting outside people's home districts. As we have seen, however, these changes did not prevent turnout from falling further at the national and local elections of 1998, nor at the European elections of 1999. Similarly, the reduction of the personal preference threshold for a candidate to be elected had a very limited effect: just one CDA candidate managed to break the party-established list-order in this way in 1998 (Koole 1999).

The second element of the Cabinet's plan for institutional renewal was to be the introduction of 'corrective' referenda, which would have permitted citizens to challenge decisions taken by the national parliament, provincial councils, or local councils. This proposal triggered long and complex debate, the VVD proving especially reluctant to approve. This was highly problematic since the reform would have required a constitutional change. When the Senator (and former VVD Minister) Hans Wiegel refused to accept the proposal in 1998, it failed to achieve the necessary two-thirds majority of the upper house. After a Cabinet crisis over the issue, it was agreed that a diluted form of the original proposal would be piloted through parliament as ordinary legislation which did not require a formal constitutional change. The principle was also accepted that referenda could be organized and would be regarded as binding by governments, although this settlement was not enshrined in a formal constitutional change.

In Belgium debate about institutional change (independent of regionalization) has been much more intensive. Particularly after 1991 and the breakthrough of the extreme-right, the 'gap' made its way into political discourse and generated plans for change within parties (Deschouwer 1999b) and political procedures. As in the Netherlands, the electoral system has often been the focus. Earlier we noted the debate about the abolition of compulsory voting, but there are other ways in which critics regard electoral procedures as hampering the (party-mediated) relationship between citizens and politics. For instance, the regional list system is believed by many to be 'too localist', and to encourage clientelism. Flemish critics tend to see the Dutch model of 'national' list-PR as a solution (which is ironic given that many Dutch politicians view it as a cause of the 'gap'). Francophone politicians— especially Liberals—would generally prefer a real majoritarian system, at least for regional elections.[6]

The electoral system is also regarded as handing too much power to party elites and managers. This is most obvious in relation to the way in which the list-order of candidates is determined. Generally, party leaderships draft electoral lists, and candidates are elected in the stated order of the list. Voters can (and almost 50 per cent of them do) cast a simple party preference, thus confirming the preset list-order. Proposals to reduce or to neutralize the weight of this list-vote abound, and the government formed in 1999 promised to give serious consideration to the issue. A related concern has emerged with respect to lists of 'successor-candidates'.

---

[6] Party political considerations may be at play here, since the Liberals sense the chance of marginalizing the Christian Democrats in Wallonia and creating a bipolar party system of competition between the Socialists and themselves.

If a member of parliament has to be replaced (usually because he or she enters government), then the first-named candidate of this separately elected list enters parliament, rather than the highest-placed 'loser' on the original list of 'effective' candidates. This procedure allows parties to control carefully the composition of their parliamentary groups. While some, such as the Flemish Liberals, would like to get rid of the system, it is very unlikely that other parties will allow this mechanism of party control to disappear.

During the 1999 elections (held at regional, federal (both houses), and European levels) a new problem appeared. Parties tended to present their most popular candidates on lists at more than one level; these individuals would often win several offices, but only take up the most appropriate, leaving the others to candidates from successor-lists. While the Flemish Liberals once again protested against this practice prior to the elections, most parties subsequently exploited it when constructing regional and federal coalitions: that is, the governing parties simply used their overall pools of office-holders to fill positions across the various levels of government. For instance, four out of the twenty-four elected MEPs (all top-placed candidates on their respective lists) resigned to take up ministerial posts at regional or federal levels, while none of the three regional Prime ministers were actually elected at the regional level. Media commentators criticized these practices heavily, but the parties found it a useful way of maintaining congruence between coalitions at different levels and managing the distribution of their office-holding personnel. Once more, however, the exigencies of managing this complex system of party politics carried a price in terms of popular legitimacy.

Certain reforms, it should be noted, have been accepted and implemented. Since 1995 voters have been allowed to cast more than one preference vote on the same list. It has had little effect, however, in that the party-defined list-order still overwhelmingly determines which candidates are elected. In addition, referenda have been introduced at local and provincial levels. Not only can political executives call referenda at these levels, but so may electors when at least 10 per cent of them petition for it. This measure was introduced in 1996, and immediately generated some ten local referenda. Although the results are not legally binding, the practice has been to regard them as such. At the national level, however, the referendum is fraught with difficulty: while the government formed in 1999 decided to investigate the possibility of consultative federal referenda, in a divided country like Belgium, such a purely majoritarian device is a potentially dangerous instrument. Issues relating to the regional divide would have to be avoided, but in reality, few issues in Belgium are *not* politicized around this fault-line.

The Belgian legitimacy crisis

It is evident from the foregoing discussion that there are some parallels between Belgium and the Netherlands, but it is equally clear that the Belgian crisis runs much deeper. Indeed, there is much more to it than declining party membership numbers and the rise of an extremist right-wing party. Overall trust in Belgian political institutions has always tended to be lower than average, but a number of events in recent years have shaken it further and provoked widespread protest against the party political establishment.

The crisis has come in waves. The first major blow was the 1991 elections, when Vlaams Blok broke through in Flanders. This was widely seen as proof that Belgian politics in general, and parties in particular, needed change and renewal. The most spectacular response came from the Flemish Liberal Party (PVV), which adopted a new name (VLD) in 1992 and sought explicitly to distance itself from the old mainstream. They fiercely attacked the two major pillarized party families, the Christian Democrats and Socialists, and promoted a number of institutional reforms. In particular, they wanted to stop patronage, clientelism and the firm hold of the two other major party families and their affiliated organizations over the public administration. Parties, they said, should defend the general interest rather than their own. However, the renewal of the Flemish Liberals failed to result in electoral gains, which undermined the momentum of this party change.

Nevertheless, the VLD was able to dominate the political agenda with its reform-oriented discourse. Moreover, the legitimacy of Belgian parties was further damaged by a number of scandals relating to party finance. These centred initially on the Walloon Socialists (PS), when investigations into the murder of the former party leader André Cools in 1991 led to the discovery of secret accounts showing considerable donations paid by the Italian firm Agusta, which (in 1988) had won a very substantial order to supply helicopters to the Belgian army. High-ranking PS officials and former Ministers had already been convicted for illegal party funding operations a few years earlier; this case, however, became much bigger, and also involved the Flemish Socialists (SP), whose former Economics Minister, Willy Claes, was obliged to resign from his current post as Secretary-General of NATO. The first arrests relating to this affair were made just before the 1995 elections, but did not immediately produce heavy electoral losses.[7] If anything, the legitimacy crisis seemed to recede.

It returned with a vengeance, however, when Marc Dutroux, the notorious serial killer of young girls, was arrested in August 1996. It quickly became clear that he could have been arrested much earlier, had the police and judiciary functioned adequately. Their blatant incompetence was not new, nor indeed was it limited to the forces of law and order, but the fact that children were its innocent victims on this occasion inspired a highly emotional and widespread popular reaction. In October 1996 some 300,000 citizens participated in Brussels' 'White March', the largest demonstration ever seen in the country. An impressive show of support for the parents of Dutroux's victims, it was also a peaceful but angry condemnation

---

[7] It was not until a few months before the 1999 elections that Claes, another ex-minister, the former PS party president and a number of their collaborators, were proven guilty of corruption by the Court of Cassation in the Agusta case.

of the Belgian state and its failing politicians, heaping the blame upon them for all
the energy they spent on the language issue and questions of institutional reform.
Not one single traditional organization (parties, trade unions, or pressure groups)
had mobilized for it.

This diverse movement did not, however, survive. Attempts were made to create
a local network of 'White Committees', but after a few months it became clear that
this would not succeed (Hooghe 1997; Walgrave and Rihoux 1997). Neither could
existing movements or parties exploit the political opportunity presented by the
protest: the most anti-establishment party, Vlaams Blok, was deterred by the fact
that one of Dutroux's supposed victims was a Moroccan girl,[8] and public sympathy was clearly extended to all the victims. One of the victims' parents decided
to form his own political party, but this polled a mere 0.2 per cent of the national
vote in 1999.

That said, this decade of turmoil and scandal has left its mark on the parties.
Initially, the mood of crisis struck Flanders, but the Dutroux case and the Agusta
affair, being centred on Wallonia, carried it easily across the language border.
When, in 1997, Marc Dutroux was able to escape from two unarmed gendarmes
(albeit only for a few hours), the angry public reaction generated plans for a
thorough reform of the police force, and the depoliticization of the judiciary. This
was perhaps the most spectacular instance of political reaction to the crisis of
legitimacy, but it was not the only example. Since 1991 many politicians have
publicly abandoned clientelistic practices, and slowly but surely appointments
and promotions in the public sector have come to be based on competence and
merit rather than party affiliation. At local level, however, change has been less
impressive in this respect (see below).

STRENGTH OF PARTY ORGANIZATIONS

The Belgian and Dutch parties have been extensively described and analysed
elsewhere (Koole and van der Velde 1992; Koole 1994; Deschouwer 1992, 1994).
It should, therefore, be sufficient to summarize and discuss the main developments,
and to highlight some striking differences between the two countries.

The Dutch parties generally have two very distinctive 'faces' (Katz and Mair
1994): the central party organization and the parliamentary party. The importance
of the latter, in particular, differentiates Dutch parties from their Belgian counterparts. Rising salaries for MPs in the late 1960s, and the subsequent subsidies given
to them in order to hire professional assistance, has inflated the size and importance
of the parliamentary group. Furthermore, the group leader is the most important
individual in the party. He or she is the number one candidate on a party's electoral

---

[8] Subsequently, it became clear that she was not in fact murdered by Marc Dutroux.

list, and is the primary candidate for governmental office, the leading spokesperson for the party, and its chief coalition negotiator. Parliamentary debates are important, even if in practice party discipline is high and decisions originate to a great extent from governmental proposals.

Central party organizations are generally less important in the Netherlands. Party presidents are administrative leaders, responsible for the relations with the membership and for internal organization. As noted, declining membership enrolment is an important fact of political life in the country, and the Dutch parties have been looking for ways of making membership more attractive, for instance, by offering individual members participatory incentives, though it remains unclear how far these initiatives will really impact on party decision-making (Koole 1999).

Central party organizations are not rich. The Dutch parties receive state subsidies for their parliamentary work, but very little money for other activities: extra-parliamentary subsidies are actually given directly to organizations whose purposes are scientific research and education. These bodies are generally very active and productive, but maintain a certain independence from the parties. Surprisingly, perhaps, in view of their dwindling numbers, party members manage to provide some 60 per cent of party incomes. Other sources of funding are scarce: donations from individuals and (especially) corporations, are not common practice, in part, perhaps, because the parties impose very strict rules designed to prohibit the potential for corruption. However, if we take income to parliamentary and extra-parliamentary organizations into consideration, the overall funding available to Dutch parties grew in real terms across the 1970s and 1980s: to compare two election years, for instance, their average income was 1,132,498 guilders in 1972, but 2,110,130 guilders in 1986 (at constant 1972 prices), a real terms increase of 86 per cent. Similarly, average expenditure almost exactly doubled, as it grew from 1,352,284 to 2,697,947 guilders at constant prices.[9]

Throughout the 1990s there was considerable debate about whether or not to raise state subsidies to political parties in the Netherlands. In 1995 a proposal to give each party a single grant to be used as it chose met with considerable criticism. The party-affiliated study centres feared that they would receive less money by such a system, as money would inevitably be channelled into campaigning rather than research, while increasing their dependence on the parties. After three years of discussion in the Cabinet and parliament, a revised system of party finance was finally introduced in 1998. This increased the total sum of state aid from 8 to 10 million guilders, and directed subsidies to the parties, while imposing strict limitations on its use: in particular, parties were obliged to deploy a fixed element on research, education, and youth organizations. These funds are

[9] These calculations are derived from figures reported in Koole and van der Velde (1992). Price deflators are taken from the World Bank's 'World Tables' 1992. The ARP, CDU and ARP are counted as a single party in order to maintain consistency with the situation in 1986, by which time they had merged into the CDA. Unavailability of data for the VVD and PSP in 1972 means that they have been excluded from the average expenditure calculations.

distributed proportionally according to the number of seats each party holds in the Lower House and not—as was suggested in the course of the discussion—on the basis of the party members (Hippe *et al.* 1995, 1996; De Boer *et al.* 1997, 1998). Overall, this revision has not changed matters greatly, although the parties have a little extra money now to finance campaigns. These seem set to become more expensive, especially as parties have been able to buy time on commercial radio and television stations during election campaigns since 1994.

Compared to Dutch parties, the Belgian parties are extremely big and rich. The parties outside parliament, and their leaders (the party presidents) are generally much more important than their Dutch counterparts. For one thing, the presidents are both organizational managers and political leaders: group leaders in the various parliaments are important politicians, but clearly subordinate to the party presidents. The presidency is therefore a critical position within each party, vital to coordinating the parties' roles in the different levels of government (see below). Imitating the procedure that was introduced in 1992 in Flanders by the Liberal Party, and that was already used by the Francophone Liberals and Christian Democrats, all party presidents are now directly elected by the members (except for the Vlaams Blok, where the first leader was a president for life, having the right to choose his successor alone): this development has only served to enhance yet further the power of party presidents (see also Koole 1999 on the Netherlands). All of this means that the presidents, their personal entourages of advisors and extra-parliamentary parties in general are inevitably well resourced.

Unlike the Dutch parties, moreover, Belgian parties are not hindered by a strict financial division between parliamentary parties and central party organizations. Although technically money arrives on different accounts, the normal practice is to pool all resources and to use them for whatever purpose seems useful. This makes the financial reports of the parties very difficult to read and compare. We will therefore not attempt to disaggregate by party, but seek instead to provide an idea of the overall resources available to the parties.

The general rule is that state subsidies are distributed proportionally. The Belgian parties receive subsidies for their parliamentary groups. They receive money and indirect subsidies for party (group) personnel that are paid directly by the Parliament. These subsidies are paid to parliamentary parties in both federal Houses and also in the regional Parliaments, totalling in excess of one billion Belgian francs (or 50 million guilders) in 1990 (Van Bunder 1993). Such payments by the state have been increased on a regular basis since first introduced in 1971 (Deschouwer 1993). Overall, there is no doubt that the total sum of money distributed to parties by the state has constantly been increasing.

After the scandals relating to party finance, the Belgian parties imposed upon themselves a very strict but also a very generous party finance law in 1991. Individual donations are now limited to a meagre 80,000 Belgian francs per year, and all other donations—which were widespread hitherto—are now absolutely prohibited. In addition to the subsidies paid to the federal and regional parliamentary groups, the Belgian state contributes a further 5 million francs and 50 francs per voter (in the most recent Lower House elections) per year to each party head office. This adds another 700 million francs per year to the total subsidies which are paid out to the parties: this equates to 35 million Dutch guilders, compared with the 10 million guilders received by the Dutch parties. This money is used for a variety of purposes, including political education and research centres, communication and campaigning, parliamentary staffing, and central party organizations. Nevertheless, the new party finance law limits very strictly the amount of money that can be used for campaign purposes, which serves to reduce the extent and cost of campaigns.

THE SYSTEMIC FUNCTIONALITY OF PARTIES

Governance and recruitment

What Katz calls the 'partyness of government' (1986) is undoubtedly very high in both countries. The cabinets are constructed by party leaders, and cabinet ministers are all leading party politicians. The parties follow closely the activities of the cabinet, and may intervene to renegotiate crucial points. Until the 1950s non-party politicians occasionally held ministerial posts in the Netherlands, but this last occurred in 1956. The last attempt to include a 'technician' in government in Belgium took place in 1991, but the minister resigned after a year in office, being unable to function within the logic of party politics. We can thus say that parties govern in the sense of monopolizing the process of recruitment to executive office (Andeweg 1988, 1992, 1996; De Winter 1993, 1996).

The electoral and parliamentary arenas are similarly dominated by party personnel. The parliamentary groups are the basic organizational structures of national assemblies, though at the sub-national level the picture of party domination has to be qualified, and differences between the Netherlands and Belgium become apparent. In general, sub-national (especially provincial) politics is not especially important in the former: Andeweg and Irwin (1993: 163) point out that, 'it is perhaps telling, that in Dutch, local politics is usually referred to as local *administration*, and that it is considered an appropriate object of study for students of public administration rather than for political scientists'. The national parties do not play such a central role in local politics in the Netherlands, where local problems usually define the agenda;[10] nevertheless, they still tend to provide the personnel of local executives since it is the norm to construct 'mirror coalitions' which allocate

[10] If anything, this has become more pronounced in recent years, with the development of a notable 'anti-national' reaction in many local councils: indeed, real local parties have started to win a significant number of seats. This phenomenon has existed for some time in rural areas—especially in the south—but has now spread to some important cities, such as Rotterdam. Moreover, a Frisian Nationalist Party has gained representation on the Frieseland provincial assembly (Andeweg and Irwin 1993: 159). This

positions in such a way as to reflect proportionally the composition of the local council. In larger cities competitive party politics plays a more significant role, but some 75 per cent of local executives still follow this proportional logic (Tops 1990). Mayors play an important role in local politics, but again they are appointed by the national government for a six-year term (the term of the council being only four years): the top executive posts are thus not at stake in local elections, but rather are derivatives of national coalitional politics. Indeed, in the more important cities the mayor is often a national politician, which further facilitates the division of spoils between parties.

The local political arena in Belgium is much more politicized and lacks the consensus flavour that is so striking in the Netherlands. The electoral formula used at local level—Imperiali divisors (see Farrell 2001: 73)—enhances the majoritarian nature of local politics in Belgium by affording leading parties good prospects of winning overall majorities on councils. While technically the federal government appoints mayors, as in the Netherlands, this is only for the term of the local council and it is usual for the local majority (coalition or single-party) to propose a candidate to the Interior Minister: unless there are legal obstacles, this nominee becomes the mayor. Thus, the highest executive position is genuinely at stake in local elections in Belgium. Furthermore, many mayors are national politicians, who combine this function with a parliamentary mandate. Overall, it is clear that national, regional, and local politics are highly inter-connected, and the connecting devices are the political parties.[11]

In general, parties are much more central to governance at all levels in Belgium. They penetrate deeper into the institutions of government and 'fuse' them, controlling both the institutions themselves and relations between them. At the federal, and only to a slightly lesser degree at the regional level, parliaments and executives are closely linked. Whereas in the Netherlands there is a more dynamic and sometimes not entirely predictable relationship between cabinets and parliamentary parties, in Belgium the parliamentary groups are very docile followers of the central party leaderships. This reflects the fact that the highly complex nature of the Belgian state obliges the parties to keep the regional and federal levels connected. In effect, both federal and regional elections are regional contests between regional parties, and in the absence of federal parties, these regional parties have to act as the link between regional and federal levels (in both executive and legislative arenas). Thus, the parties control the drafting of the election lists, decide who will accept which seat and who will be in which government. Whatever happens at one level impacts on the other. Whether a matter is discussed in one of the

shows that at the political levels where party penetration has traditionally been weaker, the national parties have been susceptible to the challenge of new and alternative parties.

[11] That said, in smaller administrative entities purely local lists are not uncommon. Typically, these are electoral coalitions which unite small parties in order to enhance their prospects of gaining representation under what is a very unproportional electoral system (Buelens 1993; Ackaert 1990).

parliaments, in one of the governments, in the formal 'Concertation Committee' between federal and regional governments, or in an informal conference on reform of the state, the crucial players will always be the parties (and primarily the party presidents).

The penetration of the Belgian parties goes well beyond the parliamentary and executive arenas. Locally, the parties remain strongly in control, although the practice of 'political' appointments is slowly fading. It is, however, a process that will take time, since incumbent employees in local administrations have mostly been recruited and promoted according to the old principle of proportional 'lottiz-zazione'. At the regional and national level depoliticization has progressed further. Nevertheless, 'ministerial cabinets' persist, and these afford each minister the support of a personal staff recruited on an almost purely party-political basis. As in France, cabinet staff are often recruited from the civil service, from which they eventually return if the minister or the party does not retain a position in office. The cabinets provide an important link between ministers and the public administration, and effectively relieve the latter of significant tasks of policy preparation and implementation. At the same time they constitute one more way of employing party staff at the expense of the state. Recent governments have attempted to reduce the size of these personal staffs, and have succeeded to some extent, but such change is slow and incremental.

This penetration of public administration by the parties is absent in the Netherlands. The Dutch administration and indeed the whole process of decision-making is functionally decentralized (Andeweg and Irwin 1993: 164), displaying a comparatively high degree of neo-corporatism. There are a large number of councils, advisory boards, and commissions in which pressure groups negotiate and meet with the administration. Formally they do not decide, but their counsel is difficult to ignore since it comes from experts and specialists. Functional decentralization is also generally a characteristic of the public administration itself, with fairly autonomous departments calling on their own specialized professionals. In this administrative patchwork, the parties have but a small role to play. Although they were once more prominent, in the days when pressure groups were often clearly linked to particular social pillars and their corresponding parties, today such connections have been eroded.

This functionally decentralized mode of decision-making has consequences for the legitimacy and credibility of Dutch political parties, as it pushes them towards an implementing rather than a decision-making role. This carries implications for democratic accountability: with the 'primacy of the political' undermined, who controls the real decision-makers? Who takes responsibility if something goes wrong with a public policy? This is a difficult problem for Dutch parties to resolve, not least because neo-corporatist practices are widely believed to be crucial ingredients of the successful 'polder model' of economic policy (see, for instance, Griffiths 1980; Scholten 1987; Wolinetz 1989; Keman and Pennings 1995).

Neo-corporatist practices in Belgium are more party-centred, with membership of commissions and advisory boards still based largely on party or pillar affiliations. Nevertheless, the system has deteriorated in respect of the main socio-economic partnerships: in particular, the once very solid ties between the two largest parties and, respectively, the Socialist and the Christian trade union federations, have become far looser and sometimes problematic. Since the 1980s governments have found it increasingly hard to associate the trade unions with their preferred economic and financial policies: repeated attempts to reach consensus on overarching strategies have failed, due especially to the reluctance of the socialist unions. As a consequence, governments have been increasingly inclined to pull social and economic policy into their sphere of real decision-making. Policies are made with the support of the unions if possible, but against them if needs be. Thus, parties have become increasingly autonomous of the unions in the sphere of governance.

One final, but highly significant, comment is needed on the decision-making power of parties (or any other actors) in Belgium and the Netherlands. Both are small countries with very export-oriented economies, and both are founder-members of the European Union (EU). In effect, the EU has become the major source of policy. Indeed, approximately 50 per cent of national legislation is constituted by the national interpretation and implementation of EU regulations. This restricts the autonomy of national governments considerably, especially in the fields of economic and financial policy. This erosion of national competences poses a major legitimacy problem for the political parties, especially in small countries that cannot even think of influencing international markets. Irrespective of which coalition governs, national policy is unlikely to change substantially. This has been amply illustrated in both countries. The centre–right coalitions of the 1980s were followed by centre–left coalitions and then by coalitions which omitted the centre and built the 'purple' arch between socialism and liberalism, but the thrust of economic policy altered little. For Belgium in particular the EU pressure has had far-reaching consequences. The EMU convergence criteria proved extremely difficult to satisfy, and an exception was made to allow Belgium membership of EMU, since it had a public debt that exceeded the country's GDP. Public expenditure cuts were imposed, first by centre–right, and then by centre–left governments. One of the richer ironies of contemporary Belgian politics is that both the Liberals and the Socialists now refer to Tony Blair as their role model for a 'third way' and an 'active welfare state'.

Linkage functions: participation, aggregation, and communication

The discussion of party legitimacy and organization shows that parties are going through hard times in the Low Countries, notwithstanding the very high 'partyness' of government and administration which endures, especially in Belgium. When we turn to societal linkages, it is apparent that parties no longer play a major role. Indeed, given the very low and still decreasing number of party members, it seems that they barely exist as societal organizations. The internal life of parties in the Low Countries typically revolves around very few people, most of them linked in one way or another to parties' governing functions within the national or sub-national state. The picture of declining turnout, in the Netherlands at least, merely serves to reinforce this sense of growing irrelevance of parties for inspiring political participation.

In both countries we have witnessed a gradual but nonetheless spectacular decline of the major centre party. The growing fragmentation of party systems in the Low Countries mean that leading parties there are now very small. Belgium's largest party is currently the VLD, polling exactly 14.3 per cent of the Belgian and 22.6 per cent of the Flemish vote. In both respects, this makes the VLD Belgium's smallest ever largest party! In the Netherlands the largest party—today the PvdA—polls just 29 per cent. This reduced size of the major parties complicates the task of interest aggregation and generates a need for increasingly inventive coalition building. Yet the parties struggle to respond to the demands of the electorate; in the Netherlands they are criticized for their 'remoteness', for the gap they leave between state and citizen, a problem which seems to generate new levels of voter apathy. In Belgium, where voters are legally disbarred from disengaging in this manner, protest parties have gained momentum, helped by the ever-problematic relations between the linguistic communities. Moreover, the ethnic cleavage has fostered state structures so complex that parties are not able to act as responsible intermediates between voters and the state. Parties find themselves caught between the rival demands of the communities as the classic consociational model comes under pressure.

Increasingly independent media add to these problems. All party press have disappeared, and radio and television are by no means under party control (Kleinnijenhuis and Scholten 1989). While the parties do have limited access to public radio and television time, such broadcasts attract very small audiences. In Belgium, the press is apt to blame the parties—those in government, at least—for the double role they play in seeking to express group interests while simultaneously building consociational alliances. The parties are given little credit for having to play such a precarious two-level game, and find themselves accused of inconsistency, a charge to which they are highly vulnerable. The ambiguities of this two-level game are not present in the Netherlands, and we have seen that the legitimacy crisis there is indeed less deep. Even so, Dutch parties are also at the mercy of an independent media. Newspapers no longer have links with parties, and the once neatly pillarized system of radio and television has gone. Although the former party- and religion-related broadcasting companies continue to exist, they are confronted by independent competitors. These are the channels through which the parties are now obliged to communicate, channels which they do not control.

CONCLUSION

On most counts, political parties have been struggling in the Low Countries. Their popular standing has been eroded in both Belgium and the Netherlands, but especially the former where a fully-fledged systemic crisis has developed. This crisis has not yet destroyed the state-derived organizational strength of Belgian parties, though it has led to its curtailment. Dutch parties have never been as wealthy as their Belgian counterparts, largely because they have squeezed fewer resources out of the state. The problems parties face in these countries reflects in part the functional challenges which confront them. These challenges are most evident in respect of the linkage functions of political communication, interest articulation and aggregation, and the mobilizing of citizen participation, none of which should surprise us in the context of depillarization and the erosion of consociationalism. On the other hand, parties remain central to processes of political recruitment and governance, though even here the challenges of Europeanization, globalization, and (in Belgium) systemic crisis have had a significant impact. For if parties wish to continue playing a central role in the political system, they have to be able to explain how and why they matter. Their capacity to make substantial differences to policy outputs being limited, they tend to rely on two other factors by which they might distinguish themselves—personality and style. This has been the strategy of both purple coalitions, especially in Belgium. The limited capacity to affect substantial policy-making may also explain the obsession with procedures (witness the endless debates about electoral reform). Yet the problem lies not so much in the manner of election, as in the great difficulty that parties have in explaining why elections really matter.

APPENDIX

List of parties

Belgium

Agalev	Anders Gaan Leven: Flemish Greens
SP	Socialistische Partij: Flemish Socialists
CVP	Christelijke Volkspartij: Flemish Christian Democrats
VLD	Vlaamse Liberalen en Democraten: Flemish Liberals
VU	Volksunie: Flemish Nationalists
Vlaams Blok	Flemish right-wing populists
PS	Parti Socialiste: Francophone Socialists
PSC	Parti Social Chrétien: Francophone Christian Democrats
PRL	Parti Réformateur Libéral: Francophone Liberals

FDF   Front Démocratique des Francophones: Brussels Francophone
                regionalists
ECOLO   Ecologistes: Francophone Greens
FN   Front National: Francophone right-wing populists

Netherlands

CDA   Christen-Democratisch Appèl: Christian Democrats
VVD   Volkspartij voor Vrijheid en Democratie: Liberals
PvdA   Partij van de Arbeid: Socialists
Groen-Links   Red–Green cartel
SP   Socialistische Partij: Left socialists
D66   Democraten 66: Left liberals
ARP   Anti-revolutionaire Partij: Reformed Protestant (merged into
                CDA)
CHU   Christelijk-historische Unie: Protestant (merged into CDA)
KVP   Katholieke Volkspartij: Catholics (merged into CDA)
GVP   Gereformeerd Politiek Verbond: Orthodox Protestant
SGP   Staatkundig Gereformeerde Partij: Orthodox Protestant

REFERENCES

Ackaert, J. (1990) 'Imperiali, d'Hondt, Niemeyer als verdelingstechnieken bij de gemeenteraadsverkiezingen'. *Res Publica* 32: 537–56.

—— and de Winter, L. (1993) 'De afwezigen hebben andermaal ongelijk. De stemverzaking in Vlaanderen op 24 November 1991', in M. Swyngedouw, J. Billiet *et al.* (eds) *Kiezen is verliezen. Onderzoek naar de politieke opvattingen van Vlamingen* (Leuven: Acco), pp. 67–82.

Andeweg, R. B. (1988) 'The Netherlands: coalition cabinets in changing circumstances', in J. Blondel and F. Müller-Rommel (eds) *Cabinets in Western Europe* (London: Macmillan), pp. 47–67.

—— (1992) 'Executive-legislative relations in the Netherlands: consecutive and coexisting patterns'. *Legislative Studies Quarterly* 17: 161–82.

—— and Irwin, G. A. (1993) *Dutch Government and Politics* (Basingstoke: Macmillan).

—— (1996) 'The Netherlands: parties between power and principle', in J. Blondel and M. Cotta (eds) *Parties and Government: An Inquiry into the Relationship Between Government and Supporting Parties in Liberal Democracies* (Basingstoke: Macmillan), pp. 128–52.

—— (1999) 'Parties, pillars and the politics of accommodation: weak or weakening linkages? The case of Dutch consociationalism', in K. R. Luther and K. Deschouwer (eds) *Party Elites in Divided Societies. Political Parties in Consociational Democracy.* (London: Routledge), pp. 108–33.

Bartolini, S. and Mair, P. (1990) *Identity, Competition, and Electoral Availability: The Stabilization of European Electorates 1885–1985* (Cambridge: Cambridge University Press).

Billiet, J. (1981) 'Kenmerken en grondslagen van het sociaal-cultureel katholicisme', in J. Servaes (ed.) *Van ideologie tot macht. Doorlichting van de bewustzijnsindustrie in Vlaanderen* (Leuven: Kritiak), pp. 29–62.

Buelens, J. (1993) 'Coalitievorming op gemeentelijk vlak'. *Tijdschrift van het Gemeentekrediet* 47: 45–66.

Bunder, D. van (1993) *Officiële inkomsten van politieke partijen en hun parlementaire fracties*. (Brussels: Centrum voor Politicologie, Vrije Universiteit Brussel).

De Boer, B., Lucardie, P. *et al.* (1997) 'Kroniek 1997. Overzicht van de partijpolitieke gebeurtenissen van het jaar 1997'. *Jaarboek 1997* (Groningen: Documentatiecentrum Nederlandse Politieke Partijen), pp. 13–90.

——, —— (1998) 'Kroniek 1998. Overzicht van de partijpolitieke gebeurtenissen van het jaar 1998'. *Jaarboek 1998* (Groningen: Documentatiecentrum Nederlandse Politieke Partijen), pp. 14–94.

De Winter, L. (1993) 'The links between cabinets and parties and cabinet decision-making', in J. Blondel and F. Müller-Rommel (eds) *Governing Together: The Extent and Limits of Joint Decision-Making in Western European Cabinets* (New York: St. Martin's Press), pp. 153–76.

—— (1996) 'Party encroachment on the executive and legislative branch in the Belgian polity'. *Res Publica* 38: 235–52.

Deschouwer, K. (1990) 'Patterns of participation and competition in Belgium', in P. Mair and G. Smith (eds) *Understanding Party System Change in Western Europe* (London: Frank Cass), pp. 28–41.

—— (1992) 'Belgium', in R. S. Katz and P. Mair (eds) *Party Organizations: A Data Handbook on Party Organizations in Western Democracies, 1960–90* (London: Sage Publications), pp. 121–98.

—— (1993) *Organiseren of bewegen? De evolutie van de Belgische partijstructuren sinds 1960* (Brussel: VUB Press).

—— (1994) 'The decline of consociationalism and the reluctant modernization of the Belgian mass parties', in R. S. Katz and P. Mair (eds) *How Parties Organize: Adaptation and Change in Party Organizations in Western Democracies* (London: Sage Publications), pp. 80–108.

—— (1999a) 'From consociation to federation: how the Belgian parties won', in K. R. Luther and K. Deschouwer (eds) *Party Elites in Divided Societies: Political Parties in Consociational Democracy* (London: Routledge), pp. 74–107.

—— (1999b) 'In der Falle gefangen. Belgiens Parteien und ihre Reaktionen auf abnehmende Wählerloyalitäten', in P. Mair, WC W. Müller, and F. Plasser (eds) *Parteien auf komplexen Wählermärkten. Reaktionsstrategien politischer Parteien in Westeuropa* (Wien: ZAP), pp. 281–314.

—— De Winter, L., and Porta, D. D. (1996) 'Partitocracies between crises and reform: the cases of Italy and Belgium'. *Res Publica* 38(2).

Dobbelare, K. (1988) *Het 'Volk-Gods' de mist in? Over de kerk in België* (Leuven: Acco).

Farrell, D. (2001) *Electoral Systems: A Comparative Introduction* (Basingstoke: Palgrave).

Griffiths, R. T. (1980) *The Economy and Politics of the Netherlands since 1945* (Den Haag: Martinus Nijhoff).

Hippe, J. and Lucardie, P. *et al.* (1995) 'Kroniek 1995. Overzicht van de partijpolitieke gebeurtenissen van het jaar 1995'. *Jaarboek 1995* (Groningen: Documentatiecentrum Nederlandse Politieke Partijen), pp. 14–91.

——, —— (1996) 'Kroniek 1996. Overzicht van de partijpolitieke gebeurtenissen van het jaar 1996'. *Jaarboek 1996* (Groningen: Documentatiecentrum Nederlandse Politieke Partijen), pp. 13–86.

Hooghe, M. (1997) *Het witte ongenoegen. Hoop en illusie van een uniek experiment* (Groot-Bijgaarden, Globe).

—— and Pelleriaux, K. (1998) 'Compulsory voting in Belgium: an application of the Lijphart thesis'. *Electoral Studies* 17: 419–42.

Huyse, L. (1987) *De verzuiling voorbij* (Leuven: Kritak).

Katz, R. S. (1986) 'Party government: a rationalistic conception', in Francis G. Castles and Rudolf Wildenmann (eds) *The Future of Party Government: Visions and Realities of Party Government*, vol. 1 (Berlin: Walter de Gruyter), pp. 31–71.

—— Mair, P., *et al.* (1992) 'The membership of political parties in European democracies'. *European Journal of Political Research* 22: 329–45.

——, —— (1994) *How Parties Organize: Change and Adaptation in Party Organizations in Western Democracies* (London: Sage Publications).

Keman, H. and Pennings, P. (1995) 'Managing political and societal conflict in democracies: do consensus and corporatism matter?'. *British Journal of Political Science* 25: 271–81.

Kleinnijenhuis, J. and Scholten, O. (1989) 'Veranderende verhoudingen tussen dagbladen en politieke partijen'. *Acta Politica* 24: 433–61.

Koole, R. (1992) *De Opuomst van de Moderne Kaderpartij. Veranderende Partijorganisaties in Nederland 1960–1990.* (Utrecht: Het Spectrum).

—— (1994) 'The vulnerability of the modern cadre party in the Netherlands', in R. S. Katz and P. Mair (eds) *How Parties Organize: Change and Adaptation in Party Organizations in Western Democracies* (London: Sage Publications), pp. 278–303.

—— (1999) 'Die Antwort der niederländischen Parteien auf die wahpolitischen Herausforderungen' in P. Mair, W. Müller, and F. Plasser (eds) *Parteien auf komplexen Wählermarkten. Reaktionsstrategien politischer Parteien in Westeuropa* (Wien: ZAP) pp. 315–52.

—— and van der Velde, H. (1992) 'The Netherlands' in R. S. Katz and P. Mair (eds) *Party Organizations: A Data Handbook on Party Organizations in Western Democracies, 1960–90* (London: Sage Publications), pp. 619–731.

Lijphart, A. (1975) *The Politics of Accommodation: Pluralism and Democracy in the Netherlands* (Berkeley: University of California Press).

Luther, K. R. (1999) 'A framework for the comparative analysis of political parties and party systems in consociational democracies', in K. R. Luther and K. Deschouwer (eds) *Party Elites in Divided Societies: Political Parties in Consociational Democracy* (London: Routledge), pp. 3–19.

—— and Deschouwer, K. (1999) *Party Elites in Divided Societies: Political Parties in Consociational Democracy* (London: Routledge).

Mair, P. and van Biezen, I. (2001) 'Party membership in twenty European democracies, 1980–2000'. *Party Politics* 7: 5–22.

Rokkan, S. (1977) 'Towards a generalized concept of Verzuiling'. *Political Studies* 25: 563–70.

Schmitt, H. and Holmberg, S. (1995) 'Political parties in decline?', in H.-D. Klingemann and D. Fuchs (eds) *Citizens and the State* (Oxford: Oxford University Press).

Scholten, I. (1987) 'Corporatism and the neo-liberal backlash in the Netherlands', in I. Scholten (ed.) *Political Stability and Neo-corporatism* (London: Sage Publications), pp. 120–52.

Tops, P. W. (1990) *Afspiegeling en Aspraak: Coalitietheorie en Collegevorming in Nederlandse Gemeenten, 1946–1986* (Leiden: Universiteit Leiden).

Voerman, G. (1995) 'De ledenaantallen van politieke partijen, 1945–1995', *Jaarboek 1995* (Groningen: Documentatiecentrum Nederlandse Poltiieke Partijen), pp. 192–206.

Walgrave, S. and Rihoux, B. (1997) *De Witte Mars, Eén Jaar Later. Van Emotie tot Politieke Commotie* (Antwerpen: Van Halewijck).

Wolinetz, S. B. (1989) 'Socio-economic bargaining in the Netherlands', in H. Daalder and G. A. Irwin (eds) *Politics in the Netherlands* (London: Frank Cass), pp. 79–98.

7

The Scandinavian Party Model at the Crossroads

Jan Sundberg

INTRODUCTION

Writing in the late 1970s, Sten Berglund and Ulf Lindström argued that Scandinavian party systems were often seen as 'ultra stable' (Berglund and Lindström 1978: 74), a view that was certainly justified between 1945 and the early 1970s. However, the general election of 1973 in Denmark signalled a new era of instability as the three major parties saw their aggregate share of the vote slashed from 73 to 47 per cent (Worre 1978: 13). It was not long before similar developments became visible in Norway, to some extent in Finland, and (a little later) in Sweden.

The main political actors in the Scandinavian democracies are organized around conflicts between labour and capital, and the rural peripheries and urban centres (Rokkan 1987: 81–95). As these cleavages were already well established by the 1920s, Stein Rokkan famously asserted that such party systems were 'frozen' in the 1960s (Lipset and Rokkan 1967: 50). The five party families of the classic Scandinavian model (social democracy, conservatism, liberalism, agrarian 'centrism', and communism) are deeply anchored in their social bases, and class in particular has been a more important determinant of party loyalty than in other west European democracies (Rose 1974: 3–25; Uusitalo 1975; Worre 1980: 299–320). However, this strong orientation towards class politics has not resulted in revolutionary acts, except in Finland. Rather, a marked proclivity for accommodation and compromise has located the Scandinavian polities close to Lijphart's ideal type of consensus democracy (Lijphart 1984: 21–36). Party leaders have displayed a commitment to national unity and democratic principles despite the presence of deep social cleavages. In particular, the mutual tolerance and moderation that parties typically accord each other in consensus democracies (Lijphart 1977: 53–5) has resulted in the creation of an extensive and well-known mixed welfare economy (Erikson *et al.* 1987: vii–ix).

However, the classic five-party model no longer provides a comprehensive account of party politics in Scandinavia: since the early 1970s a variety of other parties, old and new, have emerged. The former category includes ethnic parties (in Denmark and Finland) and Christian parties, while the latter includes Green and Progress parties. These changes have led some to doubt whether the Scandinavian party systems remain distinctive. Certainly, they conform to certain trends apparent in other west European multi-party systems, including an increase in the number of parties contesting elections and a growing sense of instability (Lane and Ersson 1999: 109–33).

An increase in the effective number of electoral parties first became apparent in Finland at the election of 1962, though change was more muted in terms of parliamentary representation. Subsequently, the turbulent election of 1970 confirmed the growth of electoral fragmentation as the populist Rural Party increased its vote from 1 to 10.5 per cent (see Table 7.1). The first substantial increases in the effective number of parliamentary parties in Scandinavia eventually transpired in Denmark and Norway in 1973 (Tables 7.2 and 7.3). The extent of change was greater in Denmark, where the election was described as an electoral earthquake: all incumbent parties lost in the election and more than a third of MPs were replaced by new members (Pedersen 1988: 257–61). For a short period the Danish party system became the most fragmented in Scandinavia. However, studies show that after the initial shockwaves subsided, the effective number of parties diminished (Pedersen 1987: 1–60; Borre and Andersen 1997: 162–5), a pattern which is confirmed by our tables: from these it is evident that since the late 1980s, the Finnish party system has resumed its position as the most fragmented in Scandinavia. By contrast, Sweden's high electoral threshold rule (introduced in 1970) helped cement the five-party system, until in 1988 the Ecological Party eventually managed to exceed 4 per cent of the popular vote and won seats in the Riksdag. Three years later, when the Ecologists slumped, the feat was repeated by the Christian Democratic Coalition and the populist New Democracy. These breakthroughs were consolidated in 1994, and as a result the Swedish party system is slightly more fragmented than before the 4 per cent threshold rule was introduced (see Table 7.4).

Despite the instability of the 1970s in particular, it remains appropriate to locate Scandinavian party systems in the category of moderate pluralism (Sartori 1976). Moreover, the average effective number of parliamentary parties is now similar to the level it was before the 1970s; even in Denmark the established parties seem to have been restored to something approaching their former pre-eminence. Small parties tend to have more volatile voters than the major parties and seek to break into an electoral market in which ideological space is crowded (Pedersen 1991: 95–114). In Sweden, the parliamentary entrance of new parties in 1988 only resulted in a modest increase in fragmentation of the party system. There and across Scandinavia the old parties persist even though some of the new ones, such as the Greens, who have deep roots in the environmentalist movement, will probably challenge them for years to come (Vedung 1991: 165–219). Thus, while the established party systems have suffered backlashes, the old parties have shown themselves to

TABLE 7.1. *Elections in Finland, 1962–99*

Year	KESK	SKDL/VAS	SDP	KOK	LKP	SFP	TPSL	SMP	SKL/POP	VIHR	Other	ENEP/ENPP	Turnout (%)
1962	23.0 / 53	22.0 / 47	19.5 / 38	15.0 / 32	6.3 / 13	6.4 / 14	4.4 / 2	2.2 / 0	— / —	—	2.2 / 1	5.9 / 5.1	85.1
1966	21.2 / 49	21.2 / 41	27.2 / 55	13.8 / 26	6.5 / 9	6.0 / 12	2.6 / 7	1.0 / 1	0.4 / 0	—	0.1 / 1	5.2 / 5.0	84.9
1970	17.1 / 36	16.6 / 36	23.4 / 52	18.0 / 37	6.0 / 8	5.7 / 12	1.4 / 0	10.5 / 18	1.2 / 1	—	0.1 / 1	6.2 / 5.6	82.2
1972	16.4 / 35	17.0 / 37	25.8 / 55	17.6 / 34	5.2 / 7	5.4 / 10	1.0 / 0	9.2 / 18	2.4 / 4	—	0 / 0	6.0 / 5.5	81.4
1975	17.6 / 39	18.9 / 40	24.9 / 54	18.4 / 35	4.3 / 9	4.7 / 10	—	3.6 / 2	3.3 / 9	—	4.4 / 2	5.9 / 5.3	73.8
1979	17.3 / 36	17.9 / 35	23.9 / 52	21.7 / 47	3.7 / 4	4.2 / 10	—	4.6 / 7	4.8 / 9	—	2.0 / 0	5.8 / 5.2	75.3
1983	17.6 / 38	13.5 / 26	26.7 / 57	22.1 / 44	—	4.6 / 11	—	9.7 / 17	3.0 / 3	1.4 / 2	1.4 / 2	5.5 / 5.2	75.7
1987	17.6 / 40	9.4 / 16	24.1 / 56	23.1 / 53	1.0 / 0	5.3 / 13	—	6.3 / 9	2.6 / 5	4.0 / 4	6.4 / 2	6.2 / 5.0	72.1
1991	24.8 / 55	10.1 / 19	22.1 / 48	19.3 / 40	0.8 / 1	5.5 / 12	—	4.8 / 7	3.1 / 8	6.8 / 10	2.3 / 0	5.9 / 5.3	68.4
1995	19.8 / 44	11.2 / 22	28.2 / 63	17.9 / 39	0.6 / 0	5.1 / 11	—	1.3 / 1	3.0 / 7	6.5 / 9	6.4 / 4	5.8 / 4.9	68.6
1999	22.4 / 48	10.9 / 20	22.9 / 51	21.0 / 46	—	5.1 / 11	—	—	4.2 / 10	7.3 / 11	6.2 / 3	5.9 / 5.2	65.3

Notes: Top figure in each cell: share of the vote; bottom figure: number of seats in lower house.
Party codes: KESK—Centre Party (Agrarian Union prior to 1990); SDP—Social Democratic Party; KOK—Conservative National Coalition; LKP—Liberal People's Party; SFP—Swedish People's Party; TPSL—Social Democratic League of Workers and Smallholders; SMP—Finnish Rural Party; SKL/POP—Finnish Christian League; VIHR—Greens. SKDL/VAS—Finnish People's Democratic League (Left-Wing Alliance since 1990); SKDL/VAS—Finnish People's Democratic League (Left-Wing Alliance since 1990).

TABLE 7.2. *Elections in Denmark, 1960–2001*

Year	SF	SD	RV	KRF	CD	V	KF	FRP	Other	ENEP/ENPP	Turnout (%)
1960	6.1	42.1	5.8	—	—	21.1	17.9	—	7.0	4.0	85.8
	11	76	11			38	32		7	3.7	
1964	5.8	41.9	5.3	—	—	20.8	20.1	—	6.3	3.8	85.5
	10	76	10			38	36		5	3.6	
1966	10.9	38.2	7.3	—	—	19.3	18.7	—	5.6	4.3	88.6
	20	69	13			34	34		4	4.0	
1968	6.1	34.2	15.0	—	—	18.6	20.4	—	5.7	4.8	89.3
	11	62	27			37	37		4	4.3	
1971	9.1	37.3	14.4	2.0	—	15.6	16.3	—	6.9	4.5	87.2
	17	70	27	0		30	31		0	4.0	
1973	6.0	25.6	11.2	4.0	7.8	12.3	9.2	15.9	8.0	6.7	88.7
	11	46	20	7	14	22	16	28	11	6.7	
1975	5.0	29.9	7.1	5.3	2.2	23.3	5.5	13.6	8.1	6.3	88.2
	9	53	13	9	4	42	10	24	11	5.9	
1977	3.9	37.0	3.6	3.4	6.4	12.0	8.5	14.6	10.6	5.6	88.0
	7	65	6	6	11	21	15	26	18	5.6	
1979	5.9	38.3	5.4	2.6	3.2	12.5	12.5	11.0	8.6	5.0	89.9
	11	68	10	5	6	22	22	20	11	5.0	
1981	11.3	32.9	5.1	2.3	8.3	11.3	14.5	8.9	5.4	5.9	87.8
	21	59	9	4	15	20	26	16	5	5.9	
1984	11.5	31.6	5.5	2.7	4.6	12.1	23.4	3.6	5.0	5.9	88.4
	21	56	10	5	8	22	42	6	5	5.3	
1987	14.6	29.3	6.2	2.4	4.8	10.5	20.8	4.8	6.5	6.3	86.7
	27	54	11	4	9	19	38	9	4	5.6	
1988	13.0	29.8	5.6	2.0	4.7	11.8	19.3	9.0	4.8	5.9	84.0
	24	55	10	4	9	22	35	16	0	5.3	
1990	8.3	37.4	3.5	2.3	5.1	15.8	16.0	6.4	5.2	5.0	82.8
	15	69	7	4	9	30	30	12	19	4.3	
1994	7.3	34.6	4.6	1.8	2.8	23.3	15.0	6.4	4.2	5.3	84.3
	13	62	8	0	5	42	27	11	11	4.8	
1998	7.5	36.0	3.9	2.4	4.3	24.0	8.9	2.4	10.6	4.8	85.9
	13	63	7	4	8	42	16	4	22	5.0	
2001	6.4	29.1	5.2	2.3	1.8	31.3	9.1	0.6	14.2	4.6	89.3
	12	52	9	4	0	56	16	0	30	4.5	

Party codes: SF—Socialist People's Party; SD—Social Democratic Party; RV—Radical Liberals; KRF—Christian People's Party; CD—Centre Democrats; V—Liberals; KF—Conservative People's Party; FRP—Progress Party; Other includes DF (Danish People's Party), ERG (Red–Green Unity Coalition) and Greenland and Faroese parties.

be more resilient than many suggested during the 1970s, and durability has been as prominent as change.

The increasing fragmentation of parliaments has affected government formation in different ways in Scandinavia. The two most fragmented party systems, Denmark and Finland, have developed in opposite directions. Finland has a long

TABLE 7.3. *Elections in Norway, 1961–2001*

Year	SV	DNA	V	SP	KRF	H	FRP	Other	ENEP/ ENPP	Turnout (%)
1961	2.4	46.8	8.8	9.3	9.6	20.0	—	3.0	3.7	79.1
	2	74	14	16	15	29		0	3.2	
1965	6.0	43.1	10.4	9.9	8.1	21.1	—	1.4	3.8	85.4
	2	68	18	18	13	31		0	3.6	
1969	3.5	46.5	9.4	10.5	9.4	19.6	—	1.1	3.4	83.8
	0	74	13	20	14	29		0	3.1	
1973	11.2	35.3	3.5	11.0	12.2	17.4	5.0	4.3	5.9	80.2
	16	62	2	21	20	29	4	1	4.2	
1977	4.2	42.3	3.2	8.6	12.4	24.8	1.9	2.6	3.8	82.9
	2	76	2	12	22	41	0	0	2.9	
1981	4.9	37.2	3.9	6.7	9.4	31.7	4.5	1.7	4.0	82.0
	4	66	2	11	15	53	4	0	3.2	
1985	5.5	40.8	3.1	6.6	8.3	30.4	3.7	1.6	3.7	84.0
	6	71	0	12	16	50	2	0	3.2	
1989	10.1	34.3	3.2	6.5	8.5	22.2	13.0	2.2	4.8	83.2
	17	63	0	11	14	37	22	1	4.2	
1993	7.9	36.9	3.6	16.7	7.9	17.0	6.3	3.6	4.5	75.8
	13	67	1	32	13	28	10	1	4.0	
1997	6.0	35.1	4.5	7.9	13.7	14.3	15.3	3.3	5.3	78.0
	9	65	6	11	25	23	25	1	4.5	
2001	12.4	24.3	3.9	5.6	12.5	21.2	14.7	4.4	6.4	74.5
	23	43	2	10	22	38	26	1	5.4	

Party codes: SV—Socialist Left Party (Socialist People's Party until 1975); DNA—Norwegian Labour Party; V—Liberals; SP—Centre Party; KRF—Christian People's Party; H—Right; FRP—Progress Party.

tradition of multi-party coalition governments. Moreover, it was long characterized by governmental instability: from national independence in 1917, sixty-seven cabinets were formed up to and including that of April 1999 (Nousiainen 1998: 243–6). In the half-century from 1937 coalitions were built around the Social Democrats and the agrarian Centre Party, and completed with parties from either right or left. The inclusion of the Communists frequently provoked a government crisis (Jansson 1992: 225–41). However, since the election of 1983, all cabinets have controlled parliamentary majorities and have survived in office for the maximum legal period between elections. Since 1995 'rainbow' coalitions have included most parties in Parliament (from the former Communists to the conservatives), except for the agrarian Centre Party and a few small parties (see Tables 7.5–7.8).

In Norway minority cabinets have been the norm since the early 1960s, as they have in Denmark since the 1970s. Sweden, traditionally the most stable Scandinavian democracy, has experienced only minority administrations since 1982, despite a long prior tradition of majority governments (Petersson

TABLE 7.4. *Elections in Sweden, 1960–98*

Year	VPK	SAP	CP	FPL	MSP	MP	KD	Other	ENEP/ENPP	Turnout (%)
1960	4.5	47.8	13.6	17.5	16.5	—	—	0.1	3.2	85.9
	5	114	34	40	39			0	3.1	
1964	5.2	47.3	13.4	17.1	13.7	—	1.8	1.5	3.4	83.9
	8	113	35	43	33		0	1	3.2	
1968	3.0	50.1	15.7	14.3	12.9	—	1.5	2.6	3.2	89.3
	3	125	39	34	32		0	0	2.8	
1970	4.8	45.3	19.9	16.2	11.5	—	1.8	0.4	3.4	88.3
	17	163	71	58	41		0	0	3.3	
1973	5.3	43.6	25.1	9.4	14.3	—	1.7	0.6	3.6	90.8
	19	156	90	34	51		0	0	3.3	
1976	4.8	42.7	24.1	11.1	15.6	—	1.4	0.3	3.7	91.8
	17	152	86	39	55		0	0	3.6	
1979	5.6	45.6	15.5	5.9	23.6	1.7	1.4	0.7	3.7	90.7
	20	166	56	21	86	0	0	0	3.7	
1982	5.6	45.6	15.5	5.9	23.6	1.7	1.9	0.2	3.4	91.4
	20	166	56	21	86	0	0	0	3.1	
1985	5.4	44.7	10.4	14.2	21.3	1.5	2.0	0.5	3.4	89.9
	19	159	44	51	76	0	1	0	3.3	
1988	5.8	43.2	11.3	12.2	18.3	5.5	3.0	0.6	4.2	86.0
	21	156	42	41	66	21	0	0	3.7	
1991	4.5	37.7	8.5	9.1	21.9	3.4	7.1	7.7	4.8	86.7
	16	138	31	33	80	0	26	25	4.3	
1994	6.2	45.2	7.7	7.2	22.4	5.0	4.1	2.2	3.8	88.1
	22	161	27	26	80	18	15	0	3.8	
1998	12.0	36.6	5.1	4.7	22.7	4.5	11.8	2.6	5.0	81.4
	43	131	18	17	82	16	42	0	4.3	

Party codes: V—Left Party (VL—Left Communists 1967–90; VPK—Swedish Communist Party prior to 1967); SAP—Swedish Social Democratic Workers' Party; CP—Centre Party; FPL—Liberal People's Party (People's Party prior to 1990); MSP—Moderate Unity Party (Right Party prior to 1969); MP—Environmental Party of the Greens; KD—Christian Democrats.

1995: 92–4). The degree of fragmentation alone cannot explain these divergent developments, but according to Damgaard (1992: 192–6), the reason lies in the ideological complexion of coalitions. Thus, while governments in Finland have often crossed ideological boundaries between the socialist and non-socialist blocs, such coalitions have never occurred in Norway, and not in Sweden since the 1950s: in Denmark the only example was a short experiment after the 1973 election (Arter 1999: 200–21). Thus, inter-bloc coalitions combined with fragmentation seem to create government instability, while coalitions which limit coalition-building to a single ideological bloc are more conducive to stability and consensus.

The hyper-stability of former years was characterized by linkages between individuals, classes, and parties. Such linkages have weakened, however, with the

TABLE 7.5. *Governments in Finland since 1962*

Year	PM's party	Governing parties	Status
1962	KESK	KOK, LKP, SFP, KESK	Majority
1963	—	Non-political technocrats	
1964	KESK	KOK, LKP, SFP, KESK	Majority
1966	SDP	KESK, SDP, SKDL	Majority
1968	SDP	SFP, KESK, SDP, SKDL	Majority
1970	—	Non-political technocrats	
1970	KESK	LKP, SFP, KESK, SDP, SKDL	Majority
1971	KESK	LKP, SFP, KESK, SDP	Majority
1971	—	Non-political technocrats	
1972	SDP	SDP	Minority
1972	SDP	LKP, SFP, KESK, SDP	Majority
1975	—	Non-political technocrats	
1975	KESK	LKP, SFP, KESK, SDP, SKDL	Majority
1976	KESK	LKP, SFP, KESK	Minority
1977	SDP	SDP, KESK, SFP, LKP, SKDL,	Majority
		Non-political technocrats	
1978	SDP	SDP, KESK, LKP, SKDL	Majority
1979	SDP	SDP, KESK, SFP, SKDL	Majority
1982	SDP	SDP, KESK, SFP, SKDL	Majority
1982	SDP	SDP, KESK, LKP, SFP	Majority
1983	SDP	SDP, KESK, SFP, SMP	Majority
1987	KOK	SDP, KOK, SFP, SMP	Majority
1990	KOK	SDP, KOK, SFP	Majority
1991	KESK	KESK, KOK, SFP, SKL	Majority
1994	KESK	KESK, KOK, SFP	Majority
1995	SDP	SDP, KOK, SFP, VIHRE, VAS,	Majority
		Non-political experts	
1999	SDP	SDP, KOK, SFP, VIHRE, VAS,	Majority
		Non-political experts	

erosion of social and partisan identities, processes which have left parties with less clear missions to fulfil in government. In this context, a notable erosion of party legitimacy has emerged in Scandinavia, a geo-political region once renowned for a profound sense of public confidence in party (Karvonen 1999: 395–415; Möller 1999: 193–221). This confidence has turned to deep scepticism in some respects, as we shall shortly see. Media commentators have tended to be the most trenchant critics, although they have been joined by some political scientists who perceive a crisis of party. Membership decline and fading party activity have fuelled such a perspective (Gidlund and Möller 1999); however, apologists have argued that parties continue to have an important stabilizing function in that democracy without parties would promote elitism and unstable leadership (Petersson *et al.* 2000). So how convincing is the evidence of weakening popular legitimacy?

TABLE 7.6. *Governments in Denmark since 1960*

Year	PM's party	Governing parties	Status
1960	SD	RV, SD	Majority
1962	SD	RV, SD	Majority
1964	SD	SD	Minority
1968	RV	RV, KF, V	Majority
1971	SD	SD	Minority
1972	SD	SD	Minority
1973	V	V	Minority
1975	SD	SD	Minority
1978	SD	SD, V	Minority
1979	SD	SD	Minority
1981	SD	SD	Minority
1982	KF	KF, V, CD, KRF	Minority
1987	KF	KF, V, CD, KRF	Minority
1988	KF	KF, V, RV	Minority
1990	KF	KF, V	Minority
1993	SD	SD, RV, CD, KRF	Minority
1994	SD	SD, RV, CD	Minority
1996	SD	SD, RV	Minority
1998	SD	SD, RV	Minority
2001	V	V, KF	Minority

TABLE 7.7. *Governments in Norway since 1955*

Year	PM's party	Governing parties	Status
1955	DNA	DNA	Minority
1963	H	H, V, KRF, SP	Minority
1965	SP	H, V, KRF, SP	Majority
1971	DNA	DNA	Minority
1972	KRF	KRF	Minority
1973	DNA	DNA	Minority
1976	DNA	DNA	Minority
1981	DNA	DNA	Minority
1981	H	H	Minority
1983	H	H, KRF, SP	Minority
1985	H	H, KRF	Minority
1986	DNA	DNA	Minority
1989	H	H, KRF, SP	Minority
1990	DNA	DNA	Minority
1993	DNA	DNA	Minority
1996	DNA	DNA	Minority
1997	KRF	KRF, SP	Minority
2001	KRF	KRF, H, V	Minority

TABLE 7.8. *Governments in Sweden since 1957*

Year	PM's party	Governing parties	Status
1957	SAP	SAP	Minority
1969	SAP	SAP	Majority
1976	CP	MSP, FPL, CP	Majority
1978	FPL	FPL	Minority
1979	CP	CP, FPL, MSP	Majority
1981	CP	FPL, CP	Minority
1982	SAP	SAP	Minority
1986	SAP	SAP	Minority
1990	SAP	SAP	Minority
1991	MSP	CP, KD, MSP, Non-political technocrats	Minority
1994	SAP	SAP	Minority
1996	SAP	SAP	Minority

THE EROSION OF PARTY LEGITIMACY?

... what is important is that the party in modern mass democracies has generally taken on an ever increasing area of commitments and responsibilities, assuring the individual's share in society and incorporating him into the community. This is no mere usurpation of power by the politicians but the natural consequence of the extension of the public domain and the constantly increasing governmental functions in a reintegrated twentieth-century society (Neumann 1956: 405).

Sigmund Neumann's assessment of party development in the postwar era approximates closely to the Scandinavian experience. Scandinavian polities aimed to provide social welfare to all in order to promote equality and economic efficacy (Esping-Andersen 1994: 75–106). As welfare provision was distributed to all categories of citizens so the mass parties radically increased their role in directing people's everyday lives. At the same time, the desire for equality in public services generated a series of amalgamations in local government (starting in Sweden in 1952, before affecting Denmark, Norway, and to some extent Finland) which resulted in the politicization of municipal government throughout Scandinavia (Sundberg 1991: 109–38). Stein Rokkan described this entry of nationally organized parties into municipal politics as a process of 'mass politicization' (Rokkan 1970: 227).

Municipal amalgamations and the expansion of the welfare state peaked around the late 1960s and early 1970s. Thereafter, however, problems appeared as social engineering began to lose its credibility. Simultaneously, signs of electoral volatility and partisan dealignment emerged, deriving in large part from the impact of social change. The modern party system was formed when Scandinavian work forces were roughly divided into three main classes: farmers, workers, and middle-class white collar workers. Each of the main parties was deeply anchored in one of these classes, the party forming and expressing the political will of its class, and in return receiving the full electoral support of that class. These mutual dependencies paid off for parties and their supporters, but only on the basis of political compromise; even prior to the War it became clear that the largest party in the system, the Social Democrats, could not win a parliamentary majority through working class support alone. Thus, partnerships were brokered between Scandinavian Social Democratic and Agrarian Parties in the years between 1933 and 1937 (Karvonen 1991: 49–81). This compromise between workers and farmers in all four countries proved to be the point of departure for the well-known welfare states of the region. Moreover, the culture of consensus it fostered effectively pre-empted all attempts at mobilizing mass support for fascism during the period.

The primacy of the class cleavage in Scandinavia from this time meant that class dealignment later in the century inevitably brought generalized electoral instability with it. The changing nature of the workforce played an important part in this process. In particular, the shrinking of the industrial working class was first noticeable in Sweden (the leading industrial nation of Scandinavia) after the 1960s, followed by Denmark, Norway and, by the 1980s, Finland (Alestalo and Kuhnle 1987: 26–9). Today the service sector predominates and women have become a major component of it. As a result, class differences are now less acute than hitherto. Furthermore, two new cleavage dimensions have become salient in Scandinavian party politics: materialism versus postmaterialism and religious morality versus secularism (Arter 1999: 127–32), not that either of these has entirely replaced the class cleavage in importance (Knutsen and Scarbrough 1995: 492–523). Thus, the traditional Scandinavian party system remains clearly discernible, but social change has fuelled electoral change and new and less stable forms of political alignment.

Studies show that the very strong patterns of class voting which once characterized Scandinavia have declined dramatically since the 1950s (Borre and Andersen 1997: 120–5), so that they now approximate those found in countries such as Austria, Germany, the Netherlands, and the UK (Lane and Ersson 1997: 179–96). This is not to say that each party does not retain a distinctive class basis to its support; most farmers still vote for the Agrarian parties, most workers for the Social Democratic parties, and the bulk of middle- and upper-class voters for the Conservative parties (Oskarsson 1994: 36–76; Aardal *et al.* 1995: 29; Gilljam and Holmberg 1995: 98–105; Sänkiaho 1996: 66–87; Borre and Andersen 1997: 118–20). However, the social changes outlined above have had an impact, such that only a minority of Agrarian (or rather, Centre) Party voters are farmers now and a considerable part of the Social Democratic electorate is middle-class. The precise measurement of class voting depends partly upon one's definition of class (Sainsbury 1987: 507–26), but it seems clear that it has declined throughout Scandinavia and particularly among working class electors.

Class dealignment has brought with it other signs of electoral instability, including the changing effective number of parties (already discussed), reduced rates of partisan identification and higher indices of electoral volatility. The most systematic long-term data on partisan identification come from Swedish studies, and reveal a decline from 65 per cent of electors who claimed some kind of partisan affinity in 1968 to just 47 per cent who did by 1994 (Gilljam and Holmberg 1995: 66–9). The corresponding decline in Norway was from 72 per cent in 1965 to 53 per cent in 1997 (Aardal *et al.* 1999: 148–56). In the other two countries the erosion of partisan identification is not nearly so dramatic, however. In Denmark, it only decreased from 54 per cent in 1971 to 50 per cent in 1973, and since then has remained stable (Borre and Andersen 1997: 163), while Finnish data show no signs of decline: 59 per cent of voters had a partisan identification in 1975, and 61 per cent did in 1991 (Pesonen *et al.* 1993: 215–19). Note too that developments are generally not spectacular in respect of the percentages of Scandinavian citizens who claim to maintain 'strong' partisan attachments. While it is true that in Sweden this figure dropped from 52 to 46 per cent in 1964, down further to 39 per cent in 1968, and to 27 per cent by 1988 (Pierre and Widfeldt 1992: 789–90), the erosion of strong attachments did not achieve statistical significance in Finland, Norway, or Denmark (Schmitt and Holmberg 1995: 126; Dalton 2000: 25).

Table 7.9 reports indices of electoral volatility across Scandinavia. Gross volatility measures the total amount of vote-switching from one election to the next at the level of individual voters, and can only be measured by surveys of electoral samples; the time-series is patchy since these surveys have not been conducted at every election in each of the countries during the period with which we are concerned. By contrast, net volatility is an aggregate-level measure of shifts in party support from one election to the next, and can easily be measured from national election results. A high level of gross volatility does not necessarily coincide with a high level of net volatility, since many of the individual-level decisions to switch support from one party to another could cancel each other out (Pedersen 1979).

Nevertheless, net volatility was generally low at the beginning of the period covered by Table 7.9 but changed rapidly with the turbulent elections of the early 1970s in Denmark, Finland, and Norway. Since then, it has on average remained at a higher level than before in the latter two countries, while diminishing slightly in Denmark (though not to pre-1973 levels). In Sweden, net volatility remained unchanged throughout the period up to the 1991 election, which seemed to demarcate a new and somewhat more volatile era. Even where electoral volatility has increased in Scandinavia since 1970, however, it should be borne in mind that it has not necessarily reached the levels experienced prior to the Second World War (Bartolini and Mair 1990; Sundberg 1996: 226–31; Mair 1997: 79–81). Moreover, the relative stability of voting behaviour is all the more striking given the substantial growth of Scandinavian electorates in the second half of the twentieth century. Overall, this growth amounted to seven million people in net terms, or nearly 40 per cent. Nationally, growth ranged from 33.6 per cent in Sweden to 44.1 per cent in Finland. Moreover, the generational turnover of voters was great in these years. Given this transformation of electorates, it can be argued that net volatility has

TABLE 7.9. *Net and gross volatility in the Scandinavian party systems after the Second World War*

Year of election	Denmark		Finland		Norway		Sweden	
	Net	Gross	Net	Gross	Net	Gross	Net	Gross
1960	11.1						3.7	7.2
1961					3.6			
1962			5.5					
1963								
1964	3.1						2.6	10.6
1965					6.8			
1966	9.6		8.1					
1967								
1968	10.9						5.7	12.1
1969					5.4	18		
1970			14.5				7.2	16.0
1971	9.6	26						
1972			4.1					
1973	21.2	40			15.9	25	8.5	16.0
1974								
1975	17.8	32	7.2					
1976							3.0	19.1
1977	18.3	31			14.7	24		
1978								
1979	10.6	28	5.8				6.5	18.1
1980								
1981	12.5	32			11.2	19		
1982							7.9	19.5
1983			10.3					
1984	10.8	33						
1985					4.9	20	8.4	19.2
1986								
1987	9.2	25	6.9					
1988	6.7	17					6.5	20.2
1989					19.1	30		
1990	13.3	19						
1991			12.4				14.9	30.0
1992								
1993					15.2	33		
1994	10.1	23					11.4	29.2
1995			11.4					
1996								
1997					16.3	33		
1998	12.0	30					15.7	
1999			9.1					
2001	12.3	—			15.0	—		

Notes: Non-voters are excluded from calculations. Between 1975 and 1987 the gross volatility estimates are weighted.

Sources: Net volatility: 1947–85, Bartolini and Mair 1990; 1986–91, Ersson 1993. Gross volatility: Worre 1989; Tonsgaard 1989: 143; Nielsen 1999: 67–81; Aardal and Valen 1995: 33; Aardal 1998: 367–81; Gilljam and Holmberg 1995: 31–2. Other entries are author's or editor's calculations. Gross volatility data for 2001 not available at time of writing.

been surprisingly low; certainly, the change in net volatility has been much lower than the rate at which electorates have expanded in Scandinavia.

Gross volatility is systematically higher than net volatility and to some extent co-varies with it. In Sweden and Norway gross volatility increased in the 1970s and since the late 1980s these two countries and Denmark have experienced similarly high levels of gross volatility. Studies show that most vote-switching occurs within the non-socialist and minor party blocs, but that the socialist/non-socialist bloc barrier has also generally become more permeable during the 1990s (Gilljam and Holmberg 1995: 31–6; Aardal and Valen 1997: 69; Borre and Andersen 1997: 162–5; Nielsen 1999: 67–81). In part, this reflects the ideological proximity of parties in a consensual system: switching between parties or even blocs does not necessarily carry the same significance as in a more polarized system. It also reflects the somewhat transitory success of populist parties in attracting the temporary support of disaffected Social Democrat supporters (Aardal and Valen 1997: 61–90).

Thus far, then, we have uncovered evidence of an increase in electoral volatility and party system fragmentation, and a limited erosion of partisan identification across Scandinavia. This hardly amounts to decisive evidence of anti-party sentiment, however. If it is true that 'politics and government are a peripheral rather than a central concern in the lives of most citizens in modern Western societies' (Milbrath and Goel 1977: 145–6), then citizens may be content to leave politics in the hands of the professionals while they concern themselves with non-political activities. Only when the professionals are perceived to have failed seriously might the voters be expected to respond with genuine antipathy, and then they have two options: either not to vote at all, or actively to support non-party or explicitly anti-party candidates, organizations, or movements. Either way, the voter rejects the party as an instrument of exercising power by gaining office through elections. So what does the evidence on electoral turnout and support for anti-party organizations suggest?

In respect of the former, it is clear that, although Scandinavian citizens often tend to leave the decision to vote until late in election campaigns turnout has generally been uncommonly high, particularly in Sweden and Denmark. That said, three of the four countries have experienced some decline in turnout (refer again to Tables 7.1–7.4). Across Scandinavia electoral turnout peaked in the 1960s and 1970s although there is some variation between the countries. When the bicameral parliament in Sweden was replaced with one chamber, and parliamentary and local elections were staged simultaneously (1970), electoral turnout rose to over 90 per cent. Electoral participation in Denmark has generally been somewhat lower, followed by Norway and Finland. Since 1970 turnout in Finnish parliamentary elections has decreased in two notable downward lurches; from a peak of around 85 per cent (in the 1962 and 1966 elections) turnout fell sharply in 1975 (to 74 per cent) and then again in 1991 (to 68 per cent). Thus, by 1999 turnout was running approximately 20 percentage points lower than in 1966. In Sweden turnout remained quite stable until it dropped by around 7 percentage points in

1998, while a similar slump afflicted Norway in 1993. Only in Denmark has the level of electoral participation remained high and stable (Thomsen 1984: 46–7): this is true even of the notoriously turbulent election of 1973. This is interesting, for it suggests that the electoral instability and party system fragmentation which we have already noted did not result from antipathy towards the political system or the political parties *per se*: if there had been real antipathy, then electoral turnout would surely have fallen equally dramatically. As it was, some of the (established) parties were subject to a degree of antipathy, while others (some of them new) enjoyed surges in support. The Danish case suggests that electoral instability on its own is not a good measure of anti-party sentiment, but when it coincides with a substantial drop in turnout it may be appropriate to infer that the electorate as a whole is expressing antipathy towards party. The more dramatic the coincidence, the greater the antipathy. Nowhere in Scandinavia is such a clearcut pattern evident. Finland reveals the starkest fall in turnout, but this is not associated with more general evidence of electoral instability.

But has electoral instability coincided with support for anti-party organizations? The short answer is no. For one thing, right-wing extremism (often associated with intolerance of pluralistic forms of politics such as party competition) did not flourish in Sweden during the 1990s despite the experiences of economic recession (early in the decade) and a relatively high proportion of immigrants. Much the same can be said of the three other Scandinavian democracies (Kaplan 1999: 205–24). This is not to say that right-wing populism has been uncommon in Scandinavia since the 1970s, as the emergence of the Progress parties of Denmark and Norway and New Democracy in Sweden show. However, while all these demonstrated antipathy towards other established parties, they did not manifest generalized antipathy towards party *per se* (or the party system); indeed, party politics was their chosen form of political expression, and they competed in the electoral arena with varying degrees of success. In a sense the rejection of party is more apparent in local politics where non-party lists have sometimes managed to break the dominance of the national parties (Wörlund 1997: 131–47). This is especially the case in Sweden, though to a lesser extent it is also true of Denmark, Finland, and Norway (Sundberg 1989; Arstein 1997; Buch Jensen 1997: 342–53).

While there is little to suggest that Scandinavians are generally dissatisfied with the way democracy works in their countries,[1] it must be said that they are more inclined to express disatisfaction with parties and MPs. Thus, in Norway the share expressing dissatisfaction stood at 58 per cent in 1973 though it had fallen a little (to 53 per cent) by 1994 (Aardal 1999: 175–7); in Sweden, however, it increased from 48 per cent of voters in 1968 to 72 per cent in 1994. In addition, the share of those

---

[1] According to a Eurobarometer survey from 1995 Danes and Norwegians are the most satisfied in Europe with the way democracy works in their countries (at 83 and 82 per cent, respectively). Satisfaction levels are lower in Sweden and Finland, where only 56 per cent of the respondents are very or fairly satisfied, but even this is close to the European mean.

who had little or relatively little confidence in politicians grew from 55 per cent in 1988 to 63 per cent in 1994 (Gilljam and Holmberg 1995: 85–7). A somewhat different indicator suggests that Danish citizens trust their politicians rather less than hitherto, moreover: before the electoral upheaval of 1973 this index of trust stood at −11 per cent, but by 1975 it had dropped to almost −30, and although the index recovered between 1977 and 1984, thereafter popular mistrust of politicians rose until it reached 1975 levels once more in the 1990s (Borre and Andersen 1997: 302–3). Unfortunately 'mistrust' is seldom problematized. Research conducted in Sweden suggests that mistrust is an ambiguous and multifaceted concept which is often exaggerated. Thus, people tend to declare their mistrust initially, only to moderate their views after consideration. Furthermore, mistrust can be 'sceptical' or 'cynical', the former variant being less pathological (and indeed, perhaps even healthy) for party democracy, while the open antipathy inherent in the latter variant poses a more profound challenge. Both, however, share a common sense of meaninglessness (Möller 2000: 185–6) associated with the perception that politics has lost importance. This, in turn, generates new levels of citizen apathy, which may have negative consequences for the quality of democracy, especially in Scandinavia, where participation and involvement have long since been cornerstones of democratic government.

Thus, it is apathy rather than genuine antipathy towards parties which characterizes Scandinavia today. This might be interpreted as part and parcel of a general decline in the associational activity of citizens in the region. Voluntary participation formed the basis upon which democracy was built in Scandinavia at the turn of the twentieth century. It now appears, however, that citizens are less inclined to join voluntary associations, and those who do join are less inclined to be active. While it is true that in the 1980s activity in grass-roots social movements and non-partisan forms of participation increased in Scandinavia (Togeby 1989), this trend began to reverse itself in Sweden over the following decade (Petersson *et al.* 1998: 48–69). More to the point, Swedish surveys suggest that participation in party activities has declined by half during the past fifteen years. In particular, it is clear that party membership has fallen across Scandinavia (Table 7.10).

The Scandinavian polities have been notable since the early days of democracy for their strong mass membership parties (Berglund and Lindström 1978; Elvander 1980; Rokkan 1981: 53–79), but membership decline has afflicted each of them, starting with Denmark in the 1960s. In the early 1960s, party membership in Denmark was approximately three times greater than it was in the mid-1990s. The causes for this early and comprehensive decline have been extensively discussed, though party scholars are unable to provide definitive answers. Proposed explanations have been offered in respect of the transformation of the social class structure (Togeby 1992: 1–19), the new media technology (Pedersen 1989: 265–78; Elklit 1991: 60–83), and the lack of material and other incentives for party members (Sundberg 1987: 17–38, 1989: 288–311). As membership faded in Denmark, it

TABLE 7.10. *Party membership trends in Scandinavia since 1960*

Country	1960s	1970s	1980s	1989/90	1997/98
Denmark					
Aggregate	598,596	489,000	276,000	231,846	205,382
M/E	21.0	13.5	7.6	5.9	5.1
Finland					
Aggregate	513,123	531,000	579,000	543,419	400,615
M/E	18.9	17.2	14.0	13.5	9.7
Norway					
Aggregate	324,000	399,000	456,000	418,953	242,022
M/E	15.5	13.4	15.6	13.1	7.3
Sweden					
Aggregate	1,092,000	1,104,000	1,429,000	506,337	365,588
M/E	22.0	19.6	23.7	8.0	5.5

Note: 'Aggregate' refers to the aggregate number of individual party members (though Swedish figures include the SAP's collective membership until the 1980s) in the national party system. 'M/E' (membership/electorate ratio) refers to the percentage of the overall national electorate constituted by party members. The figures relate to the first election held in each decade in the respective countries, prior to 1997/98, the latest date for which complete figures are available.

Sources: Katz *et al.* 1992; Widfeldt 1999; Mair and van Biezen 2001.

was not initially clear that this would be a pan-Scandinavian phenomenon since parties in Finland, Norway, and Sweden recorded more members than ever before. Aggregate membership peaked in Finland during the 1970s and 1980s, and a few years later in Norway and Sweden. Since then, however, membership decline has set in at an unprecedented rate. It has been most dramatic in Sweden, a consequence of the Social Democratic Party's decision to abolish collective membership. In the mid-1980s, membership of the party exceeded one million, but by 1991 it had fallen to 260,346 (Widfeldt 1999: 304). The Social Democrats in Norway followed the Swedish example and repealed collective membership by 1997 (Svåsand *et al.* 1997: 91–123). However, membership in the country was in decline prior to this crucial decision, and affected the other established parties as well. In Finland, membership started declining slightly in the 1980s, and more dramatically during the 1990s, leaving overall membership levels very similar to those in Sweden. The massive Centre Party organization accounts for a large part of this total, whereas all other established parties have lost members. Rapid decline in Norway has brought its membership level down nearly as far as Denmark's.

In addition, membership densities (i.e. membership as a proportion of the registered electorates) have declined. This leaves parties more vulnerable to shifts from one election to another, since members are generally more loyal to their parties than other voters. Whether membership decline has actually contributed directly to increased levels of electoral instability is hard to determine, but in principle it would seem to represent a clear threat to the established parties since their electoral position is generally best sustained in their membership strongholds (von Beyme 1985: 170–1).

In summary, then, we may say that there is considerable evidence of developments such as electoral instability, partisan erosion, membership decline, and weakened electoral participation across Scandinavia. Even so, it would be an exaggeration to suggest that Scandinavian parties face a full-blown crisis of legitimacy. Although mistrust of politicians is relatively high, parties *per se* have not been rejected by the voters. The three major established parties of the Scandinavian party system remain predominant. New parties have emerged to challenge them, but this implies that parties remain *the* platform for collective political action. While citizen participation in party politics may have declined, this is true of other forms of associational activity too, and there is no evidence to suggest that it heralds a generalized disillusionment with democracy.

PARTY ORGANIZATIONAL STRENGTH

Political parties require two basic types of organizational resource: material and human. Each of these categories can be further subdivided. Thus, material resources can comprise party-owned property and income derived from private sources (memberships fees, donations, loans, sales of party merchandise and publications, rent and interest charges) and public sources (various types of state subsidy). Human resources consist of both voluntary labour (usually supplied by members and affiliated organizations) and professional assets (paid party bureaucrats, external consultants, and elected politicians). In this section we examine a variety of these material and human resources as they relate to Scandinavian parties.

Finance

There can be little doubt that overall Scandinavian political parties have become far better off in real terms since 1960 (although they may have slipped back a little since 1980 (Farrell and Webb 2000: 117)). Table 7.11 reports financial trends in respect of the wealthiest parties in the Danish, Norwegian, and Swedish systems, the Social Democrats. On average, prices grew by a little over 100 per cent from the 1960s to the 1980s in Denmark, while the party's income grew by 390 per cent. In Sweden and Norway prices rose three-and-a-half times in the same period, while the Social Democrats' incomes rose by approximately nine times in each case. As inflation rates generally fell during the 1990s, these parties continued to enjoy spectacular financial growth.

In short, then, Scandinavian parties tend to be well resourced, and there is absolutely no doubt that the advent of state funding has done much to bring about such a situation. In Sweden, the incomes of non-socialist parties (at national level)

TABLE 7.11. *Total income and public subsidies to Social Democratic parties in Scandinavia*

Country	Income	Subsidies	Subsidy as % of income
Denmark			
1960s	4,648,143	—	—
1970s	9,530,800	1,945,878	20.4
1980s	24,493,500	8,810,140	36.0
1990s	56,050,750	27,349,307	48.8
Norway			
1960s	1,910,113	—	—
1970s	9,593,719	5,874,244	61.2
1980s	17,489,394	15,727,012	89.9
1990s	57,523,000	37,389,950	65.0
Sweden			
1960s	9,457,047	—	—
1970s	32,766,679	18,659,531	56.9
1980s	82,396,280	36,486,081	44.3
1990s	135,258,450	44,940,761	33.2

Notes: All figures are averages stated in Danish, Norwegian, and Swedish Krone, respectively. Danish figures for 1990s are based on data for 1990, 1992, 1994, 1996, and 1998 only. Norwegian figures for 1990s are based on 1995 and 1997 only. Swedish figures for 1990s are based on 1990 and 1996 only. No figures available for Finnish Social Democrats in the 1990s.

Sources: Katz and Mair 1992; Allern and Heidar 2001; Bille and Christiansen 2001; Worlund and Hansson 2001.

doubled in the mid-1960s while the Social Democrats enjoyed a trebling of their income during election years and an extraordinary eight-fold increase between the elections (Gidlund 1983: 243–4). In Norway, the income of the Social Democrats more than doubled in the early 1970s (Svåsand 1994: 197–205), as it did for all Finnish parties enjoying parliamentary representation in 1967 (Sundberg and Gylling 1992: 309–10). In Denmark, where subsidies have generally been substantially lower, their impact has been enjoyed mainly by small parties lacking alternative sources of income (Bille 1997: 163–91).

The value of subsidies has steadily increased since they were introduced, in real as well as monetary terms. Moreover, their impact is not felt at national level only. Currently, regional and local subsidies to Swedish parties combine to outstrip national subsidies by more than three times. In Norway too the total value of sub-national party subsidies outweighs that of national party subsidies. In Denmark, however, the opposite is true, thanks in no small measure to the particularly high value of state support to parliamentary party organizations; by 1995 parliamentary parties received 65 per cent of the total public subsidy awarded to Danish parties (Bille 1997: 377), a proportion that far outweighs that found elsewhere in Scandinavia. Overall, Denmark and Finland direct the greater part of their subsidies to central rather than to sub-national party structures, though Finland (unlike Denmark) channels public money mainly towards national party head offices rather than parliamentary organizations.

Private assets have by no means lost their significance with the introduction of public subsidies. The balance between public and private income is determined by the electoral cycle, the level of party organization, and the type of party. In particular, the demand for money is dictated by the electoral cycle since far more money is needed during campaigning than afterwards; indeed, spending far outstrips the supply of public subsidies during election campaigns. Not surprisingly, a Swedish study has shown that subsidies covered only 50 per cent of total party income during election years (during the period 1966–80), but fully 64 per cent in non-election years (Gidlund 1983: 243–52), a situation similar to that found in the other Scandinavian democracies. All this points to the continuing challenge which Scandinavian parties face to generate income from private sources.

The level of party organization also shapes the pattern of public/private funding. Thus, in Sweden, where local subsidies are the highest in Scandinavia, research has shown that about two-thirds of party branches have more than 90 per cent of their activities covered by subsidy in non-election years, though this is not true of election years (Gidlund and Gidlund 1981: 51–5). At regional level public funding accounted for between 40 and 70 per cent of the party incomes in the early 1980s (Gidlund 1991a: 45). Income from private sources such as donations and transfers from interest organizations seems to be directed more towards national party organizations. In Denmark, where the local and regional subsidies are much smaller, fundraising and membership fees are even more important, of course, especially at election times (Jensen 1997: 51–7). In general, it is clear that private sources predominate in supplying local party organizations in Finland and Denmark.

In respect of party types, it is evident that big parties are generally less dependent on public subsidies than small ones. Indeed, some small parties receive in excess of 80 per cent of their income from the state (Gidlund 1991b: 184), which is hardly surprising given that they have relatively few members, no related interest organizations and not many donors. By contrast, the big established parties can usually rely on either wealthy donors or long-term support from interest organizations. Studies reveal that membership income has lost importance compared to donations from interest organizations and industrial corporations (Gidlund 1991a: 42–52; Wiberg 1991: 80–98; Svåsand 1994: 197–206; Bille 1997: 163–91). Thus, established parties are financially more autonomous of the state than smaller ones. However, as Table 7.11 illustrates, even Scandinavia's social democratic parties have come to rely on the state to a substantial degree.

Members

As we saw in the section on party legitimacy, memberships have shrunk across Scandinavia, something which carries implications for party organizational capacity in a number of ways. Clearly, it impacts on the supply of potential recruits for elective public and party office at national and sub-national levels, and deprives parties of a valuable source of voluntary labour, particularly in the context of election campaigning. However, the members' voluntary contribution to their parties is not only dependent on their number, but also on their age and rates of activism. There is a tendency for old party members and some external observers alike to recall with nostalgia the good old days, when levels of activism were far higher. For instance, a pessimistic evaluation of developments in the Danish Social Democratic Party illustrates the point:

Steps were taken to reinvigorate party organization in the late 1960s, but to no avail. In Denmark, the party organization is dying, both figuratively and literally. Today, party clubs cater primarily to old-age pensioners (bingo games and coffee), and once the old-generation members die, so will the clubs. This means that party organizations will cease to function as a meaningful tool for electoral mobilization and organizational penetration into the new-generation electorate   (Esping-Andersen 1985: 118).

However, this description of an ageing membership whose social and leisure needs are catered for by the parties is not entirely borne out by the evidence of survey research, as Table 7.12 demonstrates. This clearly shows that, in Denmark at least, there was no dramatic change in the age profile of party members between 1970 and 1990. That said, studies do show that rates of activism among party members declined during the same period, whereas their participation in non-partisan forms of political participation increased (Togeby 1992: 1–19).

Though membership levels are considerably higher in Finland, essentially similar trends are visible. Thus, the majority of Finnish party members do not attend party meetings and the proportion of activists among members decreased from 45 per cent in 1975 to 33 per cent in 1994. Moreover, activism has decreased most

TABLE 7.12. *The age profile of party members in Denmark,*
1971–90

Age	1971	1977	1979 (*a*)	1979 (*b*)	1981	1988	1990
<30	20	24	23	24	25	22	21
30–49	39	31	38	44	35	43	40
>50	41	45	39	32	40	35	39
Total	100	100	100	100	100	100	100
N	218	204	198	210	101	109	207

Note: All figures are percentages.
Source: Kongshøj Larsen 1998.

TABLE 7.13. *The age profile of party members in Norway, 1957–93*

Age	1957	1965	1969	1973	1977	1981	1985	1989	1993
<30	8	8	9	5	14	16	15	14	11
31–49	45	43	41	28	32	38	38	38	39
>50	47	49	50	67	54	46	47	48	50
Total	100	100	100	100	100	100	100	100	100
N	238	218	231	218	267	267	329	273	218

Note: All figures are percentages.

Source: All figures derived from national election studies. Collective membership is included (DNA only).

amongst the young (Borg 1997: 35–65), and there is evidence too of the ageing of memberships in Finland: for instance, while 38 per cent of Social Democratic Party members were more than 50 years old in 1977, 70 per cent were in 1996. The situation is not much better for the other established parties (Sundberg 1996: 117–19). On average, Finnish party members are 53 years old, the socialist parties having the oldest members (with a mean age of 57) and the Greens having the youngest (43). Survey research suggests that some 9 per cent of the adult population claim to be party members now, but that there is some potential for the parties to do better in recruiting among the young (Borg 1997: 35–65). Finnish parties have succeeded neither in maintaining their memberships nor in attracting new generations of members.

Norway shows similar trends. In 1957, some 23 per cent of survey respondents reported membership of a political party (Rokkan 1970: 371–3), but by 1991 only 13 per cent did. The latter survey also revealed that the established parties (Social Democrats, Conservatives, and the Centre Party) and the Christian People's Party had the oldest memberships, while the populist Progress Party and the Socialist Party had the youngest (Heidar 1994*a*: 162–5). Table 7.13 shows that Norwegian party memberships have long since tended to be relatively old and that there has been little change in their age profile over time.[2] As in the Finnish case, the turnover of party members is high and activism levels are low. Thus, in 1990 some 53 per cent of the members had never attended any kind of party meeting or function (Heidar 1994*b*: 61–86); however, as no time-series information exists about activism levels, it is not safe to infer that these have declined over time (Svåsand *et al.* 1997: 109–10).

---

[2] The 1973 election reveals a notable deviation from the other figures in the time-series. This was a disastrous election for most of the established parties, but especially for the Social Democrats (DNA). These parties suffered a dramatic, but largely temporary, exodus of members between 1973 and 1977 (Selle and Svåsand 1982: 62–7), and it is implicit in Table 11.12 that those who abandoned their parties during this period were primarily young and middle-aged activists while older members remained loyal in the face of political turbulence.

In Sweden, survey data suggests that party membership declined from approximately 15 per cent of the electorate in the early 1980s to 8 per cent by 1997 (Widfeldt 1999: 117–23; Petersson *et al*. 1998: 58). Again, party memberships are not only declining, but also ageing, the average age rising from a little below 50 in the mid-1980s to 53.4 years in 1994 (Widfeldt 1999: 197–207). While all types of political activism decline over the same period (particularly amongst the young), it seems that this is especially true of partisan forms of participation. For instance, 46 per cent of Swedish party members had attended at least one party meeting in the six months prior to being surveyed in 1981, but only 34 per cent had done so in 1994 (Widfeldt 1999: 148).

With some variation of scope and magnitude, it is clear that membership is generally becoming a problem for Scandinavian parties. Numbers are dwindling, and those that do retain party membership are on average older and less active than hitherto. Such passive memberships can hardly fulfil the function of legitimating their parties (Scarrow 1994), nor can they be so effective a source of voluntary labour. Even more problematic is the fact that the passivity of contemporary memberships has made the recruitment of candidates for public office very problematic for the parties. This is most evident in local elections where the demand for candidates is usually higher than the supply of those actively seeking office. If this trend continues, parties may be obliged to recruit their candidates from outside the rank and file of their own organizations. It should be said that little of the parties' new-found wealth has been invested in recruiting new members, which gives the impression that voluntary assets are not valued as highly as they once were or as highly as professional staff now is. Indeed, Scandinavian parties—especially the larger ones—have substantially increased the size of their bureaucracies since the 1970s, generally in their national headquarters and parliamentary organizations (Farrell and Webb 2000: 117), although a few parties, such as the Centre parties in Finland and Norway, have more decentralized structures. The growth of party bureaucracies has undoubtedly been facilitated by the introduction of public subsidies (Gidlund 1991*b*: 173–86). More specifically, parties have become increasingly inclined to invest in the services of external specialists on limited-term contracts.

Overall, we can conclude that Scandinavian parties have more resources at their disposal than ever before, which is an obvious indication that they are not in a state of organizational decline. While voluntary assets (the members) and private income from fees and donations may have diminished, the effects of such developments have been more than offset by the considerable growth of professional and public assets. Although the major parties have less control over the mass media than hitherto (see the section on political communication), this has served to enhance the need for certain types of professional expertise. This change in the resources at their disposal may in a sense have altered the nature of Scandinavian parties, for it signifies the widening gulf between political elites and voters. In the 1950s and 1960s this division was still blurred as many voters were active in local politics; now, politics is to a greater extent the province of a small and largely professional minority.

THE SYSTEMIC FUNCTIONALITY OF
POLITICAL PARTIES

Governance

In so far as the long ascendancy of Social Democrats in the region has had an undeniable impact on policy outcomes, Scandinavia exemplifies the importance of parties for government. In particular, few could doubt that Social Democratic-led governments played a major part in shaping the postwar welfare states of Scandinavia (Castles 1978). That said, however, detailed research has shown that the consensual nature of Scandinavian politics has ensured that other parties are also able to exert influence, albeit mainly in other policy sectors (Klingemann *et al.* 1994: ch. 9). This is perhaps not a simple model of 'party government', but it does imply that parties are nevertheless important for the policy outcomes generated by governments. Moreover, the growing fragmentation of party systems and the emergence of minority governments only serves to entrench further the need for consensus democracy.

The era of Social Democratic dominance was characterized by stable coalitions and control of parliaments. However, the first sign that Social Democratic dominance would erode came with the election result of 1961 in Norway, which left the Social Democrats running a minority administration. Subsequently, the Swedish Social Democrats lost power to a non-socialist coalition in 1976, ushering in a new and less stable period of government. In Denmark and Finland it had generally been the norm to govern with minority or relatively large and unwieldy coalition administrations (Damgaard 1992: 191–205); the latter in particular were subject to considerable instability (Jansson 1992), though Finland has enjoyed more stable coalition governments since 1983. Thus, party effects have increasingly been brought to bear through the subtle influences of consensus democracy throughout Scandinavia.

A factor that should not be overlooked in all this is corporatism: seen one way, this might be portrayed as an obvious challenge to the governing power of parties since it appears to privilege the policy-making and policy-implementing roles of interest groups which can bypass parties in parliament. Yet, although it has traditionally been strong in Scandinavia (Wilson 1990: 72–3; Siaroff 1999: 175–205), it is not clear that corporatism has necessarily weakened the governing significance of parties in such a way. If anything, it has served to bolster the power of the parties in government. The classic model of the Scandinavian party system links parties closely to interest organizations so that, for instance, the Social Democrats have been empowered by the potential of union-organized industrial action; similarly, the Agrarian parties have drawn on the implicit disruption to food supplies which could be brought to bear by farmers' interest organizations (Rokkan 1987: 95–100). This mode of coordinated action through the party and corporate channels has been characteristic of Scandinavian politics; moreover, setbacks in one channel (for instance, via disappointing electoral performance) could be compensated to some extent by the continuing influence of a social group through the other channel: hence Stein Rokkan's (1966) well-known statement that 'votes count, resources decide'.

However, the erosion of the class cleavage and the consequent changes in Scandinavian political life have undermined some of these longstanding linkages between party and corporate channels. Most notably, 'collective' membership of the Social Democratic parties of Sweden and Norway by affiliated union members was abolished in 1990 and 1997, respectively. This was indicative of the grow-ing autonomy of the unions from the parties. Studies show that, quite contrary to the claims of some party theories, it is the unions rather than the parties which have been motivated to break the link. The unions are bigger and better resourced; governments are no longer so clearly Social Democratic as hitherto; the state bureaucracy has become more important in delivering public services; and the European Union has brought a new dimension of activity to Scandinavian politics. Today, fewer than half of all union members vote for Social Democrats in Scandi-navia, the degree of overlap in party and union leaderships has eroded, and union representation in Social Democratic parliamentary parties has declined. Social Democrats and unions still maintain informal relationships, but these bind them together more loosely than previously (Sundberg 2001: 161–82). In such a context it is perhaps not surprising that Scandinavia's fabled corporatism has eroded. This flows in part from the inability of unions to fulfil the growing demands of their mem-bers, a development that has generated growing dissatisfaction and decreasing trust in the political system (Lewin 1992). Observers are now of the opinion that corpor-atism is gradually being replaced by a limited form of pluralism characterized by more conflict between interest organizations and greater recourse to lobbying, a less formal and less institutionalized form of political pressure (Micheletti 1994: 154–63); certainly, this contention appears to be supported by empirical studies of Denmark and Norway (Christiansen and Rommetvedt 1999: 195–220).

None of this necessarily implies that parties are less important to the process of governance than hitherto, but their impact is less likely to be felt in the same way. Whereas the classic Scandinavian model emphasized the leading role of Social Democratic parties which was founded on a symbiotic relationship with organized labour, and mollified by a consensual but powerful form of corporatism, this has gradually been replaced by an emerging alternative in which parties in parliament have become more central to policy outcomes, and to which competitive pluralistic lobbying by interest groups adds a significant, if subservient, input.

Political recruitment

The recruitment of politicians at the national level is dominated by political parties. The exact process varies from one party to another and from one electoral system to another. Generally, though, parties seek candidates who have political skills, attract voters, and are socially and geographically representative. With the decline of party memberships across Scandinavia, finding candidates who can fulfil all these criteria has become more problematic. Members tend to have more formal education but do not necessarily have better political skills. Thus, the search for recruits now takes in sympathizers as well as members of the parties and their ancillary and affiliated organizations.

Finland tends to have a more candidate-centred system of political recruitment than its Scandinavian neighbours because of the nature of the electoral system which pits candidate against candidate as well as party against party. The system makes it possible for personalities from the worlds of sport and entertainment to compete, although the overwhelming majority of candidates come from more traditional political backgrounds. In Denmark, Norway, and Sweden the parties have generally exercised tighter control over the candidate-selection process, although various reforms have afforded voters greater influence in recent years, especially in Denmark and Sweden. National government itself continues to be mainly the preserve of party politicians, although 'non-political experts' have been drawn into five Finnish governments since 1960 (including the last two) and one in Sweden during the 1990s (see Tables 7.5 and 7.8).

At the local and regional levels, party politics has become more important to political recruitment since the 1970s. Especially important to politics at these levels are the full-time professional politicians who play leading roles. In Denmark, for instance, every municipality now has an elected mayor who is a full-time party politician. The biggest cities have more than one full-time politician. In total, there are approximately 300 elected full-time local politicians in Denmark,[3] while the corresponding number in Sweden is 550 (Kommunalt Förtroendevalda 1992), and in Norway (where the municipalities are smaller), the number is a little over 300 (Johnsen 1996: 18–21; Gravdahl and Hagen 1997: 60). In addition, all chairmen of regional authorities are professional politicians, and they are selected according to the strength of the parties in the elected councils. Thus, except for Finland, local and regional government in Scandinavia has become professionalized and partified, twin processes which have been spurred on by waves of municipal amalgamation.

At the level of non-elective officials, party political recruitment in Norway, Sweden, and Denmark is restricted to certain elite positions in central, regional, and local state bureaucracies. While studies conducted in the late 1960s suggested that the long Social Democratic incumbency was associated with relatively high levels of political support for the party from within the ranks of central government ministries, this did not reflect a deliberate recruitment strategy. It is likely that social democratic sympathizers were more prone to work in the ministries than non-socialists, or that bureaucrats simply adjusted to the political realities of working

---

[3] I am grateful to Søren Sass Pedersen of the National Association of Local Authorities (Denmark) for providing this information.

with social democratic ministers at this time. However, the Cabinet Office is filled with experts and political secretaries appointed by the governing parties, even though this is not strictly provided for by the constitution. In 1988, there were between sixty and seventy political experts working in the Cabinet Office, plus a number of state departmental heads and county governors who were former politicians (Söderlind and Peterson 1988: 160–3). Even so, Sweden, Norway, and Denmark do not operate genuine spoils systems at the national level.

In Finland political recruitment follows different principles. During the late 1960s when the Social Democrats formed a cabinet together with the Communists and the Centre Party the prevailing system of recruitment to the public administration was criticized and changed. The two left-wing parties argued that the public administration as a whole was unrepresentative of the electorate in so far as it was overwhelmingly bourgeois in terms of social background and attitude. As a result, the Social Democrats and Communists actively sought to fill the ministries with sympathetic appointees. Eventually, other coalition partners followed suit and the system became widespread within the public sector. This new approach to public appointments combined with a rapid expansion in the size of the public sector to produce a considerable increase in the numbers recruited by the political parties (Heiskanen 1977: 245–53; Ståhlberg 1984: 237–47). In effect, party membership became a ticket to social mobility, and almost all elite positions within the public administration depended on party affiliations. Moreover, this pattern applied as much to sub-national government, although it seems likely that the politicization of the local state has gradually eroded at non-elite levels since the 1970s.

In summary, it is evident that parties remain central to the recruitment of parliamentary and governmental elites in national politics across Scandinavia, and that they have become more significant for the recruitment of elected officials in sub-national government since the 1970s. In addition, they generally have a limited role to play in recruiting to the public administration in Sweden, Denmark, and Norway, but since the 1960s, a far more extensive one in Finland.

Interest articulation and aggregation

Three developments we have already encountered in this chapter tell us something of the capacity of parties to articulate and aggregate interests: first, the growing fragmentation of party systems in Scandinavia since 1970 implies that the established parties are less able to aggregate broad social coalitions of support than hitherto; second, the decline of class voting in the same period implies that the parties' effectiveness in articulating social group interests has been eroded; and third, some of the evidence of popular disaffection with parties could be taken to indicate that voters are less than satisfied with the way in which parties articulate their concerns. The breakthrough of populist anti-establishment parties is particularly significant in the latter respect. As early as 1966, the Finnish Rural Party won a seat in parliament but in the following parliamentary election four years later the number rose to eighteen. In 1973, two populist parties (the Centre Democrats and the Progress Party) succeeded in gaining forty-one seats in the Danish parliament, while the leading three parties lost 20 per cent of the votes. In the same year, the Norwegian Progress Party broke through as the Labour (Social Democratic) Party sustained heavy losses. In Sweden the established parties (assisted by the effects of a high representational threshold imposed by the electoral system) managed to resist populist newcomers until the 1988 election (Sundberg 1999: 221–41). However, although the assault by populist protest parties may have come relatively late to Sweden this does not imply that the country's citizens were especially satisfied with established political order. In brief then, the capacity of parties to articulate and aggregate social group interests has in some respects weakened in Scandinavia, though this is far from saying that they now play an insignificant role in either sense.

Political participation

We have already seen a certain amount of evidence to suggest that parties in Scandinavia might not be fostering political participation as satisfactorily as they once did. First, electoral turnout has declined significantly in each of the countries bar Denmark. Second, party memberships have fallen dramatically in all four countries. Third, activism has dropped off among those who do remain party members. However, this should not be taken to imply that citizens are necessarily replacing traditional forms of participation in party politics with alternatives. For instance, Swedish research suggests that, while participation in party work has declined to an alarmingly low level, this is part of a broader pattern of participatory stagnation or decline (Peterson *et al.* 1998: 48–62).

Even so, the evidence is not universally gloomy for parties. The Finns tend to engage less than other Scandinavians in alternative forms of political participation (Togeby 1989). Moreover, while the voluntaristic side of participation in party life may have declined, it is abundantly clear that participation as paid professional work is prospering in all four Scandinavian democracies (Sundberg 1999: 103–30). In addition, it is inappropriate to regard single-issue groups and movements as an 'alternative' to parties. For one thing, it is clear that memberships of parties, interest groups, and social movements overlap. For another, the latter two seek to utilize a range of political outlets in order to get their message across, including the media, the public administration, and the parties themselves. Thus, single-issue groups and movements need parties in order to be effective. What is more, the relationship can work as much to the benefit of parties, since movements provide new opportunities for building social support. Finally, it should be noted that there is some evidence to suggest that parties have responded to the decline of activism by extending to their members greater incentives to participate in internal processes of candidate and leadership selection (Scarrow *et al.* 2000: 139, 151–3).

Political communication

The established parties in Scandinavia have historically all owned or controlled newspapers which have helped them to set the political agenda and control debate. These roles were especially crucial in the context of election campaigns. The non-socialist parties held the advantage of controlling the oldest press organs with the biggest circulations and advertising revenues. However, as in the case of the trade unions, formal organizational links with the parties have gradually been eroded; one by one the newspapers have come to regard their party links as a burden rather than an advantage. Symptomatic of this trend was the moment when the oldest pro-labour newspaper in Sweden, *Arbetet*, adopted a position of independence in the autumn of 2000. The paper was not in financial difficulty, but the dominant view within the labour movement was that it should compete in the market unencumbered by formal links with parties or unions (Nurmi 2000).

During election campaigns the media obviously plays an essential role in transmitting party propaganda and shaping public opinion. Studies show that, as is the case elsewhere, TV broadcasts are the most influential type of media in Scandinavia (Siune 1984: 132–47; Esaiasson 1990: 398–410; Bjørklund 1991: 279–302; Sundberg 1995: 45–65). Until the early 1990s the broadcasting companies were owned or controlled by national governments, giving the leading political actors the potential—in theory—to manipulate to their benefit the rules allocating TV time to those contesting parliamentary elections. In reality, however, the major parties have tended not to use their position in order to discriminate against political rivals. Rather, a belief in free and equal access to broadcasting facilities for political purposes has been the norm across all four Scandinavian democracies. Thus, in Denmark and Finland, all parties contesting elections are given equal access to TV; this is provided for by unofficial convention in Denmark, but is enshrined in law in Finland. In practice, this means that each party is entitled to be represented by one spokesperson in each broadcast which, given the fragmentation of party systems since 1970, has led to a proliferation of party representatives taking part in such transmissions. This tends to limit the capacity for genuine 'debate' and instead offers each party an opportunity to set out its position. Even so, there is no doubt that, in practice, parties in government generally receive far greater publicity than those in opposition.

In Norway, the rules on access to broadcasting have been relaxed since the early 1990s: until that time any party wanting access had to have been represented in Parliament in at least one of the two most recent parliamentary periods, had to nominate candidates in a majority of constituencies and had to maintain a national organization (Svåsand 1992: 743–4). Since it was generally agreed that these rules made it difficult for new parties to break into the political arena, they now apply only to the televised debate between party leaders; in all other programmes on both channels politicians are invited to participate on the basis of journalistic evaluations alone. In Sweden, the national broadcasting corporation follows criteria similar to those operating in Norway, though there is a greater range of political programming and the focus is trained more narrowly on the main political actors (Pierre and Widfeldt 1992: 791). Thus, debate centres on the leaders of the main parties of government and opposition, often taking on a Social Democrats-versus-the-rest aspect. Small parties and newcomers are effectively denied any role in these programmes.

Prior to the early 1990s viewers were restricted to a choice of just one (Norway) or two (Sweden) national TV channels, which helped confine broadcasters to a role of somewhat passively transmitting the political messages of the main parties. Since then, however, the TV broadcasters have become important actors in their own right and now find that they can play a more active part in setting the political agenda. This has been facilitated by the massive expansion of non-partisan information flows that has accompanied the birth of new commercial and satellite broadcasting. Political programming on these new channels cannot be controlled as it traditionally was on the national channels; the latter, moreover, have had to change in response to their new competitors. Thus, a media revolution has undermined the state monopoly of political broadcasting and weakened the agenda-setting capacity of the parties.

CONCLUSION

Democracy in Scandinavia is alive and well but the form it takes has altered considerably during recent decades. The major political parties established their position through the combined influence of electoral and functional channels, a mode of operation which enabled them to become effective and to endure. However, such arrangements require hierarchical corporatist structures and stable party-voter linkages and these things began to erode with the onset of electoral change and culminated in a loss of stable party governments dominated by Social Democracy. Related interest organizations are now more autonomous of parties, a development best exemplified by the abolition of collective (trade union) membership by the Swedish and Norwegian Social Democrats. In conjunction with the loss of (active) individual members in all four democracies this signified the end of the mass membership party in Scandinavia.

Yet this does not mean that Scandinavian political parties have declined overall. For one thing, they have more resources at their disposal than ever before. Voluntary work has been replaced by professional work and private incomes have been replaced with public subsidies. Political work has to a greater extent become a job with career opportunities. While it is true that voluntary activism still dominates in sub-national government, even here professionalism has spread since the early 1970s.

Non-partisan forms of political participation have for many years offered 'alternatives' which have particularly attracted younger, more educated, and often female citizens; however, even though such activities are sometimes more dramatic and visible than routine party work, they too have shown signs of stagnation and have never come remotely close to replacing political parties in the political arena. At best, their role has been to complement parties. However, the mass media constitute a cluster of independent actors that have undoubtedly come to challenge the agenda-setting function of parties. This development has perhaps contributed to the downgrading of party members' roles as channels of political communication. Thus, indirectly the media have promoted the growth of professionalism within the parties.

None of these changes imply that party members have lost all their traditional purposes. Though less central to the financing and general operation of parties than before, they remain central to the process of candidate-selection at local, regional, national, and supranational levels. But parties now put more effort into winning votes than recruiting members. Votes and seats bring money to the parties through public subsidies, while a big membership may bring as many costs as benefits. It is, however, exclusively in the hands of the members to decide whether to maintain or abolish the membership party, as all parties in Scandinavia operate some kind of system of internal democracy. No signs are yet visible that the members are ready to abolish themselves.

So parties in Scandinavia remain the primary actors in the political arena just as they did at the beginning of the twentieth century. To be old does not automatically imply that the party as a form of political organization is obsolete and ought to be replaced. The oldest car makers in the world are of more or less the same antiquity as the oldest parties in Scandinavia, yet nobody has questioned the capacity of these organizations to renew their models. The same is true for political parties. As with car makers, parties do not generate the same products that they did in the early part of the twentieth century. They have developed their organizations and adapted their policies to a changing environment, an environment, moreover, which is partly a product of their own activities in government.

REFERENCES

Aardal, B. , Valen, H. and Berglund, F. (1995) Valgundersøgelsen 1993. *Dokumentasjonsrapport* (Oslo: Statistisk sentralbyrå).

——, —— (1995) *Konflikt og Opinion* (Oslo: NKS-forlaget).

——, —— (1997) 'The Storting elections of 1989 and 1993: Norwegian politics in perspective', in K. Strom and L. Svåsand (eds) *Challenges to Political Parties* (Ann Arbor: The University of Michigan Press).

—— (1998) 'One for the Record – the 1997 Storting Election'. *Scandinavian Political Studies* 21.

——, ——, Narud, H.M. and Berglund, F. (1999) *Velgere i 90-årene* (Oslo: NKS-Forlaget).

Alestalo, M. and Kuhnle, S. (1987) 'The Scandinavian route: economic, social, and political developments in Denmark, Finland, Norway, and Sweden', in R. Erikson, E. Hansen, S. Ringen, and H. Uusitalo (eds) *The Scandinavian Model* (London: M. E. Sharpe).

Allern, H. E. and Heidar, K. (2001) 'Partier og intresseorganisasjoner i Norge', in J. Sundberg (ed.) *Partier och intresseorganisationer i Norden* (Copenhagen: Nordisk Ministerråd Nord 8), pp. 103–39.

Arstein, T. (1997) *Gøy på landet? Bygdelister i norsk lokalpolitikk 1945–1995* (Bergen: Institutt for Sammenliknende Politikk, Univeristetet i Bergen (unpublished thesis)).

Arter, D. (1999) *Scandinavian Politics Today* (Manchester: Manchester University Press).

Bartolini, S. and Mair, P. (1990) *Identity, Competition, and Electoral Availability: The Stabilization of European Electorates 1885–1985* (Cambridge: Cambridge University Press).

Berglund, S. and Lindström, U. (1978) *The Scandinavian Party System(s)* (Lund: Studentlitteratur).

Beyme, K. von (1985) *Political Parties in Western Democracies* (Aldershot: Gower).

Bille, L. (1997) *Partier i Forandring* (Odense: Odense Universitetsforlag).

—— and Christiansen, F. J. (2001) 'Partier og intresseorganisationer i Danmark', in J. Sundberg (ed.) *Partier och Intresseorganisationer i Norden* (Copenhagen: Nordisk Ministerråd Nord 8), pp. 29–77.

Bjørklund, T. (1991) 'Election Campaigns in Postwar Norway (1945-1989): From Party-Controlled to Media-Driven Campaigns' *Scandinavian Political Studies* 14.

Borg, S. (1997) 'Kiinnostus puoluejäsenyyteen ja jäsenaktiivisuus puolueissa', in S. Borg (ed.) *Puolueet 1990-Luvulla* (Turku: Turun Yliopisto, Valtio-opillisia tutkimuksia, 53).

Borre, O. and Andersen, J. G. (1997) *Voting and Political Attitudes in Denmark* (Århus: Aarhus University Press).

Castles, F. (1978) *The Social Democratic Image of Society: A Study of the Achievements and Origins of Scandinavian Social Democracy in Comparative Perspective* (London: Routledge).

Christansen, P. M. and Rommetvedt, H. (1999) 'From corporatism to lobbyism?', *Scandinavian Political Studies* 22.

Dalton, R. (2000) 'The Decline of Party Identification', in R. Dalton and M. Wattenberg (eds) *Parties without Partisans: Political Change in Advanced Industrial Democracies* (Oxford: Oxford University Press).

Damgaard, E. (1992) *Parliamentary Change in the Nordic Countries* (Oslo: Scandinavian University Press).

Elklit, J. (1991) 'Faldet i medlemstal i danske politiske partier'. *Politica* 23.

Elvander, N. (1980) *Skandinavisk arbetarrörelse* (Stockholm: Liber Förlag).

Erikson, R., Hansen, E., Ringen, S., and Uusitalo, H. (1987) *The Scandinavian Model* (London: M. E. Sharpe).

Ersson, S. (1993) 'Stabilitet och förändring i de nordiska partisystemen'. *Paper presented at the Nordic Political Science Congress*, Oslo.

Esaiasson, P. (1990) *Svenska valkampanjer 1866–1988* (Stockholm: Allmänna Förlaget).

Esping-Andersen, G. (1985) *Politics against Markets: The Social Democratic Road to Power* (Princeton: Princeton University Press).

—— (1994) 'Jämlikhet, effektivitet och makt', in P. Thullberg and Östberg, K. (eds) *Den Svenska Modellen* (Lund: Studentlitteratur).

Farrell, D. M. and Webb, P. D. (2000) 'Political parties as campaign organizations', in R. J. Dalton and M. P. Wattenberg (eds) *Parties Without Partisans: Political Change in Advanced Industrial Democracies* (Oxford: Oxford University Press), pp. 102–28.

Gidlund, G. (1983) *Partistöd* (Lund: CWK Gleerup).

—— (1991*a*) 'Public investments in Swedish democracy', in M. Wiberg (ed.) *The Public Purse and Political Parties* (Helsinki: The Finnish Political Science Association).

—— (1991*b*) 'Conclusions: the nature of public financing in the Nordic states', in Wiberg, M. (ed.) *The Public Purse and Political Parties* (Helsinki: The Finnish Political Science Association).

—— and Möller, T. (1999) *Demokratins Trotjänare* (Copenhagen: Demokratiutredningen).

Gidlund, J. and Gidlund, G. (1981) *Ty Riket är ditt och Makten* (Stockholm: Kommundepartementet, DsKn 15).

Gilljam, M. and Holmberg, S. (1995) *Väljarnas Val* (Stockholm: Norstedts).

Gravdahl, H. P. and Hagen, T. (1997) *Ny kommunelov, Ny Organisering? Organisasjon og Arbeidsformer i Kommuner og Fylkeskommuner i 1996.* (Oslo: NIBR-notat 105).

Heidar, K. (1994*a*) 'Hvorfor partimedlem?', in L. Svåsand and K. Heidar (eds) *Partierne i en Brytningstid* (Bergen: Alma Mater).

Heidar, K. (1994*b*) 'The polymorphic nature of party membership'. *European Journal of Political Research* 25: 61–86.

Heiskanen, I. (1977) *Julkinen, Kollektiivinen ja Markkinaperusteinen* (Helsinki: Valtioopin laitos. Helsingin Yliopisto, Deta 31).

Jansson, J.-M. (1992) *Från Splittring till Samverkan* (Helsingfors: Söderström & Co).

Jensen, R. B. (1997) 'Valgkampens organisering og ressourcer', in J. Elklit and R. Buch Jensen (eds) *Kommunalvalg* (Odense: Odense Universitetsforlag).

Johnsen, V. (1996) *Kommunal Organisering: En Spørreundersøkelse til Kommuner og Fylkeskommuner* (Oslo: NIBR-notat 107).

Kaplan, J. (1999) 'The Finnish new radical right in comparative perspective', in K. Pekonen (ed.) *The New Radical Right in Finland* (Helsinki: The Finnish Political Science Association).

Karvonen, L. (1991) 'A nation of workers and peasants: ideology and compromise in the interwar years', in L. Karvonen and J. Sundberg (eds) *Social Democracy in Transition* (Aldershot: Dartmouth Publications).

—— (1999) 'Demokrati och samhörighet i Norden. Har vi en lysande framtid bakom oss?', in L. Karvonen and E. Ljungberg (eds) *Nordisk demokrati i förändring* (Sundsvall: Mid Sweden University).

Katz, R. S. and Mair, P. (1992) *Party Organizations: A Data Handbook on Party Organizations in Western Democracies, 1960–1990* (London: Sage Publications).

——, —— et al. (1992) 'The membership of political parties in European democracies'. *European Journal of Political Research* 22: 329–45.

Klingemann, H. D., Hofferbert, R., and Budge, I. (1994) *Parties, Policy and Democracy* (Boulder, CO: Westview Press).

Knutsen, O. and Scarbrough, E. (1995) 'Cleavage Politics', in J. van Deth and E. Scarbrough (eds) *The Impact of Values* (Oxford: Oxford University Press).

Kommunalt Förtroendevalda (1992) *Parti och Kön, Arvoden, Partistöd* (Stockholm: Svenska Kommunförbundet).

Kongshøj, L. E. (1998) *Kontinuitet eller forandring? Et survey baseret studie af udviklingen i de danske partimedlemmers køns-og aldersfordelning fra 1971 og frem* (Copenhagen: Copenhagen University Press).

Lane, J.-E. and Ersson, S. O. (1997) 'Parties and voters: what creates the ties?'. *Scandinavian Political Studies* 20.

—— —— (1999) *Politics and Society in Western Europe* (London: Sage Publications).

Lewin, L. (1992) *Samhället och de Organiserade Intressena* (Stockholm: Norstedts).

Lijphart, A. (1977) *Democracy in Plural Societies* (New Haven: Yale University Press).

—— (1984) *Democracies: Patterns of Majoritarian and Consensus Government in Twenty-One Countries* (New Haven: Yale University Press).

Lipset, S. M. and Rokkan, S. (1967) 'Cleavage structures, party systems, and voter alignments: an introduction', in S. M. Lipset and S. Rokkan (eds) *Party Systems and Voter Alignments: Cross National Perspectives* (New York: The Free Press).

Mair, P. (1997) *Party System Change: Approaches and Interpretations* (Oxford: Oxford University Press).

—— and van Biezen, I. (2001) 'Party membership in twenty European democracies, 1980–2000'. *Party Politics* 7: 5–22.

Micheletti, M. (1994) *Det Civila Samhället och Staten* (Stockholm: Fritzes).

Milbrath, L. and Goel, M. L. (1977) *Political Participation* (Chicago: Rand McNally College Publishing Company).

Möller, T. (1999) 'Ett förbrukat förtroende? Om misstron i skandinavisk politik', in L. Karvonen and E. Ljungberg (eds) *Nordisk demokrati i förändring* (Sundsvall: Mid Sweden University).

—— (2000) *Politikens Meningslöshet* (Malmö: Liber).

Neumann, S. (1956) 'Toward a comparative study of political parties', in S. Neumann (ed.) *Modern Political Parties* (Chicago: The University of Chicago Press).

Nielsen, H. J. (1999) 'The Danish election 1998'. *Scandinavian Political Studies* 22.

Nousiainen, J. (1998) *Suomen Poliittinen Järjestelmä* (Helsinki: WSOY).

Nurmi, K. (2000) 'Inte vilken tidning som helst'. *Journalisten*, 26.

Oskarsson, M. (1994) *Klassröstning i Sverige* (Stockholm: Nerenius and Santérus).

Pedersen, M. (1979) 'The dynamics of European party systems: changing patterns of electoral volatility.' *European Journal of Political Research* 7: 1–26.

—— (1987) 'The Danish working multiparty system: breakdown or adaption?', in H. Daalder (ed.) *Party Systems in Denmark, Austria, Switzerland, The Netherland, and Belgium* (London: Frances Pinter Publishers).

—— (1988) 'The defeat of all parties: the Danish Folketing election of 1973', in K. Lawson and P. Merkl (eds) *When Parties Fail* (Princeton: Princeton University Press).

—— (1989) 'En kortfattet oversigt over det danske partisystems udvikling'. *Politica* 21.

—— (1991) 'The birth, life and death of small parties in Danish politics', in F. Mueller-Rommel and G. Pridham (eds.) *Small Parties in Western Europe* (London: Sage Publications).

Pesonen, P., Sänkiaho, R. and Borg, S. (1993) *Vaalikansan äänivalta* (Helsinki: WSOY).

Petersson, O. (1995) *Nordisk Politik* (Stockholm: Allmänna Förlaget).

—— Hermansson, J., Micheletti, M., Teorell, J., and Westholm, A. (1998) *Demokratirådets Rapport 1998* (Stockholm: SNS Förlag).

Petersson, O., Hernes, G., Holmber, S., Togeby, L., and Wängnerud, L. (2000) *Demokrati utan Partier? Demokratirådets Rapport 2000* (Stockholm: SNS Förlag).

Pierre, J. and Widfeldt, A. (1992) 'Sweden', in R. S. Katz and P. Mair (eds) *Party Organizations: A Data Handbook* (London: Sage Publications), pp. 781–836.

Rokkan, S. (1966) 'Norway: numerical democracy and corporate pluralism', in R. A. Dahl (ed.) *Political Oppositions in Western Democracies* (New Haven: Yale University Press), pp. 89–105.

—— (1970) *Citizens, Elections, Parties* (Oslo: Universitetsforlaget).

—— (1981) 'The growth and structuring of mass politics', in F. Wisti (ed.) *Nordic Democracy* (Copenhagen: Det Danske Selskab).

—— (1987) *Stat, Nasjon, Klasse* (Oslo: Universitetsforlaget).

Rose, R. (1974) *Electoral Behaviour: A Comparative Handbook* (NYC: Free Press).

Sainsbury, D. (1987) 'Class voting and left voting in Scandinavia: the impact of different operationalizations of the working class'. *European Journal of Political Research* 15.

Sänkiaho, R. (1996) 'The social basis for party support', in S. Borg and R. Sänkiaho (eds) *The Finnish Voter* (Helsinki: The Finnish Political Science Association).

Scarrow, S. (1994) 'Politicians against parties: anti-party arguments as weapons of change in Germany'. *European Journal of Political Research* 29: 297–317.

—— Webb, P. and Farrell, D. (2000) 'From Social Integration to Electoral Contestation: The Changing Distribution of Power within Political Parties', in R. Dalton and M. Wattenberg (eds) *Parties without Partisans: Political Change in Advanced Industrial Democracies* (Oxford: Oxford University Press).

Schmitt, H. and Holmberg, S. (1995) 'Political parties in decline?', in H.-D. Klingemann and D. Fuchs (eds) *Citizens and the State* (Oxford: Oxford University Press).

Selle, P. and Svåsand, L. (1982) 'Partiorganisasjon og valgresultat: En drøftning av ulike sammenhenger', in D. Anckar, E. Damgaard, and H. Valen (eds) *Partier, Ideologier, Väljare* (Åbo: Meddelanden från Stiftelsens för Åbo Akademi forskningsinstitut nr 77).

Siaroff, A. (1999) 'Corporatism in 24 industrial democracies: meaning and measurement'. *European Journal of Political Research* 36: 175–205.

Siune, K. (1984) 'Bestemmer TV valgresultetet?', in J. Elklit and O. Tonsgaard (eds) *Valg og Vælgeradfærd* (Århus: Forlaget Politica).

Söderlind, D. and Petersson, O. (1988) *Svensk Förvaltningspolitik* (Uppsala: Diskurs Förlag).

Ståhlberg, K. (1984) 'Diskriminerande drag i utnämningspolitiken'. *Förvaltningsforskning Årsbok* 2.

Sundberg, J. (1987) 'Exploring the basis of declining party membership in Denmark: a Scandinavian comparison'. *Scandinavian Political Studies* 10.

—— (1989) 'Premisser för politiskt massmedlemskap: partierna i Danmark i en nordisk jämförelse'. *Politica* 21.

—— (1991) 'Participation in local government: a source of social democratic decentralization in Scandinavia?', in L. Karvonen and J. Sundberg (eds) *Social Democracy in Transition* (Aldershot: Dartmouth Publications).

—— (1995) 'Women in Scandinavian party organizations', in L. Karvonen and P. Selle (eds) *Women in Nordic Politics* (Aldershot: Dartmouth Publications).

—— (1995*b*) 'Organizational Structure of Parties, Candidate Selection and Campaigning', in S. Borg and R. Sänkiaho (eds) *The Finnish Voter* (Helsinki: The Finnish Political Science Association).

—— (1996) *Partier och Partisystem i Finland* (Esbo: Schildts Förlag).

—— (1999) 'The enduring Scandinavian party system'. *Scandinavian Political Studies* 22.

—— (1999*b*) 'Massmedlemskapet: en tillgång eller belastning för partierna i Norden', in L. Karvonen and E. Ljungberg (eds) *Nordisk demokrati i förändring* (Sundsvall: Mid Sweden University).

—— (2001) 'Partier och intresseorganisationer i Norden: från nära integration till relaterad autonomi', in J. Sundberg (ed.) *Partier och Intresseorganisationer i Norden* (Copenhagen: Nordisk Ministerråd, Nord 8).

—— and Gylling, C. (1992) 'Finland', in R. S. Katz and P. Mair (eds) *Party Organizations: A Data Handbook* (London: Sage Publications), pp. 273–316.

Svåsand, L. (1992) 'Norway', in R. S. Katz and P. Mair (eds) *Party Organizations: A Data Handbook* (London: Sage Publications), pp. 732–80.

—— (1994) 'Partienes finansieringsmønster: Fra medlemmenes lommebøker til statsbudsjettet', in L. Svåsand and K. Heidar (eds) *Partierne i en Brytningstid* (Bergen: Alma Mater).

——, Strøm, K., and Rash, B. (1997) 'Change and adaption in party organization', in K. Strøm and L. Svåsand (eds) *Challenge to Political Parties: The Case of Norway* (Ann Arbor: The University of Michigan Press).

Thomsen, S. R. (1984) 'Udviklingen under forholdsvalgmåden (1920–84)', in J. Elklit and O. Tonsgaard (eds) *Valg og Vælgeradfærd* (Århus: Forlaget Politica).

Togeby, L. (1989) *Ens og Forskellig: Græsrodsdeltagelse i Norden* (Århus: Forlaget Politica).

—— (1992) 'The nature of declining party membership in Denmark: causes and consequences'. *Scandinavian Political Studies* 15.

Uusitalo, H. (1975) *Class Structure and Party Choice: A Scandinavian Comparison* (Helsinki: University of Helsinki Research Group for Comparative Sociology Research Report No. 10).

Vedung, E. (1991) 'Miljöpartiet, nedfrysningsteorin och den järnhårda oligarkilagen', in B. Gustafsson (ed.) *Människa Miljö Samhälle* (Uppsala: Samhällsvetenskapliga fakulteten, Uppsala universitet).

Wiberg, M. (1991) 'Public financing of parties as Arcana Imperii in Finland', in M. Wiberg (ed.) *The Public Purse and Political Parties* (Helsinki: The Finnish Policial Science Association).

Widfeldt, A. (1999) *Linking Parties with People? Party Membership in Sweden 1960–1997* (Aldershot: Ashgate).

Wilson, F. L. (1990) 'Neo-corporatism and the rise of new social movements', in R. Dalton and M. Kuechler (eds) *Challenging the Political Order* (Cambridge: Polity Press).

Worre, T. (1978) 'Partistabilitet og vælgervandringer', in O. Borre, J. Nielsen, S. Sauerberg, and T. Worre (eds) *Vælgere i 70'erne* (København: Akademisk Forlag).

—— (1980) 'Class parties and class voting in the Scandinavian Countries'. *Scandinavian Political Studies* 3.

—— (1989) 'Folketingsvalget 1987', *Økonomi og Politik* 62.

Wörlund, I. (1997) 'Hur förklara lokala partier?', in S. Lindberg and Y. Mohlin (eds) *Festskrift till Sten Berglund* (Vasa: Pro Facultate Nr 2).

—— and Hansson, D. (2001) 'Partier och interesseorganisationer i Sverige', in J. Sundberg (ed.) *Partier och Interesseorganisationer i Norden* (Copenhagen: Nordisk ministerrad Nord 8), pp. 141–60.

8

Party Politics in Ireland

Regularizing a Volatile System

R. J. Murphy and David M. Farrell

Party politics in Ireland provides wonderful copy for the comparativist. For long, perhaps, sidelined as 'sui generis' and, therefore, as unsuitable for inclusion in comparative frameworks (Whyte 1974; Carty 1983), in recent times the political science community has been more inclined to embrace the Irish case, celebrating its peculiarities. And with good reason. After all, here we have a party system that was without any 'social basis'—seen as the principal reason for describing Irish party politics as 'unique'—long before parties in other countries started worrying about declining rates of social class attachment (Eijk and Franklin 1996). And yet, for all this, the system was inherently very stable, with governments tending to last for three- to four-year terms (including two periods when Fianna Fáil was in power for sixteen consecutive years, from 1932 to 1948 and then again from 1957 to 1973).

Furthermore, from Stein Rokkan onwards, scholars had great difficulty in trying to fit the Irish case into the accepted cleavage categories. Perhaps the best attempt so far has been made by Sinnott (1995), who manages, with some imagination, to shoe-horn it into the 'centre–periphery' cleavage, in which the two principal parties, Fianna Fáil and Fine Gael, are historically divided (as 'peripheral' parties) over the modalities of Irish secession from Britain at the start of the 1920s. Two features which could be singled out in all of this were, first, the weakness of the left, whose combined vote only just achieves double-digit proportions, and, second, the predominant position of Fianna Fáil, whose hold over Irish party politics set the tone for electoral competition, revolving as it did around the tension between Fianna Fáil and the 'rest' (chiefly Fine Gael and the smaller Labour Party). Apart from the brief period of multi-party politics in the 1950s, Ireland could very safely be categorized as a two-and-a-half party system (Farrell 1970).

An important institutional feature to mention when considering the peculiarities of the Irish case is its electoral system, the Single Transferable Vote (STV), used by just one other country for lower house elections (Malta). Of course, a major feature of STV is that, as a preferential electoral system, it tends to encourage a high degree of candidate-centred politics and decentralized party organizations

(Katz 1980). Despite being a proportional system, however, until quite recently it rarely produced the kind of coalition governments common under other PR regimes.

For a long time, and, indeed, until as recently as the mid-1970s, the accepted shibboleths of Irish party politics were its unchanging nature as a two-and-a-half party system, and the dominance of Fianna Fáil. The last quarter of the twentieth century has seen dramatic alterations to this tranquil picture (Table 8.1). This is evident in a number of developments. First, the 1970s heralded the arrival of electoral change. This meant that the certainty of government incumbency—one of the hallmarks of Fianna Fáil's status as the predominant party—ended: whereas in almost four decades from 1932 to 1969, governments changed just four times, by contrast, in the past thirty years no incumbent government has been fully returned to power. As Table 8.2 shows, this reached a point by the end of the 1980s when even Fianna Fáil was unable to form single-party government, and Irish government has since become coalition government, more in keeping with the normal experience of PR electoral systems. Indeed, the 1997 election marked the first occasion when Irish voters were offered a clear choice between two competing coalitions: Fianna Fáil and the Progressive Democrats (PDs) versus the outgoing 'rainbow coalition' of Fine Gael, Labour, and Democratic Left.

Electoral change was also shown by the host of new parties that entered the system, starting with the splits in Republicanism at the end of the 1970s and the emergence of the Workers Party (later Democratic Left), followed in the mid-1980s by splits in Fianna Fáil and Fine Gael, which generated the PDs, and culminating at the end of the 1980s in the arrival of Green politics and the election of the first Green Party TDs. Creeping up almost insidiously during all these changes has been Sinn Féin, moreover, which won its first Dáil seat in modern times at the 1997 general election.

More recently, the party system has seen some rationalization. In January 1999, there was a formal merger between Labour and Democratic Left. The prospect of this had been publicly touted since a Labour leadership change in 1997. The narrowing of policy differences between the two parties, complemented by the new-found status of Democratic Left as a coalitionable party in the 'rainbow coalition' of 1994–97 meant that a united left in parliament was attractive to both parties; it was seen as offering the prospect of an electoral boost and the possibility of challenging the two larger Irish parties. In the event, however, there is no sign of any immediate electoral benefits to the Labour Party as a result of this merger, as revealed by disappointing results in the 1999 local elections. Further, it could be argued that the merger of the two main leftist parties has raised the prospect of anti-system parties, such as Sinn Féin, sweeping up an urban protest vote.

If the Irish party system in recent times has become more unpredictable, and hence for the political establishment less controlled, it has also shown signs of becoming more regulated. As we shall see, in the light of recent legislative reforms,

TABLE 8.1. *Irish election results, turnout, volatility, and effective numbers of parties: 1961–97*

Year	Election results														Turnout (%)	Volatility	ENEP	ENPP
	Fianna Fáil		Fine Gael		Labour		PDs		WP/DL		RP/SF		Others					
	%V	#S	%V	#S	%V	#S	%V	#S	%V	#S	%V	#S	%V	#S				
1961	43.8	70	32.0	47	11.6	16	—	—	—	—	4.2	1	6.8	10	70.6	8.2	3.3	2.8
1965	47.7	72	34.1	47	15.4	22	—	—	—	—	0.8	1	2.1	2	75.1	9.0	2.7	2.6
1969	45.7	75	34.1	50	17.0	18	—	—	—	—	—	—	3.2	1	76.9	2.4	2.8	2.5
1973	46.2	69	35.1	54	13.7	19	—	—	—	—	2.0	0	3.0	2	76.6	3.0	2.8	2.6
1977	50.6	84	30.6	43	11.6	17	—	—	—	—	1.8	0	5.5	4	76.3	6.9	2.8	2.4
1981	45.3	78	36.5	65	9.9	15	—	—	1.7	1	2.5	2	4.2	5	76.2	7.5	2.9	2.6
Feb 1982	47.3	81	37.3	63	9.1	15	—	—	2.2	3	1.0[a]	0	3.1	4	73.8	4.0	2.7	2.5
Nov 1982	45.2	75	39.2	70	9.4	16	—	—	3.1	2	—	—	3.2	3	72.9	2.8	2.7	2.5
1987	44.1	81	27.1	51	6.4	12	11.8	14	3.8	4	1.9	0	4.9	4	73.3	11.1	3.5	2.9
1989	44.1	77	29.3	55	9.5	15	5.5	6	5.0	7	1.2	0	5.4	6	68.5	7.0	3.4	3.0
1992	39.1	68	24.5	45	19.3	33	4.7	10	2.8[b]	4	1.6	0	8.1	6	68.5	13.0	4.0	3.5
1997	39.3	77	27.9	54	10.4	17	4.7	4	2.3	4	2.6	1	12.8	9	65.9	9.4	4.1	3.0

Notes: PDs: Progressive Democrats, WP/DL: Workers' Party/Democratic Left, RP/SF: Republican parties/Sinn Féin, ENEP: Effective number of electoral parties, ENPP: Effective number of parliamentary parties.

[a] Sinn Féin from February 1982 onwards.

[b] Democratic Left party in 1992–97. In 1992 the remnants of the Workers' Party (included in 'Others') received just 0.7% of the vote. In 1997 its vote dropped to 0.4%.

Source: Coakley 1999; Sinnott 1995; election returns.

TABLE 8.2. *Irish governments, 1961–97*

Year	Party(ies) in government	Taoiseach (Prime minister)
1961	Fianna Fáil	Seán Lemass
1965	Fianna Fáil	Seán Lemass;
		Jack Lynch (1966)
1969	Fianna Fáil	Jack Lynch
1973	Fine Gael, Labour	Liam Cosgrave
1977	Fianna Fáil	Jack Lynch;
		Charles Haughey (1979)
1981	Fine Gael, Labour	Garret FitzGerald
Feb. 1982	Fianna Fáil	Charles Haughey
Nov. 1982	Fine Gael, Labour	Garret FitzGerald
1987	Fianna Fáil	Charles Haughey
1989	Fianna Fáil,	Charles Haughey;
	Progressive Democrats	Albert Reynolds (1992)
1992	Fianna Fáil, Labour	Albert Reynolds
1994[a]	Fine Gael, Labour,	
	Democratic Left	John Bruton
1997	Fianna Fáil,	
	Progressive Democrats	Bertie Ahern

[a] The Reynolds government was replaced mid-term by the Bruton government.

Irish parties are coming to resemble public bodies in terms of financial transparency, state regulation of their internal workings, and state subsidization. To a degree, this gradual transformation can be seen as the obvious response of a more vulnerable 'cartel' party system, wishing to shore itself up with state support (Katz and Mair 1995). As will become apparent, the growing regulation of Irish party politics has, for the most part, also been forced on the political parties by a spate of recent scandals.

The last few years of the twentieth century were not happy ones for the established parties (although the same could not be said of the lawyers). Following the discovery of payments to a senior Fine Gael politician by a supermarket tycoon, a tribunal of inquiry was established in 1997 to investigate secret payments to politicians, during the course of which evidence was uncovered of very large sums of money having been made available over the years to former Fianna Fáil Taoiseach (prime minister) Charles J. Haughey. There followed a series of other tribunals which revealed how a number of senior politicians (principally in Fianna Fáil and Fine Gael), and prominent businessmen, held deposits in offshore accounts to avoid tax liabilities. Tribunal fever continues unabated: currently the Moriarty and Flood Tribunals are investigating further allegations of payments to politicians, land re-zoning scandals in North County Dublin, and the full nature of the relationship between big business and politics in Ireland.

PARTY LEGITIMACY

Given the recent scandals, this is a highly appropriate time to be assessing the question of party legitimacy in Ireland. The growth of cynicism, anti-party sentiment, and general disillusionment with the integrity of Irish politicians have been noted by many political commentators, and are undoubtedly matters of some concern for the political parties. There are various sources of empirical evidence to suggest that the public are becoming disillusioned with politicians and with parties in general.

One piece of concrete evidence is the declining rates of voter turnout (Table 8.1), which in the last three elections has fallen below the 70 per cent mark, and in 1997 was less than 66 per cent, the lowest rate of turnout since the early days of the new state in the 1920s. Turnout in recent presidential and local elections has reached even more alarmingly low levels: both the 1997 presidential election turnout of 47 per cent and the 1999 local election turnout of 50 per cent were the lowest ever. This problem of declining voter turnout was further highlighted in November 1999, when a Dublin city by-election registered the worst turnout in any Irish election, with a derisory 27.8 per cent voting (Donnelly 1999: 29). The dangers of such trends are recognized by the established political parties, with, for instance, politicians calling for a move to weekend voting as one possible means of trying to address the problem.

Another feature of the problems Irish parties currently face is the declining rate of partisan attachment, which potentially represents a long-term challenge to the ability of political parties to structure the vote in Ireland. An examination of Eurobarometer trends is illustrative. Eurobarometer data provide the only time-series available on Irish partisan attachment. Unfortunately, the series ends in 1994, when the question ceased being asked on a regular basis. As Table 8.3 reveals, over the fifteen-year period from 1978–94, the proportion of voters declaring any identification with Irish parties virtually halved: down from 65 per cent in 1978 to a low of 35 per cent in 1991, before picking up slightly to 39 per cent in 1994. Similarly, there was a dramatic drop in the proportion of voters claiming strong attachment with parties, down from 14 per cent in 1981 to 6 per cent in 1994 (see also Sinnott 1995: 153–4; Marsh and Sinnott 1999). The 1999 European elections study, using the same question format, reveals further drops to record low levels: less than 28 per cent declared any identification, and only 4.8 per cent claimed a strong attachment. Concomitant with this declining trend in partisan attachment has been a marginal increase in the support for micro-parties and independents at both local and national level, and the rise of single-issue groups, such as the 'anti-superdump' protest groups which have proliferated in recent years. As a result of the shortage of landfill sites for rubbish in all Irish county councils, proposals to site new 'superdumps' near communities have aroused serious hostility, generating lengthy legal arguments, protests at council meetings, and the highlighting of such

R. J. Murphy and David M. Farrell

TABLE 8.3. *Irish partisan attachment, 1978–94*

Year	Very strong identifiers (%)	All identifiers (%)
1978	13.7	64.5
1979	9.6	62.5
1980	9.0	61.4
1981	8.7	60.3
1982	8.0	53.6
1983	7.5	53.6
1984	5.7	47.4
1985	7.8	47.7
1986	4.8	42.8
1987	7.7	44.7
1988	6.1	45.3
1989	6.0	41.2
1990	8.0	40.4
1991	8.0	35.2
1992	7.2	36.3
1993	6.3	36.4
1994	5.7	39.4
1999	4.8	27.8

Note: Data from Eurobarometer Spring 1978 and Autumn 1981 are not included, because the questions were not comparable; question no longer asked after 1994.

Sources: Eurobarometer 1978–94; European Elections study 1999.

problems, particularly during elections. This is part of a wider 'NIMBY' ('not-in-my-backyard') phenomenon, where communities across the country have united to oppose the siting of (itinerant) 'travellers'' halting sites, mobile phone masts, and microwave satellite television masts close to particular areas.

Irish voters are more volatile than twenty or thirty years ago. As Table 8.1 reveals, average levels of volatility leapt in 1987 to just over 11 per cent (in large part reflecting the emergence of the PDs). In 1992 volatility figures reached what for recent times are record proportions of 13 per cent. Although average volatility levels declined somewhat in the 1997 election, the volatility figure of 9.4 per cent still represents the third most volatile election since 1961. Average volatility measured at constituency level reveals further levels of instability. For instance, 1997 showed an average volatility by constituency of 16.4 per cent, which is 'slightly more volatile than 1992 (15.6), markedly more volatile than 1989 (12.4) and rather less volatile than 1987 (18.2)' (Gallagher 1999: 126). Block volatility trends—assessing volatility across the divide between Fianna Fáil and the rest—paint a more stable picture, with the exception of the 1992 election when Fianna Fáil's core vote was substantially eroded (Sinnott 1995: 110–11).

By the end of the 1990s it was apparent that 'the terms of reference of Irish politics have finally changed, and for now, at least, the party system seems largely unstructured' (Mair 1999: 149). This is highlighted in particular by the increased support for independents and micro-parties who between them attracted 13 per cent of the vote in 1997, unprecedented in recent times, capturing in the process a mixture of 'left-wing support, voters disenchanted with the established parties and concerned about honesty and integrity, and, finally, those concerned about the issue of abortion' (Marsh and Sinnott 1999: 177). The steady increase in support for smaller parties and independents is reflected in the trend in the effective number of electoral parties, which has been rising pretty consistently since the early 1980s, reaching 4.1 in 1997 (Table 8.1).

From all this evidence, it would appear that the Irish electorate has lost a certain amount of respect for the established parties. A case could be made for a potential 'crisis of trust' in political parties and politicians in Ireland, presaging a decline in party legitimacy. Although mindful of the 'methodological booby-traps and theoretical pitfalls' (Poguntke 1996: 319) associated with trying to address such an issue, we can attempt to map some of the possible indicators of a decline in party legitimacy.

Certainly, it would appear that politicians are in little doubt that their profession has suffered considerable damage as a result of the seemingly endless revelations, financial scandals, and allegations of corruption that emerged throughout the latter part of the 1990s. A cursory glance at the political discourse reveals a fear amongst politicians that they are in danger of losing the electorate's trust altogether. This is illustrated by the following comments in a Labour Party policy document:

The damage that has been done to politics as a practice and a profession by the actions of those that introduced and benefited from a culture of corruption is immense. Such actions damage a political system that is already fragile for a number of reasons. The damage occurs at a time of corrosive cynicism, public apathy and a drift away from democratic accountability. (Higgins 2000: 1)

Of course, any assumption about the corrosive effect of recent political scandals on the legitimacy of political parties ought to be treated with caution. It should be borne in mind, for instance, that whatever changes there have been in popular attitudes towards parties in general, this has not so far resulted in a significant vote for anti-party candidates. That said, we have seen that support for micro-parties and independent candidates has increased in the past decade.

Moreover, recent survey evidence suggests that the politicians' fears of deep-seated public cynicism are not entirely misplaced. Scrutiny of public opinion polls indicates a recent dramatic decline in the perceived honesty/integrity of politicians, and in the confidence in which they are held. Although we are unable to track the trends in any systematic sense— because of the lack of adequate data— nonetheless a simple comparison of polls over time is instructive. The earliest evidence of voter attitudes about politicians is from a 1976 survey, commissioned by Irish television (RTÉ). Given that this poll coincided with the arrival of electoral volatility, and that it preceded the recent scandals, it provides a useful benchmark. At this point, 46 per cent of respondents found politicians 'honest and reliable'; by contrast, 17 per cent felt they were 'incapable' and 36 per cent judged them to be 'insincere' (IMS/RTÉ survey 1976). Though it is a slightly different indicator, it is interesting to contrast this with the responses to a survey of the professions in 1991, in which 68 per cent of respondents expressed a lack of confidence in politicians, the lowest figure for all professions (IMS/*Irish Independent* survey 1991). By the end of the decade, confidence in Irish politicians had sunk still lower: in a repeat of the same question in 1998, the proportion of respondents lacking confidence in politicians increased to 77 per cent (IMS/*Sunday Independent* survey 1998).

When pressed about specific issues, such as corruption or political donations, the voters expressed widespread distrust in politicians. For instance, in a 1996 survey a bare 5 per cent of respondents believed politicians' explanations when they claimed payments to them were political donations without any strings attached (IMS/*Irish Independent* survey 1996). And when asked, in a 1997 survey, about corruption allegations against Charles Haughey, the former Taoiseach, only 8 per cent believed his explanations (MRBI/*Irish Times* survey 1997). On the basis of this survey evidence, therefore, it can reasonably be surmised that recent developments regarding allegations of corruption and payments to politicians have played some role in the erosion of popular legitimacy of the mainstream political parties.

Irish party organizations have not been immune from the recent changes at the electoral level, as revealed by trends in party membership levels. Reliable data are hard to come by, but allowing for all the usual caveats about the accuracy of the parties' own reported figures, it is nonetheless possible to track trends for all the main parties since the mid-1980s. Table 8.4 reports the figures for all the parties over time (not including the Greens) indicating declining trends across the board. A comparison of membership totals between 1986 and 1998 shows a sharp decline from 138,726 in 1986 to 95,724 in 1998, a 31 per cent drop in a little over a decade. The final column of Table 8.4, which reports the number of party members as a proportion of the electorate, shows membership declining, by about a third, from an already low figure of 5.65 per cent to just 3.49 per cent over the same period.

The raw Fianna Fáil membership figures need to be treated with caution. While the party established a membership database in 1994 (Holmes 1999), the data currently provided are only rough estimates. The figures may, indeed, show a substantial decline in claimed members; however, it is worth noting that a possible slowing down in the rate of decline appears to have occurred after the mid-1990s as a result of organizational reforms associated with its new party leader, Bertie Ahern, which saw a revitalization in the numbers of party branches (Holmes 1999: 32).

The Fine Gael figures suggest a return to the low levels of membership of the 1970s, which preceded the party's extensive organizational reforms of the

TABLE 8.4. *Irish party members, 1976–98*

Year	Fianna Fáil	Fine Gael	Labour	Progressive Democrats	Workers' Party/ Democratic Left	Total no. of members	M/E (%)
1976	NA	NA	4461	—	NA		
1977	NA	20,000	4389	—	NA		
1978	NA	20,000	4329	—	NA		
1979	NA	27,000	4471	—	NA		
1980	NA	32,847	6009[a]	—	1700		
1981	NA	39,000	5285[a]	—	NA		
1982	NA	36,000	5635[a]	—	NA		
1983	NA	31,000[a] 5364[a]	—	NA			
1984	NA	30,000[a] 5858[a]	—	NA			
1985	NA	42,000	7324	—	2000		
1986	80,000	34,000[a]	7001	15,000	2725[b]	138,726	5.65
1987	89,000	25,777	8017	12,000	3450	138,244	5.65
1988	89,000	22,401	11,424	9000	3125[b]	134,950	5.52
1989	89,000	20,693	10,781	9000	2800	132,274	5.40
1990	75,000	20,700	7028	7500	2800	113,028	4.57
1991	75,000	25,000	7400[c]	7000	1000	115,400	4.55
1992	75,000	25,000	10,000[c]	7000	1100[d]	118,100	4.62
1993	75,000	25,000	6522	8000	1100	115,622	4.52
1994	75,000	25,000	7000[c]	8000	1400	116,400	4.43
1995	70,000	20,000	5502	8000	1400	104,902	3.99
1996	65,000	21,000	5708	7000	1400	100,108	3.76
1997	65,000	25,000	5632	7000	1400	104,032	3.79
1998	65,000	21,800	5324	4000	1400[e]	95,724	3.49

Notes: All Fianna Fáil, and Worker's Party/Democratic Left figures (apart from 1980 and 1985) are from *Irish Political Studies*, which are estimates provided by the parties. From 1996–98, Fianna Fail claims 30,000 'active members', the rest of whom are 'associate members'. The source for all other parties from 1976–90 is Farrell (1992). Unless otherwise indicated, the Labour figures for subsequent years have been supplied to the authors by the party. In all other cases, and for all other parties, the post-1990 figures are from *Irish Political Studies*.
[a]In these cases data were not available on ancillary members (youth and women's sections).
[b]Democratic Left figures for 1986 and 1988 are calculated as averages of preceding and following years.
[c]*Irish Political Studies*.
[d]Democratic Left from 1992.
[e]Estimate by authors.
Sources: Farrell (1992); *Irish Political Studies* (1991–99), figures supplied by the Labour Party.

1980s (Farrell 1994). The 1998 Labour figure reported in Table 8.4 predates the Labour–Democratic Left merger, indicating that the party membership figures remained static at best; however, according to more recent party estimates, post-merger (in 1999) the membership numbers increased to 6200. The PDs, for all their threatening to 'break the mould' of Irish politics, have seen their membership decline significantly from the dizzying heights of 1987. At their 1999 conference, the party leader spoke of the need for 'root and branch' reform in order to revitalize the party organization. The figures supplied by the party almost certainly represent a substantial exaggeration of the real figure. Their current organizational weakness is indicated by a fall-off in the numbers of branches—down from 273 to 41—but also by the party's failure to nominate any candidates for the 1999 European elections, or in many constituencies for the local elections held during the same year.

Figures for Democratic Left membership, prior to its formal dissolution, also remained static. Dunphy's (1998) analysis of Democratic Left's prospects for the future predicted that the party would probably fade away, and he emphasized the organizational weakness of the party. By 1997 the membership consisted of a small number of Dublin activists supporting four party notables (that is, its remaining TDs), along with a few bases outside Dublin and isolated members in other parts of the country.

Sinn Féin membership figures have not been accurately recorded, and are not reported here. But given the recent growth of the party electorally in the Republic of Ireland, and anecdotal evidence of increased grass roots activism, there is an impression at least of growing organizational strength. In a recent newspaper interview, the party's General Secretary claimed that it was attracting '50 new members a month' and currently had 5000 'active members' in 400 branches—in both cases more than double the previously reported figures (*The Sunday Business Post*, 13 January 2000).

This review of the evidence regarding Irish party legitimacy provides stark evidence of a party system in crisis. This is evident from aggregate and individual-level figures, as well as in terms of party membership trends. A glance at some of the aggregate indicators, culled from the tables considered so far, shows a picture of voters who increasingly turned off politics. For instance, average voter turnout in the 1960s was 74.2 per cent; in the 1990s it declined to an average of 67.2 per cent. In the same period, voter volatility doubled from an average of 6.5 per cent to 11.2 per cent. Much of this electoral instability worked to the disadvantage of the established 'civil war' parties (Fianna Fáil and Fine Gael). They attracted an average vote of 79.1 per cent in the 1960s (representing 58.7 per cent of the electorate); by the 1990s that had dropped to 65.4 per cent (43.9 per cent of the electorate). The picture is much the same at the individual level. In the space of just two decades, the proportion of party identifiers plummeted (from 64.5 in 1978 to 27.8 per cent in 1999). Moreover, our review of the poll evidence reveals a recent sharp decline in voter perceptions of the honesty and integrity of Irish politicians. Finally, not only are parties losing the support of the average voter; even more seriously, in the space of just one decade, they have lost just short of one-third of their dues-paying members. By any standard, these are all major changes. They are indicative of a very different political environment in which the parties operate, and they reveal some serious problems of legitimacy for Irish political parties at the turn of the millennium.

PARTY ORGANIZATIONAL STRENGTH

There may be signs of problems for Irish parties at the electoral level, as witnessed by the increase in electoral volatility, the apparent crisis of legitimacy in party politics, and the erosion of the membership base, but as we shall see, in organizational terms Irish parties have been showing admirable resilience.

Party finances

Party politics in Ireland, as elsewhere, has become very expensive, not least because of the need to embrace organizational professionalization and new campaign styles. Until relatively recently, it was not possible to do more than guess about the sources of Irish party finance, because the whole process was 'shrouded in secrecy' (Laver and Marsh 1999: 157). Given the fact that the parties are not required to produce audited accounts, this means that, inevitably, the quality of the figures actually provided by the parties is likely to be variable: as a result a warning note needs to be attached to the trends reported in Table 8.5. Despite this, some interesting trends are worth noting. For instance, consistent with the view that party politics is becoming more expensive, we can see in the last row of the table how expenditure growth has for the most part outstripped income growth over time. The big growth period for the parties was during the 1980s—for Fianna Fáil at the start of the decade, for Fine Gael towards the end. In part, this reflected processes of campaign and organizational professionalization, which were undoubtedly at their most intense in that period (Farrell 1994), but it also reflected the high level of electoral volatility throughout the decade, requiring the parties to work harder, and spend more for their votes. Note, however, that the 1997 entry in Table 8.5 provides salutary evidence of the difficulties of relying on data provided by the parties. This is shown particularly by the dramatic jump in Labour's finance figures from the 1992 trends, which bizarrely places it ahead of Fianna Fáil in terms of expenditure and especially also in terms of income. The Labour Party stands by these figures, which are audited: according to the party, in part these reflect the fact that it was defending an unusually large number of seats in 1997.

For some years, the parties have been in receipt of disparate sources of public funding which, while certainly not insignificant in terms of their annual budgets (Farrell 1994), were not as generous as the amounts of state support common elsewhere in Western Europe. The centre-piece is a party leader's allowance, known as the 'Oireachtas grant', which in the past accounted for a significant proportion of funding to political parties, weighted in favour of the opposition parties. The payments used to discriminate against minor parties (Farrell 1992), but since 1996 they have taken account of the numbers of TDs each party has. The amounts involved are quite substantial: in the late 1990s, Fine Gael received annual subsidies of over IR£650,000, Fianna Fáil about IR£540,000, Labour just

TABLE 8.5. *Irish party head office income and expenditure: 1961–97 (IR£)*

Year		FF money terms	FF real terms	FG money terms	FG real terms	Labour money terms	Labour real terms	PDs money terms	PDs real terms	WP/DL money terms	WP/DL real terms	Total money terms	Total real terms
1961	y	NA	NA	14,066ᵃ	15,094	3217	3452	—	—	—	—	NA	NA
	x	NA	NA	12,208	13,100	3219	3454	—	—	—	—	NA	NA
1965	y	NA	NA	22,395	24,357	4958	5392	—	—	—	—	NA	NA
	x	NA	NA	22,438	24,404	4958	5392	—	—	—	—	NA	NA
1973	y	71,286	81,908	NA	NA	21,247	24,413	—	—	1305	1499	NA	NA
	x	73,264	84,180	NA	NA	28,064	32,246	—	—	905	1040	NA	NA
1977	y	189,899	243,640	79,263	101,694	40,687	52,201	—	—	8170	10,482	318,019	408,018
	x	188,799	242,229	78,388	100,572	40,688	52,203	—	—	7452	9561	315,327	404,565
1981	y	455,000	677,950	237,176	353,392	100,083	149,124	—	—	23,930	35,656	816,189	1,216,122
	x	446,995	666,023	295,080	439,669	91,450	136,261	—	—	24,022	35,793	857,547	1,277,745
1982	y	457,000	422,472	304,233	272,593	111,498	95,888	—	—	40,160	35,984	912,891	817,950
	x	448,224	401,609	421,816	377,947	117,384	106,176	—	—	38,000	34,048	1,025,424	918,780
1987	y	640,000	1,139,200	615,592	1,095,754	185,250	329,745	576,170	1,025,582	189,148	336,683	2,206,160	3,926,965
	x	616,818	1,097,936	726,338	1,292,762	308,355	548,872	682,408	1,214,686	178,172	317,146	2,512,091	4,471,522
1989	y	690,000	1,262,700	739,911	1,354,037	299,311	547,739	624,774	1,143,336	348,860	638,414	2,702,856	4,946,226
	x	719,875	1,317,371	726,271	1,329,076	315,082	576,600	569,573	1,042,319	348,308	637,404	2,679,109	4,902,769
1992	y	NA	NA	761,718	1,454,881	385,585	736,467	NA	NA	NA	NA	NA	NA
	x	NA	NA	735,426	1,404,664	329,229	628,827	NA	NA	NA	NA	NA	NA
1997	y	462,014	462,014	1,618,400	1,618,400	900,289	900,289	466,547	466,547	NA	NA	NA	NA
	x	626,801	626,801	1,524,001	1,524,001	910,330	910,330	361,316	361,316	NA	NA	NA	NA
Change 1977–97 %	y	+143	+90	+1942	+1491	+2113	+1625			NA	NA	NA	NA
	x	+232	+159	+1844	+1415	+2137	+1644			NA	NA	NA	NA

Notes: All years selected are election years. No information was available for any of the parties in 1969. For real term figures 1997 price index = 100; 1992 = 91.09; 1989 = 82.8; 1987 = 77.9; 1982 = 57.5; 1981 = 49.1; 1977 = 28.3; 1973 = 14.9; 1965 = 8.7; 1961 = 7.3.
ᵃ 1962 figures.

Sources: Farrell (1992); information supplied by the parties.

under IR£300,000, Democratic Left IR£100,000, and the PDs IR£65,000 (Laver and Marsh 1999: 156).

In 1997–98, the political funding of Irish parties was revolutionized by legislative reform which, largely in consequence of the scandals over party finance, was designed both to police the processes of party funding better and to resource the parties better. The 1997 and 1998 Electoral Acts had a number of important effects. First, qualified parties—those winning at least 2 per cent of the vote in the previous election—are entitled to a share of approximately IR£1 million annually in state funding to help maintain their organizations. Referred to as the 'Exchequer grant', this is in addition to the allowance they receive under the terms of the Oireachtas grant. The amount of money each registered party receives is determined by calculating each qualified party's first preference vote as a proportion of the total number of first preference votes received by all registered parties. As a result of the Exchequer grant and the mid-1990s' expansion in payouts under the Oireachtas grant, there has been a dramatic increase in the public funding of Irish parties (Table 8.6). In 1989 total state funding was just under half a million pounds: ten years later, this funding had increased fourfold to more than IR£2 million. This represents a 337 per cent increase in real terms over the period. Indeed, measured in real terms, state funding of Irish parties has increased by an incredible 26,625 per cent since 1960.

The expansion in state funding also takes account of the parties' election campaign expenses. Under the 1997 Electoral Act parties and their candidates are entitled to reimbursement of expenses, provided they win a minimum proportion of the vote. Election expenses are reimbursed (to a maximum of IR£5000) to a candidate who is either elected or gains a quarter of a quota. Although the scheme was not implemented in time for the 1997 election, Laver and Marsh (1999: 157) estimate that the overall amounts of such expenses in that election would have amounted to IR£550,000 for Fianna Fáil, IR£400,000 for Fine Gael, IR£190,000 for Labour, IR£100,000 for the PDs, and IR£50,000 each for the Greens, Democratic Left, and Sinn Féin.

The reimbursement scheme is intended to remove (or, at least, reduce) the incentive for politicians to rely on political donations for election expenses. Furthermore, parties are now required by law to make full disclosure of payments and political donations. While there is no ceiling on the amount of donations they can receive, the Act does set limits on the amount parties and their candidates can spend in elections, based on the number of seats in a given constituency (IR£14,000 in a three-seat constituency, IR£17,000 in a four-seat constituency, and IR£20,000 in a five-seat constituency). Parties are allowed to contribute to a validated party candidate's expenditure, and spending limits of a party's set of candidates is then aggregated nationally to specify how much a party can spend on its total election campaign. This upper limit on campaign expenditure is perhaps one of the most crucial aspects of the legislative reforms, and is bound to have a profound effect on election campaigns, particularly by the larger parties, constraining further steps towards capital-intensive campaigning.

TABLE 8.6. *State subventions to Irish parties, 1960–99 (IR£)*

Year	Oireachtas grant	Education officer scheme[a]	Exchequer grant	Totals	Real totals
1960	4500			4500	8694
1961	4500			4500	8672
1962	4500			4500	8672
1963	5040			5040	9702
1964	5040			5040	9677
1965	5040			5040	9657
1966	5040			5040	9647
1967	5040			5040	9631
1968	15,000			15,000	28,605
1969	15,000			15,000	28,500
1970	15,000			15,000	28,500
1971	15,000			15,000	28,350
1972	15,000			15,000	28,080
1973	35,000			35,000	64,890
1974	38,523			38,523	70,613
1975	50,169			50,169	90,154
1976	55,164			55,164	97,144
1977	61,937			61,937	107,027
1978	75,998			75,998	129,806
1979	85,498			85,498	107,027
1980	86,499			86,499	140,906
1981	209,026			209,026	319,392
1982	246,746			246,746	351,613
1983	238,446			238,446	330,812
1984	253,702			253,702	338,946
1985	265,930	28,000		293,930	382,403
1986	275,257	28,000		303,257	386,652
1987	313,546	28,000		341,546	427,274
1988	366,635	28,000		394,635	696,531
1989	414,035	28,000		442,035	532,210
⋮					
1997	1,355,000	28,000	1,000,000	2,383,000	3,336,200
1998	1,355,000	28,000	1,000,000	2,383,000	2,423,511
1999	1,295,500	28,000	1,000,000	2,323,500	2,323,500

Notes: See Table 8.5 regarding calculation of real figures.

[a] A grant (not index-linked) from the Department of Education which supports the employment of party youth education officers.

Sources: Farrell 1992; Public Offices Commission; information supplied by political parties.

As a result of the disclosure rules new data on political donations over IR£400 have been published by the Public Offices Commission for the first time. The main findings here are that, on the basis of donations received in 1998, Fianna Fáil and Sinn Féin rank as the most privately endowed parties in the Republic. Fianna

Fáil received IR£432,501 in private donations in 1998; Sinn Féin was next with more than IR£230,000, the bulk of this from US donors, collected via the Friends of Sinn Féin fund-raising support group. The amounts for the other parties were significantly lower, ranging from IR£63,528 for Fine Gael, down to as little as IR£5000 for the PDs (Public Offices Commission 1999).

When we examine information on donations (over IR£500) to individual politicians (TDs, Senators, and MEPs), the amounts involved have declined from a total of IR£279,068 in 1998 to IR£173,514 in 1999, a drop of some 38 per cent. In part this may simply reflect reluctance on the part of some donors to have payments to politicians disclosed; nevertheless, there are indications that large payments to political parties have declined substantially based on these figures (Public Offices Commission 2000). This is all the more interesting given that 1999 was an election year (local and European) and the expectation would be that donations should rise. Of further note is that the proportion of donations made to Fianna Fáil politicians also dropped, from 51 per cent of total political donations in 1998 to 38 per cent in 1999.

The identities of the individual donors are also very revealing. Thirty-one of the thirty-six donations made to Fianna Fáil were from the business sector, including well-known hoteliers, builders, and other commercial interests. The picture is quite similar, albeit on a smaller scale, for Fine Gael and the PDs. The Greens' only donations were from its two MEPs, each contributing IR£6540. Similarly, the sole Sinn Féin TD contributed IR£24,750 (which was in addition to the $256,000 received from the Friends of Sinn Féin fund-raising support group in the USA). Labour's reliance on the trade union movement is also shown by these figures: just under 19 per cent of the party's donations come from this source. However, this financial support has been falling as a proportion of Labour's annual income overall. Analysis of the party's financial reports reveals that union affiliation fees generally account for between 4 and 13 per cent of the party's income. For example, in 1991, affiliation fees amounted to 9.9 per cent of income, rising to 12.8 per cent in 1992. However, in 1996 affiliation fees declined to 9.14 per cent of income, and in 1997 they plummeted to 3.7 per cent (Labour Party 1991, 1995, 1997, 1999); this is partly explained by the fact that this was an election year in which the party broadened its fund-raising efforts. Donations disclosed by individual Labour politicians also reveal union support in terms of providing constituency offices for a number of TDs. Thus, we can see that apart from supplying individual active Labour trade unionists, the union movement still plays a vital role in the financial viability of the party as a whole.

The parties are required to report on their use of the Exchequer grant. As Table 8.7 shows, apart from two exceptions, most parties allocated the bulk of their Exchequer grant to general administration. The exceptions were Fine Gael and the Greens, both of which were the only parties to allocate any of these funds towards the cost of research and training. Fianna Fáil was the biggest spender on branch organization (29 per cent). The lack of spending on research or policy

TABLE 8.7. *Use of public funds by Irish parties in 1998*

	Total funding (IR£)	General administration (%)	Research education & training (%)	Policy formulation (%)	Coordination of branch & members' activities (%)	Promotion of women & youth (%)
Fianna Fáil	449,437	62.5	0	0	29.4	8.1
Fine Gael	317,257	46.0	19.6	15.5	8.2	10.7
Labour	118,799	76.8	0	10.2	8.1	5.0
Prog. Democrats	54,475	87.7	0	0	0	12.3
Green Party	31,529	10.7	76.0	12.9	0	0.4
Sinn Féin	29,159	93.1	0	5.1	0	1.8
Democratic Left	28,644	65.5	0	2.2	21.9	10.5
Total/average	1,029,300	63.2	13.7	6.5	9.7	7.0

Note: These figures relate only to the Exchequer grant.

Source: Public Offices Commission.

formulation by Fianna Fáil may be partly explained by the fact that, currently, as a government party it can utilize the research capabilities of civil servants. A second explanation is found in its 1999 conference report which showed that the Exchequer funding was concentrated on head office expenditure, which would have included salaries for research staff (Fianna Fáil 2000: 17). Naturally, since the financial outlays reported in Table 8.7 represent only a fraction of the funding obtained by political parties, we must be cautious in the conclusions we draw from them.

Overall, then, the last few years of the twentieth century witnessed fundamental change in the role of the Irish state in subsidizing political parties as integral institutions. The legislative requirements of disclosure of financial expenditure, donations, and campaign expenses, combined with the impact of Freedom of Information legislation introduced in 1998 (Connolly and O'Halpin 1999), mean that we now have more information than ever before on the financing of Irish political parties. This analysis reveals that Irish parties are gaining an increased level of subsidies from the state, with the *quid pro quo* that they are required to act more like public bodies in terms of accountability. In addition, the 1997 and 1998 Electoral Acts have potentially changed the nature of campaigning in Irish politics by introducing financial strictures, guidelines, and regulations to which political parties are expected to adhere; if anything, these changes will benefit smaller parties the most given that they are unlikely to fall foul of ceiling limits on expenditure. The main contribution of these Acts, however, is in terms of the bank balances of the parties, making Irish parties far wealthier than heretofore.

Staff

Clearly the recent expansion of state funding of parties has yet to impact on the parties' staffing policies. To date, there has been little sign of any major increase in the numbers of party staff, and comparatively speaking, staffing levels remain fairly

TABLE 8.8. *Irish party staff, 1960–99: five-year averages*

Year	Fianna Fáil	Fine Gael	Labour	Progressive Democrats
1960–64	NA	8	3	
1965–69	6	10	3	
1970–74	8	NA	5	
1975–79	14	16	4	
1980–84	20	17	6	
1985–89	25	25	9	11
1990–94	15	13	5	4
1994–99	19	20	8	4

Note: Staff working in head office only.

Sources: Farrell (1992); *Irish Political Studies* (various years).

low (Farrell and Webb 2000). Reflecting the fact that staffing patterns generally are cyclical, based on anticipated election timetables, Table 8.8 provides five-year summary averages, which suggest a gradual 'downsizing' by the parties after the intense volatility of the 1980s. Needless to say, there are shifts in staff size from year to year. For instance, in the lead up to the 1997 election, Fianna Fáil employed 21 full-time staff, a figure which dropped to 18 in 2000; in 1997, Fine Gael drafted 15 additional employees into head office (Holmes 1999: 36). Increases in Labour staff in 1999–2000 were accounted for solely as a result of the merger deal with Democratic Left.

While Irish party headquarters remain quite weak in terms of resources, there has been a trend towards hiring outside professionals during election campaigns. All the major parties make use of outside agencies for advertising, polling, and public relations. The first occasion this occurred was in 1977, when Fianna Fáil emulated a number of campaign techniques of the US Democrats (from the 1976 Carter campaign). The other parties soon followed suit, and by the end of the 1980s, Irish parties were well up to international standards in terms of the adoption of modern campaign techniques and the use of campaign professionals (Farrell 1990, 1993; Holmes 1999). By 'contracting out' to specialist agencies and campaign consultants (including, in some prominent cases, the use of overseas political consultants), the parties have avoided the need to swell their staff sizes to meet the demands of organizational professionalization in a modern age. This is consistent with comparative trends towards greater fluidity in the staffing policies of political parties (Farrell and Webb 2000).

Members

From one perspective, it may seem as if the trend towards the nationalization and centralization of campaigns is occurring at the expense of the party membership.

The professionalization of political parties is manifest in more competitive, expensive, and nationalized marketing campaigns which make full use of the mass media of communications. There is a view that the role of the traditional activist is less important, and that 'the intensity of door-to-door canvassing might also be declining' (Holmes 1999: 46). In addition, vote-management strategies, designed to maximize the 'efficiency' of the election result under the STV electoral system, require nationally coordinated campaigns. Yet vote-management techniques are only successful if the national party can persuade the local constituency organization and membership as to its value. Furthermore, considering the strongly localist political culture and clientelistic nature of Irish politics (and the constituency-based electoral system), caution needs to be exercised when referring to a seemingly irreversible nationalization of election campaigns. Emphasis is still placed upon local election battles in terms of campaign expenditure on local advertising, tailored campaign literature, and so on.

Although, to date, there has been no systematic study on levels of party member activism in Ireland, the general impression is that it has been declining (Laver and Marsh 1999). Certainly, the argument can be made that some traditional methods of campaigning, which require dedicated activist volunteers, are fading away. For instance, annual national collections, whereby the traditional party members convened at church gates to collect money for the local branch, are declining both as a practice and in terms of total revenues raised. Church-gate meetings, another traditional campaign method, also appear to be on the decline, in urban areas at least (though see Flanagan and Breathnach 1999).

Almost all the parties have a problem with paper branches, set up and/or supported for the most part by local TDs with the principal aim of helping to maintain their control of selection conventions. Although attempts have been made at various stages of party re-organization to eradicate paper branches—particularly by Fine Gael in the late 1970s and early 1980s (Farrell 1994)—it is clear that they are extremely difficult to extinguish completely (Laver and Marsh 1999), as revealed, for instance, in an internal Fianna Fáil document, produced at the end of the 1990s, which purportedly called for a major organizational overhaul. Indeed, Fianna Fáil's most recent organizational changes, passed at its 2000 conference, signal efforts to streamline the party's structure. Traditionally, the party kept few records of individual party members, reflecting the role of the branch as the party's basic unit. In the early 1990s individual party members were permitted to register with head office. Further reforms in 2000 included the creation of a new 'registered supporter' who pays a small annual sum to party headquarters, but is not expected to play an active part in the party. These registered supporters do not have voting rights, but they are allowed to attend party meetings as observers, or offer an input in policy terms. These changes have facilitated the development of a centralized database of registered supporters. Undoubtedly, this reform is appealing both for the party and its inactive supporters, allowing Fianna Fáil to maintain contact with loyal supporters while, at the same time, recognizing that many people today are simply unwilling to sacrifice time and energy to active politics.

The Labour Party is the only party with a corporate membership. In 1999 there were ten affiliated unions, representing about 44 per cent of the Republic's union membership (Coakley 1999: 283). In 2000 the number of affiliated unions was eight, with the total number of registered Labour corporate members totalling 213,875, a slight reduction in the proportion of the Republic's union membership to some 41 per cent. The Services, Industrial, Professional, and Technical Union (SIPTU) provides the main source of union financial support to the Labour Party, although members of affiliated unions are certainly not consistent Labour voters. For instance, if the total affiliate membership actually voted for the party, this would represent twice the vote received by the party in the local elections in 1999.

Access to/control of the media

There has never been the sort of 'party–press' tradition in Ireland that is evident in other European countries. Historically, the *Irish Press* came closest. It was founded in the 1930s as a paper sympathetic to the recently formed Fianna Fáil party, and for a long time it retained a close ideological association with the party, albeit somewhat less so in recent times. Similarly, the *Irish Independent* tends to follow a supportive line towards Fine Gael; though, not in the most recent 1997 election, when—in part reflecting an anti-Labour bias, and therefore a dislike of the rainbow coalition—it published an editorial supporting Fianna Fáil. Apart from these two instances, there is a long-held tradition of relative impartiality in the reporting of party politics among the Irish-owned newspapers, a position emulated by the fast-growing market of British-based newspapers which publish special Irish editions. Certainly, there is none of the anti-Socialist tabloid campaigns that have been so prominent in recent British elections.

The Irish electorate's first experience of television was beamed in from Britain. The first Irish-owned television station was opened in 1961, but to this day the competition from Britain remains considerable. For instance, in 1997 approximately 70 per cent of households had access to Britain's four terrestrial channels (Coakley 1999). Since the late 1980s the competition has been even more intense due to the introduction of cable and satellite television channels. The most important recent development in the Irish media has been the loss by the state of a monopoly on domestic radio and television broadcasting. Prior to 1988, broadcasting was under the sole auspices of the state-controlled operator, Radio Telefís Éireann (RTÉ), which runs three television channels, and three national, and a host of local radio stations. Modelled very closely on the British tradition of impartiality and political balance, RTÉ has always striven to ensure fair coverage of parties, proportionate to their electoral strength. The establishment of the Independent Radio and Television Commission in 1988 led to a proliferation of independent broadcasters, with the creation of twenty-eight new local radio stations, one national radio station, and a further commercial television channel. The independent commercial stations are instructed to maintain an impartial broadcasting position during election campaigns. As with the state television and radio channels, they are obliged to provide the parties with free election broadcasts during elections. This ensures that the tradition of balanced (proportionate) coverage has been retained despite the ending of the era of state monopoly over broadcasting. Having said that, however, the creation of commercial radio, has opened up new avenues for potential links between politicians and the media. For instance, the Flood Tribunal has investigated aspects of the relationship between certain prominent politicians and one of the new radio stations.

Although this expansion of communications networks in Ireland means that parties have a greater opportunity to communicate with the electorate at a local level, it also requires the parties to devote extra resources to monitoring these expanding local networks. One account of the 1997 general election—the first time local radio was available as a campaign medium—partly attributes Fianna Fáil's electoral success to its heavy concentration on local radio as a means of conveying its political message (Holmes 1999: 32). A further indication of the desire of the political parties to control the political content of the local media was the establishment in 1998 of a Government Communications Unit, which was given responsibility for the monitoring of all local and national broadcasting.

The overall impression, therefore, is of a considerable expansion of party access to broadcasting media (especially local radio) and, in consequence, recent efforts by the parties to monitor and to attempt to influence media content. However, in the latter case it would clearly be going too far to suggest that party control of the media has increased. Indeed, if anything, the breaking of the broadcasting monopoly and the greater competition provided by local radio and satellite television must amount to reduced partisan control if only because there are more outlets for political coverage without any attendant increase in the scope for political influence over them.

In general, then, our checklist of the state of Irish parties gained from this assessment of their organizational strength is, for them, far less worrying than were the trends relating to questions of party legitimacy: the parties have shown themselves to be resilient, as well as capable of adapting to a changing climate. And now that Irish parties have joined the club of well-resourced, state-funded parties, the potential for further organizational reform is considerable. The question now to be considered is what this all means for the role and function of parties in the contemporary political system.

THE SYSTEMIC FUNCTIONALITY OF PARTIES

Governance

Traditionally, any discussion of the function of Irish parties in the area of governance could be quite legitimately summarized in terms of the 'Westminster model', involving a highly centralized administrative structure (and very weak local government), with governmental power residing at the top of the political ladder, centred in and around the Taoiseach and his (so far all taoisigh have been men) cabinet, and an independent, strictly non-partisan, civil service (Farrell 1988; Connolly and O'Halpin 1999; Elgie 1999). One important development here has been the greater use of political advisers by government ministers: this dates largely from the early 1990s and appears to have coincided with the institutionalization of coalition governments (O'Halpin 1995).

Consistent with the Westminster model, levels of intra-party discipline and cohesion are high by comparative standards (Bowler *et al.* 1999). Parliamentary cohesion is maintained by the operation of a whipping system, and particularly in the past when single-party government was common, the government maintained a tight hold over the legislative agenda. According to Gallagher (2000: 109) TDs (MPs) 'almost invariably vote *en bloc*. Deviations from party solidarity are very rare, and are met with a draconian response.' Furthermore, parliamentary faction-hopping by TDs is rare, in no small part a reflection of the fact that politicians who hop often face uncertain electoral futures (Mair 1987*a*). Party control also extends into ministerial appointments, although this need not be the case. Under the Constitution, the Taoiseach is given the power to appoint eleven Senators (members of the upper chamber). This allows him the possibility to use this route as a means of bringing a non-party-political figure (perhaps a technocrat) into the cabinet. However, this possibility has virtually never been used. About the only time was in 1981 when the then-Taoiseach, Garret FitzGerald, used this procedure to hand-pick his own foreign minister, a move which was not popular with his senior politicians (TDs) at the time.

If the picture of governance Irish-style shows strong evidence of party influence at all levels, the same cannot be said of policy output. For instance, there is very little evidence that 'parties matter' in terms of the determination of public policy objectives. For one thing, given Ireland's size as a small-open economy (and polity, see Keatinge and Laffan 1999), and therefore its vulnerability to global pressures, the ability of Irish governments to steer public policy has always been constrained. A further set of factors worth noting when considering the governance role of Irish parties are the institutional constraints they face from the existence of a written constitution—which can only be amended by referendum—and an influential and independent supreme court, with powerful judicial review functions.

Also of relevance is the fact that since Irish party politics has traditionally lacked a social basis this has tended to produce little dramatic change in public policy from one government to the next. Traditionally there was less to distinguish the main parties in terms of macro-economic policy than is apparent in other European countries in which the class cleavage is more dominant. While clearly it would be going too far to label Irish parties as 'programatically indistinguishable' (Carty 1983: 85), nonetheless, analysis of Irish party manifestos over time reveals some quite striking internal shifts in policy direction by the main parties (Mair 1987*b*; Garry and Mansergh 1999), indicating great freedom to roam across the policy divide.

There have been two significant developments in recent years which can be said to have affected the governance role of Irish parties. The first of these has been the coalitionalization of Irish governments since the 1970s. Not only has this coincided with greater degrees of governmental (and hence parliamentary) instability (Mitchell 1999), particularly in periods when the governments were minority or bare majorities (notably in an eighteen-month period during 1981 and 1982), it has also been seen to affect the policy profiles of the parties in election campaigns, probably best exemplified in 1997 when for the very first time Irish voters were presented with a clear choice between two different coalitions. This move towards regular (and now competing) coalition governments could, in time, be suggestive of a growing party effect on government, but at this juncture it is too early to draw any firm conclusions.

Given the new patterns of government formation, and in particular the tighter legislative arithmetic which governments face, there has been an undoubted effect on the issue of governability in Ireland, which may also have had some role in making Irish politicians more susceptible to the sort of improper practices referred to in the introduction to this chapter. This is in the sense that the politicians have to fight all the harder to win seats, while the party leaders have to work all the harder (or, at least, bargain all the more vigorously) to win office, and such tendencies must (and, indeed, the evidence from the tribunals to date, is indicative of this) provoke the dangers of improper practice. Indeed, in some respects one could argue that Irish party politics in the 1990s began to look a little less like the stately and reserved Westminster-style of British politics, and instead began to take on some of the more chaotic colours of Italian-style politics, personified among other things by the paradox of a strong economy (which, arguably, has little to do with the economic management skills of Irish political leaders, and more to do with the strengths of long-term political administration by bureaucrats) coinciding with governmental instability, and charges of corruption in high places.

The second main development of note in recent years has been the growing prominence of single-issue politics (Murphy 1999), most especially with regard to the demands of right-wing Catholic groups, both in terms of their fielding candidates at elections and in terms of their role in influencing the calling of referenda. Given Ireland's written, 'fixed' constitution, referenda are required to change, insert, or delete any of its articles, and these referenda must be initiated via Dáil bills. There is no right of public initiative. But this has not prevented the increasingly vociferous interest groups from bringing pressure to bear on the politicians, thereby influencing the calling of referenda. Almost half of the twenty-two referenda which have been called since 1937 took place in the 1990s. And of the fourteen referenda held in the past twenty years, six have been about moral issues. On the face of it, such developments indicate a growing politicization of the 'confessional' dimension and the increasing activity of groups organized in this area. In this sense, one can speak of a 'threat to party'. Against this, however, there is the fact that, to date, groups organized around single issues have yet to make a breakthrough in general elections, causing Sinnott (1995: 295) to posit 'the existence of an alternative channel for the resolution of the most contentious problems in this area . . . insulating the party system from the full brunt of secular-confessional issues by providing an alternative channel for the expression of this cleavage.' Furthermore, it should be noted that, in the case of most referenda, the parties maintain an organizational focus, on some occasions (such as over European Union matters) with the larger parties fighting on the same side; on other occasions (such as over certain moral issues) with the parties fighting on different sides. The important point, however, is that the parties maintain a central position; for the most part, they are not by-passed in times of referenda.

Political recruitment

Political recruitment to appointed public office is still largely channelled through the political parties, with appointments to public bodies being determined by the government of the day. Much as in other countries, the only development of note here is the growing number of such bodies in recent years.

The parties also retain a tight hold over recruitment to elective public office. As we shall see below, the process of candidate selection within most Irish parties has undergone some fundamental changes over the past decade or more, but the bottom line remains distinctly Schumpeterian, with candidate selection by the established parties being the principal, and certainly most effective, route to elective office. Notwithstanding this, however, recent successes by micro-parties and (often single-issue) independents (as discussed above) has opened up the realistic possibility of alternative routes of entry to elective office by budding politicians. As discussed earlier, an indication of this trend is illustrated in Table 8.1 by the monotonic rise throughout the 1980–1990s in the proportion of votes received by 'Others'.

Interest articulation and aggregation

The professionalization of Irish campaigning has not been without some cost to the process of interest articulation. The fact that the parties pay more attention to (and dedicate more resources to the tracking of) public opinion when designing their campaign messages, is of itself indicative of a general shift from a politics of 'leading' public opinion, towards one of 'following' it. This is, of course, consistent with trends in other advanced democracies (Farrell and Webb 2000).

As in many other countries, in recent decades there has been an increase in the number and range of what Murphy refers to as 'cause-centred' groups (Murphy 1999: 274). Updating his evidence slightly, we can report the following trends as of 2000: 65 arts organizations; 86 health organizations, 23 Irish language organizations, 47 youth organizations, and some 300 other organizations representing various social, political, and cultural causes (Institute of Public Administration 2000). Although these numbers may seem impressive, they are not especially high by international standards, nor, for that matter, is there much evidence of any dramatic increase in the number of groups in recent years. Indeed, according to the World Values survey, the claimed membership of voluntary organizations in Ireland in the early 1990s was lower than in Austria, Belgium, Britain, Denmark, Finland, Iceland, the Netherlands, Sweden, and Germany (Murphy 1999: 274).

The rise of cause-centred interest groups may not be especially noteworthy numerically, but as we have seen, they have still been able to play an important role over the past two decades, particularly in the realm of 'the politics of morality', both in terms of influencing the calling of, and the result of referenda, but also in terms of the ability to influence the policies of minority governments. This capability was first, and perhaps most strikingly revealed in 1981, when the Society for the Protection of the Unborn Child applied intense pressure on a vulnerable Fine Gael–Labour coalition government, and managed to have the abortion issue placed high on the public agenda, resulting in 'a decade of social division, whose effects have not yet disappeared' (Murphy 1999: 280).

The established parties have also been subject to pressure from groups, independents, and new parties which have sought the electoral route to political influence. These have included what comparativists would see as the 'usual suspects', such as the neo-liberal PDs and the Greens. More recently, they have also included Irish home-grown varieties, principal among which is Sinn Féin, which has proven very adept at picking up pockets of local support in working-class areas, particularly among inner-city communities (Walsh *et al.* 2000). Of course, while the entry of these newer parties may represent a greater degree of competition for the established parties, in no way can this, of itself, be construed as a threat to party *per se*.

In short, then, the established parties in Ireland have been facing growing competition both from new parties as well as from the growing vociferousness of single-issue interest groups—the latter particularly prominent during certain referendum campaigns. But, for all this, so far the established parties remain the predominant players in the political system; for the most part, they remain firmly in control of the public agenda. The political environment may have become more cluttered of late, but so far there is little sign of the parties losing their capacity as the main articulators and aggregators of the public interest.

Political participation

The evidence reported above of declining numbers of party members and the rise of single-issue groups would seem to point to a weakening of parties as conduits of participation. Certainly, they are suggestive of a trend whereby party membership is seen to go out of fashion, in part, reflecting the general process of social change, but, in part, also indicative of problems with the state of organization within the parties themselves. In the light of this, it is useful to explore what efforts, if any, are being made by the parties to reform themselves, perhaps to allow greater scope for membership participation. It is also interesting to see to what extent the parties are becoming any more representative of the general population.

Little substantial evidence is yet available on the sociological profiles and levels of activism of Irish party members. At the time of writing, a survey of Fine Gael members is being conducted, but the results are not yet available and it is, therefore, not possible to highlight any particular trends at this point, apart from the fact that some efforts have been made in recent years to address the low levels of participation by women in parties, particularly from the 1980s onwards. However, while all the main parties have appeared proactive in this respect, this has tended to be aspirational rather than actually generating firm measures. For instance, apart from Labour's modest quota of 25 per cent for internal and electoral elections, there has been little effort by the other parties to introduce quotas, and '[a]lthough the proportion of women selected as candidates has increased over time, in 1997 it still remained stubbornly below 20 per cent of all those standing for election' (Galligan 1999: 308).

The record has been somewhat better with regard to level of informal participation by women within the parties. According to Galligan, women now comprise between a third and a half of Irish party membership, although this increase is not reflected in the positions of power within the parties. This is not to deny that the trend has been upwards, but it has not been steep. In 1983, for instance, the representation of women in the national executives of the main parties was as follows: Fianna Fáil: 17 per cent; Fine Gael: 24 per cent; Labour: 8 per cent (Farrell 1992: 444). By 1998 the proportions were for the most part higher, though this hardly represented a transformation: Fianna Fáil: 30 per cent; Fine Gael: 22 per cent; Labour: 26 per cent. It was left to the relatively new PDs to show the only case of something approaching parity, at 47 per cent (Galligan 1999: 300). As Galligan shows, the record is even less impressive for the representation of women in constituency-level officer positions within parties.

One area of significant change within many of the parties (though, notably not so far including Fianna Fáil) has been over the rights and powers of the members, and this is most evident with regard to candidate selection (Laver and Marsh 1999). After a period of growing centralization (or, at least, the greater involvement of the centre) in candidate selection in the 1970s and 1980s (Gallagher 1988; Farrell 1994), the 1990s saw steps towards an opening-up of the process to allow the grass roots members greater involvement (and, in line with Mair's 'paradox' (1994), thereby usefully sidelining the activists because of the reduced influence of constituency selection conventions). Consistent with a more inclusive style, the Green Party was the first to move, in 1989, when it introduced a postal ballot allowing all constituency members a say in candidate selection. So far none of the other parties have gone all the way towards using postal ballots, preferring instead to use the method of membership hustings. Fine Gael established an internal party commission in the early 1990s which recommended the use of one-member, one-vote ballots (OMOV). Ultimately the party adopted a system of 'hustings' (constituency conventions) at which those members (of eight weeks standing and belonging to a branch which has been registered for three months) who attend may vote (Mockler 1994). The PDs changed their party rules to allow flexibility for the national executive in determining what rules to apply for candidate selection; increasingly this has entailed OMOV selection conferences.

The election of the party leader, which traditionally has been the exclusive preserve of the elected politicians has also come under scrutiny in some parties. In 1989 Labour adopted a postal ballot system, which to date has yet to be used. Fine Gael considered moving over to an electoral college system, which would have given its members 40 per cent of the vote, but this was rejected on grounds of cost (Mockler 1994). There has been no movement towards greater powers for members in the area of policy-making—which is evermore under the control of the leadership (Garry and Mansergh 1999). Furthermore, according to Laver and Marsh, the national conference has become 'a large and unwieldy body meeting infrequently, usually once a year, and its meetings tend to be major social and political occasions' (Laver and Marsh 1999: 154).

Overall, then, in terms of membership participation, the general picture in Ireland is much as elsewhere in western Europe (Scarrow *et al.* 2000). Efforts are being made by the party leaderships to give members a greater input into leadership election and candidate selection (which, in part, helps to reduce the influence of activists); however, the leaderships prefer to maintain a tight hold over formulation of party policy, and particularly over the drawing up of the party manifesto. This unwillingness to surrender control over policy can be seen as a concomitant of campaign and organization professionalization, and the demands of a more competitive media market.

Political communication and education

Given the processes of campaign and organizational professionalization over the past few decades, it is no surprise that developments in Irish political communication are entirely consistent with international trends, not least in terms of the greater resourcing by the parties of their press operations, and the wide-scale adoption of modern means of political communication. We have already seen how the ending of the state monopoly over broadcasting has involved an explosion in the range of alternative broadcasting outlets for parties. On the plus-side obviously is the fact that there is greater scope for parties to sell themselves across this larger range of media outlets; but the corollary of this is that there has been a reduction in the ability of the parties to influence the political agenda.

There is little if any evidence of Irish parties attempting to play a role in political education. About the only case of this in terms of internal party politics, was the democratic centralist practice which used to operate in the old Worker's Party, in which new members went through a transitional period of education and training (Farrell 1994). In terms of the wider education of voters, the parties have had little if any role. Traditionally there are no party foundations or institutes, although, as we have seen, with the move towards public funding of parties in 1998 and the introduction of budget lines on research, education and training, policy formulation, and the promotion of women and youth, the establishment of party institutes in the future cannot be entirely ruled out. Indeed, if recent media reports are to be believed, Fianna Fáil appears to be giving serious consideration to the possible establishment of one (named after its founder, Eamon deValera) as the Party's archive and for the promotion of academic study (Rafter 1999). Since 1995, the Labour Party has run annual summer schools, and in 2000 it instituted a more regularized Labour Youth College, consisting of a series of political development classes. It also holds fortnightly meetings of its Dublin Group, which mainly serves as both a recruitment ground for new members in the Dublin area, and also as a means of educating younger members.

In short, then, there is scope for parties to put the generous new state resources they receive to good use, extending their links into civic society and, perhaps, even playing some sort of educative function for the citizens. Whether, in fact, they will actually do any of this is unclear, and certainly past experience would not suggest so.

In general, our review of Irish party politics in terms of functionality indicates quite a mixed picture. For instance, on a positive note we can see some faltering steps towards addressing the problem of declining political participation, as shown by the (limited) efforts towards improving the representation of women at various levels throughout party ranks, or as shown more significantly by the greater say given to party members over candidate and leadership selection (although these latter reforms are offset by a far more interventionist role being played by head office). On a somewhat less positive note, we have seen how the coalitionization of Irish party politics has had corrosive influences on the behaviour of (certain) politicians and has had consequences for Irish governability. Furthermore, the rising prominence of single-issue politics, and its attendant effects on the greater regularity of referenda, has had important consequences for the agenda-setting abilities of the parties.

CONCLUSION

Irish electoral politics at the turn of the century is far more volatile and the terrain more crowded than thirty years ago. The cosy convention of two-and-a-half party politics was shattered in the 1980s with the arrival of new parties, which in large part have, so far, endured. In more recent years they have been joined by a spate of new micro-parties, single-issue pressure groups, and assorted independents. Not all the challenges to the established parties have been exogenous, however. The on-going tribunals of enquiry are gradually, painstakingly, unravelling a web of improper and inappropriate links between prominent politicians and businessmen, feeding a frenzy of negative media coverage and a growing sense of cynicism in the body politic.

But it is a moot point as to whether we should conclude from all of this that the future for Irish parties looks bleak. Turnout may be declining, volatility rising, and party members leaving in droves, but in a number of other respects the Irish party organization remains a strong and well-resourced entity which (so far, at any rate) seems fully capable of riding out the storms. Legislative reform may have been necessary to regularize the nature of party organization in Ireland—not least in terms of disclosing financial donors and capping campaign expenditure—but it has brought with it an explosion in the level of public funding of Irish parties. The recency of this latter development makes it impossible to predict the full implications for the functions of parties. For instance, it would be interesting to see if the parties make significant moves towards the establishment of institutes, and for greater involvement in efforts at promoting political education. All that can be stated with some certainty is that in 2000 Irish parties are better placed to take such steps, and more in need of doing, than at any time in their history.

REFERENCES

Bowler, S., Farrell, D., and Katz, R. (1999) *Party Discipline and Parliamentary Government* (Columbus, OH: Ohio State University Press).

Carty, R. K. (1983) *Electoral Politics in Ireland: Party and Parish Pump* (Dingle: Brandon).

Coakley, J. (1999) 'The foundations of statehood', in John Coakley and Michael Gallagher (eds) *Politics in the Republic of Ireland*, 3rd edn (London: Routledge).

Connolly, E. and O'Halpin, E. (1999) 'The government and the governmental system', in John Coakley and Michael Gallagher (eds) *Politics in the Republic of Ireland*, 3rd edn (London: Routledge).

Donnelly, S. (1999) *Elections '99: All Kinds of Everything* (Dublin: Donnelly).

Dunphy, R. (1998) ' "A group of individuals trying to do their best": the dilemmas of Democratic Left'. *Irish Political Studies* 13: 51–75.

Eijk, C. van der and Franklin, M. (1996) *Choosing Europe? The European Electorate and National Politics in the Face of Union* (Ann Arbor: University of Michigan Press).

Elgie, R. (1999) 'Political Leadership: the President and the Taoiseach', in John Coakley and Michael Gallagher (eds), *Politics in the Republic of Ireland*, 3rd edn., (London: Routledge).

Farrell, B. (1970) 'Labour and the Irish political party system: a suggested approach to analysis'. *Economic and Social Review* 1: 477–502.

—— (1988) 'Ireland. The Irish Cabinet System: More British than the British Themselves', in Jean Blondel and Ferdinand Müller-Rommel (eds), *Cabinets in Western Europe* (Basingstoke: Macmillan).

Farrell, D. (1990) 'Campaign strategies and media coverage', in Michael Gallagher and Richard Sinnott (eds) *How Ireland Voted 1989* (Galway: Centre for the Study of Irish Elections).

—— (1992) 'Ireland', in Richard S. Katz and Peter Mair (eds) *Party Organizations: A Data Handbook on Party Organizations in Western Democracies* (London: Sage Publications).

—— (1993) 'Campaign strategies', in Michael Gallagher and Michael Laver (eds), *How Ireland Voted 1992* (Dublin: Folens and PSAI Press).

—— (1994) 'Ireland: centralization, professionalization and competitive pressures', in Richard S. Katz and Peter Mair (eds) *How Parties Organize: Change and Adaptation in Party Organizations in Western Democracies* (London: Sage Publications), pp. 216–41.

Farrell, D. M. and Webb, P. D. (2000) 'Political parties as campaign organizations', in R. J. Dalton and M. P. Wattenberg (eds) *Parties Without Partisans: Political Change in Advanced Industrial Democracies* (Oxford: Oxford University Press), pp. 102–28.

Fianna Fáil (2000) *Árd-Fheis Clár 2000* (Dublin: Fianna Fáil).

Flanagan, C. and Niamh B. (1999) 'On the campaign trail' in Michael Marsh and Paul Mitchell. (eds) *How Ireland Voted 1997* (Colorado: Westview Press).

Gallagher, M. (1988) 'Ireland: the increasing role of the centre', in Michael Gallagher and Michael Marsh (eds) *Candidate Selection in Comparative Perspective: The Secret Garden of Politics* (London: Sage Publications).

—— (1999) 'The results analysed', in Michael Marsh and Paul Mitchell (eds) *How Ireland Voted 1997* (Boulder, CO: Westview Press).

—— (2000) 'The relatively victorious incumbent under PR-STV: legislative turnover in Ireland and Malta', in Shaun Bowler and Bernard Grofman (eds) *Elections in Australia, Ireland and Malta Under the Single Transferable Vote* (Ann Arbor, Michigan: Michigan University Press), pp. 81–113.

Galligan, Y. (1999) 'Candidate selection', in Michael Marsh and Paul Mitchell (eds) *How Ireland Voted 1997* (Boulder, CO: Westview Press).

Garry, J. and Mansergh, L. (1999) 'Party manifestos', in Michael Marsh and Paul Mitchell (eds) *How Ireland Voted 1997* (Boulder, CO: Westview Press).

Higgins, M. D. (2000) *The Space of Politics Recovered* (Dublin: Labour Party).

Holmes, M. (1999) 'Organizational preparation and political marketing', in Michael Marsh and Paul Mitchell (eds) *How Ireland Voted 1997* (Boulder, CO: Westview Press).

Institute of Public Administration (2000) *2000 Yearbook and Diary* (Dublin: Institute of Public Administration).

Katz, R. S. (1980) *A Theory of Parties and Electoral Systems* (Baltimore, MD: Johns Hopkins University Press).

Katz, R. S. and Mair, P. (1995) 'Changing models of party organization and party democracy: the emergence of the cartel party'. *Party Politics* 1: 5–28.

Keatinge, P. and Laffan, B. (1999) 'Ireland: a small open polity', in John Coakley and Michael Gallagher (eds) *Politics in the Republic of Ireland*, 3rd edn (London: Routledge).

Labour Party (1991) *Report to National Conference 1989–1991* (Dublin: Labour Party).

—— (1995) *Report to National Conference 1993–5* (Dublin: Labour Party).

—— (1997) *Report to National Conference 1995–1997* (Dublin: Labour Party).

—— (1999) *Labour Party Report 1997–99* (Dublin: Labour Party).

Laver, M. and Marsh, M. (1999) 'Parties and voters', in John Coakley and Michael Gallagher (eds) *Politics in the Republic of Ireland*, 3rd edn (London: Routledge).

Mair, P. (1987a) 'Party organization, vote management, and candidate selection: toward the nationalization of electoral strategy in Ireland', in Howard Penniman and Brian Farrell (eds) *Ireland at the Polls 1981, 1982, and 1987: A Study of Four General Elections* (Durham, NC: Duke University Press).

—— (1987b) *The Changing Irish Party System: Organisation, Ideology and Electoral Competition* (London: Frances Pinter).

—— (1994) 'Party organizations: from civil society to the state', in Richard S. Katz and Peter Mair (eds) *How Parties Organize: Change and Adaptation in Party Organizations in Western Democracies* (London: Sage Publications), pp. 1–22.

—— (1999) 'Party competition and the changing party system', in John Coakley and Michael Gallagher (eds) *Politics in the Republic of Ireland*, 3rd edn (London: Routledge).

Marsh, M. and Sinnott, R. (1999) 'The behaviour of the Irish voter', in Michael Marsh and Paul Mitchell (eds) *How Ireland Voted 1997* (Boulder, CO: Westview Press).

Mitchell, P. (1999) 'Coalition discipline, enforcement mechanisms, and intraparty politics', in Shaun Bowler, David Farrell, and Richard Katz (eds) *Party Discipline and Parliamentary Government* (Columbus, OH: Ohio State University Press).

Mockler, F. (1994) 'Organisational change in Fianna Fáil and Fine Gael'. *Irish Political Studies* 9: 165–72.

Murphy, G. (1999). 'The Role of Interest Groups in the Policy Making Process', in John Coakley and Michael Gallagher (eds), *Politics in the Republic of Ireland*. 3rd edn. (London: Routledge).

O'Halpin, E. (1995) 'Partnership programme managers in the Reynolds/Spring coalition 1993–94: An Assessment'. *DCUBS Research Papers*. No. 6. http://www.dcu.ie/business/research_papers/no6.html.

Poguntke, T. (1996) 'Anti-party Sentiment: Conceptual Thoughts and Empirical Evidence: Explorations into a Minefield', *European Journal of Political Research*, 29.

Public Offices Commission (1999) *Annual Report 1998* (Dublin: Public Offices Commission).

—— (2000) 'Disclosure on political donations received by TDs, senators and MEPs during 1999' (press release), (Dublin: Public Offices Commission).

Rafter, K. (1999) 'Fianna Fáil Group Says Party Needs Overhaul', *Irish Times*, September 23.

Scarrow, S. E., Webb, P. D., and Farrell, D. M. (2000) 'From social integration to electoral contestation: the changing distribution of power within political parties', in R. J. Dalton and M. P. Wattenberg (eds) *Parties Without Partisans: Political Change in Advanced Industrial Democracies* (Oxford: Oxford University Press), pp. 129–53.

Sinnott, R. (1995) *Irish Voters Decide: Voting Behaviour in Elections and Referendums since 1918* (Manchester: Manchester University Press).

Walsh, L., Corless, D., Smyth, K., and Lehane, M. (2000) 'Looking up: The rise and rise of Sinn Féin'. *Magill*, March.

Whyte, J. (1974) 'Ireland: politics without social bases', in Richard Rose (ed.) *Electoral Behaviour: A Comparative Handbook* (New York: The Free Press).

9

Spain

Building a Parties State in a New Democracy

Ian Holliday

Spain has made a number of experiments with democracy, sham and actual, but only since the mid-1970s has it succeeded in grounding a democratic system. Then 'the very model of the modern elite settlement' (Gunther 1992) generated a peaceful transition from Franco's authoritarian regime to a democratic polity, and established the conditions in which competitive party politics could develop. Those conditions were not neutral. Rather, strenuous efforts were made to ensure that parties would come forward to take charge of Spain's new democracy (Gunther *et al.* 1988). The result turned out to have two key aspects. Synthetic parties were created, and a parties state was built.

Spanish parties are synthetic in the sense that they are supported more from above than below. It is true that in recent years all parties have attempted, with some success, to extend their social reach. However, they remain chiefly dependent on the state for survival. This reflects the circumstances of the Spanish transition, when memories both of a failed democratic interlude in the Second Republic of the 1930s, which met all the conditions of polarized pluralism (Sartori 1976), and of the one-party authoritarian state that took its place, promoted a culture not simply of consensus but also of commitment to making sure democracy actually worked this time around. Parties, being a key element of democratic experience the world over, were given a privileged position in the state largely for this reason.

Spain is a parties state in the sense that since the transition many core institutions of government have been colonized and are substantially controlled by parties. As democratic procedures were introduced at all levels of the new polity—central (1977), local (1979), and regional (1980–83)—so parties became the institutions through which much political power flowed. The many protections given to parties, and the vast amounts of patronage placed in their hands by the creation of democratic institutions at national, regional, and local levels, ensured that they became central actors in the new state.

In the early stages of the transition the precise configuration of parties that would emerge was unclear. On the right a rather loose coalition of former Francoists was confident it would take the leading role through its Alianza Popular (AP). On the left

TABLE 9.1. *Spanish national election results, 1977–2000*

	1977		1979		1982		1986		1989		1993		1996		2000	
	Vote (%)	Seats N	Vote (%)	Seats N	Vote (%)	Seats N	Vote (%)	Seats N	Vote (%)	Seats N	Vote (%)	Seats N	Vote (%)	Seats N	Vote (%)	Seats N
PCE/IU[a]	9.4	12	10.8	23	4.0	4	4.5	7	9.1	17	9.6	18	10.6	21	5.5	8
PSOE	29.3	103	30.5	121	48.4	202	44.6	184	39.9	175	38.8	159	37.5	141	34.1	125
UCD	34.6	165	35.0	168	6.5	2										
CDS					2.9	—	9.2	19	7.9	14	1.8					
AP/PP[b]	8.8	16	6.1	9	26.5	106	26.3	105	25.9	106	34.8	141	38.8	156	44.5	183
CiU	2.8	2	2.7	8	3.7	12	5.1	18	5.1	18	4.9	17	4.6	16	4.2	15
PNV	1.7	2	1.5	7	1.9	8	1.6	6	1.2	5	1.2	5	1.3	5	1.5	7
Other	13.4	28	13.4	11	6.1	2	8.7	6	11.0	10	8.9	10	7.2		10.2	12
Turnout	78.8		68.0		80.0		70.5		69.7		76.4		77.4		70.0	
ENEP	4.16		4.16		3.33		3.57		4.16		3.53		3.28		3.13	
ENPP	2.85		2.77		2.32		2.63		2.77		2.70		2.72		2.48	
TNV	—		10.8		42.3		11.9		8.9		9.5		4.4		9.9	
BV	—		2.2		6.7		2.4		1.7		1.7		1.7		7.0	

Notes: ENEP: Effective Number of Electoral Parties; ENPP: Effective Number of Parliamentary Parties; TNV: Total Net Volatility; BV: Block Volatility.

[a]The PCE stood its own candidates in the 1977, 1979, and 1982 elections. In 1986 and 1989 the IU comprised an electoral coalition focused on the PCE. In 1993, 1996, and 2000 the IU comprised a federation of parties dominated by the PCE.

[b]The AP changed its name to PP at the IX party congress of January 1989 (ahead of the 1989 general election). In the 1982 and 1986 elections the AP was the dominant partner in the Coalición Popular electoral coalition.

Source: Based on Montero (1998: tables 1, 2, 3, 4).

the Partido Comunista de España (PCE) and the Partido Socialista Obrero Español (PSOE), both of which had maintained some sort of clandestine existence during the Franco years, had good reason to believe they would now be rewarded for their opposition to authoritarianism. In the centre, the Unión de Centro Democrático (UCD), formed around transition premier Adolfo Suárez, was an obvious candidate for early control. But many other parties were created to contest the first elections. In the event the UCD was the leading force in Spain's rather inchoate and fluid early party system, emerging as the leading party in the 1977 and 1979 elections and forming minority governments. In 1982, however, it went down to spectacular defeat and within six months had been wound up as a political organization. In this election the PSOE under Felipe González emerged as the controlling party in a predominant party system, and maintained this position until the 1990s. Then, the rebranding and rebuilding of the AP, which in 1989 became the Partido Popular (PP), generated sufficient electoral competition to make the Spanish party system moderate pluralist. The PP took office on a minority basis in 1996, with José María Aznar as Prime Minister, and followed up by winning a clear majority in 2000. The other parties with at least some national profile have been the Izquierda Unida (IU), formed around the PCE in 1986, and the Centro Democrático y Social (CDS), formed by Suárez to contest the 1982 elections and effectively moribund since 1993 (Tables 9.1 and 9.2).

Alongside the national party system Spain has regional sub-systems. While most of Spain's seventeen regions now have distinctive parties, only in two are they sufficiently developed to generate anything approaching regional party systems. In Catalonia Convergéncia i Unió (CiU) is the dominant force on the centre–right,

TABLE 9.2. *Spanish government complexion, 1977–2000*

Start date	Premier	Party
June 1977	Adolfo Suárez	UCD
March 1979	Adolfo Suárez	UCD
February 1981	Leopoldo Calvo Sotelo	UCD
October 1982	Felipe González	PSOE
June 1986	Felipe González	PSOE
October 1989	Felipe González	PSOE
June 1993	Felipe González	PSOE
March 1996	José María Aznar	PP
March 2000	José María Aznar	PP

Note: The first two González governments (1982–86 and 1986–89) had parliamentary majorities. The third (1989–93) held exactly half the 350 seats in parliament, but had a working majority because four Herri Batasuna deputies declined to take their seats. The second Aznar government (elected in 2000) also had a parliamentary majority. All other governments had a minority of parliamentary seats. From 1993 to 2000 governments operated on the basis of formal or informal legislative (but not executive) coalitions with the CiU and, to a lesser extent, the PNV.

pushing the PP into third place and half-party status. Here the party system is a little more fragmented than at national level, but remains moderate pluralist. In the Basque Country the Partido Nacionalista Vasco (PNV), a conservative and Catholic party, is the leading player, though it faces challenges for the Basque nationalist vote from Eusko Alkartasuna (EA), a more radical breakaway party from the PNV, and Herri Batasuna (HB), the political wing of the terrorist organization Euskadi Ta Askatasuna (ETA). Here fragmentation of the party system has been accompanied by tendencies towards polarization. In both regions the PSOE remains the major party of the centre–left, and the PP, though weakened, has a significant presence. The extent of Spain's distinctive regional party systems should not, therefore, be exaggerated. Nowhere is there a disjuncture to match that between Northern Ireland and the rest of the UK. Partly for this reason, though more importantly for lack of space, Spain's regional party systems are not analysed here.

To explain how Spain's synthetic parties developed, and how its parties state was built and now functions, this chapter looks at the institutional framework that had such a shaping effect on party politics, and at standard measures of party performance in the domains of legitimacy, organizational strength, and systemic functionality. To conclude, the viability of Spain's parties state is assessed, and its experience of democracy is analysed comparatively.

INSTITUTIONAL FRAMEWORK

Spain took Stepan's path 4a to democracy: 'redemocratization initiated by the civilian or civilianized political leadership' (Stepan 1986: 73–5). During the process of transition, an institutional framework for competitive party politics emerged in stages. In the period culminating in promulgation of a democratic constitution on 27 December 1978, the most important initiatives were the decree law on electoral practice of 18 March 1977 and the law on political parties of 4 December 1978. However, a good deal of elaboration still needs to be undertaken, and the process of democratic consolidation is widely held to have lasted until 1982 (Gunther *et al.* 1995: 10). By this stage, of course, parties were well in charge of proceedings. Indeed, throughout the development of an institutional framework for Spain's parties state, parties themselves featured as both independent and dependent variables. Even in the very early stages the elite figures who managed the transition were mainly either already party political figures or had aspirations to develop a party political base (Gunther *et al.* 1988: 395). Only the king, Juan Carlos, and his immediate advisers do not fit into one of these two categories. This is not, then, a simple case of an institutional framework being developed *for* parties. That framework was developed at least as much *by* parties, even though in the early stages they were highly underdeveloped. The key elements of the institutional framework are the basic constitutional provisions, the electoral system, and the rules governing parliamentary group organization and party finance.

Constitutional provisions

Many aspects of the 1978 constitution have a bearing on party politics: the distinct electoral systems for the Congreso and the Senado, the pre-eminence of the Congreso, the creation of directly elected regional councils, and so on. This section examines only general provisions relating specifically to political parties.

Taking lessons from other countries with difficult democratic pasts, such as West Germany, Italy, and Portugal, the constitution brought parties within its parameters, thereby extending a measure of protection to them (Martín Rebollo 1996: 20). The relevant articles may look rather insubstantial, but the sheer fact of constitutionalizing political parties was an important step in Spain, as it had been in West Germany and elsewhere. Article 1.1 is part of this exercise in that it makes political pluralism one of the core values of the Spanish state. Parties are then linked to that core value by Article 6, which identifies them as the key agents in generating political participation and pluralism. Article 6 also makes parties free agents within the law, and mandates only that their internal structures and operations be democratic. Subsequent articles deal with the many broader aspects of the Spanish state with which parties have been forced to deal. One worth mentioning here is the constructive vote of no confidence in the Congreso (Article 113), borrowed from the West German Basic Law. The law of December 1978 and the organic laws of June 1985 and July 1987 all built on these constitutional provisions and filled them out. The 1978 law defined a political party as an association listed (with full statutes) in an open Registry in the Ministry of the Interior (del Castillo 1989: 184). It created a set of regulations relating to political parties that were reaffirmed and updated by the subsequent laws.

Electoral system

The Spanish electoral system was devised in advance of the constitutional settlement to regulate the June 1977 elections to what was effectively a constituent Cortes, or parliament. The critical period was the set of months following transition Premier Suárez's July 1976 commitment to hold free elections by the end of June 1977 (Heywood 1996: 147). In these months a compromise was worked out between two major sets of interests: a reformist right committed to some form of majoritarianism it believed would both favour its own interests and promote firm government within a stable state; and a reformist left committed to some form of proportionality it believed would advance its interests and contribute to a deconstruction of Franco's centralized state. The result was the decree law of 18 March 1977. Spanish electoral arrangements are described in very loose terms in the constitution itself (Articles 68 and 69). They were given full legal status in the organic law of 19 June 1985.

The 1977 decree law identified Spain's fifty provinces (plus its Moroccan holdings in Ceuta and Melilla) as electoral districts, and established in them a D'Hondt highest averages closed list system with a 3 per cent hurdle for elections to the 350-seat Congreso (lower chamber), and a modified plurality system for elections to the Senado (upper chamber). In practice a minimum of three and an average of seven deputies, plus four senators, were to be elected from each province. Since 1977 these two systems have not been materially changed. Indeed, the D'Hondt system has become the dominant electoral system in Spain, also being used for elections to local and regional councils, and to the European Parliament (EP). However, for local and regional elections districts are mostly (though not uniformly) larger than for national elections, and for elections to the EP Spain is treated as a single constituency.

The impact of Spain's electoral laws on party development can be gauged from the structuring effect of each system. Two linked provisions make the system used for elections to the Congreso effectively majoritarian. One is the division of the country into fifty electoral districts, each of which elects at least three deputies. The result is that substantially fewer votes are needed to elect a deputy from a small province than from a large one (Gunther 1989: 838). The second is the impact of this division on the operation of the D'Hondt system, which becomes less proportional as district size decreases (Rae 1971). In Spain 19 districts elect seven or more deputies. However, seven elect only three, eight elect four, and thirteen elect five (Gunther 1989: 839). The result is that Spain's electoral system is strikingly disproportional in its effects. Whereas Rose's index of proportionality gives an average score of ninety-five for systems of proportional representation in Western Europe, it gives a score of eighty-one for the Spanish election of 1977. That figure has since increased somewhat, but on Rose's and other, more recent, indices Spain remains closer to the UK, which has a majoritarian system, than to most other West European states (Gunther 1989: table 3). The use of closed lists was a deliberate attempt to give parties, rather than personalities, a prominent role in the political process; its effect was to place significant power in the hands of party managers who drew up the lists, and to increase substantially the possible cost of internal party dissent. The modified plurality system used for elections to the Senado is also majoritarian. The comparatively large districts frequently used with the D'Hondt system locally and regionally, and the single national constituency used for European elections, are all more proportional in their effects.

Rules governing parliamentary group organization

Spanish parties have also been shaped by the organizational rules drawn up by the Cortes (particularly the more important Congreso). These further party discipline and create strong party groups in parliament. Until 1982 parliamentary groups could be as small as five deputies in number, and the rules governing their creation were fairly lax. Since 1982, when new standing orders were adopted, parliamentary groups must in most circumstances have a minimum of fifteen members. Individual deputies must join the party groups for which they were elected, unless in the first five days of a parliamentary session they are accepted by a different group, or subsequently they join the 'mixed group' *(grupo mixto)* of effectively non-aligned deputies. The significance of these rules can only be fully understood when the central importance of the groups to Congreso operations is described. It is little exaggeration to say that all parliamentary business runs through the groups: parliamentary time, speakers, questions, motions, amendments, committee posts and funding are all controlled by them, such that the scope for individual initiative is very close to zero. Parliamentary groups are mandated to vote *en bloc*. The key figure in each group is the spokesperson *(portavoz)*, and the Junta de Portavoces, which brings these figures together, is the main arena for managing parliamentary business (Sánchez de Dios 1999: 150–1).

Rules governing party finance

Below, we shall review in some detail the contribution made by the state to Spanish party resources, but first it is important to consider the legal context of such provision. The decree law of 18 March 1977 that established an electoral law for Spain also developed a set of regulations for party finance as well as a system of state subsidies for electoral expenses. In July 1978, state subsidies were extended to parties putting up candidates in local elections. In the law on political parties of 4 December 1978 annual subsidies were granted to parties to help fund their routine activities. Other laws sought to regulate contributions to political parties and to impose on them a disclosure requirement. None of these arrangements was fully thought through. Rather, each was 'improvised piecemeal in response to pressing political exigencies of the moment' (Gillespie 1998: 75). The organic law of 19 June 1985 synthesized, and marginally extended, the rather *ad hoc* provisions developed in the first years of the transition. The organic law of 2 July 1987 dealt specifically with party finance. The system described here applies to parliamentary elections. Similar systems apply to elections to other tiers of Spanish government (del Castillo 1989: 172, 183–4).

To receive a state subsidy, the key qualification is representation in the Cortes. The 1977 law established a formula whereby parties were given a fixed electoral subsidy for each vote secured in each district in which they had won at least one seat: 45 pesetas per Congreso vote, 15 pesetas per Senado vote. Parties were also given a fixed sum of one million pesetas per parliamentary seat won (in either house). This system was in place for the 1977, 1979, and 1982 elections. In later years the sums awarded were increased in line with inflation, and parties were allowed to seek a partial advance on their probable subsidy one month before the holding of an election. State subsidy of routine party activities was introduced in 1978. Here the formula is based on votes (two-thirds of total subsidy) and seats (one-third) obtained in the most recent Congreso elections. All votes in electoral districts where an eligible party has surmounted the 3 per cent hurdle are taken into account. The total amount to be distributed is determined by the government and included in the annual budget (van Biezen 2000*a*: 331). Finally, state subsides are also advanced to political parties 'in kind', chiefly through free campaigning slots on state television channels, free space for displaying campaign posters, free use of public meeting places for campaign rallies, and a reduced postal rate for campaign mailings. Each of these subsidies was introduced in 1977 and reaffirmed in 1985 (del Castillo 1989: 176–9, 182–3). All subsidies are awarded to party headquarters, thereby reinforcing the power of central party managers (Sánchez de Dios 1999: 145).

In terms of prohibitions, the 1977 regulations outlawed two types of contribution, from the public sector and from abroad. The former prohibition learned from Italy, where a law was passed in 1974 to prevent public-sector enterprises from contributing money to political parties (notably the DC). The 1985 law restated each of these prohibitions, and set limits (initially of 1 million pesetas, currently of 10 million pesetas) on the amount of cash a party could legally receive from one individual or corporation. This law also imposed limits on electoral expenditure, establishing a ceiling of 20 million pesetas per electoral district plus 40 pesetas per voter registered in the district. These limits have subsequently been raised in line with inflation (del Castillo 1989: 180–1).

Finally, in terms of disclosure, the 1977 law required parties after each general election to submit a set of accounts to the electoral commission, the Junta Electoral Central. Initially, this procedure was observed only minimally. In 1985 the disclosure regime was tightened, with the main regulatory function being passed to the audit tribunal, the Tribunal de Cuentas. This is an independent 12-member body charged by the constitution (Article 136) with examining and controlling all public-sector accounts (Newton 1997: 184). In addition, the 1985 law created an electoral administrator to oversee campaign activities. It also required all individuals who make a donation to a political party to disclose a certain amount of personal data (del Castillo 1989: 181–2).

PARTY LEGITIMACY

Standard measures of the popular legitimacy of political parties include party membership strength, levels of electoral turnout, degree of electoral volatility, evidence of popular assessments, and nature of party–voter ties. Each is analysed in this section in order to determine the extent to which parties have taken root in Spanish society.

Party membership

On the eve of its transition to democracy, Spain had virtually no political parties worth the name. For more than two decades from the early 1940s, Franco's

Movimiento Nacional registered official membership figures of close to one million (Bardavió 1969: 117–18). However, by the early 1970s, like much of the rest of the regime, it was in a state of disintegration. In any case, it was always seen by Franco as a 'great anti-party' (Franco 1975: para. 225), and was never intended to promote party political activity on the competitive, democratic model. Other parties were banned. In the early stages of the transition the Movimiento was dissolved by its former head, Suárez, acting in his new incarnation as transition premier, and its remaining assets were transferred to the state.

Although Franco's was really a 'no-party' state (Gunther 1980), both the PCE and the PSOE maintained some form of organization in these years, and with the PNV and two minor Catalan parties, provide the only instances of party political continuity from the 1930s to the 1970s. Under Franco the PCE pursued a cellular existence within Spain, whereas the PSOE was mainly a party in exile. It is hard to say how many members each party had by the start of the transition, but 15,000 militants for the PCE and 4000 for the PSOE are the best estimates (van Biezen 1998: 48). There were also some stirrings of party political mobilization in the Basque Country and Catalonia during the Franco years. But that was about the extent of Spanish party politics at the time of the dictator's death.

Once the transition had started to take place a number of forces came together to promote party-building. It has already been said that the elites who managed the transition intended that parties should emerge to govern the new polity. Within Spain there was also mobilization from below as the social protests of the late Franco and early transition years began to take party political form (Carr 1987: 3). From outside Spain there was not only general support from the western democracies including, importantly, a promise of EC membership if Spain could build and sustain a democratic order, but also specific transnational party cooperation (Pridham 1996). German parties and party foundations were notably active at this time, with the SPD in particular providing all kinds of assistance (including cash) to the PSOE. While the PCE was also able to secure external support, parties associated with the Franco regime, such as the AP, found it much more difficult to develop transnational links.

However, not all the relevant factors in the late 1970s pointed in the direction of party political mobilization. At the mass level, civil society was only slowly re-emerging from Franco's 'culture of evasion'. Built on a bedrock of spectacular economic growth from 1961 to 1973, which took Spain to the position of tenth industrial power in the world, this culture saw the TV age sweep Spain to such an extent that, by 1977, 90 per cent of Spaniards had access to a television (Linz 1986: 658). One consequence of the limited development of civil society was that while, in 1975, 80 per cent of Spaniards were in favour of free trade unions, only 52 per cent believed the country needed free political parties (Fundación Foessa 1976: 1171). At the elite level, most of the key figures who managed the transition may have been either actual or aspirant party leaders, but their primary concern was to get right the institutional framework within which party competition would take place. Beyond this, the very supportive environment created for parties in the new state, combined with the coming of the TV age, meant that much of the need to build a mass base was removed (Barnes *et al.* 1986: 69). Things have changed a little in recent years, but even today a party with access to state resources need not see its membership base as having primary importance.

The relevant data are not entirely reliable, in large part because they are generated by the parties themselves and subject to very little external check. However, what they show is that Spanish parties have never developed much social penetration (Table 9.3). Adding together the figures claimed by the major national parties, membership as a proportion of the electorate did not reach 2 per cent before the 1990s, and had only climbed to 2.4 per cent by 1996. Members of smaller national parties and regional parties must swell these figures a bit, but it seems unlikely that they reach 4 per cent today. This is towards the lower end of social penetration registered by Western democracies (Mair and van Biezen 2001), although the modest growth experienced does provide a contrast with most other countries.

Among individual parties, the first membership surge was made by the PCE, which in 1977 claimed more than 200,000 members. The fall-off from this peak was, however, both rapid and substantial as the PCE followed other Eurocommunist parties to the margins of the political system. By 1986 the PCE's membership total had been cut by almost two-thirds to 70,000. Another ten years on it had fallen by a further half to 35,000, before recovering somewhat thereafter. Membership

TABLE 9.3. *Spanish major party membership data, 1977–2000*[a]

Year	PCE[b]	PSOE[c]	UCD[d]	AP/PP[e]	M/E
1977	202,000	52,000	10,000	50,000	1.3
1979	168,000	101,000	70,000	50,000	1.5
1982	132,000	119,000	144,000	85,000	1.8
1986	70,000	185,000		202,000	1.6
1989	49,000	215,000		240,000	1.7
1993	45,000	351,000		327,000	2.3
1996	35,000	365,000		376,000	2.4
2000	70,000	410,000		602,000	3.4

[a]Membership data are by no means exact, notably in the early years of the transition. The figures cited here are those which gain most support in the literature. It should nevertheless be noted that different figures will be found elsewhere.

[b]Most figures are given for slightly different years, as shown here in brackets: 1979 (1978), 1982 (1981), 1986 (1985), 1989 (1988), 1993 (1991), 1996 (1995).

[c]Figure given for 1993 is from 1994.

[d]Figure given for 1982 is from 1981.

[e]Figures given for 1977 and 1979 are from 1978; figure given for 1996 is from 1994.

Sources: del Castillo 1989: 187; Fundación Foessa 1994: 634, 641; van Biezen 1998: 48; Mair and van Biezen 2001.

figures in the PSOE and PP followed a reverse trajectory, with both parties building their mass bases into the mid-1990s. The greater early growth was registered by the PSOE, as much as anything else because it was the first to register good prospects of moving into government and then, in 1982, it actually did so. This made it an obvious 'magnet' for individuals on the left who wanted to back a winner, and placed it in an ideal position to incorporate under-performing socialist parties (Gunther *et al.* 1988: 159). Many of the members who joined the PSOE in the early 1980s were immediate beneficiaries of the patronage power that electoral success at all levels of the political system gave the PSOE at this time. The data on AP/PP membership reveal two bursts of growth, between 1982 and 1986, and between 1989 and 1993. The first of these periods reflects the demise of the UCD (which was the fastest growing party in Spain until it dropped off the electoral map in 1982), the consequent emergence of the AP as the main party of the centre–right, and its capture of many former UCD members. For both the 1982 and 1986 elections, the AP set itself at the centre of an electoral grouping of parties, the Coalición Popular. The second follows the more successful name change—to PP—and rebranding of the party in 1989, and the drive under a new leadership to challenge PSOE hegemony.

Once PSOE–PP rivalry had become established as the central party political tension in Spain by the early 1990s, both parties could claim genuinely national membership bases. The existence of a vibrant tier of regional government and of politicized local councils aided this process, for it enabled these parties to register electoral successes outside the national arena, extended the patronage available to party elites, and gave individuals additional reasons for joining. Despite this, the membership statistics registered by the major parties remain comparatively low.

Electoral turnout

Levels of electoral turnout were of major concern to political commentators during the transition to and consolidation of democracy, with many believing Spain to be characterized by voter apathy and congenitally unsuited to democracy (Justel 1995). Although there are good reasons in Spain's past for this concern (Cuadrado 1969), there appears to be little contemporary justification for it. Indeed, even in Spain's past the main experience of democratic disaster in the 1930s stemmed not so much from voter apathy as from excessive voter engagement. However, in the wake of the Franco regime, which prided itself on depoliticizing Spain, evidence of a vibrant political culture is widely sought. In response to Franquist propaganda claiming that political apathy was healthy for Spain, democrats in the transition hoped to show both that Spaniards were politically engaged and that a polity could be sustained on this foundation.

If electoral turnout is a valid measure of political engagement, they would seem to have a strong case. The first five transition elections (1977, 1979, 1982, 1986, 1989) returned participation rates averaging 73.3 per cent, officially deemed 'satisfactory' (Hualde 1995: 4). An early high point was 1977, with 78.6 per cent, and an early low point 1979, when *el desencanto* (disenchantment with the transition) saw participation fall to 68 per cent. However, this apparent transition fatigue actually came to very little and, once a military coup against the new democracy had been aborted on *23-F* (23 February 1981), Spaniards rallied to the new polity and turned out in the highest numbers ever registered for the 1982 election (Table 9.1). Subsequently there were some worries along the way—the European elections of 1989 saw turnout fall to 54.8 per cent, the local elections of 1991 were not a great deal better at 62.8 per cent—but even articles written to explore abstention rates in Spain were forced to conclude that there was no real problem here. 'To tell the truth, in the short but intensive democratic electoral history of our country, the moments of crisis in participation have been . . . rather exceptional' (Hualde 1995: 3). The relatively low turnout rate of 70 per cent for the 2000 general election is explained by the decision of many on the left to stay at home at a time of disillusionment with the PSOE and IU.

Even those parts of Spain that returned the most worrying participation rates in the early stages of the transition soon stopped doing so. The classic case is Galicia, which in the transition and immediate post-transition periods consistently voted in smaller numbers than the rest of Spain (Montero 1986). In 1979, for instance, only 49 per cent voted there, compared to 68 per cent across the country as a whole. The Canary Islands returned poor figures too. In the first six national elections (1977–93), these two regions registered the lowest participation rates in all elections except 1986 (when Galicia was still the worst performer, but the Balearic Islands had a marginally lower figure than the Canaries). Usually Galicia in particular was lowest by some distance. By 2000, however, Galicia was participating at almost the national average, with 69.5 per cent turning out. In the Canary Islands participation rates remained low (61.6 per cent), but not disastrously so.

Electoral volatility

Measures of electoral volatility in Spain need to be interpreted with caution, chiefly because the 1982 election meets all the conditions of a political earthquake with the hitherto governing UCD falling from 35 to 6.5 per cent of the vote, and from 48 to 3.4 per cent of parliamentary seats. Competitor parties duly profited from the catastrophe. In this election, total volatility is put at 42.3 per cent, and block volatility at 6.7 per cent (refer again to Table 9.1).

If, however, 1982 is treated as the year in which the Spanish party system moved from the fluidity that inevitably characterized its early development to the more structured and institutionalized format visible ever since, then volatility levels are modest. When the character of the UCD itself is taken into account, this seems the correct interpretation to adopt. This never was a political party in the full sense of the term, more an electoral coalition, largely of former Francoists, whose main aim was to retain some hold on power. This it successfully did during the constituent phase of the Spanish transition. Once, however, that phase was over the UCD began to break up into its component factions. The resignation of Suárez in January 1981 signalled the party's terminal decline (Heywood 1995a: 175). More generally, party system instability in democratic Spain is really a case of volatile parties and stable voters. 'It has been parties that have been unstable in Spain; voters have quickly acquired general political orientations, though linking these to parties has been difficult due to changes in parties' (Barnes *et al.* 1986: 56).

Popular assessments

Satisfactory levels of electoral participation and modest degrees of electoral volatility are not reflective, however, of popular affection for parties. In Spain, politicians and parties have almost always registered lower levels of approval even than an institution such as the military, which was consistent in its support for the often repressive Franco regime. The low scores recorded by political parties in Table 9.4 are not especially unusual in comparative terms. What they do show is that Spanish parties have failed to make up in popular esteem what they lack in membership base when compared with the other democracies surveyed in this volume.

Criticism of political parties became particularly great in the early and mid-1990s, when a series of corruption scandals enveloped the González government and spread from there to infect all other major parties. In the mid-1990s corruption was the dominant issue in Spanish politics, just as it was in Italy. Scandals had in fact surfaced well before the 1990s, and some were even linked to key party political activities. In 1984, for example, the PSOE was alleged to have been funded illegally by the SPD, with the Flick holding company acting as intermediary. However, only with the declining popularity of the PSOE, the emergence of a more

TABLE 9.4. *Indicators of popular disaffection/distrust in Spain, 1987–92*

	12/87	6/88	5/90	6/91	11/91	2/92	10/92
(*N*)	2488	2500	2895	2471	2498	2490	2499
Small/medium enterprises	7.07	6.47					6.66
Press			5.76	5.75		6.41	
Church	5.60	5.38	5.30	5.15	4.85	5.34	5.26
Parliament				5.57	5.20	4.98	5.08
Trade unions	4.05	4.01	5.48	5.06	5.47	5.10	4.22
Judiciary			5.23	5.06			4.61
Army	4.86	4.51	4.73	4.83		4.95	4.58
Big business			4.84	4.56		4.84	
Banks	4.57	3.68					3.66
Political parties	3.71	3.75	4.59	4.06	3.80	4.09	3.43

Note: All figures are mean scores on scales running from 0 (low) to 10 (high).

Source: Fundación Foessa (1994: table 4.48, p. 648).

robust opposition, and the development of a 'post-transition' media culture, did scandal come to dominate the news (Jiménez 1998). The first big case, of January 1990, focused on Juan Guerra, brother of deputy prime minister Alfonso Guerra, who was eventually forced to resign because of the kickbacks allegedly received by his sibling. Subsequently, one of the most controversial scandals focused on the Grupos Antiterroristas de Liberación (GAL), state-sponsored anti-terrorist death squads operating in the Basque Country in the years 1983–87 that were investigated with most determination in the mid-1990s. The greatest wave of scandal hit Spain in spring 1994, when as a result of a series of revelations (including those related to GAL) five PSOE ministers eventually resigned. These scandals spread from the PSOE into many elite institutions and into the other main political parties. While the PSOE clearly suffered more damage than any other party, the biggest impact of the widespread political corruption unearthed in the early 1990s may well have been its discrediting of the political class as a whole (Heywood 1995*b*).

Overall, Spaniards are not especially interested in politics. Those claiming to be very or somewhat interested have never constituted more than 30 per cent of the electorate, and not more than 25 per cent since 1983. However, it seems that they are especially uninterested in party politics. Thus, more Spaniards claim to be interested in what municipal (62 per cent), regional (49 per cent) and national government (48 per cent) does, in international issues (35 per cent), in what goes on in parliament (29 per cent) and in trade union activities (24 per cent); by contrast, only 22 per cent claim to be very or somewhat interested in election campaigns and only 21 per cent in party political activities (Centro de Investigaciones Sociológicas 1996).

Party–voter ties

In comparison with many other West European states, party–voter ties do not look strong in Spain. In a televisual polity, one of the first in the world, relatively few people belong to parties or take much interest in what they do (Puhle 1986: 342–3). At 73 per cent, Spain had easily the largest percentage of dealigned voters found by the *Beliefs in Government* research team (Biorcio and Mannheimer 1995: table 7.2). Similarly, Spanish citizens are amongst the least likely in the EU to claim a partisan attachment of any kind (Schmitt and Holmberg 1995: 126–7), although this percentage did climb modestly (from 39 to 47 per cent) between 1985 and 1994. However, party–voter ties are not confined to the linkages that predominate in northern Europe. In particular, as in other states in southern Europe and elsewhere, the links that do exist are often clientelistic. Moreover, public financing of political parties and substantial institutional change, notably in the creation of an entirely new tier of government at the regional level, have generated opportunities for parties to exploit these sorts of links with voters (Mény and Rhodes 1997: 99–105). The result is that many individuals are tied to parties in a very particularistic way. They may profess not to like this, and they may express disapproval when cases of overt corruption come to light, but they often retain their links and use them to their own advantage. It cannot be denied that in this way parties perform a certain function within the political system. They also serve in some sense to legitimize it, even while at the same time undermining it when instances of corruption are revealed.

Evaluating party legitimacy

In Spain, as in other third-wave countries of southern Europe, democracy attracts widespread support but the parties required to make it function are less strongly favoured. The *Beliefs in Government* team found entirely acceptable levels of support in Spain for the idea of democracy (95.5 per cent) and democracy as a form of government (77.8 per cent) (Fuchs *et al.* 1995: table 11.6). But the *New Southern Europe* project concluded of third-wave states in the region that 'parties seem to be regarded as an unavoidable necessity, rather than as institutions supported by high levels of popular sympathy' (Morlino and Montero 1995: 259). It would be wrong to exaggerate the problem of party legitimacy. Compared with many other transition and post-transition countries—such as Russia and a number of Latin American states—Spain is doing well. Nevertheless, when compared with the other parts of Western Europe analysed in this volume, there is an issue here (Mainwaring 1998). 'In terms of some aspects of the quality of democracy ... there is considerable room for improvement' (Gunther *et al.* 1995: 22).

PARTY ORGANIZATIONAL STRENGTH

Institutionalization of Spanish parties since the 1970s fully reveals the top-down nature of their creation. In a number of cases, the 'parties' that ran candidates in the June 1977 election were little more than electoral vehicles for established elite figures. The UCD is the pre-eminent instance, being constructed as an electoral coalition around the person of Prime Minister Suárez a matter of weeks before the 1977 election, and only developing into a (highly fractious) political party in office (Gunther *et al.* 1988: 92–112, 127–45). It is also substantially true of the AP, created as a quasi-federal party by seven former Francoists *(los siete magníficos)* in October 1976. On the left, even the PSOE, nearly 100 years old, was in a considerable state of organizational flux in the mid-1970s, and was still being refashioned around a new leadership team as the 1977 election approached. A perhaps greater problem for parties of the left was that they were not granted legal status until very late in the day: 18 February 1977 in the case of the PSOE, 9 April 1977 in the case of the PCE (Gillespie 1989: ch. 5). Since party development was often top-down, the appropriate way to analyse party organizational strength is by looking first at the parliamentary party, then at the wider mass party, and finally at party finance and 'goods in kind' received by the parties. Throughout, this section is conceived mainly in terms of party institutionalization, reflecting the transitional nature of the Spanish case for much of the period under review. Lack of reliable data means that it is not possible to look in any detail at party staffing levels.

Parliamentary party organization

The rules partially developed in the late 1970s and fully codified in 1982 ensure that parliamentary groups are strong and cohesive in Spain. There are three potential tiers of organization within parliamentary parties: the *portavoz*; a wider executive committee; and a general assembly of all backbench deputies.

In all parties, the key figure of the *portavoz*, the rough equivalent of the chief whip in the Westminster system, is elected. However, the ways in which this election is managed differ by party. In the PP the leadership is formally dominant, and proposes a candidate for election by the parliamentary group. In the PSOE this was the case until 1993, when party divisions stretching into the leadership group itself meant that elections were contested by right- and left-wing factions. On the right were *liberales* or *renovadores*, who supported the pro-market policies of prime minister González and minister of the economy Carlos Solchaga. On the left were *guerristas*, who supported the more traditional socialist platform of former deputy prime minister Guerra. In the CiU and PNV the mass party participates in this election. In the IU the parliamentary group remains the electorate (Sánchez de Dios 1999: 155). Despite these differences, the actual functioning of all these parties shows that the leader plays a major role in the selection of the *portavoz*.

The two main parties have wider executive committees that formally govern the parliamentary groups. In the PSOE this committee is usually controlled by the party leadership. Alongside it stand two further executive committees engaged in monitoring and disciplining deputies. The PP has a rather larger executive committee drawn both from the parliamentary group and the wider party. However, it often meets as an inner core drawn only from the parliamentary group. Again, monitoring and disciplinary functions are undertaken by this committee. In all parties fines can be imposed on deputies who miss key votes or vote contrary to party instructions. The executive committee can sit as a court of appeal against sanctions that have been imposed (Sánchez de Dios 1999: 156–7).

Finally, in all the major parties general assemblies of backbench deputies meet from time to time. In the PSOE the cycle is about three times per month. In the PP it is once a month. When either party is in government the meeting acts as an information exchange between ministers and backbench deputies. In opposition, general assembly meetings are more likely to debate issues on the parliamentary agenda, though the tendency to do this is greater on the left (PSOE and IU) than on the right (PP) (Sánchez de Dios 1999: 155–6).

Spanish parliamentary parties tend to be tightly controlled by their leadership groups. In the PSOE, IU, and PNV, deputies' wages are even fixed by the party hierarchy. This central control is supplemented by an important legacy of the Franco years, a weak tradition of parliamentary debate. The result is that few challenges to party elites are made through parliamentary parties. Only when the dominant coalition starts to fragment from the top, as in the cases of the UCD in the 1980s and PSOE in the 1990s, does the parliamentary party begin to play a significant role.

Mass party organization

It would be misleading to hold that party members are a major source of party organizational strength in Spain. Spanish parties are so heavily dominated by the party in office that the wider party simply cannot assume this importance. Nevertheless, the balance should not be tipped too far in the other direction. To argue that 'party membership is not significant' (Sánchez de Dios 1999: 141) or that, in the case of the PSOE, 'membership and militants are now of little importance' (Colomé 1998: 279), is to exaggerate the extent to which the wider party is marginalized. Indeed, when in 1989 the AP became the PP and embarked on a major programme of organizational development, one of the main tasks it set itself was to build a membership base to rival that of the PSOE. Even in Spain, then, members do still matter, if only to a limited extent.

Ever since its re-emergence in the mid-1970s, the PSOE has had a formally decentralized structure, building from the bottom up through local, provincial, regional, and national levels (Colomé 1998). Article 14 of the party statutes states that it is 'a political organization with a federal character', and each regional party has its own version of the national structure (congress, executive committee, general secretary), its own programme and sometimes its own name: PSOE-A in Andalusia, PSC-PSOE in Catalonia, PSG-PSOE in Galicia, and so on (Newton 1997: 192). In part, this strong regional dimension reflects party commitments made as long ago as 1917, in part the high profile of sub-nationalist pressures during the transition. In practice, however, for most of the past twenty-five years the party has been controlled from the centre (Morlino 1995: 341), with only a very distinctive region like Catalonia making anything of a divergence from the national line. The emergence of González as general secretary at the 1974 party congress (held in Suresnes, France) and the promotion of his 'interior group' to key positions within the party led to some tensions in the mid-1970s (Gillespie 1989: ch. 5). The rapid growth of the party around the time of the 1977 election generated very low levels of party institutionalization (Gunther *et al.* 1988: 165). However, the events of 1979 resolved the central dividing issues for more than a decade, and were the foundations on which the party was constructed. At the XXIII party congress held in May 1979, González's attempt to deradicalize the party was defeated and he resigned the leadership. At an extraordinary party congress held in September the reformist platform was victorious, and González regained control. His sweeping victory in the 1982 general election confirmed his position as unassailable. For much of the 1980s, it was chiefly from outside the party that challenges to the leadership came, notably the UGT trade union, with which the PSOE was once closely allied but from which a decade of neo-liberal reform distanced it. In the 1990s, however, corruption scandals and the approaching end of the González era re-opened divisions in the party itself between the *guerristas* and the *renovadores*. The protracted search for a successor to González once the 1996 general election had been lost revealed the extent to which the PSOE, without his charismatic leadership, remained a factionalized party. Following the substantial election defeat in March 2000, Joaquín Almunia, González's successor as general secretary, resigned. At the subsequent XXXV party congress, held in July 2000, José Luis Rodríguez Zapatero was unexpectedly elected his successor, narrowly beating regional baron and favoured candidate, José Bono.

Only in the 1990s has the AP/PP sought to develop a decentralized structure to fit the structure of Spain's democratic polity. In the transition proper the AP was an extremely fluid organization. It is often said to have started life as a federation of parties, though this is to stretch the concept of party almost beyond recognition. In the beginning the AP was essentially a loose grouping of Francoist factions (Montero 1988: 146). In the period of the constituent Cortes it became a party composed of six federations with a semi-presidential structure. At this time a national steering committee (Junta Directiva Nacional) and a national executive committee (Comité Ejecutivo Nacional) were created, and have survived to this day. However, real party institutionalization came only in the wake of the III party congress of December 1979. Then the party's regional organization began slowly to develop, partly as regional elections were held and the AP gained representation on regional councils. However, the main development of the 1980s was reinforcement of the centre, through creation of a national headquarters in Madrid and centralization of membership files. At the party's IV congress in January 1989, a further complete transformation was agreed as the party changed its name from AP to PP. A new media section was created, fresh links with key social groups and relevant experts were instituted, and an attempt to build a younger membership was made through the youth organization, Nuevas Generaciones (NNGG). The party also sought to develop a clearer regional focus, and to build a viable organization in all parts of Spain. At national level, its headquarters staff were boosted to around 200 (Lòpez-Nieto 1998).

There is now a certain organizational strength to Spain's two main mass parties, and they have clearly come a long way in little more than twenty years. Moreover, that strength operates principally as a leadership resource, rather than as a constraint on it. In both parties, key matters like candidate selection are strongly controlled from the centre, though upsets are still possible as the 2000 election of Zapatero to lead the PSOE showed. Indeed, one indicator of fragility in Spanish parties as mass political organizations is the difficulties they have experienced in managing leadership successions. The UCD in the early 1980s, the AP in the late 1980s, and the PSOE in the late 1990s all had problems in replacing established leaders. In the case of the AP, Manuel Fraga was even asked to resume the leadership for a while (Heywood 1995*a*: 191). However, it could be argued that the UCD was a very special case, that the PP has much more organizational strength than its forerunner the AP, and that González was a very hard act to follow as leader of the PSOE. Spanish parties clearly retain a degree of immaturity and under-institutionalization, but they are not devoid of organizational strength.

Party finance

The rules set in place in the very early years of the transition have ensured that the state is a major contributor to the large amounts of money spent by Spanish parties. This is chiefly because nascent parties in a transitional democracy were not thought likely to be able to tap funds from other sources. In the event, the most viable ones did, looking notably to banks in Spain and fraternal parties elsewhere (chiefly in West Germany, Sweden, and the Soviet Union) for aid. They also began to develop something of a membership base. Despite this, the state remains the major financer of Spain's leading political parties.

The subsidy regime established in the late 1970s falls into two main categories. The first element, created as the June 1977 elections loomed, is state subsidy of parties' electoral expenditure. The lack of a satisfactory disclosure requirement means that even semi-reliable data are only available from the mid-1980s onwards. Even then, official data published by the Tribunal de Cuentas are heavily reliant on parties' own reports, and are very slow to appear. Existing figures (Table 9.5) show that for Spain's biggest and electorally most successful parties, state funding covers at least 50 per cent of election expenditure. For the PSOE, AP/PP, PCE/IU, CiU and CDS (while still operative), the proportion has usually been above 90 per cent. For the PNV it has generally been smaller, though by 1996 it had risen to 78 per cent. The rules for distribution of this subsidy mean that very few other parties are eligible, as parliamentary representation is the key qualification. This was one key factor in driving some promising parties out of business in the late 1970s and 1980s.

State subsidy of routine party expenses is allocated on a similar, though not identical, basis. Here, data are again partial and yet more unreliable, being wholly self-generated by the parties. What the figures reveal is that state subsidy is again the critical component of party funding (Table 9.6). For the PSOE and AP/PP, it totalled around 90 per cent of running expenses in the late 1980s, before falling into the 75–85 per cent band in the 1990s. For the CDS, PCE/IU, and CiU it has always been above 60 per cent, and usually considerably so. For the PNV, it has been more erratic. This subsidy comprises three components. The most important is the ordinary state subvention. The other two components are state funding of parliamentary groups and state funding of public office holders.

For the major parties, all other sources of national funding pale into insignificance in comparison with that provided by the state. Only rarely does funding generated by the party itself play anything other than a minor role in election

TABLE 9.5. *Major party electoral campaign income and expenditure in Spain, 1986–96*

	PSOE	AP/PP	CDS	PCE/IU	CiU	PNV	Average
1986							
exp (m pts)	2651	1924	153	428	332	126	935.7
inc (m pts)[a]	1843	811	111	186	141	172	544.0
% inc: state	86	91	100	23	98	35	72.2
% inc: party	14	6	0	77	2	65	27.3
1989							
exp (m pts)	2263	1816	1044	414	381	154	1012.0
inc (m pts)[a]	1629	1030	101	140	213	186	549.8
% inc: state	100	95	100	96	82	27	83.3
% inc: party	0	2	0	0	8	73	13.8
1993[b]							
exp (m pts)	2819	2378	91	1584	363	220	1242.5
inc (m pts)[a]	3294	2731	18	1019	340	258	1276.7
% inc: state	78	86	0	90	97	44	65.8
% inc: party	22	10	100	10	0	56	33.0
1996[b]							
exp (m pts)	2512	2550		1204	406	157	1365.8
inc (m pts)[a]	3163	3375		1110	534	201	1676.6
% inc: state	93	96		95	100	78	92.4
% inc: party	7	4		5	0	22	7.6

[a]Excluding bank loans.
[b]Estimates based on legal provisions and pre-election advances.

Source: van Biezen (2000*a*: table 3).

campaigns; usually its contribution is under 10 per cent (Table 9.5). Similarly, membership dues usually cover no more than a small proportion of routine expenses, again falling below 10 per cent in most cases. The contribution of donations is hard to gauge, chiefly because the figures supplied by parties and endorsed by the Tribunal de Cuentas are not necessarily reliable. Funding scandals, often centred on the PSOE, also make it clear that official data are frequently designed to mislead. At the regional level, parties receive funds directly and indirectly from the institutions of regional government (such as money for the functioning of regional parliamentary groups), and thereby gain some resilience and autonomy.

Overall, it is clear from Tables 9.5 and 9.6 that the main Spanish parties have grown wealthier: in the decade 1986–96, average income to party election funds grew by some 208 per cent (125 per cent in real terms) while election expenditure increased by 46 per cent (28 per cent in real terms); and in the years between 1987 and 1992, non-election income increased by 52 per cent (39 per cent in real terms) while non-election expenditure burgeoned by 497 per cent (373 per cent in real terms). Despite this, however, and notwithstanding the particular generosity of

TABLE 9.6. *Major party regular income and expenditure in Spain, 1987–92*

	PSOE	AP/PP	CDS	PCE/IU	CiU	PNV	Average
1987							
exp (m pts)	1044	466	509	331	153	74	429.5
inc (m pts)	4829	NA	810	345	NA	135	1529.0
% inc: state[a]	86	NA	96	74	NA	53	77.3
% inc: dues	8	NA	4	2	NA	47	15.3
1988							
exp (m pts)	5994	1452	1286	491	379	194	1632.7
inc (m pts)	5341	1823	871	430	629	198	1548.7
% inc: state[a]	81	93	83	63	77	79	79.3
% inc: dues	11	6	17	4	23	13	12.3
1989							
exp (m pts)	7252	4911	2045	1387	901	573	2844.8
inc (m pts)	5634	2139	1136	719	727	763	1853.0
% inc: state[a]	77	91	64	63	69	23	64.5
% inc: dues	13	NA	16	1	24	13	13.4
1990							
exp (m pts)	4350	4801	1184	1171	914	653	2178.8
inc (m pts)	4535	2991	927	855	815	303	1737.7
% inc: state[a]	92	90	70	85	65	56	76.3
% inc: dues	3	5	5	2	33	5	8.8
1991							
exp (m pts)	6829	3750	677	1102	1210	1258	2471.0
inc (m pts)	5901	3357	703	1023	819	862	2110.8
% inc: state[a]	76	83	95	78	70	25	71.2
% inc: dues	13	NA	4	2	26	14	12.0
1992							
exp (m pts)	7121	4671	706	1071	765	1047	2563.5
inc (m pts)	6182	3692	786	1068	1108	1102	2323.0
% inc: state[a]	77	83	88	76	54	19	66.2
% inc: dues	14	NA	12	3	22	21	14.4

[a] Ordinary state subvention plus funding of parliamentary groups plus funding of public office holders. Of these, the ordinary state subvention is usually by far the largest, accounting in most instances for at least two-thirds of party income.

Source: van Biezen (2000*a*: table 1).

the state, all major Spanish parties are considerably indebted, mainly to domestic banks. This, plus the allegations of illicit funding that periodically surface in corruption scandals, means that reform is again on the agenda (Gillespie 1998).

'Goods in kind' received by parties

The main 'goods in kind' received by all parties are free campaigning slots on state television channels, free space for displaying campaign posters, free use of public meeting places for campaign rallies, and reduced postal rates for campaign mailings. Governing parties have routinely supplemented these goods by turning the state television network, RTVE, into a propaganda machine. In the 1970s, Suárez (in the late Franco years director-general of RTVE) and the UCD did this. Their efforts were, however, surpassed by those of González and the PSOE in the 1980s, who were widely criticized for their cynical exploitation of power. In a society in which newspaper readership has always been low and television viewing correspondingly high—surpassed in the EU only by Portugal—this level of control is of obvious importance to governing parties. However, the advent of commercial channels at the start of the 1990s has made control of RTVE a less potent governing party resource (Heywood 1995*a*: 76).

Evaluating party organizational strength

Spanish parties are chiefly held together from the top, which is what gives them a rather synthetic character. Nevertheless, at the national level the attempt to build parties has to be considered successful. There have been problems along the way, and splits have taken place. But two major national parties are now in place and look established. At the sub-national level the picture is rather more complex, with regional and local splits being more common. Spain does not have the mass political parties developed in many other West European states, including Italy, in the immediate postwar years. Instead, it has developed 'catch-all parties, in which leaders play extremely important roles while the significance of members and organizations is relatively slight' (Morlino 1995: 341).

THE SYSTEMIC FUNCTIONALITY OF PARTIES

Spanish parties do not have a positive popular profile, and much of their organizational strength comes from the state rather than from civil society. However, they may still perform the role of central actors in a democratic polity for which they were always intended. This section analyses parties' role in governance, political recruitment and patronage, interest articulation and aggregation, political participation, and political communication and education.

Governance

The role of parties in actually governing democratic Spain has not been uniform. At the start of the transition their role was necessarily limited by the time it took for democratic institutions to be created at all levels of the state. In the initial stages they were also fragile and elite-focused. Nevertheless, even then the PCE and PSOE in particular played a key role by 'making it possible to demobilize activists in order to stabilize the political environment' (Gunther 1992: 80). This was as much the case with socio-economic deals—like the Moncloa Pacts of October 1977—as it was with constitutional agreements. Subsequently, as parties established elementary organizations and colonized the newly democratic state, they became yet more important. Since the late 1970s it is clear that the Katz (1986: 43) criteria for party government have been broadly met in Spain. All major governmental decisions are taken by people chosen in competitive elections, or by individuals appointed by and responsible to them. Policy is determined within the governing party. Key politicians are selected within parties and are responsible to the mass of the people through them. Beyond this, the strong parliamentary party discipline that exists in Spain generates close approximation to the party government model. Usually party groups in the Congreso speak through their *portavoces* with a single voice. The many controls on individual activity in the Congreso also substantially enhance party discipline (Sánchez de Dios 1999: 150–1).

Parties have thus been central actors in Spain's democracy. Tarrow (1995: 229) holds that one consequence of their role in stabilizing the transitional political system has been government 'through elite transaction and consociational bargains' focused on parties. Somewhat in contrast to this, Heywood (1998) argues that the Spanish political system is properly seen not as (neo-)corporatist, but as a liberal market economy in which a considerable amount of power is concentrated at the heart of the state. Still, however, parties are key, with the governing party controlling access to the policy process. Indeed, Spain's parties are often criticized precisely for the extent to which they now govern. Heywood (1995*a*: 214) cites as a problem the fact that 'parties have tended to ignore public opinion in their policy formulation, preferring to deal directly with powerful economic interest groups while parliamentary debates are reduced to a banal and trivial level'. This is indeed problematic, but it also makes the point that parties are critical to Spanish governance. Do parties make a difference in contemporary Spain? Certainly they do. There is no significant evidence of a challenge to party from, say, candidate-centred politics.

Political recruitment and patronage

Despite this predominance of party government, not all elite political recruitment takes place strictly through party channels. In large part this reflects the unconstrained powers vested in the prime minister, who in making cabinet appointments is under no obligation to restrict his choice to members of the Cortes. Indeed, successive prime ministers have chosen to appoint from outside the ranks of party politicians, even to the key position of minister of finance, which González in the 1980s occasionally filled with leading officials from the Bank of Spain. The Aznar premiership has been marked by the inclusion in government of several independents, among whom are some from the left. On the whole, however, leading cabinet posts have been filled by members of the governing party.

Indeed, as Spain's parties have gradually colonized the democratic state, so they have exploited the extensive patronage opportunities open to them (Morlino 1995: 356). This was particularly true of the PSOE in the mid-1980s, when sweeping electoral success at national, regional, and local level enabled it to place people in many parts of the public sector. The expansion of PSOE membership in the 1980s can be partly explained by this. A similar pattern was visible in the PP in the 1990s.

Interest articulation and aggregation

In most democratic systems parties have been on the retreat as articulators and aggregators of interests. In their places have stepped established pressure groups, new social movements and single-issue campaigns. Spain's rather enervated civic culture—described in the mid-1980s as a 'near-*tabula rasa* of associational life' (Barnes *et al.* 1986: 61)—means that as a general rule there is less articulation of interests across the entire political system than in many other states. Linz has argued that one key reason for this is that prolonged periods of political stability are needed for pressure groups to establish themselves. In Spain, not only has this condition not been met, but for much of the twentieth century—under the dictatorships of Generals Primo de Rivera and Franco—the state has also tried to substitute its control for associational activity (Molins and Casademunt 1998). The result is that even political spheres like environmental policy, which frequently prompt mobilization, are comparatively unorganized in Spain (Holliday 1997). Taking all this into account, the relative performance of Spanish parties is probably little different from that witnessed elsewhere.

Indeed, it could be argued that they are doing comparatively well, for much new mobilization has in fact taken party political form. When Heywood analysed the rise of challengers to 'mainstream' parties, the organizations he listed were regional parties, green parties, and campaigning organizations built around maverick tycoons (Heywood 1995a: 187–8). However, while this counts as interest articulation by political parties, it does not generate much interest aggregation. In most parts of Spain the problem is not particularly great, for both regional and national parties have tended to contain potentially divisive and separatist demands within the mainstream political system. In the Basque Country this has not been the case, however, as successive splinters from what began life as an integrated nationalist movement focused on the PNV have shown. The regionalist demands voiced in the Basque Country in the past thirty years are particularly intractable, however, and it is by no means to Basque parties' discredit they have not been able fully to control them. One question that nevertheless remains concerns the continued ability of parties to tie militant regions into a greater Spain (Hopkin 1999: 229).

Overall, Spanish parties play an important aggregation role in a rather under-developed civil society. From the start they have pursued broad catch-all strategies.

Indeed, the UCD's strategy was so broad that it eventually fragmented into a series of constituent parts. The PSOE and PP have clearer social bases, but nevertheless seek to attract support from broad swathes of the political spectrum. It has been persuasively argued that statewide parties played a particularly key role in holding together a potentially fractious country in the first general election of 1977 (Linz *et al.* 1995: 90).

Political participation

Article 6 of the Spanish constitution explicitly identifies parties as a 'fundamental instrument' in developing political participation. In the classical terms surely intended by the framers of the constitution, the way in which Spanish parties have developed has made this one of their lesser roles: their membership bases are comparatively slight, and the extent to which they hold the attention of Spaniards is limited. On the whole, these are electoral parties of professional politicians (Morlino 1995: 345). However, the point made earlier about Spain's clientelistic political culture can be made again here: political participation takes additional forms and provides alternative ways for parties to offer linkage to their supporters. Beyond that, anyone with a concern about participation in Spain would have to note that participation rates in the central forums of Spanish democracy—elections—are not dangerously low. Overall, political participation within Spanish parties seems to be developing as the parties themselves, and the party system, mature. The kinds of pressures that led even the British Conservative Party to enhance the participatory role of rank-and-file members are also at work in Spain. One result is that the PSOE now uses a primaries system for selecting the party leader, thereby giving party members a clear role.

Political communication and education

Again, the political communication and education in which Spanish people are most likely to want parties to engage are of the level-playing-field variety in which all elements of (acceptable) opinion get a decent chance of being heard. The extent to which governing parties have sought to control the overwhelmingly important medium of political communication—television—indicates that this has not been one of their primary aims or achievements. Moreover, the tight leash on which parliamentary parties are held by their respective leaderships means that debates in the Cortes and Senado have been consistently anodyne. In these circumstances, the non-state media has become the main instrument for political communication and education. In the transition period the press—the 'paper parliament'—was a major promoter of democracy, with *El País,* founded in May 1976, playing an important role (Sánchez-Gijón 1987: 126). Thereafter, the press lost some influence to television and radio. However, it remains a leading defender of the core precepts of democracy: it is no accident that it unearthed most of the corruption scandals of recent years. While many newspapers have party political links, it would be stretching a point to say that this gives parties a key role in political communication and education. Unlike classic mass parties, Spain's electoral-professional parties have not taken one of their major roles to be the political education of their adherents.

Evaluating the systemic functionality of parties

As desired by the founding fathers, parties are central actors in Spain's democratic polity. In comparison with parties in more established democratic states, they look rather unimpressive on several measures of systemic functionality. They are better at governance and recruitment than at representative or participatory linkage. Nevertheless, even at a time when the Basque problem remains unsolved, the role of statewide parties in tying potentially secessionist regions into a greater Spain should not be overlooked.

CONCLUSION

The argument made at the start was that the circumstances of the Spanish transition generated synthetic parties and a parties state. Neither was necessarily intended. The constitutional framers would presumably have been delighted if parties had established strong bases in civil society and a limited reliance on the state. They would also have been perfectly happy if parties had chosen not to exploit their powers of patronage quite so extensively in appointing to positions within the state. However, the central issue on which they agreed was that Spain was to become a democracy, a democracy required parties, and if parties did not emerge from civil society they would be laid on by the state. As has been shown here, this is largely what happened, in part because the incentives with which parties were faced were so heavily skewed in this direction. The two main questions that arise in conclusion are how stable and viable this system is, and how it compares with other democratic experiences.

In answering the first question it is worth noting that the Spanish case conforms closely to the cartel party thesis (Katz and Mair 1995). The widespread lack of interest in participation that has characterized Spain since the transition has indeed seen parties turn to the state, from which they have secured substantial funding and privileged access to the electronic media. Here, democracy has been very much 'a service provided by the state for civil society'. And since democracy is currently held to require political parties, 'the state also provides (or guarantees the provision of) political parties' (Katz and Mair 1995: 22). It is precisely this synthetic character that Spanish parties have. Reasons can easily be given for this. Spain's partial and difficult experiences with democracy in the twentieth century mean that its party system development has been very patchy. The mass party phase was never substantial, and resulted in the searing experience of civil war from which Spain emerged as an authoritarian state committed to the abolition of all vestiges of competitive party politics. When this phase in turn came to an end the dominant historical memory of civil war fostered the political culture of inter-party cooperation and accommodation that is an ideal breeding ground for cartelization. Politics duly became more self-referential, more professional, and more secure for those parties on the inside track. The cartel was constructed, and assumed a clear form from 1982 onwards. It has ragged edges, notably at the sub-national level. In regional and local party systems fragmentation and party splits have been witnessed on a number of occasions. Nevertheless, at the dominant national level it is fixed in place.

For this analysis the particular interest of the Katz–Mair thesis is that it contains the prediction that in due course the world will make a further turn and cartel parties will face challenges from 'breaking the mould' parties and interest groups. To date this has not happened on a significant scale in Spain, and there is reason to believe that in the absence of real crisis it may not happen in the foreseeable future. Like their counterparts in much of southern Europe, Spaniards seem happy to value democracy in a rather abstract way, at the same time revealing the alienation from politics that Almond and Verba picked up in Italy some four decades ago (Montero and Morlino 1993). They particularly distrust parties, criticize them, and yet leave them largely to their own devices. They would like parties to stop spending quite as much public money as they do, to clean up their affairs and to act more responsibly, but they show no inclination to challenge their central role in Spain's parties state.

Comparative analysis of other 'third-wave' democracies reinforces this conclusion (Huntington 1991). Mainwaring and Scully (1995: 1) argue that 'the critical difference among Latin American party systems is whether or not a competitive party system is institutionalized'. As a subsidiary point, they hold that number of parties and ideological distance can be important too. The best-case scenario for democratic stability is an institutionalized two- or two-and-a-half-party system. Others have built on this analysis. Norden (1998) states that the nature of inter-party competition is also an important factor: moderate competition tends to foster stability, whereas both combative and collusive arrangements tend to undermine it. Coppedge (1998) maintains that the substance of party politics and the extent of party system change also have to be taken into account. 'Sufficiently ideological' parties—neither dominated by nor devoid of ideology—come out well in his analysis. It is hard to make any generalizations about really volatile party systems.

In applying all this to Spain, the first key issue is what is meant by 'institutionalization'. Mainwaring and Scully hold that 'an institutionalized party system implies stability in inter-party competition, the existence of parties that have somewhat stable roots in society, acceptance of parties and elections as the legitimate institutions that determine who governs, and party organizations with reasonably stable rules and structures' (Mainwaring and Scully 1995: 1). In passing, they later state that a case like Spain shows that 'democracy can function reasonably well without [an] extreme institutionalized party [system]' (Mainwaring and Scully 1995: 22). But another way of looking at all this is to use a rather weaker notion of institutionalization by means of which some of the Mainwaring–Scully conditions are partially relaxed (Norden 1998: 429). Then Spain becomes what might be called 'sufficiently institutionalized' to meet the first condition of stability. Add in the rest of what is known about Spain and stability seems highly likely. It does not have too many parties, and if anything the trend is downward. The effective numbers of electoral and parliamentary parties registered in the 2000 election are at historically low levels (Table 9.1). The decade averages for electoral parties fell from 4.16 in the 1970s to 3.69 in the 1980s to 3.32 in the 1990s. For parliamentary parties they fell from 2.81 in the 1970s to 2.57 in the 1980s before rising slightly to 2.63 in the 1990s. Moreover, even within Spain's essentially cartelized system, political debate is characterized by moderate competition between sufficiently ideological parties. Certainly PP–PSOE competition seems to be increasingly structured by class (Torcal and Chhibber 1992). Add the further dimension of a supportive external environment, and the possibility that the Spanish party system will retain its current features for a good while to come seems very strong.

A further comparison to be made is with the emergent parties and party systems in East–Central Europe. Here there is ample evidence of similarity (van Biezen 2000*b*). Parties in Spain, like their counterparts in the post-1989 democracies, are much stronger parliamentary than social actors. Indeed, Spain turns out to be a neat fit for Ágh's party parliamentarization thesis, which states that parliamentary groups provide the core around which party institutionalization takes place (Ágh 1999; Sánchez de Dios 1999: 141). At the same time, they are of course critical actors in what has, after all, been characterized here as a parties state. One key difference between Spain and East European transition states is, however, the considerable unity of its parliamentary parties, which contrasts with the faction-hopping found in much of eastern Europe, and particularly Hungary (Ágh 1999; Sánchez de Dios 1999: 152). Institutional factors, notably the rules developed by the Cortes, play an important part in generating parliamentary party cohesion in Spain.

The parties state and synthetic parties found in Spain represent a kind of halfway house between established and new experiences of party politics. In common with other southern European states of the third wave, Spain has a partially institutionalized party system that is not as strong as its counterparts in other parts of western Europe but not as weak as its counterparts in eastern Europe and Latin America (Mainwaring 1998). Parties have quite limited legitimacy and rather unimpressive organizational strength. However, as dominant forces in an underdeveloped civic environment, Spain's electoral-professional parties play a key political role.

REFERENCES

Ágh, A. (1999) 'The parliamentarization of the East Central European parties: party discipline in the Hungarian Parliament, 1990–1996', in Shaun Bowler, David M. Farrell, and Richard S. Katz (eds) *Party Discipline and Parliamentary Government* (Columbus, OH: Ohio State University Press), pp. 167–88.

Astorkia, H. and María, J. (1995) 'Evolución de la abstención electoral en España: 1976–1991', in Pilar del Castillo (ed.) *Comportamiento Político y Electoral* (Madrid: Centro de Investigaciones Sociológicas), pp. 3–18.

Bardavío, J. (1969) *La Estructura del Poder en España: Sociología Política de un Pais* (Madrid: Iberico Europea de Ediciones).

Barnes, S. H., McDonough, P., and Pina, A. L. (1986) 'Volatile parties and stable voters in Spain'. *Government and Opposition* 21: 56–75.

Biezen, I. van (1998) 'Building party organisations and the relevance of past models: the Communist and Socialist parties in Spain and Portugal'. *West European Politics* 21(2): 32–62.

—— (2000*a*) 'Party financing in new democracies: Spain and Portugal'. *Party Politics* 6: 329–42.

—— (2000*b*) 'On the internal balance of party power: party organizations in new democracies'. *Party Politics* 6: 395–417.

Biorcio, R. and Mannheimer, R. (1995) 'Relationships between citizens and political parties', in Hans-Dieter Klingemann and Dieter Fuchs (eds) *Citizens and the State* (Oxford: Oxford University Press), pp. 206–26.

Carr, R. (1987) 'Introduction: the Spanish transition to democracy in historical perspective', in Robert P. Clark and Michael H. Haltzel (eds) *Spain in the 1980s: The Democratic Transition and a New International Role* (Cambridge, MA: Ballinger), pp. 1–13.

Castillo, P. del (1989) 'Financing of Spanish political parties', in Herbert E. Alexander (ed.) *Comparative Political Finance in the 1980s* (Cambridge: Cambridge University Press), pp. 172–99.

Centro de Investigaciones Sociológicas (1996) *Barómetro de abril 1996 (Estudio 2212)* (Madrid: CIS).

Colomé, G. (1998) 'The PSOE: the establishment of a governmental party', in Piero Ignazi and Colette Ysmal (eds) *The Organization of Political Parties in Southern Europe* (Westport, CT: Praeger), pp. 270–80.

Coppedge, M. (1998) 'The dynamic diversity of Latin American party systems'. *Party Politics* 4: 547–68.

Cuadrado, M. M. (1969) *Elecciones y partidos políticos de España (1868–1931)*, 2 vols (Madrid: Taurus).

Franco, F. (1975) *Pensamiento político de Franco: antologia*, 2 vols (Madrid: Ediciones del Movimiento).

Fuchs, D., Guidorossi, G., and Svensson, P. (1995) 'Support for the democratic system', in Hans-Dieter Klingemann and Dieter Fuchs (eds) *Citizens and the State* (Oxford: Oxford University Press), pp. 323–53.

Fundación Foessa (1976) *Estudios sociológicos sobre la situación social de España 1975* (Madrid: Fundación Fomento de Estudios Sociales y de Sociología Aplicada).

Gillespie, R. (1989) *The Spanish Socialist Party: A History of Factionalism* (Oxford: Clarendon Press).

—— (1998) 'Party funding in a new democracy: Spain', in Peter Burnell and Alan Ware (eds) *Funding Democratization* (Manchester: Manchester University Press), pp. 73–93.

Gunther, R. (1980) *Public Policy in a No-party State: Spanish Planning and Budgeting in the Twilight of the Franquist Era* (Berkeley, CA: University of California Press).

—— (1989) 'Electoral laws, party systems, and elites: the case of Spain'. *American Political Science Review* 83: 835–58.

—— (1992) 'Spain: the very model of the modern elite settlement', in John Higley and Richard Gunther (eds) *Elites and Democratic Consolidation in Latin America and Southern Europe* (Cambridge: Cambridge University Press), pp. 38–80.

—— Puhle, H.-J., and Diamandouros, P. N. (1995) 'Introduction', in Richard Gunther, P., Nikiforos Diamandouros, and Hans-Jürgen Puhle (eds) *The Politics of Democratic Consolidation: Southern Europe in Comparative Perspective* (Baltimore: Johns Hopkins University Press), pp. 1–32.

—— Sani, G., and Shabad, G. (1988) *Spain After Franco: The Making of a Competitive Part System* (Berkeley, CA: University of California Press).

Heywood, P. (1995a) *The Government and Politics of Spain* (Basingstoke: Macmillan).

—— (1995b) 'Sleaze in Spain'. *Parliamentary Affairs* 48: 726–37.

—— (1996) 'The emergence of new party systems and transitions to democracy: Spain in comparative perspective', in Geoffrey Pridham and Paul G. Lewis (eds) *Stabilising Fragile Democracies: Comparing New Party Systems in Southern and Eastern Europe* (London: Routledge), pp. 145–66.

—— (1998) 'Power diffusion or concentration? In search of the Spanish policy process'. *West European Politics* 21(4): 103–23.

Holliday, I. (1997) 'Living on the edge: Spanish Greens in the mid-1990s'. *Environmental Politics* 6: 168–75.

Hopkin, J. (1999) 'Spain: political parties in a young democracy', in David Broughton and Mark Donovan (eds) *Changing Party Systems in Western Europe* (London: Pinter), pp. 207–31.

Huntington, S. P. (1991) *The Third Wave: Democratization in the Late Twentieth Century* (Norman, OK: University of Oklahoma Press).

Jiménez, F. (1998) 'Political scandals and political responsibility in democratic Spain'. *West European Politics* 21(4): 80–99.

Justel, M. (1995) *La abstención electoral en España, 1977–1993* (Madrid: Centro de Investigaciones Sociológicas).

Katz, R. S. (1986) 'Party government: a rationalistic conception', in Francis G. Castles and Rudolf Wildenmann (eds) *The Future of Party Government: Visions and Realities of Party Government*, vol. 1 (Berlin: Walter de Gruyter), pp. 31–71.

—— and Mair, P. (1995) 'Changing models of party organization and party democracy: the emergence of the cartel party'. *Party Politics* 1: 5–28.

Linz, J. J. (1986) 'Consideraciones finales', in Juan J. Linz and José R. Montero (eds) *Crisis y cambio: electores y partidos en la España de los años ochenta* (Madrid: Centro de Estudios Constitucionales), pp. 645–62.

—— Stepan, A., and Gunther, R. (1995) 'Democratic transition and consolidation in Southern Europe, with reflections on Latin America and Eastern Europe', in Richard Gunther, P. Nikiforos Diamandouros, and Hans-Jürgen Puhle (eds) *The Politics of*

Democratic Consolidation: Southern Europe in Comparative Perspective (Baltimore: Johns Hopkins University Press), pp. 77–123.

Lòpez-Nieto, L. (1998) 'The organizational dynamics of AP/PP', in Piero Ignazi and Colette Ysmal (eds) *The Organization of Political Parties in Southern Europe* (Westport, CT: Praeger), pp. 254–69.

Mainwaring, S. (1998) 'Party systems in the Third Wave'. *Journal of Democracy* 9(3): 67–81.

—— and Scully, T. R. (1995) 'Introduction: party systems in Latin America', in Scott Mainwaring and Timothy R. Scully (eds) *Building Democratic Institutions: Party Systems in Latin America* (Stanford, CA: Stanford University Press), pp. 1–34.

Mair, P. and van Biezen, I. (2001) 'Party membership in twenty European democracies, 1980–2000'. *Party Politics* 7: 5–22.

Martín Rebollo, L. (1996) 'La Constitución de 1978: Elaboración, significado e incidencia en el ordenamiento jurídico general', introductory essay to *Constitución Española* (Pamplona: Aranzadi), pp. 15–59.

Mény, Y. and Rhodes, M. (1997) 'Illicit governance: corruption, scandal and fraud', in Martin Rhodes, Paul Heywood, and Vincent Wright (eds) *Developments in West European Politics* (Basingstoke: Macmillan), pp. 95–113.

Molins, J. M. and Casademunt, A. (1998) 'Pressure groups and the articulation of interests'. *West European Politics* 21(4): 124–46.

Montero, J. R. (1986) 'La vuelta a las ureas: participación, movilización y abstención', in Juan J. Linz and José R. Montero (eds) *Crisis y cambio: electores y partidos en la España de los años ochenta* (Madrid: Centro de Estudios Constitucionales), pp. 71–124.

—— (1988) 'More than Conservative, less than Neoconservative: Alianza Popular in Spain', in Brian Girvin (ed.) *The Transformation of Contemporary Conservatism* (London: Sage Publications), pp. 145–63.

—— and Morlino, L. (1993) 'Legitimidad y democracia en el sur de Europa'. *Reis* 64: 7–40.

Morlino, L. (1995) 'Political parties and democratic consolidation in Southern Europe', in Richard Gunther, P. Nikiforos Diamandouros, and Hans-Jürgen Puhle (eds) *The Politics of Democratic Consolidation: Southern Europe in Comparative Perspective* (Baltimore: Johns Hopkins University Press), pp. 315–88.

—— and Montero, J. R. (1995) 'Legitimacy and democracy in Southern Europe', in Richard Gunther, P. Nikiforos Diamandouros, and Hans-Jürgen Puhle (eds) *The Politics of Democratic Consolidation: Southern Europe in Comparative Perspective* (Baltimore: Johns Hopkins University Press), pp. 231–60.

Newton, M. T. (with Donaghy, P. J.) (1997) *Institutions of Modern Spain: A Political and Economic Guide* (Cambridge: Cambridge University Press).

Norden, D. L. (1998) 'Party relations and democracy in Latin America'. *Party Politics* 4: 423–43.

Pridham, G. (1996) 'Transnational party links and transition to democracy: Eastern Europe in comparative perspective', in Paul G. Lewis (ed.) *Party Structure and Organization in East-Central Europe* (Cheltenham: Edward Elgar), pp. 187–217.

Puhle, H.-J. (1986) 'El PSOE: un partido predominante y heterogeneo', in Juan J. Linz and José R. Montero (eds) *Crisis y cambio: electores y partidos en la España de los años ochenta* (Madrid Centro de Estudios Constitucionales), pp. 289–344.

Rae, D. (1971) *The Political Consequences of Electoral Laws* (New Haven, CT: Yale University Press).

Sánchez de Dios, M. (1999) 'Parliamentary party discipline in Spain', in Shaun Bowler, David M. Farrell, and Richard S. Katz (eds) *Party Discipline and Parliamentary Government* (Columbus, OH: Ohio State University Press), pp. 141–62.

Sánchez-Gijón, A. (1987) 'The Spanish press in the transition period', in Robert P. Clark and Michael H. Haltzel (eds) *Spain in the 1980s: The Democratic Transition and a New International Role* (Cambridge, MA: Ballinger), pp. 123–37.

Sartori, G. (1976) *Parties and Party Systems: A Framework for Analysis* (Cambridge: Cambridge University Press).

Schmitt, H. and Holmberg, S. (1995) 'Political parties in decline?', in H.-D. Klingemann and D. Fuchs (eds) *Citizens and the State* (Oxford: Oxford University Press).

Stepan, A. (1986) 'Paths toward redemocratization: theoretical and comparative considerations', in Guillermo O'Donnell, Philippe C. Schmitter, and Laurence Whitehead (eds) *Transitions from Authoritarian Rule: Comparative Perspectives* (Baltimore: Johns Hopkins University Press), pp. 64–84.

Tarrow, S. (1995) 'Mass mobilization and regime change: pacts, reform, and popular power in Italy (1918–1922) and Spain (1975–1978)', in Richard Gunther, P. Nikiforos Diamandouros, and Hans-Jürgen Puhle (eds) *The Politics of Democratic Consolidation: Southern Europe in Comparative Perspective* (Baltimore: Johns Hopkins University Press), pp. 204–30.

Torcal, M. and Pradeep C. (1995) 'Elites, *cleavages y* sistema de partidoes en una democracia consolida: España (1986–1992)', Reis 69, 7–38.

10

Parties at the European Level

Simon Hix

Since the 1970s, academic interest in 'parties at the European level' has gone full circle. The story began in the 1970s, in the wake of the decision to hold direct elections to the European Parliament (EP), with widespread expectation of the coming of transnational European parties. In the 1980s, when it was apparent that European elections would not produce European parties, and that transnational party activity would be restricted to the 'party groups' in the EP, a period of scepticism towards transnational parties set in. As a result of the retarded development of parties at the European level in this early period, attempts to explain their behaviour and adaptation tended to see them as *sui generis* phenomena, to which traditional ('comparative') theories of party organization and competition could not be applied (see, for instance, Pridham and Pridham 1981; Niedermayer 1983).

Nevertheless, since the 1990s, with the 'party article' in the Treaty on European Union, the new role of 'party leaders' summits' and the emergence of rival party-political agendas for the single market (Hix 1995*a*), there is renewed discussion of the desirability and feasibility of Euro-parties as a way of connecting voters' preferences to the European Union (EU) policy process. These recent arguments have emerged from such diverse sources as Italian professors of political science (Attinà 1992) and *Demos*, a British think-tank with links to the New Labour government (Leonard 1997). Moreover, as these Euro-parties have taken on the organizational characteristics and pursue the same goals as political parties in similar institutional settings, their evolution and behaviour can more easily be explained using concepts and theories from the comparative study of political parties (cf. Hix and Lord 1997).

The roots of the contemporary European parties go back to 1972, when the heads of government of the then European Communities (EC) agreed to introduce a system of direct European-wide elections to the EP. The implementation of this decision was delayed until 1979. In the intervening period, three 'transnational party federations' were established in the expectation that European-wide elections would require and facilitate the creation of pan-European political parties. These party organizations were the Confederation of Socialist Parties of the EC, established in April 1974; the Federation of Liberal and Democratic Parties of the

EC, established in March 1976; and the European People's Party (EPP), which federated Christian Democratic Parties, established in June 1976. These original European party federations were joined by the European Coordination of Green Parties in April 1984.

In the 1970s it was fashionable to predict that the coming elections would usher in a new era of party political democracy at the European level. For example, Walter Hallstein (1972: 74), the then President of the European Commission, expected that:

[European elections] will force those entitled to vote to look at and examine the questions and the various options on which the EP would have to decide in the months and years ahead. It would give the candidates who emerged as victorious from such a campaign a truly European mandate from their electors and it would encourage the emergence of truly European political parties.

However, the reality was quite different. In all European elections the European party federations and the EP party groups have played a marginal role. It was not until the second elections, in 1984, that the Christian Democratic, Socialist, and Liberal party federations were all able to agree to common manifestos for the elections. Moreover, these manifestos represent bland lowest-common-denominator documents, which are ignored by national parties in their election campaigns. Hallstein, in fact, could not have been further from the truth: rather than Europe's voters choosing between rival parties, with competing agendas for European political action, 'truly European political parties' have, in fact, been conspicuous by their absence in these contests.

Nevertheless, despite the (lack of a) role of European level parties in EP elections, the party federations experienced a 'renaissance' in the late 1980s and early 1990s (Hix 1996). The main characteristics of this re-birth were a new organizational strategy and an increased awareness of and involvement in the work of the party federations by national party elites. First, in terms of the organizational strategy, the party federations developed a fundamentally new forum of transnational party activity—the party leaders' summits. There had been informal meetings of national party leaders under the auspices of the party federations in the 1970s and early 1980s. However, in the early 1990s, these meetings were formally institutionalized in the statutes of the party federations as the key executive decision-making bodies—usurping the previous dominance of the committees of International Secretaries. This development was driven by two factors.

On the one hand, as the governance of the EU became an increasingly central part of domestic policy making, there was a positive incentive for national party elites to interact with senior officials from sister parties elsewhere in the EU, to borrow policy ideas and develop common party policies towards various EU issues, such as economic and monetary union. On the other hand, party leaders' summits began to be organized immediately before, and usually in the same location as, the six-monthly meetings of the European Council. The idea was to bring together party leaders holding the office of Prime Minister, who sit in the European Council, with opposition party leaders, in an effort to shape the agenda of the Council meeting. The impact of this new strategy was first demonstrated at the Rome European Council of 27 October 1990, which was to set the agenda for the upcoming Intergovernmental Conference (IGC) to prepare the Maastricht Treaty. Two days before the Rome European Council, the EPP party leaders met, and unanimously agreed to support a fixed timetable for Economic and Monetary Union in the European Council. The British Conservative government had already stated that it would oppose any such move. However, the use of qualified majority at the Rome summit for setting the IGC agenda enabled the Christian Democrats (in coalition with the Socialist leaders) to force their agenda on a reluctant Margaret Thatcher. In her memoirs, Thatcher recalls that her advisors had underestimated the importance of the EPP meeting:

What I did not know was that behind the scenes the Italians had agreed with a proposal emanating from Germany and endorsed by Christian Democrat leaders from several European countries at an earlier caucus meeting   (Thatcher 1993: 765).

The Socialist party leaders immediately copied this organizational innovation.

The second factor in the rebirth of the party federations in the 1990s was their internal institutional development as a result of a new 'party article' in the Maastricht Treaty. The new article stated that:

Parties at the European level are important as a factor for integration in the Union. They contribute to forming a European awareness and to expressing the political will of the citizens of the Union   (Treaty on European Union, Article 191).

In response to the party article, the Secretaries-General of the Socialist, Christian Democrat, and Liberal federations presented a joint paper on the *Political Follow-Up to Article 138A*, which called for a 'European Political Party Statute'. An EU Party Statute is still in the pipeline, but will be part of plans for a uniform electoral procedure for EP elections—specifying which transnational groups qualify as a 'European Party', and even adding a line to the EU budget (independent of the EP budget line) to subsidize the organization of these parties. In the meantime, in November 1992 the Confederation of Socialist Parties was transformed into the Party of European Socialists (PES); in June 1993 the Green Coordination was dissolved and the European Federation of Green Parties (EFGP) was established; in December 1993 the Federation of Liberal, Democratic, and Reform Parties became the European Liberal, Democratic, and Reform Party (ELDR); and in October 1995, the European Free Alliance—a loose and informal grouping of regionalist parties—was transformed into a more formal 'party at the European level', with explicit institutional reference to Article 138a.

These new 'Euro-parties', as they have begun to be called, pursue the more common goals of domestic political parties. First, they have increasingly clear 'policy goals', developed through networks of committees, which are comprised of representatives from the national member parties, from the EP party groups, and even sometimes from inside the Commission and Council (such as from the Commission's Forward Studies Unit—where there are several prominent European Christian Democrat and Socialist figures). An example of this was the PES's 'Larsson Report', which was adopted by the PES leaders' summit in December 1993 (Party of European Socialists 1993). This report was drafted by a PES working group, comprising personal representatives from the private offices of the party leaders, and was chaired by Allan Larsson, the former Swedish Employment and Finance Minister. The Larsson Report was drafted in parallel to the Delors' White Paper on *Growth, Competitiveness, and Employment*, and its proposals were articulated by Socialist Prime Ministers and Foreign Ministers in a series of European Council meetings. It was not by chance, therefore, that the final version of the Delors' White Paper, which was adopted by the European Council in December 1993, contained many of the proposals (and even some of the same phrases) as the Larsson Report.

Second, the party federations have begun to pursue 'office goals'. This has primarily involved the coordination of the activities of national party leaderships to influence the behaviour of party office-holders in the EU institutions. Most obviously, the party leaders' summits monitor the policies, strategies, and performance of their EP party groups. As discussed, efforts have also been made to put pressure on the national member parties in the European Council, and this has sometimes extended to lower meetings of the Council of Ministers, as evidenced by the PES attempts to bring together Socialist Finance Ministers and opposition party finance spokespersons before meetings of the Council of Economic and Finance Ministers (EcoFin). This strategy has even stretched to the involvement of Commissioners in PES and EPP leaders' summit meetings and the emergence of an informal PES caucus amongst the nine Socialist Commissioners in the Santer Commission.

By the mid-1990s, then, parties at the European level had ceased to be weak transnational umbrellas, which existed mainly for the purpose of adopting vague manifestos for the EP elections (that were subsequently ignored!). Rather, they have evolved the trappings of domestic political parties—constitutions, secretariats, leadership structures, biennial party congresses, budgets, majoritarian decision-rules—and now pursue the classic party political goals of influencing office-holders and securing policy objectives through both the legislative and executive branches of government at the European level: in the EP, through the EP party groups; and in the Council and the Commission, through the party leaders' summits. However, the ability to turn these objectives into outcomes is severely limited by the institutional environment of the EU, the dominance of 'national' rather than partisan representation in the key EU decision-making institution (the Council), and the vested interests of domestic political parties that will always sacrifice European level party goals if they conflict with domestic parties' pursuit of national governmental office.

PARTY LEGITIMACY

Very few people know of the existence of parties at the European level. This is not only true amongst the general population but also amongst 'middle-level party elites'—the activists of the national member parties of the party federations (Reif *et al.* 1980). A case could consequently be made that European parties have no *direct* legitimacy in the eyes of the electorate. Nevertheless, the activities of political parties at the European level do have a kind of *indirect* legitimacy in two ways, in a similar way that legitimacy is secured for domestic parties through the operation of parliamentary democracy and 'party government'.

First, the legitimacy of parties at the European level is linked to public acceptance and support for the EP. Despite party activities beyond the EP, the success or failure of parties at the European level is ultimately linked to the key political arena that is dominated by partisan organizations, alignments, conflicts, and coalitions: the EP. This is comparable to the connection between the legitimacy of domestic political parties and public perceptions of national parliaments. For example, 'anti-party sentiment' in the domestic arena in Europe—such as public criticism of *partitocrazia* in Italy and the phenomenon of *politikverdrossenheit* in Germany—has gone hand-in-hand with declining trust in national parliaments (Kaase and Newton 1995).

Second, the legitimacy of parties at the European level is also related to how voters behave in EP elections. Are these elections being fought by European parties? Are they fought on European issues? Do they produce a democratic mandate for European level party organization and competition? Or, do they reinforce the dependence of the party groups in the EP and the party federations on national party organizations and conflicts, and hence actually undermine the legitimacy of a nascent European party system?

Legitimacy via the European Parliament

Since the early 1970s, European-wide opinion surveys have been conducted every six months by independent polling agencies, on behalf of the EC. These surveys ask a wide variety of questions relating to European integration, and provide a rich data set for cross-time and cross-national study of public support for the EU. Figure 10.1 shows public opinion trends since 1987 concerning the EP and EU. The data illustrate several things. First, support for the EU has been in decline since 1991. This has been called the 'permissive consensus' (Eichenberg and Dalton 1993; Niedermayer 1995) and the 'uncorking' of public opposition to the EU in the process of ratifying the Maastricht Treaty (Franklin *et al.* 1994).

Second, however, Fig. 10.1 shows that support for a 'European government responsible to the European Parliament'—in other words, the national model of parliamentary democracy transplanted to the European level—has not followed the

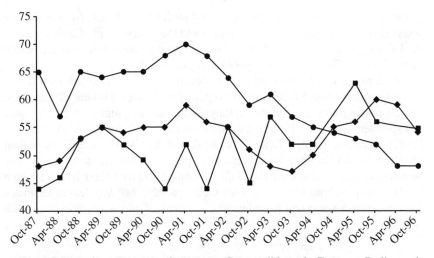

—◆— Support for a 'European Government Responsible to the European Parliament'
—●— Support for EC/EU Membership
—■— Awareness of the Parliament ('Aware')

FIGURE 10.1. Public support for the European Parliament across time

Notes: The precise question wordings are:
1. What is your opinion on the following proposal: the formation, for the EU, of a European Government responsible to the European Parliament?
2. Generally speaking, do you think that [YOUR COUNTRY'S] membership of the EU is a 'good thing', a 'bad thing', 'neither good nor bad', or 'don't know'?
3. Have you recently seen or heard in the papers, or on the radio or TV, anything about the European Parliament, that is the parliamentary assembly of the EU?
The data show the percentage of responses of 'good thing' to the membership question, 'for' to the European government responsible to the EP question, and 'yes' to the awareness of the EP question.

Sources: Eurobarometer Trends 1974–94; Eurobarometer surveys Nos 43, 44, 45, and 46.

same trend as general support for the EU. Until 1991 support for EU parliamentary democracy rose as support for EU membership rose, and between 1991 and 1994 support for EU parliamentary democracy fell as support for EU membership fell. However, after 1994, support for EU parliamentary democracy started to rise, while support for EU membership continued to fall.

Part of this is explained by the changing level of awareness of the EP amongst the electorate. Up to 1994 attitudes towards a genuinely democratic EU followed the pattern of support for the EU. However, as the figure shows, after 1994 they followed the pattern of awareness for the EP. In other words, as awareness of the EP rose in the early 1990s, support for making the EU more accountable via the EP also began to rise. Given voters' experience with democratic institutions at the national level in Europe, it is reasonable for voters to assume that the lack of effectiveness and accountability of the EU may, in fact, be resolved by giving more powers to the only genuinely democratic EU institution—the EP. Although many voters may still be relatively uninformed about the current level of importance of the EP, they assume the possibility of projecting the national democratic design on the European level (Niedermayer and Sinnott 1995).

This across-time pattern of relative support for the EP is also confirmed across the nation-states of the EU. Figure 10.2 reports public support for the EP relative to that expressed for other institutions. Italy, Spain, and Belgium are the only states whose voters trust the EP more than their national parliaments. Also, voters in France, Germany, Greece, Ireland, Portugal, and the UK trust the EP more than the Commission (as does the average EU voter across all member-states). The Netherlands and Luxembourg prefer the Commission to the EP, but have very high levels of trust in both EU institutions. Consequently, that only leaves Denmark and the member-states that joined in 1995—Austria, Finland, and Sweden—with

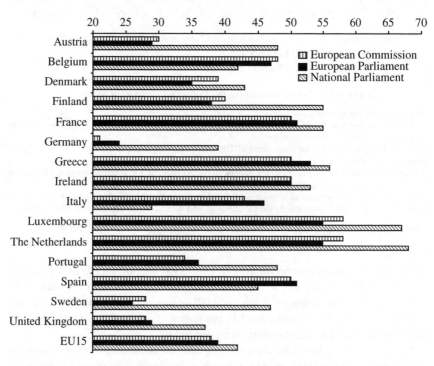

FIGURE 10.2. Support for EP relative to the Commission and national parliaments

Notes: The data show the percentage of responses of 'can rely on it' to the trust in political institutions question. The precise question wording is: To what extent do you feel you can rely on each of the following institutions to make sure that the decisions taken by this institution are in the interest of people like yourself: the European Commission, the [NATIONALITY] Parliament, the European Parliament (etc.)? Response: 'can rely on it', 'cannot rely on it', 'don't know'.

Source: Eurobarometer No. 44.2bis, Spring 1996, the 'Mega-Eurobarometer' (*N* = 65, 178).

low levels of support for both EU institutions, and a low level of support for the EP relative to the Commission.

In sum, these data do not suggest a direct source of legitimacy for parties at the European level. But, they do show a growing awareness and trust in the EP, and rising support for a more democratic EU via the EP. This consequently suggests that an EU party system based primarily on the party groups in the EP has an indirect source of legitimacy. Furthermore, it points to popular acceptance of the principle of party government at the EU level.

Legitimacy via European elections

This claim of EU party legitimacy via the EP was made by early theorists of parties at the European level (for instance, Marquand 1978; Pridham and Pridham 1981), and is often made by contemporary scholars of the EU 'democratic deficit' (Williams 1991; Lodge 1996b). However, this claim is also based on the assumption that party activity in the EP is connected to, and hence legitimized by, voters' choices in EP elections. However, this assumption does not hold in practice.

A first problem is that turnout in European elections is low, and has fallen considerably since the first direct elections, in 1979. As Table 10.1 shows, voter turnout in European elections fell from almost 75 per cent in 1979 to just below 50 per cent in 1999. In fact, despite a rise in turnout between the 1984 and 1989 elections in some member-states, voter turnout was lower in 1999 than in 1979 in almost all member-states. In all cases, the novelty of the first European elections

TABLE 10.1. *Turnout in European elections*

Member-state	1979	1984	1989	1994	1999
Austria	—	—	—	67.7	49.0
Belgium	91.4	92.1	90.7	90.7	90.0
Denmark	47.8	42.3	46.2	52.5	50.4
Finland	—	—	—	60.3	30.1
France	60.7	56.7	48.7	52.7	47.0
Germany	65.7	56.8	62.3	60.1	45.2
Greece	—	77.2	79.9	71.2	70.1
Ireland	63.6	47.6	68.3	44.0	50.5
Italy	84.9	83.4	81.5	74.8	70.8
Luxembourg	88.9	88.8	87.4	88.5	85.8
Netherlands	57.8	50.6	47.2	35.6	29.9
Portugal	—	—	51.2	35.6	40.4
Spain	—	—	54.6	60.0	64.3
Sweden	—	—	—	41.6[1]	38.3
United Kingdom	32.3	32.6	36.2	36.4	24.0
Total EU turnout	63.0	61.0	58.5	56.8	49.4

Source: Lodge (1996a), http://www2.europarl.eu.int/election/results.

quickly wore off. Ironically, only in Denmark, where the main political parties are deeply divided on the issue of Europe, did voters take slightly more interest in the 1999 elections than they did in the first contests.

A second problem is that EP elections are not really *European* contests. Rather, they are 'second order national contests' (Reif and Schmitt 1980). The main political goal of national political parties is to capture national governmental office. Consequently, all other electoral contests are 'dry-runs' for the 'big one': the national general and/or presidential election. Hence, national parties use European elections like regional or local elections (or like Congressional elections in the United States), as referenda on the performance of the party(ies) that won the last national general election. Ironically, the opportunity to test the support for the party(ies) in government is simply too great for national parties to allow European issues to interfere in European elections. The result is that elections to the EP are fought by national parties rather than the transnational party federations, and on issues relating to national politics rather than to the agenda of the EU or EP.

At the level of individual voters, there are two main impacts of this second-order phenomenon: (1) because second-order contests are less important than first-order elections, there is less incentive for people to vote in European elections; and (2) because the elections are really about the performance of national governments, the people who do vote will vote differently than they would if a national election were held at the same time—people will either vote sincerely instead of strategically ('vote with the heart') or will try to punish governing parties ('put the boot in') (Oppenhuis *et al.* 1996). Either way, the likely result is that governing parties and large opposition parties will lose votes, and small parties and protest parties will gain votes. To test these arguments, the European Elections Study Group surveyed 36,000 people immediately after the 1989 elections and 13,500 immediately after the 1994 elections (van der Eijk and Franklin 1996; Marsh and Norris 1997). The results of this research are summarized in Table 10.2.

The outcomes in 1989 and 1994 consequently confirm the impact of the second-order phenomenon on individual voters. First, in terms of electoral turnout, there were significantly lower levels of turnout in all EU member-states where national elections were not held concurrently (as in Ireland in 1989 and Luxembourg in 1989 and 1994) or where voting is not compulsory. Second, individual voters clearly behave differently in European elections than in national elections. Approximately 20 per cent of voters in all member-states vote in European elections for parties they would not have voted for if it were a contest for national government office. The partial exception to this rule is Denmark in 1989 and 1994 and France in 1994, where the party systems in EP elections were different to those in national elections (having, for example, large anti-European movements specifically established for EP elections). However, even in these cases, there was evidence that voters acted strategically to influence the national (rather than European) political process, to punish governing parties, or to reward opposition parties.

TABLE 10.2. *The 'second-order' phenomenon in European Parliamentary elections*

Member-state	Turnout compared to previous national election (%)		Voting differently to hypothetical national election[a](%)	
	1989	1994	1989	1994
Belgium[b]	−2.7	−3.3	12.6	18.5
Denmark	−38.3	−36.2	35.4	42.9
France	−17.4	−25.3	27.2	40.8
Germany	−22.0	−17.8	11.8	14.2
Greece[b]	−3.8	−8.8	8.1	12.4
Ireland	−0.2[c]	−24.2	28.7[c]	23.8
Italy	−10.1	−11.3	19.7	20.7
Luxembourg[b]	−2.6[c]	+0.2[c]	15.0[c]	14.3[c]
Netherlands	−38.3	−43.1	12.4	19.6
Portugal	−21.5	−33.4	9.7	12.7
Spain	−15.9	−17.6	22.2	12.5
United Kingdom	−38.8	−41.3	13.0	16.0
Average, all member states	−17.6	−21.8	18.0	20.7
Average, excluding cases of concurrent national elections and compulsory voting	−25.3	−27.8	—	—

[a]The data in the last two columns are derived from responses to two questions that were asked in public opinion surveys in every member state immediately prior to the European elections: (1) how do you intend to vote in the European elections? And (2) how would you vote if a general election were held tomorrow? The table shows the percentage of voters in each member state who said that they would vote for a different party in the European elections than they would if it were a general election.
[b]member states where voting is compulsory.
[c]cases were national elections and European elections were held concurrently.

Sources: Adapted from data in Mackie and Rose (1991); Koole and Mair (1995); van der Eijk and Franklin (1996).

Consequently, the prospects of indirect legitimacy for parties at the European level via the classic parliamentary democracy/party government model are mixed. On the one hand, there is growing awareness of the EP, and support for more accountability of executive power at the European level through the EP. In the party–government model, this suggests support for European level parties as the essential 'linkage' between executive power and a parliamentary majority. On the other hand, European elections (as national contests) actively restrict the potential of the party system in the EP to reflect a European-wide party-political majority. As European elections are fought by national parties, the re-election of MEPs is not dependent on the performance of the EP party groups, but rather on the performance of national political parties. Hence, the other essential 'linkage' in the party–government model, from voters' to representatives, is missing.

PARTY ORGANIZATIONAL STRENGTH

Organizational and behavioural cohesion

Parties at the European level are relatively weak organizations in comparison to national parties. The political leaderships have few resources to enforce their wishes on their party members holding political office. For example, the party federations cannot enforce leaders' summit decisions on the Commissioners from their member parties, or on the Ministers in the Council from their member parties. The party organizations that really 'pull the strings' are the sub-units of the party federations, the national member parties.

The situation is somewhat different, however, in the EP. It is true that the leaderships of the EP party groups are organizationally weak compared to the national delegations of the national member parties; for example, unlike domestic parliamentary leaderships in many systems (except the United States), the EP group leaders cannot prevent unruly MEPs from standing in the next EP election—this, in most cases, is the preserve of national party leaderships. Nevertheless, the EP group leaderships do possess other resources that can be used to enforce party organizational discipline. Thus, the EP groups determine the allocation of committee chairs, the assignment of rapporteurships on key pieces of legislation, and the chances of being promoted within the EP group and to the offices of the EP, such as the EP President and EP Vice-President. Also, the EP groups have gradually developed a system of 'whipping'. The group leaderships issue voting instructions to their members on how to vote on individual amendments and the whole text of a piece of legislation and indicate which issues are most important for the party group (a number of groups have taken up the British tradition of denoting votes as one-, two-, or three-line whips). The main party groups also have 'party whips' to monitor which MEPs adhere to the party line. MEPs who regularly break from the official party position, or refuse to attend on key votes, can be withdrawn from committee assignments (Corbett *et al.* 1995: 92).

The result is that the EP party groups have a relatively high level of cohesion in legislative votes. Table 10.3 shows 'Index of Agreement' scores for the party groups in the 1984–89 and 1989–94 parliaments. The data show that the levels of cohesion for the main party groups increased considerably between the two periods. These figures are lower than in most domestic parliaments in Europe; however, they are considerably higher than the levels of cohesion of the Democrats and Republicans in the US Congress (Raunio 1996: 136–8).

In other words, the EP party groups are important organizations in structuring the legislative agenda of the EU. Consequently, as the EP gains more power in the

TABLE 10.3. *Party group cohesion in the European Parliament*

Party group (left to right)	1984–89	1989–94
Left Unity (Orthodox Communists)	—	93.8
European Unitarian Left (Radical Left)	71.2	92.3
Greens (Greens & Allies)	—	87.5
Party of European Socialists (Socialists)	62.2	78.6
Rainbow Group (Regionalists)	67.8	69.5
Liberal, Democratic and Reform Party (Liberals)	69.5	85.7
European People's Party (Christian Democrats & Conservatives)	84.1	88.2
European Democratic Alliance (French, Irish, & Portuguese Conservatives)	75.7	64.5
European Democratic Group (British Conservatives)	82.9	92.2
European Right (Extreme Right)	96.1	88.9
Average	76.2	84.1

Note: The scores are what are called 'Indices of Agreement' (IA). An IA is a measure of the relationship between the three modalities of votes—in favour, against, and abstention—cast by the members of a party group, and in relation to the total number of votes cast by the members of a group. Formally:

$$IA = \frac{\text{highest modality} - \text{sum of the other two modalities}}{\text{total number of votes cast by the group}} \times 100.$$

In other words, the index is equal to 100 if all the members of the group vote the same way, and is equal to 0 if exactly half the members of a group vote one way and the rest vote another way. Scores = means for each parliament.

Sources: Attinà (1990), Raunio (1996).

EU legislative process, through the Maastricht and Amsterdam Treaty reforms, the organizational impact of parties at the European level is likely to increase. But, increased power may also produce increased internal divisions between different national parties, who are represented in the other chamber of the EU legislature—the Council. In other words, EP party group cohesion in the 1984–89 and 1989–94 parliaments may in fact, be a function of the relative unimportance of the EP to the interests of domestic parties before the Maastricht and Amsterdam Treaty reforms.

Finance

Until the mid-1980s the majority of the operating budgets of the party federations came from their party groups in the EP. The national parties were required to pay yearly subscriptions, but these were small compared to the size of the direct contributions of the party groups. Since the end of the 1980s, however, all the party federations have asked approximately equal subscription fees from the member parties and the EP groups. The EP groups are funded out of the budget of the EP, which is part of the overall EU budget. For example, in the PES, the member parties and the PES group in the EP were both required to pay 7.2 million Belgian Francs in the 1992 budget and 10.2 million in 1995. The total budget of the PES thus increased from 14.4 million Belgian Francs in 1992 to 21.4 million in 1995 (Hix 1995*b*).

However, the total PES budget in 1994 was 26.8 million Belgian Francs. This was more than in 1995 because it was an EP election year. Consequently, the PES allocated an extra 5 million Belgian Francs to the regular annual costs to fight the election campaign. The size of this extra money for the 1994 election campaign is interesting for two reasons. First, this constituted only 26 per cent of the total PES budget, whereas in 1979 the campaign expenses constituted 78 per cent of the total budget of the Confederation of Socialist Parties of the EC. Second, in 1994 almost an equal amount was allocated for the organization of the PES party leaders' summits.

Compared to the total budgets of parties at the national level, these amounts are very small. In fact, contributions to the party federations are so insignificant that only a few national parties report them in their annual budgets (Bardi 1994). Nevertheless, directly comparing the party federations' budgets with the total budgets of national party organizations is an inappropriate comparison. The size of the budget of a party organization at a particular level of government (local, regional, national, European) is relative to the political power and resources (budget) of that level of government. In other words, the party federation budgets as a proportion of EU expenditure should be compared with the domestic party central office budgets as a proportion of central government expenditure. In 1993, therefore, the budgets of the PES and ELDR were, respectively, 0.0000011 and 0.0000008 per cent of the total EU budget. This, in fact, compares favourably with the central office budgets of parties in federal systems. For example, as a percentage of German federal government expenditure in 1989, the Head Office budgets of the SPD, CDU, and FDP were, respectively, 0.0000043, 0.0000023, and 0.0000002 per cent (Poguntke and Boll 1992). Also as a percentage of the budget of the US federal government in 1989, the budgets of the Democrat and Republic National Committees were, respectively, 0.0000005 and 0.0000014 per cent (Kolodny and Katz 1992). Thus, in relative terms, the budget of the PES office in Brussels was approximately a quarter that of the head office of the SPD, ten times that of the head office of the FDP, and twice that of the national committee of the US Democrats.

Staff

As Table 10.4 shows, although the number of staff of the party federations approximately doubled between the mid-1980s and mid-1990s, the absolute number of full-time staff in the party head offices in Brussels remains small. Each of the parties has a permanent Secretary-General, with two or three permanent assistants. The other members of staff are seconded from the offices of the national member parties or from the EP party groups for temporary periods. These secondments

TABLE 10.4. *Average number of
full-time staff in the party federation
head offices*

Year	EPP	PES	ELDR
1979–84	5	5	4
1985–89	7	7	6
1990–94	10	13	6
1994–99	10	12	7

Sources: Bardi (1992); party federations.

are usually either to learn about the work of the party federations or to help on a specific project, such as a policy report or organizing a party leader's summit.

In contrast, the EP party groups have much more substantial secretariats. Under the rules of the EP, each party group is allowed two full-time administrative posts (A grade), and a further full-time administrative post for every four MEPs in the group. The groups are then entitled to an additional number of assistant (B grade) and secretarial (C grade) posts in proportion to the total number of A positions to which they are entitled, with 1.4 B and C posts funded for each A post. Thus, for example, in 1994 the PES group in the EP had 159 full-time staff (Corbett *et al.* 1995: 87–8).

Moreover, the total staffing of the EP party groups has increased considerably: from 285 positions in 1982 to 477 in 1994. This, then, indicates the growing organizational resources of the EP groups, particularly in contrast to the minimal resources of the 'extra-parliamentary' party federations. Nevertheless, much of the administrative work of the party federations, such as organizing party leaders' meetings or the biennial party congresses, is undertaken by the International Secretaries of the national member parties.

Members

The membership of the party federations is corporate rather than individual: the national political parties. According to the party statutes, there are essentially two types of corporate membership: 'full membership' for parties from the EU member-states, which for the PES includes parties from member-states who have begun accession negotiations; and 'associate members' and/or 'observers', from states with association agreements with the EU (such as Norway, Switzerland, and the countries of Central and Eastern Europe). Associate member/observer parties can attend and address certain meetings of the party federations, such as the executive bureaux and the party congresses, but are usually disqualified from formally participating (voting) in making party decisions or adopting party policies.

TABLE 10.5. *Political families and membership of the 'Euro-Parties' and EP party groups*

	Extreme Left parties and UEL Group membership		Regionalist parties and ERA Group membership		Green parties and EFGP/Green Group membership		Socialist parties and PES membership		Liberal parties and ELDR membership		Christian Democrat parties and EPP membership		Conservative parties and EPP(E) or UFE(U) Group membership		Extreme Right/Anti-Europe parties and I-EN Group membership	
	Party	Joined	Party	Joined	Party	Joined	Party	Joined	Party	Joined	Party	Joined	Party	Joined	Party	Joined
Aus.					**GA**	1990	**SPÖ**	1990	**LF**	1993	ÖVP	1995			FPÖ	(1995)
Bel.			VU	(1984)	AGA ECO	1984 1984	SP PS	1974 1974	VLD PRL	1976 1976	CVP PSC	1976 1976			VB FN	(1989) (1994)
Den.	SF	(1979)			DG	1989	SD	1974	V RV CD	1976 1976-78 & 92 —	KRF	—	KF[E]	1995	FmEF JB JB	(1979) (1994) (1994)
Fin.	V	(1995)			VIHR	1993	SDP	1992	KESK SFP LKP	1995 1995 1995	SKL	—	KOK[E]	1995		
Fra.	PCF	(1979)			V GE	1984 —	PS	1974	RAD MRG[a] PR	1976 1976-7 1976-94	CDS	1976	RPR[U] PR[E]	(1979) (1994)	NF AE	(1979) (1994)
Ger.					G	1984	SPD	1974	FDP	1976	CDU CSU	1976 1976				
Gre.	KKE SAP	(1981) (1981)			EA	1989	PASOK	1989	HLP	1983						
Ire.					CG	1989	LP	1974	PD Indep.	1988 (1979)	FG	1976	ND[E] PolAn[U] FF[U]	1983 (1994) (1979)		
Ita.	RC	(1979)	LN[b] LP	— (1984)	FV	1989	PDS PSI PSDI	1992 1974 1974-94	PRI PRL Rad	1976 1976 (1984-94)	DC/PPI CCD Segni SVP	1976 1994 (1994) (1979)	FI[U]	(1997)	AN	(1994)

The 'Euro-Parties'

TABLE 10.5. *Continued*

The 'Euro-Parties'

	Extreme Left parties and UEL Group membership		Regionalist parties and ERA Group membership		Green parties and EFGP/Green Group membership		Socialist parties and PES membership		Liberal parties and ELDR membership		Christian Democrat parties and EPP membership		Conservative parties and EPP(^{E}) or UFE(^{U}) Group membership		Extreme Right/Anti-Europe parties and I-EN Group membership	
	Party	Joined	Party	Joined	Party	Joined	Party	Joined	Party	Joined	Party	Joined	Party	Joined	Party	Joined
Lux.					**GA/G**	1984	**POSL**	1974	**DP**	1976	**PCS**	1976				
Net.					**GL**	1984	**PvdA**	1974	**VVD**	1976	**CDA**	1976			**SGP**	(1979)
					DG	1989			D'66	1994					**GPV**	(1979)
Por.	CDU	(1986)			OV	1989	**PS**	1979	PSD	1986–96	**PSD**	1996	PP^U	(1979)		
											CDS	1986–88				
Spa.	IU	(1986)	CEP	(1984)	LV	1989	**PSOE**	1979	**CDC**	(1986)	UDC	1986	PP^E	1991		
									CDS	1985	PNV	1986				
									FORO	1993	PDP	1986–89				
Swe.	VP	(1995)			**MP**	1984	**SAP**	1992	**FPL**	1995	KDS	1995	MS^E	1995		
									CP	(1995)						
UK			SNP	(1984)	GP	1984	**LP**	1976	**LD**	1976			CP^E	(1992)	**DUP**	(1979)
							SDLP	1976	APNI	1984			OUP^E	(1979)		

Notes: The parties in bold are represented in the 1994–99 EP. The dates in brackets show that a national party sits in the party group of the party federation in the EP, but is not a member of a party federation. UEL = Unitarian European Left Group, ELDR = European Liberal, Democrat and Reform Party, ERA = European Radical Alliance Group, EPP = European People's Party, EFGP = European Federation of Green Parties, UFE = Union for Europe Group, PES = Party of European Socialists, I-EN = Group of Independents for a Europe of Nations.
[a] MRG are members of the ERA Group.
[b] LN are members of the I-EN Group.

Source: Adapted from Hix (1995b).

The issue of introducing individual membership was discussed by the party federations following the Maastricht Treaty. The EPP introduced a new article in their statutes to allow for individual membership. In contrast, the PES and the ELDR decided that such a provision was unnecessary as individuals who are members of the national member parties are indirect members of the party federation—just as a German socialist who is a member of the Bavarian SPD is an indirect member of the national SPD.

Table 10.5 shows the national member parties of the party federations, and which parties sit in the other EP party groups. As stated in the statutes of the party federations, MEPs from the national member parties of the PES, ELDR, EPP, and EFGP party federations are automatic members of the EP party groups of these federations. MEPs from non-member parties can also join these party groups, but they must have the approval of the party federations at the highest political level, from a leaders' summit and a party federation congress. For example, this was the case with the British Conservative MEPs, who wanted to sit in the EPP Group in the EP after the 1989 EP elections, but the British Conservative Party did not intend to become a member of the EPP party federation. The final approval was given by an EPP leaders' meeting in 1992.

Media

Neither the party federations nor the EP party groups have any direct access to the media. The party groups of the EP publish their own newsletters, which are circulated to the press corps in Brussels and to the member parties. However, as with all coverage of EU news, the gate-keepers of party-political news from Brussels are the national political elites rather than European level political elites. As a result, if an EP party group has been successful in passing or blocking a major piece of EU legislation, it is the national political parties that inform the national media of this fact, and so claim the credit. This is unlikely to change until there is widespread coverage of EU politics in national television and print news independent of the national party and governmental press offices. In Britain, for example, the only major newspaper that comes close to this model is *The Financial Times*. *European Voice*, which was launched as a weekly newspaper by *The Economist*, is the most widely read newspaper with an exclusive focus on EU politics, and considerable coverage of the EP party groups and party leaders' summits. However, its circulation is small compared to national media coverage of domestic party politics or EU news filtered through national party leaderships.

Overall, therefore, parties at the European level are weak organizations. However, after over twenty years of activities, they are relatively institutionalized. Party leaders' summits have become regular dates in the diaries of all domestic party leaders, Prime Ministers and Commissioners of the member parties of the PES, EPP, and ELDR party federations. Similarly, the EP party groups are central organizers of the political agenda, individual MEPs' behaviour and coalition-formation in an increasingly powerful institution in the EU legislative process.

THE SYSTEMIC FUNCTIONALITY OF PARTIES AT THE EUROPEAN LEVEL

Governance

Plainly, party government does not operate at the European level. Those who advocate it as a solution to the EU's democratic deficit are under attack from two sides. First, in fear of repeating the naïve predictions and prescriptions about transnational parties of the 1970s, contemporary enthusiasts of parties at the European level tend to accept that parties will not be the main organizational forces in the EU system. Instead, scholars prefer to emphasize the weakness of the party federations and the problems in the structure of party organization and the party system in the EP, and accept the institutional constraints of second-order EP elections on the ability to link European level parties to voters (e.g. Bardi 1994; Anderweg 1995; Pedersen 1996).

Second, an influential body of scholars of the EU actively argue that party competition in majoritarian institutions would actually undermine the legitimacy of the EU. In this view, partisan majoritarianism would replace the consensual and deliberative style of EU governance with a competitive bargaining style, that would inevitably lead to an unacceptable transfer of resources or values from 'losers' to 'winners' (Obradovic 1996; Jachtenfuchs 1997). Parties at the European level would also lead to a politicized Commission, which could no longer be a provider of 'independent expertise' and would not be capable of facilitating pareto-efficient outcomes (cf. Dehousse 1995; Majone 1996).

As a result, two solutions to the democratic-deficit have been proposed as alternatives to the classic parliamentary democracy/party government model: (1) interest groups as organizers of functional and territorial interests in a system of Euro-pluralism or Euro-corporatism; and (2) the use of mechanisms of direct democracy, such as European-wide referenda or even the direct election of the Commission President. These proposals echo the advocates of corporatism in Scandinavia, of referenda in Switzerland, Italy, and Belgium, and presidentialism in the Madisonian model of democracy in America and De Gaulle's design for the French Fifth Republic, and of the direct election of the Prime Minister in Israel. Note that these alternative models of representation and accountability have traditionally been proposed to undermine party government that has gone too far.

First, with the establishment of the EU single market there has been an explosion in the activities of interest groups at the European level. As Table 10.6 shows, in 1995 the *European Public Affairs Directory* reported that over 1600 firms and organizations have offices in Brussels for the specific purpose of monitoring and

TABLE 10.5. *Types and numbers of private interests in Brussels, 1995*

Type of interest	Number
Individual companies	561
European interest associations	314
Private lobbyists (e.g. political consultants, public affairs companies, and law firms)	302
Miscellaneous interest groups (mostly public interest)	147
International organizations and non-EU state bodies	101
National interest associations	93
Regions	80
Chambers of commerce	47
Individual trade unions	21
Think-tanks	12
Total	1,678

Source: Adapted from Wessels (1997*a*: 18).

influencing the EU policy process. In the classic pluralist model of government, this volume of activity should produce 'countervailing' forces on either side of any policy debate, that should guarantee that all affected interests are represented in the EU policy process (Mazey and Richardson 1993). However, certain groups naturally have more resources to influence the policy process, such as private businesses in comparison to environmental and consumer groups. To overcome this problem the Commission has pursued a 'neo-pluralist' strategy, of deliberately funding under-represented groups (Greenwood 1997), and has introduced elements of corporatism into the EU system, for example, through the privileged role of the two sides of industry in setting the EU social policy agenda (Falkner 1997). Nevertheless, most critics see the EU policy process as dominated by the interests of big business (Streeck and Schmitter 1991; Green Cowles 1995).

Second, a growing body of academics argue that because of the second-order problem in European elections, elements of direct democracy could be introduced to legitimize the EU political system. For example, Philippe Schmitter (1996) and Joseph Weiler (1997) *inter alia* advocate European wide referenda to propose legislative initiatives or block existing legislation. Their underlying reasoning is that direct democracy is the only solution where voters cannot 'throw the government out', as in the Swiss system. Alternatively, if EP elections cannot be fought on rival candidates for the Commission President, the only way to link an electoral majority to executive power is through the direct election of the Commission President (for instance, Bogdanor 1986; Laver *et al.* 1995).

Nevertheless, as in the critiques of 1950s American pluralism, interest groups are not a substitute for the 'mobilization of bias' through party competition, where every member of the electorate participates as an equal player (Schattschneider 1960). Similarly, direct democracy is not a substitute for party democracy, where it does not already exist. Rather it can only be a safety valve against overbearing partisan cartels, in a system where partisan organizations already exist to structure the debate and translate voters' choices into political action. In other words, these alternative models of accountability can only work as a supplement to, rather than substitute for, partisan democracy at the European level.

Interest articulation and aggregation

Parties at the European level face a dilemma when trying to articulate the interests of their natural constituents in the domestic party systems. To illustrate this point, consider Fig. 10.3, which shows the approximate location of social class interests in the EU political space, where the Xs mark the mean positions of the social classes in response to two questions: (1) where they place themselves on a Left–Right spectrum; and (2) whether they think their country benefits from EU membership. The positions of the social classes reveals that the EU political market is fragmented. Intra-class alliances—such as manual workers/skilled workers, white collar workers/professionals, or employers/small business owners—may hold together on Left–Right issues in EU politics, such as the level of social regulation of the single market. But, once issues on the Pro-/Anti-Europe dimension come into play, for example, on how far the European integration process should be developing, these alliances are no longer sustainable.

This consequently presents problems for political parties. For example, on the Left, as the traditional constituency of Social Democratic parties (manual workers) has declined, these parties have built alliances with groups that are close on the Left–Right dimension (such as white collar employees, students, and the liberal professions). However, because of the differing attitudes of these groups towards European integration, this cross-class alliance cannot hold together on the Pro-/Anti-Europe dimension. Thus, by taking a pro-European position, the PES can hope to attract the votes of white-collar workers and professionals; by contrast, the European Unitarian Left group in the EP is pulled in the opposite direction, in order to attract the votes of unskilled and manual workers and the unemployed.

As a result, parties trying to organize at the European level are forced to pursue one of two strategies to ensure that there is no party competition on this dimension of EU politics (Hix 1999*a*): (1) parties can refuse to differentiate themselves from each other on this dimension, by taking up identical (usually moderately pro-European) positions; or (2) parties can play down the differences between them on this dimension, by refusing to address the question of European integration in domestic electoral contests. Either strategy reduces the saliency of the Europe integration cleavage, but undermines the ability of parties at the European level to organize cohesively in order to articulate the interests of cross-national social interests.

Political participation

We have seen that EP elections fail to mobilize high turnouts, notwithstanding the developing institutionalization of parties at the European level. Moreover,

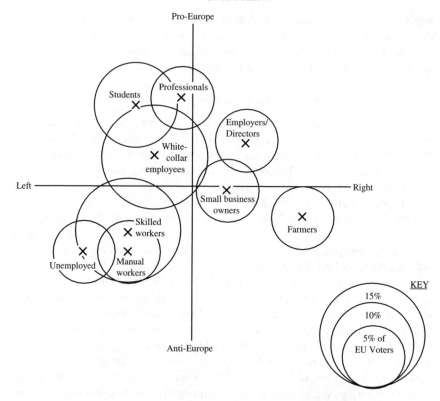

FIGURE 10.3. Location of class interests in the EU political space

Notes: The X's represent the mean responses of each occupational group to two questions asked in the 1996 Eurobarometer survey (of 64,000 European voters): (1) Do you think your country benefits from EU membership (answer: 'benefit', 'don't know', 'not benefit')?; and (2) Where would you place yourself on the following Left–Right scale (from 1 to 10)? For the first question, the location of each group is calculated as the percentage of 'benefit' responses minus the percent of 'not benefit' responses in each group. For example, if 100 per cent of a social group responded that they 'benefit' from the EU, the social group would be off the scale at the top of the diagram, and conversely, if 100 per cent responded that they do 'not benefit' the social group would be off the bottom of the scale. The ovals represent the range of preferences of approximately 15 per cent of each occupational group, as a proportion of the standard deviation of each social group on each question (i.e. the range of 100 per cent of each group would be too large to represent). Since the Eurobarometer survey is a sample of the EU population, the size of the ovals is relative to the size of each occupational group as a proportion of the total EU population.

Source: Hix (1999*b*). Calculated from data in Eurobarometer 44.2bis, 1996.

given the indirect nature of membership of the European parties (in other words, individuals are members of European parties by virtue of their membership of a national party), participation at the mass level in the work of the European parties is extremely limited. There are a few European party membership groups in cities with large populations from other EU member-states, such as the PES associations

TABLE 10.6. *Participation in European party leaders' summits*

	Average no. of party leaders' meetings per year		Percentage of leaders' meetings close to a European Council		Average turnout of party leaders (%)	
	1985–89	1990–94	1985–89	1990–94	1985–89	1990–94
Socialists (PES)	1.6	3.4	25.0	70.6	67.4	73.3
Liberals (ELDR)	1.8	1.8	11.1	77.8	59.5	55.8
Chr. Democrats (EPP)	1.8	3.0	11.1	66.7	72.1	84.9
All parties	1.7	2.7	15.4	70.7	66.5	72.9

Source: Calculated from data in Hix (1995*b*).

in London, Paris, and Bonn. However, these are usually informal gatherings, and often only involve individuals who are members of national member parties of the party federations in member-states other than the one in which they reside: for example, French Socialists in London.

Nevertheless, at an elite level, there has been a growing participation of senior national party figures in the work of the party federations. In the 1980s many national party leaders sent their foreign affairs spokespersons to party leaders' summits, arguing that they could not spare the time out of domestic party competition. However, as Table 10.7 shows, in the 1990s, as party leaders' summits began to be held more frequently and began to be organized immediately before or after European Council meetings, the record of attendance of party leaders increased for the PES and EPP. This was not the case for the ELDR. However, this anomaly is explained by the fact that in the early 1990s there were few Liberals in the European Council, so there was less of an incentive for Liberal leaders in government to coordinate their policy agendas, or for party leaders out of government to seek to influence the agenda of the European Council via the back-door of the party leaders' meetings. In other words, this exception confirms the theory.

Furthermore, because party leaders' meetings began to be such large media jamborees, with the presence of over 100 national and European party officials, in 1993 the PES began to organize special 'conclaves', which are attended only by the party leaders, with no assistants, substitutes or even translators. Not surprising, eager not to miss an intimate exchange with like-minded political leaders in other EU member-states, the record of leaders' participation in these gatherings is very high. Similar meetings have been organized by the EPP, with the same results.

Political recruitment

Parties at the European level are not directly responsible for the recruitment of political leaders to executive office in the EU institutions in the same way that national political parties place their leaders in national governmental positions.

The President of the Commission is chosen by a unanimous agreement in the European Council, and the individual members of the EC are chosen by the national governments. The Maastricht Treaty introduced a provision that the European Council's nominee would be subject to a simple majority vote in the EP. However, evidence from the July 1994 EP vote on Jacques Santer suggests that because of the imposition of a cross-party coalition in the EP (of the governing parties who back the nominee for Commission President in the European Council), the EP party groups will find it very difficult to organize a coherent partisan alliance for or against the European Council's nominee (Hix and Lord 1995).

Nevertheless, most governments choose to nominate Commissioners with previous experience in European party activities. As Table 10.8 shows, in the Santer Commission, 65 per cent of Commissioners from the non-new EU member-states (11 out of 17) had either been MEPs or had been a President, Vice-President or regular attendees of the leaders' summits of the party federations. Santer had, in fact, been President of the EPP party federation and, an MEP, and a senior figure in the EPP Group in the EP.

Furthermore, in 1994, the EP introduced a new procedure of 'hearings' in the EP committees, between the ratification of the Commission President and a final

TABLE 10.7. *European commissioners' links to the Euro-Parties (Santer Commission)*

Previously involved in the EP Party Groups	Previously involved in the Party Federations	
	YES (i.e. Pres/VP/LS)	NO
YES (i.e. MEP)	Santer (EPP-Pres)	Oreja (EPP)
	Van Miert (PES-VP)	Cresson (PES)
	Papoutsis (PES-VP)	Bonino (ELDR)
	Bangemann (ELDR-VP)	
		Bjerregaard (PES)
		Wulf-Matthias (PES)
NO	Van Den Broek (EPP-LS)	Brittan (EPP Group)
	Marin (PES-VP)	Flynn (UFE Group)
	Kinnock (PES-LS)	Monti (UFE Group)
	Pinheiro (ELDR-LS)	De Silguy (UFE Group)
		Fischler (EPP)
		Gradin (PES)
		Liikanen (PES)

Notes: Pres: President of a party federation; VP: Vice-President of a party federation; LS: regular attendance at party leaders' summits. For each Commission, the European party federation affiliation of their national party, or EP Group membership for parties that are not members of a party federation, is indicated brackets. The Commissioners in italics are from the member states that joined the EU in 1995, and hence could not have been involved in a party group or the party federations before joining the Commission.

Source: Adapted from Hix and Lord (1997: 213).

EP vote on the Commission as a whole. These hearings were designed to test the political expertise of the governments' nominees. Also, without experience either in the EP or in a party federation, Commissioners Bjerregaard and Flynn were publicly embarrassed in front of a confrontational EP, which was determined to impress upon the new Commissioners the importance of support from the EP.

In other words, parties at the European level cannot place their leaders in executive office positions. But, they can be influential in determining which figures are most likely to be chosen for the task, and a Commissioner is more able to be effective if he or she can already command the support of partisan constituents in the EP and the Council: direct experience of party politics at the European level is an important means of gaining such support.

Political communication and education

The Maastricht party article claims that 'parties at the European level ... contribute to forming a European awareness'. However, neither the party federations nor the EP party groups have the means or resources to achieve this goal. In the build-up to European elections, the EP party groups publish information leaflets and glossy brochures about their policies, their role in the EP, and their influence on the political agenda of the EU. The individual MEPs also have access to funds from the EU budget to organize educational trips to Brussels for members of national parties and individuals from their constituencies, regions or member-states. The proportion of the EU population involved in these trips is small. However, a growing number of school children and university students across the EU have visited the EU institutions under such schemes.

Nevertheless, these events tend to be more about promoting information about the EU, in general, and the role of the European Parliament, in particular, than about the political agendas of the European parties and the EP party groups. As discussed, the EP party groups may benefit from increased political awareness of the EP. But, without access to larger financial resources for purely party political purposes, a European media that understands and discusses the differences between the European parties, and the backing of domestic parties to distribute and advertise such information, there is little the EP party groups can do to communicate their policies and behaviour to Europe's voters.

CONCLUSION

In sum, depending on where one looks, parties at the European level have either changed little since their humble beginnings in the 1970s, or they have developed into institutionalized vehicles for the expression of partisan agendas for the EU political system. From one perspective, parties play a minor role in the governance of the EU. The party federations remain weak organizations, dependent on the resources, support, and commitment of the national member parties. Without the ability to determine the chances of MEP re-election, the EP party groups are also slaves to the interests and demands of the national party delegations in the EP. Also, because European elections remain essentially national contests over national governmental office, there is little chance for transnational parties to connect directly with the European electorate, and seek a democratic mandate for transnational partisan competition and coalition-formation.

From another perspective, however, parties are increasingly central to the governance of the EU, as organizers of policy positions, agendas, actors' behaviour, and coalitions. Through the growth in the significance of party leaders' summits, and the organization of these meetings around the European Council, national party leaders (particularly in the Socialist and Christian Democrat party families) have begun to develop coordinated policies towards the EU, which national party leaders can use in domestic party competition as their 'European policies'. Moreover, the EP party groups have developed considerable administrative resources, can enforce party discipline through the control of committee assignments and coalition formation in the EP, and are able to secure partisan goals through the growing power of the EP in the EU legislative process and in EP–Commission relations. Finally, as Europe's public becomes increasingly aware of the EP, and public support grows for a more powerful EP as a way of reducing the democratic deficit in the EU, the EP party groups can claim an indirect source of legitimacy for their actions.

In a comparative theoretical context, parties at the European level are somewhere between the American 'parties as empty vessels' (Katz and Kolodny 1994) and the European 'cartel parties' (Katz and Mair 1995) or 'modern cadre parties' (Koole 1996). As in the American system, parties at the EU level exist primarily as parliamentary 'coalitions'. These coalitions exist to serve the office and policy interests of the various sub-units of the parliamentary organizations (national parties in the EU setting, and state parties in the US Congress). They do not promote a clearly defined collective ideology, upon which the careers of the member parties and politicians are made or broken. Also like American parties, parties at the European level have to compete with highly organized private interest groups to influence the policy agenda, and hence it is often difficult to see a party-political imprint on legislative outcomes.

However, as in many party systems at the domestic level in Europe, parties at the European level are dominated by a cohesive parliamentary elite. In many domestic systems, the role of the rank-and-file party member has declined as the party/parliamentary leadership has secured state-funding for party activities and direct access to the public through television and other forms of modern campaigning. In the EU, the party groups in the EP do not need their member parties to finance their activities, as they secure ample funds from the EU budget. Like most domestic parliamentary parties, the EP group leaderships control the internal agendas of the parliamentary parties and committee assignments and other office-opportunities of their parliamentary members. Consequently, as the EP gains more power under the legislative procedures of the EU, the European party leaderships are able to exert an increasing influence on legislative outcomes from the EU system. Like domestic 'cartel parties', the elites of the EP party groups collude to promote the institutional interests of the European Parliament and the collective organizational interests of European parties (as in the joint Euro-party proposal for the 'party article'). But, as turnout in legislative votes in the EP increases under new internal EP rules, this collusion has given way to competition between the rival party elites in the day-to-day legislative agenda. Where this occurs, the EP party groups are more like 'modern cadre parties'.

Nevertheless, the role of parties at the European level in increasing the legitimacy of the EU has been marginal. The so-called 'party article' of the Maastricht Treaty makes the claim to the contrary, which has led to argument about how to translate these aspirations into reality. For example, the leadership of the ELDR has suggested that as a result of Article 191:

A 'Political Party at the European Level' should be partially financed from the Community's budget, [if it] . . . is represented by member parties in at least 50 percent of the EU member-states, . . . fights European elections on a common programme, [and] . . . is open to individual membership (European Liberal, Democrat, and Reform Party 1992: 2–3).

Nevertheless, such developments are being resisted by many national parties, who are jealous to defend their existing power within the party federations and the EP party groups, and to prevent European level parties being able to appeal over their heads to 'their' voters.

Having said this, until recently the legitimacy of the EU project has been guaranteed by *national* parties. Since the beginning of the European integration process political elites have generally been more in favour of European integration than the mass public. However, elites cannot simply do as they please, despite public opposition to the EU. Party leaders must compete in national and European elections. If a national party competes in an election campaign on a strongly pro-European platform and the median voter in their country is anti-European, they will lose support. This 'electoral connection' consequently presents a powerful incentive for political elites to behave 'as if' they share the opinions of their voters. As a result, national parties' manifesto promises about European integration tend to correlate very closely with voters' preferences about the EU (cf. Carrubba 1998).

Nevertheless, this system of legitimacy via national parties collapsed in the wake of the Maastricht Treaty—with growing opposition to the EU revealed in public opinion surveys, votes for anti-European parties in the 1994 European elections, and support for anti-European movements against pro-European governments in referenda in Denmark, France, Austria, Finland, and Sweden. In this post-permissive consensus world, there is renewed interest in the possibility of parties at the European level being the vehicles for structuring elite competition over the direction of the EU policy agenda, and over who holds executive office at the European level (such as the Commission President).

But this does not mean supplanting the system of legitimacy through national parties. Rather it implies 'fusing' national political elites into transnational alliances with common partisan affiliations, policy preferences, and voting constituencies, in the same way that there has been a fusion of the behaviour and preferences of national and European bureaucratic and administrative elites in the various policy sectors of the EU (Wessels 1997*b*).

The result would be a mix of two models of party-based democracy. First, parties at the European level would fulfil the classic social integration function of political parties at the domestic level in Europe, through the supply of representation by internally democratic party organizations. This could be achieved through the connection of national political parties in party leaders' summits and in the EP party groups to executive office-holders at the European level (in the Commission) and the legislative agenda of the EU. Second, parties at the European level would facilitate an American-style (Schumpeterian) model of competition between rival political elites over who gets to monopolize the political agenda and control governmental office. For example, this could be achieved through a genuine 'European' electoral contest such as a reformed system of EP elections or through an election for the Commission Presidency. Parties at the European level are still some way from this model, but they are much closer than they were at the low point of transnational party cooperation in the early 1980s.

REFERENCES

Anderweg, R. (1995) 'The reshaping of national party systems', in J. Hayward (ed.) *The Crisis of Representation in Europe* (London: Frank Cass).

Attinà, F. (1990) 'The voting behaviour of the European parliament members and the problem of Europarties'. *European Journal of Political Research* 18: 557–79.

—— (1992) 'Parties, party system and democracy in the European Union'. *International Spectator* 27: 67–86.

Bardi, L. (1992) 'Transnational party federations in the European community', in R. S. Katz and P. Mair (eds) *Party Organizations: A Data Handbook on Party Organizations in Western Democracies, 1969–90* (London: Sage Publications).

—— (1994) 'Transnational party federations, European parliamentary party groups, and building Europarties', in R. S. Katz and P. Mair (eds) *How Parties Organize: Adaptation and Change in Party Organizations in Western Democracies* (London: Sage Publications).

Bogdanor, V. (1986) 'The future of the European community: two models of democracy'. *Government and Opposition* 22: 344–70.

Carrubba, C. (1998) 'The electoral connection in European Union politics' (unpublished mimeo), Stony Brook: Stony Brook College.

Corbett, R., Jacobs, F., and Shackleton, M. (1995) *The European Parliament*, 3rd edn (London: Catermill).

Dehousse, R. (1995) 'Constitutional reform in the European community: are there alternatives to the majority avenue?', in J. Hayward (ed.) *The Crisis of Representation in Europe* (London: Frank Cass).

Eichenberg, R. C. and Dalton, R. J. (1993) 'Europeans and the European community: the dynamics of public support for European integration'. *International Organization* 47: 507–34.

European Liberal, Democrat and Reform Party (1992) *ELDR Council's Stance on Article 138A of the Treaty on European Union Pointing to the Importance of 'Political Parties at the European Level'* (Brussels: European Liberal, Democrat and Reform Party).

Falkner, G. (1997) 'Corporatist governance and Europeanization: no future in the multi-level game?', *European Integration On-line Papers*, 1, 11, http://eiop.or.at/eiop/texte/1997-011a.htm.

Franklin, M., Marsh, M., and McLaren, L. (1994) 'Uncorking the bottle: popular opposition to European unification in the wake of Maastricht'. *Journal of Common Market Studies*, 32, 4, 101–17.

Green Cowles, M. (1995) 'Setting the agenda for a new Europe: the ERT and EC 1992'. *Journal of Common Market Studies* 33(4): 501–26.

Greenwood, J. (1997) *Representing Interests in the European Union* (London: Macmillan).

Hallstein, W. (1972) *Europe in the Making* (London: Allen & Unwin).

Hix, S. (1995a) 'Parties at the European level and the legitimacy of EU socio-economic policy'. *Journal of Common Market Studies* 33(4): 527–54.

—— (1995b) *Political Parties in the European Union System: A 'Comparative Political Approach' to the Development of the Party Federations*, PhD thesis (Florence: European University Institute).

—— (1996) 'The transnational party federations', in J. Gaffney (ed.) *Political Parties in the European Union* (London: Routledge).

—— (1999a) 'Dimensions and alignments in European Union politics: cognitive constraints and partisan responses'. *European Journal of Political Research* 35: 69–125.

—— (1999b) *The Political System of the European Union* (Basingstoke: Macmillan).

—— and Lord, C. (1995) 'The making of a President: the European parliament and the confirmation of Jacques Santer as President of the Commission'. *Government & Opposition* 31: 64–76.

——, —— (1997) *Political Parties in the European Union* (London: Macmillan).

Jachtenfuchs, M. (1997) 'Democracy and governance in the European Union'. *European Integration On-Line Papers*, vol. 1, http://eiop.or.at/eiop/texte/1997.002a.htm.

Kaase, M. and Newton, K. (1995) *Beliefs in Government* (Oxford: Oxford University Press).

Katz, R. S. and Kolodny, R. (1994) 'Party organization as an empty vessel: parties in American politics', in Richard S. Katz and Peter Mair (eds) *How Parties Organize* (London: Sage Publications).

—— and Mair, P. (1995) 'Changing models of party organization and party democracy: the emergence of the cartel party'. *Party Politics* 1: 5–28.

Kolodny, R. and Katz, R. S. (1992) 'The United States', in R. S. Katz and P. Mair (eds) *Party Organizations: A Data Handbook on Party Organizations in Western Democracies, 1969–90* (London: Sage Publications).

Koole, R. (1996) 'Ledenpartijen of staatspartijen? Financien van Nederlandse politieke partijen in vergelijkend en historisch perspectief', *Jaarboek 1996* (Groningen: Documentatiecentrum Nederlandse Politieke Partijen) pp. 156–82.

—— and Mair, P. (eds) (1995) 'Political Data Yearbook 1995'. *European Journal of Political Research* 28: 4.

Laver, M. J., Gallagher, M., Marsh, M., Singh, R., and Tonra, B. (1995) *Electing the President of the European Commission*, Trinity Blue Papers in Public Policy: 1 (Dublin: Trinity College).

Leonard, M. (1997) *Politics Without Frontiers: The Role of Political Parties in Europe's Future* (London: Demos).

Lodge, J. (1996a) 'Introduction: de-mythologizing the European parliament', in J. Lodge (ed.) *The 1994 Elections to the European Parliament* (London: Macmillan).

—— (1996b) 'The future of the European parliament', in J. Lodge (ed.) *The 1994 Elections to the European Parliament* (London: Macmillan).

Mackie, T. T. and Rose, R. (1991) *The International Almanac of Electoral History* (London: CQ Press).

Majone, G. (1996) *Regulating Europe* (London: Routledge).

Marquand, D. (1978) 'Towards a Europe of the parties'. *Political Quarterly* 49: 425–45.

Marsh, M. and Norris, P. (1997) 'Political representation in the European parliament'. Special Issue of *European Journal of Political Research* 32: 2.

Mazey, S. and Richardson, J. (1993) *Lobbying in the European Community* (Oxford: Oxford University Press).

Niedermayer, O. (1983) *Europäischen Parteien? Zur grenzüberschreitenden Interaktion politischer Parteien In Rahmen: der Europäische Gemeinschaft* (Frankfurt: Campus).

—— (1995) 'Trends and contrasts', in O. Niedermayer and R. Sinnott (eds) *Public Opinion and Internationalized Governance* (Oxford: Oxford University Press).

—— and Sinnott, R. (1995) 'Democratic legitimacy and the European parliament', in O. Niedermayer and R. Sinnott (eds) *Public Opinion and Internationalized Governance* (Oxford: Oxford University Press).

Obradovic, D. (1996) 'Policy legitimacy and the European Union'. *Journal of Common Market Studies* 34: 191–221.

Oppenhuis, E., van der Eijk, C., and Franklin, M. (1996) 'The party context: outcomes', in C. van der Eijk and M. Franklin (eds) *Choosing Europe? The European Electorate and National Politics in the Face of Union* (Ann Arbor: University of Michigan Press).

Pedersen, M. N. (1996) 'Euro-parties and European parties: new arenas, new challenges and new strategies', in S. S. Andersen and K. A. Eliassen (eds) *The European Union: How Democratic Is It?* (London: Sage Publications).

Poguntke, T. and Boll, B. (1992) 'Germany', in R. S. Katz and P. Mair (eds) *Party Organizations: A Data Handbook on Party Organizations in Western Democracies, 1969–90* (London: Sage Publications).

Pridham, G. and Pridham, P. (1981) *Transnational Party Co-operation and European Integration: The Process Towards the Direct Elections* (London: Allen & Unwin).

——, —— (1981) *Transnational Party Co-operation and European Integration: The Process Towards the Direct Elections* (London: Allen & Unwin).

Raunio, T. (1996) *Party Group Behaviour in the European Parliament: An Analysis of Transnational Political Groups in the 1989–94 Parliament* (Tampere: University of Tampere).

Reif, K., Cayrol, R., and Niedermayer, O. (1980) 'National political parties' middle level elites and European integration'. *European Journal of Political Research* 8: 91–112.

—— and Schmitt, H. (1980) 'Nine second-order national elections: a conceptual framework for the analysis of European election results'. *European Journal of Political Research* 8: 3–45.

Schattschneider, E. E. (1960) *Semisovereign People: A Realist's View of Democracy in America* (Hinsdale: Dryden Press).

Schmitter, P. C. (1996) *How to Democratize the Emerging Euro-Polity: Citizenship, Representation, Decision-Making*, unpublished mimeo, Madrid: Juan March Institute.

Streeck, W. and Schmitter, P. C. (1991) 'From national corporatism to transnational pluralism: organized interests in the Single European Market' *Politics and Society*, 19, 133–64.

Thatcher, M. (1993) *The Downing Street Years* (New York: Harper Collins).

van der Eijk, C. and Franklin, M. (1996) *Choosing Europe? The European Electorate and National Politics in the Face of Union* (Ann Arbor: University of Michigan Press).

Weiler, J. H. H. (1997) 'The European Union belongs to the citizens: three immodest proposals'. *European Law Review* 22: 150–56.

Wessels, W. (1997*a*) 'The Growth and Differentiation of Multi-Level Networks: A Corporatist Mega-Bureaucracy or Open City?', in H. Wallace and A. R. Young (eds) *Participation and Policy-Making in the European Union* (Oxford: Clarendon).

—— (1997*b*) 'An ever closer fusion? A dynamic macropolitical view on integration processes'. *Journal of Common Market Studies* 35: 267–99.

Williams, S. (1991) 'Sovereignty and accountability in the European community', in R. O. Keohane and S. Hoffmann (eds) *The New European Community: Decision-making and Institutional Change* (Boulder, CO: Westview Press).

11

Still Functional After All These Years

Parties in the United States, 1960–2000

John C. Green

There is no doubt that the American party system has experienced considerable change since 1960. The meaning of this change is, however, the subject of much debate, at the core of which is a basic question: how functional is the American party system after four turbulent decades? Depending on the evidence considered, scholars offer different answers to this question, ranging from a loss of functionality due to party 'decline' to potential gains from party 'revival.' This disagreement occurs in the context of considerable nostalgia for previous eras, either the 'golden age' of partisanship in the 1950s or the 'golden age' of party organization at the turn of the century.

This chapter reviews these arguments and assesses changes in key aspects of the American party system between 1960 and 1996. We find some merit to both the 'declinist' and 'revivalist' points of view. Popular support for, and participation in, the party system has declined since 1960, weakening but not replacing the two-party context for American politics and government. During the same period, the major party organizations have become stronger and more ideological, increasing but not recasting the coherence of American politics and government. This mixed pattern of change has not altered the basic features of the party system—for good and for ill. On balance, the major parties are still functional, serving now, as in the past, as organizers of the context politics and government. However, the major parties exercise little direct control over politicians or policy, and thus are not a consistent source of cohesion in politics and government. Put another way, the United States has highly *partisan* government, but very little *party government*. Many scholars wish for the latter, of course, under the assumption that the system would then function better than it does (White and Mileur 1992).

THE AMERICAN 'TWO-PARTY' SYSTEM

There is a contradiction at the heart of the American party system and the debate over its functionality. On the one hand, the 'two-party' system is nearly *comprehensive*, in that it encompasses almost all citizens, activists, and office-holders. Such comprehensiveness allows the major parties to dominate the context of politics and government. On the other hand, the 'two-party' system is deeply *fragmented*, since it is composed of numerous and largely autonomous units, with a variety of ideological positions. Such fragmentation frequently yields a low degree of coherence in politics and government. Put another way, the functions performed by the major parties do not neatly match the forms which parties and partisanship take.[1]

The best evidence of the comprehensiveness of the party system is a nearly universal attachment to the two major parties, the Democrats and Republicans. Although such partisanship varies in intensity, it extends to most of the mass public and is especially common among political activists and office-holders. It is rare for anyone to be elected to public office without a major party label and little government takes place at the federal or state levels outside the context of the major parties. Even organizational rivals to the parties, such as interest groups and social movements, largely operate within the confines of the two-party system. Thus, nearly everyone recognizes the outlines of the party system and can place themselves within it. This comprehensiveness has led some scholars to model American parties in Downsian terms, as two rival teams of office-seekers competing for votes across a unidimensional issue space (Schlesinger 1985). While this model is quite useful in describing the most salient results of party politics, it implies a degree of unity that the major parties rarely achieve.

The best evidence of the fragmentation of the party system lies with the major party organizations. The Democratic and Republican 'parties' are actually composed of numerous, separate organizations. Some units are defined by level of government (federal, state, local), others by type of office (executive, legislative), and still others by activity (electoral, governmental). In addition, there are a host of candidate committees, interest groups, and social movements that lie outside of the major party organizations and yet regularly operate in concert with them. Such fragmentation extends to ideology, where the major parties are given to issue-based factionalism. If nearly everyone has a place in the party system, then there are clearly many places to be. This 'amorphous' or 'polymorphous' system (Katz and Mair 1992: 876) has prompted controversy over the definition of 'party,' the most common resolution of which is a three-fold distinction: party-in-the-electorate, party-as-organization, and party-in-government (Beck 1997: 9–13). While frequently criticized, this 'tripod' captures the peculiar functioning of this comprehensive yet fragmented system.

---

[1] This peculiar system arises from the structure of the American constitution and is amplified by the legal regulation of elections (Epstein 1986). On the impact of separation of powers, federalism, and single-member plurality elections on American parties, see Harmel and Janda (1982); on the impact of legal regulation of elections, see Bass (1998).

Thus, from the point of view of organizing the context for politics and government, the United States has a strong 'two-party' system. But from the point of view of producing coherence in politics and government, the United States might fairly be said to have six, one hundred, three thousand—or a 'no party' system at all. Indeed, Katz and Kolodny's (1994) description of the major American parties as 'empty vessels' accurately captures one-half of this reality. The 'two-party' system can indeed be thought of as a set of vessels through which nearly all of American politics ultimately flows. However, such vessels are hardly empty: they are chock full of citizens, activists, and office-seekers in search of greater coherence in politics and government. However, the exact arrangement and impact of such amalgams within the vessels is contingent on the political process itself. For this reason, the major American parties are often labeled as 'pluralist-organizational' (Nakamura and Sullivan 1979), 'pragmatic' (Orren 1982), 'catch-all' (Kirchheimer 1966) or 'constituent' (Lowi 1975). Although this system can exhibit coherence to match its comprehensiveness, much of the time it does not. Or put another way, the elements of the 'tripod' are not linked to one another in any necessary way (Ranney 1963).

The contradictory features of the American party system are well illustrated in Table 11.1. These data clearly reveal the comprehensiveness of the two-party system: the Democrats and Republicans dominated all of these elections, despite some noted 'independent' campaigns for president (1968, 1980, 1992, and 1996) and for Congress (1972, 1976, and 1980), as confirmed by the effective numbers of electoral parties. Major party dominance is even clearer when one considers the number of presidential electors and congressional seats won. The only minor party effort to garner more than a token number of presidential electors was George Wallace's 1968 campaign; minor parties did even more poorly for congressional seats. These results reveal a strong institutional bias in favour of the winning party. For example, the Democratic presidential candidate in 1960, John F. Kennedy, received just under 50 per cent of the popular vote, but won 56 per cent of the presidential electors. In the same year, the Democrats received a little over one-half of the popular vote cast in House and Senate contests, and yet won about two-thirds of the seats in both houses of Congress.

Despite this tendency to produce 'artificial majorities' in the Electoral College and Congress, elections have been very competitive since 1960. If one counts as 'close' elections those won with 55 per cent or less of the popular vote, then only three presidential races (1964, 1972, and 1984) and three congressional elections (1964 for the House and Senate, and 1976 for the House) have produced 'big' wins. Indeed, the major parties have become increasingly competitive since 1960 at the federal (Beck 1997: 5–59) and state levels (Bibby and Holbrook 1995).

In contrast, the pattern of election results for particular offices illustrates the fragmentation of the system. Overall, the presidential and congressional vote do not follow each other closely. For example, the Democrats won five and the

TABLE 11.1. *Elections and control of government in the USA, 1960–2000*

Year	Presidency					House of Representatives					Senate				
	Dem	Rep	Other	Control	ENEP	Dem	Rep	Other	Control	ENEP	Dem	Rep	Other	Control	ENEP
1960	*49.7*	*49.5*	*0.8*	*Dem*	*2.00*	*53.9*	*44.4*	*0.7*	*Dem*	*2.03*	*54.5*	*45.4*	*0.1*	*Dem*	*1.99*
	56.4	40.7	2.9	Kennedy		67.0	33.0	0.0			65.0	35.0	0.0		
1964	*61.1*	*38.4*	*0.4*	*Dem*	*1.93*	*56.7*	*41.7*	*0.6*	*Dem*	*2.01*	*56.9*	*42.1*	*1.0*	*Dem*	*1.99*
	90.3	9.7	0.0	Johnson		67.8	32.2	0.0			68.0	32.0	0.0		
1968	*42.7*	*43.4*	*13.9*	*Rep*	*2.57*	*50.0*	*48.4*	*0.2*	*Dem*	*2.07*	*48.7*	*48.3*	*3.0*	*Dem*	*2.12*
	35.5	55.9	8.6	Nixon		56.3	43.7	0.0			57.0	43.0	0.0		
1972	*37.5*	*60.7*	*1.8*	*Rep*	*1.96*	*50.7*	*46.4*	*0.9*	*Dem*	*2.12*	*45.5*	*52.3*	*2.2*	*Dem*	*2.07*
	3.2	96.6	0.2	Nixon		55.6	44.1	0.3			56.0	42.0	2.0		
1976	*50.1*	*48.0*	*1.9*	*Dem*	*2.08*	*55.4*	*41.8*	*2.8*	*Dem*	*2.07*	*54.4*	*45.2*	*0.4*	*Dem*	*2.00*
	55.2	44.6	0.2	Carter		67.1	32.9	0.0			61.0	38.0	1.0		
1980	*41.0*	*50.7*	*8.3*	*Rep*	*2.31*	*50.0*	*47.4*	*2.6*	*Dem*	*2.10*	*51.0*	*46.0*	*3.0*	*Rep*	*2.12*
	9.1	90.9	0.0	Reagan		55.8	44.2	0.0			46.0	53.0	1.0		
1984	*40.6*	*58.8*	*0.6*	*Rep*	*1.96*	*51.8*	*46.9*	*1.3*	*Dem*	*2.08*	*48.7*	*50.4*	*0.9*	*Rep*	*2.04*
	2.4	97.6	0.0	Reagan		57.9	41.8	0.0			47.0	53.0	0.0		
1988	*45.6*	*53.4*	*1.0*	*Rep*	*2.03*	*52.4*	*45.1*	*2.5*	*Dem*	*2.09*	*52.2*	*46.4*	*1.6*	*Dem*	*2.05*
	79.1	20.7	0.2	Bush		59.5	40.5	0.0			55.0	45.0	0.0		
1992	*43.0*	*37.4*	*19.6*	*Dem*	*2.75*	*51.0*	*45.8*	*3.2*	*Dem*	*2.12*	*49.7*	*48.7*	*1.6*	*Dem*	*2.06*
	68.7	31.3	0.0	Clinton		59.3	40.4	0.3			57.0	43.0	0.0		
1996	*49.2*	*40.7*	*10.1*	*Dem*	*2.39*	*48.5*	*48.9*	*0.6*	*Rep*	*2.09*	*47.8*	*49.4*	*0.8*	*Rep*	*2.09*
	70.5	29.5	0.0	Clinton		47.6	52.1	0.3			45.0	55.0	0.0		
2000	*48.4*	*47.9*	*3.7*	*Rep*	*2.15*	*47.9*	*47.9*	*4.2*	*Rep*	*2.17*	*49.5*	*48.5*	*2.0*	*NOC*	*2.08*
	49.8	50.4	0.0	Bush		48.7	50.8	0.5			50.0	50.0	0.0		

Notes: NOC: No Overall Control, ENEP = Effective number of electoral parties. Italicized rows represent periods of unified party government. For each year, the first row of figures reports the percentage of the popular vote and the second row the percentage of presidential electors won (in the Electoral College) or the percentage of congressional seats won (in House and the Senate).

Sources: Statistical Abstract of the United States; http://www.agora.stm.it/elections/election/new.htm.

Republicans six of the presidential contests in the table, but the Democrats prevailed in nine of the eleven House elections and seven of the Senate elections, with one tied. Indeed, the Democrats controlled the House of Representatives until 1994, and the Senate during the same period except for an interlude between 1980 and 1986. Thus, one minimal condition for 'party government,' unified control of the executive and legislative branches, has only been met around 40 per cent of the time since 1960, with Democrats holding the federal government after 1960, 1964, 1976, and 1992. The Republicans came close to party control in 1980, 1984, and 1996, when they held two of three federal 'houses.' In 2000, they secured the Presidency and the House, but faced a tied Senate which rendered support for President Bush's legislative ambitions precarious.[2] In the remaining years, Republican presidents faced Democratic Congresses—a situation that reversed itself after 1994, with Democrat Bill Clinton facing a Republican House and Senate. In this regard, the post-1960 period presents something of a contrast to other eras of American history (Brady 1988).

Other kinds of fragmentation operated in these rare periods of unified party control, however, with presidents regularly facing opposition from factions among their co-partisans in Congress and sometimes having to rely on support from the rival party to govern (Rae 1998; Shelley 1983). Indeed, only one of the periods of unified control in Table 11.1 was characterized by the extensive enactment of a party programme (the 'Great Society' of Lyndon Johnson after 1964). Interestingly, one period of split party control also produced something like the wholesale passage of a party programme (the 'Reagan Revolution' after 1980). In sum, then, nearly all electoral and governmental activity flowed through the major party vessels during this period, but this flow often failed to produce a high degree of coherence.

PARTY DECLINE AND REVIVAL

The patterns reported in Table 11.1 have provided the basis for an intense debate over the functionality of the American party system. To many scholars, the increased incoherence of the system since 1960 resulted from the 'decline' of party. Various bodies of evidence have been advanced to support this thesis, relating to party-as-organization, party-in-the-electorate and party-in-government (for a good summary of this debate, see Patterson 1996: ch. 2).

To party 'declinists,' party-as-organization seemed to lose its vitality after 1960. For example, the fabled urban party 'machines' finally disappeared, taking with

---

[2] In fact, in May 2001 Senator Jim Jeffords of Vermont renounced his Republican Party membership to become an independent. This deprived Vice-President Dick Cheney of his right to use a casting vote in the Senate in order to break the 50/50 deadlock which had prevailed since the previous November, and effectively ended a brief period of unified Republican government.

them their cadre of local party workers. This loss of vitality reduced the traditional influence of party leaders in nominations and campaigns (Ware 1985). Elections became less 'party-centred' and more 'candidate-centred' as individual candidates for federal and state office won nominations on their own in primary elections, conducted general election campaigns largely independent of party organizations, and pursued individualized issue agendas once in office (Wattenberg 1991). The expansion of modern communications technology, especially television, aided candidate-centred politics by providing citizens with information unmediated by party-as-organizations. Meanwhile, the growth of interest groups and social movements abetted candidate-centred politics by providing individual candidates with non-party resource alternatives (Crotty and Jacobson 1980; Goldman 1994).

However, the rise of competing organizations was only part of the problem. In many cases, these competitors became participants within party-as-organization itself (Ranney 1978). On the one hand, traditional party 'professionals,' who focused on winning elections and gaining material rewards from control of office, were largely replaced by issue-oriented 'amateurs' and 'purists,' who were concerned more with ideology than control of the personnel and perquisites of government (Kirkpatrick 1978). On the other hand, traditional party leaders were also replaced by a new breed of technical experts, including campaign consultants, pollsters, and fundraisers (Agranoff 1972; Salmore and Salmore 1989). The reform of party rules, federal campaign finance laws, and congressional procedures accelerated these trends.

Faced with competitors from without and new participants from within, party-as-organization became less effective, contributing to the decline of party-in-the-electorate and party-in-government. Indeed, these effects constitute a second line of evidence of party decline and have received the most attention. After 1960, the identification of citizens with the major parties decreased, producing electoral 'dealignment,' which in turn helped produce a reduction in voter loyalty (Wattenberg 1998). Straight-ticket voting (voting for presidential and congressional candidates of the same party) decreased, election outcomes became more volatile, and turnout plummeted (Ladd 1970, 1978; Cain *et al.* 1987).

The decay of mass partisanship and voter loyalty exacerbated the effects of candidate-centred politics. Unified party control became less common, generating 'divided government' and 'gridlock' (Fiorina 1992). Policy making was further immobilized by party factionalism and increased activity by interest groups (Rauch 1994). Some writers went so far as to declare a 'governability crisis' in the United States (Bennett 1991). When partisan dealignment and gridlock in government failed to produce the long-awaited 'realignment' in the electorate, some scholars began to question the long-term functionality of the party system itself (Burnham 1970).

Not all scholars accepted these arguments, however, especially the notion that party-as-organization had declined in vitality. While few disputed the changes in party-in-the-electorate and party-in-government since 1960, some argued that the major party organizations actually grew stronger and more coherent over the period (Cotter and Bibby 1980). Two lines of evidence were advanced to support party 'revival,' one based on increased organizational resources and the other on increased ideological coherence among party elites.

First, the 'revivalists' argued that the major party organizations were actually quite weak in the postwar era and that they gained strength after 1960 (Bibby 1998*a*). By the 1980s, the national units of the major parties had acquired extraordinary resources by historical standards, including funds, paid staff, and technical expertise (Reichley 1985; Herrnson 1988, 1995). State party organizations also registered impressive gains in this regard (Cotter *et al.* 1984), while some local parties made similar improvements and others enjoyed continued vitality (Gibson *et al.* 1985; Frendreis *et al.* 1990). These new resources allowed the major parties to adapt to candidate-centred politics (Frantzich 1989).

Second, there was also evidence of greater ideological coherence among office-holders and party activists. These changes appeared in congressional voting, support for presidential programmes, and party platforms (Patterson 1996). Parallel trends were noted in the party activist corps, including members of interest groups and social movements allied with the parties (Baer and Bositis 1988). While not entirely unprecedented, these changes marked a departure from the 'non-programmatic' and 'irresponsible' character of the major parties (Beck 1997: 364–5, 385–96). Still other scholars argued that the negative effects of dealignment and divided government were overstated (Mayhew 1991), and some even advanced alternatives to the concept of realignment, suggesting that a dealigned system could be coherent nonetheless (Aldrich 1995). The combination of new organizational strength and ideological coherence suggested that the party system was functioning fairly well under difficult circumstances, with prospects for future improvements.

The progress of this debate can be traced by the titles of prominent books, from the *Party is Over* (Broder 1971) and *Parties and Elections in an Anti-Party Age* (Fishel 1978) to *The Party Goes On* (Kayden and Mahe 1985) and *The Party Has Just Begun* (Sabato 1988). By the 1990s, the debate had reached stasis, with each side having made valid points (see, for instance, the exchange between Coleman (1994) and Frendreis (1994)). What follows is a review and updating of some of the key evidence presented by each side, relating to popular legitimacy of the major parties, party organizational strength, and the systemic functionality of the party system.

THE POPULAR LEGITIMACY OF AMERICAN PARTIES

How has popular support for the American party system changed since 1960? Identification with the major parties declined among the mass public after 1960, along with partisan voting and positive evaluations of parties as institutions. Thus, the party system is now somewhat less comprehensive than hitherto at the mass level, but with a majority of Americans still firmly within its grip (Mayer 1998).

Table 11.2 reports common measures of partisanship and party loyalty in 1960, 1980, and 1996. The first item is the standard seven-point measure of party identification utilized by the National Election Studies.[3] These data show a significant erosion of public identification with the major parties. Thus, in 1960 almost two-fifths of the electorate thought of themselves as 'strong' Democrats or Republicans, a figure that fell to less than one-quarter in 1980, and recovered to just under one-third by 1996. Adding 'strong' and 'weak' partisans together reveals the same pattern: in 1960 Democrats made up almost one-half of the electorate and about two-fifths in 1980 and 1996. The analogous figures for Republicans were less than 30 per cent in 1960 and 1996, with a dip to just over 20 per cent in 1980. A similar pattern holds for 'independents' and 'leaners' who together comprised just over one-fifth of the electorate in 1960, but one-third in 1980 and 1996.[4] So, in total a little more than one-tenth of the electorate moved from partisan to independent categories between 1960 and 1996. Over the period, 'strong' and 'weak' Democrats showed the largest decrease (10.6 percentage points in combination), though the biggest gain was among independents who 'leaned' Democratic (7.7 percentage points). Republicans showed smaller changes, largely because there were fewer of them to begin with in 1960. Interestingly, the 'pure' independents actually decreased over the period, after expanding in 1980. Overall, the data suggest considerable fluctuations in partisanship within this time span, with the strongest decreases occurring in the 1970s (Beck 1997: 380–1).

Another measure of party loyalty is mean 'thermometer' ratings of the two major parties. These can range from 0 to 100 'degrees' and measure how 'warm' or 'cold' respondents feel towards each major party. These measures were first available for 1964, which is thus the initial time point in Table 11.2. Over the period, the mean rating fell thirteen 'degrees' for the Democrats and six for the Republicans; if 1968 is used as the starting point, the reductions were more even (7.6 degrees for Democrats and 8.9 for Republicans). By 1996, the mean rating for both parties stood at a little above the mid-point of the scales. These and other

---

[3] Unless otherwise indicated, the data in the tables come from the National Election Studies, conducted by the Center for Political Studies at the University of Michigan and made available by the Inter-University Consortium for Political and Social Research. The interpretations offered here are the sole responsibility of the author.

[4] The conceptual status of partisan 'independents' is somewhat problematic in the American context. While such individuals surely have a tenuous cognitive attachment to the major parties, those who claim to 'lean' towards one of the parties often behave in a more partisan fashion than their 'weak' co-partisans (Keith *et al.* 1992). Indeed, if one sums all three partisan groups together ('strong', 'weak', and 'leaners'), the proportion of the population with a major party identification has remained essentially the same since 1960. Put another way, Democratic identifiers writ large were about as numerous in 1960 as in 1996, but in 1960 'strong' Democrats accounted for more than two-fifths of the total, and in 1996 a little better than one-third.

TABLE 11.2. *Partisanship and loyalty in the US electorate,*
selected years

Self-identified partisanship (%)	1960	1980	1996
Strong Democrat	23.7	17.7	18.4
Weak Democrat	24.9	23.1	19.6
Leans Democrat	5.8	11.4	13.5
Independent	9.4	14.2	8.2
Leans Republican	6.5	10.2	11.5
Weak Republican	14.3	13.9	15.8
Strong Republican	15.3	8.5	12.8
Mean 'warmth' toward[a]	1964	1980	1996
Democratic Party	71.6	61.0	58.0
Republican Party	59.4	57.0	53.4
Voter loyalty (%)	1960	1980	1996
Straight-ticket voters[b]	55.3	47.2	44.0
Inter-election stability[c]	69.5	46.3	64.4
Electoral volatility[d]	1964	1980	1996
Presidential elections	11.5	9.1	9.5
House elections	2.8	5.6	4.1
Senate elections	3.3	3.4	1.7
Average	5.9	6.0	5.1

[a] Mean thermometer rating, 0–100 degrees.
[b] Vote for presidential and congressional candidate of same major party.
[c] Vote for presidential candidate of the same party in present and preceding election.
[d] Electoral volatility is Pedersen's index of total net volatility.

Source: National Election Studies.

data suggest that parties had become less relevant to the political thinking of many voters (see Wattenberg 1998 on this point).

These shifts in partisanship were associated with reductions in voter loyalty (Beck 1997: 156–9). First, there was a decline of straight-ticket voting, falling from over half of all voters in 1960 to somewhat more than two-fifths in 1996. Another measure of party loyalty did not decline as much over the period, although it did show more volatility: support for the same party's presidential candidates in two successive elections. Better than two-thirds of voters backed the same party's candidate for president in 1956 and 1960, not many more than did so in 1992 and 1996. At the aggregate level, it should be said, there was no trend towards higher levels of electoral volatility across the period (Table 11.2). However, voter turnout declined sharply (see Table 11.14).

As one might imagine, these indicators are interconnected. From 1960 to 1996, strong party identifiers were the most likely to feel 'warm' towards their party, vote a straight-ticket, and remain loyal between elections. For instance, in 1960 and 1996 some three-quarters of 'strong' Democrats voted a straight ticket; by contrast, only two-fifths of those who 'leaned' towards the Democrats did so in 1960 and only half of them did so in 1996. The magnitude of change for all these measures is similar, involving an aggregate shift of between one-eighth and one-tenth of the electorate over four decades. These changes led Paul Beck (1998) to conclude that the United States had two electorates in the 1990s, one highly partisan and engaged in politics, and the other less partisan and highly volatile at the ballot box.

What about the public's regard for parties as institutions? Table 11.3 presents some fragmentary evidence on this point, comparing popular evaluations of political parties from 1968, 1980, and 1996 (see Dennis 1975; Owen *et al.* 1998). Unfortunately, only one of these indicators is directly comparable across the period, and this shows a 10 percentage point decline in the number of respondents feeling that parties 'care about voter opinion'. While more than half saw either general or specific value in parties (i.e. they were 'needed by the system' or helpful in 'getting government's attention'), a far less impressive proportion felt parties could be trusted to 'keep their promises' or do 'a good job' generally. Similarly, only one-fifth admitted to harbouring 'warm' sentiments towards the parties.

Greater stability of measuring instruments enables us to obtain a clearer picture of declining trust in party government over the period. Thus, the proportion of respondents believing that elections 'help get the government's attention' declined from approximately three-fifths to two-fifths between 1968 and 1996, while general trust in government and a belief that government is 'run for the interests of all' were halved. Thus, political parties appear to have lost less ground in public esteem than the broader political system.

TABLE 11.3. *Evaluations of political parties in the USA, selected years*

	1968	1980	1996
Evaluation of parties			
Parties care about voter opinion	47.6	37.7	37.5
Parties help get government's attention	60.9	—	—
The US needs political parties	—	56.6	—
Parties are needed to make system work	—	—	55.0
Parties keep their promises	32.3	—	—
Political parties are doing a good job	—	20.9	—
Feel 'warm' toward political parties	—	—	21.6
Evaluation of government			
Elections help get government's attention	61.8	51.8	43.0
Trust government always/most of the time	62.1	25.7	30.2
Government run for benefit of all people	56.4	23.0	28.3

Note: All figures are percentages of respondents agreeing with statement.

Source: National Election Studies.

TABLE 11.4. *Support for the two-party system and alternatives in the US, 1996*

	Continue two-party system	Encourage candidate system	Develop multiparty system
All	41.1	31.2	27.7
Strong Democrat	57.1	16.8	26.1
Weak Democrat	37.6	35.3	27.1
Leans Democrat	22.7	45.4	32.0
Independent	23.4	51.4	25.2
Leans Republican	26.4	41.1	32.5
Weak Republican	43.9	27.8	28.3
Strong Republican	59.7	16.9	23.4

Source: National Election Study, 1996.

Table 11.4 offers evidence on public support for the 'two-party' system itself. In the 1996 National Election Study respondents were asked about the kind of party system they would like to see in the abstract. One option was a continuation of the two-party system; another was to have candidates running 'independent' of parties (essentially a 'candidate-centred' system); and the final option was a multiparty system ('development of one or more parties to challenge the Democrats and Republicans'). Overall, two-fifths of the public expressed support for the two-party system, just under one-third wanted a non-partisan candidate-centred system, and a little over one-quarter favoured some sort of multiparty system. The rest of the table reviews the distribution of these options by party identification. Not surprisingly, the strong party identifiers were the most supportive of the two-party system. Nevertheless, roughly one-quarter of strong and weak Democrats and Republicans favoured a multiparty system. Presumably these represent issue-oriented voters who 'have no other place to go' in a two-party system. Independents tend to favour a candidate-centred system, especially the pure independents, while Democratic and Republican 'leaners' also show strong support for a multiparty system.

These figures are interesting, but not entirely surprising. After all, the support for the two-party system was just a bit larger than the number of strong partisans in 1996 (refer again to Table 11.2), and the candidate-centred and multiparty results fit with the well-known 'anti-party' tradition in the United States (Goldman 1994). Although a comparable question was not asked in the 1960s or 1980s, some evidence suggests that public opinion may not have changed that much over the period. For example, a Gallup poll in 1968 found that 27 per cent of the respondents wanted 'a new political party ... whose principles were more in line with your point of view.' Other questions from that time suggest that there was considerable support for voting for 'the man, not the party'.[5] In the 1980 National Election Study, some

[5] These data were made available by the Roper Center. The 'new party' question was USGALLUP.769.Q13a (26 September 1968), while the item on voting for 'the man, not the party' was USGALLUP.768.Q13 (19 September 1968).

30 per cent of respondents agreed it would be better if 'candidates ran without party labels,' and almost as many claimed to feel 'warm' (top one-third of a thermometer scale) to a third party. Thus, it may be that there were comparable levels of support for alternatives to the two-party system throughout the period under consideration.

In sum, public support for the 'two-party' system was less comprehensive among the mass public in the 1990s than in 1960. There seem to have been significant decreases in the identification with, and evaluations of, the major parties and the party system as a whole. 'Declinists' thus have a case for a loss of legitimacy of the party system, and this loss helps account for the patterns in Table 11.1. However, these changes are more modest than one might imagine given some of the claims made by declinists, and partisanship is still an important factor in mass political behaviour (Miller 1998). In addition, Americans are almost as likely to see political parties to be as valuable institutions as in 1960 and there may well have been considerable support for alternatives to the 'two-party' system throughout the period. The loss of popular legitimacy may be both less severe and less novel than is often assumed.

ORGANIZATIONAL STRENGTH OF AMERICAN PARTIES

What has happened to party organizational strength since 1960? Evidence on party finance and paid staff shows gains at the federal and state levels, and these changes suggest some reduction in the fragmentation of major party organizations. Estimates of 'party membership,' a problematic concept in the United States, reveal a more complex picture, but with an accent on continuity. However, all such gains have occurred in the context of candidate-centred politics, the expansion of interest groups, and a growth of minor party activity. Since 1960, the major party organizations have become better competitors in a more competitive environment (Bibby 1998a).

Table 11.5 reports the expenditures by the largest major party units in 1960, 1980, and 1996 (in 1996 constant dollars). These units include the three major federal organizations: the Democratic and Republican National Committees (the traditional 'presidential' wings of the major parties and the closest thing to 'national' party in the United States); and the Democratic and Republican Senatorial and Congressional Committees (the campaign organizations of the congressional parties).[6] Clearly, major party funding has increased dramatically since 1960. Total

---

[6] A few caveats about these data are in order. The 1980 and 1996 figures include only 'hard money' expenditures, that is, funds raised and expended under the federal campaign finance laws. 'Soft money' is excluded because it operates on the fringes of the federal campaign finance regime; its exclusion also makes the comparison with 1960 more appropriate. The 1960 numbers must be viewed with caution since the requirements for financial disclosure in 1960 were quite different than in 1980 and 1996 and were very poorly enforced. The 1980 and 1996 data are from the Federal Election Commission. The

TABLE 11.5. *Major party expenditures in the USA, selected years*

	1960	1980	1996
Democrats			
DNC	14,490	25,982	105,584
DNSC	1210	2774	30,797
DCCC	1320	4850	26,412
State/local[a]	13,530	15,013	88,886
Net total	30,050	48,619	214,306[b]
Per 100,000 voters	285	309	1093
Republicans			
RNC	21,820	130,033	192,362
RNSC	3020	36,376	66,000
RNCC	10,790	59,376	73,613
State/local[a]	39,370	55,815	120,000
Net total	75,000	81,888	408,537[b]
Per 100,000 voters	701	1794	2084

Notes: All figures are in thousands of US dollars, constant at 1996 prices.
DNC: Democratic National Committee; DNSC: Democratic National Senatorial Committee; DNCC: Democratic National Campaign Committee; RNC: Republican National Committee; RNSC: Republican National Senatorial Committee; RNCC: Republican National Campaign Committee.
[a]Estimates of expenditures in federal elections by state and local party committees.
[b]Total funds exclude transfers among committees.

Sources: See text and notes for details.

Democratic party expenditure swelled from some $30 million to $214 million over the period. The Republicans started with a larger base but still posted large gains, from some $75 million to $408 million. These impressive changes remain when population is controlled for (see expenditure per 100,000 eligible voters in Table 11.5); by this measure, total Democratic spending rose nearly four-fold, while Republicans enjoyed a three-fold increase. These figures suggest that the Democrats made some relative gains over the period: in 1960 they spent about two-fifths of the Republican total and by 1996 this ratio had grown to about one-half.

The major parties also spent some $266 million in 'soft money' in 1996 (Corrado 1997), funds raised via state parties outside of the federal restrictions but spent in aid of federal elections; these figures would expand party resources by another 42 per cent (see also Nelson 2002). If we assume that the value of local party efforts directed towards federal campaigns in 1960 (by the still active party 'machines')

1960 data have been estimated from records of the Clerk of the House of Representatives (now filed in the National Archives). A good summary of the 1960 data is provided by Alexander (1962). Much of the state committee data was missing and the total was estimated by a means used by Heard (1960: 372). The GNP price deflator was used to calculate 1996 constant dollars.

was comparable to soft money in 1996, we could add another $70 million to the 1960 estimates of total party spending. But even with this addition, total party expenditures would have doubled per hundred thousand eligible voters over the period (from $2289 to $4530).

One thing that has not changed much is the source of funds for the major parties (Sorauf and Wilson 1994). In 1960, 1980, and 1996 the great bulk of party funds were raised from individual donations. In all probability, the parties depended more on large donations from wealthy people in the 1960s, although the advent of 'soft money' in the 1990s may have allowed the wealthy to regain prominence in the 1990s. After 1960, first the Republicans and then the Democrats added direct mail solicitation of small individual donations as a major source of funds. The political action committees (PACs) of interest groups accounted for a small portion of party funds (about 5 per cent in 1996), although corporate and labour organizations also made substantial direct donations to soft money accounts in the 1990s. Organizational donations may also have played a significant role in party finance at the state and local level in 1960.

Public money also played a role in party finance. In 1996, the major parties received some $12 million to help finance their national conventions (in addition to lavish support by private donors and interest groups). Some state and local parties also received public funds under state-level public financing and benefited from tax deductions for party donations. In the 1960s and 1980s, federal tax deductions, now repealed, constituted a further source of public subsidy to parties. After 1976, the major role for public money lay in the financing of presidential campaigns; in 1996 this involved a $61.8 million grant to the Democratic and Republican candidates, and a $29 million subsidy to Ross Perot's Reform Party. In fact, the financial gains of the major party organizations resulted in part from having the burden of presidential campaigns lifted from their shoulders after 1976 (Bibby 1994: 23).

What did all this new money buy? For one thing, it purchased highly professional campaign organizations (Pomper 1971). One measure of such professionalism is the number of paid staff, estimates of which are given in Table 11.6 for the three national party organizations and all state party committees combined.[7] National and state committees had already acquired considerable paid staff by 1960, and these levels of staffing have been maintained or increased since then. Note, however, that the pattern of change is uneven, reflecting in part the fluctuating fortunes of particular committees. In addition, two trends are at odds in these data. On

---

[7] The data on paid staff come from numerous sources. The author would like to thank Robin Kolodny and John Bibby for making available data relevant to the 1960s; also consulted were Katz and Mair (1992) and Cotter and Hennessey (1964). The author would also like to thank Paul Herrnson for help with data at the federal level for 1980; Herrnson (1988) was also consulted. The 1980 state-level staff figure was estimated from data collected by Cotter *et al.* (1984). The 1996 data come from a telephone survey of national and state party committees conducted by the Bliss Institute at the University of Akron.

TABLE 11.6. *Major party paid staff in the USA,*
selected years

	1960	1980	1996
Democrats			
DNC	375	40	264
DNSC	3	26	38
DCCC	NA	20	64
State committees	164	178	228
Total	—	264	594
Republicans			
RNC	352	350	271
RNSC	3	40	150
RNCC	35	30	64
State committees	498	592	333
Total	888	1012	818

Sources: See text and fn. 7 for details.

the one hand, increased expenditures have allowed for more staff. But on the other hand, modern technology has reduced the need for staff. In all probability, the paid staffs of today are more productive than their counterparts in 1960 and even 1980. The major parties have also become employers and organizers of campaign consultants who work for their party's candidates. Contrary to expectations, campaign consultants by and large operate within the context of one of the major parties, although they are usually answerable to candidates rather than party leaders (Kolodny and Logan 1998).

The well-financed and professionalized federal and state party organizations of today perform many of the same tasks as their counterparts in the 1960s, including voter registration and mobilization drives (Herrnson 1994). By the 1990s, these traditional programmes had become quite sophisticated, integrating national, state, and local organizations in highly effective 'coordinated campaigns' on behalf of the party's slate of candidates (Bibby 1998*b*). However, the biggest area of increase has been the provision of services to the parties' candidates. Some of this help was in the form of direct financial aid to candidates, but the greater portion came in the form of 'in-kind' services: technical training and assistance, polling, opposition research, and indirect 'coordinated' expenditures (Herrnson 1988, 1995; Aldrich 1995). By the mid-1990s, court rulings allowed major party committees to expend essentially unlimited sums in the form of 'independent' and 'issue advocacy' advertising on behalf of their candidates (Herrnson and Dwyre 1998). Overall, these new resources have allowed the major parties to reduce their organizational fragmentation somewhat. Indeed, John Bibby (1998*c*) describes major party activity as consisting of: '*integrated networks of national–state party units*, allied groups and issue-oriented activists' (emphasis added).

TABLE 11.7. *Estimates of party 'membership' in the USA, selected years*

	1960			1980			1996		
	All	Dem	Rep	All	Dem	Rep	All	Dem	Rep
Financial donors to									
Parties	11.6	4.0	7.1	3.6	0.8	2.8	6.3	2.7	3.4
Candidates	—	—	—	5.9	2.1	3.6	5.5	1.4	3.2
Groups	—	—	—	6.7	3.6	2.6	5.6	2.5	2.5
Meeting attenders	8.3	3.2	4.7	7.5	3.5	3.5	6.1	2.3	3.5
Campaign workers	5.7	2.0	3.2	3.6	1.3	1.2	2.8	1.5	1.3

Source: National Election Studies.

What has happened to the traditional, local party work forces? The patronage-based cadres of local party workers have declined since 1960, a trend well underway before then (Ware 1985). These workers have been partially replaced by paid professionals and the capital-intensive campaign technologies they direct, and partly by ideologically oriented volunteer activists (Frantzich 1989). Table 11.7 offers some evidence on the number of volunteer activists since 1960 using National Election Study data. Each of these categories of activists can be thought of as proxies for 'party membership' in the absence of formal party membership in the United States.[8] Measuring party 'members' this way is problematic since different survey questions have been asked at different times, reflecting changes in the variety of political activity. The figures in italics in Table 11.7 report new categories of political activism alongside the most comparable questions asked across the years.

The largest category of activists throughout has been financial donors. In 1960, about one-tenth of the population reported making a donation to a party; by 1980 this figure had fallen to less than one-twentieth and rose again in 1996 to about one-sixteenth. However, roughly one-tenth of the population reported giving a donation to a candidate or an issue group in 1996, most of which were probably linked to the major parties. If combined with those who are explicit party donors, the 1996 figure is roughly equal to the proportion who were party donors in 1960 (11.8 to 11.6, respectively). Since the 1960s data lacked questions on candidate and group donations, it is difficult to tell for sure if there has been an increase in contributing over the past forty years, although many scholars believe there has been (Verba *et al.* 1995). The Republicans had an edge in donors in 1960, which they maintained in 1996, albeit by a smaller margin.

---

[8] The closest thing to formal party membership in the United States is the declaration of party during voter registration. However, this practice has always varied from state to state, and has become much less common in recent decades. Social clubs loosely affiliated with the major parties sometimes have formal membership requirements, which is one source of the 'group membership' reported in Table 11.7.

TABLE 11.8. *Total expenditures by major US parties,*
House candidates, and PACs, selected years

	1960	1980	1996
Major parties	105,000	130,500	622,843
House candidates	36,900	196,800	500,000
PACs	13,352	222,800	429,800

Note: All figures are in thousands of US dollars, constant at 1996 prices.

Source: See text and fn. 6 for details.

Another way of measuring 'membership' activism is to gauge attendance at political meetings and rallies, many of which are sponsored by the major parties. Such 'attenders' accounted for about one-twelfth of the population in 1960 and declined steadily to one-sixteenth in 1996. Similarly, the numbers engaged in campaign work for a party or candidate declined even more sharply over the period, from about one-sixteenth to one-thirtieth of the adult population. Overall, membership of all kinds of 'political groups' seems to have fallen since 1960, but especially that of party-related groups. For instance, NES data suggest that membership of single-issue groups was twice as high as that of party groups in 1996, whereas the contrary was true in 1964.

While all these measures of party 'membership' must be interpreted with caution, it appears that the activist corps associated with the major parties has remained roughly the same size over the period under consideration. However, there have been major changes in its composition. Traditional party activists have declined in number and been replaced by candidate and interest group activists, many of whom are clearly allied with, but not formally part of, the major party organizations. These changes reflect, in part, the increased use of technology and the effects of expanded party finance. Perhaps in order to fund the more candidate-centred and capital-intensive forms of politics which prevail today, party 'membership' is more likely to consist of relatively passive financial donating.

Thus, the major parties have gained organizational strength since 1960 and maintained their 'memberships' as they have adapted to an increasingly competitive environment. It is important, however, to put these data in perspective. Table 11.8 compares the aggregate level of party spending with the aggregate spending of candidates for the House of Representatives and interest group PACs for 1960, 1980, and 1996 (in real terms). Once again, the data for 1960 must be viewed with caution because of poor reporting.[9] In addition, these figures overlap somewhat, with the party funds including donations to candidates and candidate spending

---

[9] As with Table 11.5, the 1980 and 1996 data come from the Federal Election Commission, and the 1960 data were estimated from documents filed with the Clerk of the House of Representatives and kept in the National Archives; see fn. 6 on estimation method.

TABLE 11.9. *Minor parties and candidates in the USA,
selected years*

	1960	1980	1996
Minor parties	12	38	53
Candidates			
Presidential	5	18	19
Senatorial	21	54	81
Congressional	96	264	450

Source: Congressional Quarterly Almanac, 1960, 1980, 1996.

donations from parties and PACs. Nevertheless, these aggregates provide a sense of the changed environment in which party organizations operated over the period. Between 1960 and 1996, the expenditures of major party candidates for the House of Representatives expanded almost fourteen-fold and PAC expenditures some 33 times. Even if one assumes that the 1960 figures grossly underestimate candidate and PAC expenditures, these increases are still impressive. By contrast, aggregate party expenditures increased just six-fold. Looked at another way, House candidate expenditures were a little over one-third of party expenditures in 1960, but rose to four-fifths by 1996. Comparable figures for PACs are about one-sixth in 1960 and two-thirds in 1996. It is worth noting that both House candidate and PAC expenditures already exceeded party expenditures by 1980. Thus, major parties have become more substantial organizations since 1960, but they have faced stiffer competition from other kinds of organization as well.

Table 11.9 confirms this picture by reviewing a modest, but increasing source of competition for the major parties: minor party and independent candidates.[10] The number of separate parties on the federal ballot showed a more than four-fold increase over the period, and there were similar gains in presidential and congressional candidacies. These changes were led by significant 'third party' presidential forays in 1968, 1980, 1992, and 1996 (refer again to Table 11.1). Indeed, Ross Perot and his Reform Party in the 1990s represent the most successful challenge to the two-party system since the birth of the modern Republican Party in the 1850s. Minor parties also made similar in-roads at state-level, where minor party and 'independent' governors have been elected in a few states in the 1990s (Collet and Hansen 1996).

These minor parties and independent candidates were a diverse lot ideologically, running the gamut from radical to reactionary (Berg 1998). Although many of these 'parties' were simply extensions of a single candidacy and otherwise poorly organized, they did pose an additional challenge to the major parties. If nothing else, these efforts, like the growth of candidate organizations and PACs, reflect some

---

[10] These data were collected from national election reports in the 1960, 1980, and 1996 *Congressional Quarterly Almanac* (Washington, DC: CQ Press).

underlying support for alternatives to the two-party system, and more importantly, dissatisfaction with the functioning of the major parties. Indeed, previous periods of minor party activity have been associated with significant alterations in the two-party system (Rosenstone *et al.* 1996).

Thus, the major party organizations have gained resources and retained a large activist corps since 1960, adapting with some success to candidate-centred politics. All of these factors appear to have modestly reduced the fragmentation of the major party organizations, during a period when the comprehensiveness of the system lessened somewhat at the level of the mass public. So, the 'revivalists' make an important point: party organizations have achieved a more significant role in national politics. But one must be careful not to overstate the importance of these trends, since new kinds of fragmentation have appeared as well.

THE SYSTEMIC FUNCTIONALITY OF AMERICAN PARTIES

Measures of popular legitimacy and organizational strength are of interest to scholars because of what they reveal about the functionality of the party system since 1960. Assessing functionality depends, of course, on what functions one expects political parties to perform (Ranney 1963). Here we consider four sets of functions typically assigned to parties: governance and political recruitment; the articulation and aggregation of interests; political communication and education; and fostering political participation. 'Declinists' argue that the party system has become less functional because it is less comprehensive, especially in the elec-torate, and they point to failures in governance and decline in voter turnout. In contrast, 'revivalists' believe the parties have become more functional because of their increasing organizational resources and ideological coherence; they focus especially on the aggregation and articulation of interests.

Governance and political recruitment

We can ask three basic questions about party-in-government since 1960. First, to what extent does party government take place in the United States? Second, do the major parties make a difference to the pattern of government outputs? And third, how effective is party-in-government? The answer to the first question is straightforward: party government has been rare since 1960. Recall from Table 11.1 that unified party control of the federal government occurred only 40 per cent of the time over this period. So a minimal condition for party government has only occasionally been met at the federal level, not to mention a comparable lack of unity between the federal and state governments or within state governments.

A closer look at common criteria for party government adds further support for this judgement (Katz 1986: 43). Although nearly all federal and state elected offi-cials were chosen in partisan elections over the period, another minimal condition for party government, an increasing number acted independently of their party organizations and some were only nominal members of the parties whose labels they acquired (White and Mileur 1992). This situation was especially noticeable when it came to staffing the government and policy making: government positions flowed most directly from electoral success and less from party support. Finally, policy rarely emanated exclusively from party organizations themselves, arising instead from a multiplicity of other sources (Beck 1997: 283–383; Goldman 1994). The decline in the popular legitimacy of the party system did not cause this situation, but it may well have exacerbated it.

However, if party government has rarely been approximated, it must be noted that the United States has had highly *partisan* government over this period (Strahan 1998). The comprehensiveness of the party system has meant that elections, government staffing, and policy making ultimately flow through the major party vessels, even if the impetus for such decisions arises from non-party sources. This point can be seen most clearly with regard to the recruitment of public officials. The most important factor involved in the recruitment of office-seekers is the ambition of the office-seekers themselves (Fowler and McClure 1989), though interest groups and social movements also play important roles (Rozell and Wilcox 1999: 35–44). However, party leaders are often actors in candidate recruitment, either by tapping candidates directly or by participating in primary campaigns. Much the same can be said about recruitment to other government positions. Cabinet officials and other administrative personnel (Mackenzie 1998) and judges are recruited from a wide variety of sources (Gitelson *et al.* 1984: 296–301). However, relatively few such appointments cross party lines and past party activity is an important factor (Beck 1997: 349–50). The extension of civil service to federal government workers has reduced the role of party patronage in staffing, but it has not disappeared (Beck 1997: 107–11).

A similar pattern occurs for policy making. Interest groups, social movements, and public bureaucracies have been important sources of public policy proposals independent of party organizations (West and Loomis 1999). The growth of these organizations in the postwar period, often in conjunction with one another, has helped produce a high degree of bipartisan and even non-partisan policy making in many areas. Numerous interest groups and many government agencies are able to bypass the party politics, assisted by the news media and office-holders who behave as 'policy entrepreneurs' (Wright 1996). Certainly, the major party organizations and their leaders exercise very little direct control over the behaviour of their office-holders in enacting policy (Brady and Buckley 1998).

Nonetheless, most policy initiatives tend to flow through the major parties on the way to enactment (Sinclair 1998). The largest and most active interest groups and social movements have strong party preferences and tend to work with one or another of the major parties (Cigler 1993; Reichley 1992). The longstanding alliance between organized labour and the Democratic Party, and manufacturing interests and the Republicans are good examples of the former; the linkage of feminists with the Democrats and Christian conservatives with the Republicans are good examples of the latter. Many of these interest groups speak for elements of the bureaucracy even if the public agencies are not directly involved in party politics. After all, the Democrats tend to be the party of 'activist government' and Republicans the party of 'limited government,' postures that have direct implications for public employees. Indeed, Democrats are to some measure a party of teachers and social workers, while the Republicans are the party of soldiers and policemen. Finally, party organizations are sometimes a source of policy proposals in their own right, via party platforms and the programmes of their presidents and congressional leaders.

In all probability, these independent sources for the recruitment of public officials and policy proposals are more potent now than they were in the 1960s (Fiorina 1992). After all, candidate-centred politics is more developed, interest groups are more numerous and better organized, and public bureaucracies are more numerous and larger. But all these trends were well underway in the 1960s, so the changes over the period under discussion may be more of degree than of kind (Patterson 1996). Here, too, the decline of popular legitimacy may have exacerbated an existing situation.

It is important to note, however, that the major parties have played a crucial role in *organizing* the context of politics and government during this period (Corrado 1996; Sinclair 1998). They have proved to be extremely useful forums for coalition-building in the electorate and in government, for debate among party elites, and for the choosing of leaders among office-seekers. In fact, the increased competitiveness of the political system may have made the major parties even more valuable in this regard (Aldrich 1995). In this sense, the party system provides the context for politics and government even if party leaders exercise little direct control over personnel, policy, or partisan elites.

Given this ambiguous role of parties as *organizers* but not *controllers* of government, one might ask: do parties make a difference to government outputs? Many scholars would argue that they did in the 1960s and continue to do so, with partisanship being the single best predictor of the behaviour of government officials and congressional representatives (Clausen 1972; Shaffer 1982). The increased organizational strength and ideological coherence of the major parties may have contributed to these trends.

Table 11.10 provides some evidence on this point by comparing roll-call voting in the 86th (1959–60), 97th (1979–80), and 104th (1995–96) Congresses for the Senate and House. The political situation was similar for the first and last points because one party controlled the White House (Republicans 1959–60 and Democrats in 1995–96) and the other party the Congress, and the congressional party had just scored a major electoral victory (the Democrats in 1958 and the Republicans in 1994). The intermediate point of 1979–80 represents a rare opportunity for 'party government', when the Democrats controlled both the federal executive and legislative branches.

TABLE 11.10. *Party voting and presidential support in the US Congress, selected years*

	1959–60	1979–80	1995–96
'Party unity' votes			
Senate			
% of all roll-call votes	42	46	67
Partisan votes as % of all votes			
Democrats	27	27	56
Republicans	29	30	60
House			
% of all roll-call votes	53	43	67
Partisan votes as % of all votes			
Democrats	38	29	54
Republicans	39	31	60
Presidential support			
Senate			
Democrats	40	65	82
Republicans	69	46	33
House			
Democrats	42	64	75
Republicans	64	54	30

Note: A 'party unity' vote is defined as one in which a majority of one congressional party opposes a majority of the other congressional party.

Source: Congressional Quarterly Almanac, 1961, 1981, 1996.

The first part of the table looks at 'party unity' votes calculated by *Congressional Quarterly* (legislative votes where a majority of one party opposed the majority of the other).[11] The table shows that the House was more partisan in 1960, about the same as the Senate in 1980, and much more so by 1996. The second part of the table shows that, throughout, Democrats and Republicans by and large supported their presidents' legislative proposals, and more so by the end of the period. There was a twenty-point gap between Democrats and Republicans at the end of the Eisenhower era, and the gap doubled by the end of Clinton's first term. The Carter era votes fall in between, with Democrats giving more support to their president than did the Republicans.

A similar pattern holds with respect to major party platforms. Contrary to the conventional wisdom, these platforms regularly contain meaningful policy statements (David 1971; Patterson 1996). These policy statements differentiate the major parties from each other (Budge 1993; Budge and Keman 1990). Even more importantly, the parties have generally made good on their promises, with roughly

[11] These data were collected from the 1960, 1980, and 1996 *Congressional Quarterly Almanac* (Washington, DC: CQ Press) and are based on yearly studies of congressional roll-call votes performed by *Congressional Quarterly*.

seven out of ten specific pledges fulfilled in one way or another (Pomper and Leder-man 1980). These differences have persisted in the 1990s and have been extended by congressional party programmes such as *Contract with America* (Republicans) and *Families First Agenda* (Democrats). Much the same can be said about presi-dential programmes over the period (Fishel 1985; Krukones 1984; Patterson 1996). These trends have led Gerald Pomper to argue, provocatively, that the United States is moving towards a system of 'parliamentary government' (Pomper 1998).

In addition, similar patterns hold for major party activists, the party 'member-ship' described in Table 11.7. Surveys of national party delegates since the 1950s have found that Democratic and Republican national convention delegates differ systematically on ideology, with the former tending to be more liberal and the latter more conservative on a range of issues (McCloskey *et al.* 1960; Kirkpatrick 1976; Jackson *et al.* 1982). These patterns hold for other activists, including campaign contributors, interest group members, and social movement activists (Green and Guth 1991; Lerner *et al.* 1996). Moreover, this ideological distance between the major party activists has persisted into the contemporary era (Jackson and Clayton 1996; Green *et al.* 1998).

Thus, despite the lack of party government in the United States, there have been persistent differences between the Democratic and Republican party office-holders and activists and these have intensified since 1960. Table 11.11 presents evidence from the National Election Studies that the mass public perceived these changes as well. This is clear, for instance, in the number of respondents claiming to notice 'important differences between the parties.' While such a figure is likely to fluctuate in a contingent fashion, it has not dropped below 50 per cent.

Of course, the policy differentiation of 'partisan' government is not regarded as adequate by everyone. Simply put, many scholars believe the major parties could, and should, make a much bigger and more systematic difference to government policy outputs (White 1995). And many observers believe the American party sys-tem is not particularly effective at managing 'separated' government (Jones 1997;

TABLE 11.11. *Public perceptions of major party issue positions in the USA, selected years*

	1960	1980	1996
There are important differences between the major parties	53.7	63.3	67.0
The Republican Party is more conservative than the Democrats	56.7	67.2	67.8
One or the other party is 'better' on policy	75.3	79.0	82.8

Note: All figures are percentages.

Source: National Election Studies, 1960, 1996.

Thurber 1991). Of course, the parties were seen as a source of ineffective government in the 1960s as well as the 1990s (Burns 1963), so such differences may also be more of degree than kind. Some scholars argue that divided governing does not prevent major policy accomplishments, though even they concede that the American system is inefficient (Mayhew 1991). If a loss of popular legitimacy has contributed to the ineffectiveness of party-in-government, the greater organizational strength and ideological coherence has probably had the opposite effect.

Interest articulation and aggregation

The absence of party government combined with often intense partisanship has prompted much criticism of the ability of the major parties to articulate and aggregate interests. It is common, for instance, to attack the major parties for not representing important groups in society, especially the economically underprivileged and culturally excluded (Reiter 1987). However, the opposite criticism is also common, namely that the parties are all too representative, serving as vehicles for the representation of a myriad of 'special interests' rather than broad consensus positions (Berry and Schildkraut 1998). The organizational fragmentation of the major parties, which renders them highly 'permeable' to outside interests, means that both criticisms can be true at the same time (Epstein 1986). American interest groups and social movements probably do a better job of articulating specific interests than the major parties, given the constraints of the two-party system. But as noted above, these groups frequently seek recognition for their interests in party politics. Some scholars take the rise of minor parties and even candidate-centred politics itself as evidence of the limited ability of the major parties to articulate important interests; the evidence in Table 11.4 on alternatives to the two-party system certainly suggests that many Americans are also sceptical of the major parties on this score.

Generally speaking, the major parties are seen as much better at aggregating interests than articulating them (Bibby 1997). American political institutions tend to create 'artificial majorities', which perforce combine disparate interests into winning combinations. These tendencies are commonly understood to encourage the building of broad-based coalitions with moderate tendencies on most issues. Indeed, the consensus-building capacities of the two-party system are regularly cited as one of its principal virtues, and in practice, the major parties and their candidates are frequently criticized for not 'moving toward the centre' in campaigns. Of course, such centrist tendencies are also targets of criticism, ranging from advocates of 'responsible' parties to advocates of multipartism (see Schramm and Wilson 1993).

Thus, the American party system has a mixed record on these matters, with stronger capacity to aggregate interests and a somewhat weaker capability to articulate interests. Table 11.12 offers a rough assessment of these tendencies

TABLE 11.12. *Ideology of major party identifiers in the USA, selected years*

Self-identified ideology	1964		1980		1996	
	Dems	Reps	Dems	Reps	Dems	Reps
Liberal	31	19	29	10	41	8
Moderate	49	39	45	29	35	23
Conservative	21	42	26	60	25	70

Note: All figures are percentages, totalling 100 per cent down the columns.

Source: National Election Studies 1964, 1980, 1996.

by looking at the ideological composition of party identifiers from 1964 to 1996 using National Election study data. For 1980 and 1996, self-identified 'liberals,' 'moderates,' and 'conservatives' are listed for Democratic and Republican identifiers in the mass public; for 1964, ideological self-identification was estimated from feeling thermometers for 'liberals' and 'conservatives.'[12] The first thing to note about these data is the ideological diversity of the major party identifiers, especially the Democrats. For instance, in 1964 one-fifth of Democrats identified themselves as conservative, while a similar proportion of Republicans claimed to be liberals. Indeed, the proportion of conservative Democrats expanded to one-quarter in 1980 and 1996; moderates were common in all years as well. Given the dominant position of the Democrats over most of the period in question, it is not surprising that their identifiers would be more diverse. Nonetheless, these data reveal the capacity of the major parties to aggregate a range of quite diverse interests and ideological perspectives.

That said, a second notable feature of the table is the increased ideological polarization it reveals over time, especially among Republicans (Abramowitz and Saunders 1998). Thus, the proportion of Republican identifiers claiming to be conservative rose from one-fifth in 1964 to three-quarters in 1996. The Democrats show a more modest increase in the number of liberals among their ranks (from one-third to two-fifths) over the same period. In short, the Republicans have become less effective than the Democrats over time in aggregating a diverse coalition of interests and ideological perspectives.

Taken together, this rough evidence illustrates the mixed capacity of the two-party system to aggregate and articulate interests. These capacities have most probably not changed much over the period in question, despite clear changes in the political content of major party coalitions. Indeed, the major parties appear to be capable of building both broad-based and issue-based coalitions under the right circumstances, and as we have seen, the results of such coalitions can be translated into public policy if the conditions are right (Patterson 1996). However,

---

[12] In all years, Democratic and Republican partisans include the respective partisan 'leaners.'

the major party organizations do not control either these coalition-building or coalition-translating processes to any great degree, serving instead as the context in which such things take place. As David Mayhew puts it, American parties are more 'policy factions' than 'governing parties' (Mayhew 1991: 199).

Political communication and education

One area of significant change since 1960 has been the major parties' role in political communication and education. Historians report that the major parties dominated communication with the voters in the nineteenth century, and even public media, such as newspapers, were largely associated with political parties (McGerr 1986). The major parties are also given credit for socializing millions of immigrants into American politics in the late nineteenth and early twentieth century (Beck 1997: 24). Much of this effort has been replaced by the impact of non-partisan news media, in the case of political communication, and by public-sector schools and voluntary associations, in the case of civic education. These changes have forced party messages of both sorts to flow through channels largely outside the direct control of the major party organizations. Many scholars believe these changes have reduced both the legitimacy and effectiveness of the major parties (Goldman 1994). In this respect, television is seen as especially problematic.

Table 11.13 presents evidence on the public's sources of information during campaigns using NES data. The entries are self-reported impressions of the importance of various media and contact by party workers. Television is by far the most common source of campaign information over the period, even in the 1960s, followed by newspapers, radio, and magazines. Party contact lags far behind all these sources in all years, and is roughly three times less common than television. Interestingly, though, the reported use of all media sources of information has declined over the period (especially newspapers), whereas reported party contact has

TABLE 11.13. *Sources of campaign information in the USA, selected years*

	1964	1980	1996
Television	87.5	85.9	76.1
Newspapers	80.0	70.9	58.3
Radio	43.2	46.9	41.1
Magazines	42.3	34.6	35.4
Party contact	22.6	24.4	29.3

Note: All figures are percentages of respondents reporting having received campaign information from various media and party sources.

Source: National Election Studies 1964, 1980, 1996.

actually increased somewhat. Clearly, party messages must travel largely through non-partisan media, but this situation was as much the case in 1960 as in 1996.

In response to these changes, the major parties have developed new strategies for communication (Herrnson *et al.* 1996). Foremost among these has been the capacity to manage relations with journalists, along with the acquisition of public relations, advertising, and media production skills. Mass party publications have been replaced by communication via the public media, including most recently cable television, satellite transmission, and the Internet. These techniques have also been applied to internal party communications, ranging from connecting party officials to one another to stirring debate among party activists (Berkowitz and Lilienthal 1996). While there are surely costs to such a situation, it is also true that the range and capacities of modern communication media give skilful partisans more ways to reach the public.

Encouraging political participation

How well does the two-party system foster public participation in politics and how has this changed over the last forty years? Table 11.14 looks at three key measures of participation: voter turnout in presidential elections, turnout in presidential primaries, and activity beyond voting. These data show a mixed pattern over the period.

The evidence on voter turnout is striking (Beck 1997: ch. 8). Participation in presidential elections has declined markedly, from just under two-thirds of the electorate in 1960 to less than one-half in 1996. The decline occurred steadily over the period, with only a few exceptions, such as a modest increase in 1992 (largely due to the impact of the Perot campaign). Turnout in non-presidential elections is typically much lower. This steady decline in voter participation is puzzling because the social and political factors usually associated with turning out have increased, including liberalization of voter registration laws, increasing levels of education, and the expansion of political competition (Brody 1978).

Most observers find the decline in turnout to be deeply troubling, raising serious questions about the legitimacy of the political system. A number of explanations for turnout decline have been advanced, ranging from the decay of 'social

TABLE 11.14. *Electoral participation in the USA,*
selected years

	1960s	1980s	1990s
Presidential vote turnout	64.0	59.2	49.1
Presidential primary vote	27.4	36.8	28.5
At least one act beyond voting	36.8	32.0	36.6

Sources: Official statistics; National Election Studies, 1960, 1968, 1980, 1992, and 1996.

capital' in a highly mobile society to the failure of campaigns to address important issues and the inadequacies of modern campaign techniques and the news media (see Teixeira 1992). Not surprisingly, declinists see the loss of party identification and party vitality as a source of low turnout, while revivalists argue that the greater resources of party organizations may have counteracted the cause of turnout decline, preventing it from decreasing still further.

The remaining data in Table 11.14 add another dimension to the situation. Voting in presidential primaries has remained roughly constant over the period, despite the increase in the number and intensity of primary contests. Likewise, the percentage of the population claiming to have engaged in at least one political act beyond voting has also remained roughly constant over the period. These patterns fit our estimates of party 'membership' in Table 11.7, which also showed a rough parity between 1960 and 1996. So, in the face of declining voter turnout, other forms of party-related participation appear to have remained more or less constant.

It seems probable that American politics has become more 'elitist' since 1960 (Verba *et al.* 1995). A substantial body of research suggests an increase in the frequency of political activities that require personal resources, such as money, time, and skill. Campaign contributing is a case in point, but these trends extend also to contacting public officials, participating in interest groups, and engaging in protest activities. These kinds of activities may make the political system more responsive to small segments of the activist corps rather than to larger aggregations of the electorate.

These trends have affected the major parties as well. As we noted above, much of this activity is directed at party politics, especially activity associated with individual candidates, interest groups, and social movements (Shafer 1998). The internal life of the major political parties has certainly become more participatory since 1960. The most important change here has been the reform of major party rules, especially those concerning the selection of delegates to national party conventions. Beginning with the Democrats in 1972 and eventually extending to the Republicans, internal party decision-making has been opened to a wider range of participants. Some of the changes require that party officials and delegates be selected via primaries and according to proportional representation; other changes mandate the inclusion of women, racial minorities, and other groups by means of quotas (Beck 1997: 219–24).

While party reform has increased the scope and intensity of participation in party affairs, it is not clear that it has made the major parties more representative of their mass identifiers or the public at large. Party activists in both parties are drawn from upper-status groups, displaying high levels of education and income. In addition, they are also more ideological and intense in their issue positions than rank-and-file party members. Thus, heightened participation does not necessarily enhance the representativeness of parties, a development which has generated a long-running debate among party scholars over the efficacy of party reform. On the one hand, party reform has helped produce more legitimate and coherent parties

(Crotty 1983), but on the other hand, it may have alienated large segments of the voting public (Polsby 1983). Whatever the final verdict, the major parties are certainly vehicles for a greater level of activism in the 1990s compared to the 1960s.

CONCLUSIONS

What can we conclude about the changes in the American party system since 1960 and the impact of these changes on the systemic functionality of the parties? First, the two-party system has become slightly less comprehensive, especially with regard to its major protagonists' popular legitimacy. This decline has contributed to the lack of party government, ineffective politics, and a sharp drop in electoral participation. At the same time, the system has become somewhat less fragmented due to increased organizational resources and greater ideological coherence among office-holders and party elites. These gains have contributed to increased partisanship in government, clearer distinctions between the parties, and enhanced participation within the major parties themselves. So, both party declinists and revivalists have valid points to make, but neither position can be sustained without concessions to the other point of view.

Furthermore, these changes in the party system have not altered its basic character, for good and ill. On a positive note, the major parties are still critical vessels through which the politics of the nation flows; on a negative note, these vessels do not guarantee a high degree of coherence in politics or government. The major parties organize the context of politics and government, but exercise little direct control over the inputs and outputs of government, making true party government rare. Of course, party government has long been rare in the United States, and is hardly less so today than in the 1960s. Instead, American government is highly partisan, more than in 1960, and often in constructive ways.

In sum, then, we can conclude that the American party system is still functional after four turbulent decades and that the major parties have found ways to adapt to a raft of major social, technological, and political changes. It is also true that American party politics could function much better than it does: despite the constraints of the American constitution, the major parties could offer more coherent programmes, govern more effectively, attract more public support, and especially, mobilize greater electoral participation. Indeed, it is the continuing functionality of party politics that makes further improvements both possible and desirable.

REFERENCES

Abramowitz, A. I. and Saunders, U. L. (1998). 'Ideological realignment in the U.S. electorate'. *Journal of Politics* 60: 634–52.

Agranoff, R. (1972) *The New Style in Election Campaigns* (Boston: Holbrook).

Aldrich, J. H. (1995) *Why Parties? The Origin and Transformation of Party Politics in America* (Chicago: University of Chicago Press).

Alexander, H. (1962) *Financing the 1960 Election* (Princeton, NJ: Citizens' Research Foundation).

Baer, D. L. and Bositis, D. A. (1988) *Elite Cadres and Party Coalitions* (New York: Greenwood).

Bass, H. J. (1998) 'Partisan rules, 1946–1996', in Bryon E. Shafer (ed.) *Partisan Approaches to Postwar American Politics* (New York: Chatham House), pp. 220–71.

Beck, P. A. (1997) *Party Politics in America*, 8th edn (New York: Longman).

——— (1998) 'The changing American party coalitions', in John C. Green and Daniel M. Shea (eds) *The State of the Parties*, 3rd edn (Lanham, MD: Rowman & Littlefield).

Bennett, W. L. (1991) *The Governing Crisis* (New York: St. Martin's Press).

Berg, J. (1998) 'Beyond a third party: the other minor parties in the 1996 elections', in John C. Green and Daniel M. Shea (eds) *The State of the Parties*, 3rd edn (Lanham, MD: Rowman & Littlefield).

Berkowitz, L. and Lilienthal, S. (1996) 'A tale of two parties: National Committee policy making, 1992 and 1994', in John C. Green and Daniel M. Shea (eds) *The State of the Parties*, 2nd edn (Lanham, MD: Rowman & Littlefield), pp. 273–88.

Berry, J. M. and Schildkraut, D. (1998) 'Citizen groups, political parties and electoral coalitions', in Anne N. Costain and Andrew S. McFarland (eds) *Social Movements and American Political Institutions* (Lanham, MD: Rowman & Littlefield).

Bibby, J. F. (1994) 'Party leadership, the Bliss model, and the development of the Republican National Committee', in J. C. Green (ed.) *Politics, Professionalism and Power* (Lanham, MD: University Press of America), 19–33.

——— (1997) 'In defense of the two-party system', in Paul S. Herrnson and John C. Green (eds) *Multiparty Politics in America* (Lanham, MD: Rowman & Littlefield).

——— (1998*a*) 'Party organizations, 1946–1996', in Bryon E. Shafer (ed.) *Partisan Approaches to Postwar American Politics* (New York: Chatham House), pp. 142–85.

——— (1998*b*) 'State party organizations: coping and adapting to candidate-centered politics and nationalization', in L. Sandy Maisel (ed.) *The Parties Respond* (Boulder, CO.: Westview), 123–49.

——— (1998*c*) 'Party networks: national-state integration, allied groups and issue activists', in John C. Green and Daniel M. Shea (eds) *The State of the Parties*, 3rd edn (Lanham, MD: Rowman & Littlefield).

——— and Holbrook, T. M. (1995) 'Parties and elections', in Virginia Gray and Herbert Jacob (eds) *Politics in the American States* (Washington, DC: Congressional Quarterly).

Brady, D. W. (1988) *Critical Elections and Congressional Policy Making* (Stanford: Stanford University Press).

——— and Buckley, K. Z. (1998) 'Coalitions and policy in the U.S. Congress: lessons from the 103rd and 104th Congresses', in L. Sandy Maisel (ed.) *The Parties Respond*, 3rd edn (Boulder, CO: Westview Press), pp. 316–40.

Broder, D. S. (1971) *The Party's Over: The Failure of Politics in America* (New York: Harper & Row).

Brody, R. A. (1978) 'The puzzle of participation in America', in A. King (ed.) *The New American Political System* (Washington, DC: American Enterprise Institute), 287–324.

Budge, I. (1993) 'Parties, programs and policies: a comparative and theoretical perspective'. *American Review of Politics* 14: 696.

Budge, I. and Keman, H. (1990) *Parties and Democracy* (Oxford: Oxford University Press).

Burnham, W. D. (1970) *Critical Elections and the Mainsprings of American Politics* (New York: Norton).

—— (1975) 'American Politics in the 1970s: Beyond party', in W. N. Chalmers and W. D. Burnham (eds.) *The American Party Systems* (New York: Oxford University Press), 308–57.

Burns, J. M. (1963) *The Deadlock of Democracy* (Englewood Cliffs, NJ: Prentice Hall).

Cain, B., Ferejohn, J., and Fiorina, M. (1987) *The Personal Vote* (Cambridge, Mass.: Harvard University Press).

Cigler, A. J. (1993) 'Political parties and interest groups: competitors, collaborators and uneasy allies', in Eric M. Uslaner (ed.) *American Political Parties* (Itasca, IL: Peacock Publishers), pp. 407–33.

Clausen, A. (1972) *How Congressmen Decide* (New York: St. Martin's Press).

Coleman, J. J. (1994) 'The resurgence of party organization? A dissent from the new orthodoxy', in John C. Green and Daniel M. Shea (eds) *The State of the Parties* (Lanham, MD: Rowman & Littlefield), pp. 311–28.

Collett, C. and Hansen, J. (1996) 'Minor parties and candidates in sub-presidential elections', in Daniel M. Shea and John C. Green (eds) *The State of the Parties* (Lanham, MD: Rowman & Littlefield), pp. 239–55.

Corrado, A. (1996) 'The politics of cohesion: the role of the National Party Committees in the 1992 election', in John C. Green and Daniel M. Shea (eds) *The State of the Parties*, 2nd edn (Lanham, MD: Rowman & Littlefield), pp. 63–83.

—— (1997) 'Financing the 1996 Elections', in Gerald M. Pomper (eds) *The Election of 1996* (Chatham, N.J.: Chatham House).

Cotter, C. P. and Bibby, J. F. (1980) 'Institutional development of parties and the thesis of party decline'. *Political Science Quarterly* 95: 1–27.

—— and Hennessey, B. (1964) *Politics without Power: The National Party Committees* (New York: Atherton).

—— Gibson, J. L., Bibby, J. F., and Huckshorn, R. J. (1984) *Party Organizations in American Politics* (New York: Praeger).

Crotty, W. J. (1983) *Party Reform* (New York: Longman).

—— and Jacobson, G. C. (1980) *American Parties in Decline* (Boston: Little, Brown).

David, P. T. (1971) 'Party platforms as national plans'. *Public Administration Review* 31: 303–15.

Dennis, J. (1975) 'Trends in public support for the American party system'. *British Journal of Political Science* 5: 187–230.

Epstein, L. (1986) *Political Parties in the American Mold* (Madison: University of Wisconsin Press).

Fiorina, M. P. (1992) *Divided Government* (New York: Macmillan).

Fishel, J. (1978) *Parties and Elections in an Anti-Party Age* (Bloomington, IN: University of Indiana Press).

—— (1985) *Presidents and Promises* (Washington, DC: CQ Press).

Fowler, L. and McClure, R. (1989) *Political Ambition: Who Decides to Run for Congress* (New Haven, CN: Yale University Press).

Frantzich, S. E. (1989) *Political Parties in a Technological Age* (New York: Longman).

Frendreis, J. (1994) 'Voters, government officials and party organizations: connections and distinctions', in John C. Green and Daniel M. Shea (eds) *The State of the Parties* (Lanham, MD: Rowman & Littlefield), pp. 339–48.

—— Gibson, J. L., and Vertz, L. L. (1990) 'The electoral relevance of local party organizations'. *American Political Science Review* 84: 226–35.

Gibson, J. L., Cotter, C. P., Bibby, J. F., and Huckshorn, R. J. (1985) 'Whither the local parties? A cross-sectional and longitudinal analysis of the strength of party organizations'. *American Journal of Political Science* 29: 139–60.

Gitelson, A. R., Conway, M. M., and Feigert, F. B. (1984) *American Political Parties: Stability and Change* (Boston: Houghton Mifflin).

Goldman, R. M. (1994) 'Who speaks for the political parties? Or Martin van Buren, where are you when we need you?', in John C. Green and Daniel M. Shea (eds) *The State of the Parties* (Lanham, MD: Rowman & Littlefield).

Green, J. C. and Guth, J. L. (1991) 'Who is Right and who is Left? Activist coalitions in the Reagan era', in Benjamin Ginsberg and Alan Stone (eds) *Do Elections Matter?*, 2nd edn (Armonk, NY: M. E. Sharpe).

—— Jackson, J. E., and Clayton, N. (1998) 'Issue networks and party elites in 1996', in John C. Green and Daniel M. Shea (eds) *The State of the Parties*, 3rd edn (Lanham, MD: Rowman & Littlefield).

Harmel, R. and Janda, K. (1982) *Parties and Their Environments: Limits to Reform?* (New York: Longman).

Heard, A. (1960) *The Costs of Democracy* (Chapel Hill: University of North Carolina Press).

Herrnson, P. S. (1988) *Party Campaigning in the 1980s* (Cambridge, MA: Harvard University Press).

—— (1994) 'The revitalization of national organizations', in L. Sandy Maisel (ed.) *The Parties Respond* (Boulder, CO: Westview Press), pp. 45–68.

—— (1995) *Congressional Elections: Campaigning at Home and in Washington* (Washington, DC: Congressional Quarterly).

—— and Dwyre, D. (1998) 'Party issue advocacy in congressional election campaigns', in John C. Green and Daniel M. Shea (eds) *The State of the Parties*, 3rd edn (Lanham, MD: Rowman & Littlefield).

—— Patterson, K., and Pitney, J. J., Jr. (1996) 'From ward heelers to public relations experts: the parties' response to mass politics', in Steven Craig (ed.) *Broken Contract?* (Boulder, CO: Westview Press), pp. 251–67.

Jackson, J. S. III, Brown, B. L., and Bositis, D. (1982) 'Herbert McClosky and friends revisited: 1980 Democratic and Republican party elites compared to the mass public'. *American Politics Quarterly* 10: 158–80.

—— and Clayton, N. (1996) 'Leaders and followers: major party elites, identifiers and issues, 1980–1992', in John C. Green and Daniel M. Shea (eds) *The State of the Parties*, 2nd edn (Lanham, MD: Rowman & Littlefield).

Jones, C. O. (1997) 'Separating to govern: the American way', in Byron E. Shafer (ed.) *Present Discontents: American Politics in the Very Late Twentieth Century* (New Jersey: Chatham House), pp. 47–72.

Katz, R. S. (1986) 'Party government: a rationalistic conception', in Francis G. Castles and Rudolf Wildenmann (eds) *The Future of Party Government: Visions and Realities of Party Government*, vol. 1 (Berlin: Walter de Gruyter), pp. 31–71.

—— and Kolodny, R. (1994) 'Party organization as an empty vessel: Parties in American politics', in Katz, R. S. and Mair, P. (eds) *How Parties Organize* (London: Sage Publications).

—— and Mair, P. (1992) *Party Organizations: A Data Handbook on Party Organizations in Western Democracies, 1960–1990* (London: Sage Publications).

Kayden, X. and Mahe, E., Jr. (1985) *The Party Goes On: The Persistence of the Two-Party System in America* (New York: Basic Books).

Keith, B. E., Magleby, D. G., Nelson, C. J., Orr, E., Westlye, M. C., and Wolfinger, R. E. (1992) *The Myth of the Independent Voter* (Berkeley: University of California Press).

Kirchheimer, O. (1966) 'The transformation of West European party systems', in J. LaPalombara and M. Weiner (eds) *Political Parties and Political Development* (Princeton: Princeton University Press), pp. 177–200.

Kirkpatrick, J. J. (1976) *The New Presidential Elite* (New York: Russell Sage Foundation and Twentieth Century Fund).

—— (1978) *Dismantling the Parties: Reflections on Party Reform and Party Decomposition* (Washington, DC: American Enterprise Institute).

Kolodny, R. and Logan, A. (1998) 'Political consultants and the extension of party goals'. *PS* 21: 155–59.

Krukones, M. G. (1984) *Promises and Performance: Presidential Campaigns as Policy Predictors* (Lanham, MD: University Press of America).

Ladd, C. E. (1970) *American Political Parties: Social Change and Political Response* (New York: Norton).

—— (1978) *Where Have All the Voters Gone?* (New York: Norton).

Lerner, R., Nagai, A. K., and Rothman, S. (1996) *American Elites* (New Haven, CT: Yale University Press).

Lowi, T. J. (1975) 'Party, policy and constitution in America', in William N. Chambers and Walter Dean Burnham (eds) *The American Party Systems: Stages of Political Development*, 2nd edn (New York: Oxford University Press), pp. 238–76.

Mackenzie, G. C. (1998) 'Partisan presidential leadership: the President's appointees', in L. Sandy Maisel (ed.) *The Parties Respond* (Boulder, CO: Westview Press), pp. 316–40.

Mayer, W. G. (1998) 'Mass partisanship, 1946–1996', in Bryon E. Shafer (ed.) *Partisan Approaches to Postwar American Politics* (New York: Chatham House), pp. 186–219.

Mayhew, D. R. (1991) *Divided We Govern: Party Control, Lawmaking, and Investigations, 1946–1990* (New Haven: Yale University Press).

McClosky, H., Hoffman, P., and O'Hara, R. (1960) 'Issue conflict and consensus among party leaders and followers'. *American Political Science Review* 54: 406–27.

McGerr, M. E. (1986) *The Decline of Popular Politics* (New York: Oxford University Press).

Miller, W. E. (1998) 'Party identification and the electorate in the 1990s', in L. Sandy Maisel (ed.) *The Parties Respond* (Boulder, CO: Westview Press), pp. 109–27.

Nakamura, R. T. and Sullivan, D. G. (1979) 'Party democracy and democratic control', in Walter D. Burnham and Martha W. Weinberg (eds) *American Politics and Public Policy* (Cambridge, MA: MIT Press).

Nelson, C. J. (2002). 'Spending in the 2000 elections', in David B. Magleby (ed) *Financing the 2000 Election* (Washington DC: Brookings Institution Press), 22–48.

Orren, G. R. (1982) 'The changing styles of American party politics', in Joel L. Fleishman (ed.) *The Future of American Political Parties* (Englewood Cliffs, NJ: Prentice Hall), pp. 4–41.

Owen, D., Dennis, J., and Klofstad, C. A. (1998) 'Public support for the party system in the United States in the late 1990s'. Paper delivered at the annual meeting of the *American Political Science Association*, Boston, MA, September.

Patterson, K. D. (1996) *Political Parties and the Maintenance of Liberal Democracy* (New York: Columbia University Press).

Polsby, N. (1983) *Consequences of Party Reform* (New York: Oxford University Press).

Pomper, G. (1971) *Party Renewal in America* (New York: Praeger).

—— (1998) 'Parliamentary government in the United States?', in John C. Green and Daniel M. Shea (eds) *The State of the Parties*, 3rd edn (Lanham, MD: Rowman & Littlefield).

—— (with Lederman, S. L.) (1980) *Elections in America*, 2nd edn (New York: Longman).

Rae, N. (1998) 'Party factionalism, 1946–1998', in Bryon E. Shafer (ed.) *Partisan Approaches to Postwar American Politics* (New York: Chatham House), 41–74.

Ranney, A. (1963) *Channels of Power* (New York: Basic Books).

—— (1978) 'The political parties: reform and decline', in Anthony King (ed.) *The New American Political System* (Washington, DC: American Enterprise Institute), pp. 213–48.

Rauch, J. (1994) *Demosclerosis* (New York: Times Books).

Reichley, A. J. (1985) 'The rise of national parties', in John E. Chubb and Paul E. Peterson (eds) *The New Direction of American Politics* (Washington, DC: Brookings Institution), pp. 175–200.

—— (1992) *The Life of the Parties* (New York: Free Press).

Reiter, H. L. (1987) *Parties and Elections in Corporate America* (New York: St. Martins).

Rosenstone, S. J., Behr, R. L., and Lazarus, E. H. (1996) *Third Parties in America* (Princeton: Princeton University Press).

Rozell, M. J. and Wilcox, C. (1999) *Interest Groups in American Campaigns* (Washington, DC: CQ Press).

Sabato, L. J. (1988) *The Party's Just Begun: Shaping Political Parties for America's Future* (Glenview, IL: Scott, Foresman).

Salmore, B. G. and Salmore, S. A. (1989) *Candidates, Parties, and Campaigns: Electoral Politics in America*, 2nd edn (Washington, DC: Congressional Quarterly).

Schlesinger, J. A. (1985) 'The new American political party'. *American Political Science Review* 79: 1152—69.

Schramm, P. W. and Wilson, B. P. (1993) *American Political Parties and Constitutional Politics* (Lanham, MD: Rowman and Littlefield).

Shafer, B. E. (1998) 'Partisan elites, 1946–1996', in Byron E. Shafer (ed.) *Partisan Approaches to Postwar American Politic* (New York: Chatham House), pp. 75–141.

Shaffer, W. R. (1982) 'Party and ideology in the U.S. House of Representatives'. *Western Political Quarterly* 35: 92–106.

Shelley II, M. C. (1983) *The Permanent Majority: The Conservative Coalition in the United States Congress* (University of Alabama: University of Alabama Press).

Sinclair, B. (1998) 'Evolution or revolution? Policy-oriented congressional parties in the 1990s', in L. Sandy Maisel (ed.) *The Parties Respond*, 3rd edn (Boulder, CO: Westview Press), pp. 263–85.

Strahan, R. W. (1998) 'Partisan office-holders, 1946–1996', in Byron E. Shafer (ed.) *Partisan Approaches to Postwar American Politics* (New York: Chatham House), pp. 5–40.

Teixeria, R. A. (1992) *The Disappearing American Voter* (Washington, DC: Brookings Institution).

Thurber, J. A. (1991) *Divided Democracy: Cooperation and Conflict Between the President and Congress* (Washington, DC: CQ Press).

Verba, S., Schlozman, K. L., and Brady, H. E. (1995) *Voice and Equality: Civic Voluntarism in American Politics* (Cambridge, MA: Harvard University Press).

Ware, A. (1985) *The Breakdown of Democratic Party Organization, 1940–1980* (New York: Oxford University Press).

Wattenberg, M. P. (1991) *The Rise of Candidate-Centered Politics* (Cambridge, MA: Harvard University Press).

——(1998) *The Decline of American Political Parties* (Cambridge, MA: Harvard University Press).

West, D. M. and Loomis, B. A. (1999) *The Sound of Money: How Political Interests Get What They Want* (New York: Norton).

White, J. K. (1995) 'Reviving the political parties: what must be done?', in John K. White and John C. Green (eds) *The Politics of Ideas* (Lanham, MD: Rowman & Littlefield).

—— and Mileur, J. H. (1992) *Challenges to Party Government* (Carbondale, IL: Southern Illinois University Press).

Wright, J. (1996) *Interest Groups and Congress* (Boston: Allyn and Bacon).

12

Canada's Nineteenth-Century Cadre Parties at the Millennium

R. Kenneth Carty

The natural form of the political party risks being corrupted into an unwholesome caricature, a machine for winning elections.
The pure and simple continuation of their own existence becomes their principal preoccupation and measure of their ideals . . .
Constituted on the British model, Canadian parties have not escaped the American contagion . . .

André Siegfried (1906)

An electoral earthquake smashed Canada's national party system in 1993. The governing Progressive Conservatives were reduced from one hundred and sixty-nine to just two seats while, at the other end of the traditional spectrum, the country's left-wing (social democratic) New Democrats also suffered a major electoral collapse, leaving the party with its smallest ever caucus: neither had enough seats to be even recognized as a party under House of Commons rules. The authors of this party system explosion were two new parties, the Bloc Québécois and Reform, both of which offered fundamental challenges to the existing parties, the existing patterns of doing politics, and indeed to the country. The Bloc, which won the fourth largest vote share but, thanks to the vagaries of the first-past-the-post electoral system, ended up with the second largest parliamentary caucus and so formed the 'Official' opposition, was a child of French–Canadian nationalism and advocated the break-up of Canada through the separation of Quebec, the second largest province. Reform combined a right-wing economic agenda, a western regional appeal, and a commitment to a populist politics that eschewed the established norms of parliamentary discipline in favour of a constituency-focused delegate style of representation. Ironically, the one party that emerged least shaken by the eruption of these new parties was the Liberal Party, long the country's dominant political force. In opposition as the forces of destruction were gathering steam, the Liberals suddenly found themselves with a new majority government, though one based on a precariously small 41 per cent of the vote and, for the first time, dependent on central, English-speaking Canada.

This electoral explosion, with its overthrow of established patterns of politics, marked the end of another cycle in Canadian party system development. The party system that it broke had emerged out of a similar fundamental reshaping of Canadian party life in the early 1960s; that party system had in its turn been created in the aftermath of an earlier party system collapse and rebuilding in the 1920s. Each of these party system transformations was about more than shifting electoral alignments and party fortunes, though each was certainly marked by them. In every case the very character of the parties, their organization and activities, was changed: new structures and organizational linkages were established, party–leader relationships were altered, different bases of party and election financing were created, and party–media relationships were restructured. These reinventions of what Canadian parties were and did flowed from the demands made upon them by changing patterns of Canadian governance. This latest collapse is but the beginning of a new cycle that is forcing the parties to evolve in ways that respond to a new set of latent functions.[1] As the country turned the millennium, the parties were struggling to invent a new party system.

Through these cycles of party system transformation the same, apparently familiar, Liberal and Conservative parties persisted and dominated the electoral map. They did so as classic examples of Duverger's (1964: 64) 'cadre' parties: 'groupings of notabilities for the preparation of elections, conducting campaigns, and maintaining contact with the candidates'. At the beginning of the twentieth century Siegfried (1906: 113) commented that they were little more than 'machines for winning elections' and little has changed in the century since. This preoccupation with electoral activity, and absence of any enduring concerns for principle or interest, leaves Canadian cadre-style parties free to organize, advocate and campaign as suits both their needs and the moment. Nestled in the confines of an ancient single-member plurality electoral system, Canadian parties are poised to enter the twenty-first century much as they left the nineteenth.

While there has been considerable variation in the formal organizational structure of Canadian parties, at heart they have all been essentially cadre-like in their structure and character. Though the New Democratic Party has something of the mass structure of other social democratic labour parties, including affiliated trade union members, it too engages its members in parochial local associations whose primary focus is basically electoral. The parties' constituency associations, rooted in the electoral districts, are the fundamental organizational units to which members are attached. It is in these local associations that members choose their electoral candidates and select delegates to national conventions that (nominally) decide policy and (more importantly) elect and remove party leaders. After a series of reforms to the electoral and party financing laws in the early 1970s, the parties

---

[1] On manifest and latent functions see Merton (1949) and his discussion of party machines.

were, for the first time, able to develop permanent national headquarters with staff devoted to research and communication. Coupled with the emergence of national television news and advertising, this stimulated both a pan-Canadian thrust to party policy and reinforced the focus on party leaders in a party system that had long made leadership a regular electoral issue and centred party organization and decision-making on national leaders.

In Canada, the core linkage problem for political parties has been one of tying an American (mobile, plural, growing, changing) society to European-style (disciplined, centralized, closed) governing institutions. The solution to this problem has been an organizational trade-off in which local autonomy is exchanged for national (parliamentary) discipline. This provides local party associations in each electoral district the freedom to run their local affairs, especially in deciding upon their candidate and managing his or her campaign, while the elected politicians support the leadership's dominance of policy-making and party decision-making in the capital. Cadre-style organization persists as the dominant Canadian party form because it provides the organizational form best suited to incorporate this fundamental local–national balance. Thus, successful parties have an organization that is akin to a modern franchise system with the national organization producing and advertising the product (leaders and policy) while the independent local outlets deliver it (candidates and local campaigns) to the voters at election time. This puts the parties in the hands of whatever local candidates, activists and volunteers they can attract and hold. Given that the autonomy for discipline bargain is inherently unsatisfactory, party organizations are inevitably unstable; given that politicians and their supporters live for electoral success, exit trumps voice and loyalty, and electoral volatility is endemic.

Table 12.1 summarizes the patterns of Canadian national party politics over the last four decades. Though three parties claimed to be national organizations, the New Democrats hardly existed in the eastern half of the country and the first-past-the-post system ensured that they would remain a minor parliamentary player. The vagaries of the electoral system produced two decades of oscillating government as both Liberals and Conservatives formed minority and majority administrations. Indeed, the Conservatives' electoral victory in 1988 marked the first instance of a majority government being returned to a second term since the early 1950s (Table 12.2) which made their electoral melt-down in 1993 all the more dramatic. This parliamentary and governmental turnover did not reflect competition between competing visions of Canada, for all three parties had adopted a pan-Canadian, accommodative approach to representation, and a commitment to a style of government that was a bilingual, Ottawa-centred approach to executive federalism, animated by the practice of 'federal–provincial diplomacy' (Simeon 1972). For most of the period big constitutional issues about the very state and shape of the federation drove the national agenda. And it was the three traditional parties' apparent uncritical consensus on these issues that eventually led to the new parties' 1993 attack on the system.

TABLE 12.1. *Canadian national election results, 1962–2000*

Year	L	PC	NDP	SC	R	BQ	O	ENEP	ENPP	Volatility	Turnout 'A'	Turnout 'B'
1962	37.2	37.3	13.5	11.7			0.4	3.2	2.9	16.6	79	73
(265)	99	116	19	30			1					
1963	41.7	32.8	13.2	11.9			0.4	3.2	2.6	4.8	79	74
(265)	129	95	17	24			0					
1965	40.2	32.4	17.9	8.4			1.2	3.3	2.6	5.4	75	70
(265)	131	97	21	14			2					
1968	45.5	31.4	17	4.4			1.7	3.0	2.3	5.8	76	68
(264)	155	72	22	15			0					
1972	38.5	35	17.7	7.6			1.2	3.2	2.8	7.5	77	69
(264)	109	107	31	15			1					
1974	43.2	35.4	15.4	5.1			0.9	3.0	2.8	5.1	71	63
(264)	141	95	16	11			1					
1979	40.1	35.9	17.9	4.6			1.5	3.1	2.5	3.6	76	68
(282)	114	136	26	6			0					
1980	44.3	32.5	19.8	1.7			1.7	2.9	2.4	6.3	69	64
(282)	147	103	32	0			0					
1984	28	50	18.8	0.1			3	2.7	1.7	18.8	76	67
(282)	40	211	30	0			1					
1988	31.9	42.9	20.4		2.1		2.6	3.0	2.3	7.2	75	68
(295)	83	169	43		0		0					
1993	41.3	16	6.9		18.7	13.5	6.6	3.9	2.4	41.6	69	66
(295)	177	2	9		52	54	1					
1997	38.5	18.8	11		19.4	10.7	0.3	4.1	3.0	7.8	66	59
(301)	155	20	21		60	44	1					
2000	40.9	12.2	8.5		25.5	10.7	2.2	3.8	2.5	9.2	61	54
(301)	172	12	13		66	38	0					

Notes: Top figure in each cell: share of vote won by each party; bottom figure in each cell: number of seats won by each party in Canadian House of Commons. Figures in paranthesis in 'year' column = total number of seats in House. ENPP—Effective number of electoral parties; ENPP—Effective number of parliamentary parties. Volatility; Pedersen index. Turnout 'A': % of registered electors voting; Turnout 'B': % voting age population voting.

Party: L—Liberal; PC—Progressive Conservative; NDP—New Democratic Party; SC—Social Credit; R—Reform (in 2000 Canadian

TABLE 12.2. *Party complexion of Canadian national governments, 1962–2000*

Election year	Dates of government		Status of government	Name and party of premier	
	From	To		Premier	Party
1962	21-06-57	22-04-63	Minority	John Diefenbaker	Conservative
1963	22-04-63		Minority	Lester B. Pearson	Liberal
1965		20-04-68	Minority	Lester B. Pearson	Liberal
1968	20-04-68		Majority	Pierre Elliott Trudeau	Liberal
1972			Minority	Pierre Elliott Trudeau	Liberal
1974		04-06-79	Majority	Pierre Elliott Trudeau	Liberal
1979	04-06-79	03-03-80	Minority	Joe Clark	Conservative
1980	03-03-80	30-06-84	Majority	Pierre Elliott Trudeau	Liberal
1984	30-06-84	17-09-84	Majority	John Turner	Liberal
1984	17-09-84		Majority	Brian Mulroney	Conservative
1988		25-06-93	Majority	Brian Mulroney	Conservative
1993	25-06-93	04-11-93	Majority	Kim Campbell	Conservative
1993	04-11-93		Majority	Jean Chrétien	Liberal
1997			Majority	Jean Chrétien	Liberal
2000			Majority	Jean Chrétien	Liberal

Note: All governments are single-party administrations.

Canada is a country where geography often overwhelms history and nowhere is this more true than in its electoral politics. This is in no small measure a consequence of the continuing use of single-member electoral districts that privilege geographic party organization and political appeals. The great electoral realignments of Canadian history have been cast in geographic rather than social structural terms, and the political equations of the successive party systems have been written geographically. From the First World War to the 1960s, the Liberals' winning formula was based on a partnership between the western prairies and French-speaking Quebec. Then, after 1960, with the west in the hands of the Conservatives and Quebec still dominated by Liberals, politics came to be centred on Ontario where national elections were won or lost. The realignment that accompanied the 1993 electoral shockwaves broke that pattern, leaving the national system regionally fragmented with Reform in the west, the Liberals strongest in the centre, and the Bloc in Quebec. Of the principal parliamentary parties, only the Liberals could plausibly claim to be a genuinely national party, but their majorities now depended on the electoral system delivering them virtually all the seats in populous Ontario.

Recent decades also saw the disintegration of the party system in a different sense as federal (which Canadians call national) politics became increasingly disentangled from provincial political life. Canadians came to live in 'two political worlds' (Blake 1985), managed by competing levels of government, which were organized by distinctive and distinct political parties and party systems. Thus, a citizen in British Columbia would have her federal party politics structured by Liberals and Conservatives while Social Credit and the New Democrats organized her provincial electoral choices. Even in provinces where a party was strong at both levels, the respective party organizations were distinct and often pursued competing goals. Provincial parties of the same name often stood for quite different ends. The result was a sometimes perplexing pattern of party activity across the country with one (regionally-varied) national and ten provincial party systems tied together in only the most tenuous fashion. During the 1988 general election the Quebec Liberal leader (and provincial premier) urged his colleagues not to support the national Liberal party; in 1998 the leader of the national Conservative party resigned so that he could be acclaimed the leader of the Quebec Liberals.

As evidence of the extent to which federal and provincial parties have become separated, the 1993 political earthquake that broke the three parties' hold on the national party system made no impact on existing provincial party systems or the parties that made them up. They continued as they were with their distinct patterns reflecting the idiosyncrasies of the separate provincial political systems (Carty and Stewart 1996). The attack on the federal party system was a complex one, for it was mounted by parties that challenged the existing practices as well as the very legitimacy of the country, while simultaneously working a major electoral realignment in the geography of Canadian national politics. As Table 12.1 indicates, the level of electoral volatility experienced in 1993 was extraordinary, greater than for any other regular democratic election in the century (Mair 1997: 79, 216), and it produced a degree of parliamentary turnover remarkable even by Canadian standards. In the decade from 1984, over 80 per cent of the country's electoral districts were represented by members of more than one party.

Clearly there is something unique about Canada's political parties and the party systems they have produced. Organizationally they are fragmented, both regionally and by level of government, resulting in a complex of organizational ties that vary over time both within and across individual parties. Individuals, be they citizens, partisans, or even activists, have multiple and shifting partisan identities. Electoral volatility is comparatively very high. But for all these striking differences from parties in most advanced democracies, Canadian parties perform the same manifest functions of nominating candidates and conducting election campaigns on their behalf. If they are so different as organizations, or in the dynamics that drives their competition, it is because the challenges of linking society to state in Canada have been different. In this essay we are concerned with identifying how Canadian parties have gone about their particular business in recent decades and assessing how they will carry these traditions into the new century.

In the early 1990s Canada's national parties began, as they had on the occasion of previous party system collapses, to reinvent themselves. New patterns of membership, organization, and leadership politics were experimented with, new communication strategies were developed, and distinctive representational practices were adopted (Carty et al. 2000). Yet, in all this change, the parties' basic cadre structure has persisted, for it continues to provide them with the most satisfactory organizational solution to the problem of tying a deeply fragmented society to a regime of disciplined party governance where a geographically based electoral system persists. The new party system is still in transition: it is not clear which of the parties will survive, or how they might do so; the parties have yet to institutionalize new structures and practices; and the new regional dynamics that echo the politics of interwar Canada have yet to be fully assimilated into national electoral competition.

A CRISIS IN PARTY LEGITIMACY?

Did the political earthquake that hit the party system in 1993 signal Canadians' wholesale rejection of party politics, or at least the political parties then dominating the system? Assessing the legitimacy of a system dominated by cadre-style parties is difficult for that organizational form is designed to maximize flexibility, facilitate shifting allegiances (by voters and politicians), and so almost inevitably stimulates political volatility, all the while operating under the façade of great parliamentary umbrellas. When one or more cadre parties give way to others it is not always clear what, if anything, has really changed.

Canadians have always had an ambivalent relationship with their national political parties. In part this comes from the fact that Canada was itself a political creation, put together by party politicians acting from party-driven motives. The first common Canadian experience was a national election, held to choose the new country's first parliament, for which political parties were required. Thus, from the very beginning state and then nation-building were deeply entwined with party-building: political parties remain among the few genuinely national institutions Canadians have. This also means that they carry a heavy load. When Canadians get disillusioned and dissatisfied with the world they find themselves in, and decide something must be done about it, their instinctive response seems to be to start by remaking their political parties. The result has been an ongoing tension between the populist impulses of a new nation and the country's dependence on parties for survival. In 1990, three-quarters of the population told a Royal Commission on Electoral Reform and Party Financing that 'we would probably solve most of our big national problems if decisions could be brought back to the people at the grass roots' but the same proportion then agreed that 'without political parties there can't be true democracy' (Blais and Gidengil 1991: 16).

Earlier transformations of the party system have been marked by crises of legitimacy in which new parties have arisen to challenge the dominance of the old, stimulate organizational innovation, and mobilize Canadians in new ways. In each, deeply populist impulses threatened old ways of doing politics but were eventually absorbed by the system. While the major parties survived eruptions in the 1920s and 1960s, they did so by reconfiguring themselves and accommodating the system to new patterns of competition. 1993 was no different. The Bloc challenged the very legitimacy of the system by advocating that the country should be broken into two; Reform argued that completely new kinds of parties, embracing populist norms and practices, were needed to transform the country's parliamentary and political life. Their success in capturing a third of the vote and dominating the opposition benches in the Commons crystallized an anti-party sentiment that had been growing for some years.

Public opinion data reveals that Canadians have become increasingly cynical about politics. The proportions that report that 'the government doesn't care what people like me think' or 'those elected to parliament soon lose touch with the people' steadily grew (by 40 per cent) over the past quarter century (Blais and Gidengil 1991: 37–8). A good deal of this growing dissatisfaction has been aimed at parties. By the early 1990s, 78 per cent of Canadians were opposed to parties disciplining MPs in parliament, 47 per cent thought they offered no choice as all parties were basically the same, 81 per cent that there was too much party squabbling for good government, and 87 per cent agreed that parties simply confused the issues. Blais and Gidengil (1991: 41–4) concluded that, despite their recognition of the need for political parties, 'the main thrust of Canadians' reactions is inescapable: they mistrust parties.' Table 12.3 illustrates this growing alienation of the electorate from the parties: the numbers reporting 'a good deal' or 'quite a lot' of respect and confidence they had in parties fell from 30 per cent of the population in 1979 to just 10 per cent by the century's end, while the average party score on a feeling thermometer (running from 0 to 100) dropped from 56 in 1968 to a failing grade of 39 in 1997. This rejection was widespread: Clarke *et al.* (1998: 4) report

TABLE 12.3. *Feelings towards Canadian parties, 1968–99*

Year	Feelings about parties[a]	Confidence in parties[b]
1968	56	—
1974	53	—
1979	53	30
1980	51	—
1984	50	22
1989	—	18
1990	47	14
1993	43	9
1995	—	12
1996	—	11
1997	39	10
1998	—	13
1999	—	11

[a] average score on a thermometer (0–100) rating scale for the parties;
[b] aggregate percentage of respondents answering either 'a great deal' or 'quite a lot' to the question 'Would you tell me how much respect and confidence you have in political parties?'.

Sources: Canadian Election Surveys; Gallup poll data.

that 'negative party performance judgments transcend demographic, partisan and various evaluative cleavages in the electorate.'

Despite this reaction against their parties, and the system of competition they fostered, Canadians' inherent ambivalence about, or perhaps dependence upon, political parties shone through for they responded by starting more of them. In Canada, as befits a country with cadre parties, a national political party is simply defined (by law) as an organization running at least fifty candidates under a common label in a general election. In 1972 there were four, by 1980 this number had more than doubled to nine and then, another ten years later, grown again to fourteen. In the aftermath of the system-shattering earthquake the number fell back to ten for the 1997 election. While many of these parties hardly registered on the electorate's consciousness (nine of them together received only 2.6 per cent of the vote in 1988, see Table 12.1), two of them were instrumental in breaking the system up in 1993. Doing so in the face of the obstacles provided by the single-member plurality electoral system was a remarkable feat, but one which spoke to the crisis of legitimacy faced by the established parties and the inherent fragility of a system of cadre-style parties.

Growing antipathy towards the national political parties was not initially reflected in any systematic decline in Canadians' willingness to vote (refer again to Table 12.1). From the 1960s through the 1980s turnout varied but averaged about 75 per cent of the registered electorate (turnout in the provincial party systems differed and varied by province). But then, in the 1990s, turnout took a precipitous drop, falling to a record low of 61 per cent in the 2000 general election. Though the voter registration system was changed in 1997 (from election period enumeration to a permanent voters' list), that did not halt the erosion in the numbers of Canadians participating: in 1997 the proportion of those of voting age who bothered to vote fell to below 60 per cent for the first time in modern Canadian history. This sharp decline occurred despite the fact that both Reform and the Bloc were offering voters new and distinctive choices with the Bloc attracting many to the polls who had previously eschewed participation in federal politics (Johnston *et al.* 1996*b*). While the crisis in the party system was driving some Canadians to new parties, it was leading many others to abandon party politics all together. The result was a majority government elected by just 25 per cent of the electorate.

The very volatility of the electorate (Table 12.1) indicates the fragility of the ties between voters and parties. The 1993 explosion of the system was but the last of several occasions in the century at which the electorate, its shifts magnified by the electoral system, reconfigured the party system. To some degree the movement of Conservative voters to Reform may have represented a shift within the same party family, but Reform also attracted votes from populist New Democrats while the Bloc was redefining the very basis of national party competition in Quebec. With such a volatile electorate these new parties could shrink as fast as they have grown as the history of earlier protest parties reveals. Determined to persist, Reform sought to reconfigure and then institutionalize a united right by folding itself into a new Canadian Alliance party in the run-up to the 2000 general election. The Conservatives' refusal to cooperate with this attempt to restructure the party system suggests that large numbers of (central) Canadians see Reform/Alliance as an illegitimate interloper into the system.

Assessing the strength of the parties through the extent and intensity of the party identifications held by the electorate is difficult. First, there is the problem of measurement, for in a parliamentary system current vote intentions and partisan identifications can easily be blurred. Panel studies in the 1970s and 1980s revealed that 30 per cent or more of Canadians switched identifications between elections but whether this reflected fundamental identification changes or was in part simply tracking changes in party popularity is not entirely clear. The second problem flows from the fact that most Canadians live in two political worlds, structured by different party systems, with the result that they may need two sets of identifications. Thus, over the decade of the 1970s only about a third of the electorate maintained a consistent partisan identification at both levels of party life (LeDuc et al. 1984). Both this instability and inconsistency suggest relatively weak ties between voters and party.[2]

But did the pattern of party identification contribute to the collapse of the party system? Table 12.4 reveals that there was a slow erosion in the proportion of 'very strong' identifiers over the last third of the century: Clarke and Kornberg (1993: 303) estimate it shrank at the rate of 0.57 per cent each year between 1965 and 1991. At the same time there was no significant trend in the incidence of non-identification, suggesting not so much a withdrawal from parties *per se* as a simple weakening of the hold that the parties had on Canadians. This left them particularly vulnerable to the appeal of new parties promising to do politics differently.

Cadre parties do not need members; they just need small groups of supporters to maintain their inter-election organizations and then larger numbers of election period activists. As a result Canadian parties have never, until the 1990s, attempted to develop national membership programmes. No two parties have organized their members in the same way, and no party is organized the same way in all parts of the country. Their basic pattern has been to enrol members through local associations organized in the electoral districts.[3] These associations have been more (Conservatives and Liberals) or less (New Democrats) permeable, but have typically grown in election periods only to shrink again in quiescent inter-election years, and both of the new parties quickly fell into this same pattern. Table 12.5 illustrates the election-year centred cycles of surge and decline as individuals renew

---

[2] There is a considerable literature on party identification and its measurement. For a recent review see Blais et al. 1999. They show that party identifications are lower in Canada than either the USA or Britain and also note that in Canada, unlike the other two countries, 'the relationship between party identification and voting for the party one identifies with is not monotonic' (Blais et al. 1999: 10).

[3] One consequence of this is that there are no direct measures of annual party membership size. The figures reported in Table 12.5 are based on surveys of local associations reported in Carty 1991 and Carty et al. 2000.

TABLE 12.4. *Federal party identifiers in Canada, 1965–97*

Year	Very strong identifiers (%)	No party identification (%)
1965	24	11
1968	26	9
1974	27	13
1979	26	13
1980	31	10
1983	23	15
1984	22	14
1985	17	20
1986	15	27
1987	18	20
1988	23	11
1989	16	16
1990	20	14
1991	13	30
1993	9	22
1997	22	25

Note: Election years indicated in italics.

Source: Clark and Kornberg 1993; C.E.S. 1993, 1997.

TABLE 12.5. *Canadian party memberships*

Year	Liberal	Conservative	New Democrat	Reform	Total
1987	148,680	132,750	180,835		462,265
	0.84	0.75	1.03		2.62
1988	279,365	312,995	193,225		785,585
	1.58	*1.77*	*1.10*		*4.45*
1989	199,715	192,930	189,390		582,035
	1.13	1.09	1.07		3.29
1990	317,125	111,510	200,010		628,645
	1.80	0.63	1.13		3.56
1992	212,695	114,460		198,535	525,690
	1.07	0.57		1.00	2.64
1993	242,195	223,610		227,150	692,955
	1.22	*1.12*		*1.14*	*3.48*
1994	139,240	84,075		148,680	371,995
	0.70	0.42		0.75	1.87

Notes: Election years indicated in italics; Membership estimates are calculated from surveys of local associations. Top figure in each cell is absolute membership, bottom figure is M/E ratio.

their memberships in order to vote in candidate nomination meetings and work in campaigns. The big Liberal growth in 1990, a non-election year, reflects this same pattern for the party had a leadership contest that year and memberships were reactivated, or taken out, just for it. In Canada's cadre parties, membership has traditionally been valued for the vote it provided—for a local candidate or national leader—but little else. These really are skeleton organizations, little more than Duverger's 'groupings of notabilities for the preparation of elections.'

The extraordinary fluidity of these patterns of party life extends to the notables themselves around whom activists are gathered. It is not uncommon for individuals wanting to become a Member of Parliament to join a party on the eve of their announcement that they are planning to contest a local nomination. For their part, the parties themselves will often scavenge the neighbourhood looking for a popular local figure who might get elected: in 1997 Reform took to advertising for candidates in local newspapers. Preoccupied with electoral advantage, the parties' openness extends to recruiting individuals previously associated with their opponents. Thus, in the 1993 landslide election 27 per cent of the established parties' candidates had once been active in some other party while the figure was much higher in the ranks of the new challengers.

Table 12.5 also reveals just how shallow is these cadre parties' penetration of the electorate. They only manage to enrol somewhere between 0.5 and 1.5 per cent of the electorate so that even in years of the greatest political activity less than 5 per cent of the electorate hold even these most nominal sorts of memberships in any national political party. In cadre parties, members are drawn to successful politicians so it is not surprising that constituency memberships are typically about twice as large in associations where there is a sitting Member of Parliament. Despite its façade of a mass membership organization, this same phenomenon has also characterized the New Democrats whose incumbents traditionally had local memberships six times the size of the party's non-incumbent associations (Carty 1991: 40). It is also important to note that the tie between local activists and the parties is a highly personalized one: over half of the local associations claim that with a different candidate they would attract a different set of volunteers (and members for the moment) to work on their election organization (Carty 1991: 175). Finally, this partisan involvement is fleeting: only half of those who worked in the 1988 general election campaign for their party had participated in the previous election four years earlier (Carty 1991: 173).

The existence of a system of income tax credits for donations to political parties means that ordinary Canadians can support parties financially without taking out membership. Table 12.6 reports the number of individuals who have made contributions to the national parties over the past two decades and provides a second measure of the extent to which the parties are rooted in the population. It indicates that only about 1 per cent of the electorate contributes to a national party in any given year, but that this too varies across the electoral cycle, typically peaking in election years. For their part, local associations report that only between one-fifth and one-third of their members make regular contributions, confirming our portrait of them as weakly tied to their party (Carty 1991: 82–4). The New Democratic Party, with its more bureaucratic mass-style structure, has developed a more consistent set of donors but that advantage has been offset by somewhat

TABLE 12.6. *Number of individuals contributing to Canadian parties, 1975–99*

Year	Liberal	Conservative	New Democratic	Reform	Bloc Québécois
1975	13,373	10,341	58,889		
1976	18,261	23,409	56,142		
1977	21,063	20,339	60,169		
1978	22,350	35,615	67,133		
1979	*13,025*	*34,952*	*63,655*		
1980	*17,670*	*32,720*	*62,428*		
1981	24,735	48,125	56,545		
1982	27,968	52,694	66,665		
1983	33,649	99,264	65,624		
1984	*29,056*	*93,199*	*80,027*		
1985	28,545	75,117	97,364		
1986	35,369	52,786	90,487		
1987	28,972	39,320	87,927		
1988	*30,642*	*53,893*	*118,390*		
1989	19,970	40,191	89,290	7360	
1990	36,361	27,702	116,448	23,462	
1991	26,396	27,391	94,080	43,176	
1992	29,025	27,823	75,213	55,760	
1993	*41,058*	*44,728*	*65,301*	*49,488*	
1994	36,880	14,532	54,446	28,970	29,084
1995	39,019	15,870	55,438	32,982	25,848
1996	37,471	18,859	48,972	66,982	17,030
1997	*34,429*	*23,352*	*50,434*	*75,587*	*18,885*
1998	32,710	17,908	45,385	55,405	10,533
1999	30,735	16,437	41,760	53,262	13,104

Notes: Election years indicated in italics. The parties use different financial systems so that the numbers may not be strictly comparable: in some parties membership fees go to local associations, in Reform they may be counted as contributions to the national party; the New Democrats' party finances are so deeply entangled that it is difficult to distinguish between contributions to their provincial and national organizations.

smaller average gifts. The 1993 collapse of the Conservatives was prefigured in the collapse of their donor base: it fell from almost 100,000 in 1983, the year before its great electoral victory, to just 28,000 in 1992. But if Canadians were no longer supporting the Conservative Party the same could not be said of the party system in general: as many Canadians (200,000) were prepared to reach into their pockets to support a major party in 1993 as had been in 1988 or 1984.

Ambivalent partisans, ambivalent because the party system is an imperfect mechanism for linking them to their government, populate Canadian parties. While the fragmentation of the party system contributes to this ambivalence it is also true that ambivalence contributes to fragility and fragmentation, as Canadians opt for exit over loyalty. The 1990s crisis in the party system was in part a legitimacy crisis, but it was also part of a process of challenge and change by which cadre parties are forced to rebuild their organizations and rethink their practices, and by which the party system reorders the shape of competition. In rejecting the pan-Canadianism common to all the parties over the third (1960–90) party system, the new parties have redefined the national political agenda and stimulated organizational innovation. What they have not done is alter the basic cadre style of Canadian party life. Indeed, their easy acceptance of this form of party organization testifies to how deeply rooted it remains.

CADRE ORGANIZATIONS

Cadre parties operate at two levels, at the local grass roots where individual members join and participate, and at the national level which focuses on the parliamentary life of the caucus. Sitting rather precariously between them are modest national offices that try to organize and coordinate local party activity in the interest of the central leadership. The relationship between these two levels of party life is uneasy. The constituency associations jealously guard their autonomy and prerogatives in the face of a national party that would like to impose common practices and be able to reach into the associations to influence their decisions. These conflicts most often arise over the constituency associations' long-standing right to choose (or remove) its local candidate. Attempts by the national party to impose its will, though sanctioned by party rules and the law, are seen as illegitimate by the membership. Too heavy a hand will simply result in members deserting. Given that serious national parties believe they must mount at least a nominal campaign in each constituency, this makes their organization heavily dependent on the enthusiasm of the local volunteers they can attract and hold. For their part, to protect themselves, incumbents work to make the party organization in their constituencies a personal one and try to keep the national office out of their affairs.

Individual party members have little to do between elections. In the constituencies there are routine tasks of organizational maintenance as well as purely local communications and policy work, but none of this takes many members. It is only at election time that the organizations spring back into life and in the process enrol large number of members: a contested nomination may see thousands registered in a matter of weeks. However, where there is no contest for the nomination, memberships may change little. Thus, membership levels can be very misleading guides to organizational strength for they often simply reflect the desire of individuals to participate in a contested party meeting. The very fluidity and openness of cadre-style organizations, coupled with minimal inter-election demands, means that membership is a relatively low priority for the parties.

Most constituencies across the country have local units of at least four of the (post 1993) national parties. Their strength and activity vary sharply across both space and time within the same party. As vote-gathering machines, a party's electoral victories stimulate healthy local associations, for access to local representatives provides members with an incentive to remain active. This is why continuing electoral success is directly related to membership strength. But does weak organization explain electoral defeats, or strength account for victories? In the case of Canadian parties the answer is more likely to be the reverse—electoral defeats produce weak organizations, wins lead to strong local associations. Thus, when the Conservatives suddenly made a breakthrough in Quebec in 1984 it quickly developed a full set of strong local organizations where none had existed for most of the century. Within a few years of the party's defeat in 1993 that organizational presence had vanished so that many local associations were not even able to find candidates on their own for the 1997 election (Woolstencroft 1997: 77).

The national party organizations maintain central offices but these are largely charged with routine organizational maintenance tasks and running the periodic national conventions. In some parties the headquarters staff manage ongoing direct mail fund-raising campaigns but in others it is assigned to separate organizations. In none of the parties is there a highly developed permanent staff of career party functionaries. For most of the country's history the parties were only able to raise funds at election time and so no tradition of strong or substantial party offices developed. Now that the parties have more resources the local associations do not want a party bureaucracy that would inevitably interfere with them, while the elected politicians have taken care of themselves (parliamentary and constituency staffs supported by the state have grown over the past two decades) and do not want to see permanent party officials who might rival their pre-eminence in the party. When the parties have lots of money party offices tend to expand but then quickly contract when revenues fall. The result is little continuity in party field workers and the absence of a permanent organizational staff whose work might transform the cadre cast of the parties.[4]

Canada's cadre parties exist to contest elections and there are three organizational corps that constitute the real sinews of their electoral machine and so are critical to their working and success. None are part of the formal apparatus of the party; all exist as informal, personalized extensions of electoral politicians. Directed and staffed almost entirely by shifting cadres of volunteers activated for a contest, they spring into life for electoral contests and then retreat into quiescence between contests. In the subtle, continually shifting networks of relationships among those who make them up lies the organizational heart of the cadre party. First are the organizational teams put together in the constituencies to fight local contests. These teams centre on the candidate and reflect his or her approach to politics and place in the constituency. Run by amateur local campaign managers, and official agents, who are appointed by the candidate and answer to him or her,

---

[4] One indication of the comparative insignificance of party staff in Canada is the absence of any study of the parties' national offices and the lack of any data on national party staffing patterns over time.

they are staffed by volunteers who are there to support the particular candidate (Carty 1991: ch. 7; Sayers 1999). Traditionally autonomous, these campaign teams are only loosely integrated into the national campaign despite the fact that together they spend more than the national party during a general election campaign. The second key organizational group is the national campaign committee and those who work for it. These are the 'war-time generals' brought in to organize the parties' national electoral campaigns in place of the 'peace-time generals' who run the party offices between elections but are displaced for the critical business of fighting elections. The chair of the campaign team, and the key members of it, are appointed by the party leader and owe their positions and influence to their personal ties to him or her. These individuals generally hold no formal position in the party but their key electioneering role, and their strong ties to the leader, make them among the most powerful figures in the nether worlds of Canadian parties. Finally, the leadership selection politics of Canadian parties forces those who aspire to become party leader, and thus dominate the national organization and parliamentary caucus, to build party-wide networks of supporters. The result is the development of personal factions within the parties, organizations that can reach well beyond the circles of the national capital down into the local organizations of as many constituency associations as possible. These highly personalized networks, defined by their loyalty to an individual, may lay dormant for long periods of time but can be quickly activated for leadership challenges or contests. It is the competing loyalties of these three sets of organizational groups, first to their patron, second to the party, that drive both intra-party and inter-party competition in Canada and leave the parties with extraordinarily fluid, candidate-centred organizations.

To all this the social democratic New Democratic Party sought to be an exception. With its mass-membership structure, and its provision for the affiliation of trade union locals, it provided for an organization that was less electorally focused and less dependent on personality. However, as a federation of provincial party organizations, its strength is dependent on the vitality of the party in the provinces, and not being a player in several of the provincial party systems has weakened its national organization significantly. Where the party was most successful it succumbed to the cadre instincts of Canadian party organization with personal machines growing up around party leaders and its incumbent politicians.

For most of their history Canadian parties were relatively poor, able to raise money at election time but then doing without during the inter-election periods. The increasing cost of electronic politics forced the parties to realize that that model of financing was no longer workable and in the mid-1970s major reforms to election and party financing were passed by parliament that: provided for state subsidies (through both direct payments and indirect tax expenditures); limited campaign (but not inter-campaign) period spending; and established a regime of public disclosure and accountability. These changes quickly changed the parties, significantly increasing their organizational strength and capacity. However, the new arrangement was limited by the decision not to regulate the financial affairs

TABLE 12.7. *Canadian party income, 1976–99*

Year	Liberal	Conservative	New Democrat	Reform	Bloc Québécois
1976	5823*	4084	2925		
1977	4587	3774	3525		
1978	5018	5465	4184		
1979	*6302*	*8376*	*6020*		
1980	*7457*	*7564*	*6101*		
1981	5592	6950	6003		
1982	6746	8521	7108		
1983	7736	14,767	8669		
1984	*11,598*	*21,979*	*10,513*		
1985	6163	15,073	10,152		
1986	10,719	15,639	14,639		
1987	8882	13,058	12,608		
1988	*16,358*	*25,231*	*18,754*		
1989	6397	14,521	13,865	13,511	
1990	12,038	11,045	15,439	2212	
1991	6776	12,037	19,933	6588	
1992	7555	11,542	13,819	8543	
1993	*14,723*	*22,276*	*18,227*	*8357*	
1994	11,764	4131	10,722	5675	2053
1995	13,229	5576	12,394	4337	1683
1996	14,113	6708	12,074	7162	1160
1997	*17,481*	*10,982*	*14,012*	*8800*	*2140*
1998	13,714	5813	5527	5772	727
1999	14,627	5140	6422	6284	1297

Notes: All figures in thousands of $Cdn.
*Includes the party income for both 1975 and 1976. Election years indicated in italics.

of the local associations or leadership contests. Given their vital importance in a cadre system, this has left a large 'black hole' in Canadian party finance and our knowledge of the parties' organizational life.

Tables 12.7 and 12.8 report the ebbs and flows of party income and expenditure since 1975 and the introduction of a partially regulated and publicly subsidized party finance regime. As Stanbury (1991) has demonstrated, the parties' finances are anything but transparent and no two of them operate in the same way so that the data have to be read with considerable caution.[5] But that said, there are several distinct features of the national parties' finances that stand out. First, there was a noticeable increase in the total amount of money in the party system beginning in the mid-1980s; this has been broadly sustained in real terms since then. This increase was led by the Conservatives' success in raising money by direct mail

[5] The impact of inflation over the period covered in the tables was considerable and this must be taken into account in assessing any trends over time. NDP finances are particularly difficult to decipher as they include provincial level accounts. On that see Stanbury 1991.

TABLE 12.8. *Canadian party expenditures, 1976–99*

Year	Liberal	Conservative	New Democrat	Reform	Bloc Québécois
1976	4707*	3497	2381		
1977	4187	4233	3105		
1978	5283	5470	3514		
1979	*2771*	*5184*	*4678*		
1980	*3702*	*4923*	*5992*		
1981	5116	7542	6491		
1982	6781	8521	4871		
1983	6277	13,199	8009		
1984	*11,999*	*20,777*	*7407*		
1985	8149	11,654	11,071		
1986	11,166	14,141	15,188		
1987	9274	13,490	14,012		
1988	*10,176*	*21,124*	*14,933*		
1989	7115	12,824	12,507	966	
1990	11,587	10,384	14,262	1721	
1991	6769	11,534	18,711	6289	
1992	6931	10,697	14,237	89,211	
1993	*15,517*	*22,197*	*13,632*	*6338*	
1994	11,707	2403	9411	2921	2053
1995	10,687	4191	14,506	5661	2001
1996	13,193	6590	13,575	7220	1289
1997	*26,664*	*21,965*	*17,397*	*11,138*	*4807*
1998	12,790	5102	10,770	6156	711
1999	12,605	5138	15,088	6246	1052

Notes: All figures in thousands of $Cdn.
*Includes the party expenditure for both 1975 and 1976. Election years indicated in italics.

from supporters, but not necessarily members, and soon emulated by the other parties. These contributions from individuals carried an income tax credit, so were effectively being partially financed by the state. This practice pointed to the distinction between supporter and member in which the former was often more valuable to the politicians.

The second regular feature of the parties' finances is the sharp increase in election years when expenditures typically double inter-election year amounts. This reflects the relative ease with which the parties are able to raise funds for election campaigns as well as the public subsidies that the state now provides for their election expenses. It is also a powerful reflection of the fact that these parties are election machines that conserve their energy for electoral activity and do not believe that their national organizations have a significant role to play in public life between elections. There are non-general election years in which a party will spend large amounts of money (e.g. the Conservatives in 1983 or the Liberals in 1990), but they too are election-centred for those instances of high spending are typically periods in which the party is seized in the throes of a leadership contest.

The third point to note is that the governing party is more successful at raising money, and hence spends more, than any of its opponents: the Conservatives were the richest party from the mid-1980s until 1993 when they were passed by the Liberals after they came to office. This pattern is surely typical of cadre parties whose principal difference, as far as many individual and corporate donors are concerned, is that one is in power, the other not. The long-standing practice of many corporations has been to give to both parties—but more to the one in government. It is also true, however, that the Liberals and Conservatives, the only parties ever to have held national office, are regularly better financed than the other parties. Despite Reform/Alliance's considerable success in displacing the Conservatives from their western parliamentary strongholds and as the principal party of the right, the country's economic establishment did not desert the Conservatives as quickly as the voters and so the Conservative Party had the resources to weather the worst fallout of the 1993 electoral earthquake.

A fourth aspect of Canadian party finances is the state's approach to regulation and subsidization. That Canadian party (and candidate) expenditures are regulated, and subsidized, only for the few weeks in the multi-year election cycle testifies to the public conception of them as cadre organizations whose only significant activity is electoral. That the parties do not attempt to exploit these long periods when they are unregulated to spend more in them testifies to their own conception of themselves as essentially vote-gathering machines. This focus on the parties' public, electoral, activity has left their internal affairs completely unregulated. The result has been leadership contests in the major parties, at which the prime minis-tership was at stake, in which the total amounts spent by the candidates exceeded those allowed the whole party in a general election, and local nomination contests within individual constituency associations in which would-be candidates spent more than the winner was then allowed to spend in the election contest itself (Carty *et al.* 2000: ch. 7). These monies do not always make their way into party accounts and it is difficult to know what the true magnitudes, or sources, are. The commit-ment to local association autonomy that has been integral to the operation of these cadre parties has meant that local finances are both unregulated and unreported. Considerable sums are believed to exist in many local bank accounts and trust funds but their size and use remains one of the mysteries of Canadian party life.

Cadre parties are focused on the politicians so it should be no surprise that the spending limits that now govern Canadian elections permit the local candidates, as a whole, to spend more than the national parties in their quest for office. In the 1997 general election, a national party's candidates could spend up to $18.8 million, about 65 per cent more than the $11.4 million allowed by the party for its national campaign. While the national parties could actually exceed those limits due to loopholes in the law (e.g. polling expenses are not considered election expenses), the bias in favour of the local campaigns, which are rarely integrated into the national efforts, is considerable (Sayers 1999). The continuing ability of many local party associations to raise more than they are allowed to spend helps them maintain their organizational independence from their party's national office. Thus, the overall pattern of party finance that has evolved in the past two decades is one that seems particularly well designed to meet the needs of the local associations and more especially the local politicians who dominate them. At the same time, the relatively modest limits on individual candidates keeps the system permeable to new entrants and so intrinsically volatile.

Canada's cadre parties have not been transformed into modern cartel party organizations (Young 1998). Though both parties and candidates receive some public subsidies to support their election expenditures, and while individuals can receive a (steeply graduated) tax credit for political donations, the proportion of public funding to both has been estimated at about a third of their total spending (Young 1998; Carty *et al.* 2000: ch. 7). This is unlikely to change as the opposition Canadian Alliance Party is opposed, in principle, to state support for political parties, although until the law is changed their politicians continue to take full advantage of it.

One hundred years ago Canadian parties were deeply enmeshed in the media but that era has long passed. In the absence of any enduring press–party linkages or support patterns, the political parties must compete with other groups and individuals for the media's attention. Between elections their national organizations (as opposed to their parliamentary caucuses which seem to live for the front page or lead story) make relatively little effort to do so. At election time they require that broadcasters provide some free-time for election broadcasts, allocated by rules agreed to by the parties and administered by a Broadcasting Arbitrator working through the independent Chief Electoral Officer, and make other time available for purchase. In recent years the parties have experimented with the private media— direct mail, the Internet—and it is clear that the use of these technologies will grow in the future. Public opinion polling is, of course, an important medium (one in which information flows upwards to politicians rather than downwards from them) and the parties have maintained their ability to use it by excluding its costs from the limits otherwise imposed on election expenditures. This is one area where the parties have established an advantage over their local associations, for the costs associated with polling continue to exceed the reach of most constituency parties.

Everything is done twice, and often differently, in Canadian political organizations, once in English, once in French. As serious national parties must reach Canadians in both major language groups this forces them to establish two distinct media communications groups in their organizations.[6] During election periods the French-speaking and English-speaking campaigns are organized quite separately from one another and develop distinctive messages for the two language communities. The very limited integration of the media in the two parts of Canada

[6] In practice the parties and their local candidates, speak to Canadians in the many different languages that they find in the electorate.

makes this possible, while the different agendas and partisan balances driving politics in the two sides of the country makes it necessary.

The portrait we have of Canadian parties' organizational strength is opaque. It is so because they remain modern examples of nineteenth century institutions. These cadre parties thrive when they win, but struggle when they do not. Indeed defeat often stimulates an 'opposition party syndrome' (Perlin 1980) in which the politicians that survive the defeat fall prey to internal factionalism and leadership conflicts, which in turn makes candidate recruitment and local organization-building difficult, leading to defeatism and the inability to present a convincing face to the electorate and so another election defeat which is then, more often than not, followed by another round of the syndrome. This is a pattern that persists because the style of party organization persists. What has changed over the years is the role Canadian parties have played in the country's governance.

CADRE PARTIES IN A MODERN POLITY

The parties' basic manifest functions remain: they continue to monopolize the task of nominating candidates and conducting election campaigns, though the latter role is being challenged by the increasing involvement, at both national and local levels, of interest groups in the electoral process. By comparison, the parties' latent functions have shifted dramatically as Canada has evolved (Carty 1997). In the early decades (1867–1920) the parties were engaged in state-building as they controlled the public service. The patronage politics that first party system produced eventually saw the parties consume the state. The succeeding party system (1920–60) forced the parties to become nation-builders, operating as the agents of national accommodation through a politics of regional bargaining and brokerage. By the end of that second era the state had consumed the party and the Liberals were left as the 'Government Party' (Whitaker 1977). The third party system (1960–93), now crushed by the earthquake of 1993, pushed the parties into the role of pan-Canadian agenda setters as the effective centre of Canadian governance was moved to the apartisan setting of the intergovernmental conference room where federal and provincial governments bargained public policy. It was the very flexibility of their cadre organizational style that allowed the parties to respond to the very different functional demands the political system made of them in each of those different periods. At issue now is the capacity of this old form to serve modern needs.

Governance

The hard question is to what extent does Canada enjoy party governance? The easy answer is that by their very nature cadre parties can provide the form, but rarely the essence, of party government. In reality, any interpretation of Canadian parties' role must be more nuanced than that simple judgement allows. In his recent book on the organization and operation of the national government, Donald Savoie argues that Canadian government is organized as prime ministerial government: the parties 'are essentially election-day organizations' incapable of even 'articulating a plan of action' let alone implementing it 'should it come to power' (Savoie 1999: 344). Bakvis' study of the role of ministers corroborates this picture for he argues that 'party is still important, but primarily as one of the arenas in which ministers jockey for position and influence' (Bakvis 1991: 286). Yet, despite consigning party to the narrowly electoral dimension of national politics, Canadian politicians persist in practising a classic Westminster form of party government. Five of the twelve elections since 1960 failed to return a parliament with a majority party but in none of those instances was a coalition government ever seriously contemplated let alone created. A strong commitment to the norm of one-party government (in the name of electoral accountability) leads party leaders to form minority governments in such situations, confident that the plurality electoral system will soon return the system to normal by delivering a majority at the next election.

The long-standing party bargain of local organizational autonomy for parliamentary discipline produces national party caucuses that are highly cohesive. Though recent studies are beginning to challenge the myth that all MPs are nothing but 'trained seals', loyalty is the overwhelming principle (Massicotte 1998; Wearing 1998). Elected members who are unhappy with their party, or the limitations imposed on their parliamentary life, are as likely to choose the exit as the voice option. The result is a relatively high turnover rate, and correspondingly short parliamentary careers (Docherty 1997), a pattern that strengthens the propensity to prime ministerial over party government. With neither the power to select nor remove the leader, the caucus can provide little in the way of a party check on the government.

Disciplined one-party majority government does mean that Canadian governments can pursue distinctive agendas and can move national public policy in their preferred direction. The Liberals demonstrated this after the 1993 election when they sharply reversed the direction of the country's fiscal policy with dramatic reductions in expenditures, which quickly turned large government deficits into surpluses for the first time in almost three decades. Whether there was anything distinctively Liberal about these policies is more contentious; it was the Liberals who had first created the huge deficits during an earlier turn in office. Canadians who voted for the Liberals in 1993 should have been surprised for they had run on a programme calling for more government spending and the abrogation of two of the then Conservative government's main policies—a new Goods and Services Tax and the North American Free Trade Agreement. In fact, they did neither and soon had embraced both. Thus, while governments can, and do, make a difference, it is rarely a party difference. It is precisely this that has led increasing numbers of Canadians to believe that those they elect soon lose touch, and provided the impetus to the rise of the Reform party.

Canadian government may be party government but it is also federal government in a country in which the national and provincial party systems have become detached. For constitutional reasons many of the areas of major (i.e. expensive) public policy require the close cooperation of both levels of government in both the instigation and implementation of public services. This has meant that over the past several decades the most significant public policy decisions have been made in a complex system of intergovernmental competition and accommodation. Besides strengthening the hands of government leaders *vis-à-vis* their own parties, this has led to something of an apartisan decision-making process. With representatives from four or five different parties inevitably involved in intergovernmental bargaining, partisan considerations must often be put aside in the interest of reaching agreement. Not only does this process drain most public policy of a distinctly partisan colouring, but it also shields most decisions from any clear process of democratic accountability. Since cadre parties seek to provide for party government in only the narrowest sense they do not see this as a problem.

There are three ways in which this modest form of party government is now under challenge. The first is from the Charter of Rights and Freedoms, which was written into the constitution in the early 1980s. It has reinforced a political discourse of rights, stimulated more Canadians to take part in politics through interest groups as opposed to parties, and inserted the Supreme Court as a major actor in the political process. The result has been that parties are no longer able to dominate, or always even to define, the national agenda, that they must compete for resources with interest groups which now actively intervene in election campaigns, and that the courts may strike down their policies or force governments to adopt policies that divide their party supporters.

The second challenge to traditional forms of party government comes from the Reform/Canadian Alliance Party with its commitment to altering the very character of parliamentary life in Canada. The party, drawing on deep-seated populist impulses in the Canadian west, argues that the very nature of representation should be changed. It seeks to replace politicians' fealty to their party with obedience to the will of their constituents. This attack on the sanctity of party discipline, which is inherently precarious in a cadre party, strikes at the very heart of party government as it has been practised in Canada for over a century. Though it has not yet been successful in its campaign against party discipline, nor does its caucus particularly practise what it preaches, the movement's electoral successes do testify to the virulence of anti-party sentiment among many political activists.

Finally, Quebec nationalism, organized by the Parti Québécois provincially, and the Bloc Québécois in national politics, provides a direct challenge to the very survival of the country. Those parties' commitment to support a series of provincial referendums on the issue of Quebec independence, until they win, has kept this fundamental issue at the top of the national political agenda, but in a way that isolates most Canadians, and hence the national parties, from the debate. In doing so it fosters a perception among many that the national government is preoccupied with Quebec and is comparatively indifferent to the interests of other regions. It is this sense that national parties, especially when in government, turn their backs on the west that contributed to the rise of Reform and the breakdown of the party system in 1993.

Political recruitment

Canada's cadre parties exist to do little more than manage elections so it is not surprising that they monopolize the routes to elected office. The parties' privileged position as the gatekeepers of the country's electoral life leaves little room for independents in Canadian politics. But their nature means that they are as much vehicles for the politically ambitious as they are disciplined recruitment agencies. Virtually all political recruitment is done through the local constituency associations that jealously guard their traditional power of nominating their parliamentary candidate. These local associations often do not have any formal search committees, or enforceable rules governing their nomination contest, so that self-selection is a dominant force in the process (Carty and Erickson 1991). Individuals, following their ambition, or the urgings of a few friends, can organize a personal campaign team, sign-up sufficient new members and win a nomination meeting vote (Sayers 1999). So deeply entrenched is this practice that even sitting MPs are not immune from challenge at the constituency party nomination meeting that proceeds every election: in 1997 four sitting MPs lost their places to individuals who recruited themselves and captured the local party nomination.

In recent years party leaders and managers have attempted to exercise more control over the recruitment process—in order to run more women and minority candidates, to defend the party against single-issue group penetration, to attract 'stars', and sometimes to defend sitting MPs. The Liberals have tried leader's appointments, the New Democrats quota systems, and Reform/Canadian Alliance elaborate screening mechanisms to do this, but none of them have been particularly successful at altering the basic pattern of recruitment. Local party associations see the right to choose their candidates as a matter of party democracy and strenuously resist interference from other parts of the party. On occasion, when the leadership has insisted, an entire local executive has resigned on the eve of an election leaving the party candidate to survive as best they might.

Local associations give the highest priority to recruiting individuals who are 'committed to the constituency', and rate qualities like 'experienced party worker', 'political experience' or 'nationally well known' at the bottom of a list of twelve qualities they look for in a candidate (Erickson 1997: 53). Primarily interested in winning, these local organizations will often recruit a candidate who has an attractive constituency profile with little consideration for his or her past party activity. In 1997, one New Democrat party association recruited a former Conservative government minister, the Liberals had former New Democrat legislators and MPs as candidates, a Conservative association nominated a former Reform MP, and both Reform and the Bloc had former Liberals and Conservatives. All this gives evidence of a very catholic approach to recruitment and the absence of a disciplined or tightly managed career ladder by the parties.

The short political lives that the Canadian parliamentary process allows most politicians (Docherty 1997: 42–7) means that the parties may be forced to recruit individuals into positions of leadership from outside the caucus, sometimes from outside the party itself. All three of the leaders of the old parties (at the end of the century) were not in parliament when they won their leadership, and some ministers of the government were drafted into the party in order to join the government. The separation of the national and provincial party systems, and the almost complete absence of party politics at the municipal government level, contributes to the difficulties that parties have in dominating the routes to political office. Whether the parties are recruiting the politicians, or the politicians are using the parties, is an open question. Seen from the perspective of the system's gatekeepers the parties appear to dominate. But on the ground, where the politicians live, the cadre style of the parties leaves the politicians comparatively free to come and go through whichever gate suits them at the moment.

Canada, like many other nineteenth-century democracies, was once governed by the politics of patronage. Most of that was done away with in the early decades of the twentieth century (though it demonstrated a remarkable persistence in several of the eastern provinces), leaving only limited traces in the governance of the country. The government still controls appointments to the Senate, as well as a wide range of public advisory boards and commissions, and enthusiastically appoints its supporters to them, especially where such individuals can do no ready harm. There is also some minor patronage (contracts, legal work, etc.) available to governing parties, but for the most part these appointments and commissions are designed to reward electoral and financial supporters, as much as to shape or control public policy and government programmes in any systematic fashion. Using these resources to recruit both people and money allows the parties to sustain their electoral vocations.

Interest articulation and aggregation

For much of the century Canada's cadre parties have specialized in finding ways to aggregate competing interests rather than articulate underlying social cleavages. This propelled them towards an accommodative style of politics dominated by the imperatives of regional brokerage. Then, as a new party system emerged after 1960, the parties adopted a new pan-Canadian approach to governing which saw them work towards building support from individual Canadians for their conception of the national agenda (Smith 1985: 31). This politics had the three national political parties adopt essentially similar approaches to issues of representation

(Carty *et al.* 2000: ch. 5) while sharply increasing the distance between federal and provincial party organizations.

In their move to establish a pan-Canadian politics the Liberal and Conservative parties did not question their long-standing cadre-organization instincts that led them to bridge cleavages and mask differences in the interest of building a broad electoral base. For their part the New Democrats traded their socialist principles for the electoral promise of populist appeals (Bradford and Jenson 1992). The consequence was that there was little difference among the parties: all adopted the same vision of a modern welfare state, all proclaimed and practised a politics of pluralism and openness in party life and public policy, all bought into a conception of Canada as bilingual and multicultural, and all sought to accommodate the constitutional demands of Quebec. Each of the national parties accepted that their ambitions for national policy initiatives clashed with the constitutional realities of the federal division of powers and so committed themselves to government by executive-federalism. But that system made it impossible for voters to hold any government, any party, electorally responsible. Inevitably this eviscerated much of the point of the parties' electoral competition and three decades of seemingly endless debate and constitutional wrangling over Quebec–Canada relations rubbed an increasingly frustrated electorate raw. The result was the collapse of the party system in the 1993 election.

Both the Bloc Québécois and the Reform parties promised a new kind of politics, a new approach to how interests ought to be promoted, and in doing so represent a fundamental attack on the very essence of the pan-Canadian party system that had existed since 1960. Their 'anti-system' messages are different. The Bloc, articulating Québécois nationalist aspirations of independence, seeks an end to the politics of accommodation between English and French speakers by breaking the country apart. But it is a second division team with its political direction being driven by the Parti Québécois and the politics of the party system in Quebec. How long the Bloc will remain in national politics, or what course it will follow, are more likely to be dictated by events in Quebec than the wider Canadian party system. The party's success at capturing the majority of Quebec seats in parliament has increased the regionalization and fragmentation of the national party system. It has meant that for the first time in the country's history a national Liberal government had to be formed without substantial support from Quebec. It has fundamentally altered and stretched the national political agenda by putting Quebec independence on the ballot in one-quarter of the country.

Reform's populist politics rejected the politics of pan-Canadian accommodation and executive-federalism in favour of simple majoritarianism practised by smaller and more decentralized government. It advocated the end of party discipline in the interest of making parliamentarians responsive to their local electorates, and it rejected a politics of interest-group pluralism and the recognition of special rights in the name of individualism and equality. It was in this, more than in its determinedly right-wing economic policies, that the party challenged the existing national political parties and broke the mould that had governed them for over three decades. Carrying this anti-system message while playing in the system has not been easy. Does the party have to accommodate to the pressures of the system to increase its chances of winning? But if it does so will it have lost its soul, and its very reason for being? Can it be the ultimate cadre party while reforming the very nature and scope of Canadian governance? The decision to reinvent itself as the Canadian Alliance reflects its belief that it can. The historical record suggests it cannot, but it also suggests that with its strong regional base the Canadian Alliance can persist as a major actor in the party system.

The eruption of these two new parties in 1993 followed a 1992 national referendum on constitutional change that had repudiated the country's political class (Johnston *et al.* 1996: 277). That referendum asked Canadians to accept a comprehensive package of constitutional amendments and it was supported by all the national parties, most provincial party leaders and leading spokespersons for business, labour, and aboriginal interests. For perhaps the first time in Canadian history since Confederation, the country's political elites were united and their defeat at the hands of the people, led by Quebec nationalists and western Reformers, signalled the growing gap between Canadian elites and masses. It is this gap that the new parties have continued to exploit. They reject the consensus that the elites of the old parties had fashioned on the constitution and bilingualism, they question the legitimacy of the rules of the game governing party and election financing, and they argue for new representational norms. Reform/Alliance and Bloc success in forcing social and economic divisions into the party system shrank the differences between the political agendas of the party elites and the mass public, but only by increasing the diversity among the party elites themselves and so expanding the range of choice offered by the party system.

Not all Canadians find cadre parties particularly satisfying political instruments for promoting their policy objectives and there has been an increase in the public and electoral activity of single-issue groups. These groups compete with the parties for resources, human and financial, and increasingly attempt to push their issues onto the agenda. The focus and discipline with which they articulate their demands makes it increasingly difficult for the parties to engage in the traditional brokerage that promises something, but rarely everything, to everyone. These groups have invaded the electoral process in at least three ways over the past decade. First, single-issue groups sometimes mobilize their members to swamp a local party's membership in order to influence the nomination of a candidate (or selection of delegates to a party convention). The parties have fought back and their leaders now veto local nominations engineered by obviously single-issue groups. Second, these groups increasingly participate in local constituency campaigns in an attempt to heighten the salience of their issue and to support or oppose particular candidates. In the 1988 general election over half the candidates of the major parties reported that some interest group had intervened in their local campaign in a deliberate attempt to influence their election or defeat (Carty 1991: 186–8). The third approach taken by interest groups has been to launch large-scale mass media campaigns during the election in an attempt to shape the national campaign agenda.

Regulating single-issue group electoral activity was not a concern when the electoral expense regime was put in place in the mid-1970s, but the recent growth in their activity now worries the political parties who see their control of the electoral process in jeopardy. Twice in the last decade they have moved to limit interest groups' activity and influence by imposing severe restraints on their spending during campaigns. Twice that legislation has been found unconstitutional. The commitment of the government to legislate for a third time in the dying months of the century indicates that the old parties are determined to try and defend their traditional electoral ground and to reassert their monopoly over the channels of electoral participation. The sheer scale of interest group life, and the courts that give them a hearing and a place in the system, are likely to thwart that ambition.

Participatory organizations?

Active participation in the life of Canadian parties is, for virtually all individual members, structured by and centred in local constituency associations. National parties believe they must maintain associations in every constituency and the reality is that many of these are little more than 'paper branches', organizations with no money, few members and are consequently inactive (Carty 1991: 98–102). Active local party organizations providing an opportunity for political activity are most likely to be found in areas of electoral strength, especially those where the party has a sitting incumbent. Given the high levels of electoral volatility, areas with an active membership can quickly be turned into participatory deserts.

Party members engage in a wide range of local activities, not all focused on national politics, but the principal tasks are those of organizational maintenance—fund-raising, social events, and annual membership drives—with a concern to be ready for the next election. Large numbers of local associations report that they have their members engaged in policy study of one kind or another, but then admit that there is very little competition among their members to be delegates to their party's national conventions where policy will be debated (Carty 1991: ch. 3). Most experienced party members realize that despite their work, opinions, or convention resolutions, party policy remains the preserve of the professional politicians and especially that of the leadership. As a result, most local associations, whatever their nominal membership, are dominated by a small core of committed activists who keep the local machine on stand-by or work to support the personal ambitions of a local MP. The high level of turnover on local executives suggests that these positions offer little in the way of influence or power in the party. Reform entered the system promising to break this pattern by giving local members a greater role in the party's policy-making and its parliamentary direction. While its local associations were very active in its early years, the leadership continues to manage its membership as easily as in the traditional parties (Flanagan 1995).

In the absence of any systematic membership data it is not possible to draw sharp profiles of just who these party members are. Studies of delegates to party leadership conventions all report that they are disproportionately middle class and well educated. They are also often young and new to the party. To the extent that these delegates reflect the membership, it is clear that a party's members are rarely typical of its electorate and that many of them do not have a record of long service or involvement in party activity.

The only good reason to join a political party in Canada is to participate in nominating a local candidate or in choosing the party leader. Membership conveys a vote and the opportunity to participate in making a decision of real, immediate, and obvious consequence. For most other partisan activity, including working on campaign teams that are appointed by the candidate, formal party membership is irrelevant. Only when there are internal party contests do Canadians join local party associations in substantial numbers, creating the membership peaks and troughs that mirror electoral cycles, their membership fees constituting little more than a party poll tax. Even these membership swells distort the extent to which there is a participatory membership, for turnout rates in party contests for candidates or leaders is normally well below 50 per cent (Carty and Erickson 1991: 125).

By the standards of a cadre party these are participatory organizations. Individual party members have a direct vote that allows them to choose, or replace, their local notable at election time. For much of this century party members have also had an indirect vote (via a delegate convention) in the selection and then removal of party leaders. By the 1990s growing dissatisfaction with the leadership convention process—its escalating costs, candidate manipulation of majoritarian delegate-selection processes, and multiple-voting provisions—led the parties (first at the provincial, then the national level) to adopt party leadership-selection processes that give every member a direct vote (Carty and Blake 1999). While a consensus has yet to emerge among the parties as to how best to organize such contests, the principle seems now firmly entrenched for all but the New Democrats who are unclear as to how to incorporate their affiliated (local trade union) members.

In 1998 the Conservatives were the first nationwide party to use a direct membership vote to select a new party leader. In fact, the vote was constrained by the party's decision to weight votes so that each constituency's membership, irrespective of its size, had an equal influence on the outcome.[7] The contest led to a large increase in the party's national membership—from 18,000 to 90,000—in a couple of months, but only half of the members actually voted in the first ballot, 40 per cent in the second. The party had recruited just 3.7 per cent of its 1997 voters in anticipation of the contest and then only 1.9 per cent of them participated. True to form the membership soon collapsed and by 1999 was back down to 18,000

---

[7] Each constituency was given 100 points to be distributed in proportion to the share won by the candidates in the vote. In this the Conservatives were attempting to mirror the logic of a national election contest in which it is the constituency that is the unit of importance.

(Stewart and Carty 2001). The Canadian Alliance followed suit in 2000 when it too chose its leader by a vote of a newly, and temporarily, inflated membership. With the country's next prime minister likely to emerge out of some sort of membership vote, the parties appear to have lost control over one of the most critical internal decisions they make, leaving parliamentary parties to adjust to a membership and leadership far removed from their world.

Despite the Conservatives' modest success, some of the provincial parties have stimulated greater participation in direct membership votes for their leadership, particularly when in office. In Alberta the governing provincial Conservative Party even allowed new 'members' to join between the two ballots, effectively eviscerating the notion of party membership and turning the contest into an American-style primary election. But this is only to recognize and extend the logic of cadre politics by making the party a loose framework within which notables conduct their leadership struggles among the electorate.

The nomination and leadership processes of the parties have remained unregulated by law and the parties have demonstrated only the most limited capacity to constrain the excesses of ambitious politicians. As it becomes clear that these are no longer private internal party matters to be settled by a disciplined membership, but are public contests open to any interested individual,[8] calls for their regulation by the state will grow. To date the parties have resisted pressures to do so, but in this the parties may yet succumb to another round of the American contagion Siegfried observed a century ago.

Political communication and education

Walter Bagehot, in his study of the English constitution published in the year of Canada's creation, argued that the education of the nation was one of the primary tasks of parliament and the party politicians who inhabit it. Since the death of the partisan press in the early decades of the twentieth century it has not been a high priority for Canadian parties. Beyond the efforts of individual campaigns, they have not sustained any regular communication programmes and few of them have managed even to maintain regular party newsletters for extended periods of time. When the 1991 Royal Commission on Electoral Reform suggested the creation of party foundations to do policy research and education work, the recommendation merely seemed to puzzle the few party politicians who read it. Party communication remains electoral campaigning. To try and do more would restrict the politicians' freedom to run on the issues of the moment, or to reverse direction to catch a prevailing electoral wind.

---

[8] Most of the parties have traditionally opened their membership (and hence party contests) to individuals who were neither of legal voting age nor Canadian citizens. Reform set a new standard when it insisted that only voting age citizens be entitled to vote in its affairs.

This narrow conception of their responsibility to political education has supported the parties in a preoccupation with regulating election campaign rules in their favour. To ensure that they have the ability to get their campaign messages to the electorate the parties have used the Election Act to require that multiple dwelling units provide them access, that the press not charge them higher than average advertising rates, and that broadcasters provide free-time and guarantee the purchase of additional paid-time. Coupled with their attempts to limit the campaign period advertising of single-interest groups, these are all designed to strengthen their hold on election agenda-setting. Once the campaign is over, Canadian party organizations retreat to their quiescent stage, adopting a largely passive and reactive response to the mass media and the shifting tides of public opinion.

Canadian parties define their biggest communication challenges as those of operating in at least two languages, though local election campaigns can often involve several more. The parties have traditionally dealt with this by having two distinct communication and campaign teams responsible for French- and English-speaking Canada. Though these teams are appointed by the leader, and report to the centre, there is often very little coordination between their activities. Preoccupied with helping politicians get elected from distinct electorates, they are not concerned with ensuring the party is speaking with one voice.

PLUS ÇA CHANGE, PLUS C'EST LA MÊME CHOSE?

The great French political geographer, André Siegfried, visited Canada at the beginning of the twentieth century and discovered a party system whose elections were characterized by unmatched 'fury and enthusiasm' (Siegfried 1906: 117). He reported that four issues dominated electoral contests: 'general prosperity', which all the parties supported; 'local advantage', promoted by each candidate seeking to be their constituency's representative; the 'race question', by which he meant the tension between French-speaking Catholics and English-speaking Protestants; and 'leadership'. With all for prosperity and local patronage, and none for inflaming the social division, electoral politics more often than not came down to questions of personal leadership. Parties were reduced to those gathered around leaders who were responsible for creating whatever national organization existed, and 'whose mere name is a programme in itself' (Siegfried 1906: 136).

If Siegfried were able to return at the beginning of the twenty-first century he might be surprised at how little elections had changed. Parties all promise to have the formula for prosperity, constituency candidates still run as local champions, the relationship between the two large ethnic communities still bedevils the country's politics, and elections revolve around the claims of party leaders. But more striking is how little the parties have changed. They remain cadre-style organizations consisting of small numbers of local activists and politicians linked together at the

centre by a party leader. These leaders now command parties with all the trappings of modern 'electoral-professional' political machines—specialized media
and campaign organizers, pollsters, computer-driven fund-raising and communication technologies—to help them fight elections, but their relationship to the
organization in the constituencies and its local notables has hardly changed.

The Social Democrats tried to build a party organization on the model of a mass
party but with limited success. While they never enrolled large enough numbers to
create a true mass base, their real obstacle was the enormous social and economic
heterogeneity of the country that made cadre forms the most efficient structure for
linking the imperatives of local diversity to the impulses of national government.
Their most successful organizations have been the local associations built by successful local MPs who epitomize the cadre notable. While party finance reforms
have made the parties' electoral resources more dependent upon the state than in
the past, there is little evidence that this has led to a cartelization of Canadian party
organization (Young 1998).

The convulsions that began to restructure the Canadian party system in the
early 1990s led to two new parties playing a significant role in parliament, to
the fragmentation and regionalization of party support for all of the parties—the
new as well as the old — and to an increased diversity in the parties' style and
approach to articulating and aggregating interests. Within the parties, new patterns
of leadership politics, giving all members a vote, began to emerge. As in past
periods of party system change, the basic underlying electoral alignments are
being reshaped producing new constellations of competition and different sets of
electoral choices for individual electors. Yet, in none of this party system change
has there been a fundamental challenge to the basic cadre form of party organization
that has persisted since the nineteenth century.

Siegfried's characterization of successful Canadian parties as 'machines for
winning elections', preoccupied with 'the pure and simple continuation of their
own existence', seems as relevant at the beginning of the twenty-first century as
it did at the beginning of the twentieth. Given shape by the imperatives of the
plurality electoral system and a majoritarian parliamentary politics, but operating in a new society, Canadian parties have fallen uneasily between their more
structured European cousins and their idiosyncratic American neighbours. They
have resisted any organizational contagion from the left and the developmental
paths of European parties (Katz and Mair 1995). If there is to be any contagion in
the new millennium then Siegfried was prescient in pointing to the south. In the
last century America's cadre parties have been transformed into a set of regulated
'public utilities' to structure democratic competition (Epstein 1986: ch. 6). With
the emergence of primary-like contests driving their internal politics, Canada's
parties seem poised to follow in that direction.

While Canada's cadre parties persist, even if reorganized and reshaped, it is clear
that the party system, defined by those same parties, has not. At the beginning of the
new millennium it is being recreated (for the second time in the last half-century) to

serve a changing political system as the patterns of Canadian governance are being reordered. The parties' primary tasks—their manifest functions—of nominating candidates and conducting elections persist; what are again changing are the latent functions they perform for the wider polity. This is not the decline of party, for the roles of the political parties are not so much in decline as they are being transformed. They must be judged in terms of the demands of a new and different system rather than compared to their practices in an old one. The genius of Canadian cadre parties has been in their ability to survive and adapt to successive political systems that have made radically different demands upon them. That is why the country is entering the twenty-first century with refurbished nineteenth-century parties.

REFERENCES

Bakvis, H. (1991) *Regional Ministers: Power and Influence in the Canadian Cabinet* (Toronto: University of Toronto Press).

Blais, A. and Gidengil, E. (1991) *Making Representative Democracy Work: The Views of Canadians* (Toronto: Dundurn Press).

————— Nadeau, R., and Nevitte, N. (1999) 'Measuring party identification: Canada, Britain and the United States'. A paper presented to the annual meeting of the American Political Science Association, Atlanta.

Blake, D. E. (1985) *Two Political Worlds: Parties and Voting in British Columbia* (Vancouver: UBC Press).

Bradford, N. and Jenson, J. (1992) 'Facing economic restructuring and constitutional renewal: social democracy adrift in Canada', in Frances Fox Piven (ed.) *Labour Parties in Postindustrial Societies* (New York: Oxford University Press).

Carty, R. K. (1991) *Canadian Political Parties in the Constituencies* (Toronto: Dundurn Press).

—— (1997) 'For the third asking: is there a future for National Political Parties in Canada?' in Tom Kent (ed.) *In Pursuit of the Public Good* (Montreal: McGill-Queen's University Press).

—— and Blake, D. E. (1999) 'The adoption of membership votes for choosing party leaders: the experience of Canadian parties'. *Party Politics* 4.

—— and Erickson, L. (1991) 'Candidate nomination in Canada's National Political Parties', in Herman Bakvis (ed.) *Canadian Political Parties: Leaders, Candidates and Organization* (Toronto: Dundurn Press).

—— and Stewart, D. K. (1996) 'Parties and party systems', in C. Dunn (ed.) *Provinces: Canadian Provincial Politics* (Peterborough: Broadview Press).

————— (2001) 'Leadership politics as party building: the 1998 conservative leadership contest', in W. Cross (ed.) *Political Parties, Representation and Electoral Democracy in Canada* (Toronto: Oxford University Press).

—— Cross, W., and Young, L. (2000) *Rebuilding Canadian Party Politics* (Vancouver: UBC Press).

Clark, H. and Kornberg, A. (1993) 'Evaluations and Evolution: Public Attitudes Towards Federal Political Parties, 1965–1991'. *Canadian Journal of Political Science* XXVI, 287–312.

Docherty, D. C. (1997) *Mr. Smith Goes to Ottawa: Life in the House of Commons* (Vancouver: UBC Press).

Epstein, L. (1986) *Political Parties in the American Mold* (Madison: University of Wisconsin Press).

Erickson, L. (1997) 'Canada', in Pippa Norris (ed.) *Passages to Power: Legislative Recruitment in Advanced Democracies* (Cambridge: Cambridge University Press).

Flanagan, T. (1995) *Waiting for the Wave: The Reform Party and Preston Manning* (Toronto: Stoddart).

Johnston, R., Blais, A., Gidengil, E., and Nevitte, N. (1996) *The Challenge of Direct Democracy: The 1992 Canadian Referendum* (Montreal: McGill-Queen's University Press).

Katz, R. S. and Mair, P. (1995) 'Changing models of party organization and party democracy: the emergence of the cartel party'. *Party Politics* 1: 5–28.

LeDuc, L., Clark, H., Jenson, J., and Pammett, J. (1984) 'Partisan instability in Canada: evidence from a new panel study'. *American Political Science Review*, 78, 470–84.

Mair, P. (1997) *Party System Change: Approaches and Interpretations* (Oxford: Oxford University Press).

Massicotte, L. (1998) 'Party cohesion in the Canadian House of Commons 1867–1945'. A paper presented to the annual meeting of the Canadian Political Science Association.

Merton, R. (1949) *Social Theory and Social Structure* (Glencoe, IL: The Free Press).

Perlin, G. (1980) *The Tory Syndrome: Leadership Politics in the Progressive Conservative Party* (Montreal: McGill-Queen's University Press).

Savoie, D. J. (1999) *Governing from the Centre: The Concentration of Power in Canadian Politics* (Toronto: University of Toronto Press).

Sayers, A. M. (1999) *Parties, Candidates and Constituency Campaigns in Canadian Elections* (Vancouver: UBC Press).

Siegfried, A. (1906) *The Race Question in Canada* (Toronto: McClelland and Stewart), reprinted, 1966.

Simeon, R. (1972) *Federal-Provincial Diplomacy: The Making of Recent Policy in Canada* (Toronto: University of Toronto Press).

Smith, D. (1985) 'Party government, representation and national integration in Canada', in P. Aucoin (ed.) *Party Government and Regional Representation in Canada* (Toronto: University of Toronto Press).

Stanbury, W. T. (1991) *Money in Politics: Financing Federal Parties and Candidates in Canada* (Toronto: Dundurn Press).

Wearing, J. (1998) 'Guns, gays and gadflies: party dissent in the House of Commons under Mulroney and Chrétien'. A paper presented to the Annual Meeting of the Canadian Political Science Association.

Whitaker, R. (1977) *The Government Party: Organizing and Financing the Liberal Party of Canada, 1930–1958* (Toronto: University of Toronto Press).

Woolstencroft, P. (1997) 'On the ropes again? The campaign of the progressive conservative party in the 1997 federal election', in Alan Frizzell and Jon Pammett (eds) *The Canadian General Election of 1997* (Toronto: Dundurn Press).

Young, L. (1998) 'Party, state and political competition in Canada: the Cartel Argument revisited'. *Canadian Journal of Political Science* XXXI, 339–58.

13

Political Parties in Australia

Party Stability in a Utilitarian Society

Ian McAllister

Very quickly the mechanism of party became the established gatekeeper of political activity: the parties monopolized politics by controlling entrance to parliament itself and by controlling the behaviour of politicians once they had arrived there. Ever since, the policy options of the Australian politics have been in the hands of the major parties and attempts to break this monopoly have been quite unsuccessful.

(Aitkin and Castles 1989: 219)

Placed in a comparative perspective, the hallmark of Australian politics is the dominance of party. The vast majority of voters identify with and vote for one of the major political parties; gaining election at the federal level is next to impossible without the benefit of one of three party labels—Liberal, National, or Labor; and minor parties have played little part in shaping the development of the party system. Within the legislature, party government operates in every sense of the word. The parties determine the legislative agenda and enforce rigid discipline among their members; conscience votes are rare and cross-party voting all but unknown. Australia is, then, a party-based polity *par excellence*. Perhaps more interestingly from a comparative perspective, it has seen little decline in the strength of the major parties in recent years, in contrast to Britain, the United States, or many of the other advanced democracies.

The explanation for the continuing strength of political parties in Australia can be traced to the origins and development of the country's political culture. Hartz (1964) has argued that the cultural development of Anglo-American colonial societies is determined by the values and beliefs that were dominant during the period in which they 'split' from the host society, Britain. In each case, the new society bears the imprint of the values and beliefs of Britain at the time that the colonial 'fragment' was established as an independent entity. In the United States the split from Britain occurred in the late eighteenth century and the fragment that took root was characterized by the libertarian ideals of the eighteenth-century Enlightenment. By contrast, Australia's split occurred in the nineteenth century so that the colonial 'fragment' was imbued with the utilitarian ideas of Jeremy Bentham and his followers. As a result, Australian political culture has been avowedly utilitarian in its orientation (Hancock 1930; Collins 1985).

The expression of utilitarianism in politics has been seen as 'the reliance on an instrumental view of the political process' (Hughes 1973: 142), so that the state exists primarily in order to resolve problems and disputes, not to preserve individual liberty. In Hancock's (1930: 69) famous words, 'Australian democracy has come to look upon the state as a vast public utility, whose duty it is to provide the greatest happiness for the greatest number.' Examples include the extensive use of the law to regulate society and ensure proper social conduct, from industrial relations to minor aspects of individual behaviour, such as parking. Perhaps the prime example of utilitarianism in politics, however, is compulsory voting. Since democracy seeks to give all citizens a role in decision-making, the utilitarian method of achieving this 'right' is through compulsion and legal enforcement. Australia is one of the few democratic countries in the world to force citizens to vote in this way.

Political parties are a necessary and important part of this utilitarian political culture. Australian parties fulfil the same functions as their equivalents in other societies—simplifying the choices of voters, educating voters and providing systemic support[1]—but ordinary voters provide little questioning of their role. Parties are viewed as an integral part of a system of political institutions which exists solely to maximize efficiency; they attract neither undue loyalty nor overt disaffection. While there is evidence of some cynicism towards parties (and even more cynicism towards politicians) there is surprisingly little criticism of parties as institutions (McAllister 1992: 42–3). At least part of this is a consequence of the identification of parties with the state, which, as we have noted, is seen as a major collective benefit to society (Bean 1991).

THE DEVELOPMENT OF THE PARTY SYSTEM

The party system has seen comparatively little change during the course of the twentieth century. The colonization and settlement of Australia after 1788 meant that it avoided most of the territorial conflicts common in mainland Europe, although it has suffered from some regional and religious conflict. The nineteenth century witnessed regional rivalry between the colonies, although in the latter part of the century colonial governments were preoccupied with security and trade issues. The patterns of religious support evident in Europe during the nineteenth century were also imported into Australian party politics, and religion has surfaced

---

[1] Excluding, of course, mobilizing the vote, which is unnecessary because of the system of compulsory voting.

periodically as an issue within the Labor Party, the best examples being the 1915 conscription debate and the 1950s opposition to communist influence in the trade unions.

The most significant impact on the party system has been industrialization. In the 1880s and 1890s, rural–urban divisions dominated political conflict, with the rural areas opposing the economic policies of the rapidly industrializing cities. This regional conflict was gradually overtaken in the early years of federation by conflicts between industrial owners and workers. In the first decade of the twentieth century, three parties dominated federal politics: the Labor Party, which was formed in 1901 from the various colonial Labor parties, and the Protectionists and Free Traders (Loveday 1977; McMullin 1995). In 1909, the Protectionists and the Free Traders settled their differences and combined to form the Liberal Party (later the United Australia Party, before re-adopting the Liberal Party title), thereby establishing the pattern of two-party competition that has been the basis of the Australian party system ever since.

Despite the dominance of the owner–worker cleavage, reflected in Labor–Liberal party competition, the rural–urban division has remained politically salient through the Country (later National) Party. Between 1914 and 1919, a sustained period of low prices for agricultural produce stimulated the rise of country parties dedicated to defending agricultural interests, and they combined to form a single party in 1920, shortly after entering into a coalition with the Liberal Party. The coalition has remained in existence since then, except for two short periods in 1973–74 and 1987. Despite the permanent nature of the arrangement, there has been little pressure for a merger; two conservative parties, one catering to urban dwellers the other appealing to farmers living in the 'bush', has suited those on the anti-Labor side of politics.

Several smaller parties have enjoyed some success in Australian politics. In 1955 the issue of communist influence within the trade union movement and Labor's response resulted in the formation of the anti-communist, and largely clerical, Democratic Labor Party (Reynolds 1974). The party drew most of its support from Victoria, where it enjoyed some electoral success, but by 1974 it had no federal parliamentary representation and became effectively moribund. The Australian Democrats, although formed by a disaffected Liberal in 1977, have largely attracted their support from ex-Labor voters and activists (Warhurst 1997). They have never won a lower house federal seat, but the proportional electoral system in the Senate means that they have had a consistent presence there since their formation, often holding the balance of power between the two major parties. In 1998 the Democrats' leader, Cheryl Kernot, defected to Labor, the highest profile defection in Australian political history. She was subsequently elected as a Labor candidate.

In April 1997 a further minor party was formed, Pauline Hanson's One Nation Party. Hanson was a former Liberal federal election candidate who had lost her party endorsement prior to the 1996 election following comments in a local newspaper concerning aborigines. Notwithstanding this, she was elected as an independent with a substantial swing of 19.3 per cent. Following a series of much publicized launches across the country, the new party won almost one quarter of the vote in the Queensland state election in June 1998, on a populist platform that combined opposition to Asian migrants and aborigines with support for gun ownership. In the 1998 federal election the party secured 8.4 per cent of lower house votes nationally, making it the third largest party in votes, although no candidate secured a lower house seat.[2] It is not yet clear if One Nation will occupy a lasting place in the party system, or if it merely represents a rural protest vote against the National Party's acquiescence to the economic rationalism of their Liberal coalition partners. In the federal election of 2001, the party suffered a setback, its vote being nearly halved (see Table 13.1).

Despite these minor incursions into the votes of the major parties, the long-term stability of the Australian party system over the course of the twentieth century sets it apart from most others. The parties that compete for electoral support at the close of the twentieth century are very much the descendants of the parties that competed at the beginning of the century. Moreover, with the exception of some comparatively minor splits and fissures, parties outside the major Labor–Liberal/National division have gained little electoral success. Of the thirty-nine federal elections that have been conducted since 1901, only eight have produced non-major party support exceeding 10 per cent of the first preference vote (though these include the last five elections[3]), and in only one federal election—1990—has a single minor party gained more than 10 per cent of the vote (see Table 13.1).[4] In the seventeen federal elections from 1961 to 1987 inclusive, the Labor and the Liberal–National parties together attracted an average of 91.7 per cent of the vote, a substantial figure by any measure, though this dropped to 85.6 per cent for the five elections conducted since 1990. It is this Labor versus Liberal–National competition which Lipson (1959) has characterized as 'a trio in form and a duet in function.'

The preferential voting system which has been used for House of Representatives elections since 1919 (between 1901 and 1917 first past the post was used) has meant that party stability has been translated into secure majorities in the lower house for either Labor or the Liberal–National coalition. Since 1960, the Liberal–Nationals have governed for a total of 26 years, Labor for 16 years (Table 13.2). Indeed, the Liberals were in government continuously from 1949 until 1972, a period of 23 years, one of the longest periods of unbroken rule in any established democracy. Robert Menzies was prime minister for 16 of those 23 years, making

---

[2] Pauline Hanson lost the Queensland seat of Blair that she had won in 1996 as an independent. The party's sole federal representation in the 1998 parliament is one senator.

[3] The elections in which minor parties have totalled more than 10 per cent of the vote were those of 1943 (16.3 per cent), 1958 (10.6 per cent), 1977 (12.2 per cent), 1990 (17.2 per cent), 1993 (10.8 per cent), 1996 (14.3 per cent), 1998 (20.2 per cent), and 2001 (19.5 per cent).

[4] In the 1990 federal election the Australian Democrats won 11.3 per cent of the first preference vote.

TABLE 13.1. *Australian election results, 1961–2001*

Year	Liberal		Country/ National		Labor		Democratic Labor		Democrat		One Nation		Other		ENEP
	V	S	V	S	V	S	V	S	V	S	V	S	V	S	
1961	33.6	45	8.5	17	47.9	60	8.7	0					1.3	0	2.8
1963	37.1	52	8.9	20	45.5	50	7.4	0					1.1	0	2.8
1966	40.2	61	9.7	20	40.0	41	7.3	0					2.7	0	3.0
1969	34.8	46	8.6	20	47.0	59	6.0	0					3.7	0	2.8
1972	32.1	38	9.4	20	49.6	67	5.2	0					3.7	0	2.8
1974	34.9	40	10.8	21	49.3	66							5.0	0	2.7
1975	41.8	68	11.3	23	42.8	36							4.1	0	2.7
1977	38.1	67	10.0	19	39.6	38							9.4	0	3.2
1980	37.4	54	8.9	20	45.1	51			6.6	0			2.0	0	2.8
1983	34.4	33	9.2	17	49.5	75			5.0	0			1.9	0	2.7
1984	34.4	45	10.6	21	47.6	82			5.4	0			2.0	0	2.8
1987	34.6	43	11.5	19	45.8	86			6.0	0			2.1	0	2.9
1990	35.0	55	8.4	14	39.4	78			11.3	0			5.9	1	3.4
1993	37.1	49	7.2	16	44.9	80			3.8	0			7.0	2	2.9
1996	38.7	76	8.2	18	38.8	49			6.8	0			7.5	5	3.2
1998	34.0	63	5.7	16	40.1	66			5.1	0	8.4	0	7.0	2	3.5
2001	37.1	68	5.6	13	37.8	66			5.4	0	4.3	0	9.3	3	3.4

Notes: V—percentage of first preferences votes won by party candidates; S—Number of seats won; ENEP—Effective number of Electoral parties.

Sources: McAllister *et al.* 1997; Australian Electoral Commission website.

TABLE 13.2. *National party governments in Australia since 1949*

Government	Period	Prime minister
Liberal, Country[a]	Dec 1949–Dec 1972	Robert Menzies (Lib), Dec 1949–Jan 1966; Harold Holt (Lib), Jan 1967–Jan 1968; John Gorton (Lib), Jan 1968–Mar 1971; William McMahon (Lib), Mar 1971–Dec 1972
Labor	Dec 1972–Nov 1975	Gough Whitlam (Lab), Dec 1972–Nov 1975
Liberal, Country[a]	Nov 1975–Mar 1983	Malcolm Fraser (Lib), Nov 1975–Mar 1983
Labor	Mar 1983–Mar 1996	Bob Hawke (Lab), Mar 1983–Dec 1991; Paul Keating (Lab), Dec 1991–Mar 1996
Liberal, National[a]	Mar 1996–	John Howard (Lib), Mar 1996–

[a]The Country Party changed its name to the National Party in 1982.

Source: As for Table 13.1.

him the longest serving Australian prime minister, enjoying office for almost twice that of his nearest competitor for the honour, Bob Hawke.

The traditional view of Australian politics is that class has formed the basis for party political divisions for most of the twentieth century. A 1974 study showed, for example, that Australia had a stronger class cleavage than any other major democracy, with the exception of Austria and the Scandinavian countries (Rose 1974: 17). This view began to be questioned in the 1970s. Aitkin argued that while there was a stable level of class voting, it was relatively weak: 'Australian politics is the politics of parties, not of classes' (Aitkin 1982: 142). Similarly, Kemp (1978) claimed that the electoral importance of class had declined significantly in the 1960s and 1970s. More specifically, Kemp argued that structural changes caused by advanced industrial society, such as the decline in traditional blue collar occupations and the growth in public sector employment, were undermining the traditional class cleavage that had formed the basis of the party system since the turn of the century (Kemp 1978: 348–9).

While it is clear that class in the postwar years was never as electorally import- ant as many believed, it is also indisputable that social class, in its many forms, still exercises a significant influence over Australian political behaviour (Jones and McAllister 1989). The changes that have taken place in the postwar years, and more particularly since the 1960s, have served to strengthen two-party hegemony rather than weaken it. The rise of post-material values, reflected in the growth of environmentalism, has been an issue that has been adopted by both major par- ties, notably following the dramatic increase in electoral support for environment groups in the 1990 federal election (Bean *et al.* 1990). The parties have been equally adaptive in responding to new social groups. For example, starting with the Whitlam Labor government in the early 1970s, Labor has been by far the most successful in appealing to non-English speaking migrants, who now make up about one in every seven voters.

PARTY LEGITIMACY

Turnout

While political culture—in the broadest sense of a set of values, attitudes, and beliefs that exists within the mass electorate—is central to ensuring the continuing legitimacy of parties in Australian politics, political institutions provide form and substance to that legitimacy. Political parties were not recognized in the constitution until 1977, when an amendment was passed to permit the filling of casual vacancies in the Senate. Among the various political institutions, parties receive their strongest support in the electoral system. In the Senate, the single transferable vote system of proportional representation was altered in 1984 to permit voters to express ticket preferences—in effect, introducing a party list system in all but name. The preferential voting system (otherwise known as the Alternative Vote) based on single-member constituencies used in the House of Representatives since 1919 has also favoured the major parties, given its well-known tendency to produce disproportional outcomes.

But more important to the parties has been the system of compulsory voting, itself a direct consequence of the utilitarian political culture. Writing nearly half a century ago, the eminent overseas observer Overacker (1951) commented that 'the character of the party battle and the behaviour of the voters are affected by the compulsory franchise and preferential voting'. The system has its origins in the introduction of compulsory enrolment for all eligible voters for Commonwealth elections in 1911, a change which was quickly copied by the states. Compulsory voting was seen as a logical (and non-contentious) extension of compulsory enrolment. It was first introduced in Queensland in time for the 1915 general election and over the next three decades the other states and the Commonwealth followed suit: the Commonwealth in 1924, Victoria in 1926, New South Wales and Tasmania in 1928, Western Australia in 1936, and finally South Australia in 1941.

In all cases, the move to compulsion was bipartisan; it suited the convenience of all parties and was opposed by none. Normally the bill to introduce compulsion was presented by a private member. This enabled the major parties to allow a major shift in the system to occur without the risk that any party machine would be blamed. In the case of the Commonwealth, the entire 1924 debate in both houses took less than three hours; no government minister commented on its merits. The effect on turnout before and after the introduction of compulsion was dramatic, as intended. In the Commonwealth, turnout increased from 58 per cent in the last election under voluntary voting, to 91.3 per cent in the first election held under compulsory voting. In effect, the increase in turnout was significant and immediate, which was the goal of the politicians who introduced it. Ordinary citizens accepted the new system with little complaint and as a consequence the system has been easy to administer.

TABLE 13.3. *Electoral participation and volatility in Australia since 1961*

Year	Turnout	Informal votes	Total volatility	Bloc volatility
1961	95.3	2.6	5.2	4.4
1963	95.7	1.8	4.0	3.9
1966	95.1	3.1	5.6	4.8
1969	95.0	2.5	7.9	6.2
1972	95.4	2.2	3.5	1.9
1974	95.4	1.9	2.4	2.4
1975	95.4	1.9	7.6	7.4
1977	95.1	2.5	6.9	4.1
1980	94.4	2.4	7.5	3.7
1983	94.6	2.1	4.8	2.3
1984	94.5	6.8	1.9	1.5
1987	94.3	4.9	1.8	1.2
1990	95.8	3.2	9.5	2.0
1993	96.2	3.0	5.6	2.8
1996	96.2	3.2	6.3	3.6
1998	95.3	3.8	9.7	3.8
2001	95.3	4.8	6.1	2.5

Note: The Liberal–Nationals are considered a block for the entire period, Labor and Democratic Labor for the elections 1961–72, and Labor and the Australian Democrats for 1980–2001.

Sources: As for Table 13.1.

Since 1960, turnout in federal elections has averaged 95.2 per cent, showing that compulsion works (see Table 13.3). However, compulsory voting also has two consequences. First, there are a large proportion of invalid (called 'informal' in Australia) votes at elections. Australia has one of the highest levels of invalid votes among the established liberal democracies and is comparable to what was found in the Netherlands in the two decades after the Second World War, which had a compulsory voting system until 1971 (Irwin 1974). Voters who spoil their votes are more likely to be immigrants from non-English speaking countries: compulsion, combined with frequent federal and state elections and differing electoral systems, results in many spoiling their ballots (McAllister and Makkai 1993). Second, the compulsory voting system advantages the Labor Party, by forcing a proportion of apathetic voters to the polls who would otherwise abstain; since these voters are disproportionately lesser educated and young, they are more likely to vote Labor. Surveys suggest that Labor gains around 2.5 per cent of the first preference vote from compulsory voting (Mackerras and McAllister 1999).

Voters express widespread support for compulsory voting and there has been comparatively little change in their views during the postwar years. Since the 1940s support has never fallen below 60 per cent, and the highest recorded support was 76 per cent, in 1970 (Aitkin 1982: 31). Moreover, surveys which distinguish degrees of strength of support show that voters who favour a compulsory system have stronger views than those who favour a voluntary system.[5] As a direct result of the utilitarian political culture, Australian voters are not only comfortable with compulsory voting, they regard it as an important part of their democratic system.

But the consequences of compulsory voting have extended far beyond merely increasing voter turnout. For the political parties, they have relieved them of the need to mobilize the vote, perhaps their most ubiquitous function in modern democracies. This has reduced the parties' operating costs, and freed resources so they can be devoted to voter conversion. Increasingly, conversion has been conducted through the electronic media, with more traditional forms of campaigning, such as door-to-door canvassing, becoming ever more rare as the organizational bases within the electorate have declined.[6] Compulsory voting has also had the indirect effect of making parties less concerned about the quality of their candidates, since the personal vote is small (Bean 1990) and candidates rely on party labels for election.

Party identification

For voters, compulsory voting has had even more important consequences. Australia has a complicated set of election systems that differ between the states and the Commonwealth (i.e. the federal level), differ between the upper and lower houses, and have changed significantly over-time. In federal elections, voters use the preferential system based on single-member constituencies in lower house elections, but a modified form of the single transferable vote in upper house elections. In the states, the voting systems also vary between upper and lower houses. Just as important, federal elections must be held every three years and every six years for the upper house; in the states, the same rule for lower house elections applies, except in New South Wales where the period between elections is four years.[7] The net effect is that the average Australian voter must attend the polls—under the threat of a court-imposed fine—around once every 18 months, an unprecedented level of voting among the advanced democracies.

In practice, voters minimize the high levels of information required of them for electoral participation by maintaining a party identification. By ensuring that they identify with a party, voters take their cue from that party and thereby reduce their

[5] For example, in the 1998 AES survey 44 per cent of respondents strongly favoured compulsory voting, 28 per cent favoured it, 18 per cent favoured voluntary voting, and 10 per cent strongly favoured voluntary voting.

[6] Unfortunately, there are no concise over-time data concerning the proportions exposed in Australia to different forms of party campaigning. Prior to 1987, when the Australian Election Study survey started, there had been no academic surveys conducted during federal elections. In 1996, 2.1 per cent of those interviewed in the AES said that they had attended a meeting or rally conducted by an election candidate.

[7] The period between upper house elections in six years. Upper house elections may be held more frequently if there is a 'double dissolution' election, whereby both houses are dissolved simultaneously. This may occur if certain constitutional provisions are met.

information costs; equally, continual visits to the polls ensure that their partisanship remains salient. Parties also play their role in reinforcing the system by providing 'how to vote cards' to their intending voters outside polling stations; in the 1998 federal election, 52 per cent said that they followed a 'how to vote' card, compared to 48 per cent who said that they decided their own preferences. Party identification is, therefore, the basis for party stability. As Aitkin (1982: 1) argues, 'the causes of stability are to be found in the adoption, by millions of Australians then and since, of relatively unchanging feelings of loyalty to one or other of the Australian parties'.

Trends in the direction of party identification in Australia demonstrate that, with the exception of the late 1960s, a period of Labor decline, no more than 4 percentage points separated the proportions identifying with the two major parties (see Table 13.4). Although the vast majority of voters identify with one or other of the major parties, there has been an increase in the proportions with no party attachment. Indeed, this group has increased threefold in size since 1987, although the most recent 1998 survey suggests a modest decline. Party identification is also expressed in strength as well as direction, and there has clearly been a decline in the strength of party identification, as the table demonstrates. Those who see themselves as very strong identifiers have declined by almost half, from 34 per cent in 1979 to 18 per cent in 1998. The net increase resulting from this weakening in partisanship has taken place among those who are 'not very strong' partisans, who now make up one half of all voters. This declining strength in partisanship is a trend that also has been apparent in Britain and the United States, where it was first evident in the 1960s, somewhat earlier than in Australia.

Viewed from an international perspective, party identification remains high in Australia, and it is undoubtedly one of the major factors contributing to political stability. Nevertheless, the decline in the strength of partisanship, and more recent increases in the proportions of those with no party attachment, may presage the

TABLE 13.4. *The direction and strength of partisanship in Australia, 1967–2001*

Year	Direction				Strength		
	Labor	Lib–Nat	Other	None	Very strong	Fairly strong	Not very strong
1967	39	50	3	8	33	44	23
1969	40	47	9	4	34	48	18
1979	45	44	3	8	34	47	19
1987	47	44	4	5	20	47	33
1990	44	41	7	8	18	47	35
1993	44	41	3	12	19	49	32
1996	37	41	5	17	19	45	36
1998	41	38	7	14	18	32	50
2001	36	41	8	15	18	48	34

Sources: 1967 and 1979 Australian National Political Attitudes surveys; 1987–2001 Australian Election Study surveys.

long-term erosion of party identification, as has occurred elsewhere. One consequence may well be a slight growth in electoral volatility since 1987: thus, the twelve elections from 1961 to 1987 produced an average total net volatility level of 4.9, whereas those since have generated an average total volatility of 7.4 (see Table 13.3). Moreover, there is little doubt that weakening partisan identification was a major factor underlying the unprecedented support for minor parties in the 1990 and 1998 federal elections. Relatedly, in the 1996 federal election, an unprecedented five of the 148 lower house members elected were independents. Closer inspection, however, reveals that two were former Liberal incumbents from Western Australia who had resigned from the party, one was a former Labor incumbent expelled for his anti-immigration views, and one the former Liberal candidate, Pauline Hanson, to whom reference has already been made. Only one of the four, then, lacked a significant party background prior to the election. There remains, therefore, little evidence to support a party decline hypothesis.

Party membership

Membership and financial information concerning the parties is difficult to find, and such data, particularly with regard to membership, are often of questionable validity. In the case of the three main parties—the Labor, Liberal, and National parties—membership records are held by the states, not by the national party. Estimates of party membership in the mid-1990s show that the Nationals have the largest mass membership, at about 110,000, followed by about 63,500 Liberal members, 56,500 Labor, and 6000 Democrats (McAllister *et al.* 1997: 40ff). This suggests that about 2.1 per cent of the eligible electorate is a current member of a political party, a figure which is corroborated by survey estimates.[8]

Overtime membership statistics, such as are available, show considerable fluctuation. The National Party, currently the largest in terms of mass membership, is the only party to have shown a consistent increase since the late 1960s. However, the Nationals are the least strict in terms of their interpretation of who is a party member, counting those who have not renewed their membership, as well as permitting family memberships which obviously inflates the estimates (Ward 1991: 158). The Liberal Party has registered a consistent decline in membership from 127,000 in 1967 to 64,000 in 1996. At its peak in 1950, the party had 89,000 members in New South Wales and Victoria alone (Ward 1991: 156). By contrast, Labor's membership has been more stable, although it too is at a historic low: on the eve of the Second World War, the party had 370,000 members, nearly seven times its current membership (Crisp 1955: 20). There are few reliable estimates of the Australian Democrats' membership; most suggest a membership in the region of 4000 to 6000 (Ward 1997: 113).

---

[8] The 1996 AES found that 2.5 per cent of voters were current members of one of the four parties. A much larger proportion, 5.9 per cent, reported that they were past party members.

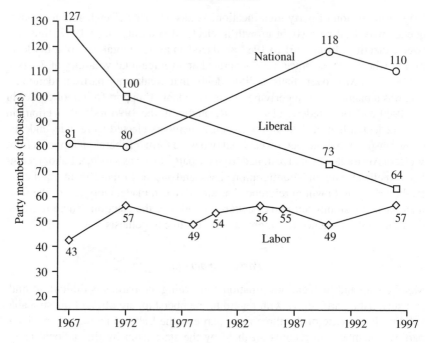

FIGURE 13.1. Party membership in Australia, 1967–96

Note: National Party estimates are inflated by family memberships.

Sources: Ward (1991); McAllister *et al.* (1997).

Attitudes towards parties

Not surprisingly given their prominence within the political system, voters see political parties as essential for the smooth and efficient operation of the democratic system. Just under half of those interviewed in the 1998 AES took a neutral stance on whether or not parties were doing a good job, but of those who did take a position, one-third had a positive view, compared to 22 per cent who were negative (Table 13.5). However, the overwhelming majority of those who take a positive view of parties—as well as those who are neutral towards them—express satisfaction with the workings of Australian democracy. By contrast, a majority of those who are negative towards parties are also dissatisfied about democratic functioning, which tends to confirm the importance to democracy of parties. Parties, then, are intimately bound up in the public mind with how the democracy operates, and how they feel about it.

Summarizing briefly the evidence on party legitimacy, then, over the course of the past twenty years, electoral volatility and minor-party support have both increased, while levels of partisanship and, probably, party membership have decreased. This suggests some distancing of electors from parties; even so, it is

TABLE 13.5. *Attitudes towards parties and democracy in Australia*[a]

	Total	Satisfaction with Australian democracy				(N)
		Very satisfied	Satisfied	Not very satisified	Not at all satisfied	
Parties do a						
Very good job	2	53	38	6	3	(34)
Good job	31	25	69	5	1	(578)
Neither	45	9	63	24	4	(847)
Bad job	16	4	37	49	10	(296)
Very bad job	6	9	11	37	43	(115)
	(1878)	(14)	(57)	(23)	(6)	(1870)

[a]Question wordings are: 'In general, do you think political parties are doing a very good job, a good job, neither a good nor a bad job, a bad job, or a very bad job for the people of Australia?'; 'On the whole, are you very satisfied, fairly satisfied, not very satisfied or not at all satisfied with the way democracy works in Australia?'

Source: 1998 Australian Election Study survey.

fair to suggest that partisan identification and turnout remain high in comparative terms, while overt disaffection with parties is fairly low, though a not insignificant minority hold negative orientations.

ORGANIZATIONAL STRENGTH

Evaluating changes in party organization in Australia is complicated by several factors. The first is the functional division between parties at the federal or national level, and at the state and territory level. Each of the major parties consists of a loose coalition composed of their respective state and territory parties, the cohesiveness of the coalition depending on the ability of the national party to exercise control over its constituent parts. In the Labor Party, some degree of central control is exercised over the state parties, largely because the party itself has been opposed to federalism (Parkin and Warhurst 1983; Galligan and Mardiste 1992). The Liberal Party is more of a federal party than Labor, depending almost entirely on its state counterparts for resources and support. Most federal of all is the National Party 'whose state branches are autonomous to the greatest degree and its national organization almost non-existent' (Jaensch 1994: 121).

The particular origins of each of the parties has helped to shape their organizational development. The Labor and National parties have their origins in mass movements existing outside parliament, in the labour and farmers' movements, respectively. In the Labor Party, this led to the dominance of the trade unions within the party, but it had fewer consequences for the Nationals, who swiftly established themselves as a parliamentary party, albeit based on a mass membership. The

Liberal Party was formed within parliament as a classic cadre party in Duverger's (1954) sense, only later branching out into the wider society to garner support. Thus, while ideology has played a major role in shaping Labor's policies, the Liberal Party has been guided more by pragmatism, expediency, and the pursuit of power (Jaensch 1994: 117).

There has been considerable change in the organizational bases of the parties since the 1960s. First, a highly organized factional system emerged in the Labor Party in the 1980s, mainly in response to the need to balance a wide electoral appeal with ideological commitment among the mass membership. There are three highly organized national factions, incorporating their own memberships, office-bearers, and holding regular conferences to discuss policy. Most Labor candidates are now factional members—indeed, factional considerations are often a major consideration in candidate selection—and in the 1994 National Conference, every single delegate was aligned with one of the three national factions (McAllister *et al.* 1997). Most parliamentarians are also factional members; in 1996, the AES showed that all but four of those responding to the survey were members of one of the four factions. The purpose of the factions is to enable the party to project as wide an electoral appeal as possible, while still maintaining its organizational integrity (McAllister 1991).

Second, in line with other labour and social democratic parties, the Labor Party has sought to reduce the influence of its trade union wing on party policy. Although the influence of the trade unions has varied from state to state, with South Australia, for example, being almost entirely dominated by the unions, traditionally any change in party policy must have union support. Until the 1960s, party policy was made by a group of six nominated by each state conference; parliamentary members of the party, much less the party leader, were excluded. These six individuals were described in a famous phrase by the Liberal prime minister, Robert Menzies, as 'the faceless men.' Criticism of this system of policy-making led to the establishment of a biennial National Conference, consisting of 190 delegates from the states and including parliamentary members: this is now the supreme policy-making body within the party.

There have also been more direct efforts to limit the power of the trade unions in the Labor Party. In 1973, a party subcommittee recommended that other elements within the party, such as women's and youth groups, should have greater representation. This proposal was defeated by the unions, but in 1980 the system was reformed to limit the unions to 75 per cent of the total votes cast at the biennial conference, a figure which was subsequently reduced to 60 per cent. Such reductions in the role played by the trade unions in the party have also been stimulated by the falling proportion of union members in the workforce; this peaked in the early postwar years, at 62 per cent, and remained at just over 50 per cent for most of the 1960s and 1970s. It declined in the late 1980s, and by 1994 just 35 per cent of the workforce were union members (McAllister *et al.* 1997: 522). Nevertheless, among the Labor candidates interviewed in the 1996 Australian

Election Study, only 14 per cent said that they had never been active in union or staff association affairs.[9]

Party finance

As with party membership figures, obtaining reliable estimates of the cost of running the parties is problematic, with the partial exception of federal election years when properly audited figures must be submitted to the Australian Electoral Commission. The adoption of modern campaigning techniques in the 1980s, mainly relying on the electronic media, has seen a spiralling of election costs for the major parties. This is now the major component of the major parties' federal election spending and has driven up their overall expenditure levels. In the 1974, 1975, and 1977 federal elections, the Liberal–National parties' spending on the campaigns did not exceed $A1.26 million, while the cost to Labor was somewhat less. The 1983 election campaign was the first in which Labor spent more than $A1 million and costs have escalated consistently since. In the 1987 and 1990 elections, Labor expenditure greatly exceeded that of their Liberal–National competitors. The 1993 election saw some reduction in costs, reflecting the problems the parties were encountering in paying off their debts.

While the inconsistency of data reporting over the years makes it difficult to be exact, we may be confident that parties are significantly better resourced in real terms than they were in the 1960s, at least during federal election years. Public funding of parties' federal election campaigns was introduced in 1984, greatly increasing the overall cost of elections to the state: thus the total state expenditure on the 1983 election was $A18.7 million whereas barely 12 months later it had leapt to $A38.4 million. In real terms, the cost to the state remained fairly constant during the 1980s, but jumped at the 1996 election to $A51.6 million at 1984 price levels (see Fig. 13.2). Moreover, the proportion of the total public bill absorbed by party funding has increased: in 1993, it was just 23 per cent, but in 1996 and 1998 it was 35 per cent. At the same time, state expenditure on federal elections *excluding* party funding has actually decreased in real terms per elector since 1984, so we may infer that it is the growth in subventions to parties which has driven the real-term increase in state spending on elections. A candidate or parliamentary group is eligible for election funding if they win at least 4 per cent of the formal first preference vote in the division or the State or Territory they contest. The amount paid is calculated by multiplying the number of votes won by an inflation-indexed funding rate; this rate stood at 162.21 cents per vote in 1998.

We have already noted the declining memberships of (some) Australian parties since the 1960s, but the parties remain sufficiently mass-based to conduct their electoral functions satisfactorily. Much of the explanation for why the

---

[9] A total of 54 per cent said that they had been 'very active' in trade union or staff association affairs, 33 per cent 'somewhat active' and 14 per cent 'not active.'

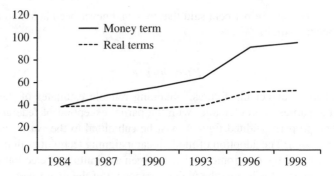

FIGURE 13.2. Total public cost of federal elections, 1984–98

Notes: Amounts reported in $A millions, holding values constant at December 1984 price levels.

Source: Australian Electoral Commission website (http://www.aec.gov.au/ results/1998/report/appendix.htm).

organizations can experience decline without any significant degradation in their performance rests with the system of compulsory voting. In general, parties mainly rely on their mass memberships to mobilize the vote; freed of this by compulsory voting, the parties use the mass media to appeal for votes. That, of course, requires finance, but few modern mass-based parties rely on their membership for the bulk of their finance. Like the Labor and Liberal parties, most are financed from corporate donors and wealthy individuals. A partial exception is the Australian Democrats, whose financial basis is heavily dependent on the fund-raising activities of their (limited) membership.

Mass media

As the foregoing has made clear, much of the parties' effort in the area of voter conversion has been aimed at political advertising through the mass media, rather than in canvassing or local campaigning. Australia has strict rules concerning political advertising in the mass media; all advertising must be authorized, with the name and address of the approving person appearing on the item, and legislation prohibits any advertising that may mislead electors into casting a vote.[10] In the broadcast media, there are three levels of political advertising. 'Political matter'

---

[10] This clause is notable for producing Amnesty International's first ever prisoner of conscience in Australia, Albert Langer. During the 1996 election, Langer urged voters to use their preferences under the alternative vote electoral system to disadvantage the major parties. Under the Electoral Act, such a strategy did not invalidate a vote, but it was illegal to publicize it. When Langer breached a court injunction brought by the Australian Electoral Commission not to place any further advertisements in national newspapers outlining his strategy, he was jailed. Similar advertisements appeared during the 1998 campaign, but Langer was not prosecuted.

is defined mainly as coverage of policy items outside the context of an election campaign; 'election matter' includes commentary, interviews, and announcements that expressly solicit votes or advocate support; and 'election advertisements' are sponsored by candidates or parties. The boundaries between the three types of political advertising remain controversial and have been the subject of several court cases, with opposition parties challenging the government's use of public money to publicize what they regard as party policy. There is no limit on the amount that the parties may spend on paid political advertising.

Despite the considerable amounts that the major parties spend on political advertising, Australian Election Survey data suggests that fewer voters are following election news in the mass media. In 1987, the first election for which data are available, just over a half of all voters said that they followed election news regularly on the television, and around three out of every ten regularly followed the election in newspapers and the radio. The trend since has shown a decline; in the most recent federal election, just 32 per cent regularly followed election news on the television, and about two out of every ten voters on the other two media.[11] The decline in the use of television for election coverage also comes at a time when it is used more consistently for debates between the major party leaders. Leaders' debates have taken place at every federal election since 1984, with the exception of 1987. In 1990, 56 per cent of voters said that they had watched the leaders' debate (then between Bob Hawke and Andrew Peacock), compared to 43 per cent in 1998 (between John Howard and Kim Beazley).[12]

The decline in the use of the mass media for election information is difficult to explain, particularly in view of the increasing levels of education within the electorate. For example, in 1967, just 3 per cent of the electorate had a university education, compared to 10 per cent in 1987 and 18 per cent in 1998. Moreover, in line with increasing cognitive mobilization, political interest has also increased: in 1967, 18 per cent said that they had 'a good deal' of interest in politics, compared to 35 per cent in 1987. However, the greater prevalence of education since 1987 does not appear to have further increased interest in politics, and in the election surveys conducted since 1987, those saying that they had 'a good deal' of interest has remained constant at an average of around 35 per cent.[13] It may be, therefore, that the impact of education on cognitive mobilization (and hence following election news) has peaked.

Overall, Australian party organizations cannot be said to show signs of serious weakening. Though their membership levels may have fallen away, this is hardly

---

[11] Nor does the internet appear to be a substitute source of election coverage. In the 1998 federal election, just 4 per cent said that they had accessed election information from the internet.

[12] In 1993 and 1996, two debates were held rather than one, making overtime comparisons difficult. Nevertheless, in 1993, 40 per cent said that they had watched both debates and 31 per cent one only; the 1996 figures were 32 and 26 per cent, respectively.

[13] Namely, 35 per cent in 1987; 36 per cent in 1990; 38 per cent in 1993; 32 per cent in 1996; and 36 per cent in 1998.

crucial in the context of compulsory voting and the investment made by parties in televisual forms of political communication with the electorate. Moreover, while it has not been possible to gather accurate data on party staffing for this chapter, it seems unlikely that this would have eroded given the growing financial capability of Australian parties.

SYSTEMIC FUNCTIONALITY

Governance

Notions of governance and accountability in Australia have followed Westminster conventions, with the British model forming the basis for the 1901 constitution that established the federation (Crisp 1965; Butler 1973). Notwithstanding this inheritance, a distinctive Australian approach to representation has been shaped by three factors. First, as already discussed, a federal system was introduced to permit the pre-1901 colonies to retain a degree of political independence. A second consideration is the size of the country. With 17 million people in an island continent that exceeds the size of Europe, elected representatives often have to travel long distances between their electorates and the federal capital in Canberra. Even within their electorates, the distances are often considerable: the Western Australian parliamentary constituency of Kalgoorlie, for example, is the largest in the world and exceeds the size of France. Within these vast territories, voters are often very remote, physically and politically, from their chosen representatives.

A third modification to the Westminster model of responsible party government is the level of discipline that the Australian parties enforce on their members. Labor was the first to achieve effective discipline at both the electoral and parliamentary levels, but the Liberals, of necessity, soon followed (Rydon 1986: 188). Dissent from the party line within the House of Representatives is almost unknown and the party machines have a variety of means by which they can enforce discipline among their members, not the least of which is the threat of 'deselection'—the removal of the person as the party candidate in a constituency. As Jaensch (1994: 239) puts it, 'legislative voting is redundant, except on the rare "conscience votes" or the rare case when a member of the Liberal or National parties has come under pressure from constituents or the local or state party base.'

The dangers of party were well understood by the founding fathers, and their solution was to establish a directly-elected upper house, the Senate. The Senate is composed of equal numbers of members from all of the original six colonies, and was intended to be a house of review equal in status to the House of Representatives. However, during the course of the twentieth century the Senate has lost many of its powers to the lower house and party political factors are at least as important in the

Senate as they are in the House of Representatives (Farrell and McAllister 1995).[14] Party control of the Senate was consolidated by the introduction of proportional representation and a doubling of the members in 1949, and more importantly by the introduction of ticket voting in 1984. About nine out of every ten Senate voters now choose the party ticket, thus consolidating party control of the chamber.

In assessing the role of political parties in governance, the functional division that exists between state and federal politics is perhaps the most important consideration. While the federal government is predominantly concerned with the 'high' politics of macroeconomic management, foreign affairs, international trade and defence, the state and territory governments deal with the day-to-day issues of social welfare, health, economic development, regulation, law enforcement, and the myriad of other responsibilities that affect the everyday lives of citizens. Although the federal government retains ultimate control of these functions through the disbursement of finance,[15] the delivery of these services, and the policies that determine how and to whom they are to be delivered, is a state matter.

There is considerable anecdotal evidence to suggest that voters make a distinction between the state and federal parties and are, on occasion, prepared to vote for different parties between the two types of election. Party control often differs between state and federal electorates, and different parties often control the state and federal governments.[16] The reality, however, is that until recently relatively few voters are prepared to change their vote between state and federal elections. Table 13.6 reveals that in 1967, 88 per cent of survey respondents said that they voted for the same party in the most recent state and federal election; in 1993, the figure was 82 per cent. Between 1993 and 1998, however, voters casting a ballot between different parties in the federal election and their most recent state election almost doubled, to 30 per cent. At the same time, the slow decline in consistent Labor voters continued. Whether this represents a continuing trend or merely a consequence of the particular circumstances of state politics must await further elections.

But even if voters are more inclined to want different party governments at state and federal levels, they still favour major-party governments. There is little evidence that minor parties and independents are making any significant inroads into the electoral support which the major parties traditionally attract across the states, at least in the lower houses. Between 1960 and 1997, lower house elections in the

---

[14] Senators are elected for six-year terms, with half retiring every three years. The method of election is the single transferable vote method of proportional representation in which a whole state forms the constituency. However, since 1984 voters have had the option of selecting particular candidates, or opting for a party ticket. This has had the effect of increasing party influence within the Senate.

[15] In the 1942 Uniform Tax case the High Court ruled, in effect, that the states were unable to levy income tax, thereby making them dependent on the federal government for finance.

[16] There is comparatively little crossover in personnel between state and federal politics. For example, unlike Britain or the United States, where local and state government, respectively, are viewed as training grounds for national office, Australian state politicians rarely move into federal politics.

TABLE 13.6. *Party support in federal and state elections in Australia, 1967–2001*

	1967	1979	1993	1998	2001	Change 1967–2001
Consistent						
Labor	50	44	40	36	34	−16
Lib–Nat	38	43	42	35	39	−1
Other	3	2	2	5	5	+2
Inconsistent	9	11	16	30	22	+13

Note: Figures are the per cent voting consistently Labor, Liberal–National or other party in the most recent state and federal election, or who changed their vote. Question wordings differ between surveys.

Sources: 1967 and 1979 Australian National Political Attitudes surveys; 1993, 1998 and 2001 Australian Election Study surveys.

six states produced no clear trend. In Victoria and South Australia, there has been no significant trend either up or down, in NSW, Western Australia and Tasmania, there has been an upwards trend, and in Queensland a substantial downward trend. In the five states which have retained upper houses, minor party representation is higher.[17] For example, in the 1995 election to the NSW upper house, seven of the 42 seats (or just under 10 per cent) were won by non-major party candidates.

There are a variety of explanations for the absence of any evidence of party decline at the state level. Most obviously, patterns of state political behaviour represent a continuation of the stable patterns found at the national level, reflected at both levels of government by high levels of party identification which is in turn reinforced by the system of compulsory voting. In addition, voters are also less likely to hold the government responsible for macroeconomic problems; 'the villain in the piece is not an effective national government, but powerful, self-interested forces outside Australia whose actions distort an otherwise robust national economy' (Mughan 1987: 73). This effectively insulates the federal government from responsibility for national economic conditions, which, admittedly, does serve to undermine the pure model of party government (Katz 1986). To be sure, voters expect their state governments to be competent financial managers—and spectacular financial disasters in three states in the 1980s produced decisive changes in government as a consequence—but this has not produced any crisis of governability (Sharman 1997). Ultimately, Australian voters retain confidence in their political system, a system in which the major parties predominate in government at state and federal levels.

---

[17] The upper house was abolished in Queensland in 1921.

Interest articulation and aggregation

In line with other advanced societies, interest groups have become more important in shaping public policy. This has been motivated by the increase in the scope of government responsibility for a wide range of liberal-egalitarian issues, ranging from gender equity and the environment, to aboriginal and consumer rights. In turn, this has emphasized the relative inability of two major parties divided on the question of economic management to accommodate such social issues on their policy agendas (Marsh 1995: 82). This has probably resulted in the decline of party memberships observed earlier, as well as an increase in the membership of single-issue groups, which have become much more visible and influential within the policy process. As in many other societies, paramount among these groups has been the environmental movement.

After a steady increase during the 1980s, public concerns for environmentalism peaked in the late 1980s (McAllister and Studlar 1993; Crook and Pakulski 1995). In line with these concerns, public support for environmental groups articulating these concerns also rose dramatically. These groups have espoused a wide variety of policies and opinions, ranging from lobbying governments on a narrow range of environmental issues, to outright hostility towards economic growth and support for a fundamental reorganization of society. While the political parties are aligned along the Old Politics dimension, these environmental groups range across the whole spectrum of New Politics concerns and demands. The diversity of the movement rests on the ambiguity which surrounds the notion of 'the environment': for some, it implies the natural environment; for others, it encompasses the human environment; and for a minority it extends to tangential concerns such as feminism (Burningham and O'Brien 1994).

The electoral influence of the environmental movement was demonstrated in the 1990 federal election, when various mainly uncoordinated groups achieved the highest third-party vote ever recorded in a federal election (Bean *et al.* 1990). Australia's preferential vote electoral system meant that most of these votes flowed to the Labor Party, which was viewed as being more favourable to the issue than the conservative Liberal–National coalition. Without these environmentalist vote preferences, it is likely that Labor would have lost the election. At the state level, too, environmental groups have seen some electoral success. In Tasmania, which hosted the formation of arguably the world's first environmental group in the early 1970s, greens have held five of the thirty-five lower house seats since 1989.

The eclecticism of the environmental movement, coupled with the general suspicion of organization and bureaucracy which is inherent in New Politics values, means that membership information for many of the groups is difficult to find.[18] The figures that are available suggest that support peaked in the early 1990s and

---

[18] In some cases this is deliberate: the concept of formal membership is rejected and activists simply participate as and when the need arises and are so inclined. In other cases, this is because none of the relevant information is collected centrally. However, several groups obtain substantial funding from

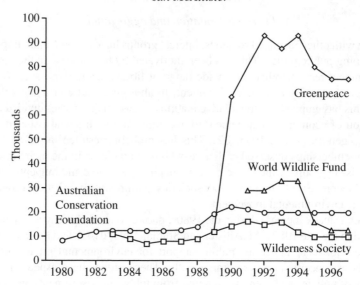

FIGURE 13.3. Membership of environmental groups in Australia, 1980–97

Sources: Papadakis (1993); Directory of Australian Associations, various years.

has either declined or remained stable since then, at least for the more prominent organizations (Fig. 13.3). In the case of the relatively moderate World Wildlife Fund, for example, membership collapsed from 33,000 in 1994, to 16,000 in 1995. Most dramatic of all is Greenpeace. Greenpeace was relatively ineffective in Australia until the early 1990s, when the international body sent one of its most experienced organizers to revitalize the local group (Papadakis 1993: 100). The overhaul of the organization, together with better publicity and a concerted attempt to advertise the movement's goals in the press, had the effect of more than doubling the membership in just three years. However, it too has suffered a recent decline, from a peak of 93,000 in 1994, to 75,000 in 1997.

Environmental groups have more than twice the active members counted by the political parties. The 1995 World Values Survey conducted in Australia found that just under 3 per cent of those interviewed said that they were active party members, compared to 7 per cent who said they were active in environment groups. However, both groups are eclipsed by the size of the active memberships of sporting, church, and arts organizations: about one in every three Australians says that he is active in a sporting organization, and about one in four in an organization associated with the arts. Only about one in eight says that he is active in a trade union, reflecting a long-term decline in union membership, not just in Australia but worldwide. There is little overlap in membership between members of parties and members

the federal government, and this means that they are required to submit membership statistics as a condition of their funding.

of environment groups. Among party members, 19 per cent say that they are also active in environment groups; among environment group members, just 7 per cent report party membership. In short, parties have struggled to articulate and aggregate the range of social interests since the emergence of New Politics activism.

Political recruitment

Legislative recruitment in Australia is party recruitment; political parties select the candidates, and without a party label, election is extremely difficult. Of the 2244 contests for the federal lower house that have taken place between 1949 and 1998, only nine—or 0.4 per cent—have been won by independents. However, four of the nine independents had previously been elected under a party label, and for various reasons resigned or been expelled from their party; only four contests, then, have been won by independents without a prior party association in the electorate. But not only is party recruitment dependent on being a party member, election candidates are drawn disproportionately from the ranks of those who have previously provided the party with party service; full-time party employees have a significantly greater chance of recruitment than party members who had not held such a position (McAllister 1997*a*). Thus, parties are a vehicle for professional political careers.

In 1996, around one quarter of the candidates for both major parties had some prior family political involvement, through having a close family member who had stood for election. Moreover, during the short six-year period for which data are available, a family background in politics appears to have become more important in ensuring recruitment within either party (Fig. 13.4). Having worked in a state or federal MP's office is also an important route for recruitment, notably within the Labor Party: in 1996, more than one in five Labor candidates said that they had held such a position at some time. However, such a route of entry into elective politics appears to have become significantly more important for aspiring Liberal–National politicians. Finally, having been employed as a party official is less important than other aspect of recruitment; nevertheless, given the relatively small numbers involved in full-time party work, the estimates suggest that a significant number of them move into an elected position.

Political participation

There have been no systematic studies of party members in Australia, beyond anecdotal works or limited surveys of particular party branches (see, for example, Simms 1997; Ward 1997). In part, this reflects the relative unimportance of the party membership in elections: voter mobilization is achieved through compulsory voting, and voter conversion is effected through the electronic media. The role of party members in elections is restricted to handing out 'how to vote' cards at polling places and distributing candidates' election addresses. In part, too, as

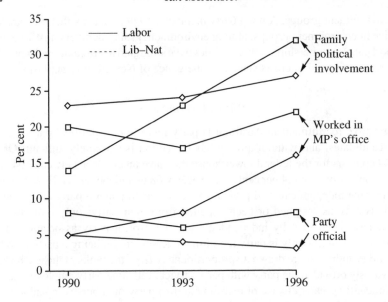

FIGURE 13.4. Party service and recruitment in Australia, 1990–96

Note: 'Family political involvement' refers to a close family member standing for state or federal election; 'worked in MP's office' refers to state or federal MP or minister; 'party official' refers to employment by state or federal party. Question wordings differ slightly between surveys.

Sources: 1990–96 Australian Election Study surveys, candidate samples.

already noted, the lack of any systematic study of party members is a practical consequence of the absence of any centralized membership records among the major parties. Compared to studies in other countries, we know comparatively little about the characteristics of Australian party members. Fortunately, we can go some way towards redressing this deficiency. The 1996 Australian Election Study survey asked a sample of voters whether they were current or past party members; while the numbers are small—123 respondents out of the total sample of 1795 fell into this category—the data do enable us to make some preliminary estimates concerning the activism and social profile of party members (see Table 13.7).

Australian party members are about as active in their respective organizations as party members elsewhere. One-third of current members reported contributing money to their party during the election campaign, while 27 per cent said that they had worked for the party or an election candidate. Among the two major parties, financial contributions are more common among the Liberals, while engaging in party work records similar levels across both parties. These levels of activism are similar to those that have been found in Britain (Seyd and Whiteley 1992; Whiteley *et al.* 1994). Members are also older than the electorate as a whole—just under 55 years, on average, compared to 45.5 years for all

TABLE 13.7. *Characteristics of party members in Australia*

| | Status | | Party[a] | | |
	Current	Past	Labor	Liberal	Electorate
Activism[b] (per cent)					
Contributed money	33*	4*	8*	17*	1
Worked for party	27*	8*	21*	19*	1
Gender (per cent male)	54	46	48	41	48
Age (mean years)	54.8	53.9*	49.4	55.2*	45.5
Australian born (per cent)	83	86	82	88	76
Tertiary education (per cent)	26	31	38	23	23
(*N*)	(53)	(72)	(41)	(44)	(1669)

*Statistically significant from the electorate at $p < 0.01$, two-tailed.
[a]Party estimates combine past and current members.
[b]The questions were: 'During the election campaign, did you do any of the following things? Contribute money to a political party or election candidate? Do any work for a political party or election candidate?'

Source: 1996 Australian Election Study survey.

voters—but unlike election candidates, they are not significantly more likely to be male than the electorate as a whole. They are, however, more likely to be Australian born. Rather as in Britain, therefore, Australian parties tend to be good only at mobilizing the direct participation of small groups of socially unrepresentative citizens.

Political communication and education

Although the data presented in Fig. 13.1 suggested that party membership in Australia had been gradually declining, some 236,000 citizens remain members of political parties—around one for every forty-eight voters. Since the average voter will know at least one party member in their social or family circle and probably more, such penetration serves to further legitimize parties in the eyes of the electorate. But perhaps more importantly, Australia's federal structure also has a major role to play in political communication. In addition to the 224 members of the federal parliament, there are 618 members of the upper and lower houses in the states and territories, the vast majority of them elected as members of the major parties.[19] Australia's total of 842 elected representatives means

---

[19] There are 148 members of the House of Representatives and 76 members of the Senate. Upper and lower house representation in the states and territories is as follows: NSW (42, 99); Victoria (44, 88); Queensland (no upper house, 89); South Australia (22, 47); Western Australia (34, 57); Tasmania (no upper house, 25); Northern Territory (no upper house, 25); Australian Capital Territory (no upper house, 17).

that there is one elected representative for every 13,300 voters. Once again, this brings parties and the whole panoply of public policy much closer to the average citizen.

The net effect of such a large number of elected representatives is to make government more accessible to voters. The 1993 AES asked a series of questions which attempted to measure the extent to which citizens had contact with their federal elected representative. Almost one in ten said that they had met the representative during the previous year, while 5 per cent had been to a meeting that he or she had addressed. Perhaps more revealingly, almost one in four said that they or someone at their home had contacted their federal MP at some stage, almost equally divided between seeking information and those seeking help. If we extrapolate these estimates to state elected representatives, it suggests that a significant proportion of the population makes contact with their elected representatives, and that these elected representatives play an important role within the mass electorate in disseminating information, opinions, and views.

The party elites, acting on a bipartisan basis, have also sought to educate the public in two ways. First, civic education has been actively promoted as a means of producing a more knowledgeable and politically active electorate. Although civic education had been an important part of the school curriculum in the years before the Second World War, its nationalist focus caused it to fall into disfavour in the 1960s and 1970s. Interest in civic education re-emerged in the 1980s, and in 1989 the Australian Education Council announced that one of its goals would be 'to develop knowledge, skills and attitudes and values which will enable students to participate as active and informed citizens in our democratic Australian society within an international context' (quoted in McAllister 1998: 10). In 1994 the Labor government established a Civic Experts Group which proposed an extensive programme of civic education which would take place in schools and tertiary institutions. This initiative was maintained by the incoming Liberal–National government in 1996.

A second example of political education, it might be argued, has been the concern among political elites to exclude race or ethnic issues from the political agenda. In a country with a large immigrant population and continuing tensions between aboriginal and white Australians, politicizing racial or ethnic issues has considerable potential to threaten the stability of the political system. Party elites have realized this and have maintained an informal bipartisan consensus that these issues should not become election issues. Almost without exception, when issues such as multiculturalism or Asian immigration have been raised, party elites have acted swiftly to stifle the debate (McAllister 1993). This bipartisan consensus was placed under considerable strain during the 1998 federal election, with the rise of Pauline Hanson's One Nation Party. The Liberals and Nationals had the most to lose electorally, but most conservative politicians refused to endorse One Nation preferences on their 'how to vote cards.' The net effect was to isolate One Nation from the established major parties.

CONCLUSION

The confluence of several events has resulted in Australian democracy becoming synonymous with party democracy—and with the continuation of this pattern of politics in the face of party decline in comparable polities. First, Australian democracy was established much earlier than elsewhere: in the late nineteenth century, Australia was a laboratory for electoral experiments in democracy, introducing manhood suffrage, votes for women, the secret ballot, payment for electoral representatives, and abolishing plural voting before every other democratic country, with the partial exception of New Zealand.[20] Second, the cleavage structure around which the party system evolved was frozen during this period of experimentation and has remained stable and salient during the course of the century since. Third, and most importantly, the political system was embedded within a utilitarian political culture, where efficiency was and is regarded as paramount. What is more efficient than mass political parties, providing accountability, policy choice, and a ready and able elite willing to hold political office?

Utilitarianism and its practical embodiment within the electoral system—compulsory voting—have ensured that Australian political parties have remained dominant and relatively unchallenged during the course of the twentieth century. Each new generation identifies with and retains a party loyalty, and that loyalty is reinforced by a regular round of state and federal elections which involve nineteen out of every twenty voters. The result has been remarkable stability in party support over an extended period, with few challenges to the integrity of the party system. Voters regard parties, along with voting, as an essential component of political competence and the vast majority see parties as central for making democracy work. Such a belief in the utility of parties sets Australia apart from the other advanced democracies.

That does not mean, of course, that the parties have not adapted and changed to retain their hegemonic position. The Australian parties have been particularly adept at responding to and incorporating incipient political challenges. In the early 1990s, it appeared that environmentalism might engender a serious challenge to the party system; both major parties enthusiastically embraced environmental protection as a majority policy priority. In the 1980s, the Labor Party adopted the free market policies espoused by conservative parties elsewhere; the resulting strains within the mass membership were effectively contained by the development of a complex and sophisticated system of intraparty factions. When change has threatened the Australian parties, they have been equal to the task of accommodating it.

---

[20] Prior to the establishment of the Commonwealth in 1901, most electoral changes had been introduced in the colonies. Votes for women was introduced as early as 1894 in South Australia (compared to 1893 in New Zealand), the secret ballot in the 1850s and payment for members in the 1890s. Plural voting was abolished in most of the colonies in the late 1880s and 1890s (McAllister 1997b: 8).

There has been some erosion of party support, in strength rather than in direction, and the mass memberships of some of the parties appear to be in decline. Both major parties have experienced a weakening in the strength of their supporters' commitment, and the mass membership of the Liberal Party, in particular, appears to be in long-term decline. Whether this forebodes any significant long-term party decline remains to be seen, and the evidence, both at the state and federal levels, is mixed. Past experience, however, suggests that unless there is a fundamental shift in the political culture that underlies the political system, the hegemony of the established parties is secure.

REFERENCES

Aitkin, D. (1982) *Stability and Change in Australian Politics*, 2nd edn (Canberra: ANU Press).

Bean, C. (1990) 'The personal vote in Australian federal elections'. *Political Studies* 38: 253–68.

—— (1991) 'Are Australian attitudes to government different? A comparison with five other nations', in Francis G. Castles (ed.) *Australia Compared* (Sydney: Allen and Unwin).

—— McAllister, I., and Warhurst, J. (1990) *The Greening of Australian Politics* (Melbourne: Longman Chesire).

Burningham, K. and O'Brien, M. (1994) 'Global environmental values and local contexts of action'. *Sociology* 28: 293–316.

Butler, D. (1973) *The Canberra Model* (Melbourne: Macmillan).

Collins, H. (1985) 'Political ideology in Australia: the distinctiveness of a Benthamite society'. *Daedalus* 114: 147–69.

Crisp, L. F. (1955) *The Australian Federal Labor Party, 1901–51* (Sydney: Longmans).

—— (1965) *Australian National Government* (Melbourne: Longman).

Crook, S. and Pakulski, J. (1995) 'Shades of green: public opinion on environmental issues in Australia'. *Australian Journal of Political Science* 30: 39–55.

Duverger, M. (1954) *Political Parties: Their Organization and Activity in the Modern State* (London: Methuen).

Farrell, D. and McAllister, I. (1995) 'Legislative recruitment to Upper Houses: the Australian Senate and the House of Representatives compared'. *Journal of Legislative Studies* 1: 243–63.

Galligan, B. and Mardiste, D. (1992) 'Labor's reconciliation with federalism'. *Australian Journal of Political Science* 27: 71–86.

Hancock, W. K. (1930) *Australia* (London: Ernst Benn).

Hartz, L. (1964) *The Founding of New Societies* (New York: Harcourt, Brace & World).

Hughes, C. A. (1973) 'Political culture', in Henry Mayer and Helen Nelson (eds) *Australian Politics: A Third Reader* (Melbourne: Cheshire).

Irwin, G. (1974) 'Compulsory voting legislation in the Netherlands: impact on voter turnout'. *Comparative Political Studies* 7: 292–315.

Jaensch, D. (1994) *Power Politics: Australia's Party System* (Sydney: Allen and Unwin).

Jones, F. L. and McAllister, I. (1989) 'The changing structural base of Australian politics since 1946'. *Politics* 24: 7–17.

Katz, R. S. (1986) 'Party government: a rationalistic conception', in Francis G. Castles and Rudolf Wildenmann (eds) *The Future of Party Government: Visions and Realities of Party Government*, vol. 1 (Berlin: Walter de Gruyter), pp. 31–71.

Kemp, D. (1978) *Society and Electoral Behaviour in Australia* (Brisbane: University of Queensland Press).

Lipson, L. (1959) 'Party systems in the United Kingdom and the Older Commonwealth: causes, resemblances and variations'. *Political Studies* 7: 12–31.

Loveday, P. (1977) 'Emergence, realignment and consolidation', in Peter Loveday, Alan W. Martin, and Robert S. Parker (eds) *The Emergence of the Australian Party System* (Sydney: Hale & Iremonger).

Mackerras, M. and McAllister, I. (1999) 'Compulsory voting, party stability and electoral advantage in Australia'. *Electoral Studies* 18/2.

Marsh, I. (1995) *Beyond the Two Party System* (Cambridge: Cambridge University Press).

McAllister, I. (1991) 'Party adaptation and factionalism within the Australian party system'. *American Journal of Political Science* 35: 206–27.

—— (1992) *Political Behaviour: Citizens, Parties and Elites in Australia* (Melbourne: Longman Cheshire).

—— (1993) 'Immigration, bipartisanship and public opinion', in James Jupp and Marie Kabala (eds) *The Politics of Immigration* (Melbourne: Bureau of Immigration Research).

—— (1997a) 'Australia', in Pippa Norris (ed.) *Pathways to Power: Legislative Recruitment in Advanced Democracies* (Cambridge: Cambridge University Press).

—— (1997b) 'National Identity', in B. Galligan, I. McAllister, and J. Ravenhill (eds) *New Developments in Australian Politics* (Melbourne: Macmillan).

—— (1998) 'Civic education and political knowledge in Australia'. *Australian Journal of Political Science* 33: 7–24.

—— and Makkai, T. (1993) 'Institutions, society or protest? Explaining invalid votes in Australian elections'. *Electoral Studies* 12: 23–40.

—— Mackerras, M., and Boldiston, C. B. (1997) *Australian Political Facts* (Melbourne: Macmillan).

—— and Studlar, D. T. (1993) 'Trends in public opinion on the environment in Australia'. *International Journal of Public Opinion Research* 5: 353–61.

McMullin, R. (1995) *The Light on the Hill: The Australian Labor Party, 1891–1991* (Melbourne: Oxford University Press).

Mughan, A. (1987) 'The "hip-pocket nerve" and electoral volatility in Australia and Great Britain'. *Politics* 22: 66–75.

Overacker, L. (1951) *The Australian Party System* (New Haven, Conn: Yale University Press).

Papadakis, E. (1993) *Politics and the Environment: The Australian Experience* (Sydney: Allen and Unwin).

Parkin, A. and Warhurst, J. (1983) *Machine Politics in the Australian Labor Party* (Sydney: Allen and Unwin).

Reynolds, P. (1974) *The Democratic Labor Party* (Brisbane: Jacaranda Press).

Rose, R. (1974) *Electoral Behaviour: A Comparative Handbook* (NYC: Free Press).

Rydon, J. (1986) *A Federal Legislature: The Australian Parliament, 1901–80* (Melbourne: Oxford University Press).

Seyd, P. and Whiteley, P. (1992) *Labour's Grass Roots* (Oxford: Clarendon Press).

Sharman, C. (1997) 'Politics in the States', in Brian Galligan, Ian McAllister, and John Ravenhill (eds) *New Developments in Australian Politics* (Melbourne: Macmillan).

Simms, M. (1997) *The Paradox of Parties: Australian Political Parties in the 1990s* (Sydney: Allen and Unwin).

Ward, I. (1991) 'The changing organizational nature of Australia's political parties'. *Journal of Commonwealth and Comparative Politics* 29: 153–74.

—— (1997) 'Party organization and membership participation', in John Warhurst (ed.) *Keeping the Bastards Honest: The Australian Democrats' First Twenty Years* (Sydney: Allen and Unwin).

Warhurst, J. (1997) *Keeping the Bastards Honest: The Australian Democrats' First Twenty Years* (Sydney: Allen and Unwin).

Whiteley, P., Seyd, P., and Richardson, J. (1994) *True Blues: The Politics of Conservative Party Membership* (Oxford: Clarendon Press).

14

Parties and Society in New Zealand

Jack Vowles

THE PARTY SYSTEM

In the two or three decades up to the 1990s, the New Zealand party system became less and less dominated by the two parties around which it had aligned in the 1930s. Of these, the National Party is at heart ideologically conservative, with a tinge of old-fashioned liberalism. Labour emerged out of the trade union movement in 1916, and by the 1980s had become a centre–left party predominantly made up of the salaried middle class. Before the 1990s, at the parliamentary level two-party politics reigned. Party competition was shaped by a first past the post (FPTP) or single-member plurality (SMP) electoral system. Electorally, dealigning trends were apparent, but had little impact on parliamentary politics. Table 14.1 shows that while the number of effective parliamentary parties remained at around or below two until 1996, the number of effective electoral parties was already just under three in 1984. Table 14.2 shows that single-party governments ruled, and that they were predominantly National. From 1990 onwards electoral demand for wider parliamentary representation and more accountable government underpinned a successful campaign for proportional representation (see Vowles 1995; Jackson and McRobie 1998).

The 1996 and 1999 elections were fought under a new mixed member proportional (MMP) electoral system. MMP produced Parliaments that differed substantially from those elected in 1993 and earlier. In 1993 four parties were represented, but National and Labour had more than 95 per cent of the seats between them. In 1996 six parties were represented in the House, and National and Labour together could muster only just over two-thirds of the seats. To Labour's left, the Alliance represented a robust belief in social democracy. A centre party, United, kept one seat due to an electoral pact with National. The newest party, the Association of Consumers and Taxpayers (ACT), took a position on the neo-liberal right of the party system. New Zealand First, a populist nationalist party aimed its appeals to the political centre. Together with the National Party, in 1996 New Zealand First formed New Zealand's first coalition government since the 1930s. That coalition

TABLE 14.1. *Elections in New Zealand, 1960–99*

Year	Labour		National		Social Credit		Alliance		Values/ Green		NZ First		ACT		United		Christian	NZ Party	Others	ENEP	ENPP
	v	s	v	s	v	s	v	s	v	s	v	s	v	s	v	s	v	v	v		
1960	43.4	34	47.6	46	8.6															0.4	2.37	1.96
1963	43.7	35	47.1	45	7.9															1.3	2.39	1.97
1966	41.4	35	43.6	44	14.5	1														0.5	2.61	2.02
1969	44.2	39	45.2	45	9.1															1.5	2.45	1.99
1972	48.4	55	41.5	32	6.7				2.0											1.4	2.43	1.87
1975	39.6	32	47.6	55	7.4				5.2											0.2	2.55	1.87
1978	40.4	40	39.8	51	16.1	1			2.4											1.3	2.87	2.01
1981	39.0	43	38.8	47	20.7	2			0.2											1.3	2.89	2.08
1984	43.0	57	35.9	36	7.6	2			0.2										12.3	1.0	2.99	1.98
1987	48.0	57	44.0	40	5.7				0.1										0.3	1.9	2.34	1.94
1990	35.1	28	47.8	68	1.7		5.2	1	6.9											2.8	2.70	1.74
1993	34.7	45	35.1	50			18.2	2			8.4	2					2.0			1.6	3.52	2.16
1996	28.2	37	33.8	44			10.1	13			13.4	17	6.1	8	0.9	1	4.3			3.2	4.43	3.76
1999	38.7	49	30.5	39			7.7	10	5.2	7	4.3	5	7.0	9	0.5	1	2.4			3.7	3.86	3.45

Notes: v = votes, s = seats; ENEP = Effective number of electoral parties; ENPP = Effective number of parliamentary parties.

Social Credit: Renamed the Democratic Party in 1985, joined the Alliance for the 1993, 1996 and 1999 elections.

Alliance: NewLabour in 1990. From 1993 to 1996 includes NewLabour, Social Credit (Democratic Party), Green Party, Mana Motuhake, and the Liberal party. By 1999 the Liberal party had been absorbed into the Alliance general membership, and the Green Party had left to stand alone.

ACT: Association of Consumers and Taxpayers, founded 1995.

Christian: Christian Heritage in 1990, 1993, and 1999: the Christian Coalition in 1996 (including Christian Heritage and the Christian Democrats).

Values: Disbanded in 1989 but immediately replaced by the Green Party, which became part of the Alliance for the 1993 and 1996 elections.

TABLE 14.2. *New Zealand party governments*

Year	Alliance	Labour	National	NZ First	Independent	Date of Election/ New Government*	Prime ministers
1960			100			November 1960	K. J. Holyoake
1963			100			November 1963	K. J. Holyoake
1966			100			November 1966	K. J. Holyoake
1969			100			November 1969	K. J. Holyoake
1972		100				November 1972	N. E. Kirk/W. E. Rowling
1975			100			November 1975	R. D. Muldoon
1978			100			November 1978	R. D. Muldoon
1981			100			November 1981	R. D. Muldoon
1984		100				July 1984	D. R. Lange
1987		100				August 1987	D. R. Lange/G. Palmer/ M. Moore
1990			100			October 1990	J. Bolger
1993			100			November 1993	J. Bolger
1996			75	25		December 1996	J. Bolger/J. Shipley
1998			94		6	August 1998	J. Shipley
1999	20	80				November 1999	H. Clark

Notes: All figures are percentages of Cabinet seats allocated to parties.
*Date of Elections 1960–93. During this period, new Cabinets were announced closely after the election, but in some cases the following month. In 1996, the coalition Cabinet was not formed until two months after the election, and it broke down in August 1998.

broke down in August 1998, but National continued to govern with support from a group of Independents who had left New Zealand First. At the 1999 election, Labour and the Alliance Party formed a minority coalition government, with parliamentary support from a revived Green Party, which had been part of the Alliance in 1993 and 1996, but not in 1999. The result of the election brought the number of parties in the House up to seven.

From 1960 until the late 1980s, three parties had been the most important and consistent electoral actors: National, Labour, and Social Credit, a party which provided a refuge for protest voters and a vehicle for the promotion of unorthodox economic ideas (Miller 1989, 1992). Prior to 1990, with the exception of Social Credit, no political parties other than National and Labour had secured representation for over half a century, and none had maintained an effective party organization for more than two elections in a row. Lacking payoffs in parliamentary representation, it was difficult if not impossible for small parties to maintain sufficient member morale and commitment. Between 1990 and 1999, however, the number of organizationally viable parties grew to at least six.

Table 14.1 provides the more detailed story. National and Labour dominated parliamentary representation until 1975, with the exception of one Social Credit member who was elected in 1966. Social Credit peaked in 1981, but could only take two seats despite gaining just over 20 per cent of the votes cast. There was a wave of party formation in the 1970s and 1980s. Values appeared in 1972 but faded during the 1980s, to be reborn in 1989 as the Green Party. In 1984 the New Zealand Party took up a brief role as a neo-liberal critic of the National government, a position in the party system reoccupied by ACT in 1995. Conservative Christianity emerged in the form of the Christian Heritage Party in 1990, and as part of a more broadly based Christian Coalition in 1996, but failed in 1996 and 1999 to cross the threshold for parliamentary representation under MMP (5 per cent or more of the party vote, or the winning of one or more constituencies). More significant was the defection of a core of left-leaning activists from the Labour Party, and the formation of the NewLabour Party in 1989. NewLabour took one seat at the 1990 election. From that platform, NewLabour provided a foundation for the construction of a left-leaning Alliance of social democrats, Greens, Maori activists, and other critics of neo-liberalism. It fought its first election as a unit in 1993. New Zealand First, meanwhile, was formed in 1993 by National Party rebel Winston Peters. In 1996 it gained substantial support among indigenous Maori voters hitherto strongly behind the Labour Party.

THEORETICAL ISSUES

The New Zealand case of party system dealignment and change is of interest for various theoretical reasons. Electoral systems shape both distributions of seats in legislatures and voting choices, although perhaps not so strongly the latter (Duverger 1954; Riker 1982). Electoral institutions therefore create incentives for political elites to adopt different strategies. The trajectories of individual political actors in New Zealand between 1990 and 1999 suggest strongly that the change of electoral system led those actors to follow different paths than those they would otherwise have taken. Had electoral system change not taken place, most of the main actors outside the two major parties in 1996 would surely have remained within the two established parties. Without the change, the number of organiza-tionally viable parties would almost certainly remain smaller. The future of all but the National and Labour parties would have remained uncertain.

The international literature debating party decline tends to focus on party sys-tems in general, although there is some focus on new parties replacing old ones, or, more recently, on old parties adapting successfully to the challenges posed by new compectititors (Bartolini and Mair 1990; Kitschelt 1994). On the surface, the New Zealand experience highlights the relative decline of the two major parties, and the rise of others. An alternative hypothesis should, however, be considered. Perhaps the decline of the two-party system in New Zealand represents a decline of parties in general. The development of new parties is recent, and their electoral support remains uncertain.

The effects of proportional representation have opened up the political market-place, and made it more difficult to maintain any hint of a two-party 'cartel', maintaining system-level rules that prevent or at least limit competition from outsiders (Katz 1996). Nonetheless political elites more dispersed between parties can still use substantial resources supplied by the state to maintain their hold on electoral politics. As elsewhere, in New Zealand popular participation and support for party activities has declined, and state support has partly filled the gap (Reiter 1989). In such circumstances political parties may be vulnerable to shifts in public attitudes that might threaten continued state-funding, or prevent its expansion, however modest present support may be.

PARTY LEGITIMACY

During the first decades of research in comparative political sociology, New Zealand acquired a reputation as an extremely stable democracy with high levels of participation, voter turnout, voter satisfaction, and an entrenched two party system (Mitchell 1969). On the institutional plane, New Zealand was described as the 'purest Westminster democracy' (Lijphart 1987). Associated with this social and political pattern has been a strong tradition of populist democratic radicalism (Vowles 1987), and comparatively strong political parties. Consistent with the expectations of theorists of responsible party government, early research into public attitudes in New Zealand indicated that New Zealand voters had high expectations that parties should make policy commitments prior to election, and that once in government, parties should then implement these commitments (Robinson 1967; Mitchell 1969).

Such judgements were based largely on the 1960s. Below the surface, however, there was more to the story even then. By the 1990s, it was a different story (Vowles 1998). While parties challenging National and Labour almost invariably promoted proportional representation, support for such parties was but one element in the campaign for electoral system change. It was public dissatisfaction with politicians in general which contributed to electoral system change by popular referendum with the objective of restoring the political responsiveness of party governments (Vowles 1995; Lamare and Vowles 1996; Jackson and McRobie 1998).

A snapshot of public impressions of political parties in the aftermath of the change to MMP can be glimpsed in data from the 1996 New Zealand Election Study (see Vowles *et al.* 1998). Immediately after the change of electoral system, nearly 70 per cent of New Zealanders believed that political parties were necessary to make the political system work, but only a quarter believed that political parties cared about what ordinary people thought. This latter finding is consistent with other data which suggests that New Zealand voters' confidence in politicians' willingness to heed their opinions has declined steeply since the 1960s (Robinson 1967; Mitchell 1969; Vowles 1998).[1] Had the questions been asked in the 1960s,

---

[1] The two questions were: where would you place your view on this scale from 1 to 5, where ONE means that political parties are necessary to make our system work, and FIVE means that political

the answer to the question about parties caring would have almost certainly been far more positive.

Survey measurement of public perceptions of political parties in New Zealand over time has been episodic and inconsistent since the 1960s, when the first surviving survey data were collected. Table 14.3 provides data on party identification trends in general, with more recent information on trust in political parties. Tracking party identification over time is difficult in New Zealand because the survey data is interrupted and there are problems of question comparison.[2] Party identification in general has declined, and particularly identification with the traditional two major parties, but this is a very recent phenomenon. Party identification apparently reached its highest point in 1987, but this may be in part an artefact of question phrasing. Leaving this aside, fairly high levels of two-party identification probably survived from 1963 until the late 1980s, with a collapse in 1990. The new parties of the 1990s appeared to be attracting somewhat increasing numbers of identifiers in 1993 and 1996, but the continuation of that process is by no means certain. Indeed, party identification may have fallen slightly in 1999.

There has been a substantial decline in the strength of party identification since 1981. Correlating identification by age shows that the tendency for older voters to identify and younger voters not to do so has been of similar proportions except for 1987, when identification may have reached a peak, and 1990, when younger voters were even less likely to identify than usual. In general, the picture of party identification in the 1990s suggests stabilization at significantly lower levels than before. On the other hand, distrust of the two major parties showed signs of decline after the 1996 election and declined even more so in 1999. A larger number of voters expressed trust in one or both of those parties than had been the case after the 1990 and 1993 elections. This improvement in one of the indicators of party legitimacy is most likely to reflect changes in the behaviour of the two main parties. Memories of the unpopular Labour government of the 1980s had faded, and Labour was apparently returning to policies more acceptable to its voters. National had also recovered from a burst of policy radicalism in 1991, and had managed to reassure at least some of its voters that it could be trusted once more to be conservative.

Trends in voter volatility tell a similar story, although evidence of a longer term dealignment is more apparent. There was a clear increase in mean electoral

parties are not needed in New Zealand? And, where would you place your view on this scale from 1 to 5, where ONE means that political parties in New Zealand care what people think, and FIVE means that they don't care what people think?

[2] Questions have varied between providing and not providing respondents with a prompt for non-identification. This difference in phrasing can be crucial, as without a prompt for non-identification the proportion of identifiers is considerably inflated (Johnston 1992). In the table, those years in bold indicate prompted non-identification, and the others indicate where there was no such prompt. As expected, the non-prompted years, 1981 and 1987, indicate the highest levels. However, given high mobilization in 1981 and the reversion to tight two-party competition in 1987 there is reason to believe that these high levels are not entirely artefacts. They may be somewhat exaggerated. For another assessment of party identification levels in New Zealand using some different data, see Bean 1996.

TABLE 14.3. *Partisan identification, trust in parties and electoral stability in New Zealand, 1960–99*

Year	Party Identification[a]					Trusts one or more[b]		Volatility[c]	
	% all	% two-party	% other party	% strong	By age (r)	Major parties	Other parties	TNV	BV
1960								4.9	4.9
1963		65						0.8	0.8
1966								6.2	6.2
1969								4.9	4.9
1972								6.2	6.2
1975	70	65	5		0.11			9.4	6.2
1978								10.1	9.3
1981	80	69	11	60	0.11			4.6	4.6
1984	81	63	16	51	0.04			16.2	13.3
1987	85	79	6		−0.01			13.6	5.4
1990	59	54	4	37	0.23	28		16.8	4.5
1993	59	51	8	41	0.15	25	30	13.7	11.8
1996	62	50	12	48	0.12	37	30	15.1	13.8
1999	55	48	7	44	0.15	50	35	16.3	13.0

[a]Party identification questions were asked without an explicit 'no party' option in 1981 and 1987, and with such an option in 1975, 1984, and from 1990 onward. % strong indicates those who expressed a very strong or fairly strong identification, or strong identification in 1984 (no strength of identity questions were asked in 1975 or 1987). 'r' = Pearson's product moment correlation coefficient for relationship between age and strength of partisan identification.

[b]Major parties National and Labour, other parties Alliance and New Zealand First only in 1993 and 1996, plus ACT in 1999.

[c]TNV: Total Net Volatility; BV: Block Volatility, where blocks are: Right (National, ACT, New Zealand Party, Christian), Centre (Social Credit, New Zealand First, United), and Left (Labour, Alliance, Values/ Greens). Social Credit/Democrats are defined as Centre until 1993, when they joined the Alliance.

Sources: 1963, 1981, 1990, 1993, and 1996 New Zealand Election Studies (see Vowles and Aimer 1993; Vowles *et al*. 1995, 1998).

volatility from 1984 onwards. In 1987 and 1990 there was more movement within left, right, and centre blocs of parties. Since 1993, there has been more movement between the blocs, mainly from both right and left into and out of the centre. Comparatively low in the 1950s and early 1960s, total net volatility (TNV) in New Zealand slightly surpassed the western European average between 1966 and 1984. Between 1987 and 1999, average voter volatility increased to about double that of the earlier period.

Trends over time in turnout and vote shares are also consistent with a story of emerging voter dissatisfaction and party system dealignment. Turnout was in decline from the 1950s onwards. And on a base of all potential voters the two main parties were losing support even more than indicated by their shares of the valid votes. Table 14.4 indicates the main trends. Both sets of data are calculated as a proportion of the eligible population. Failure to vote is therefore taken as both a function of non-enrolment and failure of some of those enrolled to vote.

TABLE 14.4. *Participation in party politics in New Zealand, 1946–99*

Year	Labour		Party memberships				All party members		Eligible voters		
			National		Social Credit				Two-party vote as % of eligible voters	Valid turnout as % of eligible voters	Minor party votes as % of eligible voters
	N	M/V	N	M/V	N	M/V	N	M/E			
1946	20,631	3.8							91.1	91.4	0.3
1949	34,547	6.8							89.2	90.1	0.9
1951	37,809	7.7							87.6	87.7	0.1
1954	30,760	6.4	250,000	51.5			280,760	21.9	75.7	85.6	9.9
1957	25,380	4.5							80.2	86.6	6.4
1960	30,520	6.0	246,000	44.2	2500	2.5	279,020	20.1	76.8	84.4	7.6
1963	13,122	2.5							74.6	82.2	7.6
1966	18,404	3.7			7500	4.3			66.9	78.6	11.7
1969	13,245	2.2			10,000	8.2			72.4	80.9	8.5
1972	12,313	1.8	150,000	25.8	2000	2.1	164,313	9.3	71.6	79.7	8.1
1975	13,997	2.2	196,000	25.7			209,997	10.5	69.9	80.2	10.3
1978	45,838	6.6	200,000	29.4			245,838	11.8	65.9	82.1	16.2
1981	49,837	7.1	200,000	28.6	22,000	5.9	271,837	12.5	64.7	83.1	18.4
1984	38,337	4.6	133,000	19.2	11,000	7.5	182,337	8.1	67.5	85.5	18.0
1987	30,701	3.5	100,000	12.4			130,701	5.5	71.3	77.6	6.3
1990	19,203	3.0							63.0	76.0	13.0
1993									53.5	76.7	23.2
1996							153,000	5.8	48.6	78.4	29.8
1999							132,890	4.8	51.9	75.0	23.1

Note: M/V = members/party voters ratio; M/E = members/national electorate ratio. National and Social Credit figures are for election years; Labour figures are for the full year immediately before the election. 1999 data was provided by personal communication; this figure includes members of Labour's affiliated unions not included in the data in 1990 and earlier. For age-eligible population estimates, see Nagel 1988, and New Zealand Electoral Commission 2000.

Sources: Gustafson 1986, 1997: 139; Miller 1989, 1992; Royal Commission on the Electoral System 1986; Vowles 1994; Harris 1997.

The two-party vote (Labour plus National) is calculated on the same basis. The difference between the two-party vote and the non-vote is the vote for other parties or candidates, almost non-existent in the late 1940s, but nearly 30 per cent by 1996. Its decline to 23 per cent in 1999 is still relatively high in historical perspective.

Turnout and the two-party vote declined to a low point in 1966. The period from 1975 to 1984 had some of the characteristics of a realigning period. The National government led by Robert Muldoon came to power on a platform of mild deregulatory change, in the aftermath of the first oil crisis, which hit the New Zealand economy hard. In response to mounting economic difficulties, the government adopted policies that offended many of its business supporters. Intensifying public dissatisfaction fed into increasing voter support for Social Credit. While the two-party vote continued to fall, turnout increased. This was a period of political mobilization. Social Credit climbed to a vote share of almost 21 per cent in 1981, and the Labour party shifted its ground toward 'new politics' issues (McAllister and Vowles 1994; Vowles 1994).

Labour came to power in 1984 at a high turnout election at which the two-party vote also made a recovery, at which a partial realignment could perhaps have been established (Vowles 1997). The two-party vote reached a post-1960s peak in 1987, but turnout fell sharply, particularly in former Labour-voting manual worker households (Vowles 1990). Just as the Muldoon government had offended National's traditional business supporters, Labour's unexpected promotion of market liberalization offended many of its traditional working class and union supporters. Attacked on the grounds that their policies had not been foreshadowed prior to the 1984 election, key Labour politicians simply challenged the assumptions behind 'mandate' theories of party government and denied that they had an obligation to keep to earlier commitments (Mulgan 1990).

Many of its former voters rejected Labour, and National was elected in 1990. Many National voters expected a slowing of the process of deregulation and market liberalization. But like Labour before it, National became widely viewed as having broken its promises in key areas of policy, and pushed ahead with further deregulatory change and expenditure cuts. Public dissatisfaction with both major parties revived support for other parties, notably on the left with the formation of the Alliance.

By 1993, New Zealanders had experienced three successive governments which had offended key elements of their voting coalitions. All three governments were perceived to have broken promises, and offended against expectations of responsible party government and populist democracy deeply embedded in New Zealand political culture. As a result, many New Zealand voters shifted to other parties than those dominant since the 1930s, and turnout declined. These trends do not necessarily reflect the development of 'anti-party' attitudes. During the electoral system referendum campaigns there was a certain amount of anti-party rhetoric. It came mainly from those who opposed electoral change, and who regarded a shift to proportional representation as enhancing the power of political parties. The greater part of the discourse of those promoting change was made up of rhetoric critical of politicians rather than parties, although it may be that many of the discontented did not distinguish between the two.

Party membership is perhaps the most obvious indicator of the strength of political parties and the depth of their organizational foundations. There is no requirement that New Zealand political parties release their membership figures to the public, and consequently that data is difficult to find. The Labour Party opened up its individual-member records fully in the early 1990s, but information was at that point collected for each year immediately before an election. National Party data has been made public for selected years, but there is not a complete series. Social Credit data is similarly incomplete. The fragments can be put together, as for most of the last half century the three parties were the only significant organizations. More recent data is available from the New Zealand Electoral Commission which, since 1995, has been responsible for the registration of political parties. While unable to release data on the membership of individual political parties, it has provided figures for total party membership in 1996 and 1999. These are the most reliable figures in the table. The National and Social Credit figures are probably the least reliable, although they almost certainly indicate trends.

Subject to these qualifications, Table 14.4 provides an estimate of total party membership in New Zealand as a percentage of the voting age population (see M/E ratios). It indicates a peak in party membership in the 1950s (just under 22 per cent). Party membership declined in the 1960s and moved even lower by the early 1970s. A period of membership recovery ensued until 1981, at which point further decline set in. The 1996 figure, however, includes membership of Labour's union affiliates not included in the data for 1990 and earlier. Unofficial estimates of Labour's combined individual and affiliate membership in 1996 were in the order of about 40,000.

The biggest change over the period has been in membership of the National Party. On bases of total voters for each party, both parties' memberships peak in the early 1950s (see M/V ratios in Table 14.4). The period of political mobilization from the early 1970s onwards affects both parties. The most remarkable feature of the data is, of course, the great difference between National and Labour. National has probably been one of the most successful centre–right parties anywhere in attracting a large mass membership (Milne 1966; Gustafson 1986). It has done so using two main strategies. First, it has maintained a very low membership fee, while also soliciting higher donations from those of its members who can afford to contribute. Whole families have been listed as members. Second, its internal processes, notably candidate selection, have been relatively open and democratic. National also benefited from deep social roots in rural areas. Many of its most prominent members and leaders have a history of activism and office-holding in Federated Farmers, although there has never been a formal relationship between that organization and the National Party.

In one sense, Labour's organizational strength is underestimated by the data up to 1990, as it excludes information on the membership of Labour union affiliates. However, until the 1990s few ordinary members of Labour's trade union affiliates were integrated into Labour Party organization in New Zealand. Union participation in Labour Party affairs was confined to the elite level. Union block votes rarely secured more than 40 per cent of votes cast at Labour Party conferences. These were traditionally cast to secure representation of trade union officials in the party organization, and, until the 1970s, to secure conference support for the parliamentary leadership. But between the 1950s and the late 1980s few union-backed candidates made their way into the parliamentary Labour Party, and the party–union linkage atrophied (Webber 1978). In 1982, 45 unions were affiliated to the party. They represented between them approximately 30 per cent of union members, 37 per cent of private sector unionists, and 12 per cent of public sector unionists, (Working Party on the Relationship Between Trade Unions and the Labour Party 1982).

The passage of the Employment Contracts Act 1991 brought an end to compulsory union membership in the private sector, prohibited any form of closed shop, and reduced unions to the status of incorporated societies. Union membership as a percentage of the workforce more than halved by the end of 1997, when estimated union density stood at 19.2 per cent, and the number of unions was much lower than the early 1980s. Decline was only a little lower than average in the traditional manual or blue-collar unions which form the historic core of Labour union affiliation. Public sector white-collar unions survived best (Crawford *et al.* 1998). But although their members provide a high proportion of Labour Party members and activists, their unions have never affiliated to the party (Vowles 1992*a,b*). As in other similar parties, union affiliation was a source of internal party conflict in the New Zealand Labour Party up to the 1990s. With fewer members and voting delegates at party conferences, unions are now weaker in the party organization than ever before. It is unlikely that the percentage of union members affiliated to the party is much above 10 per cent of the much lower number of union members in the late 1990s. However, this lower level of affiliation of unions and their members to the party is probably more meaningful than in the past. Numbers are no longer swelled by involuntary members. Members of a union not wishing to be associated with the Labour Party are no longer counted as members for purposes of affiliation. In the late 1990s, the major part of Labour's union affiliate members came from two of the largest unions, the Service Workers (15,000 members), and the Engineering, Printing, and Manufacturing Union (40,000) (New Zealand Council of Trade Unions 1997). Despite fewer members, by the late 1990s unions had nevertheless re-established a key role in the Labour Party, most clearly indicated by an increase in the number of former union members and officials in Labour's parliamentary party.

Overall, then, our review of the relevant evidence points to a number of indicators of declining party legitimacy in New Zealand. Partisanship and party membership have declined fairly decisively, as, to a lesser extent, have electoral turnout and public confidence that parties care or listen to voters. Electoral volatility has increased. However, parties are not exactly experiencing a full-fledged crisis of popular legitimacy, for two-fifths of electors remain strong partisans and, somewhat paradoxically, general trust in parties has risen.

PARTY ORGANIZATIONAL STRENGTH

Party finance

The study of party finance in New Zealand has been practically non-existent, because parties do not release data for public scrutiny. As Mitchell put it in 1962 (p. 77), the parties have 'an obsessive concern with shrouding their finances in secrecy'. This attitude survives forty years on. Political parties in New Zealand, with few exceptions, regard themselves as private organizations with no obligation to reveal their sources of income and their expenditures. Given this, analysis of party finances in New Zealand has to be based on unofficial sources and impressions rather than on hard data. Milne's account of the Labour Party in the 1960s emphasized its financial weaknesses (Milne 1966: 191). National, on the other hand, seemed to have a much more solid financial base (Mitchell 1962: 78). Members usually receive annual reports that disclose a certain amount of information, and some of these find their way into the public domain, with occasional commentary, but there has as yet been no systematic analysis. Such material is at times available, but at other times not. Another reason for the lack of analysis of this data has been the normal exclusion from such reports of information about the costs and expenditures associated with national election campaigns.

Affiliation fees from unions long provided a consistent source of income to the Labour Party, enabling it to run its national office. In the early 1980s Labour began to use members' pledges to donate on a regular basis through bank transfers (Strachan 1985: 167). However, the party was in financial difficulties in the early 1980s and was forced to both sell its national headquarters in Wellington and its Auckland offices, although it retained use of part of the former on a lease-back arrangement. In general, Labour's organization became more professional and effective from the early 1980s onwards.

In 1987, the Labour Party spent New Zealand's largest budget on a national election campaign: $3.5 million, on top of which television time funded by taxpayers was also provided. Most of this came from business people and firms who supported Labour's policies of market liberalization on the expectation that these would be continued. In 1987 National's normal sources of campaign donations had dried up so much that the party was unable to afford to do more than very limited polling during the election campaign. Commentary on the size and sources of Labour's 1987 expenditure began the debate on campaign limits and disclosure that led to the establishment of a first effective regulatory regime in 1995.

Data on the expenditure of individual candidates has been available for many years, and such expenditure has been subject to limits which, if exceeded, can lead to prosecution. However, in isolation this data has been of little substantive interest for assessment of party finances. But with the establishment of the Electoral Commission (Harris 1997), limits have been set on national party campaign expenditure and annual public disclosure of significant donations and expenditures is now required. There is a maximum cap of $2.3 million per party for national campaign expenditure.

Table 14.5 summarizes the information available for 1996 and 1997. Full data for the 1999 campaign was not yet available when this chapter was being completed. At all levels, the 1996 campaign cost just over $11 million, of which a little less than a fifth was made up of public funds in the form of the Broadcasting allocation. In terms of size, the very small parties relied on public funds most heavily (for up to 40 per cent of their campaign costs). However, for ACT, the broadcasting allocation made up only 4.5 per cent of its expenditure. The two biggest spenders were National and ACT, followed by Labour. The data on donations are not comprehensive. In 1996 and 1999 the law obliged parties to disclose those exceeding $1000 at the level of a single constituency, or a national donation exceeding $10,000. The total figures for donations below those figures were not disclosed. Furthermore, the sources of donations made anonymously above those figures could not be disclosed, although their amounts appear in the data. Some parties enjoy quite high levels of anonymous donation, and parties also receive significant income from their membership fees, and from money-raising activities conducted by their organizations between elections. Trade union contributions to the Labour Party are also largely hidden in the form of affiliation fees. Given all this, the data on donations are incomplete and give little indication of party incomes. Evidence from the 1999 election suggests a decline in party capacity. On a nominal basis, national party expenditures for the 1999 election were nearly 11 per cent lower than in 1996. With allowance for 3 years' inflation, the real decline is likely to be closer to about 15 per cent.

Staff

Again, data on party staffing is fragmentary. No consistent records exist which enable the researcher to construct a continuous time-series. Gustafson observes that the largest professional staff employed by the National Party was probably in 1954, with ten staff nationally, and eighty-seven deployed throughout New Zealand, with additional paid part-time staff for accounting and canvassing (Gustafson 1986: 206). In 1960, National had seventeen headquarters staff, with about forty-seven organizers employed throughout the country. The party's five regional divisions also employed somewhat over twenty administrative and

TABLE 14.5. *Party campaign funding and broadcasting allocations in New Zealand, 1996–97*

	1996 national spending	1996 broadcasting allocation	1996 electorate spending	Total 1996 expenditure	1996 donations	% of donations from known sources	1997 donations	% of donations from known sources
ACT	1,653,169	93,740	352,735	2,099,645	352,500	17.7	37,868	34.0
Alliance	558,059	251,949	538,570	1,348,579	62,060	100.0	57,579	97.5
Democrats					92,592	100.0	22,000	100.0
Labour	843,480	436,400	665,749	1,945,628	329,073	29.4	300,172	74.7
National	1,426,067	540,377	942,713	2,909,157	170,427	92.0	64,500	61.2
Natural Law	24,208	35,371	18,813	78,392	10,060	100.0	19,900	0.0
NZ First	858,255	250,055	553,425	1,661,736	100,075	93.4		
Christian	313,407	92,953	102,394	508,735	165,450	100.0		
United	49,120	93,406	142,754	285,280		100.0		
Other	186,671	260,543	149,729	596,944	19,519			
Total	5,912,438	2,054,796	3,471,934	11,434,096	1,301,757		502,019	

Source: New Zealand Electoral Commission.

clerical staff (Weeks 1961). From the 1960s onwards, the capacity of the party to pay so many salaries declined. In 1964 National Party headquarters staff had fallen to fourteen (Milne 1966: 180).

By contrast to National, in 1960 Labour's staffing was minimal, and not well organized. In 1960, Labour Head Office staff were only six, with one organizer based in Auckland. Before 1957, Labour had employed up to five organizers but, in government until 1960, had not replaced them (Weeks 1961). By the mid-1960s it had re-established the positions of four organizers (Milne 1966: 189). National had eight or nine times more staff employed than Labour in 1960. Neither organizational assistance from Labour's affiliated unions nor voluntary work offset Labour's disadvantage. In the early 1960s, Labour's staffing and organization were manifestly inadequate. Even those staff employed were not used effectively. For example, in the final week of the 1960 election campaign Labour's General Secretary was engaged in jury duty, and clerical staff were knitting during working hours. Shortage of funds was one reason for the deficit, but the parlous state of Labour's organization itself made fund-raising difficult outside of Labour's core trade union networks (Weeks 1961).[3]

Increasingly, New Zealand political parties have come to rely on taxpayer funding for policy development, staffing, and organizational support, although levels of funding remain meagre by standards set elsewhere. The National Party organized its own research in the 1940s and 1950s, but Labour had virtually no resources other than its parliamentarians for policy development. At best, one member of the party's Head Office staff was conducting part-time research in 1960. After an inquiry into these matters, Parliamentary Research Units were set up for each party in 1970, with salaries for five researchers and backup staff for each parliamentary party. In 1973, the numbers were doubled. The size of the two units remained the same into the late 1990s, although by 1997 another eight researchers were distributed among three other parliamentary parties (McLeay 1997; Klincum 1998).

Parties in government have the institutional resources of government to support them, and some of those resources are of course indirectly or directly deployed for party political purposes. Otherwise, ordinary members of Parliament relied on only a limited amount of secretarial support until the 1980s. It was not until the early 1970s that the leader of the Opposition's Office was given significant staffing, with three employed in 1973, and the number of staff only reached double figures in 1989 (Hunn and Lang 1990). The budget for the leader of the Opposition's Office in that year was about $700,000, although not all costs are included in the estimate. With the increase in the numbers of parties in Parliament, all parties now have parliamentary offices. Some commentators allege that such parliamentary

---

[3] Requests for information for this study were made to all significant political parties in New Zealand. Repeated requests in writing and by telephone were made to the National and Labour parties, but in both cases no information was forthcoming a full year after the initial requests were made.

resources are used not only to service the party in Parliament but also the party organizations outside as well (McLoughlin 1997).

By 1996 funding for party offices within Parliament was allocated in monetary terms. Parliamentary offices for all the parties, including research personnel, were costing the New Zealand taxpayer just over $6.7 million. This figure does not include funds allocated to individual members of Parliament for the purposes of servicing their constituents, which include provision for secretarial and organizational assistance. Members are free to allocate some of this for the use of their parties collectively if they wish. Neither do the figures include travel expenditures for individual members and their families. While probably not comparable to the support given to political parties in other countries, these resources are significant compared to the likely size of party budgets derived from donations and other non-state-funded income.

For the newer parties represented significantly in Parliament for the first time due to proportional representation, the resources are crucial in underwriting their consolidation and organizational development. Funding for offices outside of Parliament is given on the basis of service to constituents, but obviously provides organizational infrastructure that will inevitably be used for party political purposes. Most of the activities of the political parties are 'bulk-funded' by the taxpayer, and no detailed staffing information is available from the funding provider, the Parliamentary Services Commission, because unlike most other government organizations it does not fall under the coverage of the Official Information Act.

Membership activity

Studies of the nature of party activism in New Zealand have been few, and from them it is difficult to construct a coherent picture of change over time. There is some evidence that as party membership has declined it has also aged, with lower recruitment of younger people (Vowles 1992a). The social background of party activism has received much attention, and, in particular, the change in Labour membership from the manual unionized working class employed in the private sector towards non-manual unionized public sector workers (Gustafson 1976; Vowles 1983, 1992a).

But perhaps of most significance, there is impressionistic evidence that the role of party membership has changed since the 1960s. Organizational changes in the Labour Party during the 1970s stemmed from the need to construct a more professional and efficient organization appropriate to lower membership levels (Strachan 1985), and similar changes in National Party organization followed a few years later (Gustafson 1986). The role of members in election campaigns has also changed. Face to face canvassing in marginal constituencies, focusing especially on voter enrolment in areas of strongest support, remained a high priority for the Labour Party into the 1970s, but has more recently been replaced with methods more appropriate to a lower membership, such as canvassing by telephone. This may be one reason for generally lower turnout and voter enrolment in the 1980s and 1990s. It is also likely that the party members who remain are less willing than those in the past to contribute time. On the other hand, they are probably more willing and more able to contribute money.

Communication of the party message to voters remains an important role for members and activists and is still encouraged by party strategists. Members are encouraged to engage in traditional activities such as writing letters to the editors of newspapers, and to participate in newer ones, such as talkback radio. However, the messages of contemporary New Zealand parties are constructed by professionals, either employed by the party nationally or contracted to provide such advice at that level, and are designed for communication through the mass media, and notably television. Public polling and focus group research are used to test party performance, policies, and party rhetoric. Ordinary members and activists play little or no role in this work (Denemark 1991, 1992, 1996).

Media

The National Party's last party newspaper folded in 1967, after many years of sub-sidization from party funds (Gustafson 1986: 198). Weekly until 1961, it became a monthly before its demise. Labour had attempted a daily paper, the *Southern Cross*, in the 1940s, but that lasted only five years. Labour's weekly, the *Standard*, ceased publication in 1959, and a monthly, the *Statesman*, continued into the 1970s, with a readership only among the party faithful (Milne 1966: 17). Labour attempted a monthly, the *New Nation*, in the 1970s, but that too folded although the name was revived for use for an internal party publication. No New Zealand political party has successfully published a paper that reached outside its own party membership since at least 1960. More generally, New Zealand newspapers have rarely adopted the overt partisanship of the press in other countries, though their editorial preferences have tended to favour the National Party overall. Weekly and monthly magazines provide some analysis of politics from various points of view.

In 1960 radio remained a government monopoly and news was neutral in the public broadcasting tradition, although there was considerable deference to the government of the day; this had largely disappeared by the 1970s. Public broad-casting survives in the form of the National programme, which provides the highest quality media coverage of politics. The key medium is, of course, television. Television broadcasting commenced at the start of the 1960s, and remained a gov-ernment monopoly until the late 1980s. National coverage over a high percentage of households was achieved by the end of the 1960s. Radio broadcasting time had been allocated to political parties during election campaigns until the beginning of the television era on criteria determined by the government with some consulta-tion with the Opposition. The same mechanisms carried through into television. Table 14.6 indicates the hours allocated at the 1963 and 1984 elections.

TABLE 14.6. *Hours of election campaign broadcasting allocated to parties in New Zealand, 1963 and 1984*

	National	Labour	Social Credit	Others	Total
1963					
Radio	9.5 (38.8)	9.5 (38.8)	5.0 (20.4)	0.5 (2.0)	24.5
TV	0.83 (36.9)	0.83 (36.9)	0.42 (18.7)	0.17 (7.5)	2.25
1984					
Radio	1.92 (32.0)	1.92 (32.0)	1.33 (22.2)	0.83 (13.8)	6
TV	1.92 (32.0)	1.92 (32.0)	1.33 (22.2)	0.83 (13.8)	6

Note: Figures in parenthesis are the percentages of total broadcast time for the medium allocated to the party.

In the 1950s about 27 hours of broadcast time had been allocated, all to the radio. When television started it initially took a two-hour bite of that allocation, but by the 1970s both media were allocated about 6 hours each. Attention rapidly switched to television. The use of the medium soon developed beyond talking heads. By the 1975 election, dancing cartoon cossacks in aggressive National Party advertisements produced by US animators Hanna Barbara were used to smear the Labour government with communism (Wilkes 1978).

The value of taxpayer-funded political advertising was estimated in 1984 at $2.3 million (Royal Commission on the Electoral System 1986). By this time criteria for its allocation between political parties had been developed by the Broadcasting Corporation of New Zealand (BCNZ). With the demise of the BCNZ and the appearance of private television, the task was handed over to the Broadcasting Standards Authority, and allocations began to be calculated financially rather than just in terms of time. Political parties were also given greater control over the timing, length, and content of their material. Increasingly they were using their own funds to contribute towards the production costs. At the 1990 and 1993 elections about $2 million of taxpayer funds were allocated.

At the 1996 election the task of allocation moved to the Electoral Commission, with a similar budget. The formula developed by the BCNZ had been incorporated into the Broadcasting Act of 1989, and tended to be weighted somewhat toward larger parties. The two main television channels also ran their own election programmes featuring debates between the political leaders, and of course covered the campaign in their news. By the 1980s and 1990s the style of campaigning had shifted away from the traditional public meetings, street corner addresses, and door to door canvassing. While traditional methods were still not uncommon, most attention was directed towards the party leaders, who toured the country in search of photo opportunities, rarely meeting voters in any but the most controlled circumstances. The 1987 election marked a new phase in the slickness and sophistication of television advertising, this time led by the Labour Party. By the 1990s television debates in front of audiences of uncommitted voters provided one of the few opportunities for ordinary people to publicly challenge party leaders face to face.

Overall, developments in party organization in New Zealand conform quite closely with classic accounts of parties in the modern era. Thus, while traditional resources such as membership activism, party presses, and radio broadcasting have dwindled, this does not necessarily weaken parties given the switch to televisual political communication, professional staff, and state funding.

SYSTEMIC FUNCTIONALITY

Governance

Political parties in New Zealand have traditionally been viewed as very strong. They remain highly disciplined, particularly in Parliament. While the major political parties may be divided on certain issues from time to time, these differences have not developed into well-defined factionalism. Only in the 1980s did the Labour Party show signs of organized factionalism on both right and left, but both factions split off to form the core of new parties to Labour's right (the ACT) and left (NewLabour). The constitutional structure of New Zealand also lends itself to decisive party government. Until the advent of MMP, single parties gained parliamentary majorities and had no difficulty in legislating, save for a brief period in the early 1980s, and after 1993 in the transitional period leading up to MMP.

In the 1960s New Zealand was in the final stages of a unique version of corporatism. This combined a highly regulated labour market, state sanctioned compulsory union membership, highly protected and somewhat inefficient manufacturers engaged primarily in import substitution, a farming sector assisted by marketing organizations underpinned by the state, and a farming peak organization reliant on funds compulsorily levied from producers by law. Until economic trends made the prevailing public policy pattern decreasingly viable, there were powerful disincentives against government policies which might disturb the complex arrangements between sectional interests negotiated over many decades.

Nonetheless, government policies did change as the two main parties alternated in office. Government expenditure rose under Labour governments more than under National, and expenditure on social security benefits rose under Labour and stagnated under National. Until the 1990s, National was more likely to increase expenditure on health and education. Labour tended to favour the manufacturing sector and the union movement, National the farming and other business sectors. The two parties converged in the 1970s on social policy matters, and adopted different positions on economic policy in the late 1980s and early 1990s. Labour's promotion of market liberalization in the 1980s took National by surprise, but even the 1984–90 Labour government allowed benefits to fall in real terms only marginally while both government expenditure and social expenditure rose significantly. Labour's expenditure cuts fell most heavily on farming and industrial subsidies. It was left to National after 1990 to deregulate the labour market, destroy the legal foundations of trade unionism, and cut social security benefits to the bone in 1991.

While the influence of organized interests apparently declined in the 1980s (Vowles 1992c, 1993) the influence of the bureaucracy increased substantially. The intellectual seeds of market liberalization were sown in the Treasury in the late 1970s and early 1980s and percolated throughout the public sector as the 1980s wore on (Easton 1989). A powerful elite consensus towards 'more market' prevailed against the preferences both of voters and many party activists. The leaders of the 1980s Labour government in particular sought to distance themselves from their own party organization. They saw it as one interest group among many, rather than as the source of their political values and the organizational focus of their voting coalition. Such dismissal of voter and party opinions fed increased public disillusion about the political process, and encouraged the cause of electoral system change.

The change to proportional representation is influencing the nature of party government in New Zealand, in ways that may be too early to assess. Until recently, party effects on governing outputs have generally been strong, but New Zealand's first MMP government proved to be an uneasy coalition of populists, conservatives, and market liberals, a frustrating mixture for those who wished to see further market liberalism as well as for those who wished to at least partly reverse the rightward trends of economic and social policy. After the 1999 election, the Labour–Alliance coalition was showing early signs of greater cohesion and more coherence in its purposes.

Interest articulation and aggregation

Perceptions of declining government accountability were a powerful force behind the campaign for electoral system change. Yet the focus of the disillusion was usually politicians or government rather than political parties themselves. Those most active in the campaign for change were often party activists, or at least had a history of party activism, and tended to distinguish between political parties and the politicians they spawned. Indeed it was the defenders of the plurality system who argued that proportional representation would excessively increase the power of political parties. Many of those arguing for change welcomed rather than dreaded the prospect that MMP might allow party organizations to have greater influence over politicians through party list selection.

Among the ordinary people who voted for change without actively promoting it, there was a general sense of frustrated populism directed more against politicians than political parties. A public sentiment even stronger than support for electoral system change in the early 1990s was a belief in the desirability of binding referenda forced on governments through an initiative process. The National government sought to defuse support for MMP by legislating in 1993 to enable initiatives to trigger non-binding referenda through the signatures of 20 per cent of registered voters. This Citizens' Initiated Referendum process was too transparent a palliative to have the desired effect. After 8 years it had been triggered three times. It is a mechanism that could see more use in future.

Linkage between political parties and their support constituencies atrophied somewhat over the forty years since 1960. Class voting has declined very substantially (Vowles 1992*d*; Vowles *et al.* 1998: 34). The role of the trade unions within the Labour Party greatly diminished, although it revived in the late 1990s. Reflecting greater political recruitment of persons with union backgrounds into the Labour and Alliance parliamentary parties during the 1990s, a number of former trade union officials were appointed to the Labour–Alliance Cabinet. National has been more consistently successful in maintaining its core support among farmers, but lost ground among urban professionals and business people in the 1980s. The relationship between membership of single-issue groups and that of political parties is, like many other aspects of political sociology in New Zealand, under-researched. Group membership in general was high from the 1960s through to the early 1980s. However, the high point of single-issue group activity in recent New Zealand history was during the late 1970s and early 1980s, when anti-nuclear, anti-racist, and environmental activism proliferated. Party membership also increased substantially over the period, indicating a process of general political mobilization, rather than a challenge of single-issue groups to parties.

Labour had a virtual monopoly of the votes of New Zealand's indigenous minority, the Maori, by the early 1970s. But at the 1996 election Maori support shifted dramatically to New Zealand First (Sullivan and Vowles 1998). In 1999 Maori shifted back to Labour, but not so much as to restore complete Labour dominance of the Maori vote. Meanwhile, ACT appeared to be carving out a constituency in National Party heartland.

In the 1990s both major parties seemed more successful in constructing policy coalitions than had been the case in the 1980s, when Labour briefly appeared to outflank National on its right. By 1996 Labour had established an economic and social policy position slightly to the left of centre, on which most of its members and political leaders appeared to have reached consensus. National had more of a problem with a persistent market liberal faction seeking to move policy rightward in the direction of the ACT. Meanwhile the Alliance, to the left, did not appear to exert the same leftward pressure on left-leaning Labour members. In short, a period of fluidity in the various parties' relations with their support constituencies characteristic of the 1980s appeared to have passed. A more stable balance appeared to have emerged, one less strongly rooted than in the past and, perhaps, one still vulnerable to the stresses and strains arising from the consequences of electoral system change.

Participation in party politics

As already noted, party membership in New Zealand has substantially declined since the 1960s. A smaller band of party members, less than 5 per cent of the adult population, continue to participate. Parties rely increasingly on the advice of professionals about voter opinions, and much less on the views and opinions of party members. Politicians tend to value party members primarily for their monetary donations, their assistance in fund raising, and their work in support of campaigns. Table 14.7 provides comparative data on participation in other associations as reported in the 1996 NZES. Party membership has a lower profile than membership of environmental and women's' groups and weekly church attendance.

As a general rule, there is more lip service paid to party members' policy preferences on the left than on the right. However, while the Alliance parties individually gave considerable policy-making power to party activists through party conferences and other mechanisms, the structure of the Alliance made this difficult because policy accommodations between member parties had to be made at the elite level. However, the Alliance has gradually been emerging as a unitary organization in its own right, a process further facilitated by the departure of the Green Party from the Alliance between 1997 and 1999.

Labour's annual conference has long been an arena for substantial policy debate, and the left of the party at various times has fought for policy to be set by conference. However, a policy committee and later a Policy Council containing representatives from Labour parliamentarians and the party organization set manifesto policies, but significant aspects of such policies were ignored by the Labour government of the 1980s. Within the National Party there has been little demand for policy determination directly by the party, although the party leadership has set policy in

TABLE 14.7. *Political participation and group life in New Zealand, 1996*

Activity	%
Discusses politics	91
Talks about how to vote	35
Attended political meetings	12
Contributed money to party	7
Worked for party	3
Has signed petition	83
Has written to a newspaper	18
Called talkback radio	11
Member environmental group	9
Member women's group	13
Member trade union	19
Weekly church attendance	14

Source: NZES 1996.

a Policy Committee with some organizational representation. Nonetheless there is a tradition of vigorous policy debate at National Party conferences, although it is rarely allowed to roam into areas damaging to the party. Since the 1980s the conferences of the two major parties have been more carefully managed, and Labour, in particular, has changed its procedures to permit the organizational leadership to more effectively control the conference agenda.

Political recruitment

All members of Parliament elected in New Zealand since 1960 were first selected as a candidate by a political party. The one independent elected, Winston Peters, was an MP who failed to win re-selection as a National candidate, resigned from the party, and fought a by-election to regain the seat. Peters subsequently went on to form a political party, New Zealand First, which he led into the 1993 election later that year. Otherwise, no independent members of Parliament have been elected to the House since the 1950s.

Parliamentary candidate selection is therefore one of the most important roles of political parties in New Zealand. Most selection procedures allow a considerable role for ordinary members, although unsuitable candidates are usually filtered out at higher organizational levels. The National Party has long been regarded as the most democratic party in New Zealand in its candidate-selection processes. This takes place entirely at the constituency level at a public meeting, with a wide franchise, and through preferential ballot. However, the National Party refused to accept sitting member Winston Peters' renomination as a candidate early in 1993, because of his policy differences with his parliamentary colleagues. As this process of approval had rarely if at all been applied on ideological grounds before, and not to a sitting member, this set a precedent and indicated the extent to which the filtering process could be used to restrict the choices of local selectorates.

Labour's candidate-selection process since 1960 has mixed central organization and local influences. Pressure to extend the influence of local members made it possible for constituency organizations with larger memberships to gain more representation on the selection committee, on which the result of a ballot of members present at the selection constitutes one vote. Nonetheless, divided local opinion frequently made it possible for candidates preferred by the central organization to win selection. The central organization naturally takes an overall rather than a local view of candidate selection. For this reason, Labour's candidates since the 1970s in particular have been more widely representative of society than National's, particularly in terms of gender.

The new phenomenon of party lists required new candidate-selection procedures for the established parties. Both National and Labour use relatively broadly based and representative regional conferences to rank list nominees, with the various regional orderings subsequently blended by a central committee. The procedures of the other parties have thus far been subject to little systematic analysis. The

Alliance, as a coalition of smaller parties, had difficulties in balancing demands of party members for democracy with the need to represent component parties appropriately in their list orderings. New Zealand First's procedure was the subject of a legal challenge by nominees who claimed that it was heavily influenced by the preferences of the party leader and therefore not sufficiently democratic, but the case was thrown out because the members concerned had left the party.

At regional and local government levels in New Zealand, political parties play a relatively small role and independent candidates, local associations, or loose coalitions of like-minded candidates are normally elected. Labour tickets have from time to time made some impact on city council and Mayoral contests in the larger urban areas, as, more recently, has the Alliance. There has been no systematic analysis of political party participation in local politics in New Zealand. Party involvement has almost always been confined to Labour and the Alliance. Fragmentary evidence suggests that national political parties usually do not fare well in local elections. Their inroads are usually temporary and while they sometimes capture Mayoralties, Council majorities are more rare. Right-leaning tickets or slates often successfully use parochial arguments against party involvement, or argue that party politics should be kept out of local government. Often, Labour MPs and constituency organizations have discouraged involvement in local politics by the party, because they see it as a distraction from the prime task of securing election of a Labour MP to Parliament. A number of Mayors elected on Labour tickets have subsequently run as independents for re-election, usually on the grounds that they prefer freedom from party pressure for accountability. For the 1998 local government elections, Labour and Alliance activists formed joint tickets with the approval of both parties, and achieved some successes. However, those Councillors are unlikely to be directly accountable to their parties, but more to those who supported and elected them.

In one sense, the penetration of parties in the state is therefore 'shallow', in that they dominate in central government but have little influence in local government. However, the influence of local government in New Zealand politics is small compared to that of central government. Given this, perhaps the incentives for political parties to contest local elections in New Zealand have not been as strong as in other countries.

Political communication and education

The Labour Party still retained a commitment to educate the public in the principles of cooperation and socialism in its constitution in 1960. In reality, Labour has attempted little or no work of that kind. Its concern, like that of National from its origins, was increasingly to secure power by appealing to the concerns of voters as they are, rather than as they might be.

Attempts at political education have revived in recent years, this time on the right. Politicians on the right increasingly seek to educate the public on the principles and practices of individualism and self-reliance. For example, the Coalition government elected in 1996 promoted a proposal for a compulsory retirement savings scheme and sought to persuade voters to support it on grounds of its economic sustainability and the need to oblige people to save for their own retirement. In 1998 the Coalition released a document on 'Social and Family Responsibility' which it sent to all households, requesting responses to a series of open-ended questions which, it assured, would be analysed by government officials. Other recent efforts at political education have tended to use the government itself and therefore taxpayer-funded resources to achieve stated goals. For example, the Human Rights Commission is charged with public education on Human Rights issues, as is the Electoral Commission with public education about electoral matters.

Parties' agenda-setting powers are limited primarily by the recently imposed limits on campaign expenditures and the process of allocation of television advertising during campaigns, which does not permit the purchase of further time from parties' own funds. This remains an area of debate, with parties with more access to funding arguing for the right to purchase extra time. The absence of a highly partisan press also limits party agenda-setting capacity. On the other hand, the increased commercialization of even the state-owned media outlets remaining has degraded the quality of television news, which is the main source of voter information on politics. Parties wishing to set agendas have learnt how to package their news releases and their political initiatives to maximize their impact under this regime. The absence of sustained political analysis on television can permit parties to employ such tactics with some success, although the impact can still be offset by a certain journalistic cynicism and commitment to political balance.

CONCLUSION

Most New Zealand voters acknowledge that without political parties it would be virtually impossible to conduct representative democracy as we know it. In New Zealand as elsewhere, political parties, most notably the Labour Party, integrated the organized working class into the political process and, somewhat later, the indigenous Maori.

The future and role of political parties in New Zealand is highly contingent on the continuing adaptation of voters and parties to the recent change in the electoral system. Hopes that the accountability and representativeness of government would be enhanced by the institutionalization of multi-party politics are now somewhat dimmed, but it is too soon to tell what the longer term consequences of electoral reform may be. The vitality of parties remains moderately high, despite their reduced memberships, and their declining ability to raise campaign funds from private sources.

The decline of the two-party system in New Zealand represents a decline of parties in general, at least in terms of the level of relatively spontaneous support they receive. The increased support that parties receive from the state makes it possible for parties to maintain their roles and institutionalize their organizations on a base of substantially lower membership than in the past. But the level of taxpayer support for parties and politicians in general is an issue in New Zealand politics, although more at the level of relatively trivial excesses in travel expenditure. The other symptom of low public tolerance for expenditure to support the political process is a campaign to reduce the size of the legislature, which increased under MMP to 120. Reduction of the size of the house received overwhelming support in a non-binding referendum held at the time of the 1999 election.

The effects of proportional representation have opened up the political market-place, and made it more difficult to maintain any hint of a two-party 'cartel', with system-level rules that prevent or at least limit competition from outsiders (Katz 1996). Nonetheless, persistent opposition to the new electoral system indicates continued support for the reimposition of a two-party cartel among some of the key actors in New Zealand politics. The implications of such a counter-revolution on public attitudes to the party system and political legitimacy in general could be far-reaching.

REFERENCES

Bartolini, S. and Mair, P. (1990) *Identity, Competition, and Electoral Availability: The Stabilization of European Electorates 1885–1985* (Cambridge: Cambridge University Press).

Bean, C. (1996) 'Partisanship and electoral behaviour in comparative perspective', in M. Simms (ed.) *The Paradox of Parties: Australian Political Parties in the 1990s* (Sydney: Allen and Unwin).

Crawford, A., Harbridge, R., and Hince, K. (1998) *Unions and Union Membership in New Zealand: Annual Review for 1997* (Wellington: Industrial Relations Centre, Victoria University of Wellington).

Denemark, D. (1991) 'Electoral instability and the modern campaign: New Zealand labour in 1987'. *Australian Journal of Political Science* 26: 260–76.

—— (1992) 'New Zealand: the 1987 campaign', in Shaun Bowler and David Farrell (eds) *Electoral Strategies and Political Marketing* (London: Macmillan).

—— (1996) 'Thinking ahead to mixed-member proportional representation: party strategies and election campaigning under New Zealand's new electoral law'. *Party Politics* 2: 409–20.

Duverger, M. (1954) *Political Parties: Their Organization and Activity in the Modern State* (London: Methuen).

Easton, B. (1989) *The Making of Rogernomics* (Auckland: Auckland University Press).

Gustafson, B. (1976) *Social Change and Party Reorganization: The New Zealand Labour Party Since 1945* (London: Sage Publications).

Gustafson, B. (1986) *The First Fifty Years: A History of the New Zealand National Party* (Auckland: Reed Methuen).

—— (1997) 'The national party', in R. Miller (ed.) *New Zealand Politics in Transition* (Auckland: Oxford University Press), pp. 137–46.

Harris, P. (1997) 'The electoral commission', in R. Miller (ed.) *New Zealand Politics in Transition* (Auckland: Oxford University Press).

Hunn, D. K. and Lang, H. (1990) *Review of the Office of the Leader of the Opposition* (Wellington: New Zealand Government).

Jackson, W. K. and McRobie, A. (1998) *New Zealand Adopts Proportional Representation* (Aldershot: Ashgate).

Johnston, R. (1992) 'Party identification measures in the Anglo-American democracies: a national survey experiment'. *American Journal of Political Science* 36: 542–59.

Katz, R. S. (1996) 'Party organizations and finance', in L. Le Duc, R. Niemi, and P. Norris (eds) *Comparing Democracies: Elections and Voting in Global Perspective* (Thousand Oaks: Sage Publications).

Kitschelt, H. (1994) *The Transformation of European Social Democracy* (Cambridge: Cambridge University Press).

Klincum, G. (1998) *Parliamentary Research Services in New Zealand, Australia, and Canada* (PhD thesis, Victoria University of Wellington).

Lamare, J. and Vowles, J. (1996) 'Party interests, public opinion, and institutional preferences: electoral system change in New Zealand'. *Australian Journal of Political Science* 31: 321–46.

Lijphart, A. (1987) 'The demise of the last Westminster system? Comments on the report of New Zealand's Royal Commission on the electoral system'. *Electoral Studies* 6: 97–103.

McAllister, I. and Vowles, J. (1994) 'The rise of new politics and market liberalism in Australia and New Zealand'. *British Journal of Political Science* 24: 381–402.

McLeay, E. (1997) 'Living "Off" politics in Wellington: an institutional analysis'. Paper presented to the *New Zealand Political Studies Association Conference*, University of Waikato, 6–8 June.

McLoughlin, D. (1997) 'Plenty to Hide'. *North and South*, June, 32–3.

Miller, R. (1989) 'The democratic party', in H. Gold (ed.) *New Zealand Politics in Perspective*, 2nd edn (Auckland: Longman Paul).

—— (1992) 'The Minor Parties', in Gold, H., (ed.) *New Zealand Politics in Perspective*, 3rd edn., (Auckland: Longman Paul), 310–25.

Milne, R. S. (1966) *Political Parties in New Zealand* (London: Oxford University Press).

Mitchell, A. (1962) 'The general result', in R. M. Chapman, W. K. Jackson, and A. Mitchell (eds) *New Zealand Politics in Action: The 1960 General Election* (London: Oxford University Press), pp. 235–98.

—— (1969) *Politics and People in New Zealand* (Christchurch: Whitcombe and Tombes).

Mulgan, R. (1990) 'The changing electoral mandate', in M. Holland and J. Boston (eds) *The Fourth Labour Government: Politics and Policy in New Zealand* (Auckland: Oxford University Press).

Nagel, J. H. (1988) 'Voter turnout in New Zealand general elections 1928–1988'. *Political Science* 40: 16–38.

New Zealand Council of Trade Unions (1997) *Biennial Report* (Wellington: New Zealand Council of Trade Unions).

New Zealand Electoral Commission (2000) *The New Zealand Electoral Compendium* (Wellington: New Zealand Electoral Commission).

Reiter, H. L. (1989) 'Party decline in the West: a sceptic's view'. *Journal of Theoretical Politics* 1: 3.

Riker, W. H. (1982) 'The two party system and Duverger's law: an essay on the history of political science'. *American Political Science Review* 76: 753–66.

Robinson, A. D. (1967) 'Class voting in New Zealand: a comment on Alford's comparison of class voting in the Anglo-American political systems', in S. M. Lipset and S. Rokkan (eds) *Party Systems and Voter Alignments* (New York: Free Press).

Royal Commission on the Electoral System (1986) *Towards a Better Democracy* (Wellington: Government Printer).

Strachan, D. (1985) 'A party transformed: organizational change in the New Zealand Labour Party 1974–82', in H. Gold (ed.) *New Zealand Politics in Perspective* (Auckland: Longman Paul).

Sullivan, A. and Vowles, J. (1998) 'Realignment? Maori and the 1996 election', in J. Vowles, P. Aimer, S. Banducci, and J. Karp (eds) *Voters' Victory? New Zealand's First Election Under Proportional Representation* (Auckland: Auckland University Press).

Vowles, J. (1985) 'Delegates Compared: A Sociology of the National, Labour, and Social Credit Conferences, 1983', *Political Science*, 37, 1–17.

—— (1987) 'Liberal democracy: Pakeha political ideology'. *New Zealand Journal of History* 21: 215–27.

—— (1990) 'Politics', in P. Spoonley, D. Pearson, and I. Shirley (eds) *New Zealand Society* (Palmerston North: Dunmore), pp. 176–90.

—— (1992a) 'Party strategies and class composition: the New Zealand labour and national parties in 1988 and beyond'. *New Zealand Sociology* 7: 36–61.

—— (1992b) 'Who joins the Labour Party and what do they think?', in M. Clark (ed.) *The New Zealand Labour Party After 75 Years* (Wellington: Victoria University of Wellington Department of Politics, Occasional Publication No. 4), pp. 73–97.

—— (1992c) 'Business, Unions, and the State: organizing economic interests in New Zealand', in H. Gold (ed.) *New Zealand Politics in Perspective*, 3rd edn (Auckland: Longman Paul), pp. 342–64.

—— (1992d) 'Social groups and electoral behaviour', in M. Holland (ed.) *Electoral Behaviour in New Zealand* (Auckland: Oxford University Press), pp. 91–118.

—— (1993) 'New Zealand: capture the state?', in Clive S. Thomas (ed.) *Interest Groups in Post-Industrial Democracies* (Westport: Greenwood Press), pp. 97–110.

—— (1994) 'Dealignment and demobilization? Non-voting in New Zealand 1938–1990', *Australian Journal of Political Science* 29: 96–114.

—— (1995) 'The politics of electoral reform in New Zealand'. *International Political Science Review* 16: 95–115.

——, Aimer, P., Catt, H., Lamare, J. and Miller, R. (1995) *Towards Consensus? The 1993 General Election and Referendum in New Zealand and the Transition to Proportional Representation*. (Auckland: Auckland University Press).

—— (1997) 'Waiting for the realignment: the New Zealand party system 1972–1993'. *Political Science* 48: 184–209.

—— (1998) 'Aspects of electoral studies present and past: New Zealand voters and "the System", 1949–1996'. *Political Science* 49: 90–110.

—— and Aimer, E. P. (1993) *Voters' Vengeance: The 1990 Election in New Zealand and the Fate of the Fourth Labour Government* (Auckland: Auckland University Press).

—— Aimer, P., Banducci, S., and Karp, J. (1998) *Voters' Victory? New Zealand's First Election Under Proportional Representation* (Auckland: Auckland University Press).

Webber, D. (1978) 'Trade Unions and the Labour Party: the death of working class politics in New Zealand', in S. Levine (ed.) *Politics in New Zealand* (Sydney: Allen and Unwin).

Weeks, K. (1961) *Political Party Personnel in New Zealand* (MA thesis, Victoria University of Wellington).

Wilkes, C. (1978) 'The great New Zealand melodrama: television and the 1975 general election', in S. Levine (ed.) *Politics in New Zealand* (Sydney: Allen and Unwin).

Working Party on the Relationship Between Trade Unions and the Labour Party (1982) *Report of the Working Party on the Relationship Between Trade Unions and the Labour Party* (Wellington: New Zealand Labour Party).

15

Conclusion

Political Parties and Democratic Control in Advanced Industrial Societies

Paul Webb

Few, if any, would deny that political parties are integral to representative democracy as we know it. And yet since the 1960s it has become increasingly commonplace to encounter references in academic literature, journalistic comment, and polemical assertion alike to the 'decline of party', a contention usually predicated on the view that parties are 'failing' in a variety of respects. We have now reviewed in some detail the contemporary state of political parties in advanced industrial democracies with respect to their standing in the electorate, their organizational development and strength, and their functional performance. It is time, therefore, to summarize as far as possible the complexity of these findings and to reflect on their implications for democracy. For the sake of comparability, this summary analysis sticks to the national cases covered by this study, and excludes the case of the European Union (EU).

SUMMARY OF FINDINGS

Party legitimacy

Table 15.1 summarizes the evidence provided by our country experts in respect of party standing in the electorate. Recall that we stated in the Introduction to this book that we did not presume all of the indicators to be simple and unambiguous measures of partisan strength in the electorate: we recognize, for instance, that falling turnout and the erosion of partisan sentiment could be explained by temporary processes of ideological convergence between the major parties in a political system. Similarly, measures of party system fragmentation like the effective number of parties could vary for reasons unconnected with declining party legitimacy; for example, the emergence of new cleavages might generate additional parties in a system. Nevertheless, it remains possible that each of these measures could, under

TABLE 15.1. *Indicators of the popular legitimacy of parties*

Country	TNV	ENEP	Turnout	Partisan identification[a]	Absolute membership	Relative membership	Anti-party sentiment	Dealignment + APS?
UK	Fluctuates	Up ('74)	Fluctuates	Down ('74)	Down ('64)	Down ('64)	Significant	Yes
Italy	Up ('92)	Up ('92)	Down ('79)	Down ('89)	Down ('79)	Down ('74)	Critical	Yes
Germany	Fluctuates	Up ('87)	Down ('87)	Down ('76)	Down ('87)[b]	Down ('83)	Significant	Yes
France[c]	Up ('81)	Up ('78)	Down ('81)	Down ('80)	Down ('81)	Down ('88)	Significant	Yes
Belgium	Up ('81)	Up ('68)	Down ('95)	Down ('80)	Down ('90s)	Down ('90s)	Critical	Yes
NL	Up ('67)	Up ('71)	Down ('71)	Down ('81)	Down ('80)	Down ('70)	Significant	Yes
Sweden	Up ('91)	Up ('88)	Down ('98)	Down ('64)	Down ('91)	Down ('91)	Significant	Yes
Denmark	Up ('73)	Up ('73)	Stable	Down ('80)	Down ('66)	Down ('66)	Significant	Yes
Norway	Up ('73)	Up ('89)	Down ('93)	Down ('90)	Down ('90)	Down ('90)	Significant	Yes
Finland	Up ('91)	Fluctuates	Down ('75)	No data	Down ('90)	Down ('90)	Significant	Lack of data
Ireland	Up ('87)	Up ('87)	Down ('82)	Down ('79)	Down ('90)	Down ('90)	Significant	Yes
Spain	Down ('86)	Down ('82)	Fluctuates	No data	Up ('82)	Up ('82)	Low	No
USA[d]	Fluctuates	Stable	Down ('72)	Down ('64)	No data	Down ('60s)[e]	Significant	Yes
Canada	Up ('84)	Up ('93)	Down ('93)	Down ('85)	Down ('94)	Down ('94)	Significant	Yes
Australia	Up ('90)	Up ('90)	Stable	Down ('87)	Down ('67)[f]	Down ('67)[f]	Significant	Yes
NZ	Up ('84)	Up ('93)	Down ('87)	Down ('84)	Down ('84)	Down ('72)	Significant	Yes
Summary	12 Up, 3 Stable or fluctuating, 1 Down	13 Up, 2 Stable or fluctuating, 1 Down	12 Down, 4 Stable, or fluctuating	13 Down	14 Down, 1 Up	15 Down, 1 Up	2 Critical, 13 Significant, 1 Low	14 Yes, 1 No

Note: Figures in parenthesis refer to the first year from which significant change is evident. 'Stable' and 'fluctuates' both imply a time-series which lacks a clear trend, but the former implies less volatility over time than the latter.

[a] Refers to % of strong partisan identifiers; [b] Refers to trend in West Germany; [c] Refers to French parliamentary rather than presidential elections, since this enables us to gauge change from 1960, the latter only having commenced in 1965; [d] Refers, where, relevant, to US Presidential rather than Congressional elections, since these tend to be regarded as most important by American voters, and show more marked variations in ENEP, volatility, and turnout; [e] 'Party membership' does not exist in the USA as it does in most European polities. This 'M/E' figure is based on survey indicators of those donating to party campaigns and claiming to belong to 'party group' (see Table 11.7); [f] This is based on McAllister's contention in chapter 13 that, although National Party membership appears to have gone up since the 1960s, the party operates a very loose system of counting members, including past members who have not renewed subscriptions; note 13.8 provides survey evidence which supports the contention that the M/E ratio has declined in Australia. 'TNV' refers to 'total net volatility'; 'APS' refers to 'anti-party sentiment'.

certain circumstances, tap the declining 'partyness' of society, and it is therefore important to see if we find evidence of consistent developments across a number of them. This would strongly suggest that party penetration of society had indeed eroded in a multifaceted and enduring fashion.[1]

The first indicator of party legitimacy reported in Table 15.1 is *electoral volatility*. This is total net volatility (the Pedersen Index) and, although we recognize the capacity of this measure to fluctuate in a manner contingent on the dynamics of party competition, it is immediately apparent that in most of the countries comprising our study (12 out of 16) the level of electoral volatility has indeed increased over time. The only case of declining volatility is that of Spain, which does not surprise us greatly in view of the fact that this is the sole example of a recently transitional democracy in the sample; it is to be expected that the early years of democratization and party system formation will be volatile, but that volatility will reduce thereafter as the party system consolidates into a stable competitive pattern. Indeed, it will become apparent, as we anticipated in the Introduction, that Spain is in many ways an 'outlier' in our sample of advanced industrial societies. This strongly suggests that these findings are shaped by a country's stage of democratic development rather than by the 'contagious' influence of neighbouring states, though we will be in a better position to confirm this after the findings of the second volume associated with this project (dealing with parties in transitional democracies) are known. The second measure we have examined is the *effective number of parties* in a system, a classic indicator of party system fragmentation. As with volatility, although we recognize the possibility that a system may become more fragmented without necessarily implying the weakening legitimacy of parties, it is nevertheless interesting to observe that the effective number of parties has grown in most of our systems (13 out of 16) since 1960: again, Spain is the only contrary case.

Electoral turnout, like electoral volatility and party system fragmentation, is once again a variable which may fluctuate over time for quite contingent reasons; nevertheless, it is striking that electoral participation has dropped in twelve of our sixteen cases, a development that would seem quite damning for parties which historically played a crucial role in mobilizing the masses. For Wattenberg this implies 'that there is less of a market for the parties' product and that party systems around the advanced industrialized world have fallen upon hard times' (Wattenberg 2000: 76). We are not yet entirely convinced that the latter half of this statement is an appropriate interpretation of declining electoral turnout, however. As Wattenberg himself says, research suggests that turnout can vary according to ideological differences between parties; the more convergent parties are, the less the voters are likely to feel it vital that they should vote. In view of this, evidence that ideological

---

[1] Note that no attempt is made to summarize 'electoral hesitancy' in Table 15.1. While some of the case-studies in this book refer to developments in electoral hesitancy, most do not due to lack of data. It is therefore rather difficult to draw general conclusions about such an indicator.

differences between left and right have generally diminished (Caul and Gray 2000) should not be overlooked as a possible factor in the apparent decline of electoral turnout around the world. Whether this means that party systems have 'fallen upon hard times' is questionable though: at most, we might say that a certain model of party—the mass party—is in decline as some of the old political cleavages and identities associated with its emergence in the nineteenth and twentieth centuries erode or diminish, a point made long ago by Kirchheimer (1966). Clearly, we now find ourselves in the midst of a period in which different models of party predominate, but this does not mean that such parties do not remain central to modern democracy in various ways, as we shall see in due course. Neither does it necessarily imply anything pathological for democracy as a whole. Nevertheless, although we cannot yet be sure that it will prove an enduring phenomenon, we would accept that parties currently seem less able to mobilize mass participation than hitherto across the world's advanced industrial democracies.

The remaining indicators that we review are generally less ambiguous measures of party penetration of society. First, and in many ways most importantly, is subjective *partisan attachment*. Wherever possible, this is measured by the classic party identification variables pioneered by the *American Voter* researchers at the University of Michigan in the 1950s (Campbell *et al.* 1960), though the precise wording varies from country to country. Table 15.1 concentrates on the proportion of voters claiming strong partisan affinities, and we see that this has declined in all thirteen countries for which our contributors have uncovered data. Note too that in eleven cases for which we have information we find a combination of weakening partisan identification and increased volatility, which is not surprising since we would expect voting behaviour to become less stable as people's partisan loyalties wane. It is hard to question the notion that *party membership* is a valid way of gauging party penetration of society, which makes the evidence very striking, for this is down almost everywhere too, both in terms of absolute numbers and relative to the size of the electorate. Once again, the only place where party memberships seem to have climbed is Spain.

Finally, our country experts sought out *survey-based evidence of anti-party sentiment*. There is, of course, no direct consistency across countries of the type of survey instruments reviewed here, but it was important to our research objectives to know if there were significant levels of citizen disaffection with parties in the countries reviewed. In two cases—Italy and Belgium—the level of popular dissatisfaction recorded is certainly more than merely 'significant' and has to be understood as part and parcel of a full-blown crisis of the political system. In all other cases bar one, there is evidence of a significant level of disaffection with, or cynicism towards, parties; what is more (although not all of our authors have managed to track this in a systematic fashion because of the unavailability of measuring instruments which are consistent across time), in some cases this dissatisfaction seems to have grown. Once again, the main exception to the rule is Spain; in addition, Vowles reports a slight increase in general trust in parties in the aftermath of the electoral reform of 1996 (see Table 14.3).

In summary, then, while parties in crisis are certainly the exception rather than the rule, it is undeniable that their popular standing has been weakened in most Western democracies. This should not lead us automatically to assume that parties and party politicians are viewed with active hostility by many citizens, though the well-known phenomenon of partisan dealignment has undeniably served to weaken party penetration of society and to leave the average voter more indifferent towards parties than his or her counterpart of forty years ago. It may be important, however, that in fourteen out of the fifteen countries for which we have data, partisan dealignment (as indicated by the erosion of partisan identification) coincides with definite evidence of significant (and usually increasing) levels of anti-party sentiment (see final column of Table 15.1). Circumstantially at least (though this can only be confirmed by detailed individual-level analysis with data which are not always available) this suggests that there may well be significant minorities in most of the countries examined who are more than merely 'dealigned' in the sense of lacking an underlying partisan affinity: they are also actively critical of parties in their countries. This has more profound implications for party legitimacy. Even so, it is interesting to discover that even in such countries, where people are asked whether parties are still important or necessary to the political system (as in Britain and France), they are overwhelmingly inclined to answer 'yes'. On balance, then, we are inclined to believe that the problems parties in advanced industrial democracies now face in terms of popular legitimacy are probably chronic but rarely acute.

Party organizational strength

The data on party organizations have often been patchier than for party legitimacy, though great strides have been taken by researchers in rectifying this over the past decade. Even so, our contributors have not always been able to gather long time-series data on party resources going all the way back to the 1960s. The attempt to summarize their findings here therefore draws on the interpretation and narrative of the chapters (and occasionally on secondary sources), as well as on the formal data tables found therein. To give one example, the conclusion that French parties are wealthier now than in the 1960s depends largely on Andrew Knapp's judgement (expressed in Chapter 5) that, despite the traditional secrecy of party funding in the country until the 1990s, it is clear that spending on campaigns and staffing must have grown very significantly in the 1970s and 1980s, a development compounded (and no doubt facilitated) by the advent of state funding in 1988. Table 15.2 attempts to summarize our overall findings in respect of two key types of party resource for which we have data in most countries: income and paid labour. Again, where possible, we attempt to give some indication of the year or the period when changes started to become apparent.

TABLE 15.2. *Indicators of party organizational strength*

Country	Income	Central staffing	Total
UK	Up ('83)	Up ('87)	2 Up
Italy	Down ('92)	Down ('92)	2 Down
Germany	Up ('72)	Up ('72)	2 Up
France	Up ('88)	Data unavailable	1 Up
Belgium	Up ('71)	Up ('71)	2 Up
NL	Up ('70s)	Up ('68)	2 Up
Sweden	Up ('66)	Up ('65)	2 Up
Denmark	Up ('75)	Up ('80)	2 Up
Norway	Up ('73)	Up ('75)	2 Up
Finland	Up ('67)	Up ('70)	2 Up
Ireland	Up ('81)	Up ('75)	2 Up
Spain	Up ('86)	Data unavailable	1 Up
USA	Up ('60s)	Up ('80s)	2 Up
Canada	Up ('84)	Stable	1 Up, 1 Stable
Australia	Up ('83)	Data unavailable	1 Up
NZ	Data unavailable	Up ('70)	1 Up
Summary	14 Up, 1 Down	11 Up, 1 Down, 1 Stable	25 Up, 2 Down, 1 Stable

Note: Changes in income are in real terms, using deflators cited in World Bank 1992; http://www.globalfindata.com; and http://www.sunshinecable.com.

Additional sources: Katz and Mair (1992, 1994).

Not surprisingly, financial and staffing trends tend to covary. In fourteen of the fifteen cases for which we have evidence, the average incomes of parties have increased in real terms; in eleven out of twelve cases for which we have been able to uncover time-series on central party staffing levels, these seem to have grown. It should be said that these findings need to be set in the context of other variables for which it is harder to gather systematic data, but which are less positive for parties' organizational strength. Thus, we know that in many places local party organizations are far less healthy than central party headquarters due to factors like the decline of membership activism: this is evident in the UK, Italy, the USA, and NZ. But we have focused especially on central party resources since these are presumed to have become more important with the advent of televisual, capital-intensive and professionalized forms of political communication and campaigning. For the same reason, the erosion of party-controlled press and publications which has occurred in a number of cases has probably not been as significant as it might initially seem. This is all the more true in view of the qualitative professionaliza-tion which many parties have undergone, and which complements the changes in quantitative resourcing (Farrell and Webb 2000; Webb and Fisher 2001). Thus, it is important to bear in mind that quantitative decline in resources need not always imply the qualitative weakening of party organizational capacity.

The changes which we have witnessed in party organizations are reflected in the well-known heuristic interpretations of party development which have been developed over the years, especially the electoral-professional and cartel party models. Whereas the former of these (Panebianco 1988) emphasizes the professionalization of party staffing, the latter (Katz and Mair 1995) is notable for explaining the financial maintenance of parties in terms of the growth of state funding. In addition, each model discusses the general shift in internal power relations within parties, with the 'parliamentary' face of organizations, and especially those parts which are intimately associated with the leadership, becoming more dominant. This is part and parcel of a shift away from parties' mass traditions (particularly symbolic in the case of the left-of-centre parties with their origins as 'social encapsulators') in which emphasis was placed upon the importance of large, activist memberships as sources of labour, finance, and communicatory linkage.

In essence, it is clear overall that the erosion of party legitimacy in the electorate does not tend to coincide with a consequent erosion of party organizational strength. On the whole parties have adapted and survived as organizations, remodelling themselves to the needs of an era in which patterns of linkage and communication between parties and social groups have been transformed.

Systemic functionality

In many ways it is intrinsically more difficult to measure parties' functional performance and it is certainly not a dimension of analysis that is susceptible to easy summary in tabular form. However, a reasonably clear sense of our country experts' general views does emerge. The summary which follows starts with those functions to which parties remain most central.

Notwithstanding the views of commentators like Dalton and Wattenberg (2000: 276), we feel that the one function which parties continue to dominate, at least in parliamentary democracies, is that of *political recruitment*. Indeed, in many instances this role has even been extended over the past 30 years as party politicization of local government has occurred in a number of countries. Moreover, political recruitment is not just a matter of finding candidates for national and local elective office, for parties in most countries maintain control over important—sometimes vast—reservoirs of patronage, from the British quangocracy to the Italian system of *lotizzazione*. Thus, recruitment of candidates for representative and related governmental functions remains virtually inconceivable without political parties. Nevertheless, it must be conceded that even here parties face challenges and difficulties. First, the reputations of parties have sometimes foundered because of their complicity in the seedier side of political recruitment. It is not necessarily that citizens would prefer less party-dominated systems of political recruitment, but in a number of countries (most obviously Belgium and Italy) they have become deeply cynical about the corruption which attends some of these patronage networks. Second, in North America parties remain the gatekeepers of political recruitment, but they do not necessarily control the much more candidate-centred systems of politics practised there: in effect, it seems that politicians use the parties as much as the contrary. As Ken Carty makes plain in his chapter, this seems to be almost as true of Canada, a parliamentary system, as it is of the USA, a presidential system. Perhaps this should not surprise us, for it is not only the race for the presidency which is candidate-centred in the US, but congressional elections too (Wattenberg 1991). It should be noted that to a lesser, though not insignificant, extent evidence is accumulating that candidate-centred forms of politics are spreading to other parliamentary systems (Poguntke and Webb, forthcoming), which suggests the possibility of a growing challenge to party as conduits of political recruitment.

In respect of *governance* our country experts considered two main questions, the first of which was whether party government was challenged by alternative models of bureaucratic power, corporatism, or individual candidate-centred government. On the whole, there seems to be agreement that parties remain central to the provision of national governance almost everywhere, despite the various constraints under which they operate. Bureaucratic power is a perennial feature of the modern state, of course, and has often been at its strongest in the context of weak 'immobilist' government, as in postwar Italy or Fourth Republic France. Recent research suggests that formally accountable political executives may be best understood as arbiters between the party organizations from which they emerge and state bureaucracies: for instance, professional bureaucrats are especially conscious of the need for the state to fulfil certain domestic and international functions, and consequently pressurize the government in their role as 'institutional guardians of these responsibilities'; on the other hand, where these commitments may be in tension with partisan mandates, parliamentary and grass roots followers exert a countervailing pressure on governments to be true to their electoral pledges. The evidence suggests that partisan influences on policy emerge as significant in most countries: paradoxically, they tend to be strongest where party domination of patronage is lowest, in countries such as the UK, Germany, and France, but weaker in 'partitocratic' systems like Italy and Belgium (Cotta 2000). In any case, neither this finding nor the evidence of this book suggests that parties are becoming 'less loyal to their policy commitments' (Dalton and Wattenberg 2000: 267).

Corporatism represents a significant challenge to party government only in the Netherlands, where functionally decentralized forms of public administration have pushed the parties towards 'an implementing rather than a decision-making role', according to Kris Deschouwer. Elsewhere, corporatism has been practised in a way that cements parties' role in government rather than challenges it; thus, its erosion in Belgium and Scandinavia is a double-edged sword for parties, since it at once renders them more autonomous of actors such as trade unions while reducing control over them. Candidate-centred politics, as we have already noted, is probably becoming more pronounced in a number of countries, though only in presidential systems such as the USA or France does it have the capacity to represent a serious challenge to party in respect of the governing function. In

France, some presidential candidates have barely been 'party' candidates in any meaningful sense, but have relied on loose and fluid organizations whose chief purpose seems to have been support for their political careers: this appears especially true of centrists like Valéry Giscard-d'Estaing or Raymond Barre. Even so, the semi-presidential nature of the French political system ensures that the head of state is not the true head of government (at least in the domain of domestic policy) unless he enjoys the support of a disciplined parliamentary majority: in the context of 'cohabitation', it is the prime minister who controls parliament and therefore the domestic governmental agenda. This underlines the continuing relevance of party government even in the French context (Duverger 1980). The USA is the paradigm case of candidate-centred politics, of course, though it is interesting to observe that even here, John Green notes 'partisan government' has emerged in sharper relief since the 1960s as the behavioural cohesion of congressional parties has grown. It should be added that a further alternative to party government which has grown in significance is direct democracy: long since practised at state level in the USA, this has become more common around the world, particularly Germany at *Land* level and Italy at national level. Even so, in none of the countries surveyed in this book does direct legislation account for a particularly large proportion of the laws enacted; it can hardly, therefore, be considered a serious rival to party government as yet.

But do parties really 'make a difference' to policy outcomes? Deschouwer emphasizes that small states such as the Low Countries and the Scandinavian polities are particularly constrained by the growing presence of the EU. In addition, recent research conducted by others (Klingemann *et al.* 1994; Caul and Gray 2000) suggests that parties are now less distinct from one another in terms of left–right ideology than was the case in 1960. One would suppose that this principally follows the decline of class politics, though it may have been further exacerbated by the developing internationalization of economic activities in the advanced industrial world. Nevertheless, notwithstanding the constraints which are undoubtedly imposed by European integration, economic globalization, and demographic change, or in some cases by endogenous factors such as lack of legislative party cohesion, most of our country experts agree that party effects can still be readily discerned and count for a lot, a point for which is there is ample secondary corroboration; notwithstanding a degree of left–right convergence in the 1960s and early 1970s, real ideological differences do persist, and overall there is 'a remarkably high congruence between the themes stressed in party election programs and the subsequent policies enacted by the parties that get into government' (Klingemann *et al.* 1994: 268). Indeed, in some countries the capacity for party effects in government may even have grown—most obviously in the case of Italy with the first alternations in power since 1945 occurring during the last decade.

Overall, therefore, our view is that there is no real case for concluding that parties' centrality to national governmental processes and outcomes has been declining. Indeed, one wonders if this is not a prime instance of an area where

Sorauf's (1964) contention, alluded to in the book's Introduction, that parties have never really dominated all of the functions usually claimed for them, is most appropriate. That is, under peace-time circumstances in liberal democracies, parties have surely always been hemmed in by a variety of constraints emanating from both their domestic and international environments. In the absence of any compelling systematic evidence that parties' scope for autonomous action has diminished we would argue that there most probably never was a Golden Age of party government, and that it is therefore a misconception to speak in terms of 'party decline' in this respect. Parties have always acted under a variety of constraints, but have nevertheless been central to key policy-making networks. It is doubtful that anything fundamental has altered in these terms, with the partial exception of the growing impact of the EU in a European context.

The *articulation and aggregation of interests* constitutes a category of representative functions in which we see evidence of yet greater challenges to party. Almost everywhere, contributors confirmed that parties' capacity to perform the *articulation* function has been challenged to some extent by the rise of interest group activity and new social movements. In an era in which fewer citizens are linked to parties by virtue of their social group identities, they are more likely to become involved in political activity in respect of particular issues which concern them. However, while conceding this to be the case, we feel it should nevertheless be set in the context of the following points. First, it should not be overlooked that parties do retain some capacity to articulate group interests. Moreover, some of our contributors also pointed out that interest-group activity did not always represent a direct challenge to party, but rather a complement to it: thus, parties and unions have often joined forces to articulate group demands in places like Scandinavia and New Zealand. This is clearly true also in respect of the emergence of Green parties since the 1970s. Finally, individual-level research suggests that the rise of single-issue group activity may even serve as a stimulant rather than an obstacle to partisan identity and involvement (Aarts 1995: 251).

The *aggregation* function is particularly interesting. Do parties succeed in bundling together the demands of their various support constituencies in a coherent and stable fashion? The answer is broadly 'yes, but the job has become harder'. In presidential and candidate-centred political systems this function is more likely to be performed by individual politicians rather than parties *per se*, though John Green notes that even in the USA, parties play an important role in aggregating interests. In parliamentary democracies, our contributors generally report that parties are still central to this function, and indeed, it is not difficult to see why: the aggregating of demands into more or less coherent programmes for governmental action cannot be done by interest groups, social movements or the media—it is a task that simply has to be undertaken by parties competing for elective office, or be left to unelected bureaucrats. This is unlikely to be a role to which many state functionaries, even the most elevated and self-confident among them, are well suited, nor one which they usually seek.

In the case of one country, Italy, Luciano Bardi reports that parties' aggregative capacity has probably increased in recent years with the emergence of broad coalitions of left and right. It is more common, however, for our authors to report that the aggregation function has become a more challenging and complicated task for parties. In some cases, this is due to the fact that parties seeking to adopt catch-all strategies after 1960 set themselves the task of aggregating a broader array of social group interests than hitherto: this was certainly true of centre–left parties that shifted from simpler class mobilizational strategies. Beyond this, however, the task of aggregation has become intrinsically more complex because of social changes which have generated incompatible demands from different components of the support base, and/or because of the emergence of new issue cleavages. This is most obvious in cases where cleavages that threaten national unity have emerged (as in Canada or Belgium), but it is not an insignificant problem in a number of other advanced industrial societies that have become more socially heterogeneous since the 1960s. In particular, the emergence of new issue agendas relating to gender, ethnicity, regionalism, environmentalism, and European integration has undoubtedly complicated the vital task of aggregation for the major parties.

Even so, parties do remain absolutely central to the aggregation function. A salutary illustration of why this is so is provided by Simon Hix's chapter on the EU, a case which is an exception to the rule. Without democratically accountable parties aggregating demands at the European level, the EU lacks democratic legitimacy. Interests are articulated at this level principally through interest groups and national governments rather than parties, and aggregation is performed by national governments and the European Commission. Neither of these agents is directly accountable to the electorate at the EU level. Consequently, they have no incentive to expose a programme for EU-wide governmental action to a European electorate, and policy action is often rendered 'invisible'; citizens have little or no sense of a programme of European government on which they have an opportunity to express their judgement. By contrast, in national political systems the process by which parties aggregate policy demands and generate rival programmes for governmental action is all too clear; citizens may or may not choose to participate directly in this process as party activists, but through the media they can follow it in as much detail as they wish and opportunities for debate and voting on programmes exist both within and between parties (in national elections). That is, democratic parties render publicly visible the process by which a plethora of group demands are aggregated into more or less coherent and manageable policy programmes. That the EU lacks such a mechanism probably goes some way to explaining the widespread perception of 'democratic deficit' which afflicts it. To be sure, this is not to suggest that the adoption of a system of parliamentary democracy and party government at the EU level is the *only* way around this problem, though some critics would clearly advocate such a model (Leonard 1997); a highly candidate-centred system focusing on the direct election of a European 'president' is an alternative way of achieving the same effect (as Hix argues in his chapter). But this is not our concern in this book: the point is simply that the EU example serves to illustrate the importance of the aggregation role played by parties in parliamentary democracies.

Parties have clearly been undermined since 1960 by the spread of non-partisan forms of *political communication and education*, especially television. The media have clearly assumed a greater role in performing the political communication function and also in assisting interest groups to publicize their demands. Few would deny that citizens rely far more on non-partisan forms of media for political information and comment than hitherto. Seldom now, as we have seen, do major parties in Europe continue to run their own press organs, accepting instead the need to compete for favourable coverage in the independent (through admittedly sometimes apartisan) media. This implies that the agenda-setting capacity of political parties has most probably been squeezed, and it certainly means that the most authoritative source of a citizen's political information is apt to be critical of any and all parties. This is likely to damage the popular status of parties as a whole. An example of the way in which the style of media treatment of party politics affects the public perception of parties can be provided by the coverage of election campaigns. It is apparent from research conducted in the USA and Britain that this focuses increasingly on the conduct of campaigns rather than substantive issues of policy or leadership. For instance, in 1992, 57 per cent of the major terrestrial television networks' news broadcasts on the British election campaign focused on party strategies and the electoral process; by 1997 this had risen to 64 per cent. The print media's concentration on the campaign rather than the issues was even greater (Norris *et al.* 1999: 73, 79). Essentially similar findings hold in respect of the 2001 election (Deacon *et al.* 2001: 107). There is something doubly dangerous about this for party legitimacy. First, it carries the potential to leave citizens frustrated with politics in general, since the media's obsession with the process of politics clearly runs contrary to the public's own preferred agenda of substantive issue concerns (Norris *et al.* 1999: 127). Second, the intimate and constant exposés of party strategies and news management techniques leave little to the public imagination, and surely serve to foster a growing—and possibly exaggerated—cynicism about parties and politicians. Not that parties are entirely blameless in this: while they can hardly be faulted for losing control of the agenda-setting process, there is evidence that the growing inclination to adopt 'negative' styles of political communication has further soured public perceptions of elite-level politics, and may even have served to depress election turnout (Ansalobehere and Iyengar 1995).

The area in which party performance seems most obviously flawed is the fostering of *political participation*. It is certainly the respect in which parties seem most likely to attract criticism, as noted in the book's Introduction. Clearly, the evidence we have already reviewed in respect of declining party membership and activism, and (more problematically since it is more likely to prove transitory) falling electoral turnout, points to an obvious weakening of party performance. A variety of reasons explaining membership decline have emerged in the literature and are neatly summed up by Scarrow (1996) as either 'supply-side' (stemming from the social changes which make citizens more reluctant to join parties) or 'demand-side' (reflecting the organizational and strategic reasons why party strategists might no longer seek to recruit members) in nature. In general, the supply-side explanations are far more convincing, primarily since there is no good evidence that parties no longer actually want members. The main supply-side factors accounting for the decline of party-oriented participation parallel those on which we have already touched in the discussion of weakening party penetration of society: at the heart of much of this is the decline of the class and denominational cleavages which underpinned social group identities. Of course, parties are reflexive institutions and have often responded to developments such as the decline of membership activism by enhancing the participatory incentives available to their members (for instance, through new rights of candidate or leadership selection, and sometimes through greater involvement in policy making). Thus, the opportunities for political influence through party membership are probably as great as they ever have been, but citizens generally seem less inclined to avail themselves of such opportunities.

To sum up this review of the systemic functions performed by parties, we have seen that parties remain central to democratic political systems, especially in respect of governance and recruitment and, albeit more problematically, aggregation. The challenges they face in respect of articulation, communication, and participation have pushed parties into more marginal, though by no means insignificant, roles within Western political systems. These are all functions in which parties are now more obliged to share the stage with other actors, principally single-issue groups and the mass media. Such changes reflect the nature of advanced industrial society, which is more affluent, leisured, privatist, and cognitively mobilized (through the joint impact of education and the communications revolution) than the industralized democratic world of 40 years ago. As a consequence, citizens are less closely bound to parties through old social group identities and less dependent on parties for their cognitive cues about public affairs. But what does this mean for democracy more generally? Are parties failing democracy?

POLITICAL PARTIES AND DEMOCRATIC THEORY

On the face of it the results of our research suggest a mixed picture in terms of parties' democratic performance: some things they do well, some less well, some things they are central to, others they are more marginal to. But it is possible to be clearer than this about the implications of our findings for democracy. For 'democracy' is not a monolith but a contested concept, subject to rival interpretations, and conclusions about parties are inevitably shaped by normative and theoretical perspectives on democracy.

Taking a cue from Ware (1987) we can identify three core elements to democracy. These receive differing emphases in the various treatments of the subject, and the different weight accorded to each element inevitably affects perceptions of party performance. Ware refers to the first democratic element as *interest optimalization*. For a political system to be democratic, he suggests (Ware 1987: 8), 'rules or procedures employed must bring about results that optimally promote or defend the interests of the largest number of people in the relevant arena'. From this perspective, there have broadly been three approaches to the role of parties in fostering democracy, all of them focussing implicitly on the articulation and aggregation of interests. None of them are likely to take a very positive view of party performance, given what we have discovered in this book.

First, there are 'market liberals' who are hostile to parties on the normative grounds that political agencies should interfere with market processes as little as possible. Strictly interpreted, this view is not widespread and therefore cannot be regarded as a serious threat to party legitimacy in advanced industrial democracies. At the risk of appearing complacent, we would suggest it can be dismissed as essentially irrelevant to an understanding of the status and functioning of contemporary political parties. Second, there are pluralists (Truman 1951; Dahl 1961) who are not intrinsically hostile to parties as agencies of representative democracy, but who see them as largely secondary to interest groups. As we have seen, there is a good deal of evidence which points to the burgeoning role of interest groups as articulators of demands, a development seemingly consistent with the pluralist perspective. Yet our evidence suggests that the classical pluralist approach tends to under-emphasize the continuing importance of parties to the tasks of aggregation and governance. Indeed, pluralists themselves have observed and noted the problems caused by an explosion of interest articulation which is unmatched by commensurate rise in a political system's aggregative capacity (Crozier *et al.* 1975), though this is not to say that they are convinced that parties are capable of fulfilling that need. Aggregation is a function which features highly in the concerns of the third group of 'interest optimizers', those who like Arrow (1951) argue that the electoral process is destined to be flawed in so far as it tends to produce voting 'paradoxes' and 'cycles'. This leads to the conclusion that it is virtually impossible to satisfy people's wants in an optimal way, unless policy is made in homogeneous and consensual communities (which advanced industrial societies are not), or in pure two-party contexts: the latter scenario simplifies programmatic choice to a binary decision-making process and thereby avoids the well-known problem of 'cyclical majorities', which arises when three or more alternatives are available. Strictly speaking, this is a requirement which relates to party *systems* rather than to parties as such, but in any case it is easy to observe that all contemporary advanced industrial democracies fail such a test: even the USA, the nearest thing to pure two-partism, does not always guarantee voters a straightforward choice between two candidates, even for presidential office. Thus, from the perspective of interest optimalization, parties may generally be regarded as either failing to aggregate effectively, or as marginal to the process of articulation of interests.

A similarly damning conclusion about parties is likely to emerge for any writer giving primary emphasis to the second element of democracy, which Ware refers to as the *civic orientation*. From this perspective, democracy is not fully realized until citizens express their shared interests as members of the same community, a theme which goes back at least as far as Jean-Jacques Rousseau. Participation in the democratic process is vital to the political education of citizens if they are to develop this civic orientation. Advocates have therefore often placed political participation and education high on their criteria for evaluating democracy and its institutions. Implicitly, too, the aggregation of demands into a general will which expresses the public interest is important to this approach. Contemporary political parties are unlikely to fare well by the civic democrat's standards, however.

On normative grounds radical civic orientationists have usually argued, in Rousseauean vein, that parties are inimical since they tend to articulate and foster narrow group interests to the detriment of the wider community: this is very different to the view of pluralists, who regard pursuit of groups interests as central to healthy democracy. It can be seen that the civic orientationist has in mind a very particular sense of 'interest aggregation', based on the pursuit of shared popular conceptions of the common good, and is most unlikely to see modern parties as satisfying requirements. Of course, this is equally true of parties at any point in time during the past century, so it should be noted that one could hardly speak in terms of 'party decline' when adopting such an approach. Moreover, insofar as parties do, or ever did, play a role in political education, there would be an obvious danger that this would consist largely of indoctrinating narrowly defined group interests. This is significant because it seems likely from some of the evidence emerging from this book and elsewhere that the educative impact of parties has generally shrunk with the decline of the mass party. As Duverger implied, political education was a classic function of the mass party, which he likened to a school with pupils (Duverger 1954: 63). But, especially in the case of class-left parties, 'political education' would have been conceived largely in terms of ideologies related to group interests. Furthermore, although it is possible to point to the increased participatory rights which many parties have offered their members, it is unlikely this would be sufficient to impress civic democrats; for them, parties can only offer an impoverished notion of participation, even if evidence of membership and turnout decline is disregarded. From the civic visionary's perspective, then, political parties are at best irrelevant, at worst downright pathological. The only way around this is to adopt a far less demanding notion of 'civic orientation', according to which any kind of community consciousness, including group identity based on region, class, religion, or ethnicity, qualifies. This hardly helps, however, given the demise of the mass party. In short, it is hard to rate party performance highly from a civic orientationist perspective.

Proponents of the third element of democracy—*popular control*—may not take such a dim view, however. They would contend that, even if participation and civic education are limited, and interests are not fully optimized, democracy is meaningful to the extent that it provides the opportunity for people to exercise a degree of choice and control over public affairs. Ware identifies two distinctive approaches within this tradition. First, there are democratic elitists such as Joseph Schumpeter who see 'popular control' as consisting of little more than the electorate's capacity to remove leaders when their governance is no longer wanted. This is probably the least demanding perspective in terms of party performance. In fact, parties may not even be strictly necessary to it, so long as there are rival candidates to contest the major elective offices of state. That said, parties are useful for democratic elitists in so far as they facilitate the necessary process of electoral competition and perform the implicit function of recruiting candidates for office. Thus, democratic elitists should have no serious criticisms of contemporary parties, and one presumes they would regard phenomena such as the decline of party membership and partisan dealignment relatively serenely. Equally, we would expect them to be indifferent to the difficulties confronting parties with respect to fostering civic education and political participation or articulating and aggregating interests, for none of these shortcomings prevent parties from furnishing voters with electoral choices.

The second approach to popular control imposes somewhat higher expectations on parties. Associated with Schattschneider (1942), this argues that meaningful control can be exerted through mechanisms of popular choice, and emphasizes three particular requirements. First, there must be a connection between the competing programmes put before the electorate and the policies a government implements. For Schattschneider the best way of ensuring this was to have a two-party system, since this would maximize the chances of single-party government, which he assumed to be less likely than a coalition to dilute its campaign promises in office. In fact, our evidence suggests that Schattschneider may have exaggerated the virtues of two-partism in this respect, for most of our authors claim that parties make a difference to public policy when in office. There is good reason to be confident that—notwithstanding a degree of left–right ideological convergence since 1960—parties do in fact continue to offer electorates meaningful programmatic choices in advanced industrial democracies, and that they generally follow through with those programmes when in office. Indeed, previous research suggests that two-party systems do not necessarily perform better in these terms than coalitional systems, except where the latter arise from very fragmented consociational polities such as the Low Countries (Klingemann *et al.* 1994: 260). Kris Deschouwer confirms as much in this book, pointing out that the difficulty that Dutch and Belgian parties have in offering distinctive policies also owes something to their countries' vulnerability to the dictates of the EU and other countries with far bigger economies. On the other hand, we have also seen that in one case in our sample, Italy, voters now have more meaningful choices of government than hitherto, given that the first alternations in power between left and right since 1945 have occurred in the past few years.

A further requirement of the popular control perspective is internally democratic parties: if parties are to be mechanisms of popular control, then it follows logically that they should not be overly elitist organizations. This is interesting, for the gradual replacement of mass parties by electoralist organizations (be they catch-all, electoral-professional, or cartel in nature) seems to imply the possibility that parties have become more top-down over time. Yet it is far from certain that this is in fact the case: we have already noted how parties have often responded to the decline of membership by offering new participatory rights in internal decision-making processes. Three of the contributors to this volume have investigated this issue systematically in previous research and concluded that 'grass-roots party members (and even non-member supporters sometimes) commonly play a significant role in selecting legislative candidates and in legitimizing election programmes, though party elites generally retain vetoes over candidate selection and enjoy considerable autonomy in shaping party policy' (Scarrow *et al.* 2000: 149).

The final requirement of popular control is that parties should have sufficient control of the state in order to implement their policies once in power. This takes us back to our findings on governance and recruitment, which are overwhelmingly reassuring in this respect: if there is one function which parties dominate it is recruitment, and we have noted relatively little evidence that bureaucratic power or corporatism represent serious impediments to partisan influence on government, though it is true that they can each act as significant potential constraints. Broadly speaking, though, we have good grounds for being confident that party penetration of the state is broadly sufficient to ensure the implementation of party programmes.

Overall, the evidence of this book in relation to the functions of governance, recruitment, and aggregation is sufficient to convince us that parties remain central to the ways in which contemporary advanced industrial democracies assure a meaningful degree of popular choice and control in public affairs. It is surely from this perspective on democratic theory, then, that observers are least likely to regard parties as failing, though it is clear that these organizations have evident shortcomings when it comes to the more demanding criteria of optimizing interests and instilling civic orientations among citizens.

CONCLUSION: PARTIES AND DEMOCRATIC REFORM

Many observers will view parties—implicitly at least—as important mechanisms of democratic choice and control. This is not to suggest, however, that everything is rosy in the garden of party politics. Given the erosion of cleavage politics and the consequent weakening of social group identities, parties maintain more of an 'arms-length' relationship with societies than in the heyday of the mass party. Moreover, the high expectations that many citizens have of the state in respect of the scope of problem-resolution, and the hyper-critical nature of political coverage by the mass media in many countries, both make it unlikely that we will witness a strong revival in partisan orientations among voters. This does not mean that parties can afford to be complacent about the way in which citizens regard them, however, and they should clearly be prepared to make reforms where these might address important problems relating to their democratic functioning and popular legitimacy. Indeed, there is evidence to suggest that parties are already generally sensitive to the need to monitor their functioning and legitimacy and do not shy away from reform where they believe it to be necessary. The scope for practical reform is necessarily limited, however: in particular, it is difficult, perhaps impossible, to conceive of reforms that would achieve the ideals of the civic visionary, or which would get around the well-known problems of interest optimalization.

However, from the popular control perspective, reform is possible and has been attempted, evidence of which is apparent in a number of ways. For instance, there are now few advanced industrial countries still lacking detailed frameworks of legal regulation for party politics. One of the most recent to develop such a framework was the UK (Webb 2001). This is increasingly important given the likelihood that popular distrust of parties stems in part from the widespread perception that they are self-interested, unduly privileged, and inclined to corruption. Nothing is more likely to generate a sense of cynicism about party elites than the feeling that politicians are narrowly utilitarian and prepared to exploit their positions for partisan or personal advantage. This point incorporates, but takes us well beyond, the domain of the patronage scandals associated with political recruitment. Indeed, it is not hard to think of a wide variety of examples over the past few years; national parties in Italy, Germany, France, Spain, Belgium, and Britain, not to mention a host of less celebrated local party elites in these and other countries, have all been tainted. Moreover, it is possible that party legitimacy has been eroded through perceptions of self-interest even when parties have not been involved in any illegitimate activity. This is a point made well by Katz and Mair (1995) in respect of their concept of the 'cartel party', which holds that leading parties, whether currently in government or not, effectively collude to establish institutional rules of the game favouring their dominant position within the system. In particular, they exploit the resources available from the state (such as financial subventions or subsidies in kind) in order to ensure their organizational survival and even growth. This leaves us with a paradox which may exacerbate the problems of waning popular legitimacy:

On the ground, and in terms of their representative role, parties appear to be less relevant and to be losing some of their key functions. In public office, on the other hand, and in terms of their linkage to the state, they appear to be more privileged than ever. (Mair 1995: 54)

This may indeed be a risk, but given the organizational need which parties have for state resources in order to function, it is most unlikely that such support will be withdrawn or substantially reduced (except in critical cases, such as Italy, where it becomes apparent that parties have blatantly exploited the state in a corrupt and self-serving fashion). In any case, there is an alternative risk to non-support by the state, which may be even more corrosive of party legitimacy: this is the danger of parties' over-dependence on particular interests for funding, a situation which can easily breed (perceptions of) 'sleazy' links between parties and certain social actors. In any case, it may be argued that state support for parties is justified in order to prevent free-riding by citizens who do not otherwise contribute to party politics, but who benefit just the same from the operation of a party system without which democracy could not function. Realistically then, there is unlikely to be any retreat from the principle of state support for political parties in democratic societies. On the other hand, it is important to craft the form that state support takes with certain considerations in mind. In particular, it is essential that parties should never be allowed to become so 'fat' on state-derived income that they lack incentives to recruit active members and raise additional income through them; thus, it is important for systems of state funding to reward parties which recruit successfully. Moreover, the price to be paid for such support is a degree of state intervention to regulate parties' internal affairs; for instance, it is particularly important to render transparent the sources of party income. Such regulation is not a panacea which will prevent all irregular or corrupt behaviour by parties, but it is surely a *sine qua non* of public confidence in them. It is perhaps not surprising, therefore, that regulatory frameworks are increasingly the norm in advanced industrial societies.

A further area in which reform should be considered is that of participatory linkage. Although mass participation in politics does not carry quite the same weight from the perspective of popular control that it does from that of civic orientation, it is by no means unimportant: as we have seen, if parties are to be mechanisms of popular control, they should not be too elitist and should enact democratically formulated party policies when placed in office by the electorate. There is no doubt that governing parties will be buffeted by events and sometimes constrained by the countervailing pressures imposed by state bureaucracies, but there should at least be a broad correspondence between the programmes that a party formulates and those which it enacts in office. Hence the need for a degree of intra-party democracy. As we have seen, many parties have already trodden this path, and have sought to introduce participatory incentives for members over the past twenty years, not necessarily because they were motivated by the sheer desire to enhance popular control, but sometimes in direct response to concerns about their waning legitimacy. Thus, the main German parties have all reacted to evidence of dealignment, 'parteienverdrossenheit' and a growing popular preference for 'unconventional' forms of political behaviour, by creating more opportunities for intra-party democracy and citizen involvement in government decision-making (Scarrow 1997, 1999).

An important point to emphasize here is that the scope of such reforms need not be and should not be restricted to parties themselves; participatory linkage and popular control can primarily be enhanced by reforms whose scope falls outside the domain of parties in the strictest sense, though such reforms are very likely to impact on parties. The German reforms illustrate this to some extent since they incorporate the direct election of mayors and the introduction of citizen-initiated ballot propositions and referenda. Indeed, it is possible to be more ambitious still in prescribing ways of enhancing citizen participation, for instance through the introduction of devices such as 'voter juries' (Fishkin 1991; Adonis and Mulgan 1994), and the possibilities of much greater citizen feedback generated by the advance of communications technology. But it is interesting to note that, while proponents of direct democracy have often been bold and imaginative in their visions, few have previously emphasized the continuing relevance that parties would have, even under such a scenario. Budge, however, has argued persuasively that the introduction of even radically more participatory models of democracy would remain absolutely contingent on precisely the sorts of linkage which parties have traditionally supplied in representative democracies. For him, 'any feasible form of direct democracy would also be run by parties'. This is largely so because of the complexity of policy detail with which citizens would be confronted across a broad range of issues; in the face of this, ordinary voters—no less than legislators in contemporary parliaments—would require parties to organize and lead debates. Thus:

... it is simply unrealistic to think that democracy could function without groupings resembling political parties... Mediating institutions, above all parties, facilitate rather than impede policy decisions and must be recognized as doing that under democracy in whatever form it occurs. (Budge 1996: 175)

If Budge is right then the introduction or extension of direct democracy across advanced industrial democracies could be expected to enhance responsiveness by party governments to electorates that they would be obliged to consult more regularly on the impact of specific policies. Note too that the role they would play in organizing and leading debate (and in responding to the outcomes of such debate) implies that parties could be central to the revival of participatory linkage without necessarily even recruiting more members. The essential message is that parties would remain at the hub of an enhanced mechanism of participatory linkage, and that such a mechanism holds out the prospect of revived party legitimacy given the redefined sense of purpose they could achieve under it. If achieved, such a vision may well appeal to those who view democracy in terms of the civic orientation it encourages in citizens as well as to those who see it more straightforwardly in terms of popular control.

Nevertheless, it would be wrong to get carried away with the prospects or potential of reform. Its impact is likely to be limited for a number of reasons. First, it should be borne in mind that parties already have often responded to their changing social and political environments by reforming themselves and the legal contexts in which they operate; yet as we have seen, it has rendered them immune neither to corrupt activity nor to a degree of popular disenchantment. Second, it should also be remembered that popular frustration with parties is likely to stem in part from the perception that they are ineffective in government. We know that in fact parties do make a significant difference to governing outputs in most systems, but they nevertheless face real constraints, especially in smaller countries which are highly susceptible to the workings of the international economy and transnational actors like the EU. This poses particular problems of accountable party government for such countries for which it is hard to see a way around. Third, the impact of any reforms which are designed to enhance participatory linkages between state and citizen will almost inevitably be limited by the degree of socio-economic equality within the societies concerned. The detail of this argument is too complex to enter into here, but it has been well rehearsed and established elsewhere. As Held (1996: 322) says:

A democratic state and civil society are incompatible with powerful sets of social relations and organizations which can, by virtue of the very basis of their operations, systematically distort democratic outcomes. At issue here is, among other things, the curtailment of the power of corporations to constrain and influence the political agenda, the restriction of the activities of powerful interest groups... to pursue their own interests unchecked, and the erosion of the systematic privileges enjoyed by some social groups.

The political and economic risks attached to any concerted attempt by a government to take on such social and economic interests present formidable obstacles. Indeed, the continuing presence of social and economic inequality may help to explain why levels of political participation and civic orientation are not higher in places where direct democracy is already well institutionalized, such as the USA.

So we conclude this book on a cautious but upbeat note. Parties are perhaps not all they might be and neither are the societies in which they operate. Nor is it realistic to suppose that either will be transformed radically in the foreseeable future. This notwithstanding, however, parties continue to perform vital tasks with a relatively high degree of effectiveness and are central mechanisms of popular choice and control. If they did not exist in the advanced industrial democratic world, somebody would undoubtedly have to invent them.

REFERENCES

Aarts, K. (1995) 'Intermediate organizations and interest representation' in Klingemann, H. D. and Fuchs, D. (eds) *Citizens and the State* (Oxford: Oxford University Press).

Adonis, A. and Mulgan, G. (1994) *Back to Greece: The Scope for Direct Democracy* (London: Demos).

Ansalobehere, S. and Iyengar, S. (1995) *Going Negative: How Political Advertisements Shrink and Polarize the Electorate* (New York: Free Press).

Arrow, K. J. (1951) *Social Choice and Individual Values* (New York: John Wiley).

Campbell, A., Converse, P., Miller, W., and Stokes, D. (1960) *The American Voter* (New York: John Wiley).

Caul, M. L. and Gray, M. M. (2000) 'From platform declarations to policy outcomes: Changing party profiles and partisan influence over policy' in Dalton, R. S. and Wattenberg, M. P. (eds) *Parties Without Partisans: Political Change in Advanced Industrial Democracies* (Oxford: Oxford University Press), 208–37.

Cotta, M. (2000) 'Conclusion: from the simple world of party government to a more complex view of party-government relationships', in J. Blondel and M. Cotta (eds) *The Nature of Party Government: A Comparative European Perspective* (Basingstoke: Palgrave), pp. 196–222.

Crozier, M., Huntington, S. P., and Watanuki, S. (1975) *The Crisis of Democracy: Report to the Trilateral Commission on the Governability of Liberal Democracies* (New York: New York University Press).

Dahl, R. A. (1961) *Who Governs?* (New Haven: Yale University Press).

Dalton, R. J. and Wattenberg, M. P. (2000) *Parties Without Partisans: Political Change in Advanced Industrial Societies* (Oxford: Oxford University Press).

Deacon, D., Golding, P., and Billig, M. (2001) 'Press and broadcasting: "real issues" and real coverage', in P. Norris (ed.) *Britain Votes 2001* (Oxford: Oxford University Press), pp. 102–14.

Duverger, M. (1954) *Political Parties: Their Organization and Activity in the Modern State* (London: Methuen).

Duverger, M. (1980) 'A new political system model: semi-presidential government'. *European Journal of Political Research* 8: 165–87.

Farrell, D. M. and Webb, P. D. (2000) 'Political parties as campaign organizations', in R. J. Dalton and M. P. Wattenberg (eds) *Parties Without Partisans: Political Change in Advanced Industrial Democracies* (Oxford: Oxford University Press), pp. 102–28.

Fishkin, J. (1991) *Deliberation and Democracy* (New Have, CT: Yale University Press).

Held, D. (1996) *Models of Democracy*, 2nd edn (Cambridge: Polity Press).

Katz, R. S. and Mair, P. (1992) *Party Organizations: A Data Handbook on Party Organizations in Western Democracies, 1960–1990* (London: Sage Publications).

————— (1994) *How Parties Organize: Change and Adaptation in Party Organizations in Western Democracies* (London: Sage Publications).

————— (1995) 'Changing models of party organization and party democracy: the emergence of the cartel party'. *Party Politics* 1: 5–28.

Kirchheimer, O. (1966) 'The transformation of West European party systems', in J. LaPalombara and M. Weiner (eds) *Political Parties and Political Development* (Princeton: Princeton University Press), pp. 177–200.

Klingemann, H. D. and Fuchs, D. (1995) (eds) *Citizens and the State* (Oxford: Oxford University Press).

—— Hofferbert, R., and Budge, I. (1994) *Parties, Policy and Democracy* (Boulder, CO: Westview Press).

Leonard, M. (1997) *Politics Without Frontiers: The Role of Political Parties in Europe's Future* (London: Demos).

Mair, P. (1995) 'Political parties, popular legitimacy and public privilege'. *West European Politics* 18: 40–57.

Norris, P., Curtice, J., Sanders, D., Scammell, M., and Semetko, H. A. (1999) *On Message: Communicating the Campaign* (London: Sage Publications).

Panebianco, A. (1988) *Political Parties: Organization and Power* (Cambridge: Cambridge University Press).

Poguntke, T. and Webb, P. D. (Forthcoming) *The Presidentialization of Democracy: A Study in Comparative Politics* (Oxford: Oxford University Press).

Scarrow, S. E. (1996*a*) 'The consequences of anti-party sentiment: anti-party arguments as instruments of change'. *European Journal of Political Research.*

—— (1996*b*) *Parties and Their Members* (Oxford: Clarendon Press).

—— (1997) 'Party competition and institutional change: the expansion of direct democracy in Germany'. *Party Politics* 3: 451–72.

—— (1999) 'Parties and the expansion of direct participation opportunities: who benefits?'. *Party Politics* 5.

——, Webb, P. D., and Farrell, D. M. (2000) 'From social integration to electoral contestation: the changing distribution of power within political parties', in R. J. Dalton and M. P. Wattenberg (eds) *Parties Without Partisans: Political Change in Advanced Industrial Democracies* (Oxford: Oxford University Press), pp. 129–53.

Schattschneider, E. E. (1942) *Party Government* (New York: Rhinehart).

Sorauf, F. J. (1964) *Political Parties in the American System* (Boston: Little Brown).

Truman, D. B. (1951) *The Governmental Process* (New York: Alfred E. Knopf).

Ware, A. (1987) *Citizens, Parties and the State* (Oxford: Polity Press).

Wattenberg, M. (2000) 'The decline of party mobilization', in R. Dalton and M. P. Wattenberg (eds) *Parties Without Partisans* (Oxford: Oxford University Press), pp. 64–76.

Wattenberg, M. P. (1991) *The Rise of Candidate-Centered Politics* (Cambridge, MA: Harvard University Press).

Webb, P. D. (2001) 'Parties and party systems: modernisation, regulation and diversity'. *Parliamentary Affairs* 54: 308–21.

Webb, P. D. and Fisher, J. (2001) 'Professionalizing the Millbank tendency: the political sociology of New Labour's employees'. *SEI Working Paper in Contemporary European Studies No. 47* (Sussex: Sussex European Institute).

Index